MICHELE **SAEE**

PHILOSOPHY AND PROCESS

CONTENTS

To Sayeh and Alisina

Editors

Nick Gillock
Alisina Saee Nazari
Julie Sinclair Eakin

Book Design

Weestar Studio

Acknowledgments

Special thanks to Xingyu Wei (Weestar) for your creativity, belief, and encouragement not to give up working on this book all these years. And to Anisa Aboutalebpour for your contributions to the design, and development of the book.

Architecture is, by its nature, the work of many people. The work of my studio has been made possible through a culmination of many voices and unique talents graciously contributing to a common vision. It has been an honor to have received the gifts of their talents, the energy of their processes, and the influence of their wisdom. These individuals include:

Joo Abranjo, Ubaldo Arenas, Anisa Aboutalebpour, Johnny Auer, Reza Bagherzadeh, Malcom Ball, Merzad Beglari, Aaron Betsky, Florence Blecher, Jillian Burt, Breanna Carlson, Miguel Castillo, Kyle Chan, Alfred Chen, Ting Hao Chen, Leo Cho, Marie Christopher, Joori Chun, J.C. Chung, Rosa Cisneros, Geoff Colin, Aurelie Comboul, Jonathen Day, Roy Dehbibi, , Miguel de la Torre, Danny Diaz, Marty Doscher, Tyron Drake, Hugh Dutton, David Ellian, Mike Fink, Michael Fouther, Michael Galluci, Armineh Gariban, Nick Gillock, Ron Golan, Saul Goldin, Nardin Golparvaran, Brant Gordon, Richard Heinz, Marty Herling, Lousine Hogtanian, Terry Hudak, Pil Hyun Hwang, Bettina Ipsen, Dave Jeffers, Jeehyun Joo, Dave Kadly, Farhad Kharestan, Hojung Kim, Tex Kim, Elmar Kleiner, Melissa La'O, Domenico La Gioia, Jooyung Lee, Thomas Leerberg, Angela Leverett, David Lindberg, James Lowder, Richard Lundquist, Arshia Mahmoodi, Eric Marable, Max Massie, Angelo Matteoni, Fiorenza Matteoni, Stefano Matteoni, John McCoy, Daniel McFarland, Emil Merzel, Rob Mothershed, Hernan M. Munayco, Yaron Naim, Kamran Namdar, Andrew Nasser, Vince Naso, Hossein Navvabi, Hien Quan Ngo, Keiko Okada, Rudabeh Pakravan, Chloe Parent, Sangmi Park, Clive Piercy, Bruno Pingeot, Elizabeh Plessen, Afsheen Raeesrohani, Sandep Rahi, Somayyeh Ramezani, Bryan Richard, Pierre Riopel, Eric Rosen, Franco Rosete, John Rotondi, Abbas Safii, Eckart Schwerdtfeger, Susi Schindlbeck, Joan Simon, John Scott, Shiraz, Tony Singaus, Sam Solhaug, Han Suh Sohn, Charles So, Barna Stubner, Emiko Teragawa, Raymond Tombokan, Tong Tong, Roland Tso, Matthew Uselman, Philippe Uzzan, Yassaman Vafai, Azin Valy, Alysia Wang, Huanran Wang, Andrew Wilcoxson, Brian Wilson, Qianqian Xing, and Hongbo Yue.

I especially would like to thank those who contributed to this monograph. Thanks for your dedication and generosity of spirit: Claude Parent, Eric Owen Moss, Luigi Prestinenza Puglisi, Nick Gillock, Alisina Saee Nazari, Julie Sinclair Eakin, Gordon Goff, and Jake Anderson.

Heaven and Hell

Michele Saee

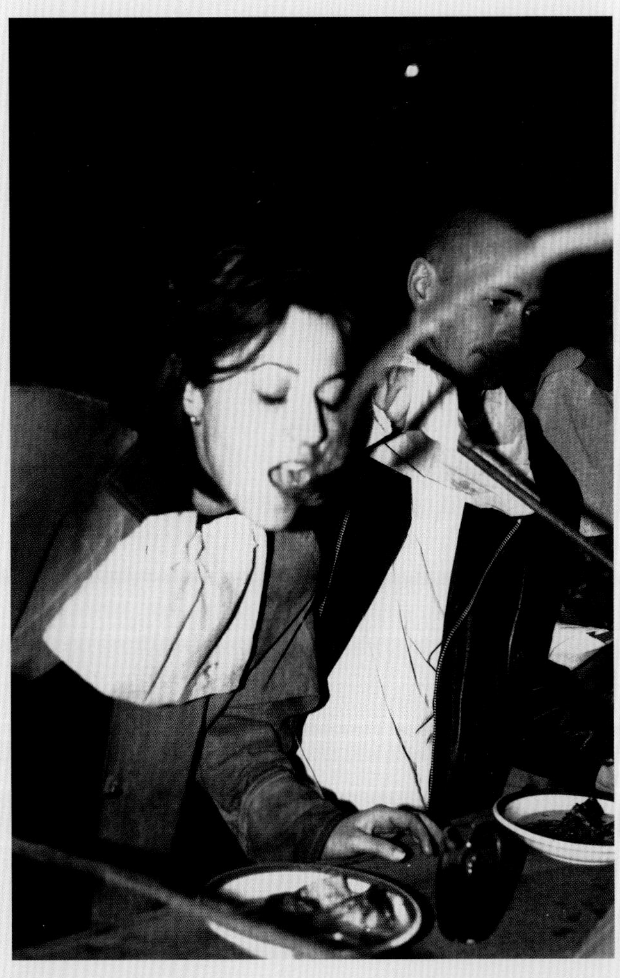

The city is dead and no amount of examining the body will tell you anything about the life it once had or where that life has gone. The form of industrial production that fed the city, as a life form, can no longer be maintained when the forms of production of its capital have been changing. This was how I discovered Belgrade after the tragedies of war in 1996. I was invited to a conference called "PROJEKT X" where one of the organizers was my Sci-Arc colleague and friend Mark Hawker.

As a student in Florence, I visited the old Yugoslavia during President Tito's administration—hailed as a glorious period of communism. It saddened me to see it again in its post-war condition. The image of the war-ravaged city is still vivid in my memories. There were artists, designers, performers, thinkers, and philosophers gathered from different parts of the world in solidarity. All looking for clues to why it was almost effortless to lose our collective humanity, to get engaged in the destruction of ourselves and others in just a few years.

I invited my class from SCI-Arc to join me. Nick, Emil, and Maryanne accepted with enthusiasm. I was uncomfortable leaving my wife Arezou, who was pregnant with our son, with our daughter, but she insisted I go. I missed our group flight because of a mistake in the ticket booking, so I had to leave the following day, which meant we'd meet in Belgrade. This was an intensely emotional time in my life because of the birth of my son, my financial difficulties, and the lack of satisfaction with my work.

I got on the plane the following day and the torturous trip began. The airports in Yugoslavia were shut down, so we had to fly to Budapest via Berlin. Once in Budapest, I had to find my way to the train station to make it to the border of Yugoslavia, and then from there who knew. My thoughts were flying aimlessly. The images of war I'd seen from the media became more and more realistic as I got closer to my destination. A force was pulling me and I could not identify it. I was filled with a sense of melancholy.

I arrived in Budapest without feeling or experiencing it. One of the most beautiful and historical cities left no impression on me. I ran to the train station and before I knew it we were traveling to the countryside. The mood aboard the train changed quickly as we were getting closer to the border. I soon realized that I was being watched and followed. Moving from one cabin to the next confirmed I was right. A middle-aged woman approached me with her thick accent and broken English asking me if I was American. I replied, "No, I am Iranian." She was curious about where I was headed and I told her I am going to Belgrade to meet friends. She cautioned me not to trust anyone and I laughed for the first time since the trip began.

The weather was piercing cold with no heat in the train. Looking out of the window I imagined people running in the opposite direction, away from the war, yet here I was going in. My fellow travelers dwindled the farther we got away from Budapest, but a handful of people took their place when we reached the border city. I got out and walked through the station searching for friendly eyes. Ultimately, that was all I could do. If I follow my destiny, eventually I'll get to Belgrade I thought.

I was walking up to people asking, "Belgrade? Belgrade?" hoping that someone would direct me to the right place. Finally, a young man pointed to an area where a group of people were gathered and responded, "Belgrade." I waited there for some time until a station wagon came by. After a few confusing exchanges and help from the young man, I got a ticket and was on the bus. It was a strange feeling not being able to speak with people in a common language, but liberating to interact with feelings, gestures and eyes. My friend, I never got his name, was a student at the University of Belgrade and was going to Hungry to buy supplies for his family. Not long after we started our trip we stopped at a border station and the guard peeked inside, gesturing that we could go.

The frigid night on the bumpy, dirt roads caused discomfort for most of our trip, but that didn't stop me from passing out for a few hours. We arrived in Belgrade early in the morning. The bus dropped us off at a piazza and a taxi then took me to the conference site where I united with my team. It was obvious that they were also in shock after their trip to Belgrade. The reality was much darker than any of us could imagine. We were witnessing lifeless, hopeless, and desperate people amongst destruction where there once stood a vibrant city filled with kind, caring, and loving people. This moment in history gave us a glimpse of the human capability to destroy the self and others.

I wanted to scream, but what would that have accomplished? I felt hopeless just like them. On the other hand, looking to the students of the University of Belgrade put fire in my belly and gave me faith. They were the hope in this terrible circumstance, working tirelessly to send a message to the rest of the world that they were alive and no war could destroy their spirit or creativity. My team and I decided to do a performance/installation before our departure to thank our hosts and show them that we stood with them in solidarity.

I recalled a story I was told by my mother based on the allegory of the long spoons. The source of the story is unknown and has become part of the folklore of different cultures. It is an inspiring story about how the survival of humanity is about caring and loving the other, which fit the moment and place we were in.

We selected a space in the sugar factory, which felt like a nave. The space was about 80 feet long, 30 feet wide, and 30 feet high. Its central part was the perfect stage for our installation. We used the debris of the dismantled factory machinery to construct the base for a 30-foot table. Meanwhile, we'd collect branches from the trees around the factory and with the borrowed spoons from the cafeteria we'd build the long spoons. The PROJEKT X organizers offered to provide the food and wine, which was greatly appreciated. The event was taking place on the night of our departure. We sent the invitation to a group of friends and new people we'd connected with, then set the table with goulash, bottles of local wine, and bread. Everyone met at a gathering spot in the courtyard where we blindfolded them and tied a spoon to each of their hands. We'd then guide them into a queue. After everyone was ready we led them into the dining space, lit with hundreds of candles, and positioned them on opposite sides of the table. Once everyone was in their position, we removed their eye covers, thanked them for their participation, and instructed them to help themselves to the food and wine we had made especially for them. It didn't take long before the first person used their spoon to feed someone on the opposite site, and immediately after the event took off.

The message was clear. As members of a global community, we need each other and we need to take care of one another if we want a better world for ourselves and future generations. Like most messages we need reminders now and then. In those few hours we all connected spiritually and hoped for a better world. Then our transportation was ready to take us to the border. After saying goodbye to our friends and team of organizers we got into the station wagon and as we were getting farther away from the sugar factory, the reality of the war-damaged country resurfaced like a nightmare. We were stopped a few times by the military guards and our passports were checked. We didn't say much during the trip as we were all processing the intense experience we just had.

The original fable goes like this: A woman dies and is going to be sent to Heaven. The day finally arrives when her guardian angel appears to take her. On their way to Heaven, they pass by Hell's gate and the woman asks if she can visit. Her angel gives her permission and they enter. She is astonished to see a beautiful field with fruit trees, milk and honey running through the streams, and the sun shining. It was divine, unlike anything she has ever seen. Finally, they approach the dinner table in the center of the field. She can hardly believe her eyes. Before her is an incredible setup with vegetables, fruits, and foods of every kind. She is perplexed and can't understand how it is that Hell could be so fantastic. Then she sees people making their way to the table. They are famished, exhausted, with faces full of sadness and bitterness. Strangely enough, she notices that there are long spoons tied to their hands. She keeps asking her angel, "Why? Why are these people, with all that surrounds them, are they so miserable?" The angel's reply is to wait and see for herself. The people keep arriving from left and right and try to start eating, but their long spoons don't allow for the food to reach their mouths. They try to throw the food in the air and to catch it with their widened jaws, but are ultimately unsuccessful. The woman is saddened and asks her angel if they can leave. Once they leave, they make their way to the gates of Heaven. The woman is even more surprised when she notices that Heaven resembles Hell to every detail. Everything is replicated. Even the same table with the same food. She sees people arriving from all directions, but something is different. The people are a lot healthier and a lot happier, even with the same spoons attached to their hands. To the woman's astonishment, she watches everyone sit down to eat, observing them using their spoons to feed each other from opposites sides of the table.
(The above story has been paraphrased from an ancient Iranian fable.)

Introduction
by Claude Parent

CLAUDE
PARENT
ARCHITECTE

Bons voeux

Je pense à vous.

à Michele SAEE et à Erozge.
Depuis L. A. j'ai choisi mon camp.

L. A.

Michele Saee first rubbed elbows with architecture when he was a very young man in Italy. He graduated with a Masters of Art in Architecture from the University of Florence complimenting Persian roots with a European art education.

By 1981, Italy had already given up on rational architecture. A long time had passed since Frank Lloyd Wright, with his love of the organic, had passed through Rome and Venice in the company of Bruno Zevi and working with the likes of Superstudio Michele was infected with the aggressive virus of the moment's rebellious modernity.

With a post-graduate degree in urban studies from the Polytechnic Institute of Milan in 1982, Michele took his notoriously probative nature to Los Angeles and began his work with Morphosis, a firm strongly committed to research in avant-garde architecture.

Student life had equipped the young architect with two major assets: his critical sense and an appetite for invention. It was a time when a mixture of Michele's own extreme sensitivity and consistently poetic solutions combined with his academic background. The result: an explosive combination requiring careful handling.

The temptation of an academic career eventually led him to take up teaching, first at the Otis College of Art and Design in 1986, and then in 1990 at the Southern California Institute of Architecture (SCI-Arc). Despite the prestige these positions afforded, the opportunity to meet some of the greatest architects of the time, and the pleasure and intellectual support he took away from it, I, nonetheless ponder what may have been lost for a maker of Michele's caliber by these diversions.

In spite of his work at this time, evidence of the embarkation of a deeply sensitive individual's dream to reconcile the interweaving of Eastern, Latin and American cultures.

Combining his education and experimental nature with a style that could be described as "out of control," Michele began to assert his ability to manifest radical work where "architecture is part of daily life and architectural production is the reflection of our needs, our desires, and our capacity to improve the quality of our relationships through our creativity and taste for adventure."

My initial admiration of his work led us to a confusing mix of English, French, and Italian that no one else could ever understand, which gave way to an exchange and acknowledgment of our primal truths and essential commitments.

The impact of his magnificent models and drawings revealed to me a fabulous imagination, and, the confluence of our ideas on architecture inspired in me a sense of total support and commitment. The overlapping of languages ultimately allowed us to seal our friendship with a type communication freed from the shackles of analytically understanding. After exhausting ourselves for hours attempting to understand one another, his projects, full of emotion and mystery, finally revealed themselves.

Let us now consider some impression's of the work of Michele Saee (both built and un-built) while leaving aside the cognizant language of critical analysis so that we may drift into a sort of daydream.

I have four impressions of Michele and his work. First: There is a gap between the discourse and the actual project. This gap is penetrated by a basic poetic element and a limitless imagination. Second: close-up, the permanent image of frozen waterfalls appear, as if the physical element had been stopped in its trajectory at a specific moment in time. This was Michele's impulsive decision. Third: all projects have traces of geological layers that give his architecture an almost monumental dimension and morphology similar to a landscape or relief. The last impression, and by no means the least, is the permanence of the staged movement of spaces and surfaces in order to attain a constant vision of imbalance. We must never forget that Michele Saee is by birth and education a child of instability and continuity.

Finally let's look at his "Publicis Drugstore" on the Champs Elysees, facing the Arc de Triomphe in Paris. From the start it seemed like an impossible task: to preserve Pierre Dufau's rigid, cubic building, while making changes to the building's surface, and keeping the workers and the businesses going inside during remodeling. One cannot dream of a more dangerous project. I would have refused to do it. But Michele was courageous and readily embarked on this impossible manifesto. Because the employees refused to lose even the slightest amount of natural lighting, the building's surface had to remain totally transparent, with no material effect of partial opacity, not even printed patterns. He chose to install a dynamic system that enveloped the original cube, a sort of intense tornado whose whirling volumes are so present that they succeed in replacing the older building despite their transparency. This basic confrontation is made subject to the sun, clouds, and the world passing by—at any moment, the building appearance subject to the whims of changing weather. Along with this acquiescence to visual elements in a continual flux, one must more readily accept an inevitable haziness in interpretation.

Yesterday, on a typical gray day for the Ile de France, I saw the Publicis Drugstore as a sail in sky-tones stretched taut by the wind. Walking up the Champs Elysees, one can choose either to become immersed as a part of the composition or to chart a path to best take in the spirals of glass and steel. To love this project you need to taste it, choose your favorite angles, become involved with it and conjure up your own imagination without any apprehension.

Claude Parent
May 26, 2006

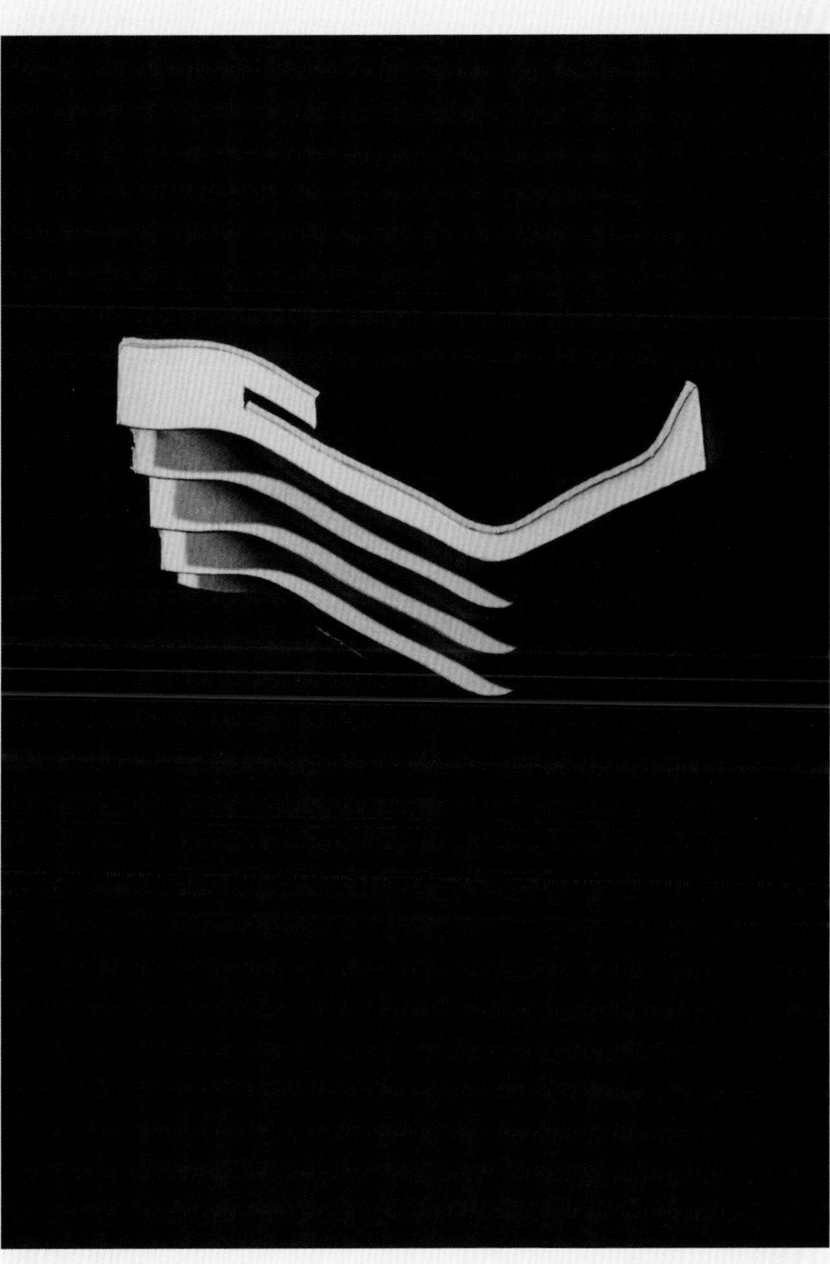

LIFE'S WORK, WORK PROCESS, AND PHILOSOPHY BY MICHELE SAEE

I started writing this book long before I actually started writing it. The experience of putting it together in its current form has been a fluid, emotional, and educational exercise in life, love, work, and architecture, providing a tool of growth for me. It has encouraged the exploration of a lifetime full of great experiences, and discoveries. Everything with a beginning has an end, and another end, and another. The design process is never-ending as long as one continues to discover and transform every day. The changes may be un-noticeable most of the time but are cumulative.

I have been blessed to be surrounded by my loving family, friends, and colleagues for the last 30-something years since I started my own studio. I will continue in this process as long as I am able in every way. This work is no longer an extension of who I am or what I do; it is me in every form and shape: my body (machine), my soul (Socrates), and everything in my life's path is a part of it.

I cherish the moments I spend in my studio designing and drawing, making the simplest and the most complex works of design. In my mind there is no difference. There is a timeline in this book that attempts to define a sequence of events but in reality I believe I am working on a lifetime project and that each experience is just another piece of a puzzle which leads me to the next. *Ars longa, Vita brevis:* "Art is long, life is short" (Hippocrates) gives meaning to this claim.

LE CORBUSIER

GAUDI

The work I have been involved in up 'til now is my life's work (or my work's life) and has been honest and pure in every way.

I have come to believe that the profession I admire and respect is misunderstood for a variety of reasons but also that it is the most noble of all. We practitioners are passionately involved in the practice of providing service in a profession that is extremely complex, broad, and time-consuming, with self-gratification, for the most part, being the best form of compensation. Our small community works hard for most of their lives to produce meaningful work that may never be understood by the general public and perhaps not even appreciated.

I believe in architecture as a part of everyday **LIFE,** and that the work of architecture reflects our needs, our desires, and our ability to improve the quality of our relationships with creativity and adventure. The work you see in this collection should convey those beliefs.

A number of recurring concepts have been developed and processed in my work, some of which continue to become fundamental elements of the work. Perhaps most significant is the role of **BODY** as form and as content in the contemplation and making of architecture. This theme has been developing in my work over the last three decades and its expression has evolved and transformed. The path from body as a function or tool with which one could inform the space taking shape (Le Corbusier 's machine); to body as the inspiration for architectural form (Gaudi); to the body's form directly translated into architectural space (Gaetano Pesce); and, finally, the body of the maker (architect) taking over and becoming the architectural space (Saee, Golzari House). The discovery of the maker's body or the rediscovery of the need for the architect to become physically involved was not a new concept but the degree to which it is important and critical has been advanced in my work. I witnessed how the work's vision

GAETANO PESCE

GOLZARI HOUSE

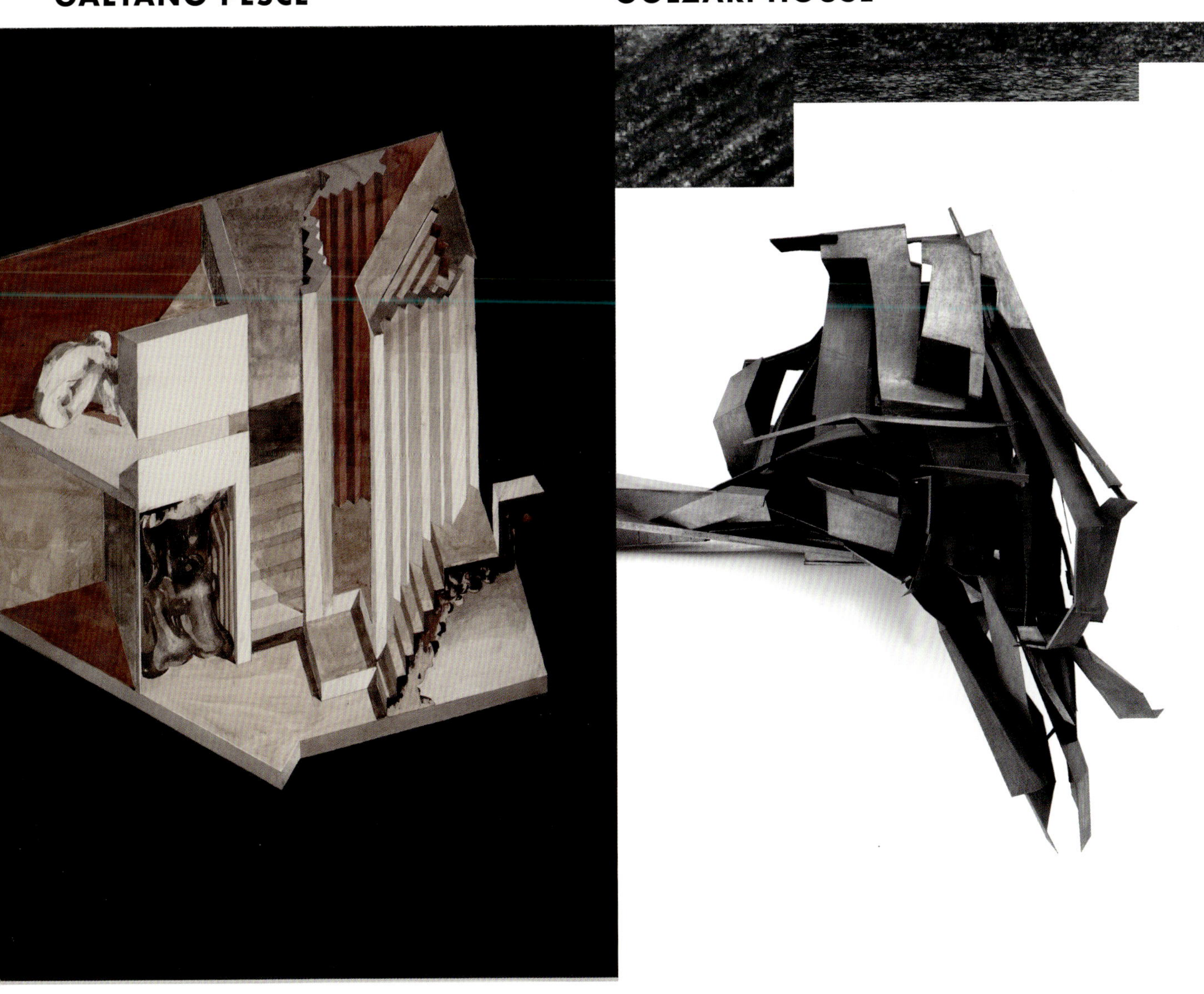

is crucial in its development and the necessity of having a personal involvement with the work.

More and more I believe that whether we automate production or make things with our hands, we produce with the body in mind. The body, ever familiar to itself, communicates to the world in a comparative way. It seeks relationships—positioning itself in terms of rank and scale in pursuit of fulfilling its needs and desires.

A few experiments helped me to understand this concept better. Two were installations, the first an event in a house by architect Paul Revere William housing an art exhibition, "Art Works For Children," where my team and I used our hands and bodies to shape half-inch steel rods into the exhibition space; and second, with the students of Florida A&M in Tallahassee, where we constructed a gathering space on the campus using a four-foot-wide role of 16 gage galvanized sheet metal shaped by using our hands and bodies. An entire process of body learning and body making was integrated into the design. The learning had its own trajectory but the architecture was immediate and the procedure informed us about the necessary degree of one's involvement for making honest architecture. The sensibility and degree of involvement, together with broader concepts based on scale, size, and the particular forms of involvement depended on the types of projects I envisioned. It was clear that this was a conceptual investigation but at the same time it hinted at very fundamental issues involved in the architectural process, in which collaboration is most important.

The concepts of **CITY and CONTEXT** have been other significant interests in my work, specifically how the environment informs the architecture of the space and vice versa. Like other living phenomena, context is a dynamic part of life and in constant

ARTWORK

FLORIDA A&M IN TALLAHASSEE

transformation. I have questioned the power of historicism since my architectural studies in Florence and wondered how the Florence of Superstudio would look if they were given the opportunity to create the contemporary context of a more cosmopolitan Italian city. In a way we can see what it would be like by referring to the work of the architects they inspired, like Rem Koolhaas and many more.

I have long been fascinated with the formation of cities as modes of production and our desires for co-habitation. Unfortunately, most of the modern urban models of the last half century have been disastrous.

The tendencies toward automated production and other technological movements demonstrate movement away from direct bodily interaction. This becomes more apparent when these devices are put in the service of seeking and expanding "market" for "consumer" goods. It is important to be aware of the self-consciousness we tend to exhibit toward technology. The sophistication with which we create patterns and systems in our cities solely for the consumption of products, especially "information" products, trick us into thinking this is a creative activity. A generic character begins to evolve in many of our cities as well as the objects and relationships that surround us. We can become seduced by a market culture as if it were an actual human being. Conversely, in my work the buildings and projects foreground some principle issues—about the body, as well as the projection of our bodies into the forms of our cities, and about the city as an entity of body itself.

CITY AND CONTEXT

I'm also focused on the role of **MEMORY** in architectural investigation, and how our perceptions of space, form, and function are linked to our experiences past, present, and future. Memory becomes the indication of the urban synthesis. I believe the memory of space is the most powerful construct in our lives that is the life of the environments we build or occupy. It is perhaps needless to say that we are in some ways products of the environments we live in and that they influence and affect us at the psychological, emotional, and physical levels of our being, which has everlasting influences in the way we live, produce, interact, select, and identify. From the moment we step into this world we occupy a space, an environment, and we are part of a community or city until we die; therefore, we both influence and are influenced by the forms and spaces we live in, projecting our perception and our vision of the world we inherited onto the next generation.

Everything takes form, even infinity.

Formal opposition is incapable of remaining calm.

The need for exploration and **EXPERIMENTATION** is another fundamental element in the making of my work. Ideas need to be challenged at every stage of their development, with boundaries examined and re-established so as to inch forward into insecure territories of experimentation. There is too often acceptance for repeating the same ideas, often due to lack of time or because of other limitations.

But our body and mind, our environment, and our livelihood depends on trying to challenge the status quo in order to grow and to improve the conditions we are struggling with everywhere in the world. This constant reaching out for something new can lead us into the unknown territories of discovery. The results will be mixed but ultimately we will uncover things that will help us grow and discover the tools we need to improve of the lives of all living creatures.

The 1960s and 70s avant-garde movements' visions and experiments are today's realities. We continue to examine concepts of controlling the environment through design, and reshaping our future through technology and the development toward new ways of inhabiting the planet, all of which have cultural, artistic, social, and political consequences. Unfortunately, as architects and designers, we are trapped in the middle of a powerful consumer society run by those who can turn architecture and any other design product into commodities and consumer goods. Opposing this reality is our ethical position as architects wanting to create meaningful work for the people.

COLLABORATION in the process of making architecture is inevitable, and navigating this territory requires a masterful ability to give different members of each team the space they need to breathe and accomplish their work. There are not two projects, two sites, two cities, or two people who are "the same," and it requires generosity of spirit and humility to accept that you don't know everything. You can't know everything about everything but you have to learn how to create a unifying language for a vision in order to realize a project and to make meaningful architecture.

Nothing is possible without **DISCIPLINE and HARD WORK!** The creative process takes time to develop and I have learned from personal experience and witnessing others that there is never a shortcut available. It is laborious and taxing and requires a serious commitment, work ethic, experience, effort, energy, vision, perseverance, and more.

TEACHING has been an important part of my architectural experience. I always loved school and I always wanted to teach. In Florence, where I studied architecture, the schools of architecture and fine arts (Belle Arti) shared some buildings in the city. The school was spread around the city, which required us to walk through the city going from one class to the next. I realized many years later what a great experience it was to learn about the history, architecture, city, and culture by walking the city and observing its finest attributes. Teaching was a great tool for me to stay current regarding the architectural discourse of the time and challenged me to question my ideological and architectural process. Schools of architecture are the sanctuaries for those resisting to sell their souls to the developers who do not care about the value of architecture and are willing to do everything in their power to increase their profit margins.

The **PROFESSION** of an architect is complex and laborious, which requires one to be engaged in the entire practice at every level. As far as I am concerned, architecture is about the entire process and the architect's expression and awareness are evident in every single work they touch. Individual experience, knowledge and memories guide our perceptions regarding the poetics of transformative qualities in our environment. Through seeing, making begins. The way of seeing invariably shapes the invention even though our capability to see is in direct relationship to our awareness of what we are seeing, our mental model of the world.

The design **PROCESS** is the product of a thought, an intention, and a desire to explore; but the process of making and seeing those thoughts in practice leads us to understand the reality of life and ourselves. In a certain way the process is even more important than the product. Designing and making architecture does not require a formula. Today we have lost our relationship with the spaces we live in. Our intimate and behavioral necessities are no longer involved in forming and making those spaces. Consequently, we need to alter our way of thinking in order to re-learn to see things inside out and inside in instead of relying on pre-programed software to do that for us.

I believe that the most important architectural **TOOLS** are pencil and paper. How can I express how I feel about something that is so fundamentally a part of architecture: **THE DRAWING**. I am always thinking through and about architecture, dissecting the methods and processes we use to bring architecture into being, and drawing and writing those notions into my sketchbooks. Sketching, re-sketching, and re-sketching, and on and on until it starts to talk back and has a life of its own, until my hands and heart can respond to its voice. This may sound like a romantic notion but to me it is very real. The complexity of architectural space requires real human interaction, real commitment, and passion in order to become useful and successful. The other important tool in my design process is building **MODELS**. The three-dimensional drawing takes a new form and jumps out from the paper. The pieces get shaped by the body. The material is shaped, cut, bent, cursed, and painted—varying intensities emerge. Like the drawing, every sketch model leads to the next and to new discoveries, with a range of potential readings revealed. These

MEMORY ANTIQUE

Experimentation
Shakespearian theater

are one-of-a-kind pieces that could only have been constructed in the way they were. They're traces of the body left in the work. This record of sketches and models begins to define a concept in development.

The use of technology as tools developed for architectural design is in its infancy, and most of what we have used in the last three decades was originally developed for industrial production. This has not stopped us from experimenting with them, with mixed results. Our culture's fascination with technology, evident in the results, seems to be more a fascination with the object of the technology itself rather than how our lives are affected.

In the process of making, the body learns. When something works we repeat it and expand upon it. Mutation emerges. Ideas develop threads, and some lead to other possibilities and some may be abruptly abandoned. The body gets tired and feels the pain of this process. The skin gets cut, muscles become sore.

The waves of transformation brought by technological advancements cause us to accept the idea that the traditional role of the human being in our cities has been excluded. Yet ultimately the body is the space which joins the electronic and physical space of the city. The aspects of urban living that we become nostalgic about rarely disappear completely, rather they shift and accommodate. Unchanged, others will fade away. But their influences remain, in some places completely and in others through traces and memories.

Collections of memories and experiences act within us. Through our bodies they appear as a single existence and emerge in what we produce, whether we intend them to or not. The work claims the signature of the maker, where these inspired points converge.

THE DRAWING

PUBLICIS

The architecture of this work betrays my attempts to take notice of the realities, agents, and interlocking systems reflected in the urban experience that creates its form and materiality, its sensory qualities, events and occurrences. Such an attitude allows us to think of form and space as a dynamic rather than static phenomena, as that which is more defined than liquid yet less defined than solid.

Achieving this state is an emergent process, reliant on the non-linear interaction of its generation for the final outcome of its form. The design involves an investigation of factors found in the larger condition of the environment in which it is contained. The site, a collection of elements in process, develops at its own rate and exists in various states as a living organisms rather than objects.

The site dynamics of the Publicis headquarters on the Champs Elysees in Paris, or Template house in a tower building development on the second ring of Beijing, or the 149-unit Tahiti apartments along the Pacific Ocean in the Marina Del Rey area of Los Angeles are very different sites. Certainly we cannot rely on the same type of investigation about the city or context to address their needs but the degree of involvement, visioning approach and sensibilities required to search for the right inspiration was quite the same.

For the Publicis building the site's history and complexity was overwhelming: its location on a corner lot across from the Arc de Triomphe was intimating. On the second ring around the Arc, in the most historic areas of Paris and fronting on one of the busiest streets in the world, the corner of the building demanded acknowledgment. The movements of the current of people, bicycles, and cars in a circle and up and down the Champs Elysees formed a dynamic swirling vortex, a geometrical veil on the building that interacts with the surroundings. The transformed building doesn't look like the buildings

TEMPLATE HOUSE

TAHITI MARINA APARTMENTS

around it but it feels in its correct place in time, and connected to many other buildings in Paris and other places in the world.

Architecture for every project has its own way of defining its connection with its context. The context as a living organism has to get involved in the process of design, which at one level requires analysis of the physical, historical, social, economic, and political conditions of the site, which could be related to or in contrast with those elements based on the analysis. On another level the architecture may introduce mechanisms based on its design necessities, which transforms the context in a fundamental way. The Publicis project was such a proposal and the first radical transformation in the city of Paris since the Pompidou Center. This proposal was conceptualized with the assistance of city officials and their support to making the first step in transforming the Champs Elysees area.

The Template House in Beijing was designed and built in just three months for the occasion of the first architectural Biennial in China. We designed a building inside a building inside another one, which was on the seventh floor of a high-rise tower development. You could have not been more removed from the context of the city than in this project but that would have been a simplistic approach because the real context was our perception of a more specific framework of cultural history that focuses on the detailed, textured viewed from within.

In contrast or reaction to the nature of the context, I imagined a living environment that serves as a place of escape; a quiet, contemplative oasis in the midst of Beijing's tumultuous racing modern growth. The design for the interior was developed in two parts; the outer container, which was the existing concrete building, and the inner container, which was entirely built out of wood like a secondary skin defining areas of the program and activities.

The site and context of the Tahiti Marina apartments is an interesting phenomena in any urban setting. The "mud flats," as they were called, is claimed land and a 19th-century real estate speculator's vision to convert wetlands into lucrative development where the land is leased by the county to the developers in a profit-sharing agreement.

The buildings in this area were speculative boxes in contrast to their amazing site. Surprisingly, in our building, some of the well-positioned units there were windowless closets or bathrooms facing the Pacific Ocean, instead of better positioned living or bedrooms. When we realized that the context is the Pacific Ocean and not the thoughtless boxes on the site or in its surroundings we were liberated to define the architecture and the future context of the area.

In the current state of architecture, the urban environment and the arrangement of the design elements are no longer hierarchical. What informs the architecture of one building may be influenced from another part of the planet. What once was an expression or manifestation of a common language is now irrelevant and meaningless. The boundaries between elements are blurred. The spaces are open and flexible, not fully defined but not undefined either. Their divisions are established by the tension between various activities which could occur in them. All these elements are contained by an exterior envelope which could be described as its starting and its ending. Ultimately, the success of the design is the reflection in its form of the inherently interconnected, pliant, and dynamic process that goes into its creation, very much like the city itself.

To enjoy all that is presented to us through our existence, we have to examine our world and touch and be touched in profound ways. This process can become the generator not only of the tools and methods employed, but also the program to which they are applied. A reconstruction of perceptual and conceptual tools and methods yields a medium for thought—often contemplative, at best mysterious and unpredictable. In order to become more simply human we must address the boundaries that we create and are presented with. What one sees is the emergence of a whole field of questions, both strange and familiar.

COINCIDENCES & ACCIDENTS 1981–1985

The Beginning
[Taking Chances]

A series of coincidences and connections led me to meet with architect Alessandro Magris, one of the five members of Superstudio (Adolfo Natalini, Christiano Toraldo di Francia, Gian Piero Frassinelli, Roberto Magris, and Alessandro Magris) and later work there for two years.

I met philosopher Fons Elders and his two sons in Florence in 1982 one Sunday afternoon by chance when he was looking for architect Piero Frasinelli on his way from India to Amsterdam and I was the only one in the office that day. It became a life changing event for all of us.

Fons was planning a competition for a housing project in Amsterdam and he was inviting Superstudio and Rem Koolhaas to participate.

1981–1983 SUPERSTUDIO

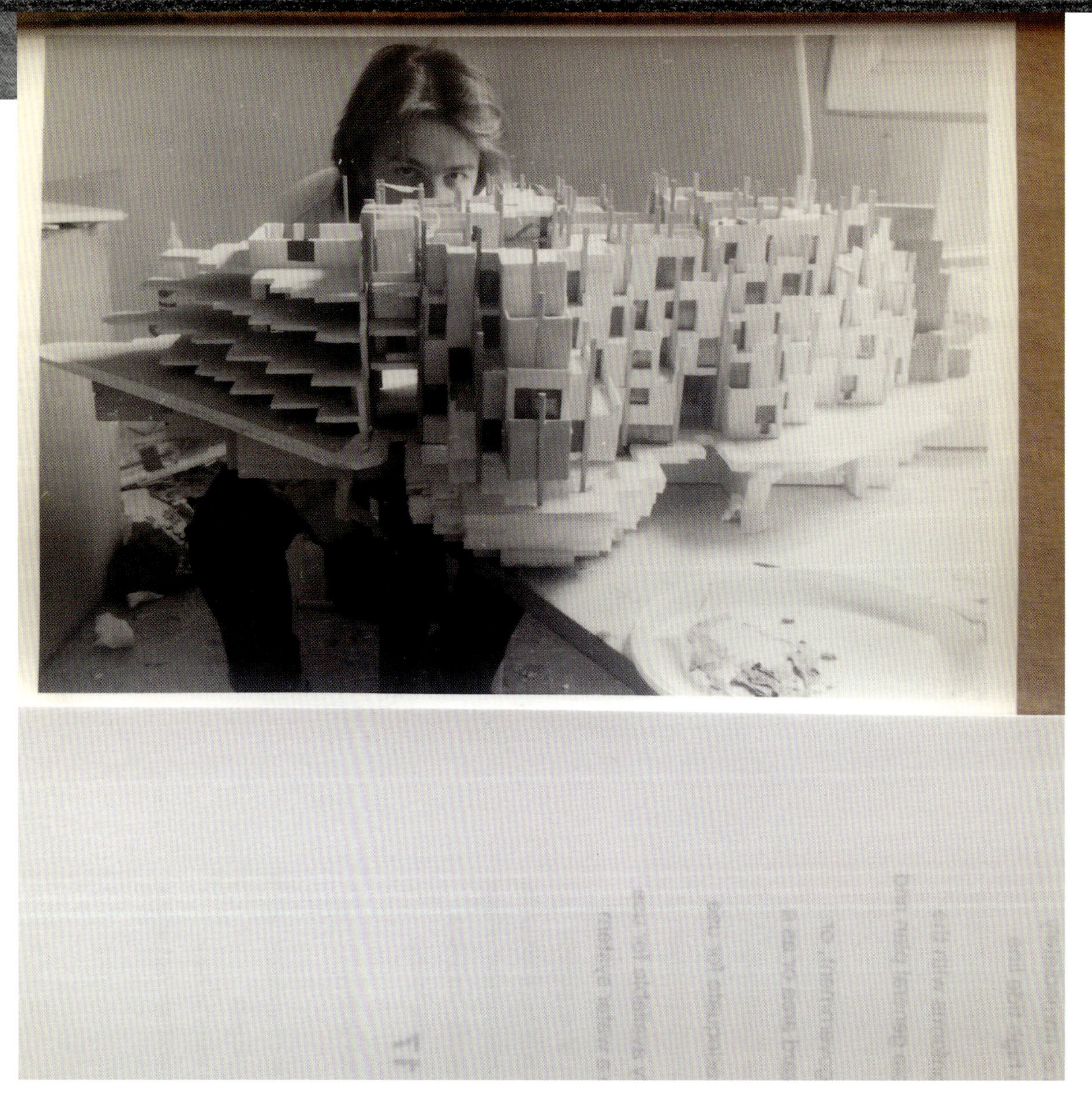

I told Piero the surprising news the next morning, which was received with skepticism when I insisted on setting up the meeting, and that we had nothing to lose.

-

I collaborated with Piero on the House of Four Winds and we won the competition. Later it was built.

I met philosopher **Fons Elders**

I walked into the Morphosis (Thom Mayne, Michael Rotondi) office, which was one of the five places I would have liked to work in Los Angeles, and felt it was the kind of place I wanted to make for myself one day. The other studios on my list were Gehry, Moss, Hodgetts/Mangurian, and Moore.

-

My interview with Thom Mayne became exciting when he saw my big role of ink drawings from Florence. He was fascinated with my previous employer, the legendary Superstudio.

-

Their energy was contagious and directness refreshing.

-

There were a few people and projects at the office and no need for an extra hand since an army of enthusiastic SCI-Arc students were ready to move in.

-

I didn't take the light rejection seriously and within a few weeks I was working there.

-

Morphosis was kind of like my post-graduate study in the U.S. and my introduction to Los Angeles.

I met **Evan Kleiman,** photographer **Marvin Rand,** lighting designer **Saul Goldin,** structural engineer **Miguel Castillo,** and steel fabricator **John McCoy**

1983–1985 MORPHOSIS

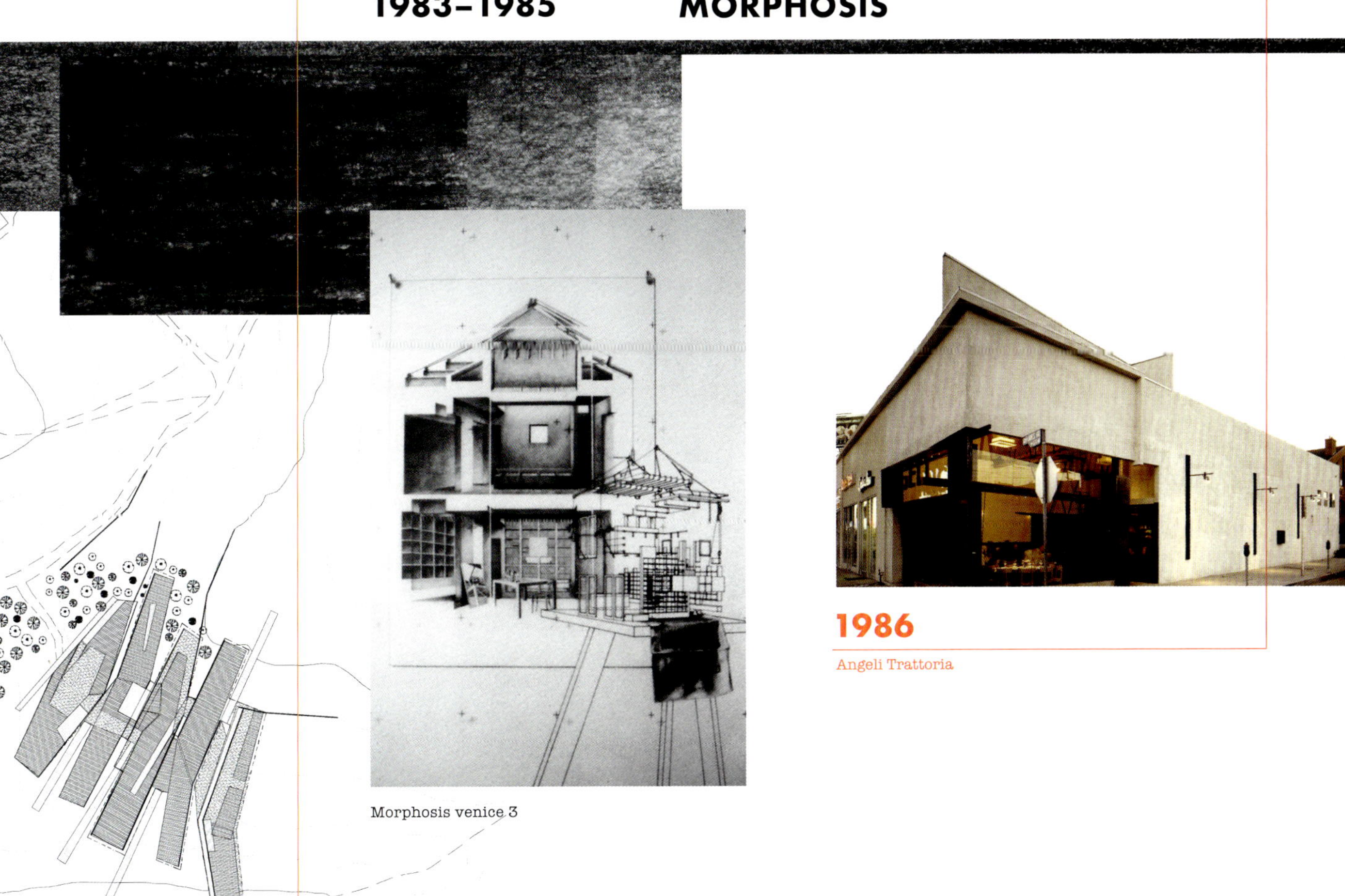

Morphosis venice 3

1986

Angeli Trattoria

2000

Hermes

ON MY OWN 1985

I needed to move on.

-

I rented my first studio on Washington Blvd., across the street from what used to be the historic Ebony Showcase Theater. I took over the lease from artist Arnold Meshes as he was moving to New York.

-

I started teaching at OTIS PARSONS.

BUILDING STUDIO

This project was inspired by the Venice houses of Morphosis; transforming an existing house with an addition in the backyard.

-

The compositional elements are fragmented in an attempt to make the whole and to connect with the existing but a strong desire to create something new contradicted the "false" intention.

SPRECHER HOUSE

As the search for projects proved to be harder than I anticipated I decided to design and build a few things on my own.

-

The steel chair and coffee table led to an exhibition at Square One Gallery, which introduced me to great creative clients for the Ecru clothing store and Design Express furniture store.

CHAIR 1985, COFFEE TABLE

SPRECHER HOUSE
(First Official Commission)

Chair

Coffee Table

I HAD DIFFICULTIES SHEDDING INFLUENCES

The reality of doing everything and learning!

I discovered L.A. through the process of design and construction.

-

A layered city with hidden treasures.

-

It's about the attitude!

Hillside House proved to be more complex than I imagined.

1985–1986

ANGELI TATTORIA

1986

BORGEN STREET HOUSE

I was hands-on, very involved in every part of the design and construction process.

-

I met many great craftspeople.

-

Architecture as a sign of an identity.

-

Los Angeles's iconic architecture.

Twenty-unit apartment building.

-

Learning the legal process.

1986–1987 ECRU MELROSE

1986–1989 434 APARTMENTS

L.A. the melting pot.

-

Introducing a Japanese fusion restaurant into the context of Los Angeles.

-

Learning about life through architecture.

1987

CAPITAINE (RESTAURANT)

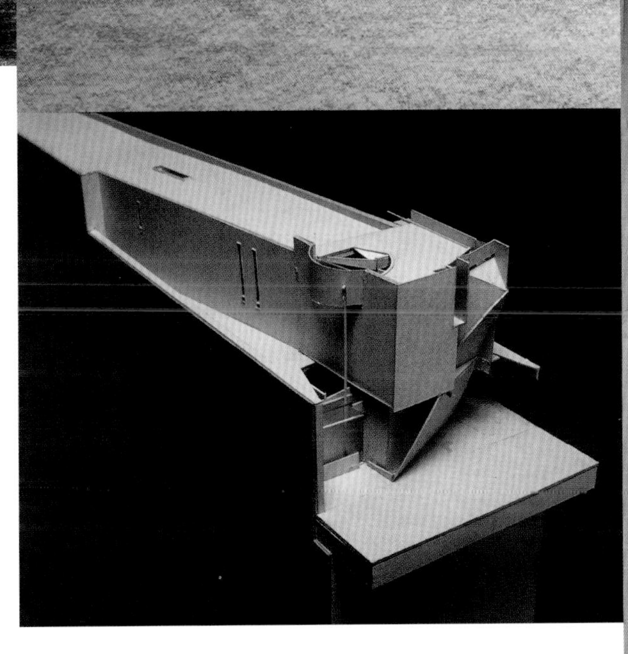

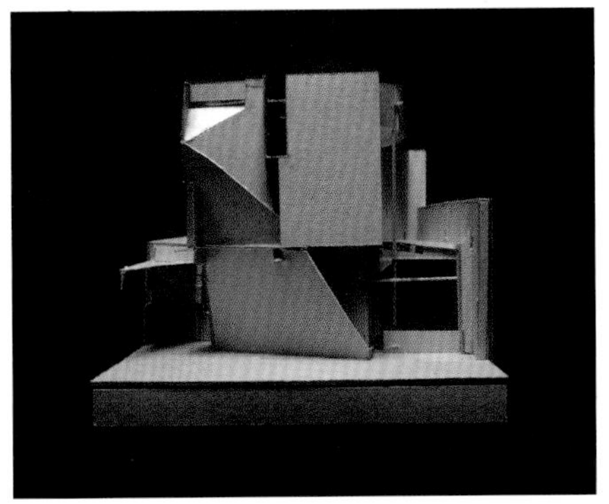

It was a great experience working with Michael Chapman, cinematographer of classic movies like *Raging Bull* and *Jaws*, and Amy Jones, screenwriter of *Mystic Pizza*.

The large industrial building was transformed to accommodate the human scale to display contemporary furniture and objects.

-

Body and space challenge.

1988

CHAPMAN JONES HOUSE

DESIGN EXPRESS

We sometimes need to hold onto concepts that define our identity.

-

For the Sun family Fung Shui made the connection they needed to their Korean origins.

1989 SUN HOUSE

BODY, ESSAY BY NICK GILLOCK, 1990

There is a quiet manifesto in the work of Michele Saee, which reverberates with violent consequence the deeper we trace it. It resonates at a frequency that is only audible if we assume the uncomfortable stance of questioning our basic assumptions and the deep cultural tradition that precedes them. The gentle nature of these disruptions is a reflection of life and the work which brought them about as a natural consequence of their evolution. The catalyst of this evolution in my work is the transformative relationship with the concept of body. The *body* with regard to architecture and architectural production can and should be understood as a complex matrix of philosophical, physical, and definitional relationships.

The body of the architect as the physical inspiration for architectural production.

The constructed body (physicality) of the building.

The body as a functional entity: for the occupant to be accommodated by the body of the building.

Each of these instances of *body* is interrelated through the activity of architecture to every other. The specific nature of these inter-relationships and their interactions is largely determined by how we choose to understand the constitution and definition of *body*.

Western intellectual cannon fundamentally assumes the Cartesian dualism between the *body* and *mind/soul*. It is crucial to understand the deep consequences of this assumption. Plato uses the impending death of Socrates in the Phaedo Dialogue to explore and expand the philosophical implications of the dialectic. Plato writes how Socrates steered his disciples along a series of philosophical arguments

and rebuttals, establishing a series of dichotomous relationships between the rational concepts of body and soul:

body - soul
dependent - independent
variable - constant
visible - invisible
mortal - divine
unintelligible - intelligible
contaminated - pure

The body and soul are thus estranged; established as discreet and opposing components, which combine in earthly life to constitute every human being. The body is objectified as a physical mechanism, which simultaneously enables the exploration of the soul and is itself an object of exploration. These latent assumptions to this day remained foundational, and largely unquestioned throughout the formation of architectural discourse within Western culture.

Le Corbusier is perhaps most responsible for introducing the body/soul dialectic into the fabric of modern architecture. He establishes this dialectic with respect to build/form, which in turn relates to humanity with the same implicit structure: the harmony (soul) of a structure (body) made evident with light (reason).

It is important to consider that Le Corbusier does not consider the body of the architect as having a significant role in the act of architectural production. He places the architect in a Platonically aloof position presuming that only the soul of the architect need be involved. The body is idealized within a series of modular proportional measures wherein the abstracted beauty of the human body is transposed as a mathematical grammar for his architecture.

The tradition continues in current speculation about the possibility that computer technology may finally make it possible for the soul/mind to escape into a world without the limitations

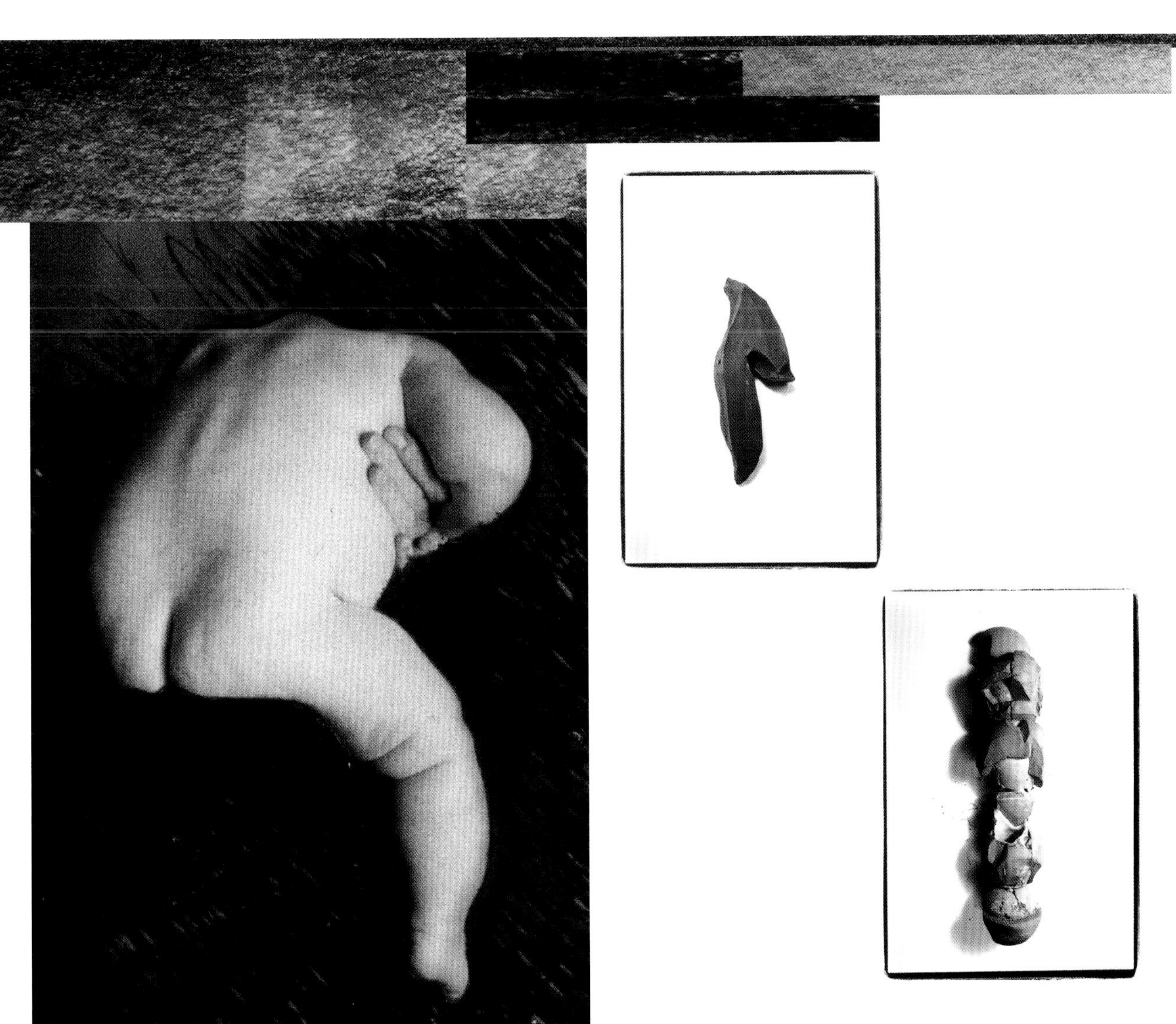

of the body. That in the words of Socrates, the soul might finally free itself of the shackles of the body.

With his 1964 postmodern manifesto *Complexity and Contradiction in Architecture* by Robert Venturi was one of the first to utilize architecture to attack this tradition in its inability to respond to the messier aspects of mass culture. Invoking the "proof of ultimate inconsistency in mathematics" by Godel and the "difficult poetry" of T.S. Elliot, Venturi seeks validation for: "forms that are impure rather than pure, compromising rather than clean, distorted rather than straight forward, ambiguous rather than articulated, allusive rather than simple, perverse rather than impersonal, accommodating rather than excluding."

Venturi advocates for the very things that fall outside of what Le Corbusier characterized as "an indefinable trace of the Absolute, which lies in the depths of our being," or in Cartesian terms, the Soul being unable to respond to the body's worldly creations.

The work of Michele Saee contained in this volume evolves toward a rupture of the body/soul dialectic, taking the discursive position that the body and soul are not separate, but are indivisible aspects of a single thing. Taking a position in architecture parallel to that which Nietzsche in *Thus Spoke Zarathustra* took with philosophy: "Behind your thoughts and feelings, my brother, there stands a mighty ruler, an unknown sage - whose name is self. In your body he dwells; he is your body. There is more reason in your body than in your best wisdom." It is this self with its implications and potentialities in contemporary culture and technology, which are the driving forces of Michele's work. It seems useful to explore the steps, which have lead up to this.

Phase I - The Modern Body

The human body is inescapably coded into the structure of all buildings. Functional concerns, ergonomics, and building code necessitate that the proportions of buildings always have an instrumental relationship to the needs of the human form. Keeping the Cartesian dialectic in mind, we can say that the body of the building has a synergistic relationship with the body of the occupant. The regime of functionalist modernism dictates that the form of the building should react (form following function) to the form of the human body. Arguing that the soul of the building and the soul of the occupant rarely have such an instrumental relation. The early work of this monograph is bound to and defined by these modernist conceptions. The body of the architect has not yet reached a state of active participation in the production of work. What pervades the work and the sketchbooks of this time is an exuberant fascination with the juxtaposition of the human form with architectural form, with a belief that the primary function of architecture is to accommodate the human body, and an obsessive fascination with the human body as a source of beauty, inspiration, and mystery.

Phase II - The Speaking Body

In Michele Saee's work as early as the ECRU Melrose project, an emerging interest in the important relationship between building form and content becomes evident. At the same time a focus on the body as a source of formal content and a growing interest in the ability of the body to convey certain latent meanings, becomes critical to the designs. Furthermore, these forms begin to establish resonant relationships with the human body, to transcend functionalist doctrine and rational explanation. In ECRU Melrose, an anthropomorphic vocabulary blends with the billboard like facades of previous projects creating a strong dialogue with the pedestrian as they pass by.

With ECRU Marina and Angeli Mare this vocabulary turns inward with each project becoming an occupiable organism. The inside of the projects in some sense becomes like the innards of a body. Each form becoming a mysterious and presumably integral organ of the building. In these projects we feel the body of the building striving to find an integration with its soul, the form responding to needs beyond the purely corporeal.

Phase III - The Body Works

In this third phase of the body of Michele's work, we find an architecture caught in the uncertainty of the present. An uncertainty composed of the residual debris of broken, but not discarded assumptions. The form-making process is now primarily concerned with the placement of the body of architecture to work. It is a time of struggling to find a new methodology of labor. Where the work began it confronted a dialectic of dialectics. Now it struggles to reconcile a triad of indivisible entities: the creative-body of the architect has joined the mind, and this new body is struggling to act in concert with the built-body and the served-body.

The work began as an unavoidable fascination; the inescapable seduction of form. A resonant expressiveness stretching beyond the realm of reason. Initially it was an exploration of the meanings contained in bodily form. The poetics of our most essential possession; our body. My body and your body. The struggle continues to resolve the question of how spaces in which the body and soul can inhabit simultaneously, inseparably, can be formulated. How can we release an imprisoned splendor trapped within, moving beyond what is merely plastic, visible, into a realm where the invisible becomes sensible?

(1/4/1997, re-edited 4/2/2019)

A research project questioning the current stage of work.

Personal exploration (therapeutic values)

-

Time of personal and professional uncertainty.

-

Wabi, a Japanese word meaning "lacking things, having things run entirely contrary to our desire, being frustrated in our wishes."

-

Individual resistance! I was finding my voice.

-

There were no more traces of the influences I have been trying to shed.

Time for the new!

-

I met Philippe Uzzan, an architect, thinker, and art and architecture gallery owner.

-

Meivsanah exhibited at Uzzan-Saddock Gallery in Paris.

1990 MEIVSANAH HOUSE

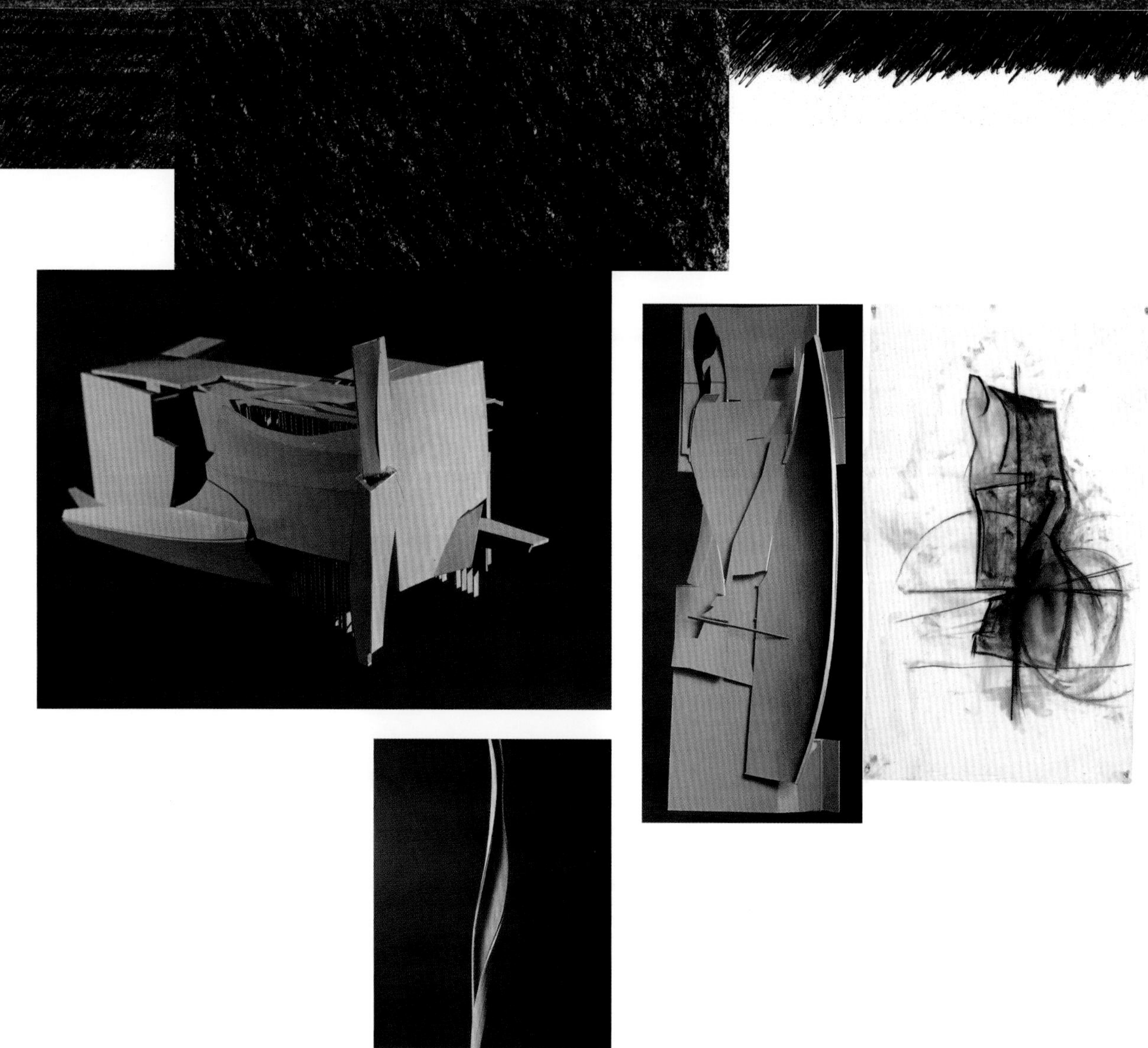

Expanding the role of the body in the form of the city is a form of resistance with optimism and hope.

The city's fictional memory becomes the inspiration for a new approach to reorganize and create a social urban space in place of a chaotic and existing urban element.

Murano glass.

PIAZZALE ROMA VENICE ITALY

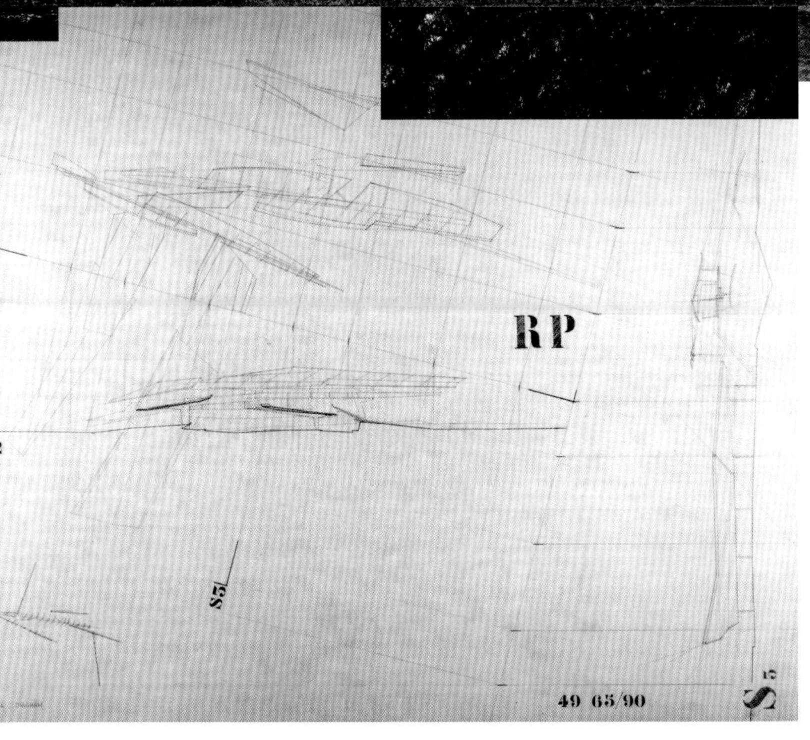

This projects and Angeli Mare were designed simultaneously and I tried to experiment with the concept of the body and space in very different ways. Ecru is a direct copy and Angeli is an interpretation of the body.

I was willing to take bigger risks.

-

What if the body in its form and concept becomes the space?

-

How does the body feel in the space, where not only the scale and proportions are directed by the body but its forms?

-

The template for the space and building section was generated from the sculpture figure of the Hindu deity Shiva.

1990 ECRU MARINA

The new Angeli was a combination of different notions of body, space, and ideas of interiority.

Found objects were created to provoke nostalgia from my personal connections to the Italian culture and architectural fascinations I had as a young man living and studying in Florence.

-

This was a new form of searching for my voice; elements were designed as a reconstructed wooden boat made for the entrance door; wine rack as a homage to Le Corbusier, or a bar shaped like Carlo Molino's nude woman collage.

-

The challenge of the project was to form a natural harmony among the obvious functional aspects of the design together with the research (my experimental hidden agenda).

-

The space of the mind can shape the experience of an architectural space in the way that its functional needs do.

1990–1991 ANGELI MARE

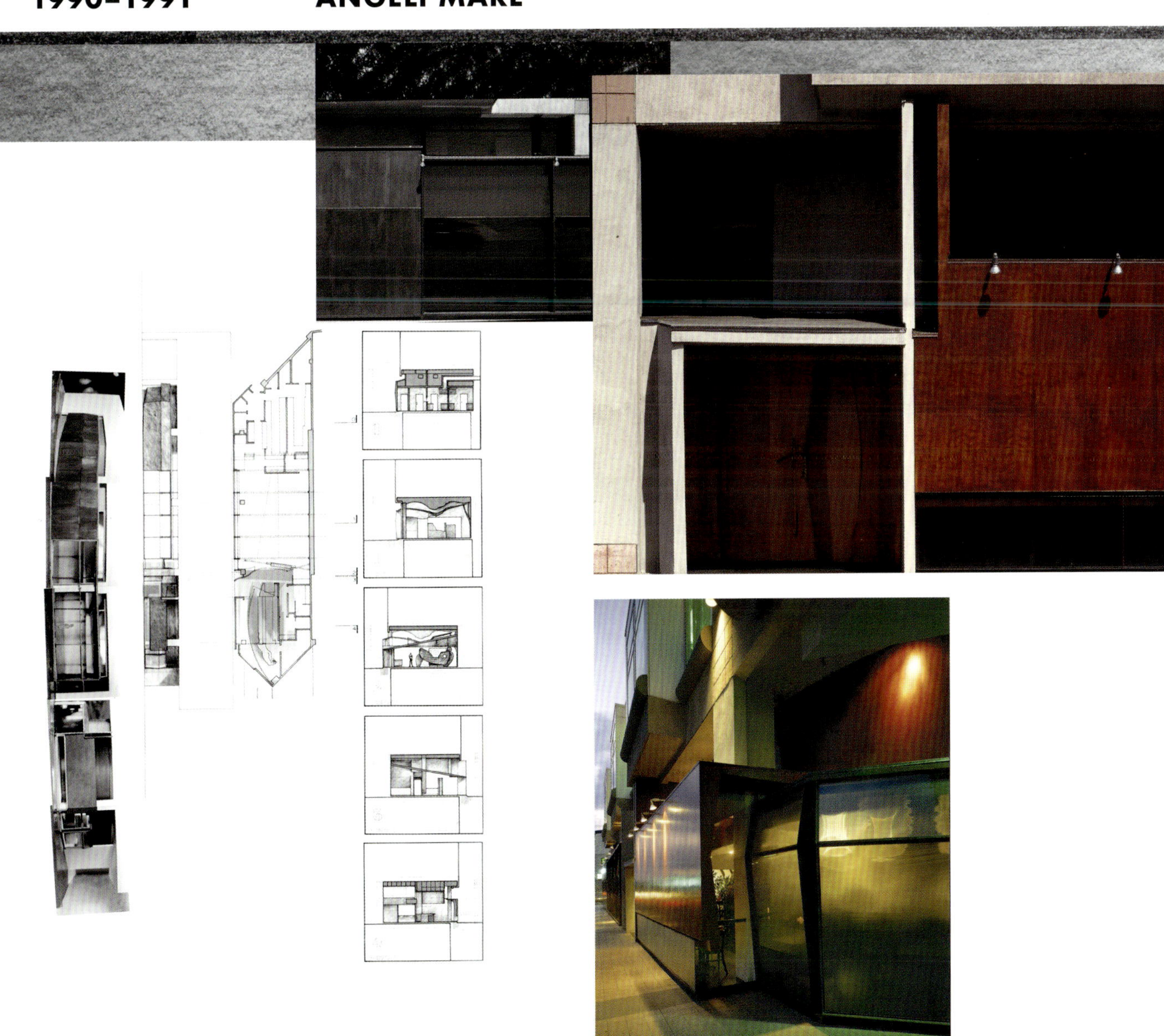

A small jewelry store crafted like a precious wooden box with precious objects of wood, steel, and glass inside.

1991

PAVE JEWELRY

New attempts are made here to evolve body and space and to innovate the design of a dental clinic.

-

The new generation of works, influenced by the experiments and explorations, shows the difference in approach and final product but I feel something is still missing.

There is a need for a structural transformation where the functional elements of the clinic become a part of the architecture of the space.

-

There is a need for a real break to create something new.

1992

COSMETIC DENTAL CLINIC

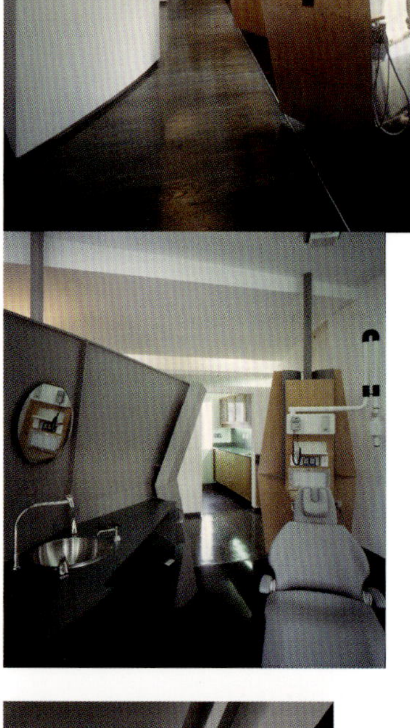

A neighborhood café in the middle of one of one of the oldest LA neighborhood known as "Frog Town" near the Los Angeles River.

My uncle Hassan Eslamipour came from Maryland and stayed with us for a few months and built this café that belong to my parents. It was next to their restaurant Osteria Nonni, an Italian restaurant.

1993

ATWATER TEA+COFFEE

This sketch book filled with drawings I made in Paris in the early nineties expresses how I felt at the time, and my thoughts about something fundamental to architecture that we take for granted - drawing. The process of making architecture and all the related subjects were in transformation at the time. This was the beginning of digital architectural production; drawings, models, programming, technology, and more. I was, as always, thinking through and about architecture searching for my own direction for the next decade of challenges, still believing in an architectural work independent of its tools. After building a series of thoughtful designs and well-constructed works that were well received, I was not satisfied with the direction of my work. So I got help from a few friends and got an apartment in Paris and moved there to think and figure things out.

(It was not scary at the time!)

-

Why drawing? I wanted to dissect my thoughts and see their shapes with the hope to find my way to develop my work of architecture. Drawing was the tool I knew but I decided to learn it in a new way. There are evolutionary moments in the process of development of every author and their life/work, moments marked by a specific event, project, text, etc. We recognize those moments reviewing our work through time; sometimes we experience them publicly and sometimes in the privacy of our struggles. These childlike sketches were not made to be architectural or buildings or urban environments and were not meant to spark inspiration or provoke imagination. I did them to help me step away from what I knew with the hope of discovering something else.

("*There are no rules that say you can't.*" P.J. Harvey)

9/16/1993 HIDES SKETCHES OF SPACE

New Beginning PARIS.

-

The work of the past seven years was gratifying but limited.

-

I wanted a fresh start.

1993

Michele Saee
9 16 93

— ... "musel sense", as it was once called, befor Sherrington investigated it & renamed it "proprioceptio—"—

It is This sense dipendent on impulse from muscles, joints & Tendons, usually overlooked because normally un conscious, it is This vital "six sense" by which The body knows it self, judges with perfect, automatic, instantaneous precision and motion of all it's movable parts, Their relationship to one anothers, Their align ment in SPACE... The sense of movment— but "PROPRIOCEPTION," less euphonious, seems an all together better word, because it implies a sense of what is "proper" That by which The body knows itself, and has itself as "property."
(Alegtostandon O.W.S P.70/71)

proprocepto— could be effected in a long period of Time under certain conditio—s which means That, conditio—s of space can effect it's relationship to space it's in.

Even Though a great deal of importance has been given to The visual qualities of architecture which has effected our perceptio— in wrong direction, AlThough our other senses very much are effectively active in The process of experiencing space & Architecture.

It take very little to come to a certain realizatio— in understanding space

I needed to move out of
LA for a short time and
question my work.

-

Sketches I made were the
beginning of the next stage
of my development—
projecting forward.

1993

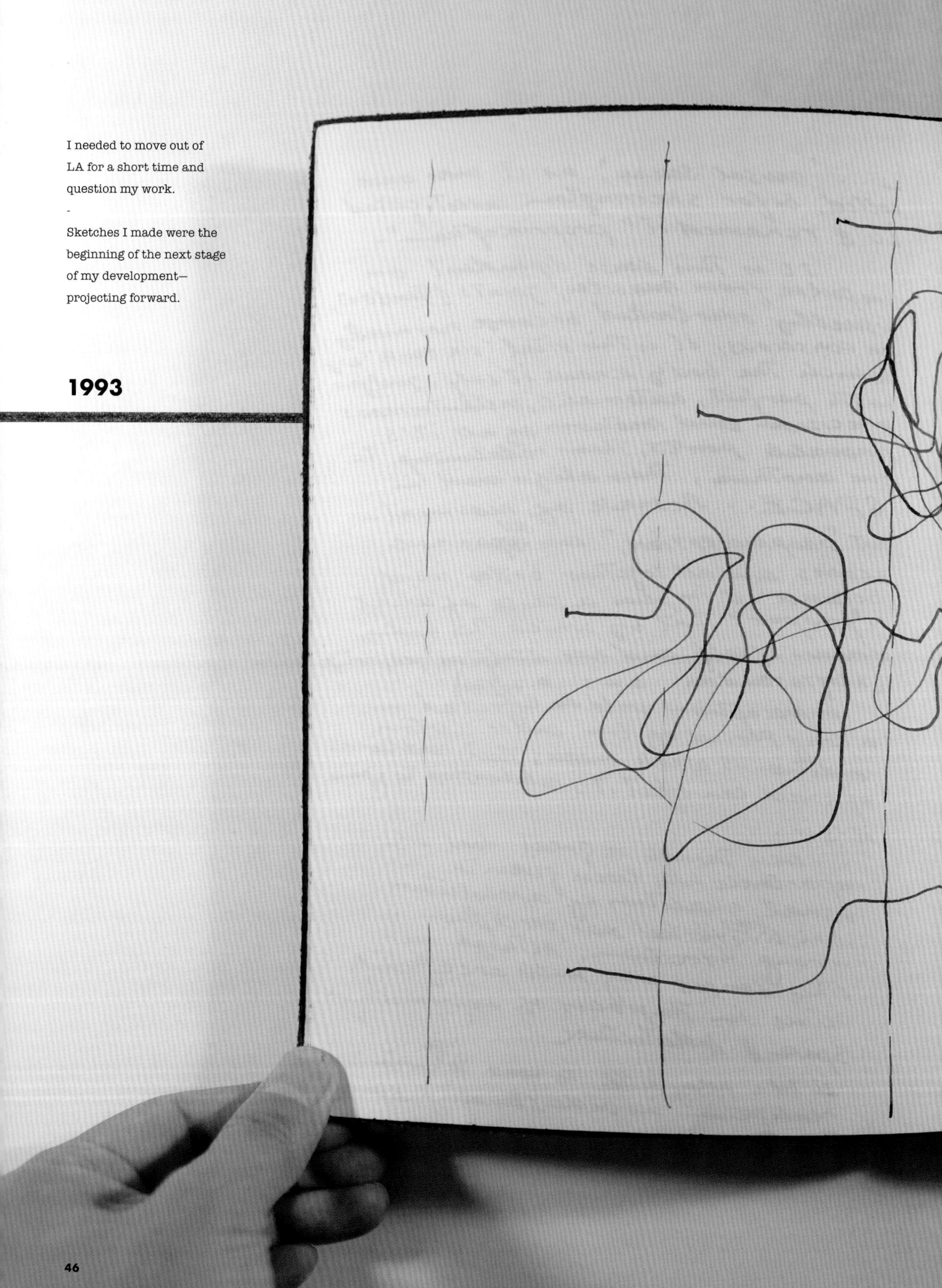

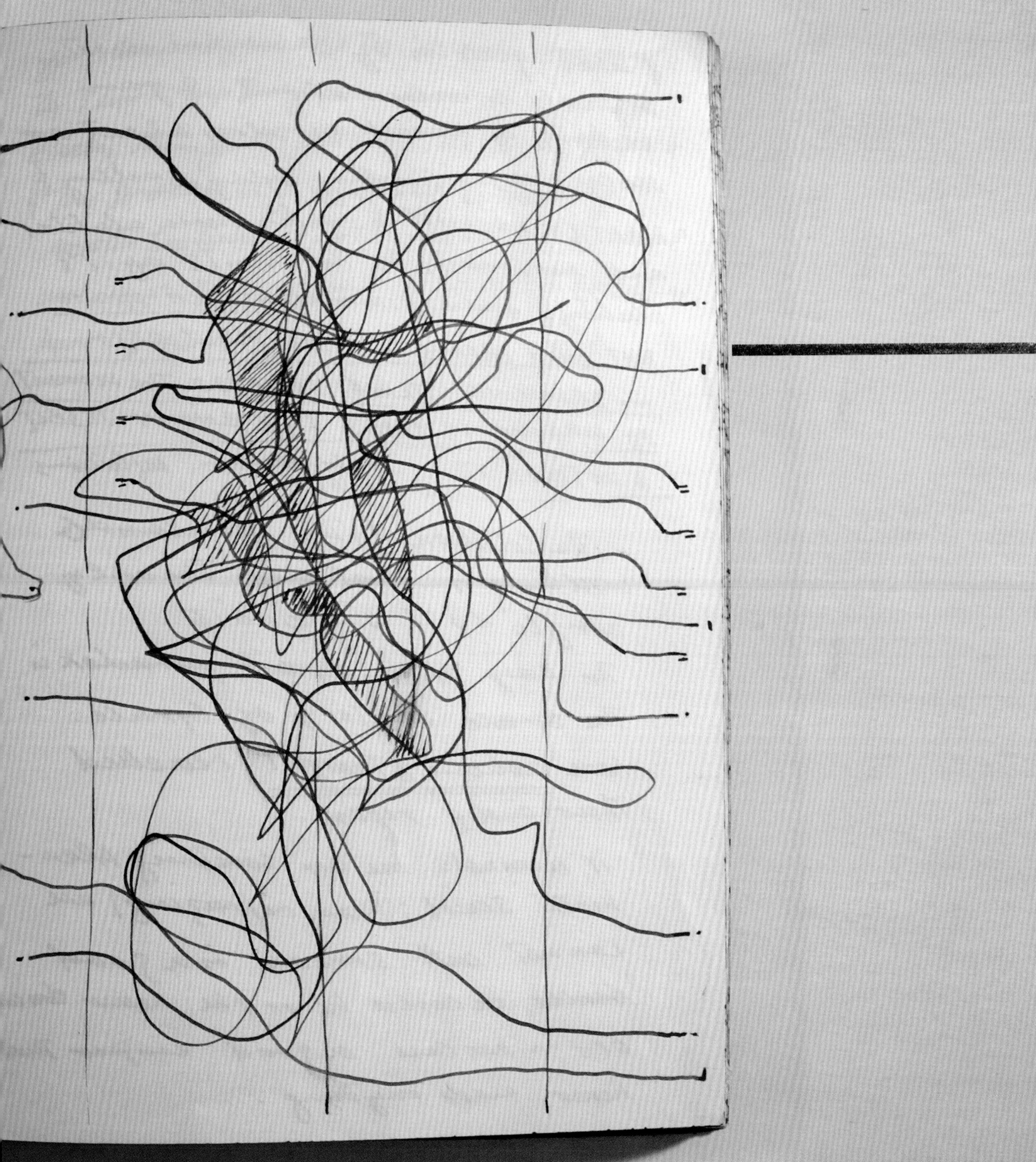

Walking the city of Paris
aimlessly; drawing,
sketching aimlessly.
-
Not searching, not looking,
and letting go.

1993

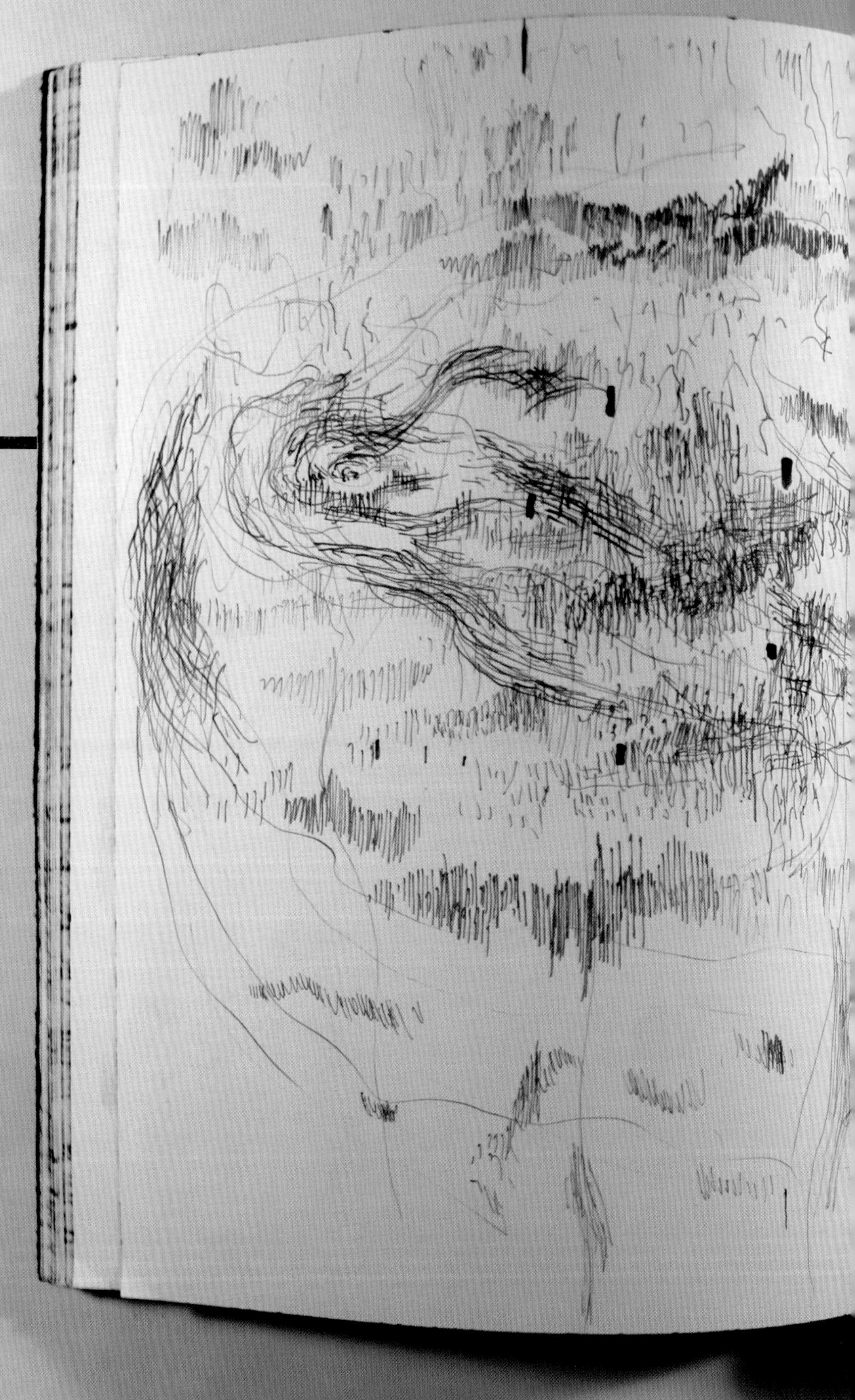

RECESSION!

I lost everything I had invested financially over the previous seven years.

1993

1993

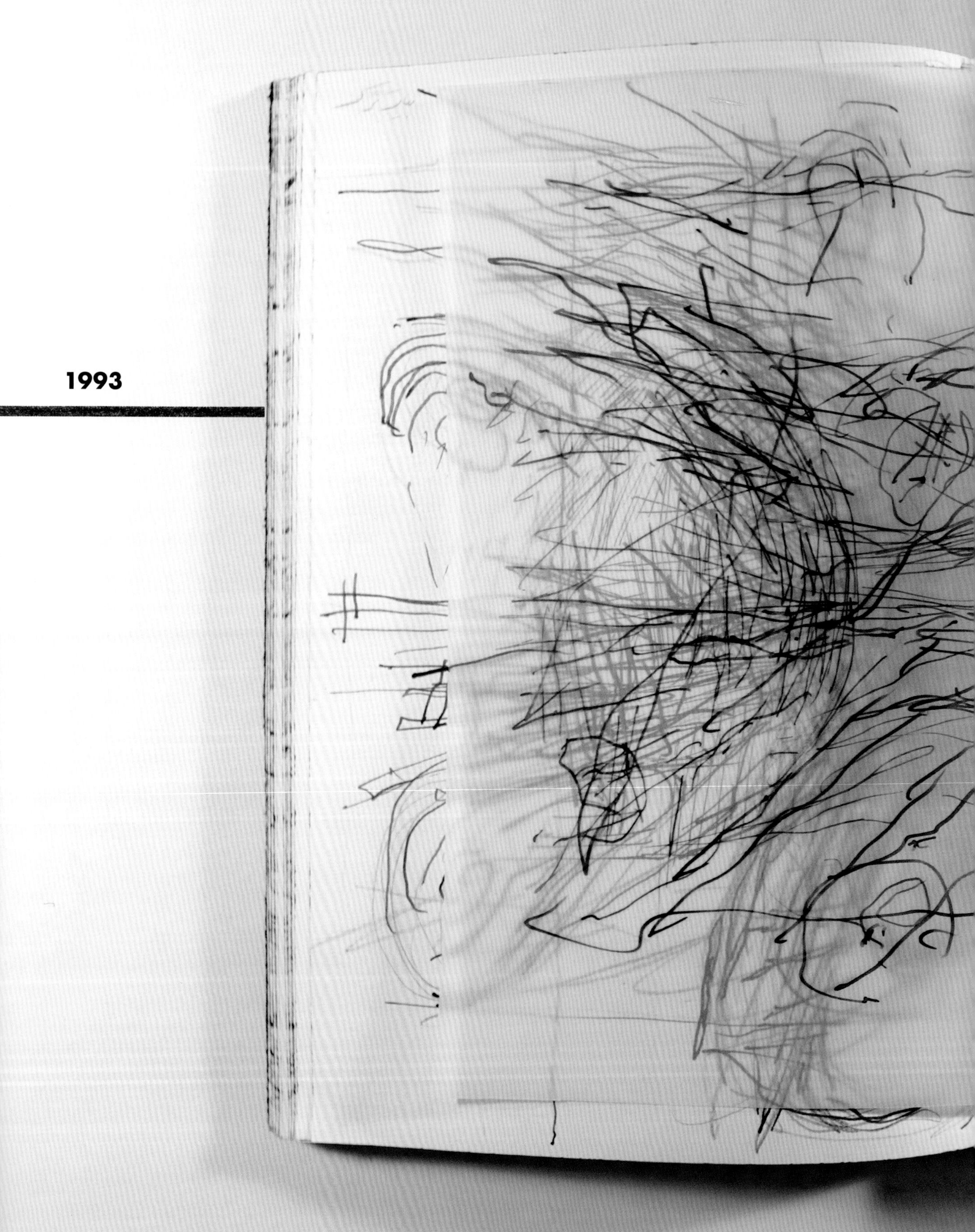

1994

Proprioception is the vital "sixth sense" by which the body knows itself and judges with perfect, instantaneous, automatic perfection all its movable parts, their relationship to one another, and their alignment in space.

This project was an attempt to step outside the constraints of economics and power to allow the built work to be influenced not by the client's financial priorities but by poetry, history, grace, and art that inspires the creation of space.

The shape of the "plus" (+) was meant to connect the two areas of the A&M University campus, but during the construction the excavators' mistake led to the cross shape which we discovered later when the aerial photos were made. We corrected this mistake with the use of Photoshop to see the picture of what could have been the actual design.

1994 PROPRIOCEPTION

Body knows itself.
-
The maker knows its body.
-
The body is a tool.

I met Paul Revere Williams in spirit and I was inspired to design an installation in a house he designed (the Petitfils house in Beverly Hills). This was for an exhibition to raise consciousness and funds for a city of Los Angeles organization that supports abused mothers and children.

This was my response to his architecture. The inner courtyard garden of the house was our stage where a group of my colleagues and friends constructed the installation using our bodies to shape the 20-foot-long, half-inch solid steel rods to form the space.

It is a continuous line like space and time. We jointed the line at each spot in order to continue. It was like sketching in space and being inside our own thoughts and drawings.

1994 ART WORKS FOR CHILDREN

The solid body of the architecture of the past was graced with the temporary soft elements of the new body like a dream.

Hopes were fading and my projections for new projects to build a new solid infrastructure seemed like a dream following the heroic breaking away from what seemed to be a secure (financially) professional line of architectural work.

I continued working on a number of experimental installation projects with less and less confidence in myself.

Where is the dream?
Where is the dream project I was hoping for?

LIFE IN TRANSITION

The dream is farther away than expected.

-

I added another layer of words/sketch to the Paris sketches and published a book titled *Hides, Sketches of Space* inspired by Miles Davis's Sketches of Spain. I am blue.

1994

I got married to Arezou, the love of my childhood, and became a father for the first time to our beautiful daughter, Sayeh (shadow). She is two years old here, born on July 22nd, 1992.

-

I moved to a new studio tucked into the back of an Indian restaurant with the camera facade and began to work with a different attitude and invented a project to work on.

This was the pivoting moment in my life's work.

This project started as an homage to Jackson Pollock. House for Jack. He freed the line and I wanted to free the space.

Our son, Alisina, was born on August 8th 1996. I was a father for a second time and the emotions were flowing like never before.

I didn't know at the time but fortunately I lost my bid for the SCI-Arc directorship, which was like getting a divorce and losing a longtime friend.

1995–1996 GOLZARI HOUSE

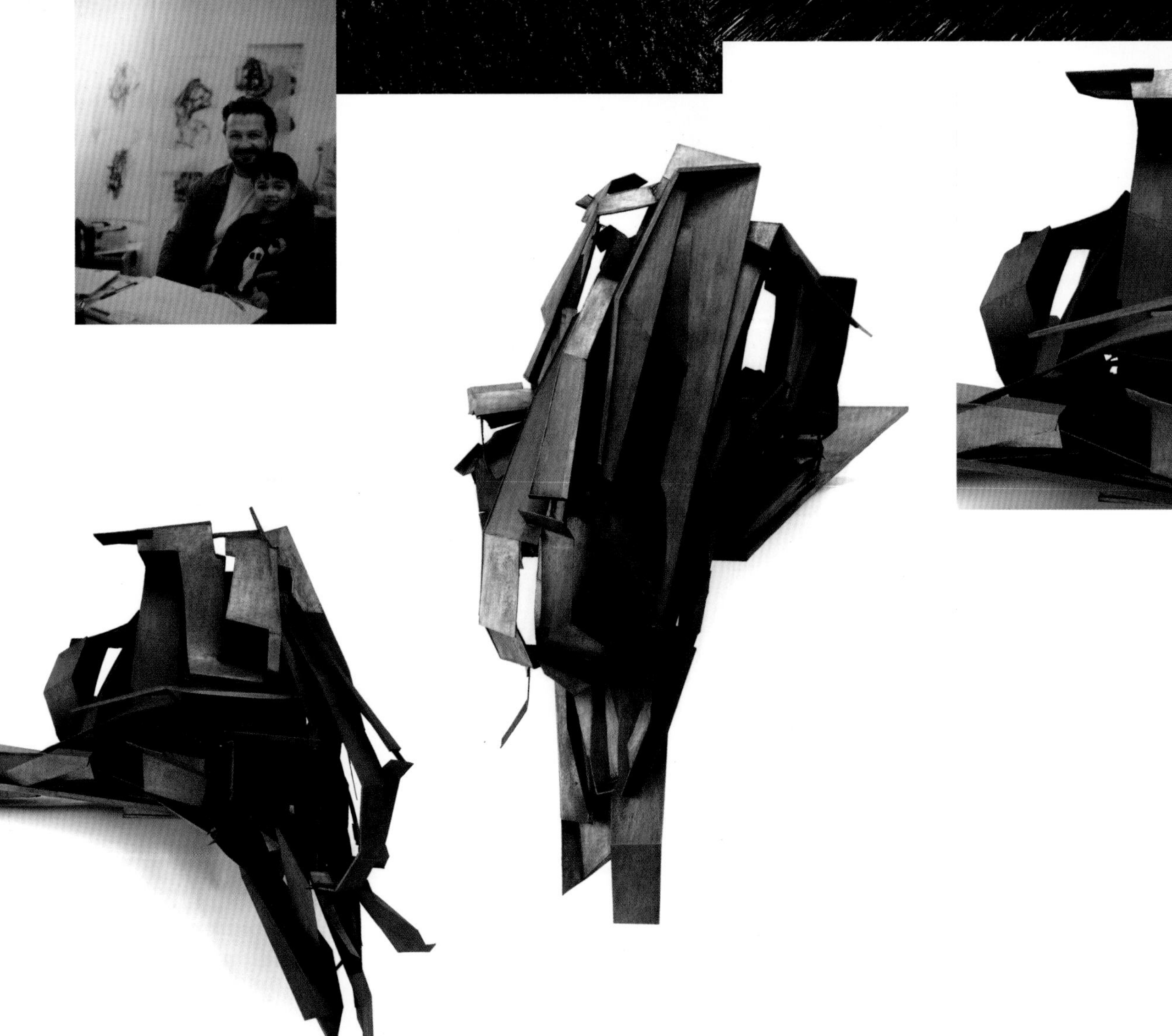

Designing the Golzari House was therapeutic, suggesting a mission to redefine my ideological position in architecture.

I was searching for a new system of order which could help the user to become more integrated with their bodies and the environment.

Personal and social simultaneously.

Architectural space with no beginning and no end.

Longing for a new relationship between body and space.

-

How can I become a part of it?

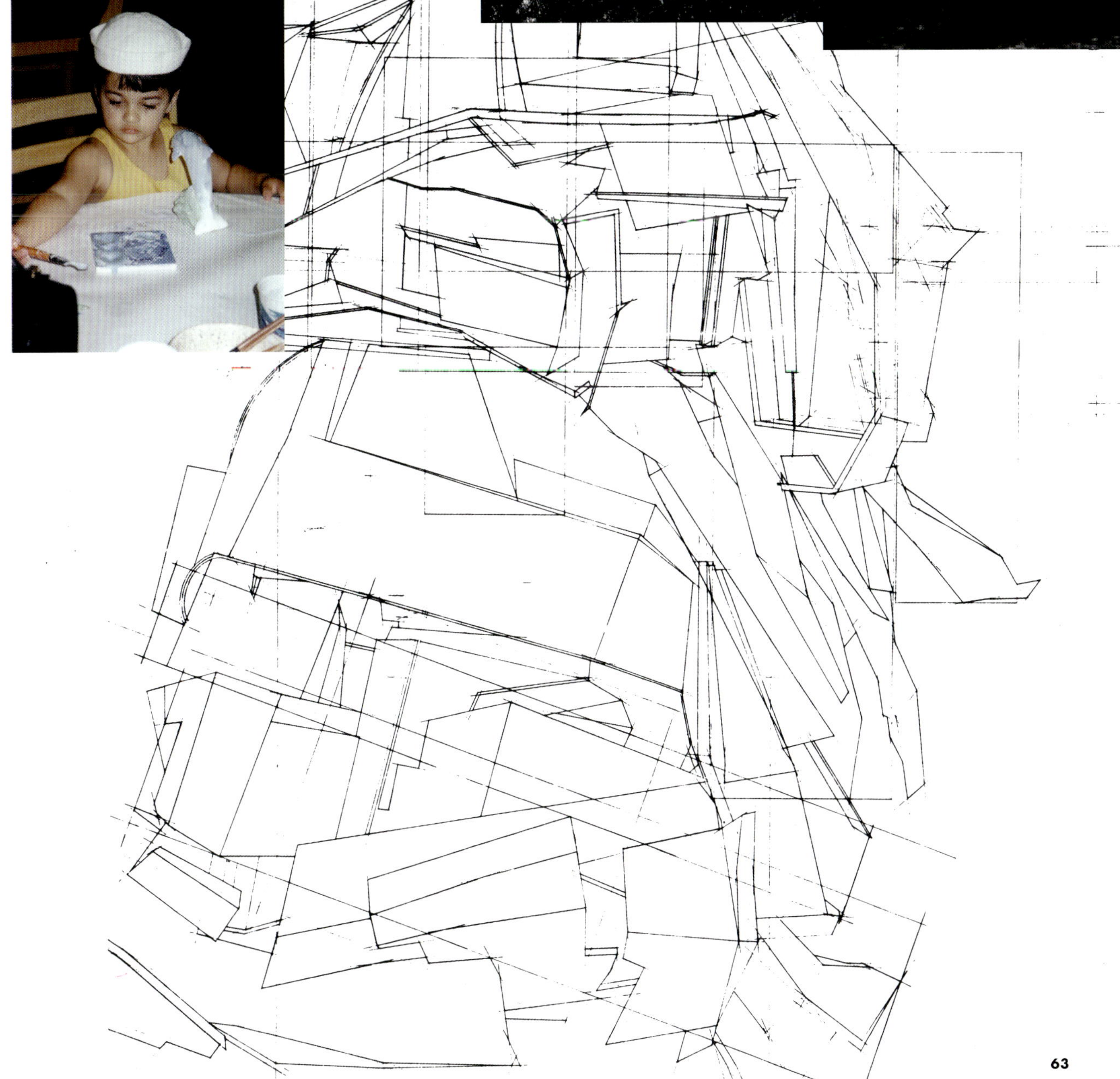

Is a park still a park if there are no plants or trees? Petrosino Park was an attempt to make a different type of park in the condensed urban context of New York City.

What if the natural elements instead—trees, plants, bushes, or grass—could be integrated into the architecture of the park's surfaces, textures, materials, and their interrelationships create shaded spaces for relaxation, gathering, and activities?

I moved forward with all my energy and gave it all I had.

1996 PETROSINO PARK

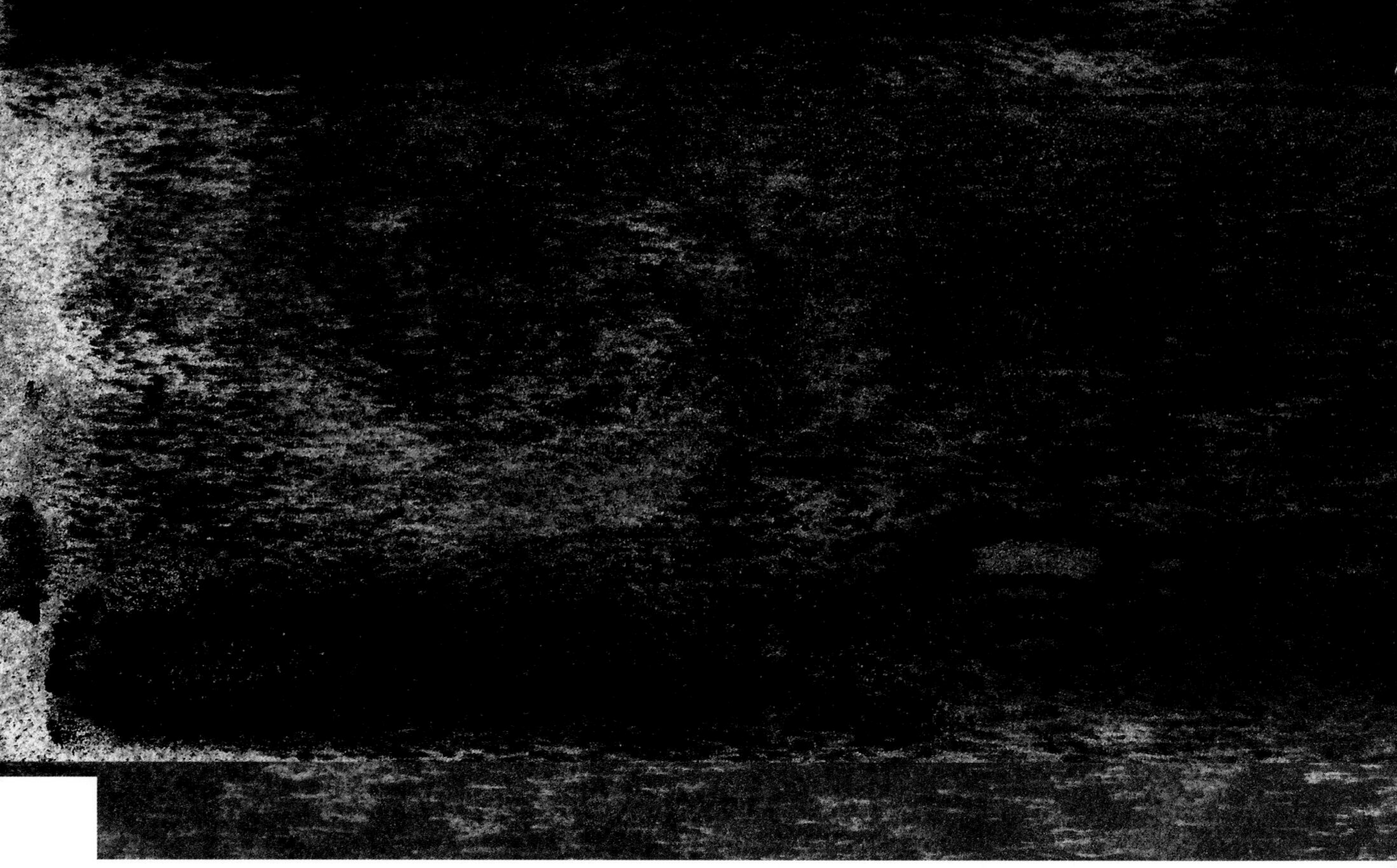

MICHELE SAEE IS NOT PART OF THE CONVENTIONAL PARLANCE

ESSAY BY ERIC OWEN MOSS

Michele Saee is not part of the conventional parlance.

The New Testament propitiously announces where *most* [design] conception originates: "In the beginning is the word."

That biblical proposition, however, is one that the architect Michele Saee has intentionally neglected, because his architecture starts from a very different vantage point.

According to Michele Saee, the beginning of architecture is the act; the word is extraneous.

In the conventional parlance of contemporary architecture, the conception of building belongs to a discourse, and that discourse associates the idea of building with any number of alternative hypotheses that precede the act of conception and design. So the essential meaning of each building is inevitably derived from a theoretical discussion, and the building becomes the constructed manifestation of that discussion.

But Michele Saee is not part of the conventional parlance.

In addition, the normative intellectual discourse automatically provides a format for interpretation of the work: the success of the project can be measured in terms of how a building conforms to the tenets of the theory it purports to sustain.

But there's nothing normative about Michele Saee's discourse.

Current theories have recognizable nomenclature, complete with architects and identifiable allegiances: Modernism, Neo-Modernism, Post-Modernism, Deconstruction, and so on.

But Michele Saee is a categorical misfit.

Recall Homer's Cyclops, who once asked the imprisoned Odysseus for a name. Odysseus replied, "My name is no name."

Ditto architecture by Michele Saee.

No labeling will suffice; no adherence to an a priori theory will explain; his projects are never the philosophical resolution of any deductive hypothesis.

Invention, for Michele Saee, comes from a step-by-step process of assembling — not a conventional, retraceable logic, or method, or sequence — and by a practiced poetic instinct.

Intentionally, that instinct leaves only a happenstance record of Michele Saee's system of design development. And as a consequence, the architecture begins to look more and more like a conjunction of emotional extremes.

Michele Saee is the architect as therapist — not society's, but his own. Schizophrenia, in this case, is curative.

His projects run an emotional gamut of form and space — assemblies of steel and glass and wood and concrete parts that are perpetually incomplete. Solids and holes *abound*, but never a conceptual whole.

Michele's architecture suggests he's assembling a puzzle he doesn't quite recognize because he's simultaneously designing the required puzzle pieces.

That's his architecture: the pieces never quite fit and the puzzle remains intentionally unfinished. How does he do it?

Indent the dent.
Resurface the surface.
Wait for weight.
Deplane the plain.
Curve and re-curve.
Increase the crease.
Un-box the box.

Michele reshapes the shape, ad infinitum, questions the questions, and *perseveres*, with only provisional answers.

What's a wall?
What's a floor?
What's a roof?
What's a window?

Michele makes a sketch. He makes a model. More sketches, more models, and sketches on the models, and more models of the sketches...

No a priori shape or space; no a priori design destination. The "thing-ness" of each project seems to grow out of Saee's implementation process: less concern with the final building and more interest in the growth process.

Like the mad gardener who drops an experimental seed in the ground without quite knowing that he will soon be obligated to cultivate, he prunes and grafts that magical beanstalk as it rises.

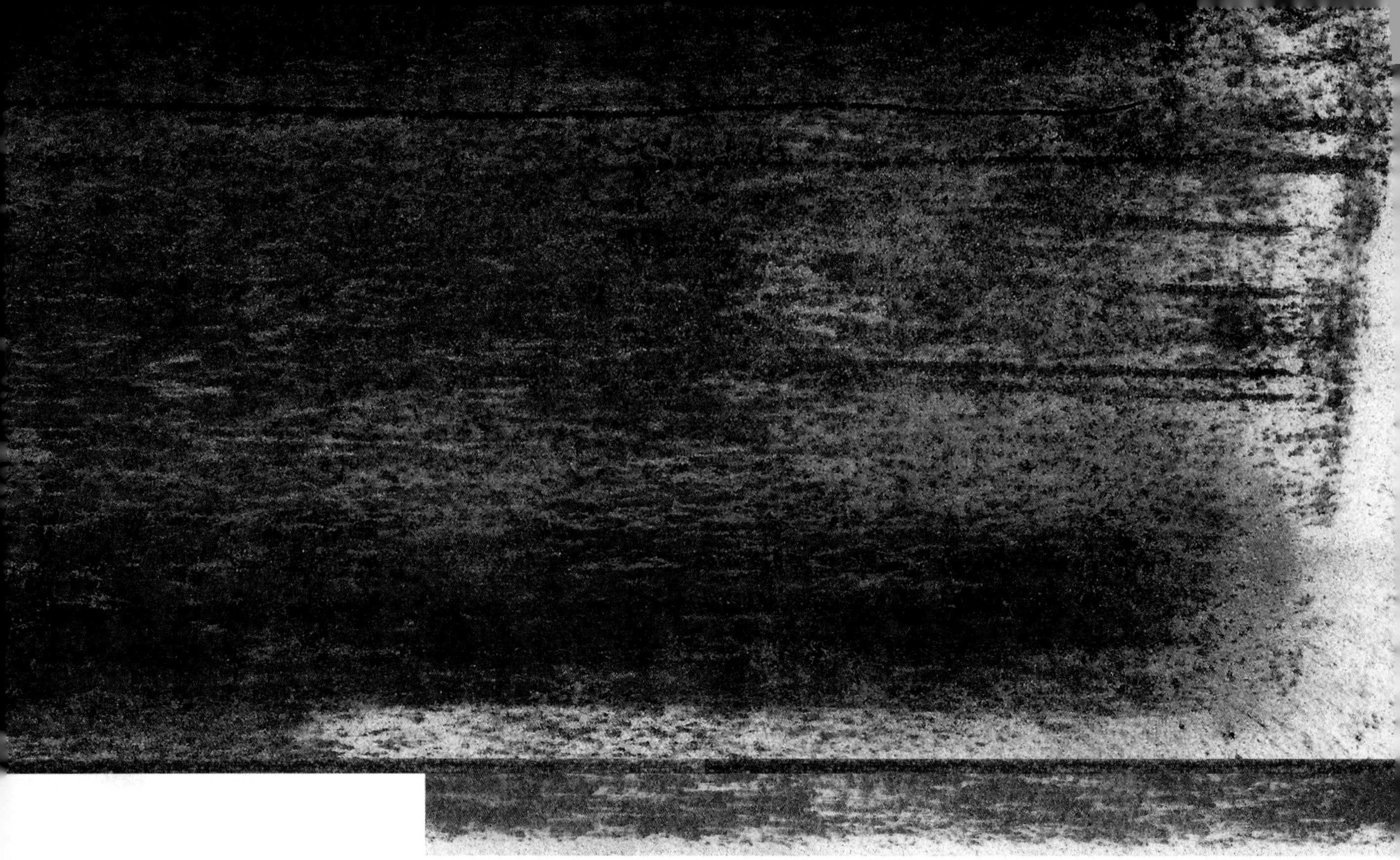

"To design is to construct," Michele Saee tells us. He invites the fabricators and their material expertise to his concept development then re-imagines the capacity of those fabricators and their definition of material expertise. And as the process of construction is re-understood, it is visually implicated in the design concept by redirecting that process: new assembly mechanisms, new technologies, all expressed in architecture.

Let's bend the glass that can't be bent.
Let's fold the steel that can't be creased.

Michele Saee's concept model ultimately includes the aggregate assembly of his newfound techniques of assembly.

Philosophically, Michele Saee is one of those architects who have contributed to the demolition of the ideal of generic space—Plato's prototype, Plato's form of the form and shape of the shape—and any appeal to an a priori essence of shape or material has disappeared. What is left, what Michele Saee gives us, are an infinite variety of privately beautiful spatial speculations.

Michele is essential for what he does, and *for* what he refuses to do.

He is not a signatory to any cultural, historic, or technical formulations or doctrines. He is no one's ideologue. He offers no manifestoes. He is his own message and messenger.

Michele speculates on architecture from [his] inside out.
So architecture, for Michele, is a private wondering,
a wandering.

And by implication, his work asks the essential question in contemporary architecture: Is there a singular architecture that belongs to the meanings the architect alone invents?

The answer is that "Michele Saee building" is both verb and noun, both the result and the process of achieving the result. No words, just the investigatory act, an act inaccessible to intellectuals in the language in which they conventionally demand a reasoned response.

Michele Saee offers no reasoned response — no theory, no discourse, no philosophy. Instead, he provides an ongoing mad dash of shape, material, and technique — to a moving finish line.

Michele Saee's reason for being is an architecture that exists solely as a critical examination of its own subject. It imagines a private world and wanders in that world. The architecture of Michele Saee records that wandering.

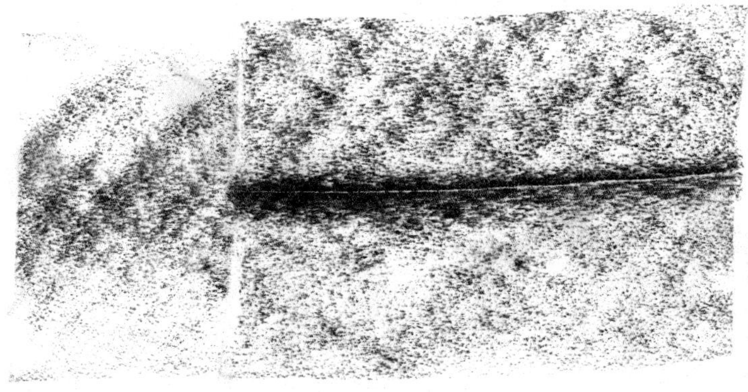

Each act of building creates a historical marker in the flow of history-taking its place in the equilibrium of the milieu.

Turku Library

The Turku Library was designed to create a socially and intellectually charged gathering place within a southwestern Finnish city that spends most of the year buried in cold weather. The proposal envisioned the library as a suspended volume only accessible via elevator and stairs that meet it from an underground parking structure or a ground-level public square. To attract thinkers and bookworms as a permanent feature of the development, the plan also includes a mixed-use component by incorporating on-site housing units.

Overlooking the grand Aura River, the design responsively engages the characteristics of the site: Turku Castle, Turku Cathedral, Vartiovuori City Park, and the Turun Sanomat Newspaper Building designed by Alvaro Alto.

I have always been curious and have challenged the concept of the city and context in my work. I believe that our understanding and reading of the context is crucial in the process of our design. In this project, I especially viewed the context as a living organism that had to get involved and inform the architecture of the building.

I believe that the context and the architecture of any building is engaged in an ongoing dialogue, influencing each other in time. Some of the effects of this dialogue

are visible through physical manifestation, while others are felt as part of the experience or memories they leave behind.

The massing and interior spaces of the Turku Library are configured to frame vistas of these landmarks, which in turn become active parts of the design. A predominantly concrete exterior contextualizes the urban surroundings and contrasts a warm, comforting interior environment, which draws on a palette of stained woods.

Turku Library

Location:
Turku, Finland

Year:
1996 competition (not built)

Program:
Library, Residential, Commercial

The Turku Library design is a challenge to the traditional paradigm of the library as a place of collective solitude. As libraries compete with other mechanisms of information distribution for the attention and patronage of today's scholars and thinkers, their survival as institutions may very well hinge on their ability to evolve into conduits for social interaction. To encourage and promote activities of collective gathering, I created bridges within the public spaces of the building to promote opportunities for engagement and interaction between patrons of the library.

The spaces of the library are structured to facilitate information exchange and modes of interaction. The entrances from Linnankatu and Kauppiaskatu Street encourage this interchange. Flowing helices of the city, the traffic, pedestrians, and the current of urban movements enter the site, intertwining with the spiraling layers of the library. The often overlooked resonant connections between the natural rhythmic formations of life and the urban topography become actualized in form. The activation of the ground plane as a socially charged environment is reinforced by the sheltering effect of the library above and the introduction of program elements such as coffee shops, presentation, and performance spaces and the Turku Library Exhibition Center.

The north side of the building includes a residential component. The apartment units on the second floor are a novel concept meant to attract a community of bookworms

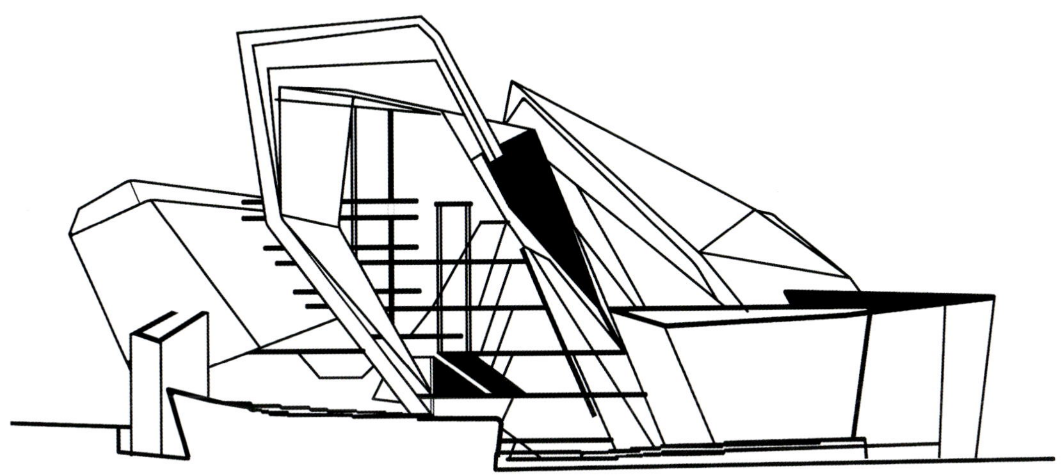

and to serve as an anchor to the library's social environment. Residents championing the new library as their home, revitalizes the space as a home away from home for the broader community.

Ultimately, Turku Library reflects a belief that the act of building can enhance and dialogically engage a city steeped in history. An expanded urban context beyond the immediate physical surroundings of the site has been interrogated, activating deep historical layerings, social structures, land forms, and hidden stratospheres unique to Turku. The nature of any library is to collect and archive the records of a civilization's cultural lineage, allowing us to engage the future while acknowledging the past. Each act of building creates a historical marker in the flow of history, taking its place in the equilibrium of the milieu. Like a ripple in a pond, The Turku Library is a landscape within a landscape, where the intricacies of modern life blend with the richness of the past.

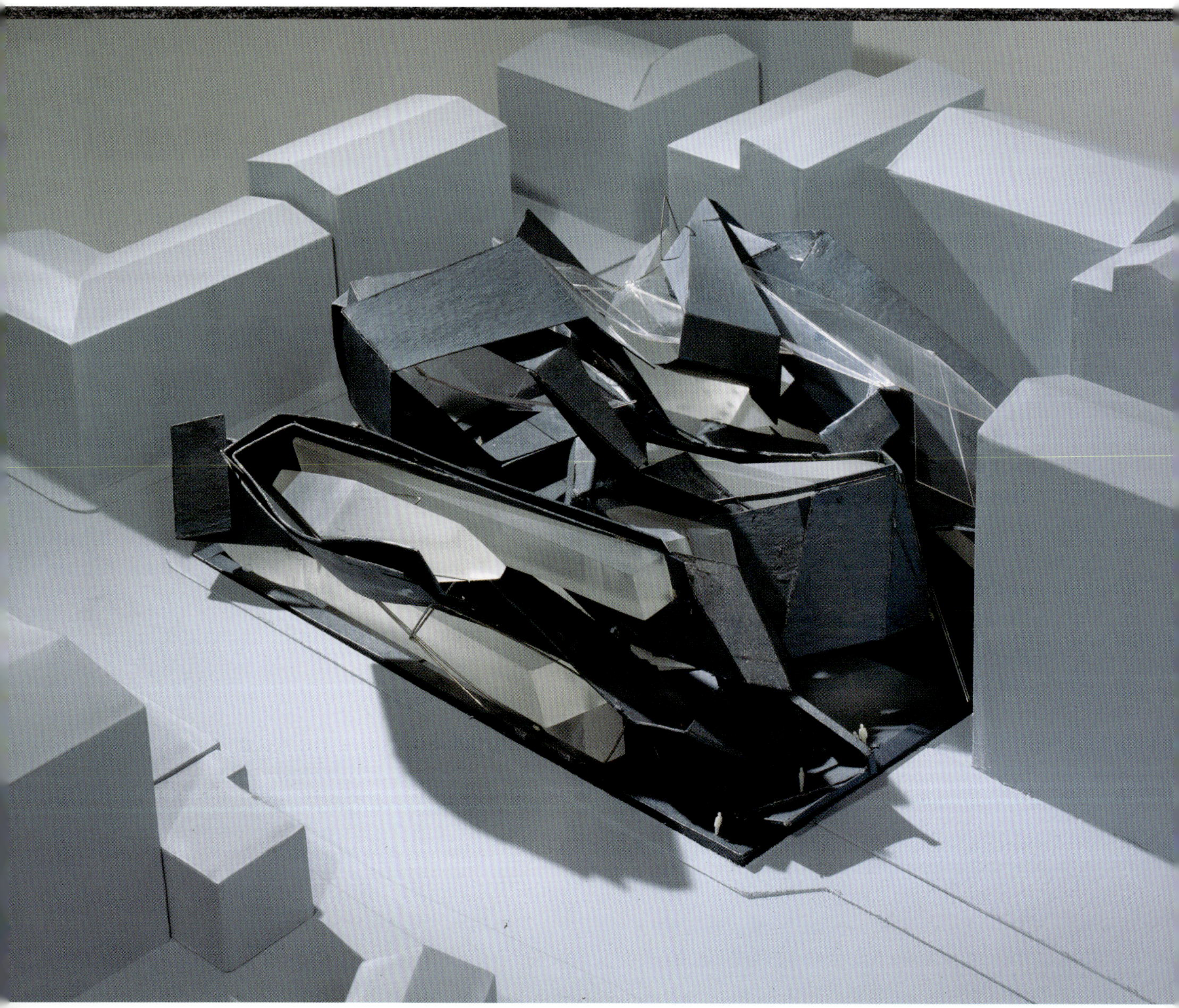

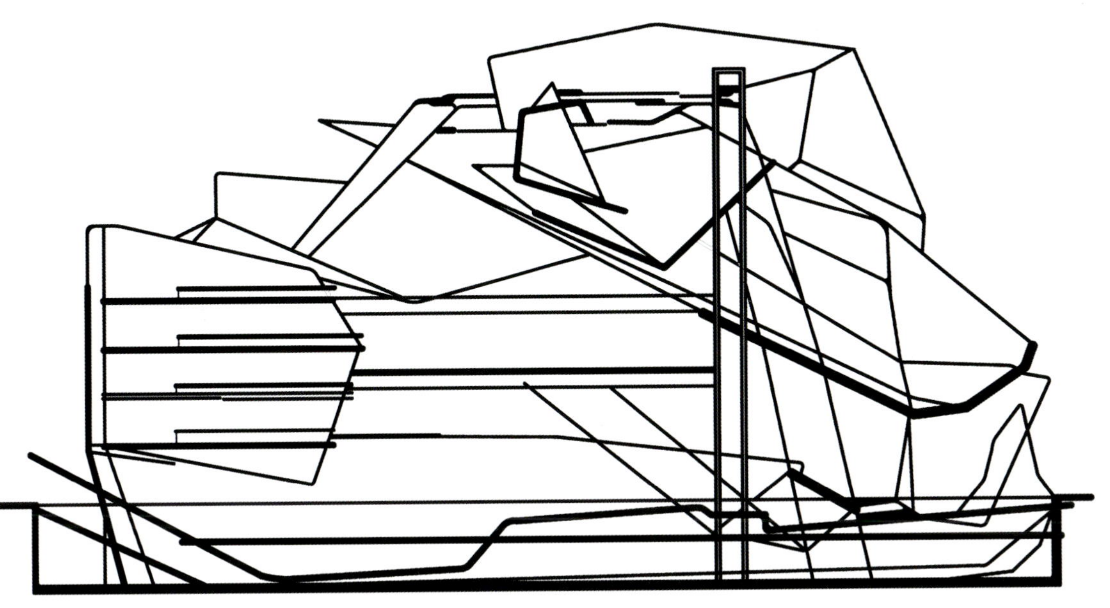

Architecture is not open and perceptive, nor does it involve intentional consciousness or a subject seen within a perspectival order.

Artist Studio

Void-Comp, Sculpture by David Lindberg

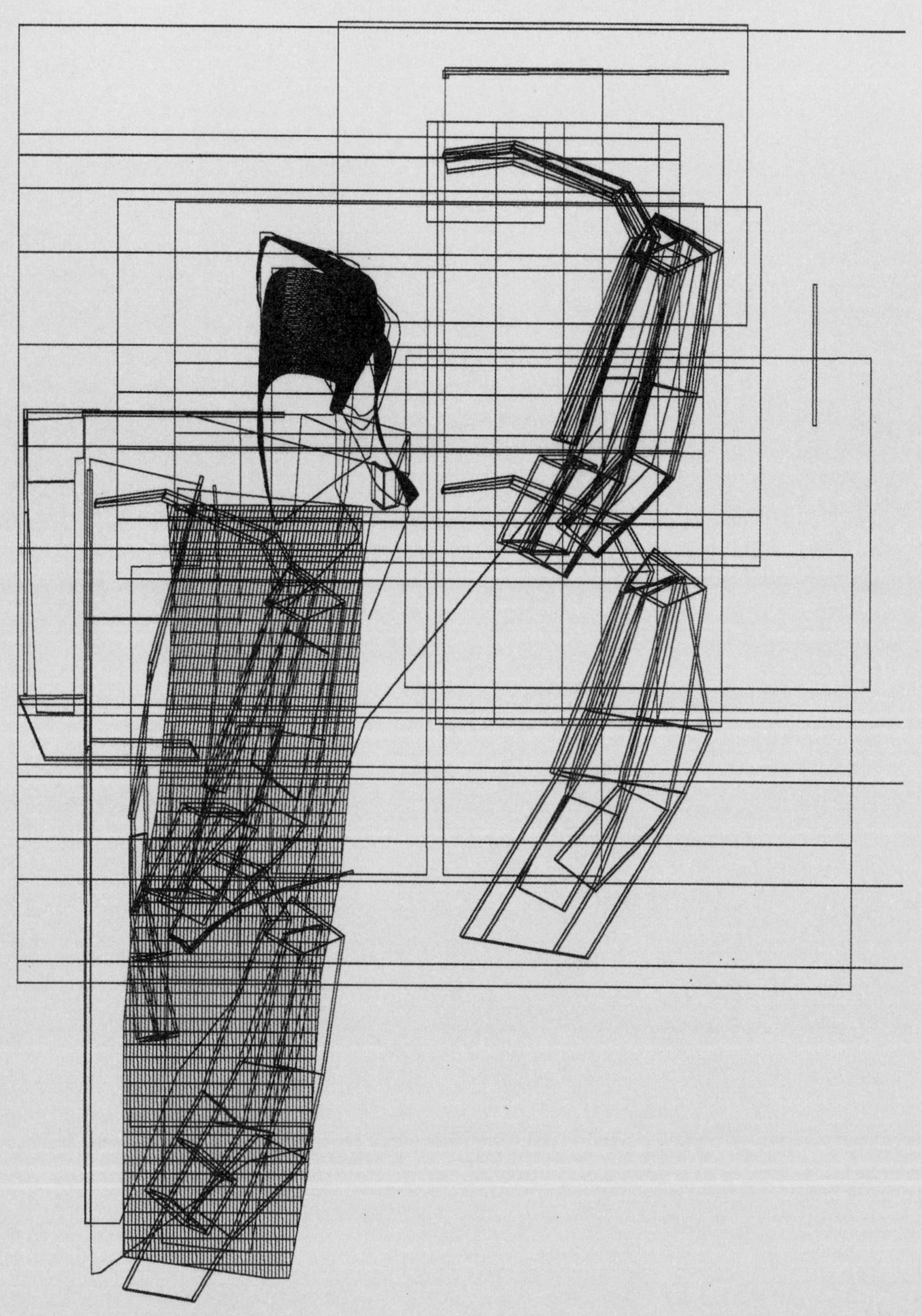

Artist Studio

Location:
Los Angeles, California, USA

Year:
1997 conceptual (not built)

Program:
**Work Studio,
Gallery and Living**

"I start to construct with the consumer object. If it doesn't work out the way I want it to?! Well, I have to deal with that. It's just like in real life: you can't go back."
— David Lindberg

I met David Lindberg when teaching at Otis Art Institute's Parsons School of Design in the mid-eighties. David was an exceptional student with astonishing talent and I wanted him to join me that summer to work as my design assistant. After a few years, his free-spirited personality was confronted by the discipline of architecture and he decided to pursue his work in the arts instead. I strongly supported his decision and we remained close friends.

David's sculptures, artwork, and creative process intrigued me, so one summer I decided to design him a studio to submit to the AIA awards. David wasn't aware of the project, but my free time grew into a period of reflection and experimentation. If I was to design a studio for anyone else, I don't know if I would've been as experimental or reflective. I took advantage of the

opportunity to create with a purpose. My purpose was defined by friendship and how it ultimately influences the architectural process creatively and spiritually.

At the time, my assistant Lucine Hogtanian and I were finishing the Turku Library competition. The library challenged me to think about the relationship between the context of the city, it's architecture, and how their interconnectedness influenced one another through time. David's studio design began with similar ideas in mind. Los Angeles is not Turku, but nevertheless a similar concept was experimented with. The question: Can an architect design a work of architecture (build it) like an artist making a sculpture?

I always saw architecture as part of everyday life because the imagination is directly related to the human condition. I never understood the creative process linearly. While others would add to a creative foundation, resolving the problems that arose, I would try to take leaps into unexpected territory. I'd search to experience something new by challenging my thoughts and work processes, which is why I decided to adopt David's philosophy. To develop the project, I needed to step beyond what I considered comfortable, which was limiting me.

We agreed to design his studio in separate, independent parts based on our reading of him and his work. We would finish with the design of one part before moving on to the next. Each piece had to functionally and compositionally work with what came before it. We started with his studio as a container vacant of context, which we could add to. Much like the objects David finds when producing his sculptures, the box develops an identity once it interacts

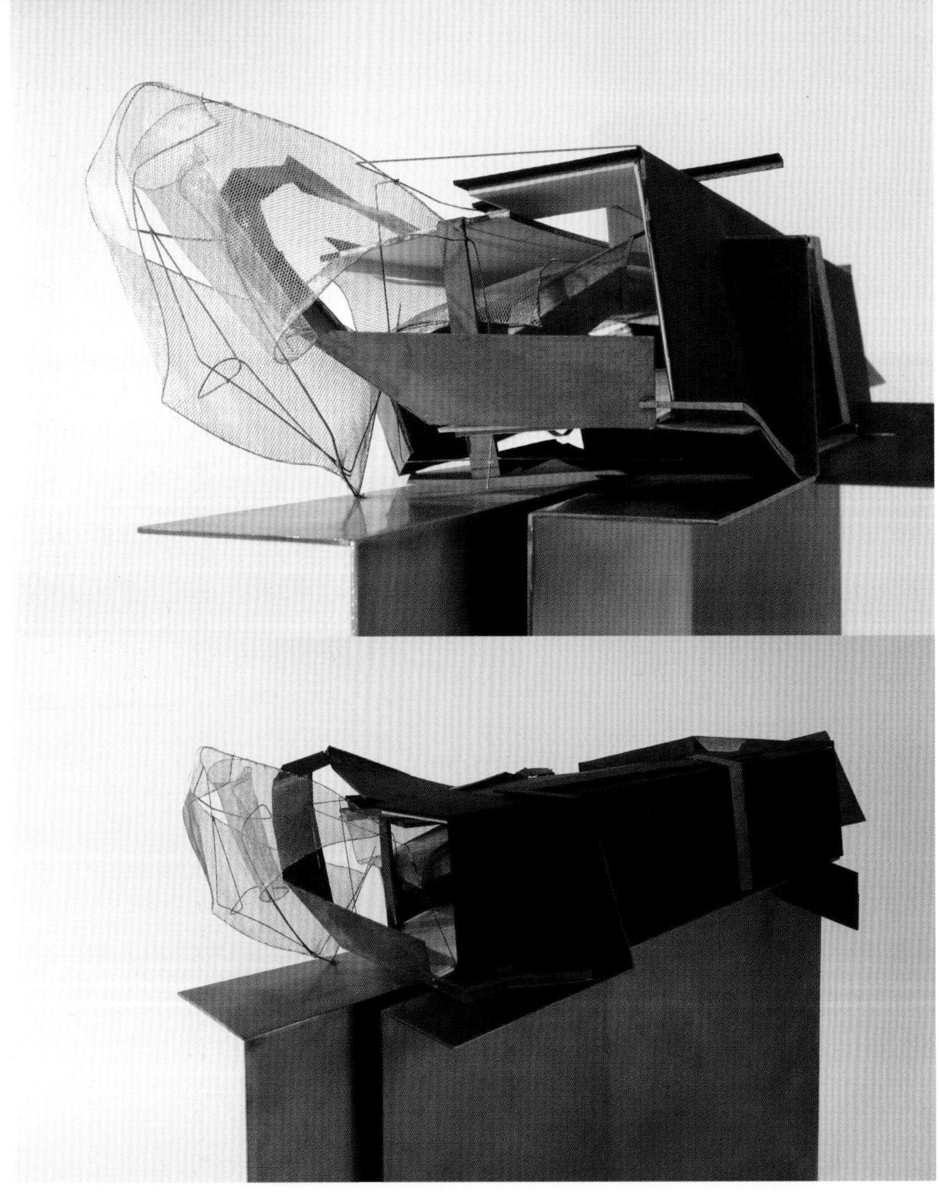

with the site and develops programmatic needs. We then would respond by adjusting the size and shape. We arrived at a lofty, rectangular working space opened on both ends with a continuous wall on one side to display his pieces. The studio space floats three feet above the ground, allowing for air circulation and simplifying installation/modification of the building systems (electrical, mechanical, plumbing, etc.). It also adds flexibility for additions of dividing walls for potential projects.

On the opposite side of the continuous wall are sliding walls that can open up to the yard, giving David the option to work inside and outside simultaneously. This also allows trucks to deliver materials or transport artwork to destinations for installation and exhibition. On the same side, we included a living quarter for David consisting of a bedroom, bathroom, and closet. Attached to the living quarter is a kitchen, dining room, and resting space, which is visually open to the studio and enclosed in a seamless glass partition. Most of the furniture is made by David or his friends using found objects. In the front, a sculptural element projects out toward the street acting as a shield to the studio and an icon celebrating the artist's studio.

Architectural design and realization is an extensive process that must be actualized before construction could even begin. The client, the architect, and their consultants, and multiple city departments' comment on the proposed project before the permits are issued and the contractors are hired. Every scenario is considered and, in most cases, multiple cost evaluations are made before breaking ground. Architecture inherently does not allow the type of flexibility and spontaneity to explore

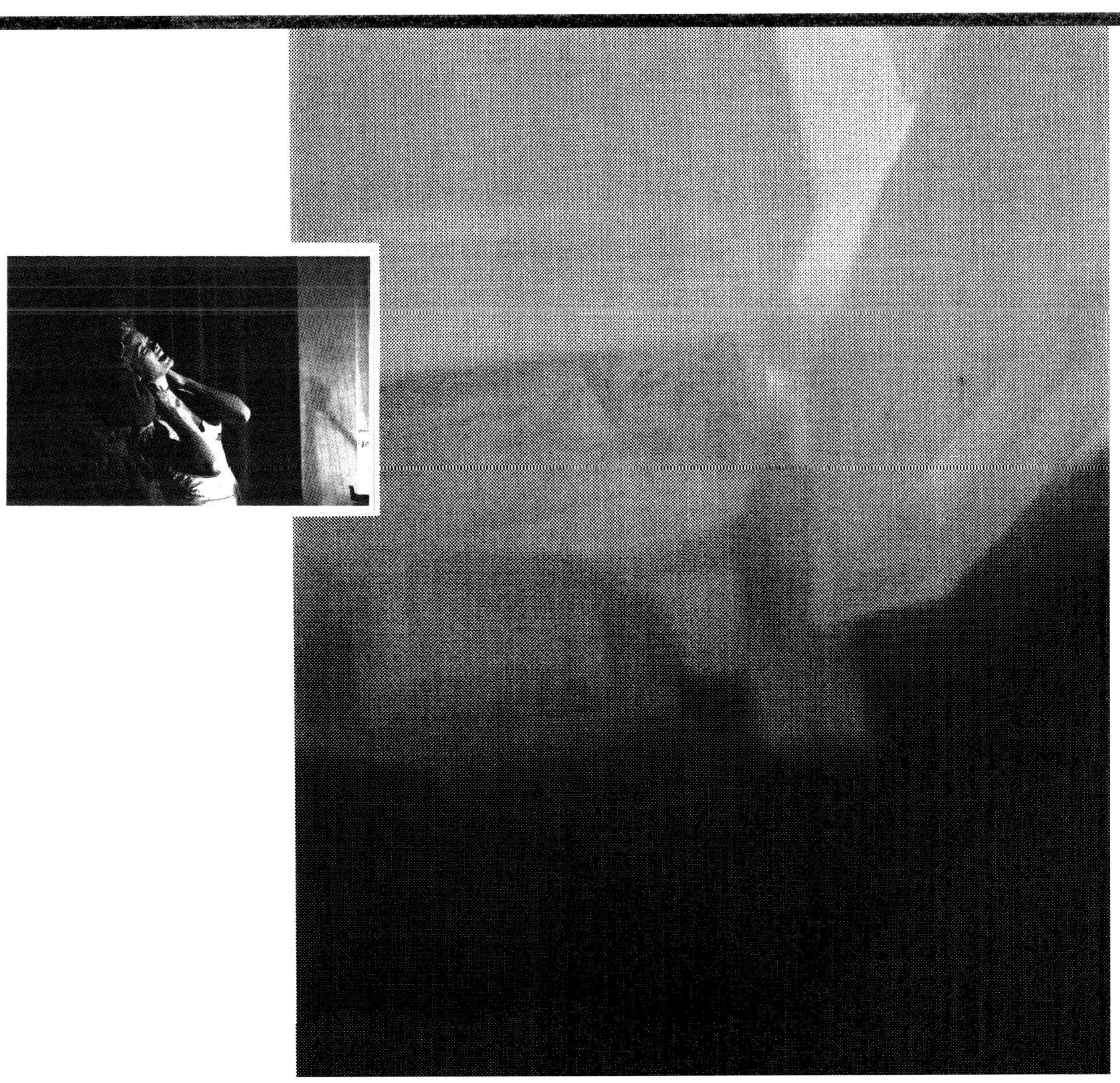

ideas since it is constantly being questioned by the numerous concerns that everyone involved might have. All these needs must be addressed in order for the work to move forward.

For David's studio, we were imagining the client's needs and taste. This may have been liberating when we started the project, but we soon realized that our equation was missing something critical. We needed the dynamic, creative interaction that the client brings to any project. After a few weeks of discussions and designing, we realized that we were conducting a different type of architectural investigation. Our "client" was not directly involved and we were projecting our assumptions, never to be sure about their validity. This sparked a dialogue about the practice of architecture as a whole and the role each of the participants play in the process.

We surprisingly concluded that the limitations and restrictions put on architects by the different forces involved wasn't a horrible burden, but rather forced us to be more creative. Having to answer to different concerns made the final result more interesting, which the work communicates consciously and unconsciously.

The act of designing David Lindberg's studio was an exploration to define different functions, volumes, and programs, which continued to influence the experience of the space. In this way our design can be customized to respond to the user or users with their specific needs. Architectural process is not about control or one person's desires and needs. It is a collaborative exploration where the compromises are as important as succeeding to realize your true vision. The outcome is the realization of our true vision.

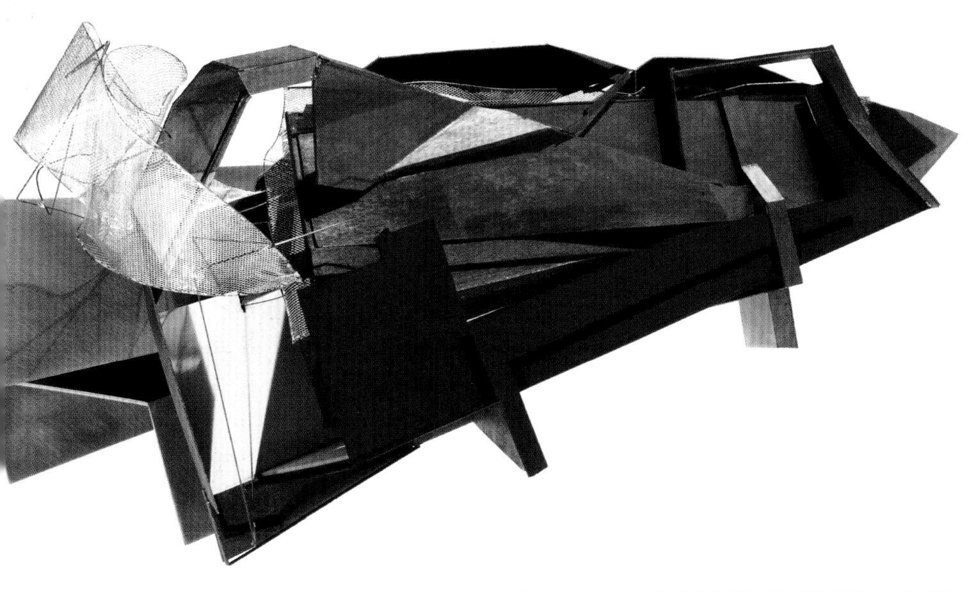

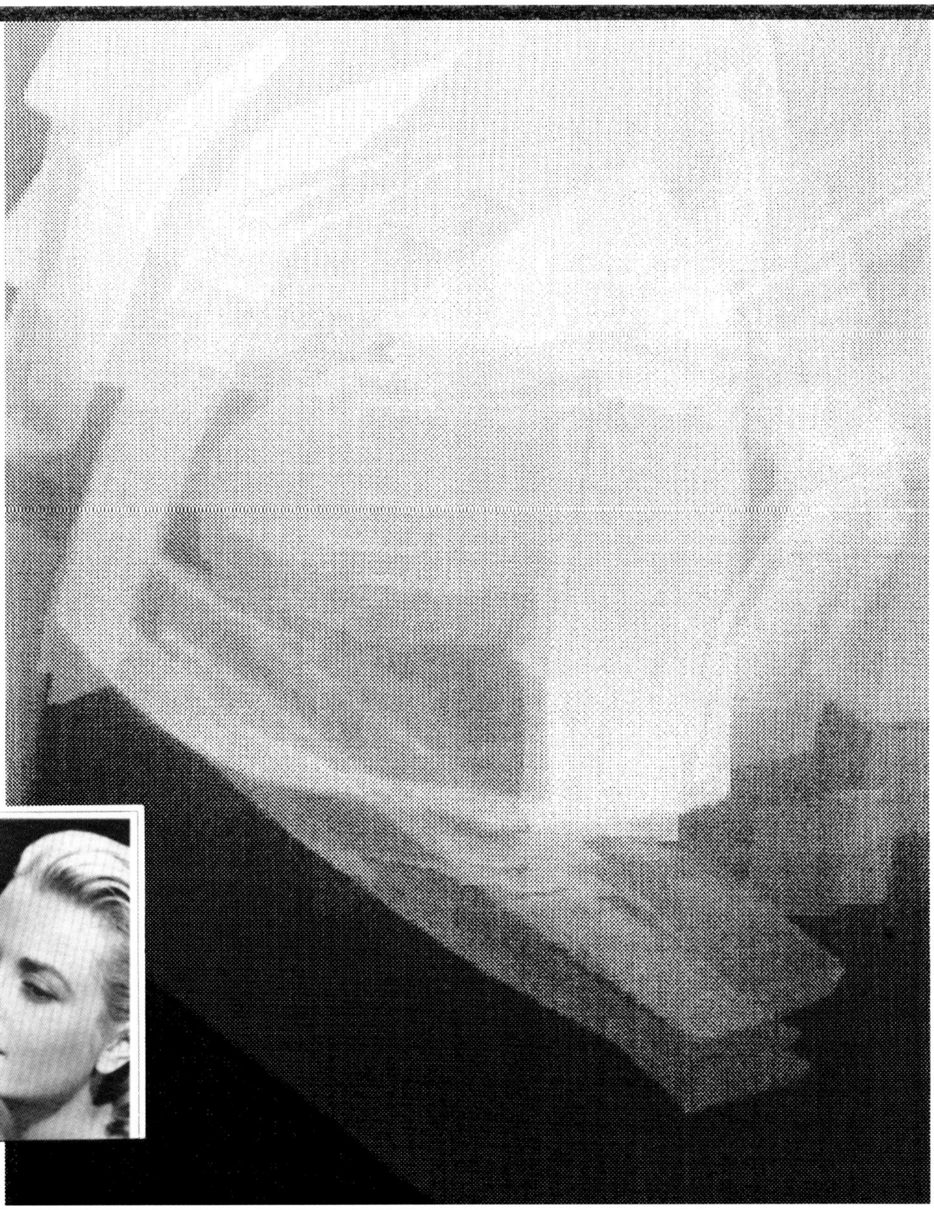

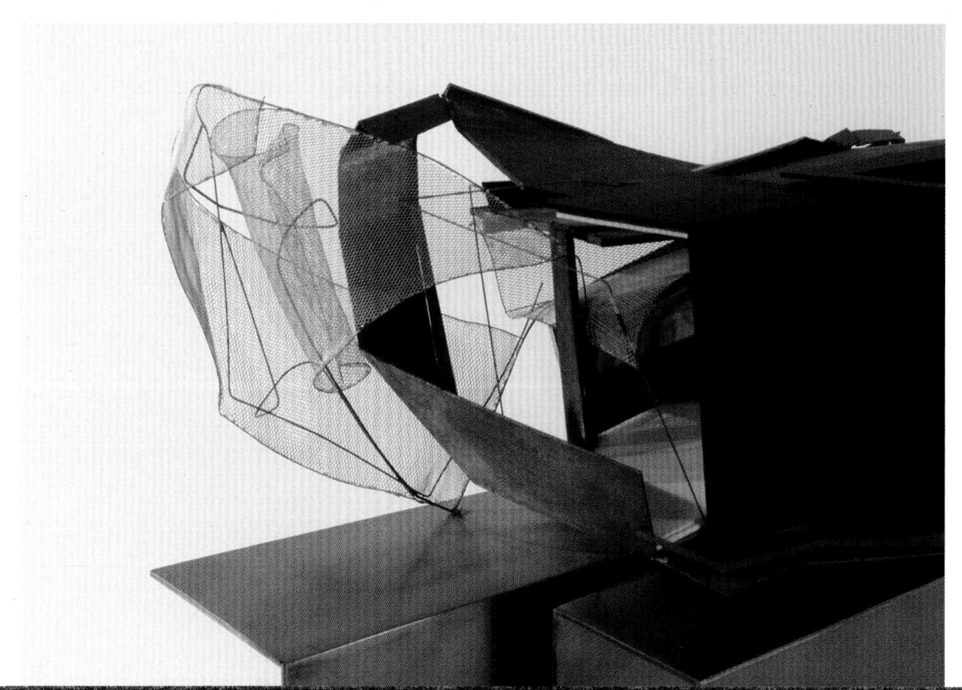

He is the god of boundaries while at the same time the god of communi-cation, the universal translator.

Hermes, International Cultural Center

I had the pleasure of meeting Fons Elders during my time at Superstudio in Florence. It was a stroke of serendipity to be the only one at the studio that fateful Sunday in the summer of 1981. I answered the intercom and heard, in a thick Dutch accent, “This is Professor Elders and I am here to meet Professor Frassinelli regarding a project.” I went to the front door, shocked to find three bald men in Sari cloth. Each was decorated with silver jewelry and I still remember the kind expression in their eyes. They’ve just returned from India and decided to stop by to meet Frassinelli without making an appointment. The surprised look on my face melted away once Fons and I sat down and talked. We connected immediately and before I knew it, we were exchanging life stories. Neither of us knew that would be the beginning of a lifelong friendship and collaboration.

The next day I told Piero Frassinelli the whole story in detail, but was confronted with cynicism and doubt. I insisted that a simple sit down wouldn’t hurt. After much persuasion, I coordinated a meeting with Elders and that same day, Superstudio was invited to compete for a housing project in Amsterdam titled “House of Four Winds.” At the time, Elders told us that it was a competition between Superstudio and OMA (Office of Metropolitan Architecture) headed by the Dutch architect Rem Koolhaas.

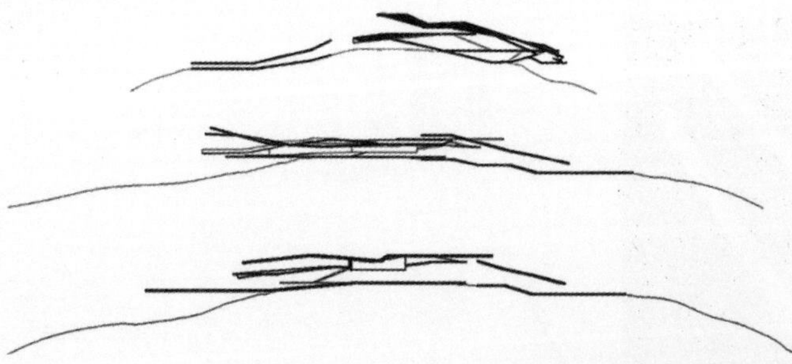

Superstudio eventually won the competition and I had the privilege of being involved in the initial stages of the project's design, which was finally built after ten years. Fons's hard work and perseverance finally paid off. Considering all the issues he dealt with surrounding the planning, designing, financing, and construction, everyone agreed it was because of him that the House of Four Winds was finally realized.

A similar faith brought Fons and I together again almost 20 years later. In 1999, Elders invited me in to compete for the Hermes International Cultural Center Project. I was to present my design to the board of his organization, Forum 2001, at their fourth symposium named "Conference of the Birds" in Sardinia, Italy.

It was soon clear that the project was going to challenge me creatively, spiritually, and emotionally. I trusted to embrace the process because I knew that Fons's creative, unorthodox mind is what makes him a great teacher, thinker, and philosopher.

Hermes, International Cultural Center

Location:
Sinalunga, Italy

Year:
1999–2002 (not built)

Program:
Cultural Center for Comparative Studies among Cultures

Fons and I exchanged emails on a weekly basis, discussing the program and his philosophical inspiration for the center. He was the teacher and I the student, taking notes about why he selected the name Hermes. The cultural center was destined to thrive and facilitate communication, coexistence between different cultures. In the words of French scholar Antoin Favivre, "Showing the path of otherness, of living diversity, of communication of souls...Hermes favors and simulates living relationships within art and literature." So, when designing a building for this grand purpose, the question then becomes, what is the spirit of interchange? As an architect, I must acknowledge the interchange between:

a. the kinetics of the land and natural foliage of the site.
b. the impulses and intentions of bodies as they occupy space.
c. the manifestations of the outside world and the built form, both of which are human-made and made by nature over the course of centuries.

I looked for an architectural solution that could coexist with the mountainous plateaus that gradually slope to the sea. At first glance, the landscape seemed calm, but after a few days I soon realized how stubborn and wild the land was with it's dark, volcanic granite. You could feel the exuberant energy that the site was projecting, which confirmed why Elders selected this location. The site's powerful nature was able to transform every human-made attempt at change, simulating the shapes and materials of the natural existing site. This was well apparent in Sardinia's granite buildings and streets lined with cork trees.

"The geographic space of Sardinia has a significant singularity both with respect to the peninsular spaces of the continent and with respect to the other islands of the Mediterranean. The central element of this identity is the dominance of nature with respect to the anthropic factors in the conformation and physical transformation of the landscape. A landscape that still has in itself, legible and often meanwhile, the original character imprinted in the telluric harshness of its forms, which shaped by an irreducible windiness, mark the slow evolution of geological history."
– Antonio Muzzetto

To better understand Fons's selection of the site, one would need to understand his humanity and his tireless search for meaning or truth. He is a philosopher, highly educated in film, theater, visual arts, urban planning, architecture, landscape, and humanities. He possesses a relentless, investigative mind and is committed to creating a community of artists, scholars, and writers from all over the world. Most importantly, he believes that he can make the world a better place if he remains confident in his vision and works hard.

Twenty years after meeting Elders, I felt maturer and more capable to influence his vision for the project. He taught me to trust my perspective, which was the product of my Iranian ancestry and spirituality. He helped me find dormant memories and stories, which connected me to a deeper consciousness and granted me insight on the spiritual journey that brought us together. Therefore, I wanted to reflect on his beliefs and the essence of his human nature, creating a dialogue between his philosophical concepts for the cultural center and for the site.

After a few attempts, my search led me to a "non-architectural" solution. Anything building-like didn't belong or felt disconnected. The site's stubborn nature was clear in it's message: leave me alone or conform to my disposition. I was desperately looking for a way to interact with the site, while emphasizing the flash of the modern intellect behind the building's architectural aspirations.

Inspiration for the design came from the land, not from the period architecture surrounding it. The hilly terrain of the site's rocky fabric is striped with ribbons of handmade stone walls looping endlessly toward the horizon. I wanted

to avoid vertical massing and rigid angular lines to reduce our footprint on the land. I worked instead to accentuate the flow of the earth to continue along with its natural progressions.

I imagined a building that draped into the land's sloping contours. As a result, a person strolling through the countryside could easily walk onto the roof of one of the building's outstretched arms before even realizing they had approached the structure. To accentuate the horizontal design that bows and bends toward the earth, we selected material and a color scheme that blends with the surroundings while adhering to the municipality's strict rules of contextualization. To meet these regulations, local volcanic stone was used for the retaining walls and all of the buildings' foundations. This rich cleft-cut gray stone identified the center with the site and created the illusion that the roofs were floating above the hillside. The roofs were made out of steel and wood beams with an exposed wood frame, which connected the inside materials with the natural environment. There are wood framed doors, windows, and glass enclosures made to connect the floating roof to the stone walls, while keeping the openness intact. The terra cotta garden roofs are utilized with the terrace and rooftop planters furthering the building's camouflage.

An important subtext of the design was to create a peaceful relationship between the site's parks and springs. That being said, the Cultural Center was envisioned upon the fundamental belief that buildings are about function as much as, if not more than, form. Therefore, I wanted to culturally transcend the project's fixed location within the central Gallura, creating an ambiance where anyone could feel that they belonged. In its final form, the building is

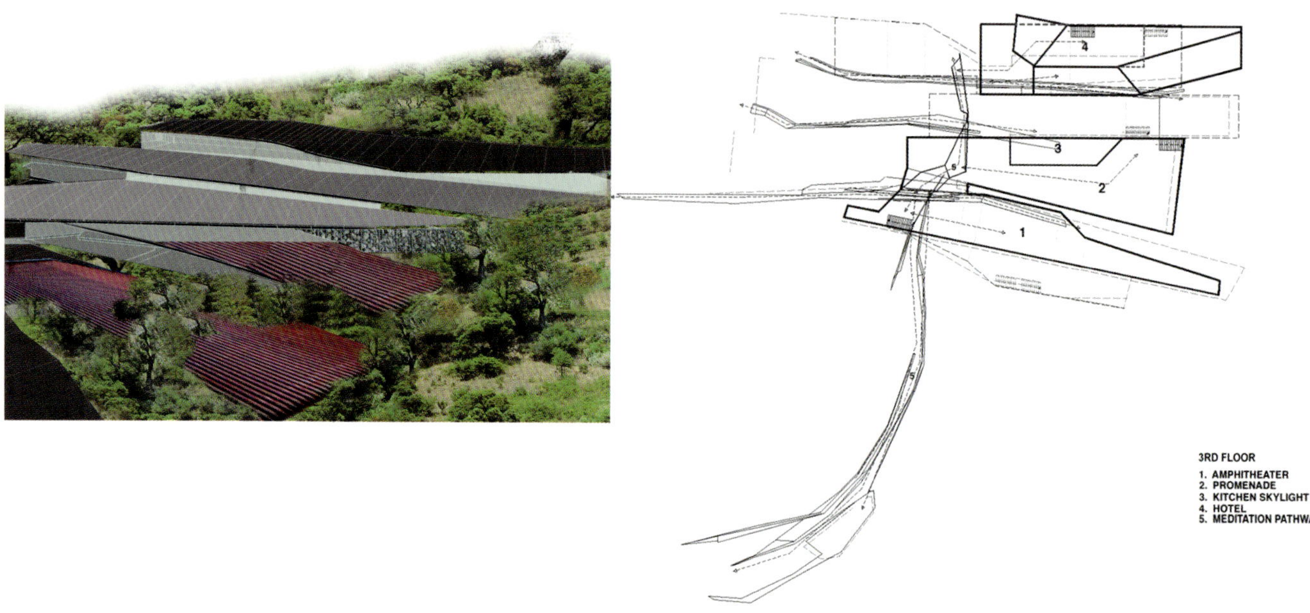

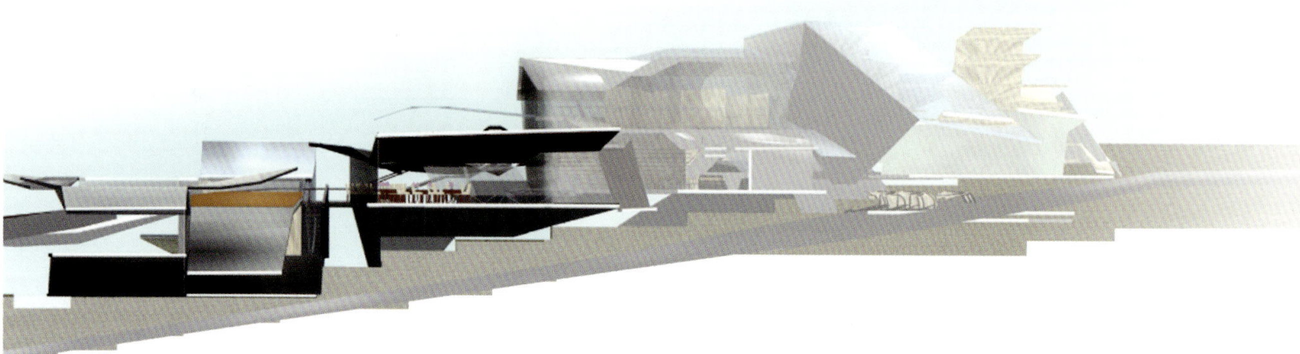

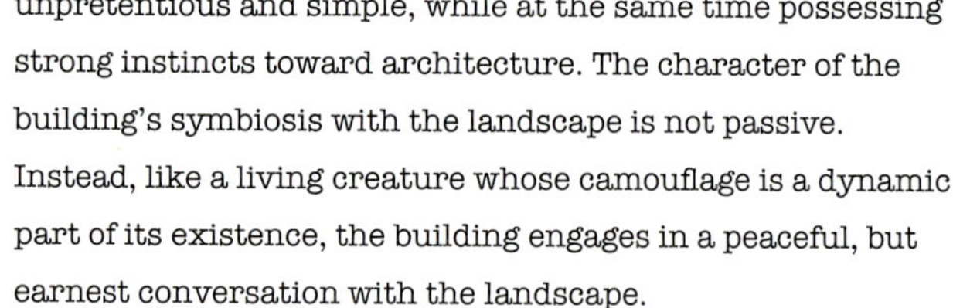

unpretentious and simple, while at the same time possessing strong instincts toward architecture. The character of the building's symbiosis with the landscape is not passive. Instead, like a living creature whose camouflage is a dynamic part of its existence, the building engages in a peaceful, but earnest conversation with the landscape.

Anticipating the corporeal patterning of the persons who pass through the space, a program was developed to fulfill the multifarious intellectual needs of the center's participants. Echoing the array of cultural, economic, and industrial backgrounds, the flexibility of the space was maximized through the incorporation of varied spatial systems.

The design encourages flexible uses of the center's many parts by defining a study and research library, an exhibition area, a multimedia room, an auditorium for conferences and seminars, a dormitory for residents, and a meditation area. As a space of interchange, the gregarious multi-cultural environment of the Hermes Centre is a space exemplifying both its founder's intentions and the spirit of its context.

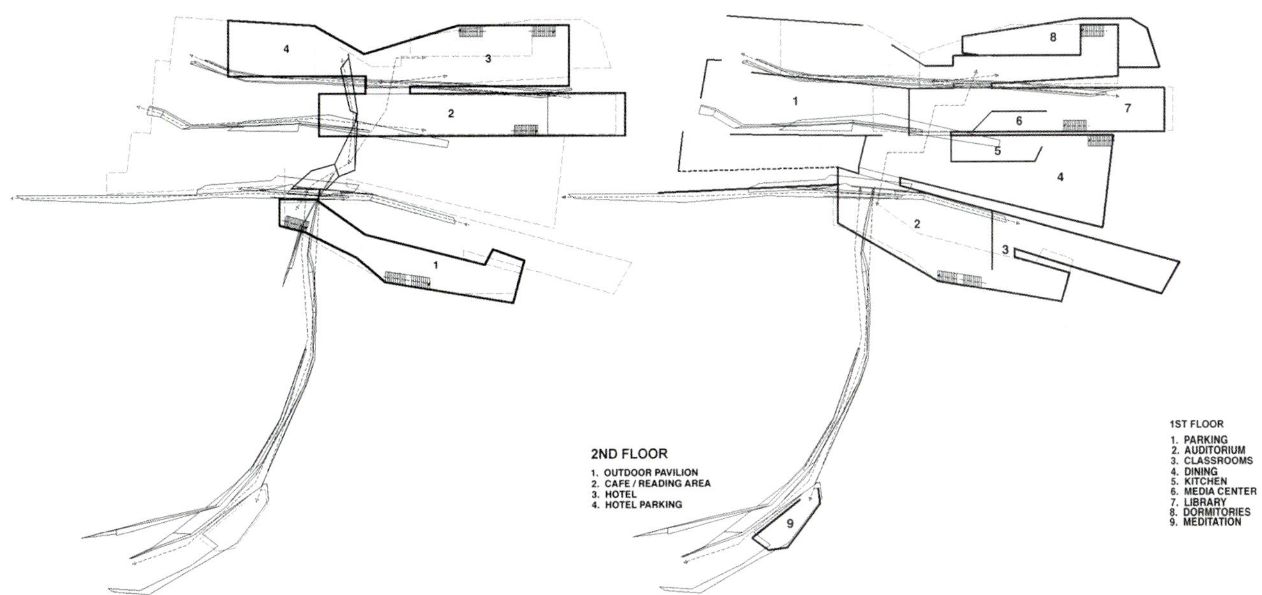

"The International Cultural Centre, a space destined to thrive in facilitating communication and coexistence between different cultures, takes its name and creative impetus from the Egyptian-Greek Mythological figure Hermes. Often identified with the Roman God Mercury and the Egyptian God Thoth, Hermes as a winged deity is the messenger and interpreter to the gods. Syncretized within the persona Hermes Trismegistus, the intervention of Hermes within human affairs often signals the states of existence that are transcendent of dialectics. In the words of Antoine Faivre: "Hermes shows the path of otherness, of living diversity, of communication of souls...Hermes favors and stimulates living relationships within art and literature.

He is the god of boundaries while at the same time the god of communication; the universal translator. In Mozart's' famous opera The Magic Flute, Hermes (Mercurius) is disguised as the character Papageno. In the role of a bird catcher Papageno embodies another of Hermes attributes, the ability to exemplify one of the major maxims of alchemy: fac fixum volatile (In other words) make fixed the volatile, and make volatile, what is fixated. These characteristics of Hermes' nature resonates with the Cultural Center's mandate: the promotion of the spirit of interchange."

– An Excerpt from a letter Fons wrote to Michele

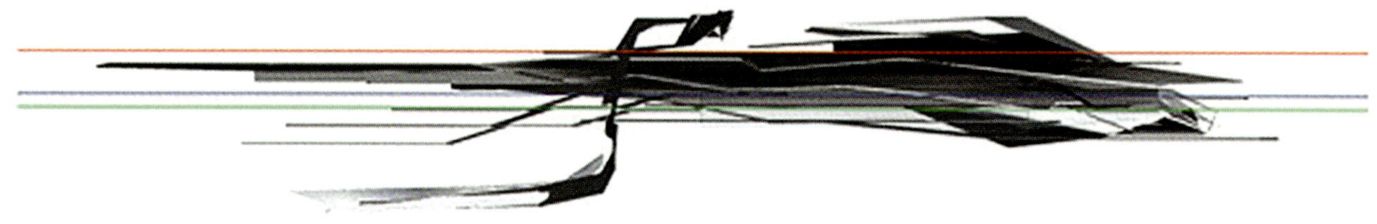

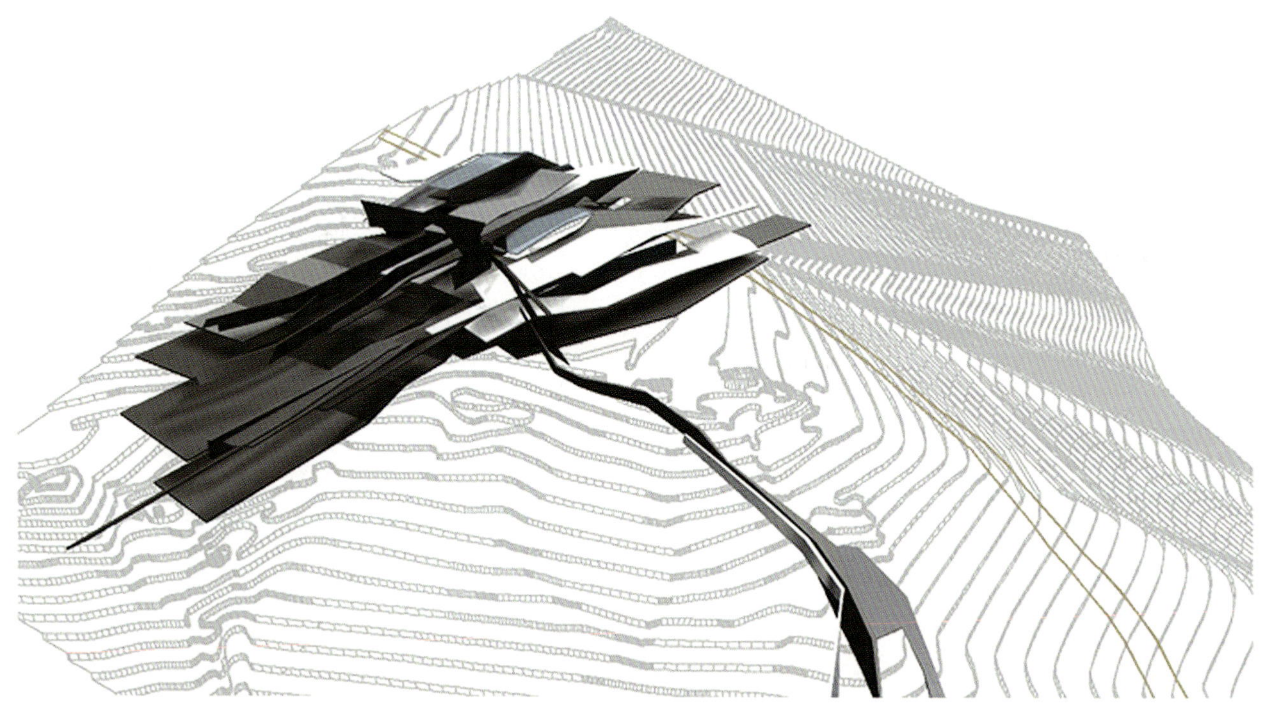

Gliding through smooth waters this home's creative inhabitants arrive where the concept of what is real becomes a choice.

Linnie House

This house located on the Linnie Canal in Venice, California is situated in a convergent space of urban contradictions, architectural experimentation, historical resonances, and social and programmatic ideologies.

At the start of the 20th century, the land south of Ocean Park Boulevard through the Del Rey peninsula, later known as the Venice Canal Historic District, was transformed into the "Venice of America," by developer Abbot Kinney. Visitors marveled at his human-made canal network, ornate Venetian-style shopping arcades, and festive entertainment pier with dance halls, bath houses, and entertainment. Despite the continuing success of Venice, the popularity of the canals waned. In 1929, a majority of the canals were filled-in and converted to public streets. It wasn't until the sixties when the remaining canals became popular again, hosting beatniks, artists, hippies, and the likes of Jim Morrison.

In 1999, Shelly Burger and Lothar Schmitz purchased a 30x90-foot lot. Both envisioned a house that would feel like an artist's loft, but functions like a traditional home; a place where they could work and create – Shelley was a lawyer who changed her career to follow her passion of writing poetry while Lothar was a research physicist at UCLA who creates sculptures inspired by science, biology, and the environment.

The design for this home needed to balance the historically significant surroundings, but more importantly it needed to satisfy the desires of two strong-minded intellectuals who had both, since childhood, dreamed of living in a futuristic, contemporary space.

Rather than starting the architectural process with drawing, I took advantage of the clients' artistic abilities and began with a collaborative exchange of ideas. I encouraged each of the clients to write a story or essay expressing their visions for the lot. Inspired by these, I then produced the initial series of sketches responding to their intentions, interrogating the site on the canal, and evoking the history of the place.

Linnie House

Location:
Venice Canal, California, USA

Year:
2000 – 2005 (built)

Program:
Single family House

Aspiring to transcend the physical limitations of the small 30x90-foot lot, the entire building's architectural design slants toward the canal, which is as an architectural response to the height limitation (as it is dictated by zoning code). The front portion of the building increases toward the back of the property, transforming and harnessing uncertainty as a generator of form. The physical limitations of the lot (the code restrictions by the planning department, building department, coastal commission, neighborhood association, etc.) became an opportunity to be more creative.

The habitable spaces of the house form with the inertia of un-programmed spaces and areas converging, diverging, and layering. Once defined, those areas were programmed to meet the needs of the house's occupants.

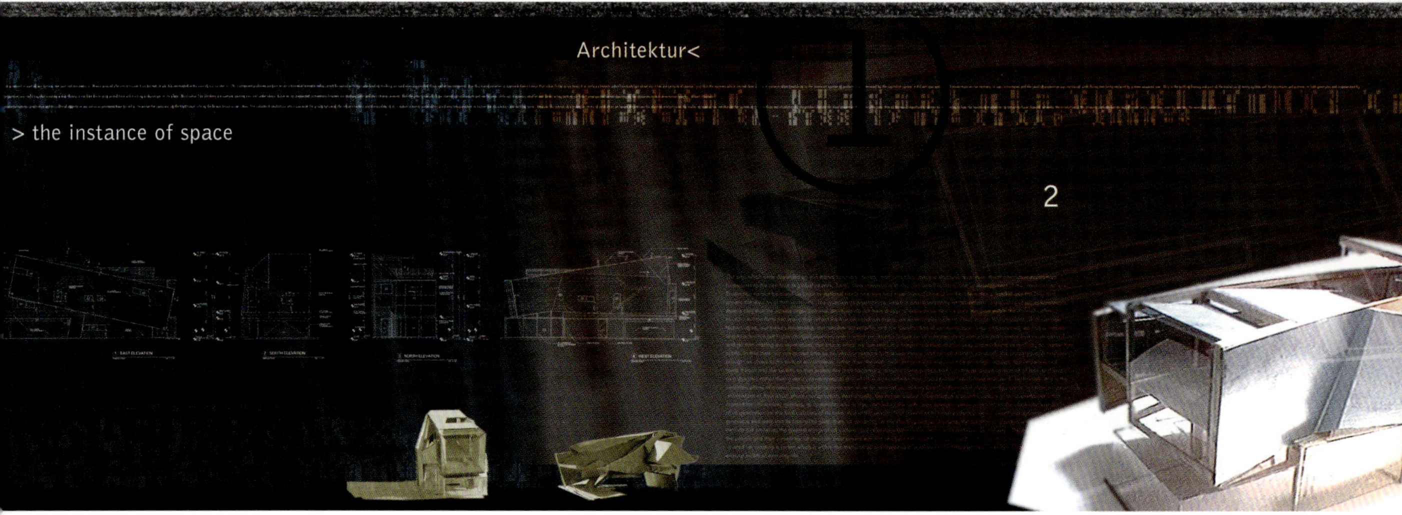

SAEE
3
>unprogrammed surface
2

>methodology of uncertainty
ng,diverging and layering across the area of the site
4
6

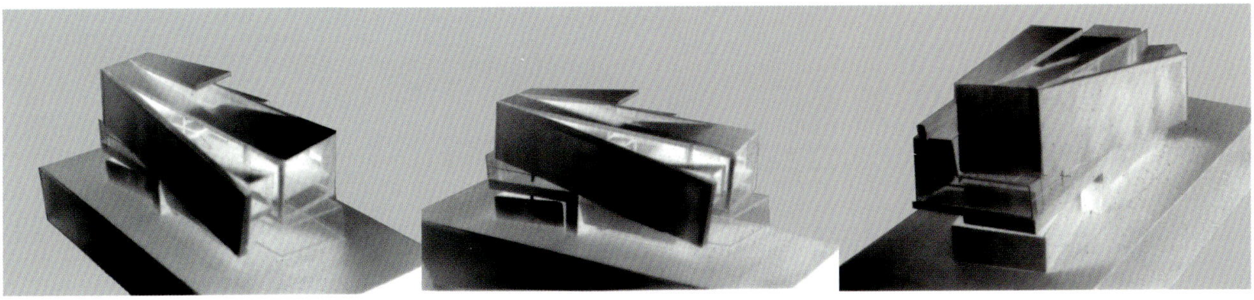

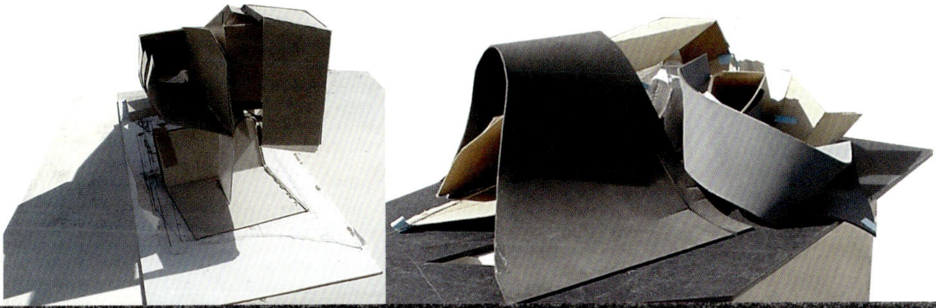

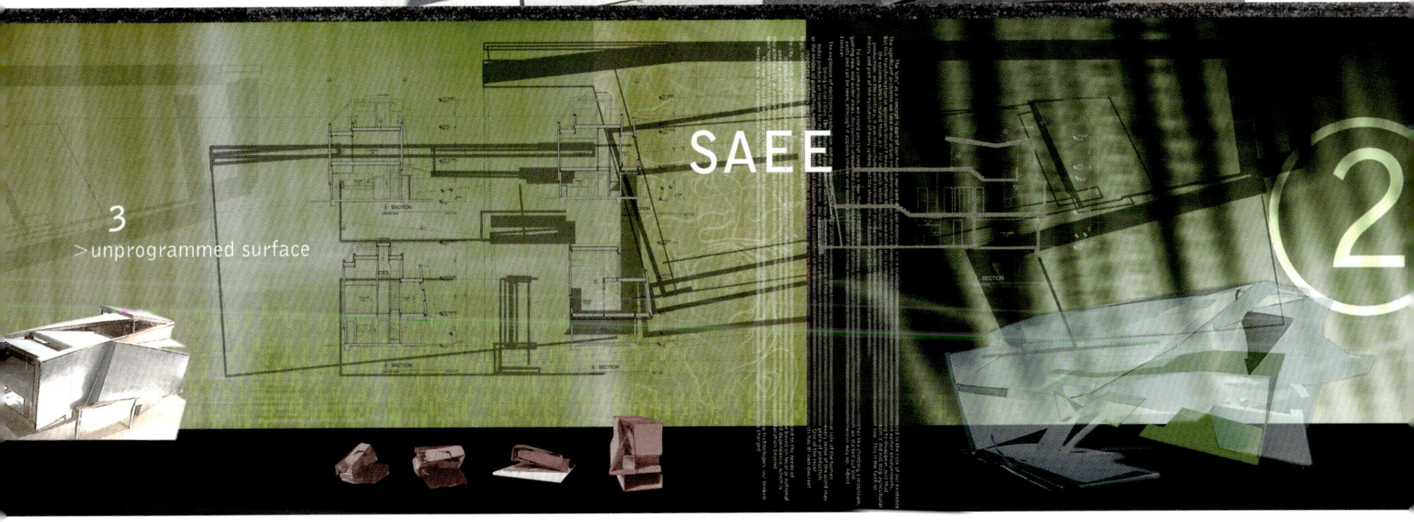

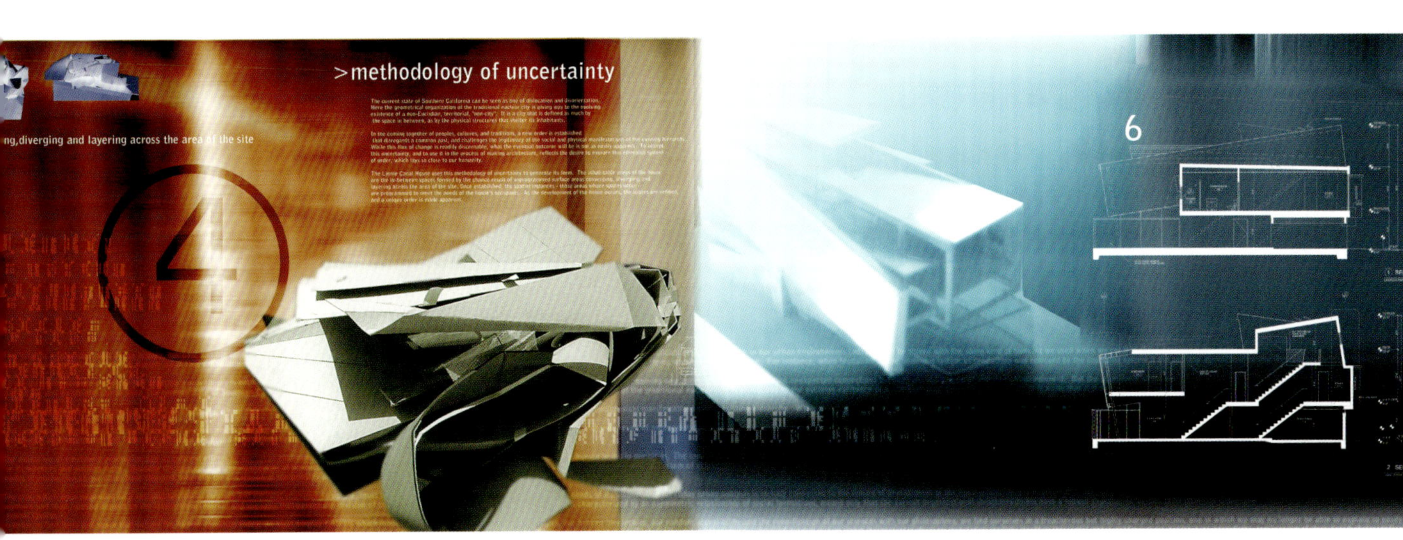

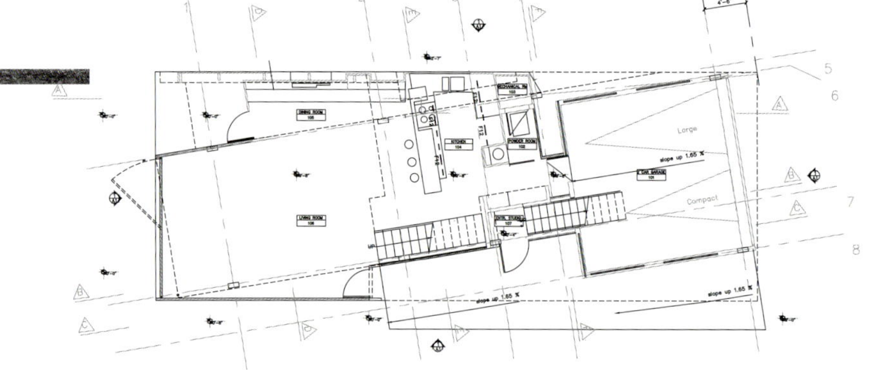

Large
Compact
slope up 1.65 %

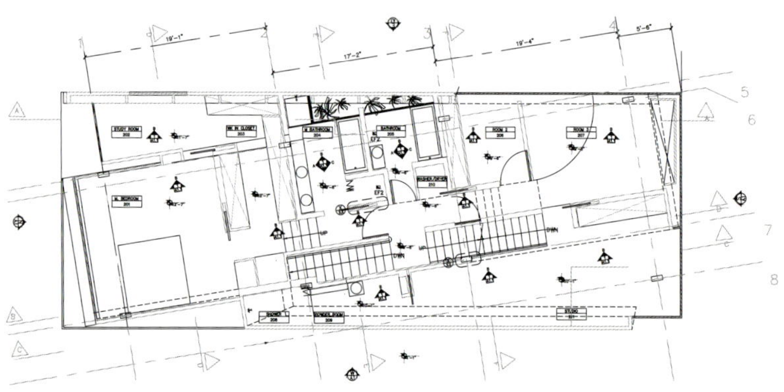

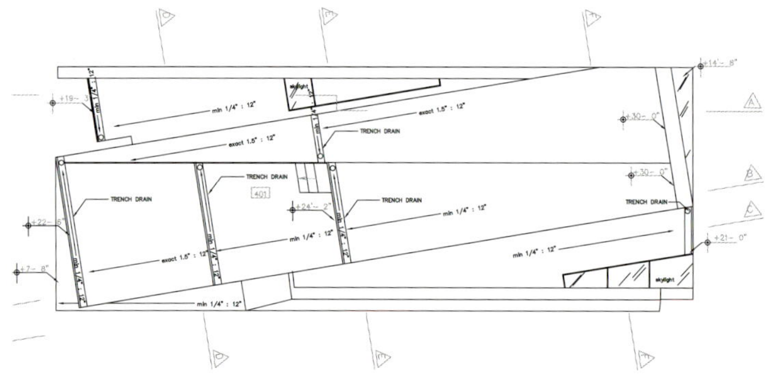

TRENCH DRAIN
min 1/4" : 12"
exact 1.5" : 12"
skylight

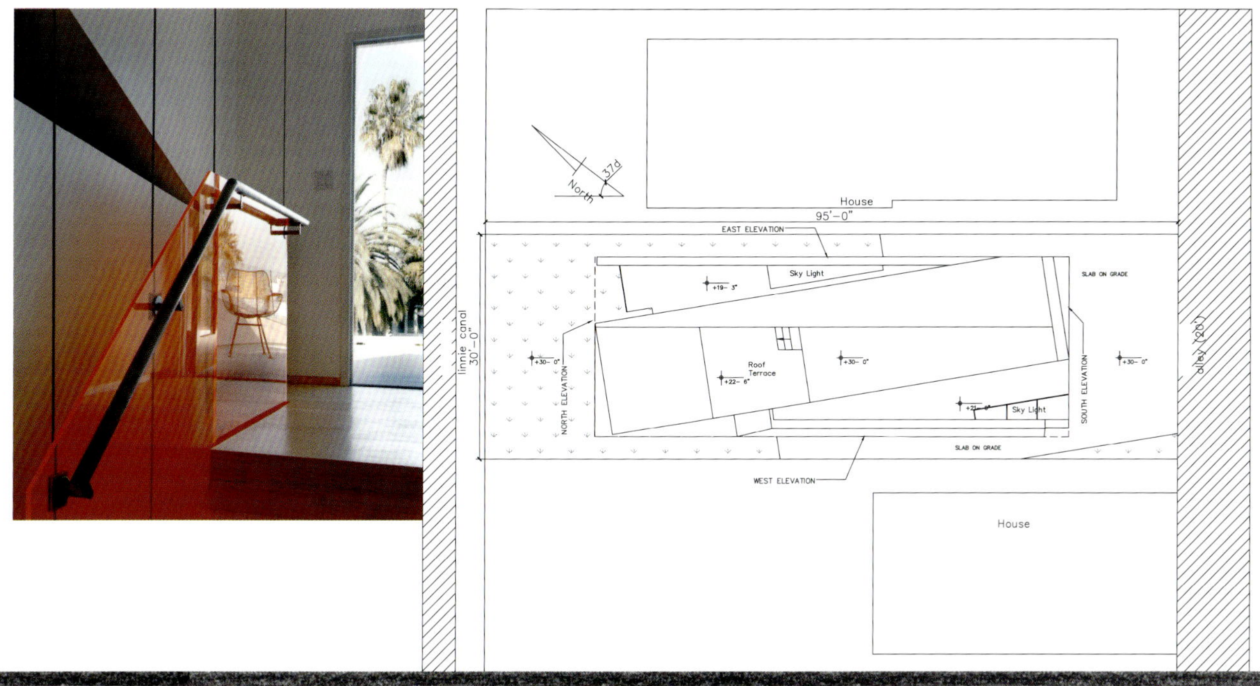

For example, the need for an additional guest bedroom or an independent rental unit were among the programs that were added to the project.

The design of the spaces and the architectural forms of the building were being developed simultaneously. Unlike the traditional approach to design known as "form follows function," in our process, form and function were

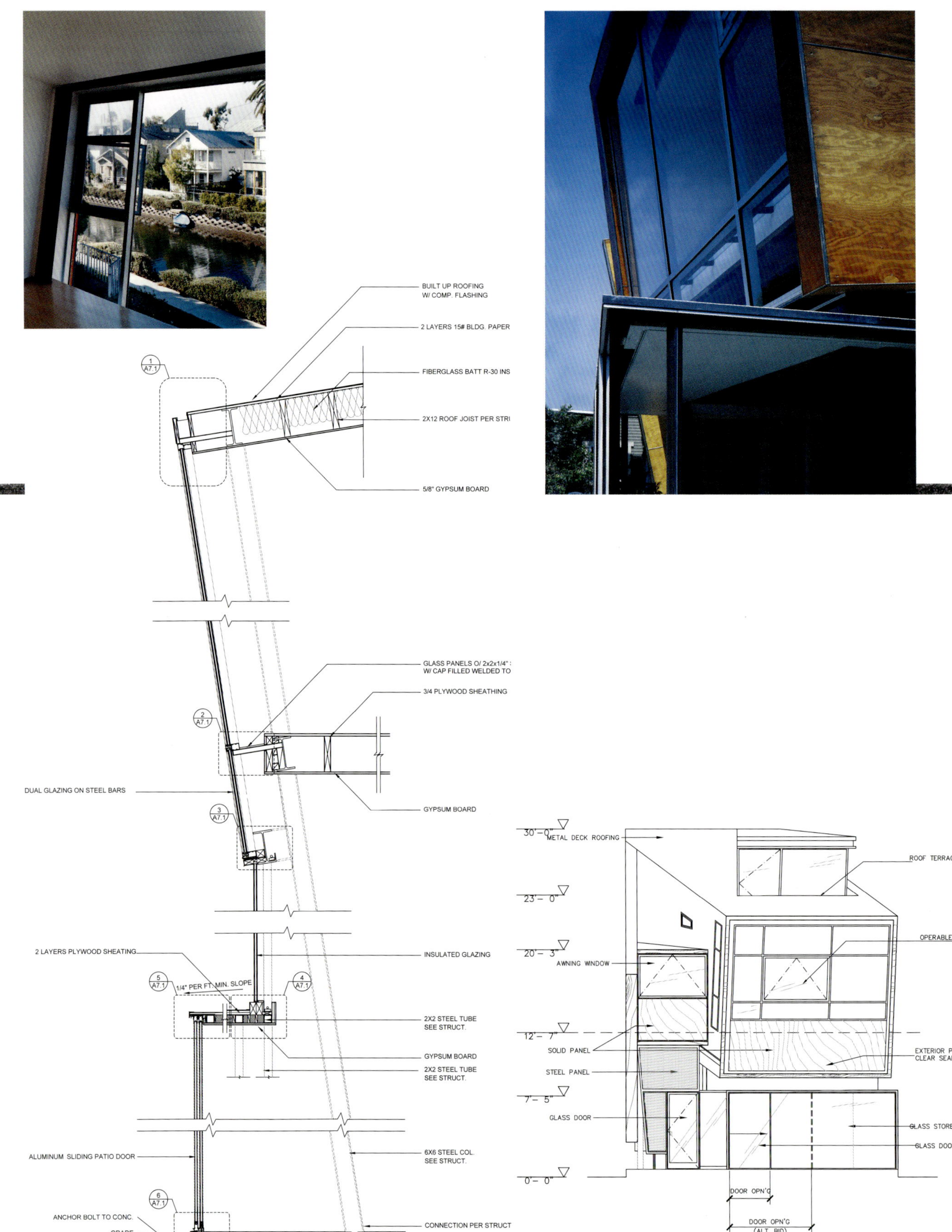

BUILT UP ROOFING
W/ COMP. FLASHING
2 LAYERS 15# BLDG. PAPER
FIBERGLASS BATT R-30 INS
2X12 ROOF JOIST PER STR
5/8" GYPSUM BOARD
GLASS PANELS O/ 2x2x1/4"
W/ CAP FILLED WELDED TO
3/4 PLYWOOD SHEATHING
DUAL GLAZING ON STEEL BARS
GYPSUM BOARD
2 LAYERS PLYWOOD SHEATING
1/4" PER FT MIN. SLOPE
INSULATED GLAZING
2X2 STEEL TUBE
SEE STRUCT.
GYPSUM BOARD
2X2 STEEL TUBE
SEE STRUCT.
ALUMINUM SLIDING PATIO DOOR
6X6 STEEL COL.
SEE STRUCT.
ANCHOR BOLT TO CONC.
GRADE
STEEL ANGLE
CONNECTION PER STRUCT
CONCRETE SLAB
POLYSTYRENE INSULATION
SAND
SAND
VAPOR BARRIER
CONCRETE FOUNDATION
30'-0"
METAL DECK ROOFING
ROOF TERRACE
23'- 0"
20'- 3"
AWNING WINDOW
OPERABLE
12'- 7"
SOLID PANEL
STEEL PANEL
EXTERIOR PLY
CLEAR SEALE
7'- 5"
GLASS DOOR
GLASS STOREF
GLASS DOOR
0'- 0"
DOOR OPN'G
DOOR OPN'G
(ALT. BID)

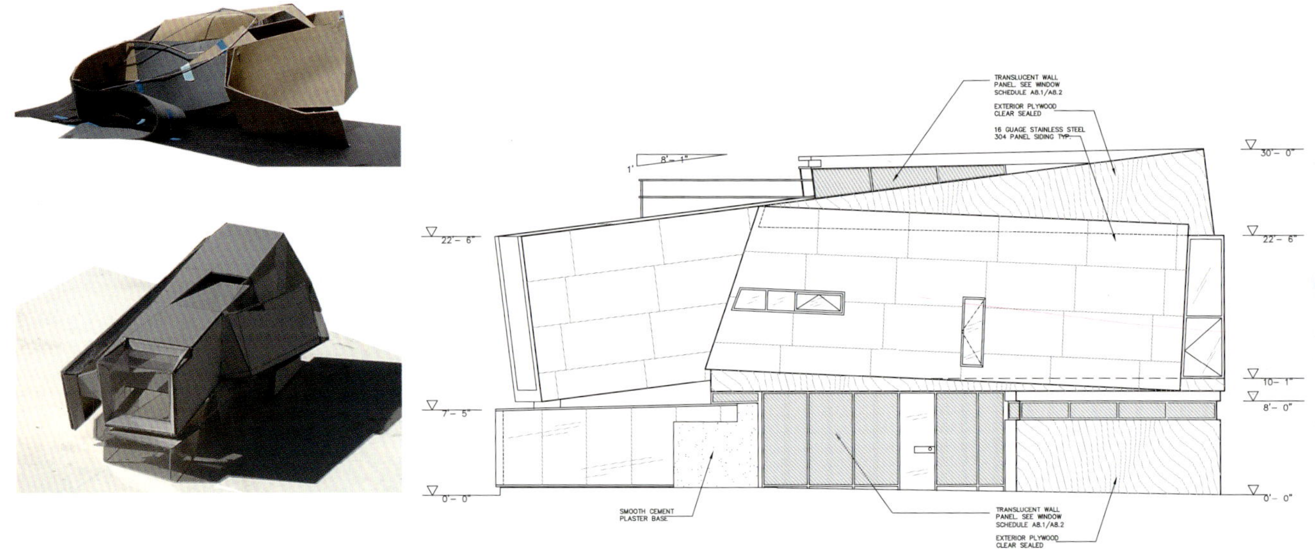

accommodating the needs of the site, clients, and myself. Further development refined the collection of spaces with the emergence of a unique spatial order and tectonic sensibility. At our regular meetings with Shelley and Lothar, we addressed their programmatic needs and sketched on the drawings to place them most suitably to their needs. Their spatial criticisms that followed were related to size, function, light, and materials. It was a dynamic process and not the easiest since, needless to say, we each had our own personalized idea of what we call home.

We supplemented the basic domestic spaces (bedrooms, bathrooms, kitchen, etc.) with two artistic spaces (a writing study and an artist's studio), a small autonomous apartment, and a two-car garage.

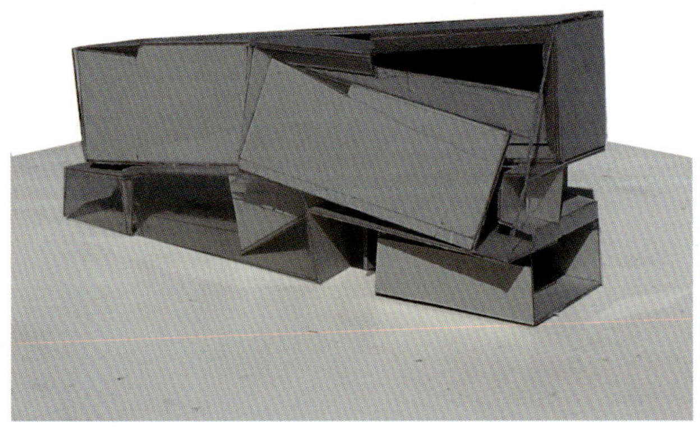

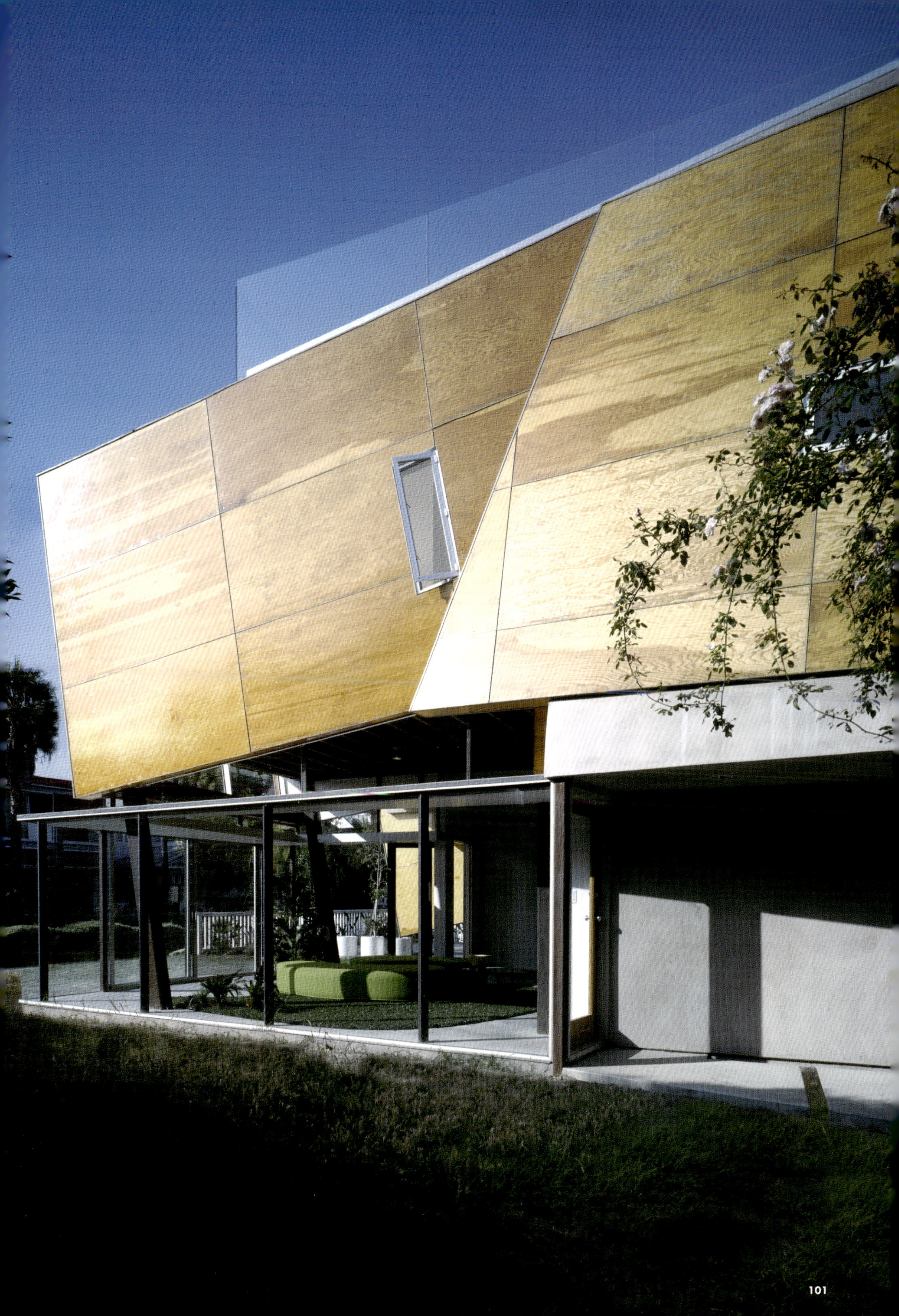

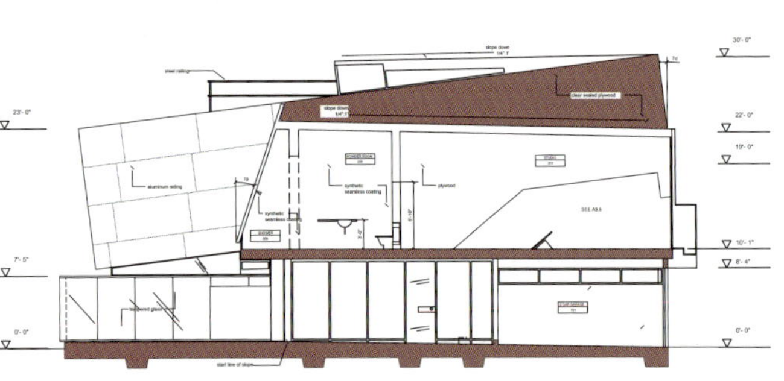

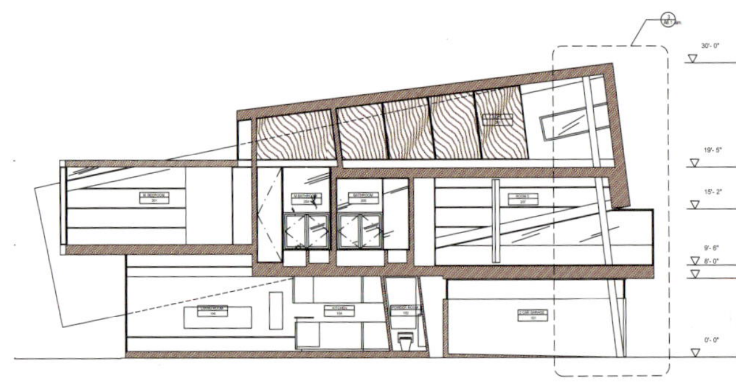

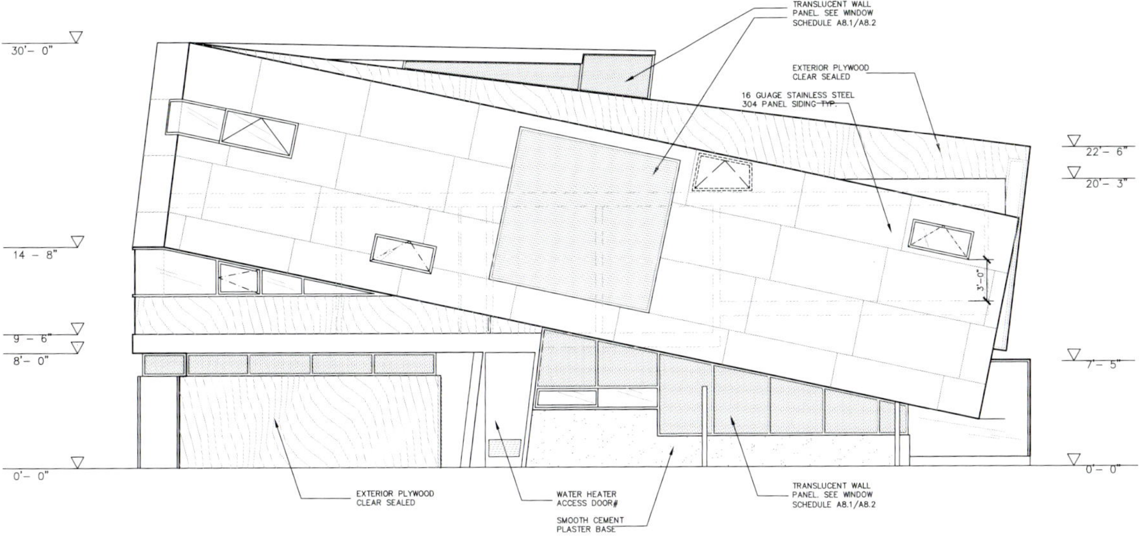

Within the resulting three-story structure, there are five levels. Functional spaces are arranged to create a psychology of continuity between the interior spaces and the canal. Opening to the front yard toward the canal, the boundaries of the living area dissolve into a transparent wall of sliding doors and fixed glass. The exterior walls slide and shear, responding to the features of the site while accommodating the functional needs of the program. This wall of glass spans the building's north and southwest borders, dissolving the corner and enhancing the perceptual extension of the interior all the way to the canal.

There are two independent sets of stairs situated back to back in the house. One brings you to the second level of the main house's bedrooms, bathrooms, through the artist studio, and finally to the roof. The master bedroom, above the living room, is on the third level, which is three steps higher than the second level. This gives the living room an elevated and more spacious feeling,

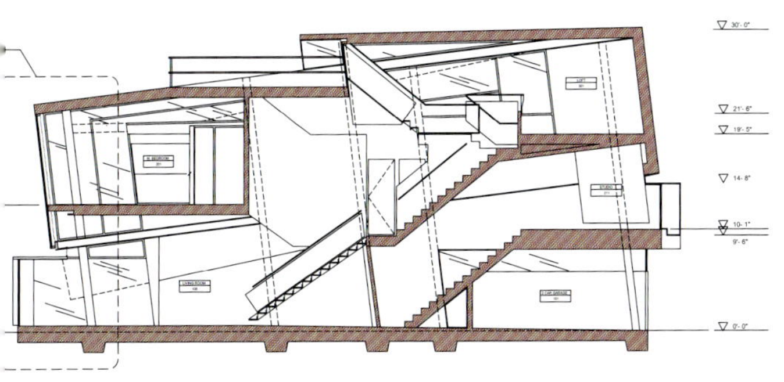

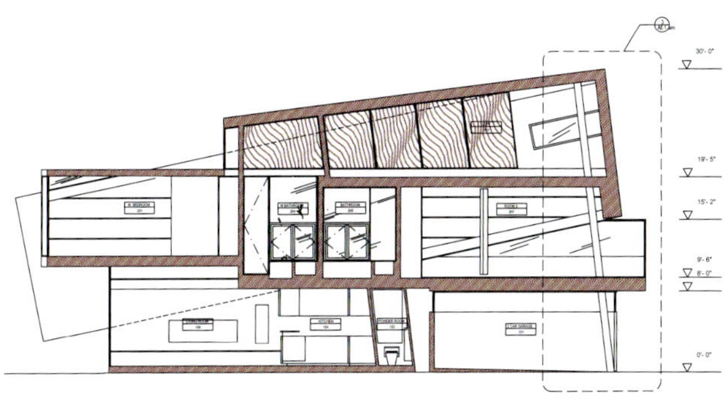

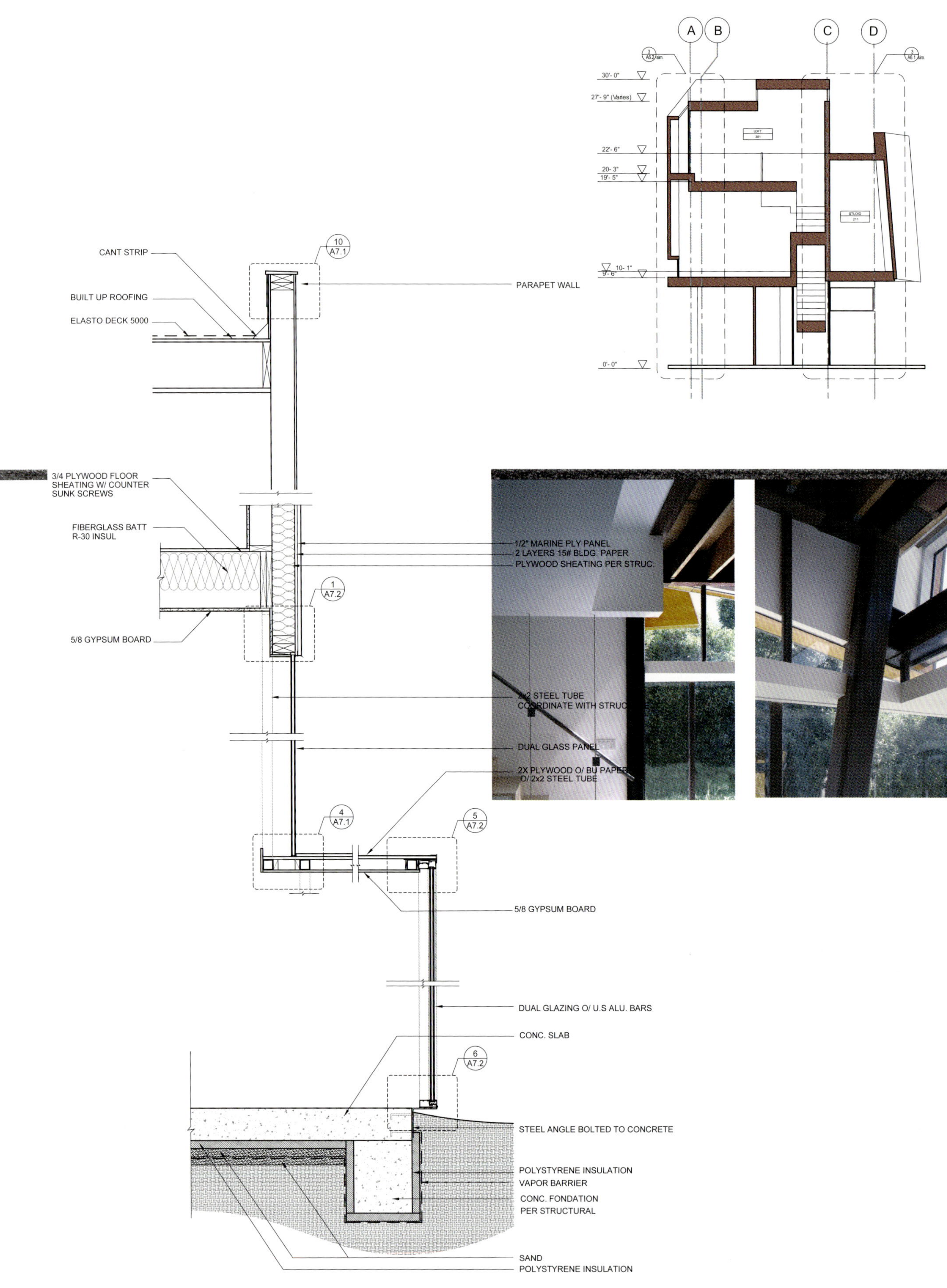
A
B
C
D
30'- 0"
27'- 9" (Varies)
22'- 6"
20- 3"
19'- 5"
10- 1"
9'- 6"
0'- 0"
LOFT
STUDIO
CANT STRIP
BUILT UP ROOFING
ELASTO DECK 5000
10
A7.1
PARAPET WALL
3/4 PLYWOOD FLOOR
SHEATING W/ COUNTER
SUNK SCREWS
FIBERGLASS BATT
R-30 INSUL
1/2" MARINE PLY PANEL
2 LAYERS 15# BLDG. PAPER
PLYWOOD SHEATING PER STRUC.
1
A7.2
5/8 GYPSUM BOARD
2x2 STEEL TUBE
COORDINATE WITH STRUC
DUAL GLASS PANEL
2X PLYWOOD O/ BU PAPER
O/ 2x2 STEEL TUBE
4
A7.1
5
A7.2
5/8 GYPSUM BOARD
DUAL GLAZING O/ U.S ALU. BARS
CONC. SLAB
6
A7.2
STEEL ANGLE BOLTED TO CONCRETE
POLYSTYRENE INSULATION
VAPOR BARRIER
CONC. FONDATION
PER STRUCTURAL
SAND
POLYSTYRENE INSULATION

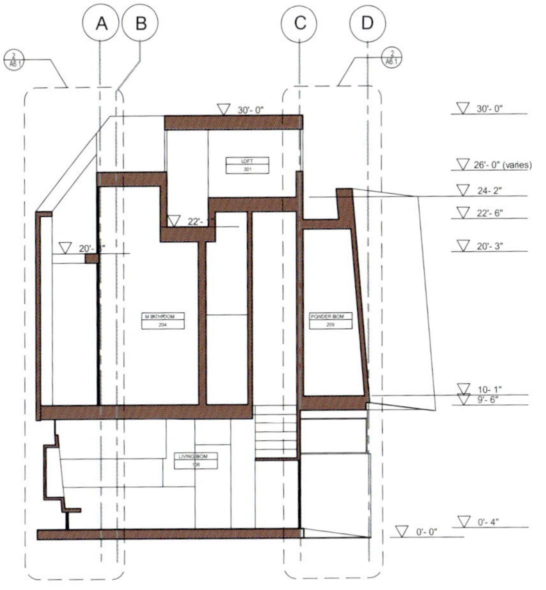

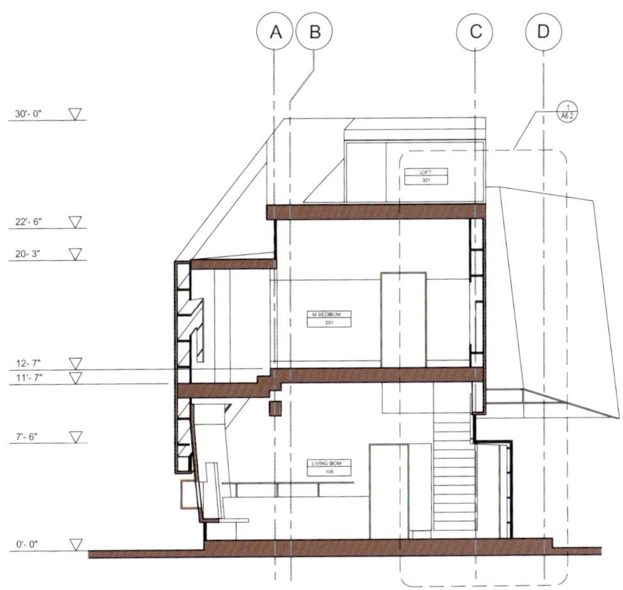

while granting more privacy to the master bedroom, which dynamically joins the interior and exterior with a slanted glass wall that draws attention to the canal and the palm trees beyond. On the north side of the bedroom, a small space opens toward the property line. Tailored for Shelley's creative escape, this compact space expands to the space of the canal with an entire wall of glass. The stairs continue up to the fourth level studio loft space, where Lothar creates and plans his installation art, and ends at the roof level (fifth level). Affording an awe-inspiring view of the Linnie Canal and the beautiful Venetian landscape, one realizes that they have been transported from the heart of one of the world's busiest metropolises to the tranquil Venice of America.

The other set of stairs brings you to a small and lengthy pie-shaped studio apartment that comprises the second floor. During the design's final stages, Shelly and Lothar expressed their financial concerns for the house. They asked if we could consider including a small, independent apartment that they could rent to others. We agreed and that's how the little pie-shaped studio came to be. It seemed to be the missing piece, once I considered the building design, plan, and the geometry of its different volumes.

The Linnie House transforms reality, propelling its occupants from the hustle and bustle of urban Los Angeles to the peacefulness of a vapor, travelling through Italian canals. This home's creative inhabitants arrive where the concept of what is real becomes a choice.

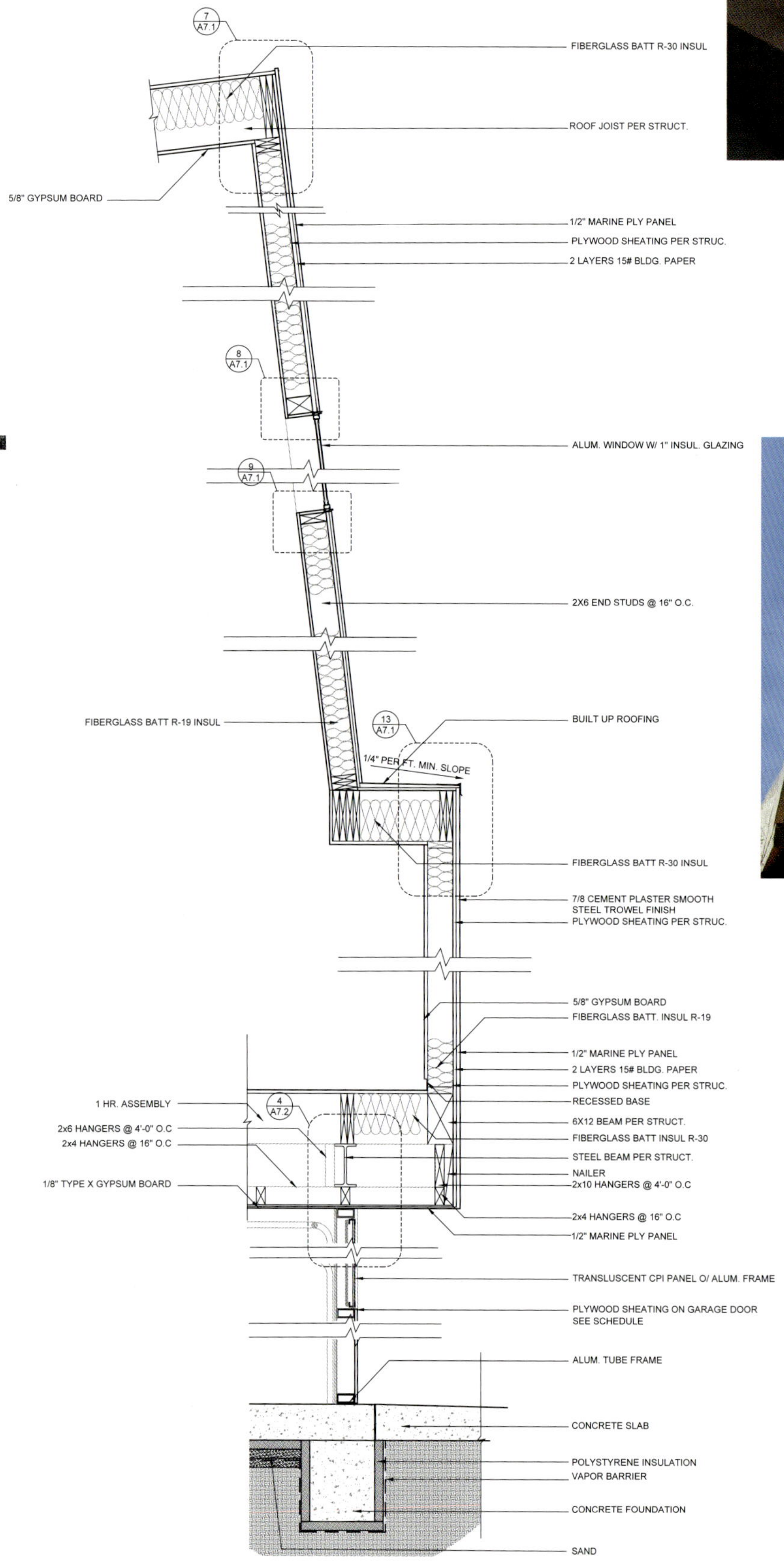

7
A7.1

FIBERGLASS BATT R-30 INSUL

ROOF JOIST PER STRUCT.

5/8" GYPSUM BOARD

1/2" MARINE PLY PANEL

PLYWOOD SHEATING PER STRUC.

2 LAYERS 15# BLDG. PAPER

8
A7.1

ALUM. WINDOW W/ 1" INSUL. GLAZING

9
A7.1

2X6 END STUDS @ 16" O.C.

FIBERGLASS BATT R-19 INSUL

13
A7.1

BUILT UP ROOFING

1/4" PER FT. MIN. SLOPE

FIBERGLASS BATT R-30 INSUL

7/8 CEMENT PLASTER SMOOTH
STEEL TROWEL FINISH

PLYWOOD SHEATING PER STRUC.

5/8" GYPSUM BOARD

FIBERGLASS BATT. INSUL R-19

1/2" MARINE PLY PANEL

2 LAYERS 15# BLDG. PAPER

PLYWOOD SHEATING PER STRUC.

RECESSED BASE

1 HR. ASSEMBLY

4
A7.2

6X12 BEAM PER STRUCT.

2x6 HANGERS @ 4'-0" O.C

FIBERGLASS BATT INSUL R-30

2x4 HANGERS @ 16" O.C

STEEL BEAM PER STRUCT.

NAILER

1/8" TYPE X GYPSUM BOARD

2x10 HANGERS @ 4'-0" O.C

2x4 HANGERS @ 16" O.C

1/2" MARINE PLY PANEL

TRANSLUCENT CPI PANEL O/ ALUM. FRAME

PLYWOOD SHEATING ON GARAGE DOOR
SEE SCHEDULE

ALUM. TUBE FRAME

CONCRETE SLAB

POLYSTYRENE INSULATION

VAPOR BARRIER

CONCRETE FOUNDATION

SAND

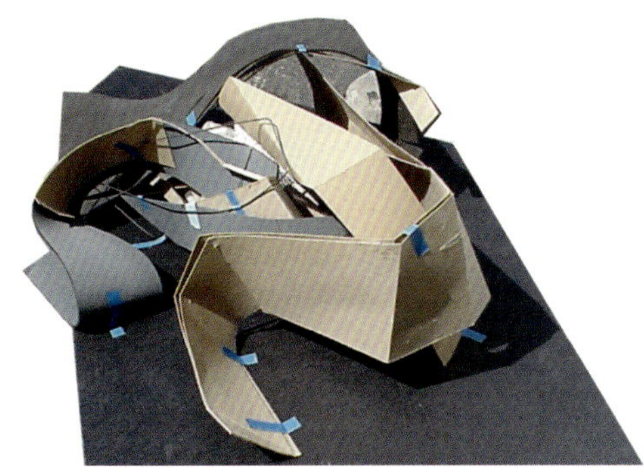

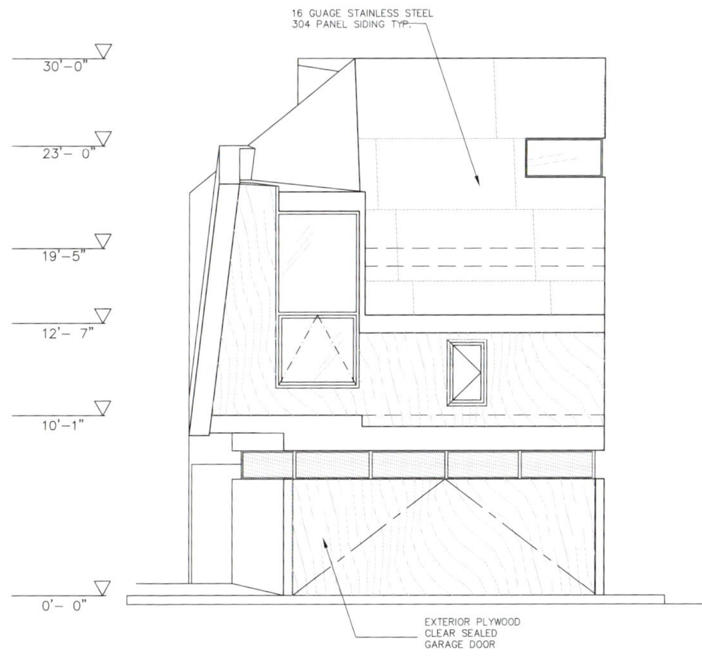
16 GUAGE STAINLESS STEEL
304 PANEL SIDING TYP.
30'-0"
23'- 0"
19'-5"
12'- 7"
10'-1"
0'- 0"
EXTERIOR PLYWOOD
CLEAR SEALED
GARAGE DOOR

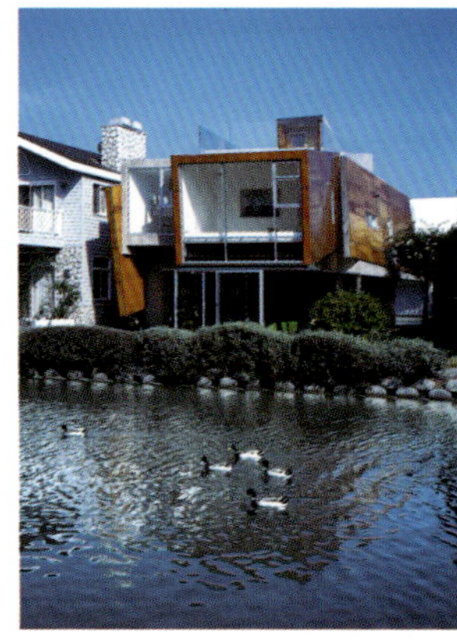

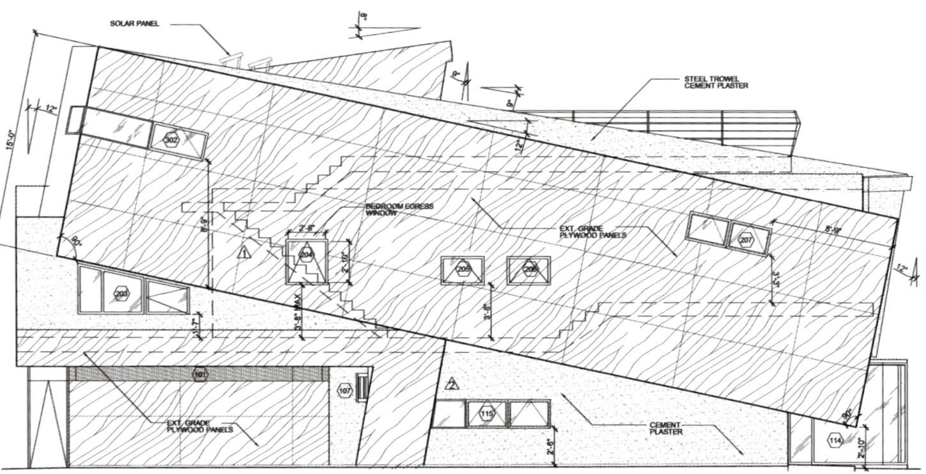

SOLAR PANEL
STEEL TROWEL
CEMENT PLASTER
15'-0"
12"
302
BEDROOM EGRESS
WINDOW
EXT. GRADE
PLYWOOD PANELS
2'-8"
204
2'-10"
205
206
207
8'-9"
3'-3"
203
3'-8" MAX
3'-8"
101
107
115
EXT. GRADE
PLYWOOD PANELS
CEMENT
PLASTER
114
2'-6"
2'-10"

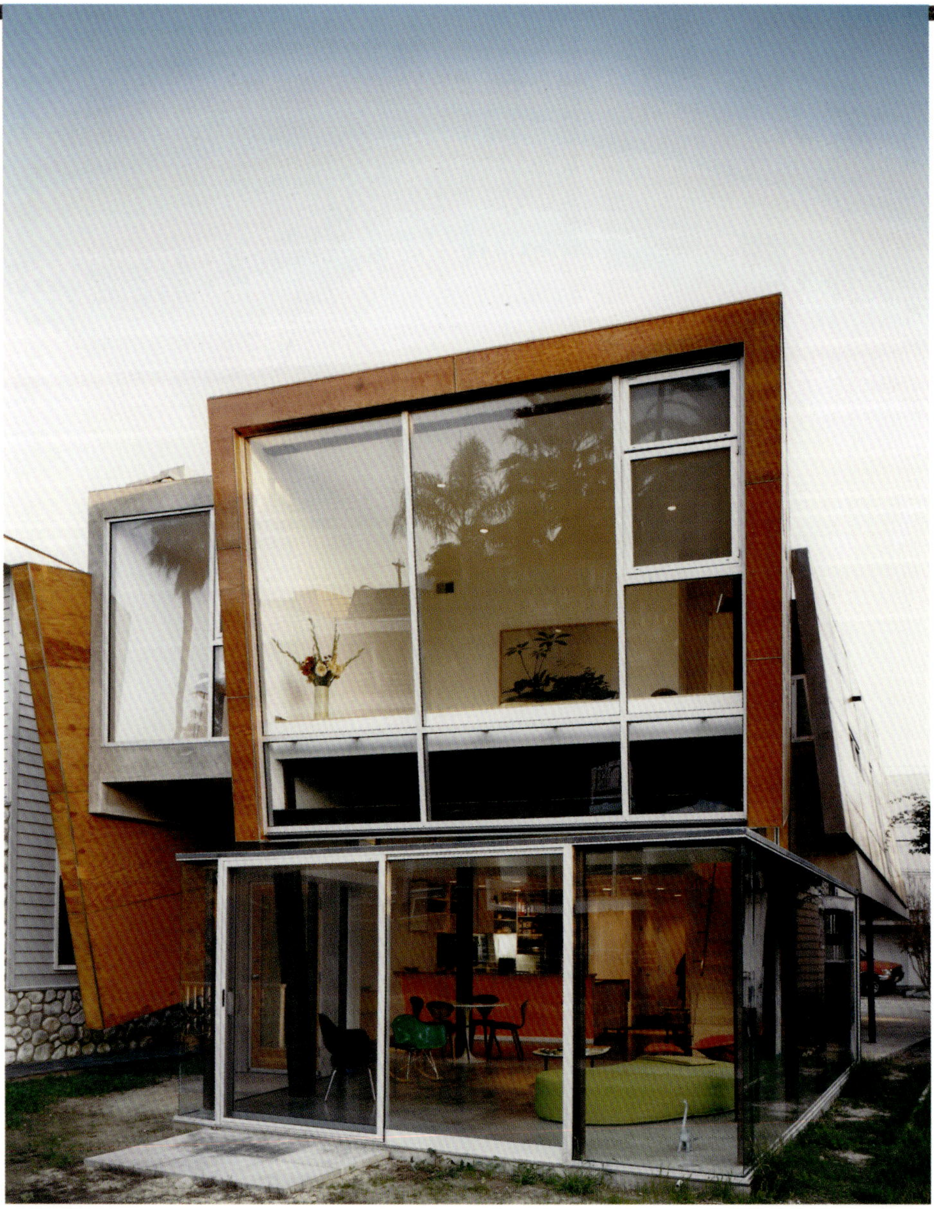

The reinvention of this Santa Monica landmark required the reconciliation of an immutable past and with a radical future.

In 2000, Cellular Fantasy rented a bank to convert it to a retail/office space for their cellular communication products. One of the two partners, Hamid Mozzafarian, was a close friend of my cousin and we would run into each other at family gatherings. He and his partner, Siamak Hodjatie started their cellular phone company in the early 90s and were met with success. Hamid liked my work and expressed how he wanted to develop a creative, innovative work environment that would reflect the fast growing nature of his company.

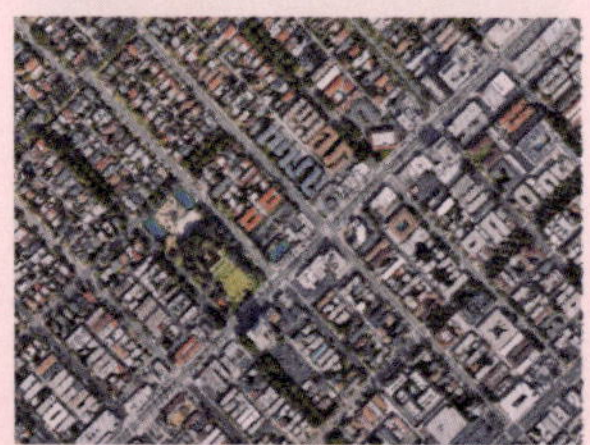

The project began as an attempt to transform the existing period architecture, but reinventing the exterior of this 30-year-old bank soon proved to be a bureaucratic impossibility. Presenting a fortress-like façade to the street, the travertine stone hovers above on the corner of Wilshire and 26th like a huge mausoleum.

Constructed of travertine stone the building was designed by Millard Sheets, a California artist, who late in life made a lucrative second career designing HSA (Home Savings of America) buildings throughout Southern California as backdrops for large pictorial murals – also of his design.

The client's goal was to completely renovate both the inside and outside. The bank's interior space needed a strong concept to engage and interact with the clients and the team of employees. Meanwhile, the outside needed softening up to divert the attention from the cold mausoleum look that dominated the building's appearance. The building's program had to be redefined for use as a commercial venue for cellular technology sales and services. To make that happen, we developed a strategy to create a building consistent with a contemporary hub of communication.

With the goal of coaxing the building away from its funeral-like appearance, we proposed to float a curtain of blue-glass in front of the travertine walls to frame the mural. The hue of the glass would accentuate the mural and the reflections in the glass would mollify the nature of the travertine cladding, giving it a softer, more penetrable feel.

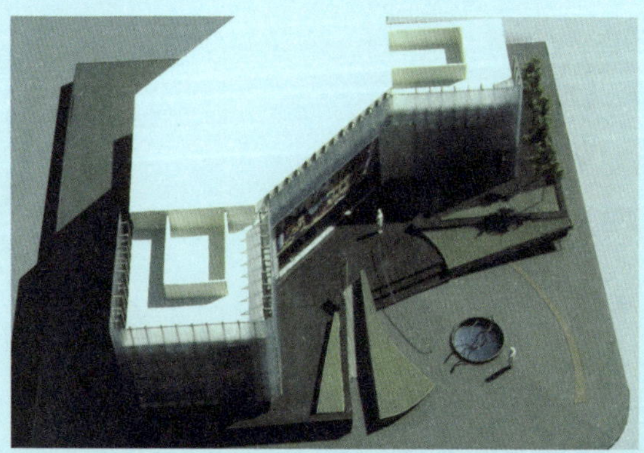

Cellular Fantasy

Location:
Santa Monica, California, USA

Year:
2001 (built)

Program:
Retail and Offices for a Wireless Company

After our design was accepted by the client, we submitted our proposal to Santa Monica's Architectural Review Board and Santa's Monica's Historical Society to "assure that the buildings, structures, signs, or other developments are in good taste, good design, harmonious with the surrounding developments, and in general contribute to the preservation of Santa Monica's reputation as a place of beauty, spaciousness, and quality."

Unfortunately, the Architectural Review Board was comprised of members who were either uneducated or misinformed about architecture and historical buildings. Each had a personal agenda that influenced their decision, therefore, our proposal didn't stand much of a chance. Following a contentious city hearing marked by disagreements, we were denied remodeling the exterior based on their conclusion that the bank was a historical building. Their verdict differed from the Santa Monica Historical Society's determination that the building was not a historical building. It wasn't even on the National Register of Historic Places. According to Diane Ghirardo, the existing structure was an "an example of Italian Fascist Architecture" and "a mediocre one at that."

Despite the subsequent rejection of the building's Historical Landmark Status, we had to return to the drawing board and conceptualize the client's program as an insertion of the program within the existing shell.

The client challenged us to abandon the normative concept of a segregated workspace/cubicle system and instead create an environment maximizing transparency and visibility within the workplace environment. We created a contemporary, cocoon-like workstation for each employee in order to reinvent the cubicle as a hybridized, architecturally furnished element.

The interior ambiance of the former bank is transformed through the layering of transparent, semi-transparent, and perforated surfaces. All three are deployed to differentiate spaces for the store and office functions, and providing modulated levels of visual privacy. A series of translucent, polyurethane shields overlap to surround each desk, giving the employees the impression of a private work environment, while maintaining visible connections between co-workers.

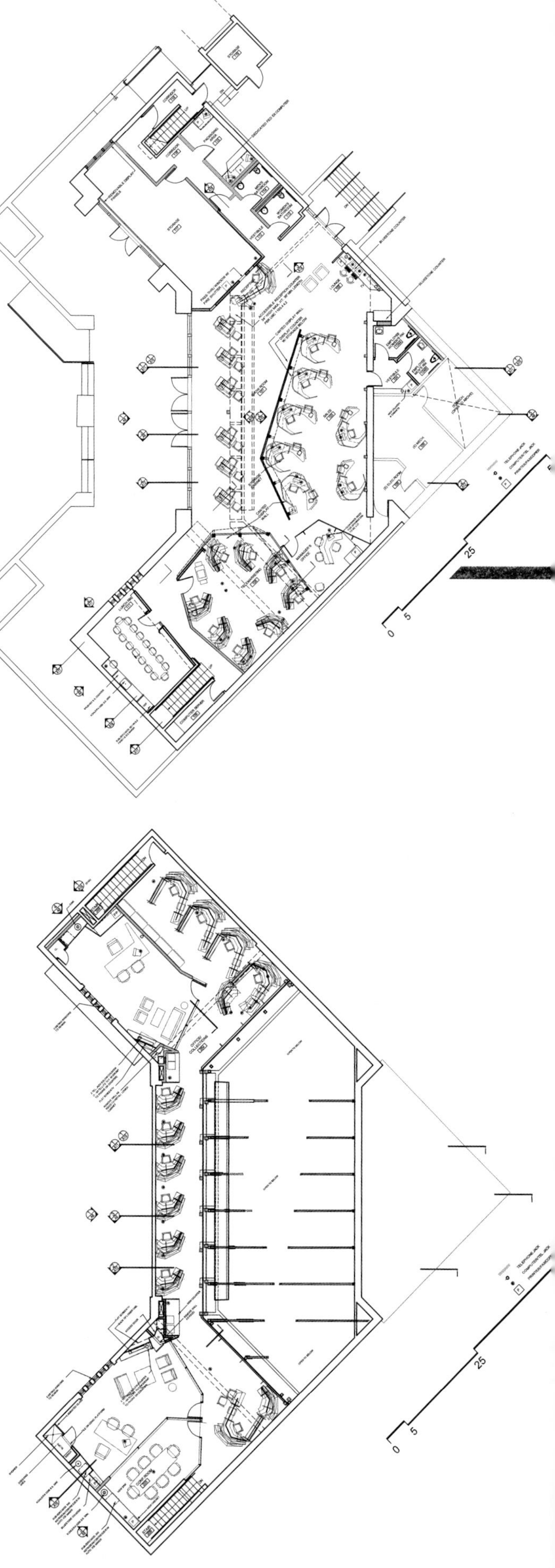

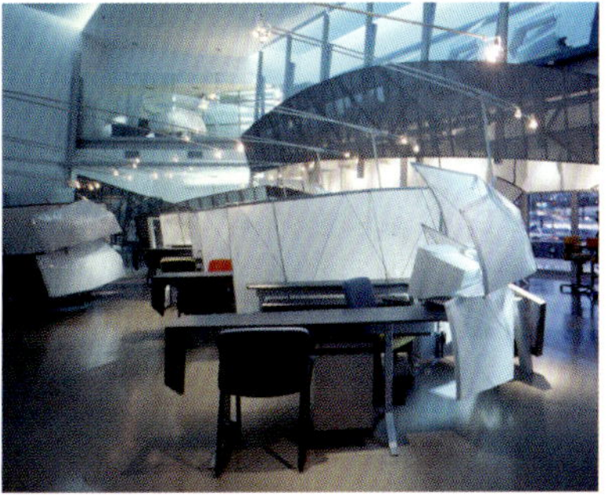

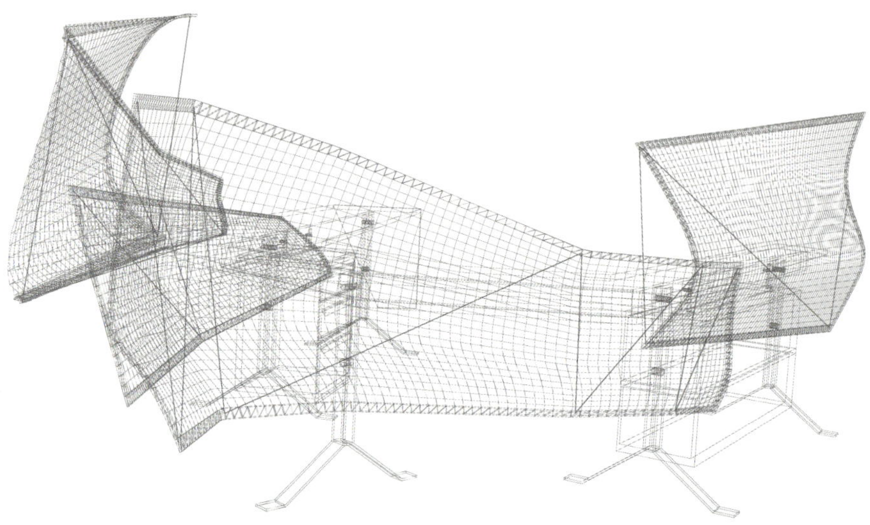

Efficiencies and communication are enhanced, creating shadows and partial sightlines through the cocoons allowing employees to maintain an apprehension of one another's presence.

Open areas between the cocoons also increase opportunities for visual connectivity. Private management offices are exposed to view on the second level of the space, but equipped with privacy features like electro-chromic glass walls that, with the flip of a switch, transform from opaque to clear.

The program demanded a space which was conducive to commercial sales. Therefore, we employed a type of space making, which avoids the creation of forcefully defined spaces. Maintaining fluidity in the extension of space, we were able to free the environment of closed and confining areas. The intervention is nestled in the belly of the space, encouraging directional spatial flows and accentuating the natural volume of the building's core. To take advantage of the enormous stained glass window that makes the building's east exterior shell, we paired with it an interior screening element composed of layers of perforated plastic fabric. Shifted to create an abstract effect, the elements wash the space with vibrant specular colored light that, like a living painting, which softens as the day progresses.

The basic envelope of the space remains untouched while at the same time is fundamentally transformed. A coalescence between the movement and volumetric play of interior elements with the existing element results in a spatial experience, which exceeds the sum of its parts and defies expectations. The reinvention of this Santa Monica landmark required the reconciliation of its immutable past with its radical future.

Once the travertine shell was restored, the new signage and landscaping were added, and the stained glass window was subtly transformed, it was clear that we had succeeded in maintaining the integrity of the past, while simultaneously stretching our perceptions to the edges of our rapidly transforming world.

A project that was originally sought to fundamentally transform a place from the outside in, has transformed its experience from the inside out.

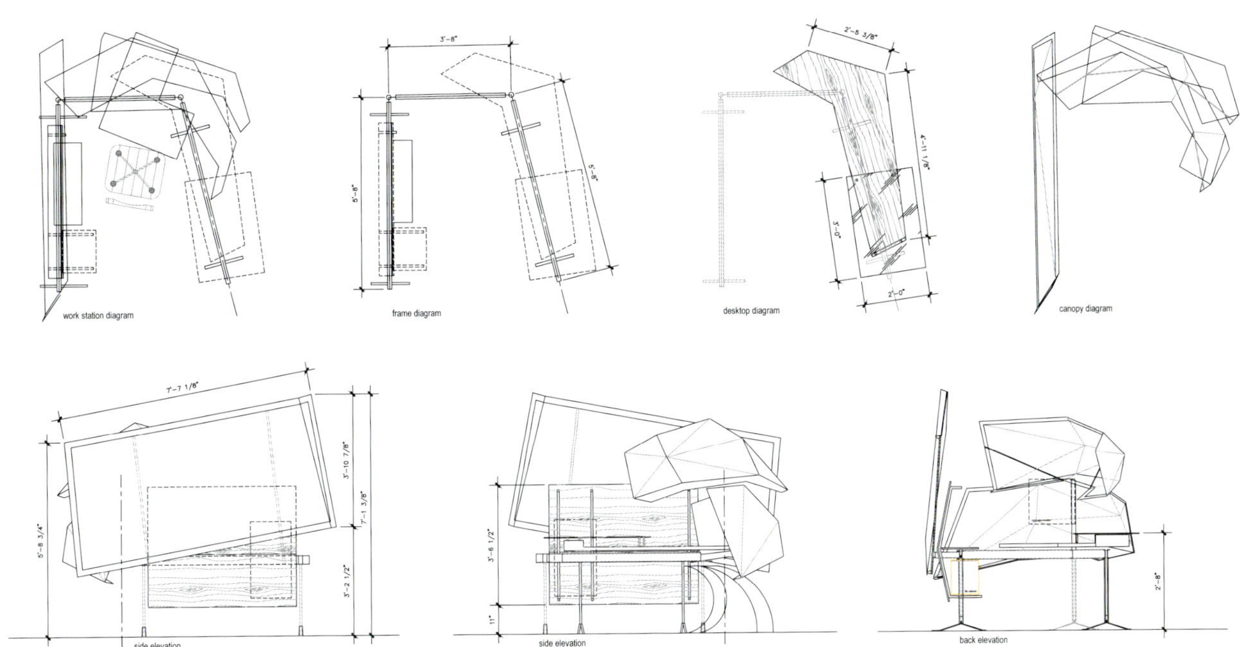
work station diagram
frame diagram
desktop diagram
canopy diagram
side elevation
side elevation
back elevation

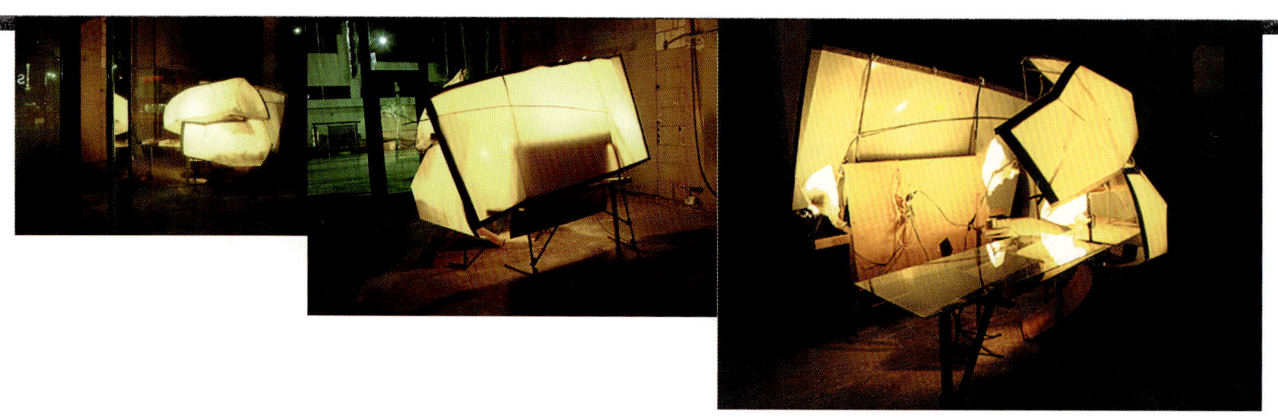

"The past sheds light on the future; the future gives meaning to the past."

Marcel Bleustein Blanchet,

Founder of Publicis

The new Publicis Drugstore arises out of itself. Rather than derived from styles or trends, the architecture is instead the metaphorical offspring of the motivating principles of the Publicis Company. In this way the character of the company is translated into the building's materials and tectonic language. The architectural vision for Publicis originated with the company's founder Marcel Bluestein Blanchet who imagined a new signature building inspired by and conveying the core principles that were crucial in the company's transformation from a family drugstore to a communication giant.

The new architecture of Publicis strongly exerts its new character while engaging the existing structure with a mutual respect and crafting a dynamic connection with the city and celebrated site of the Arc de Triumph. Revealing a fragile character of light and transparency that is at the same time strong the old and new elements of the façade embrace the city and its history. Far from ignoring the past, old and the new meet in a gesture of celebration and regeneration; collectively contributing more as a cohesive whole than they ever would have been able to individually.

As a physical embodiment of Publicis company the new Publicis Drugstore restructures zones of diverse activities to create an open and united space of commerce and discovery. Flowing naturally within the space are intense zones of architectural movement that give expression to the symbolic core of the multi-faceted business entity.

The program area for the renovation encompassed the façade and street-level drugstore, as well as four subterranean floors below the existing building. Inspired by the spirit of "La difference," the architecture aims for an integration where concept and structure are mutually supportive and where a particular set of symbolic, practical, social, and technical concerns are imprinted in the innovative fabric of a place of reinvention.

When I first came to the office of Publicis, peering through the glass entry I was intrigued to see a simple wooden door displayed and suspended at an angle. Out of interest I took a photo of it and later learned that it was the original door to the office of the founder of Publicis. Marcel Bleustein-Blanchet a self- made man, kept it proudly as a reminder of his modest beginnings. On the flight back to Los Angeles I sketched and wrote about my observations, unable to get the door out of my mind. When I developed my film the next day, the photo of the door offered a wonderful surprise: reflected in the glass was my enthusiastic face looking in with the camera; behind me was a view of the Champs-Elysees and the city of Paris. Layered within this single poignant image was both inspiration and harbingers of things to come.

The door, which now holds a prominent place in the new building's design, symbolizes the suspended past, poised at an angle and pointing toward the Arc de Triumph behind the clear glass screen, it reflects the city and swings in both directions, inviting entry to the past and future.

Following a fire in 1970 in which the original Haussmann and structure burned down before Mr. Blanchet's eyes the current structure was built in 1972. In place of the original building was an aluminum-framed concrete building clad in a copper-colored mirrored glass skin was erected. Per its classifications as a high-rise structure it was constructed to meet all of the security, fire, and building code standards of the time. Within the fabric of it's Parisian surrounding the building's envelope abstractly mirrored its internal programs with little regard for its immediate surroundings.

Situated on a corner lot at the end of a large block, the '70s building turned inward despite its frontage on three bustling streets and proximity to the world's best known monuments. On the east elevation the building presents an unadorned and detached facade toward the famous Avenue des Champs-Elysees. To the South the building's façade responds to the curve of Rue Parkesburg, which as part of the second circle around the Arc de Triumph traces a circle emanating from the Arch. Finally, despite its seeming unimportance, a narrow tertiary street known as a Rue Vernet plays a crucial arterial role in the day to day functioning of Publicis: as both the main employee entrance and primary conduit for deliveries.

Despite it's obvious shortcomings I came to appreciate the relationship which my clients had developed with the existing building in the 30 odd years they had been there. The intervention would have to acknowledge this lineage while at the same time fulfilling the building's fertile opportunity to dynamically connect the building with its environment.

Publicis Drugstore

Location:

Paris, France

Year:

2000–2004 (built)

Program:

Multi-Functional Retail, Commercial, and Communication Space

1973–75 Original building
by architect Pierre Dufau

1960 with mom at the
Arc de Triomphe

2000

Excited about the prospects of making a piece of architecture at one of the most amazing sites in the world I looked throught the glass doors of Publicis to find the door the founder, Marcel Bleustein-Blanchet left as the simbol of his modest begining.

The door and this image became my source of inspiration.

I was reminded of Marcel Duchamp's door on Rue Larrey 1972
"A door half open half shut."

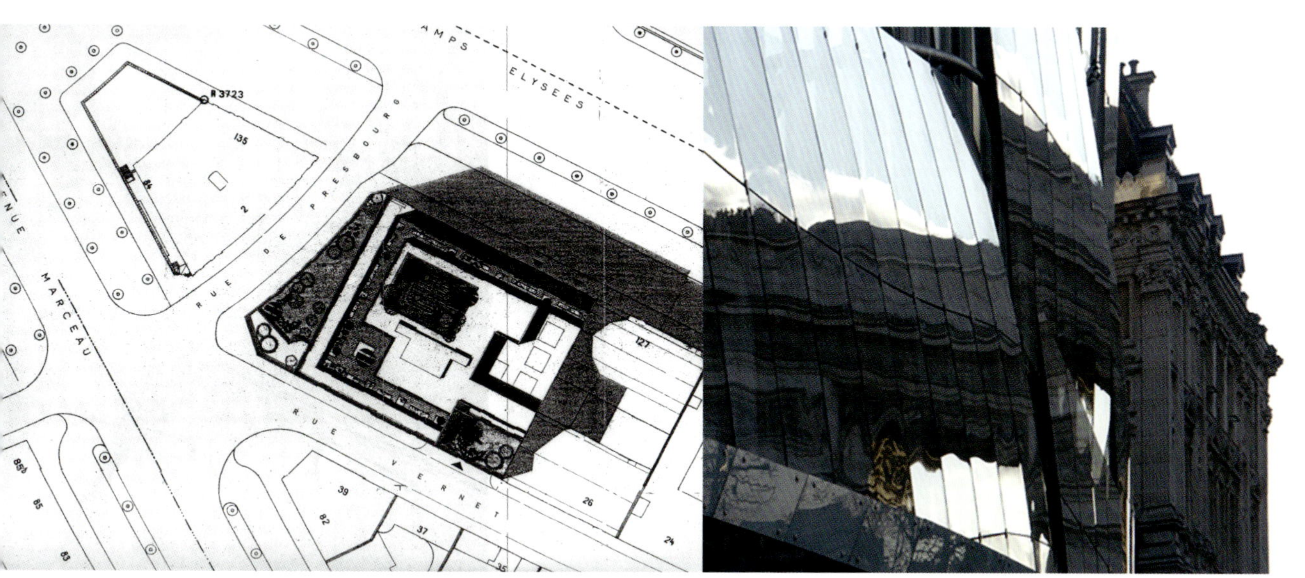

In navigating this territory we also obligated ourselves and the architectural forms to activate a commentary on the paradigm shifts characterized in order and distinguish our current global culture from those that preceded it. Discussing quantum mechanics in a book titled Other Worlds author Paul Davies instructively describes this philosophical evolution:

"In the old Newtonian picture, the universe consists of a collection of things, located here and in other places at this moment. Relativity, on the other hand, reveals that 'things' are not always what they seem, while places and moments are subject to interpretation. The relativist's picture of reality is a world consisting of events rather than things... a new language and geometry is required which takes into account the observer in a fundamental way. Newton's concepts of space and time were a natural extension of our daily experiences. Relativity theory on the other hand requires something more abstract, but also many believe, more elegant and revealing."

In our exploration of this new territory we proposed a geometric organization that acknowledged the existing building, its relationship to its surroundings, and the site's circumscription by strong currents of human and automobile traffic. Responding to this field of disparate conditions while maintaining focus on echoing the core principals of the Publicis Company, the form of the architecture transcends traditional expectations. The introduction of a bold swirling vortex of energy initiates the building's interface with its surroundings. Charges with the expansive openness of a daring sculptural form this spatial attractor is further energized by the trajectories of pedestrians and vehicles as they move along through and around the building. At the eye of these centripetal elements is embodied the spirit and soul of the new Publicis.

The new building's new façade is transformed with wrapping curved-glass screens that contrast with both the columns and strictly mirrored fenestration of the existing building. Partially veiled with the shifting and overlap of the glass panels, the entire surface achieves qualities of both depth and lightness reflecting the cinematic collage of the new and original elements with the activity of the building, the activity of the street, message, and signage.

The primary arching steel structure of the main façade orients the corner of the building along the Avenue des Champs-Elysees, Rue Presburge, and Rue Vernet, and is tied back to the vertical columns of the existing building. The secondary façade structure of custom-made extruded steel forms a dancing lattice that marches across the main structure anchoring the curved-glass panels. A force of momentum rises toward the corner with a kinetic spiral structure both announcing the architecture and celebrating its relation to the Arc de Triumph.

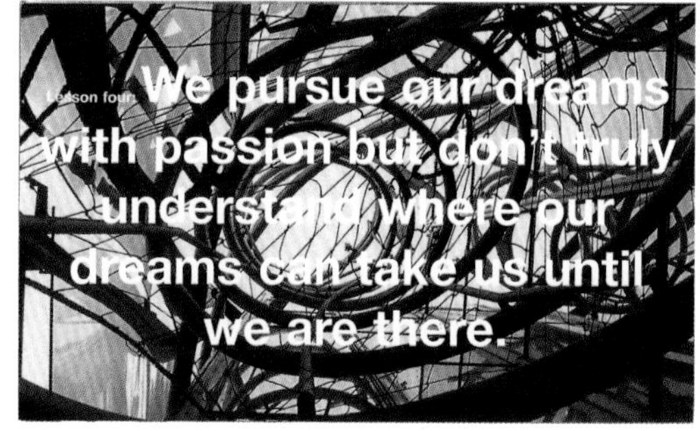

Aspiring to defy the forces of gravity and geometry I had imagined a new face for Publicis heading skyward like an angel; weightless and airborne with its wing stretched outward toward the Arc de Triumph, limbs of glass and steel dynamically impaling a capacity for flight.

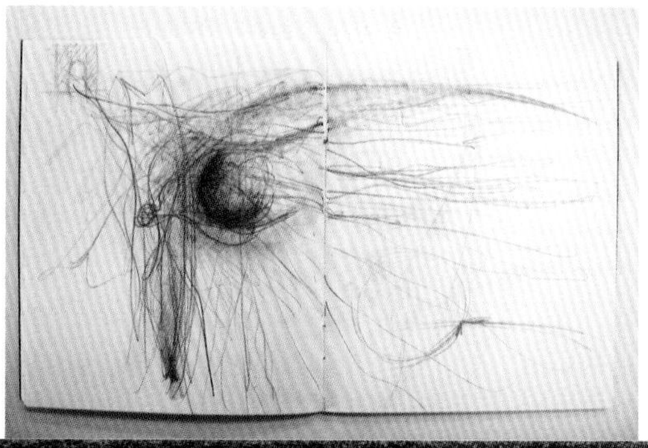

We pursue our dreams but we don't truly understand where our dreams can take us until we are there.

During my third year at the University of Florence, a group of us made a trip to Paris for the opening of the Pompidou Center. We arrived by train and walked to the building along hundreds and then thousands of other people to visit this architectural phenomenon. As we got closer the crowd grew denser and denser to the point where we were walking in each other's arms. I distinctly remember the newness when encountering the building, its structure and programs. Our steps were its first.

We finally reached the escalators, which took us to each floor. With each level we rose, the city was revealed to us again, and again, giving the experience a sense of discovery and excitement. I felt like a child overjoyed by everything I saw. I watched as waves of people rushed toward the building. It felt almost spiritual. Pressed against the curved glass at the top of the escalator landing, I paused for hours and watched people march. I imagined, I hoped, I dreamed. I am not sure why I didn't share my thoughts with my friends. Maybe because I was afraid to verbalize it or to hear what they would think.

I sometimes want things not really knowing what they are or how they would affect my life. I can't exactly describe the feeling, but I know standing in front of Publicis for the first time felt like being at the top of the Pompidou center. We go after our dreams not knowing what they mean until we are actually there. I didn't have the project yet, but that was the first time I was so close that I could actually taste it.

2000 first competition entry

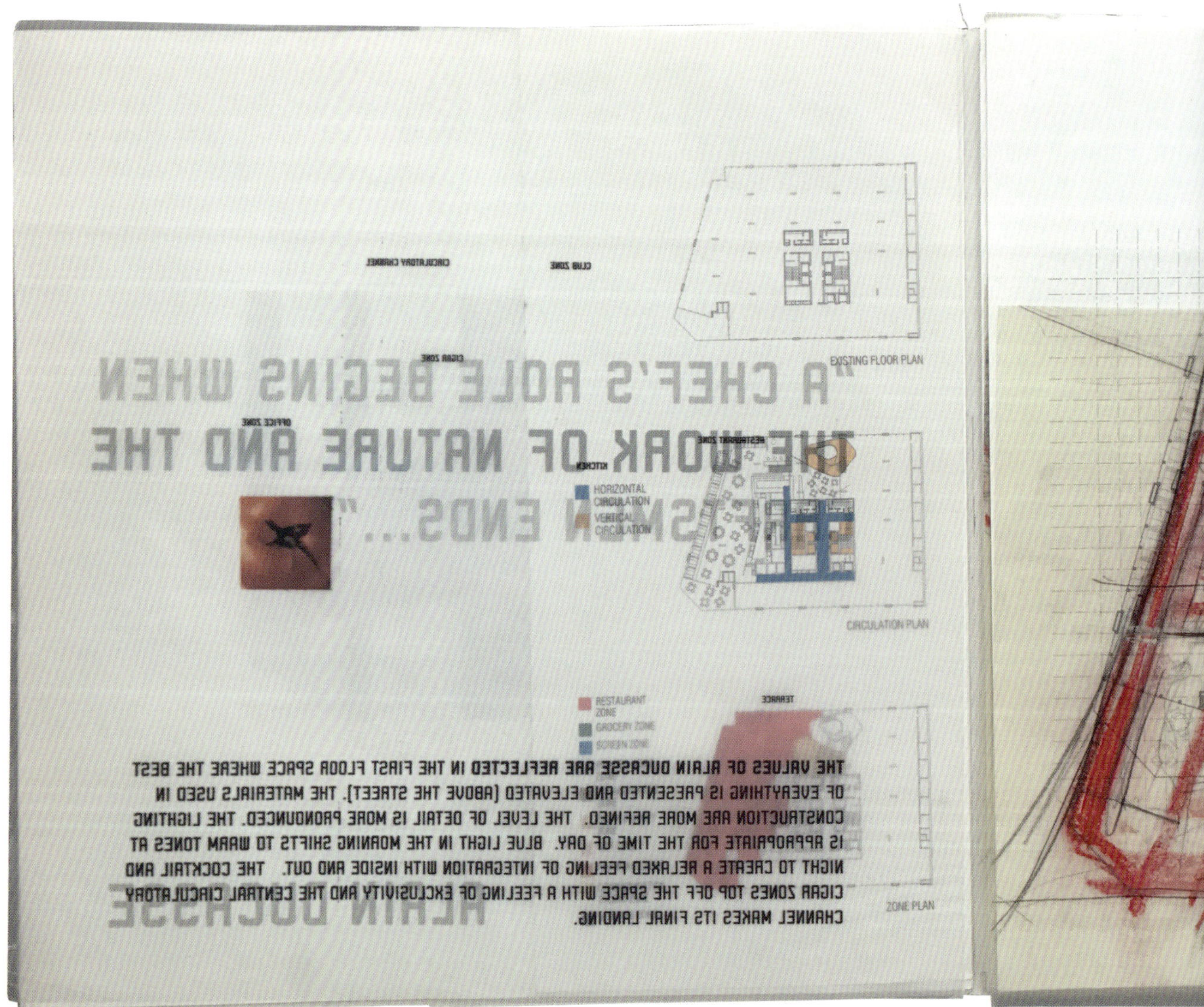

Here I was in Paris with the Arc de Triomphe in the background, presented with the possibilities to create something in one of the most iconic sites in the world. The Arc felt much bigger than I remembered. My ideas were bursting and there wasn't any way I knew how to stop them or slow them down. Wouldn't it be problematic to just change the storefront without changing the building, considering its sensitive location? Will I imitate the existing storefront system to maintain the building's integrity? Shouldn't I just design the facade? My passion was fueling my creativity. I had everything to gain and nothing to lose and that was the kind of energy I was going to bring to this work. I felt truly focused in a spiritual way and felt I had the right to the project. I could see my vision for Publicis materialize in front of my eyes.

It was just a few weeks earlier when my friend, Philippe Uzzan, called from Paris. I met Philippe in the early nineties when he visited LA to promote his Paris gallery for art and architecture. A young talented man with passion and love for architecture, we bonded right away. An architect himself, he decided to start the first private architecture gallery in Paris, which changed public perception about architectural drawings and models. Philippe was hired by Publicis Group to make a shortlist of international architects for the renovation of the Publicis drugstore and to become the point person on behalf of client to explore the transformation of the building with the city authorities.

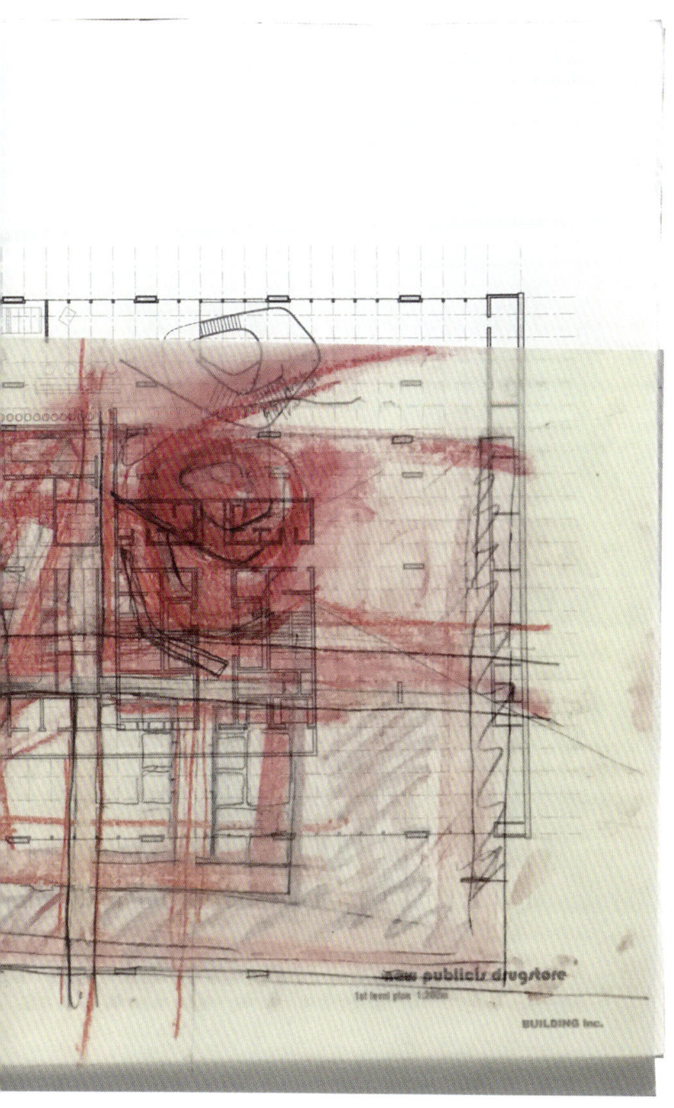

It was the afternoon. I was exhausted after a balancing act to keep everyone on my team hopeful about the unpredictable future. Philippe invited me to send in my portfolio (RFI) for the Publicis Drugstore renovation competition, but made sure I didn't get my hopes up. He knew my work and admired my designs, but thought I had "very little chance" to seize an opportunity with the fifth largest advertising company in the world. Either way Philippe said, "It's good for you to participate in this kind of competition." I am sure his intensions were good and what he said was meant to protect me in case of disappointment but the call made me feel empty. Invisible. The next morning I reluctantly sent my Rizzoli book to Paris. A few days later I had a surprising call from Philippe. We were shortlisted! *Merd!*

I was afraid of losing everything even though I didn't really have anything yet.

I had the opportunity to work with Madam Elisabeth Badinter and Monsieur Maurice Levy. Madam Badinter was a noted intellectual, a feminist philosopher, author, and daughter of the founder of Publicis, Mr. Marcel Bleustein-Blanchet. She was also married to Mr. Robert Badinter, the Minister of Justice during the presidency of Mitterrand and the abolishment of the death penalty. Mr. Maurice Levy was the CEO of Publicis, having joined in 1971 as an IT director.

FAIL SAFE

SOCIAL CENTER
WALLS MAKE SPACES PEOPLE MAKE PLACES

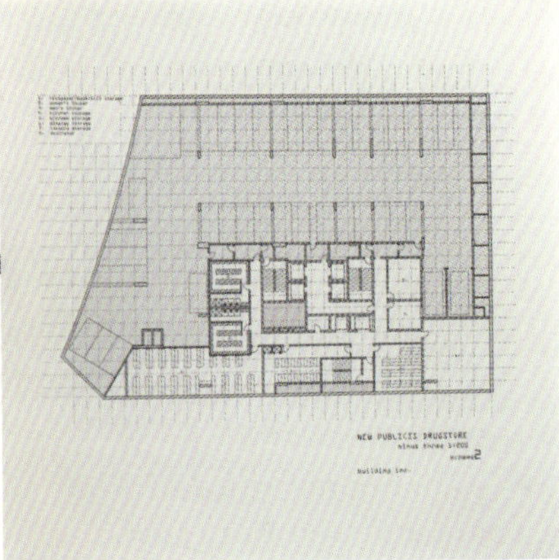
NEW PUBLICIS DRUGSTORE

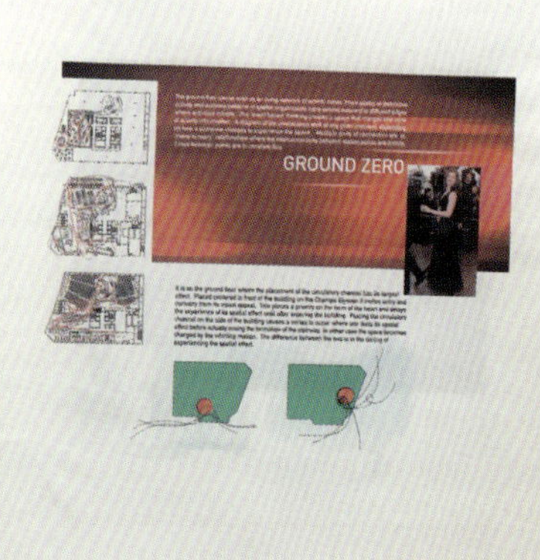
GROUND ZERO

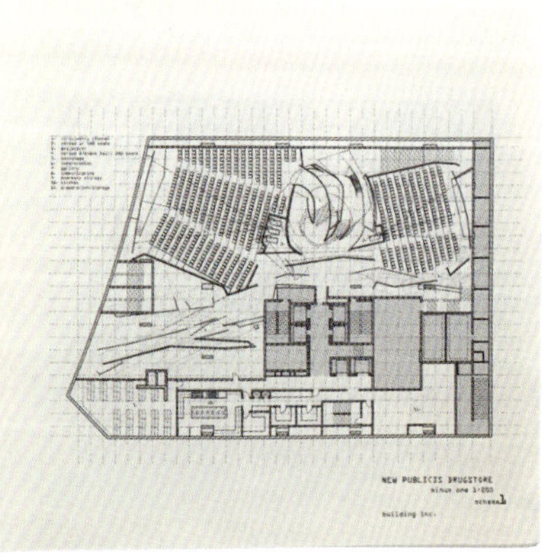
NEW PUBLICIS DRUGSTORE

In 1972, donning the fireman's leather jacket and helmet he found in a nearby truck, Mr. Levy rushed inside a burning Publicis headquarters and saved the magnetic tapes holding the firm's precious computer files. The founder trusted Mr. Levy to take over the company's direction when he retired, something that has only happened once since its formation in 1926.

Madam Badinter, with Mr. Levy, planned to remodel the Publicis drugstore in tribute to her late father, Mr. Marcel Bleustein-Blanchet. Located on the second ring around the Arc du Triumph, Publicis had everyone's interest. The competition would be a battle. The initial team was formed, but grew with the project. The process was brutal. Not many continued due to extensive working hours and how creatively demanding it became.

The competition team was made mainly of my friends and students; most of which were unable to continue and be a part of the project after we got the project because the competition took such a long time and Publicis almost cancelled the project a few times considering their options. I am forever grateful to Hans, Terry, David Lindberg, Reza, Emil, and Nick to name a few.

Every aspect of the project had its own complexity. The pressure and fear of failure loomed over me, yet some indescribable force got me out of bed day after day and brought me to the studio, giving me the strength to fight. I was competing for the most important project of my life to date.

With my young family a new learning process began where my love for my family had to be balanced with my work. I felt guilty pursuing my dream wondering if I was compromising their needs and their lives. I became more than aware of the constructive struggle between living life and following one's dreams, yet grew to accept the vulnerability of this life and my life choices. I had to surrender to my process of architecture like a farmer to their land. I will give my blood, sweat, and tears to a piece of land with the hope of harvest. Everything is great, everyone is happy, but all of a sudden there is a thunderstorm and it all falls apart. I wait for the storm to pass, evaluate, return to the land, and start over. This was the life I chose for myself, but I knew it's not easy living with someone who's pursuing this dream.

The practice of creating architecture, like poetry, gives new meaning to some of the words we loosely use to describe the work: schematic design, design development,

construction documents, etc. Yet, I don't believe that these words give us the essence of the process in its actuality. We must surrender to our practice, accepting the fragility and unpredictability of life's process. Accepting the limits to our abilities without losing our creativity. Everything and everyone is susceptible to change in a drastic or violent way and creativity can be the vehicle of this transformation. Challenging our perception and changing our ways of life. Some changes are gradual, but some are fast and unpredictable.

Compared to Florence where it almost feels like nothing changes, Los Angeles was constantly evolving, exposing me to fast transformation. Eventually, China showed me the violence behind this practice. Nothing was safe anymore. Developing architecture or buildings is an inherently violent act because the land is destroyed. Every living organism is removed to make place for construction. Building infrastructure to create urban life is the same, scarring the land and the environment.

Change is unavoidable. Publicis is no exception, burning down to the ground in the devastating fire of September, 1972. Yet we continue to rise from the ashes. Violent transformation can lead to the creation of something far more captivating than ever expected. It is unpredictable, almost distracting, and for most people emotionally unbearable if it is a part of their everyday life. How an architect comes to grips with this is influential to how the project develops.

When I broke the glass

Alone in a small conference room, I was waiting my turn to present to Madam Badinter and Monsieur Levy. I needed to relax and put my thoughts in order. This was a critical moment in my life where my dream could become reality, but more importantly I could provide a better life for my family.

I was shortlisted for the Publicis project and since then my credit card debt was piling up. Three months passed before I began asking for help from friends and loyal students. My hunger for Publicis showed. As my close friend Terry would later put it, I was absolutely "shameless." I pushed my team for longer hours. No days off. Our work schedules reflected nothing other than architectural glory. I was acting as if this was my only chance to step up to the plate and do the unimaginable.

The hot and thick air surrounded me in that little, windowless conference room. I could feel the perspiration build up on my neck and forehead. I loosened my tie and sipped on my Perrier, trying to calm down by thinking about Sayeh and Alisina. It wasn't working. Why was I shortlisted? What if I don't get this project? I was 20 when I had dreams to produce meaningful architecture; when I started trying to make a name for myself. At the time I was forty-four. Will I have another chance like this? I have never done anything in Paris. Do I have the experience needed to develop a building in such a historical part of the city? I don't even speak the language! Yet my friend and client Sia would force me to ask myself; why not me?

As I was battling with these thoughts someone knocked on the door. It was the director of the Publicis Drugstore, Thierry De la Brosse. "It's your turn Michele, let's go," he says. I jolted up, feeling all the blood rush to my heavy feet. I pulled myself together and followed him to the other small conference room where my models and drawings were

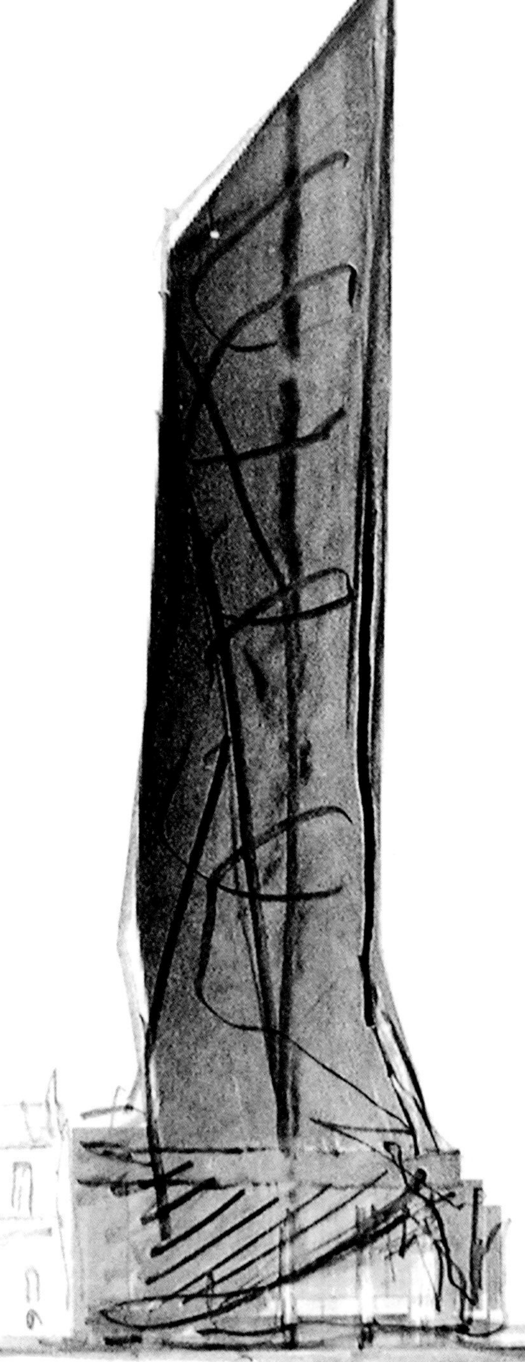

displayed on the floor. The room was spinning. Seated on the opposite side of me were Madam Badinter and Monsieur Levy with whom I was meeting for the first time. They were cold but cordial as we were introduced. Thierry then asked me to start my presentation.

I began telling the story of my first visit to Publicis and the building. How I saw the famous door of the founder's first humble studio and how impressed I was by his determination and abilities to create an iconic place in the heart of Paris. I was deep in my philosophy as to how the door resembles a similar work of Marcel Duchamp's door on Rue Larrey (1927). "A door half open half shut." But by their facial reactions, Badinter and Levy appeared to be puzzled and not very interested in what I was trying to say. Therefore I switched gears into talking about the relationship of the existing building and its context: The Arc de Triomphe and so on. Yet again they seemed even less interested, looking at me with their discontent eyes. I kept moving forward onto the next topic, describing the existing building's short comings and its inappropriate interaction with the street, blah, blah, blah.

Thierry then stopped me as he was looking at his watch and said, "Okay Michele, you have twelve more minutes." I could not believe it. What did he just say? I haven't even begun describing my design yet. I have ten minutes to describe more than two months of work!? Nobody told me about the time limit.

My mouth was as dry as if I had eaten a handful of sand. My body was hot and damp from desperate perspiration. Not knowing what to do next, I grabbed the models and put them in front of them. I began focusing on two of the most important features of my design:

(1) The heart of project is an undulating circular glass staircase that unifies the entire program. It connects five different levels within the existing building;

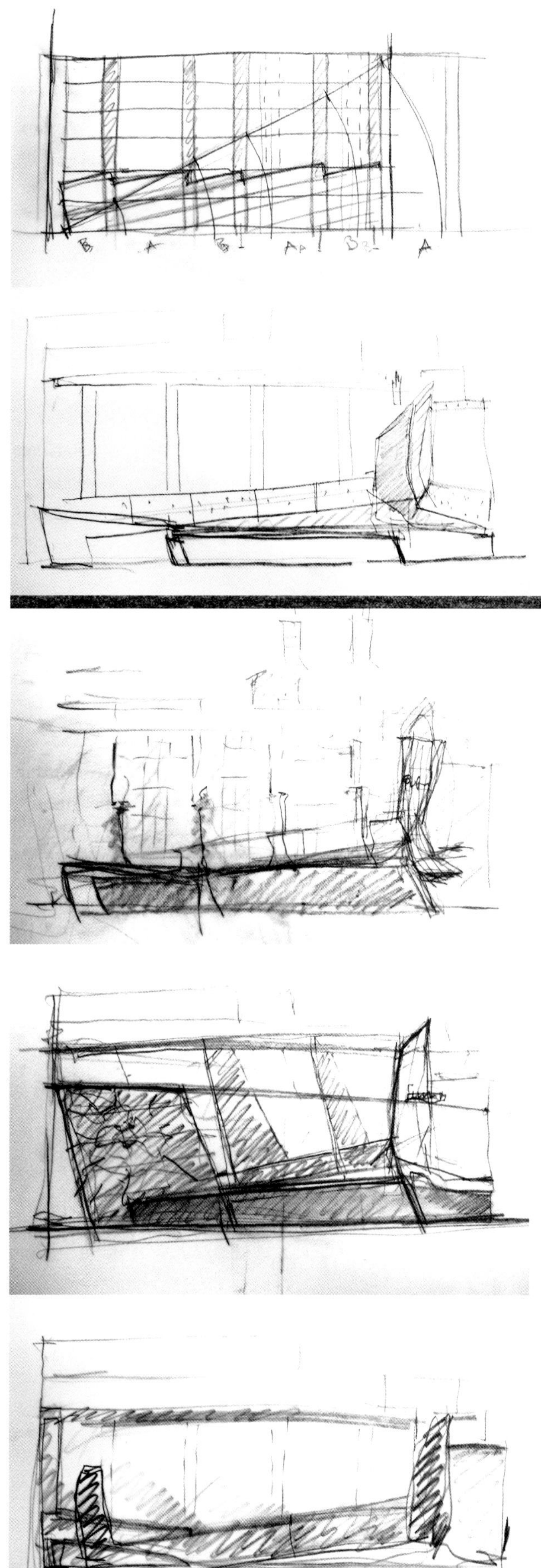

and (2) the new façade, which was not included in the competition brief, but I thought to be fundamental for a company like Publicis. I explained how the façade is the door between the existing building and the city and the new image of the company based on its founder's dreams and aspirations re-connecting Publicis with Paris.

I was talking fast and moving even faster. My models and drawings flying back and forth. In a split second, I moved one of the models closer to Madam Badinter and pushed her glass of Evian over the Brazilian blue marble table top. The glass shattered, spilling the water all over the drawings, models and papers. My heart sank and yet all of a sudden I had a sense of relief. In that bizarre moment all I thought about was the fountain at our house in Tehran. I was only a few years old when I fell in through the ice one winter and the neighbor mistook me for the family cat. Sharif, my mother, screamed and ran to my rescue because we didn't have any pets.

I am not sure why I didn't panic, but I know that life sometimes reveals its miracles in mysterious ways.

I was calm, collected as if I had nothing to lose. My world ended in that split second yet I was still standing, presenting my ideas to one of the largest advertising companies in the world. Just then, I realized I have something to offer. They need me as much as I need them. With newfound confidence I continued my presentation and did not let the incident derail me as they got closer to my models.

Monsieur Levy then asked me if I had any material samples for my design, so I pulled a piece of low iron crystal glass and blue stone out of the base of the model. I persisted with how I thought it was too early for material selection, but how these two materials would be my vision for Publicis. One shall represent the past, pointing at the blue stone, and the future, pointing to the crystal. Monsieur Levy asks, "How does that represent the past?" but before I could reply Madame Badinter asserts, "its *blue stone* Maurice," alluding to Marcel Bleustein-Blanchet.

I had grabbed their attention. I opened the models to show different levels of the program, no longer worried about time. They would stop me when they had enough. We reached the -1 level in the model where the cigar club was located and for the fun of it I placed a couple of Cohiba cigars inside the cigar room—Monsieur Levy's favorite. The presentation ended after a few questions and answers, but before I left Monsieur Levy asked me to make sure to smoke the Cohiba before I got home. Cuban cigars were still illegal in the US back then.

The image of the curved shards of glass on the Brazilian blue granite table remains vivid in my memories to this day. After I left the building I felt that my chances were pretty slim to get this project. Their reaction to my presentation was not clear, and unsettling at best. Disappointed and exhausted I lit up the Cohiba cigar and sat on a bench behind the Publicis drugstore thinking about calling Arezou or my team. I knew they were desperately waiting for my call but I couldn't. I thought, no news is sometimes better than bad news. It would have been a horrible day if I didn't get the project. I called Philippe. When he heard my voice he said; "You better come to our house tonight. I'll order

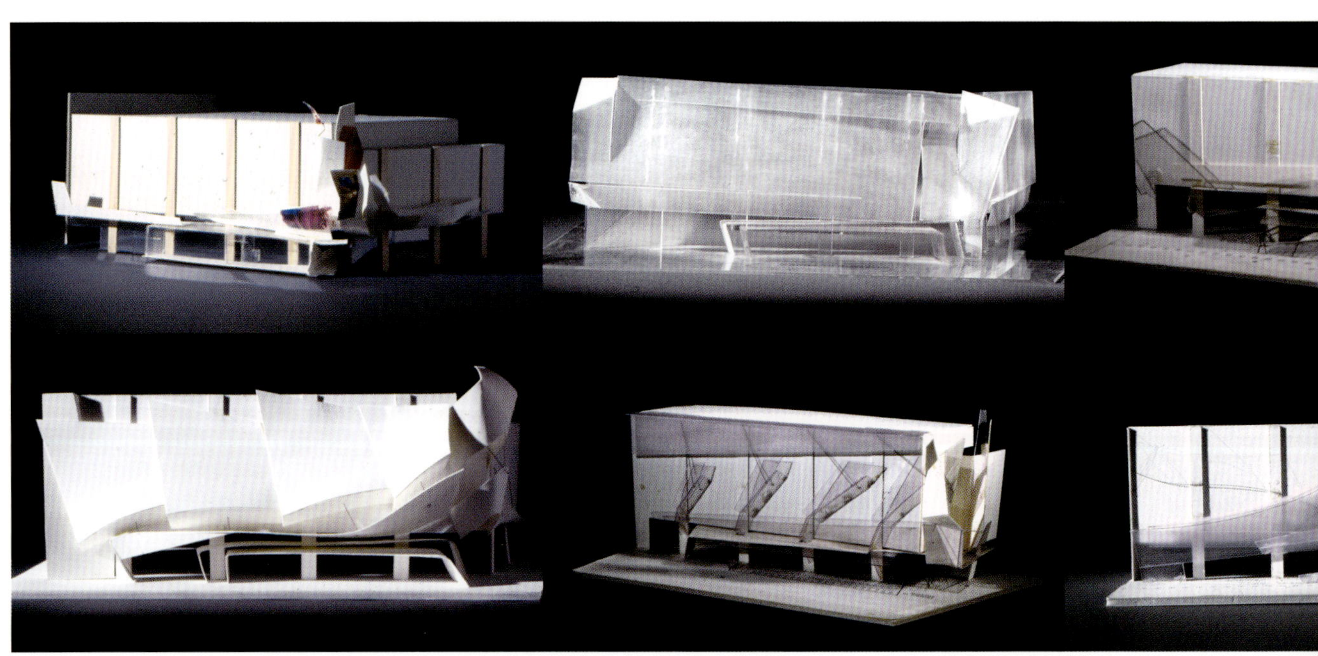

Chinese food." This was a routine event during this period; when Philippe and his wife Amaya lovingly tried to make me feel better and encourage me to continue.

The competition process was a roller coaster with new requests and comments from everyone involved. Its end came when I received a phone call from my wife during a lunch with two clients. I should expect a call from Mr. de La Brosse, she warned. I couldn't believe it! I was ecstatic. I wanted to scream, to cry. It was an extraordinary feeling, but coupled with an underlying fear of what is next. Am I ready? Arezou was so happy and proud that I could sense it in her tone. A few minutes later Thierry called and said, "I wanted to congratulate you Mr. Architect! You were selected and we need to set a time to discuss what the next stage is going to be." I had an out of body experience.

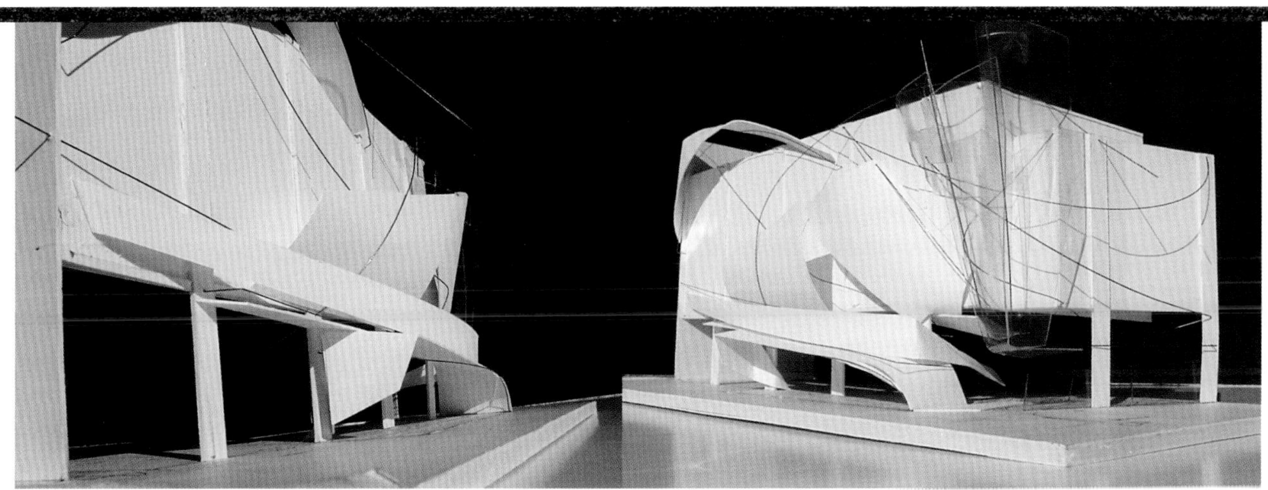

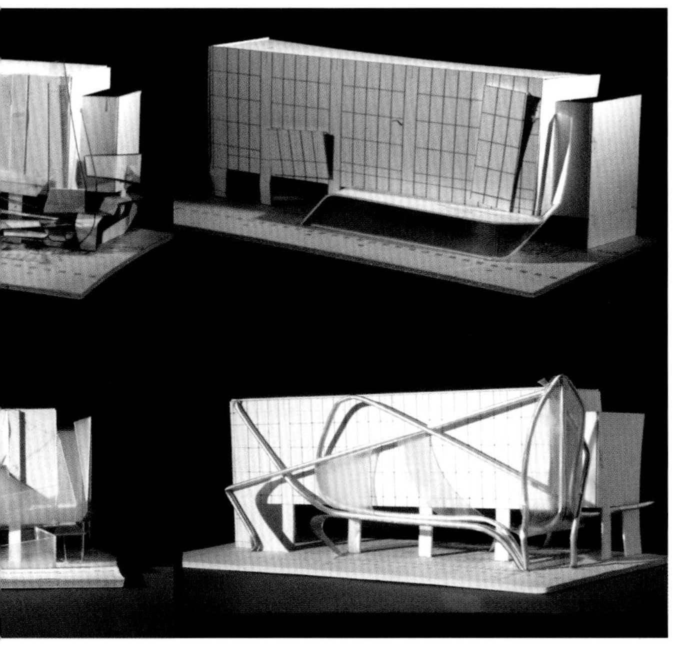

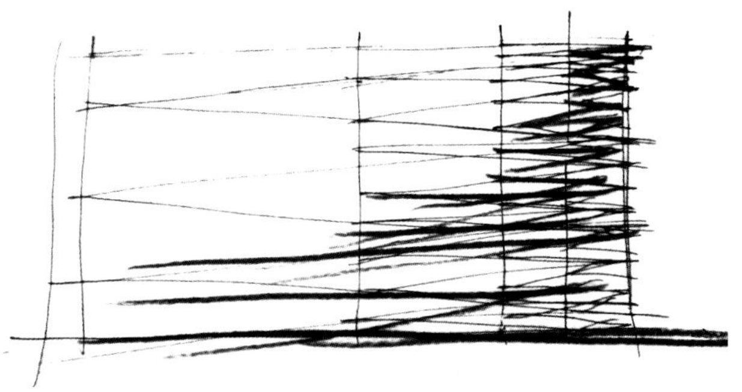

"Do you think we can build it?"

Alain Collon was pivotal in the development of the building's redesign. In the early stages of development, Collon made it clear that this undertaking will be a case study for succeeding projects not only on the Champs-Elysees, but other historical areas with similar sensibilities and importance. He recognized my design's attributes and its influence on the future development of the area. This favor of my proposal gave it the legitimacy it needed to be considered by other city officials and for it to continue.

It was apparent Mr. Collon was a man with strong convictions whose passion for the project almost felt like a responsibility to the Champs-Elysees and the state of architecture in France. We would have open dialogues about the design of Publicis in its complicated context, agreeing that the new building had to maintain its own integrity while it interacts with its surroundings.

Things changed rapidly as we got the project and had to form a new team. After a long search and overcoming different obstacles, French architect Bruno Pingeot joined us as our local architect in Paris. We rented a small studio on Rue de Saintonge in Marais area and set up shop to do this great project. We were working day and night on different projects in LA, Paris, and Tempio. We spent 12 hours a day producing different proposals based on our site analysis

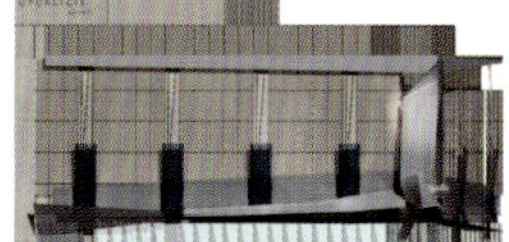

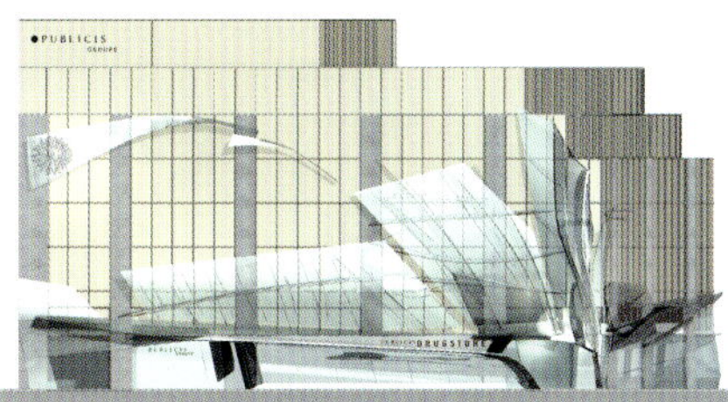

context, context, program, our interactions with the site and its patrons, etc. This was a very dynamic and exciting time full of great energy and productivity. We worked through six or more different ideas at the same time.

It was like having our own competition in the studio. Everyone was motivated. Our workplace was filled with piles of drawings, sketches, and models. We couldn't part with anything and it felt good to produce work that we were proud of. I was concerned about whether they would understand my vision or even like it. I was concerned about being away from my family or whether my young team would be able to pull through and rise to the occasion, but I had to remain confident. I had to trust this process if I was to have any hope of great results—the faint light at the end of the tunnel.

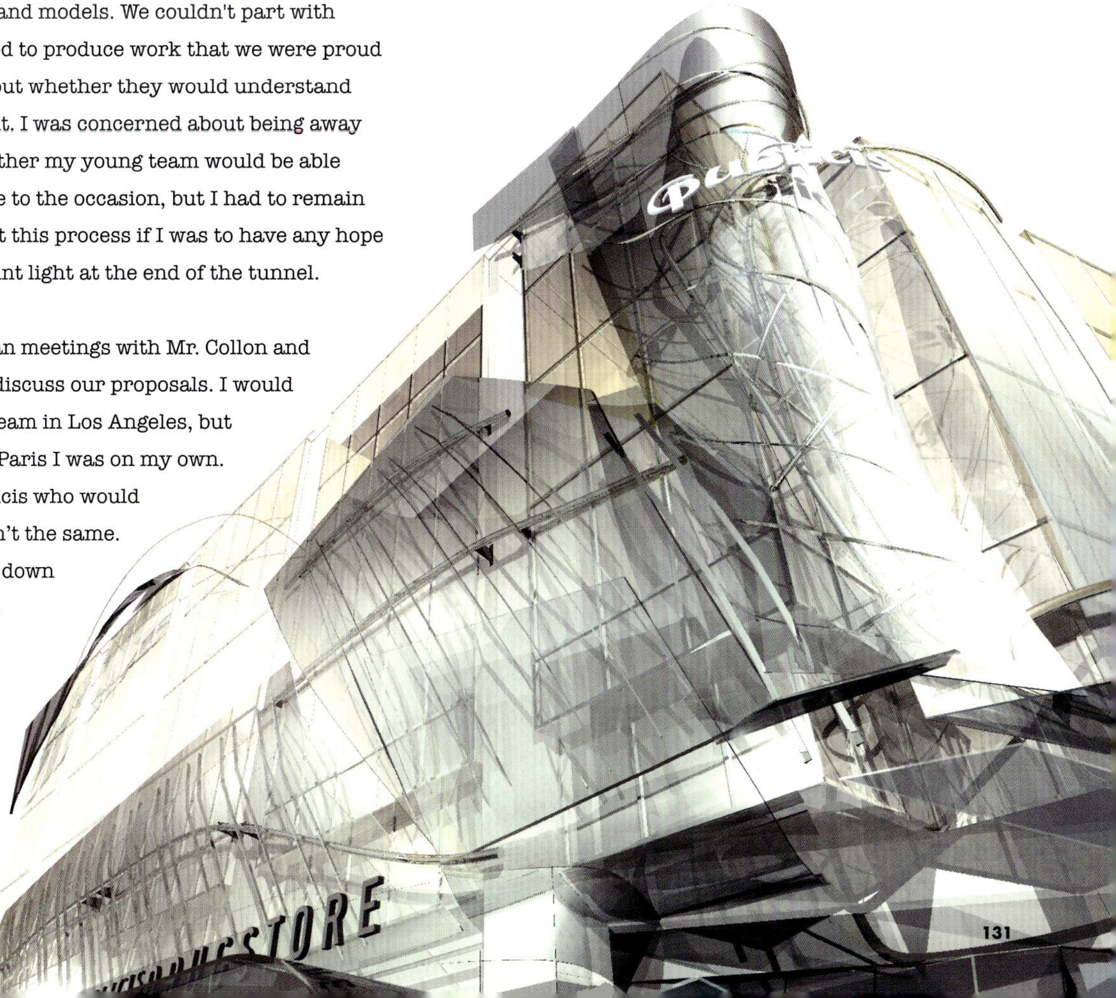

Every few weeks I'd plan meetings with Mr. Collon and his team of experts to discuss our proposals. I would be surrounded by my team in Los Angeles, but the minute I landed in Paris I was on my own. I had people from Publicis who would support me, but it wasn't the same. I couldn't let my guard down around them. Mr. De la Brosse was kind and generous with a great sense of humor, but he was strict and disciplined like a military man. He was the director of the drugstore and was brought in specifically for the development of the project and building. I learned a great deal about the French work ethic from him.

I would arrive with Thierry de la Brosse and Philippe Uzzan to a large meeting room with a huge square-shaped table in the middle. Then Mr. Collon and his team would appear and keep coming until the room was almost full. Each meeting started with Thierry presenting the general state of affairs and then introducing me, following the formal French tradition. I've heard from many colleagues about the difficulties dealing with the L'architecte des Batiments de France (ABF), but I couldn't share their sentiments. These were meetings that I looked forward to.

Mr. Collon would study my moves on the development of the project very carefully. So carefully, he could read my emotional state when reviewing the project, which was unusually heartwarming and encouraging. I especially remember how Alain would check on me when I was depressed. When the clients were expressing doubts moving forward with my design, Alain was supportive. Our mutual respect and interest created an amicable environment of trust.

Publicis decided to renovate their building in order to keep Marcel Bleustein-Blanchet's legacy alive. On the other hand, the current design was nostalgic to the time Mr. Blanchet founded Publicis, therefore there was a fine line between destroying his legacy and preserving it. I argued that the new facade would be the door separating the founder's creation and the future of the company, but this process was personal and emotional, especially for Mrs. Badinter— who questioned the extent to which her father's building would be transformed.

The project went on hold for a few months because of this. Mr. Collon called me one day asking about the status of production. Upon hearing that it has stopped, he set to meet with Madam Badinter and Publicis to explain how important it was to continue. Blanchet's relationship with the company and the city he loved influenced how important the project was for Publicis and the Champs Elysse's transformation.

Alain's compelling argument to Madam Badinter, Robert Badinter, and me brought the project back to life. Collon saw how the Publicis design would affect the immediate area, contrasting buildings from the seventies, leading many to be renovated or rebuilt. Luckily Publicis had the means to make this intervention possible from a logistical point of view, but more importantly it's interest in recreating this building was unorthodox. Mr. Collon was focused on establishing a precedent. Traditionally in France, works of architecture or buildings of significance were done by the government and not private companies or entities unless you were Cartier or Louis Vuitton. In this case it was an initiative that the city wanted to set an example and encourage other companies to follow suite.

At the studio, our work was moving forward with full force. The atmosphere was packed with different types of glue, paper, cardboard, soldering material, and takeout food. All of us were on a mission to narrow down our designs and announce a winner. Energy levels were high and everyone was particularly sensitive about their work. At this juncture I was pulling forward different design proposals, collaborating with different members of my team. I committed to each design idea until they were fully formed in order to have the best design solution available, but had to eventually face the harsh reality of selecting one.

During the selection process I was just hoping that Collon will agree with my decision in order to move forward. My team and I spent weeks evaluating and making additional physical and digital models until, finally, I saw it. The selected design, with a few others, were presented to Collon the following week. Thankfully he gravitated toward my favorite. Now it was time to convince Badinter and Levy.

I went back to LA with great news and fire in my belly. We were one step closer, but we were on a different path now and the need to hire consultants was pressing. Our next step was to develop the design and to prepare the presentation to meet with Mrs. Badinter and Mr. Levy. I was concerned and doubtful about their reaction and the future of the project.

Everything was falling into place. I could feel that we were on the right path with the design and I was making sure to stay positive. We built a new model out of plexiglass, cardboard, and piano wires and were back in Paris a few weeks later. I took a taxi to Publicis directly from the airport since I couldn't carry the big box to the hotel. Thierry was expecting me and the replica delivered to his office. I was not sure what to expect. I was especially nervous to see their reactions once they saw it. As I pulled it out of the box, Thierry's face was exceptionally alarming. He looked confused and insecure about the design before he said anything, or maybe that's what I was projecting. Thierry told me he has scheduled a meeting with Mr. Levy that night, but suggested that we only present the drawings to evaluate his reaction and then present the model at another meeting. I agreed.

The meeting with Mr. Levy was mostly short and anti-climactic. Levy was expecting more, so before we ended Thierry told him that I had brought a model and he would have someone bring it upstairs if he wanted to see it. "Not necessary," Mr. Levy said, "Let's go there now." He left and we followed. I was ready for everything and anything in that moment.

As we entered Thierry's office, Mr. Levy sat in front of the model for more than ten minutes, staring. I was standing by his side in agony, not saying a word until he raised his head and asked me, "Do you think we can build it?"

"Of course." I said. I'm internally screaming "He liked it!" which meant two down and one to go. I needed to convince Madam Badinter.

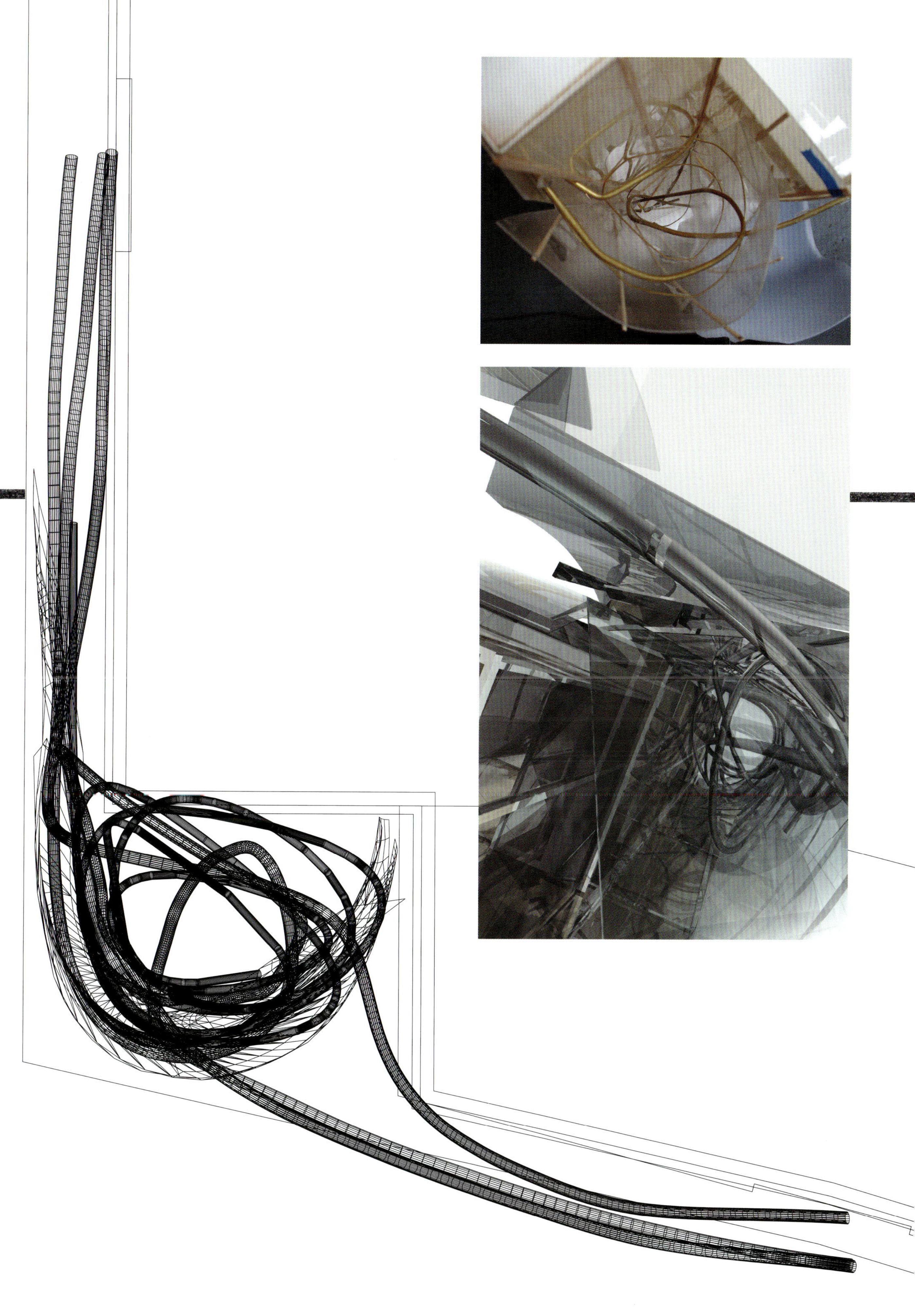

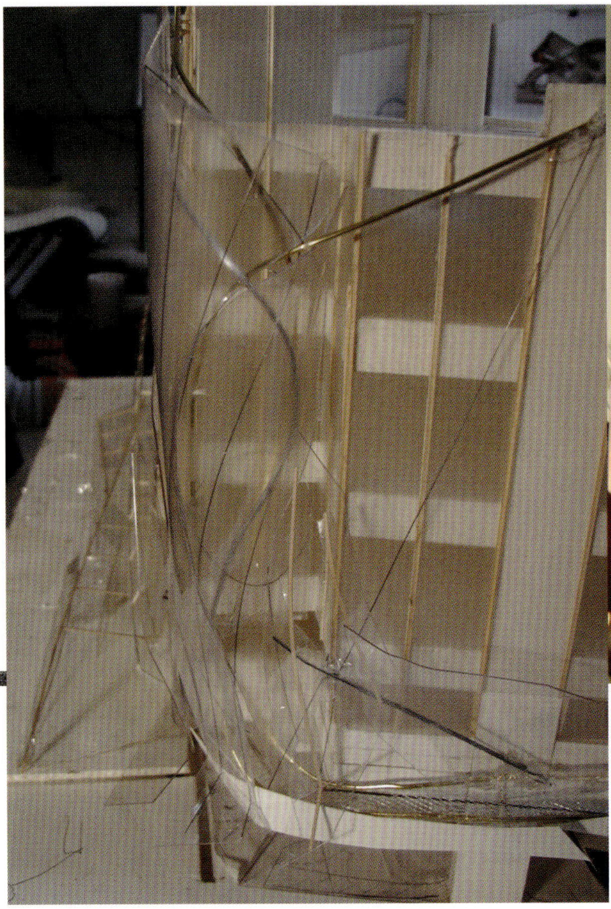

When I thought I had it everything fell apart.

The nature of architecture is collaborative. An architect takes on multiple roles to coordinate and maintain a certain vision during the development of the project. They are not only responsible for their team, but also to serve as the liaison for the clients and their own team of consultants. Not only does it require involvement, but the harmony of numerous people at each level of its development is essential. Therefore, architects don't work in a vacuum. My studio, alone, consisted of 15 people. Then there was the design team, movie theater consultants, sound consultants, material consultants, furnishing consultants, lighting consultants, etc. Publicis had their own team of consultants ranging from the food

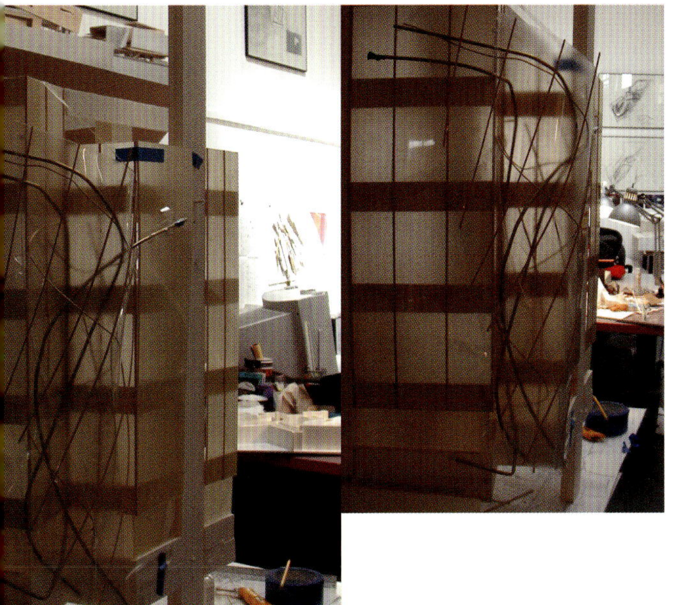

Lesson two: Never be too sure.

Han Suh Sohn
Reza Bagherzadeh

industry to graphic design and construction. An important figure from the Publicis team had to be Alain Ducasse. The French-born Monégasque chef served as their food consultant; I had to try to reach consensus with many other creatives. For example, if Publicis would like their theater to be used for conferences, then it was up to me to work with the movie theater, sound, and lighting consultants of both teams to make sure this was feasible all the while maintaining an aesthetic that Publicis and I were content with. Once I'd reached an agreement with the client, I would then need to cooperate with city officials amongst multiple departments and agencies, contractors, subcontractors, and sub-sub contractors. There are sometimes hundreds of people involved in a modest-sized project.

Every builder in Paris wanted the project or at least a piece of it, mainly because of Publicis group's affluence and the exposure the project had in the city of Paris. Due to their pre-existing relationship and the assurances they received, Publicis finally selected Coteba, one of France's leading companies concentrated on project management of large-scale buildings. Yet, soon after they were signed, Coteba's attitude changed and I was slowly pushed away. Cut from the inner circle. I wasn't surprised nor convinced that they understood the design and its complexity. I'd express doubts if they were qualified for such a project, but every time I was reassured, "Don't worry Michele. They are a large company. They will use all their resources to ensure the success of your design." All the more alarming.

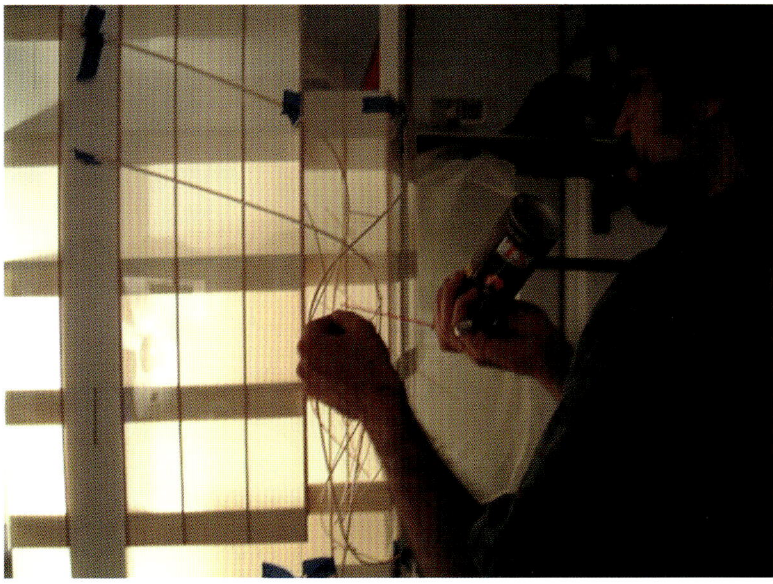

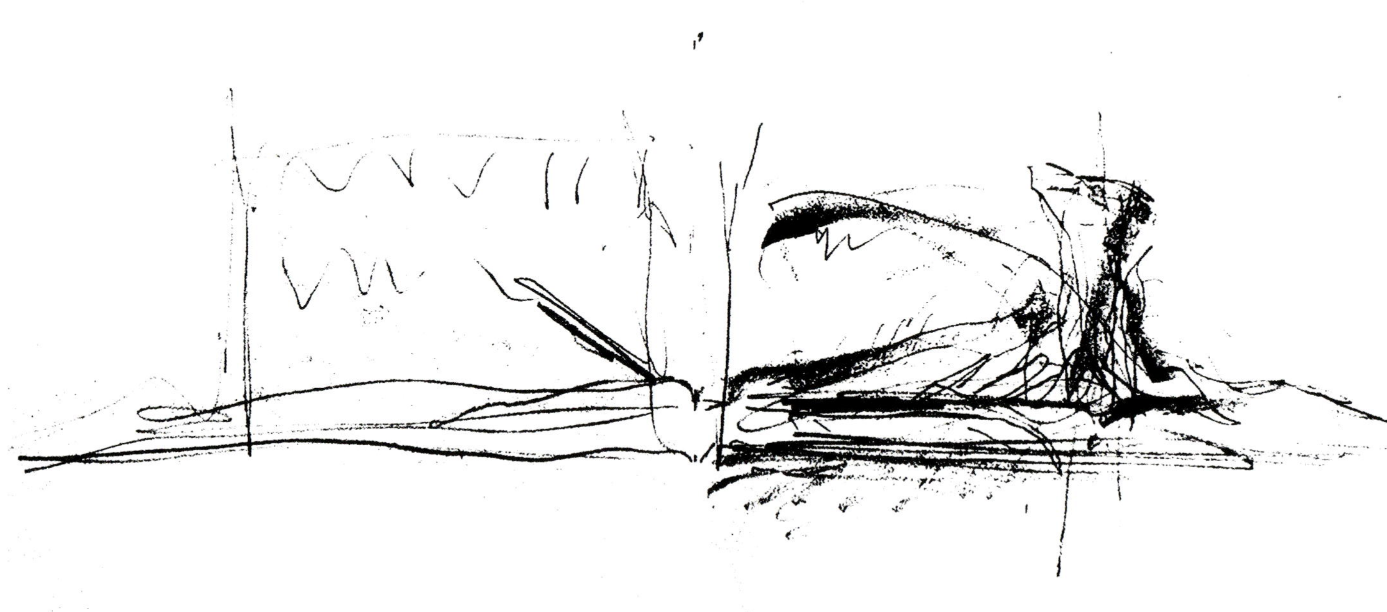

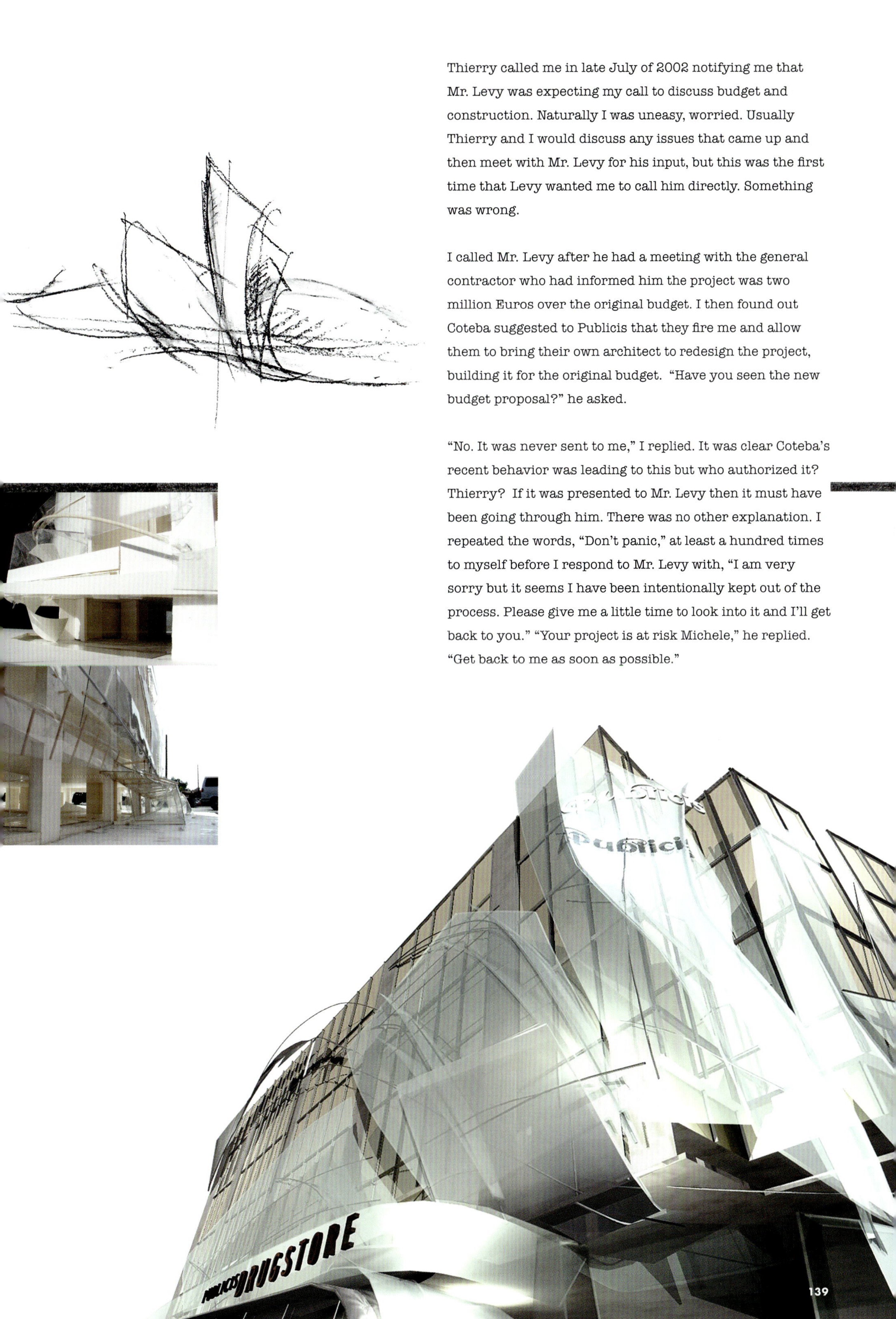

Thierry called me in late July of 2002 notifying me that Mr. Levy was expecting my call to discuss budget and construction. Naturally I was uneasy, worried. Usually Thierry and I would discuss any issues that came up and then meet with Mr. Levy for his input, but this was the first time that Levy wanted me to call him directly. Something was wrong.

I called Mr. Levy after he had a meeting with the general contractor who had informed him the project was two million Euros over the original budget. I then found out Coteba suggested to Publicis that they fire me and allow them to bring their own architect to redesign the project, building it for the original budget. "Have you seen the new budget proposal?" he asked.

"No. It was never sent to me," I replied. It was clear Coteba's recent behavior was leading to this but who authorized it? Thierry? If it was presented to Mr. Levy then it must have been going through him. There was no other explanation. I repeated the words, "Don't panic," at least a hundred times to myself before I respond to Mr. Levy with, "I am very sorry but it seems I have been intentionally kept out of the process. Please give me a little time to look into it and I'll get back to you." "Your project is at risk Michele," he replied. "Get back to me as soon as possible."

PUBLICIS
LANCEL
BOUTIQUE

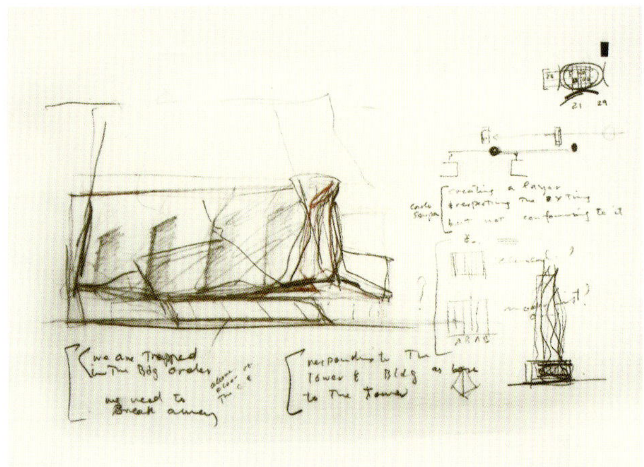

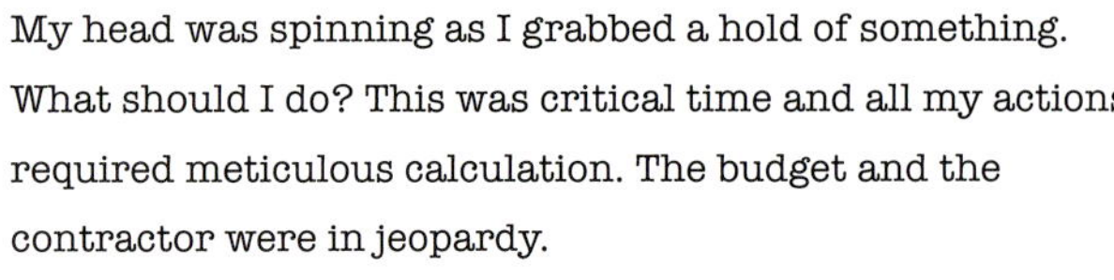

My head was spinning as I grabbed a hold of something. What should I do? This was critical time and all my actions required meticulous calculation. The budget and the contractor were in jeopardy.

At this time I discovered that one of my assistants, whom I trusted (I had long term plans to make him my partner), not very honest about his activities. He was presenting himself as an independent architect and using my projects to promote himself for work opportunities. I found the letter and resume he sent to potential clients in the trash bin of our studio computer in Paris. It shocked me to see him presenting himself as one of the founders of the studio I started in 1985.

I couldn't trust anyone nor the budget Coteba presented to Mr. Levy, so I reached out to a professional cost estimator in Paris. We signed a confidentiality agreement for them to work with my office and prepare an estimate of the cost of our project based on the complexity of the design, materials, and assemblies. In secrecy I traveled to Paris to meet with them and in a few weeks had a document signed by a reputable company. I called Mr. Levy's office to set a time for a meeting in mid-August. Paris was relatively quiet during this time; the Parisians were on vacation. On the day of the meeting I contacted Thierry to join us, which caught him off guard. This was a critical meeting for me and the project.

One certainty: I was not going to give up. I never forget the look on their faces when I handed them the cost estimate booklet signed and stamped by the economist. I always thought the French hid their emotions well, but it was not the case that day when I explained that I hired the cost estimator privately and paid for it for the benefit of the project. It showed we are within our budget based on itemized spreadsheets. Mr. Levy was pleased and asked me to get more actively involved in the search for a "new contractor."

Publicis

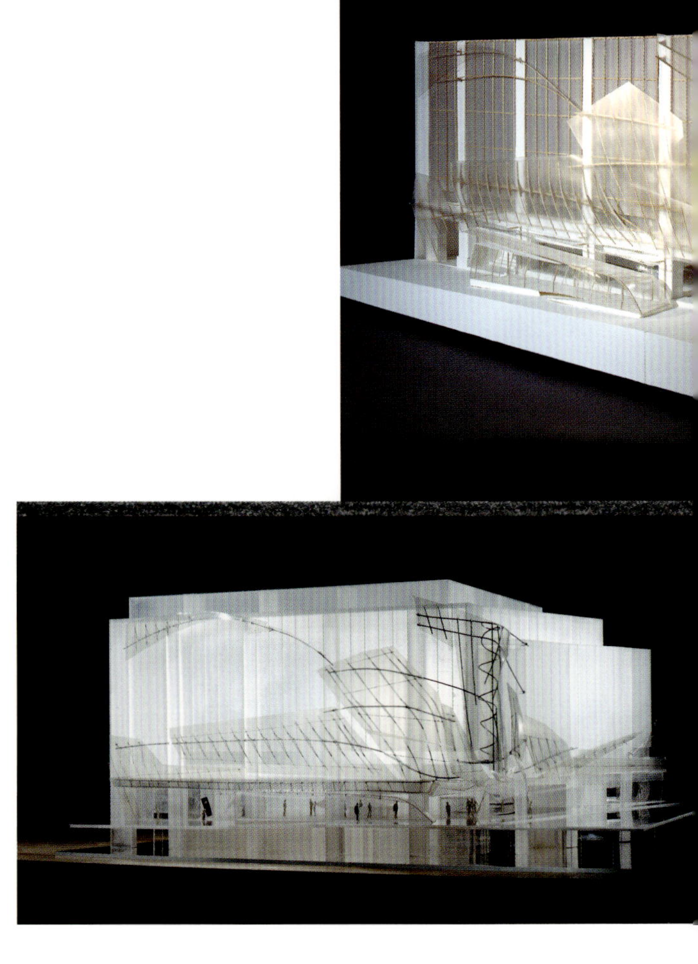

I later found out Mr. Levy's meeting with Coteba was more dramatic than I presumed. Apparently when Coteba suggested to fire me and change the design, Mr. Levy threw them out of his office. His response was that Coteba was arrogant and unprofessional to suggest that Publicis was willing abandon two years of investment, studies, research, design and city approvals because they lacked the abilities to make it work for a 10-15% difference in cost. We, our collective teams and the project which has taken a life of its own, entered a new phase. I learned that Mr. Levy was the man with the vision.

Removing one obstacle didn't mean we were safe. Now that the budget was taken care of, we had to find a new contractor. The project needed the same creative approach in every aspect of its making and that included selection of the contractor, method of construction, etc. People involved need to share the same vision which is the backbone of the entire process. I also realized that most people are fearful of the design because they (the city, the contractors, the consultants) weren't able to "see" it in the way I, and the people around me, did. This would translate to the fear of cost, the construction, and installation of the façade. I also have to mention how my lack of experience contributed to this fear. I did feel like I'd bitten off more than I could chew, but it forced me to rise to the occasion because there wasn't any other option. Everything was at stake.

There were only a few companies in France who could do the job well and their prices were very high for our budget. I revisited those companies to try to negotiate the price and a common ground by offering my involvement to facilitate the job, but to no avail. I needed a new approach.

The idea of a single General contractor for the project was questionable at this juncture. We needed to:

• separate the construction of the façade from the interior of the project and

• take additional steps to present the façade in a simpler way that was easier to understand.

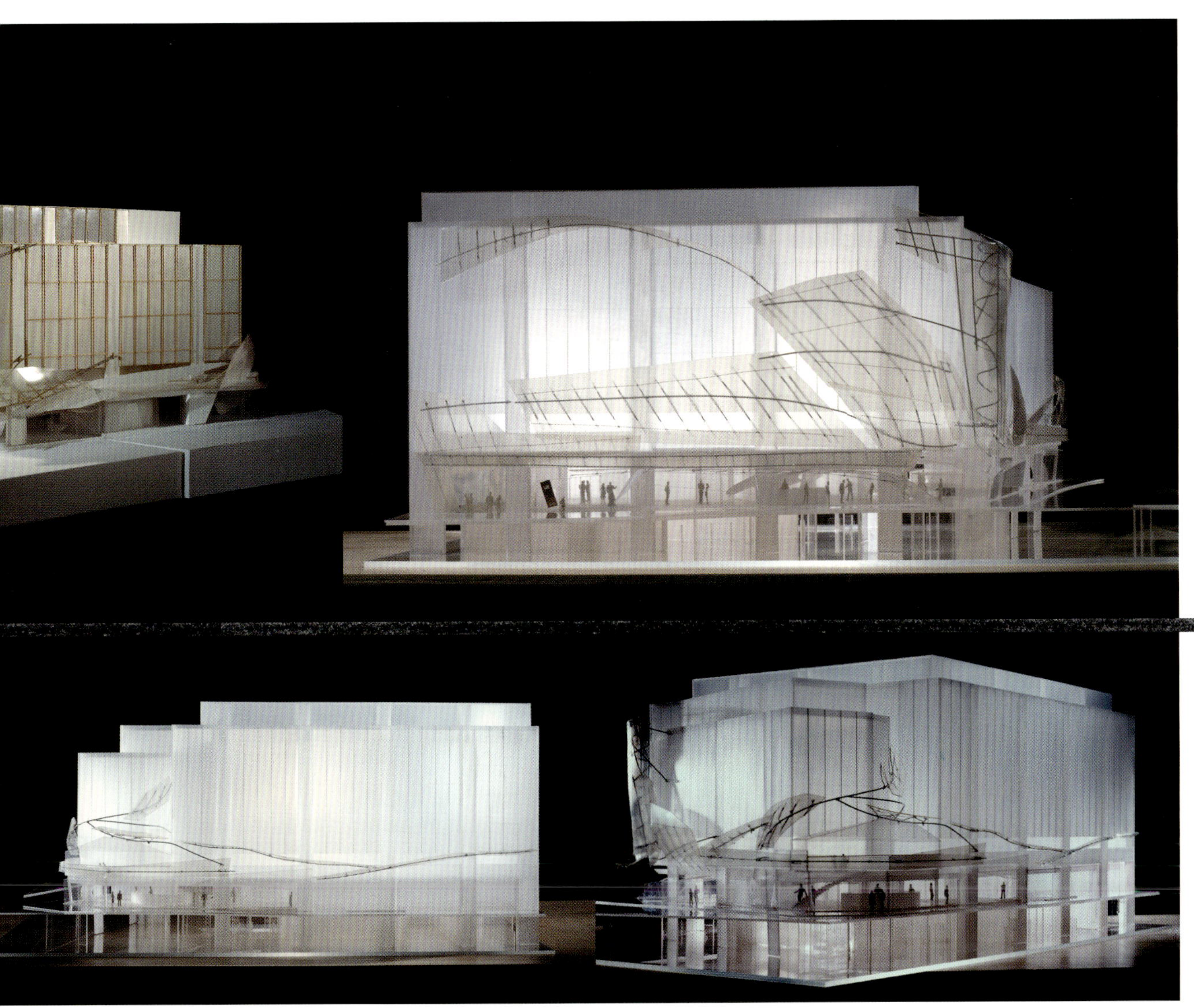

Therefore, instead of the façade as one complex construct we methodically cut it up diagrammatically in order to ease the study of it. For example, the structural frame or the glass as separate parts and following the same logic we could study the corner as an individual piece of the frame and the rest as wings that are similar in their shape with the same curve, etc. Once we altered our perception, focusing on individual parts rather than the whole, it became easier to see and understand the project.

After a number of meetings in France, I reached out to Thom Mayne and Frank Gehry's offices for advice and they put me in contact with companies in Italy, Spain, and Germany. Hugh Dutton knew Gartner in Germany so we set an appointment to meet and discuss the project with them. Gartner is an expert in creating custom-made building envelopes in steel and aluminum with an impressive resume of work all over the world. The question was if they would take on a relatively small project with a complex design, difficult location, and moderate budget. The meeting with them was refreshing and encouraging. They were transparent and direct about their capabilities and what it would take for them to produce a well-finished product. Hugh and I brainstormed with them all day. We visited their factory and met people from each of their departments. I noticed that they are mainly builders of structural frames and skeletons of the skeletons and that we could outsource the glass component for our project.

On the way back to Paris I remembered Saint Gobain Glass Company being a client of Publicis. In terms of color and clarity, their low iron glass is some of the best in the world. We were in contact with Gartner the following week and the overall reactions were positive. Meanwhile I was exploring the glass companies with acceptable bending techniques in Germany and France to avoid ripple effects and strange distortions in the curved glass. At this stage I was giving it my all, reaching out to as many people and places as possible. Inspired by Gehry's Condé Nast Cafeteria in New York City, I reached out to C-Teck in Los Angeles, but learned that Publicis would be too big for them. Their method of building individual ceramic molds was too time consuming and expensive. This was happening during a time of breakthroughs in glass technology that came with a boom in glass buildings that served as precedent for our project.

The Cricursa Curved Glass Company in Barcelona, Spain was highly recommended for their quality. I called and caught the next flight to visit them. They were very secretive and sensitive about their facilities, but were kind and hospitable. We discussed the project for hours and when I left the next day, I believed I could create my building within the budget.

I knew Gartner was undergoing a global transition, so they liked the idea of doing this exposed project in the heart of Paris. Saint Gobain was providing the glass for their long time PR Company Publicis, and Cricursa was the company to cut and curve the glass. In this way we were able to demystify the project and reduce the risk for everyone involved while saving two million Euros.

I presented the idea to Mr. Levy with Hugh at my side and we got his approval to move forward. There we were, back on track with Gartner and Cricusa as the façade contractors and Saint Gobain producing the glass. It was a very creative and exciting time. I was finally dealing with knowledgeable, skilled contractors. In order to begin production we still needed:

- geometrical survey of the façade of Publicis;
- convert our Rhino model into Catia (3D modeling software);

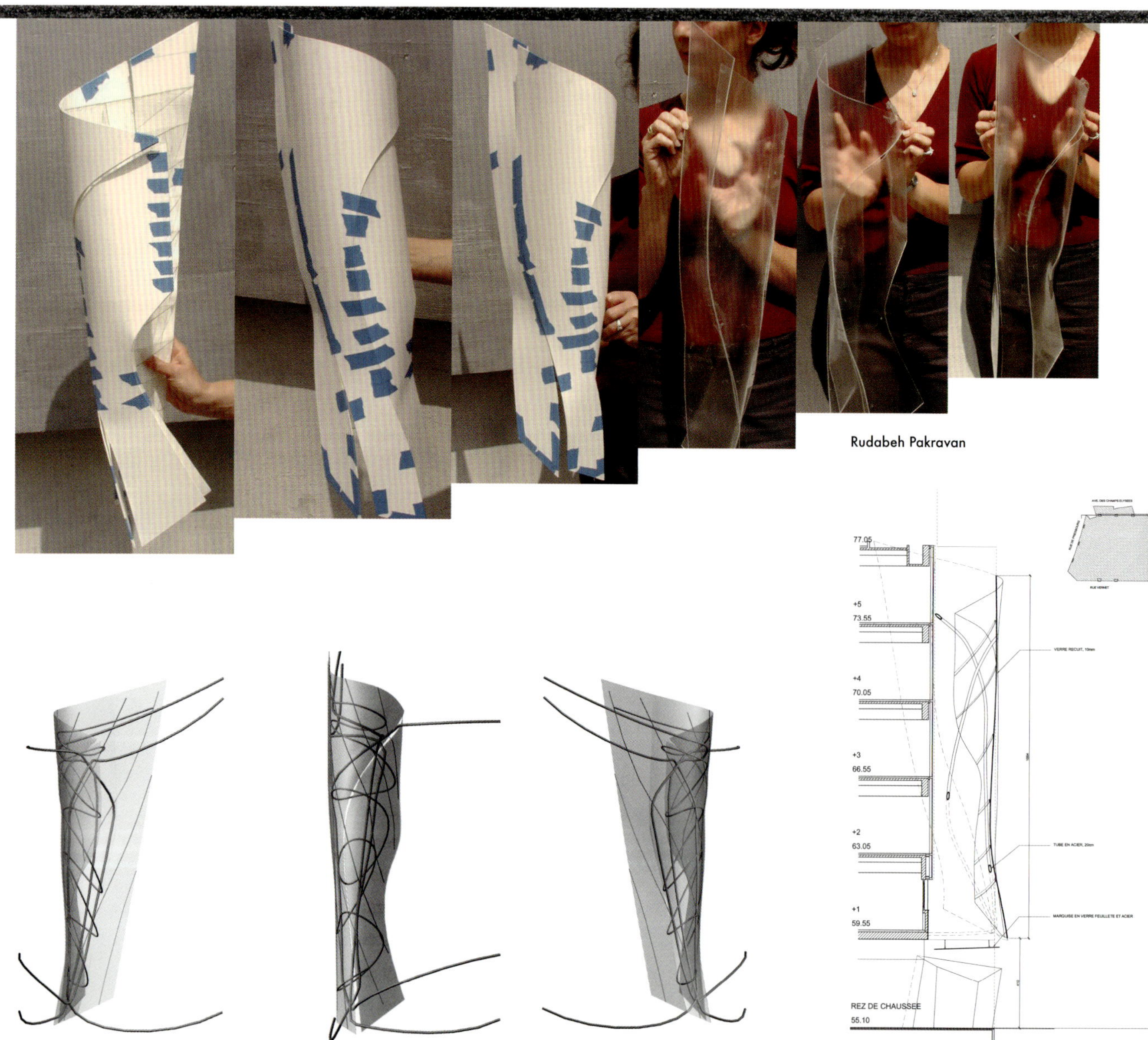

Rudabeh Pakravan

• to developing the Catia model, adjusting it based on building survey;
• Identifying main points of connection on the building and install connection hardware.

From this point everything had to be precise to make sure it fit exactly where the connections were made. Gartner constructed the entire façade in their large facilities, horizontally using steel stick-like pins. Amongst the two types of pins, one was for steel and the other for the glass with rigid rubber tips. Both were designed to hold the glass at the precise distance from the steel frame where the specially tested glue caulking would be injected. The pins were tall enough for the builders to work under and around them. First the primary structure was constructed. The custom-made tube elements were extruded at their facility, then the secondary structures that carry the glass. The Catia model provided the size of each piece of glass size, curve and location. This document was sent to Cricursa for them to build the molds for each piece of glass on the façade.

The entire façade became one unique piece consisting of multiple, complex elements— the pieces, the connections, and the location. Hugh and I travelled back and forth during the construction of the façade to review the fabrication and solve some of the problems that require adjustments to the design.

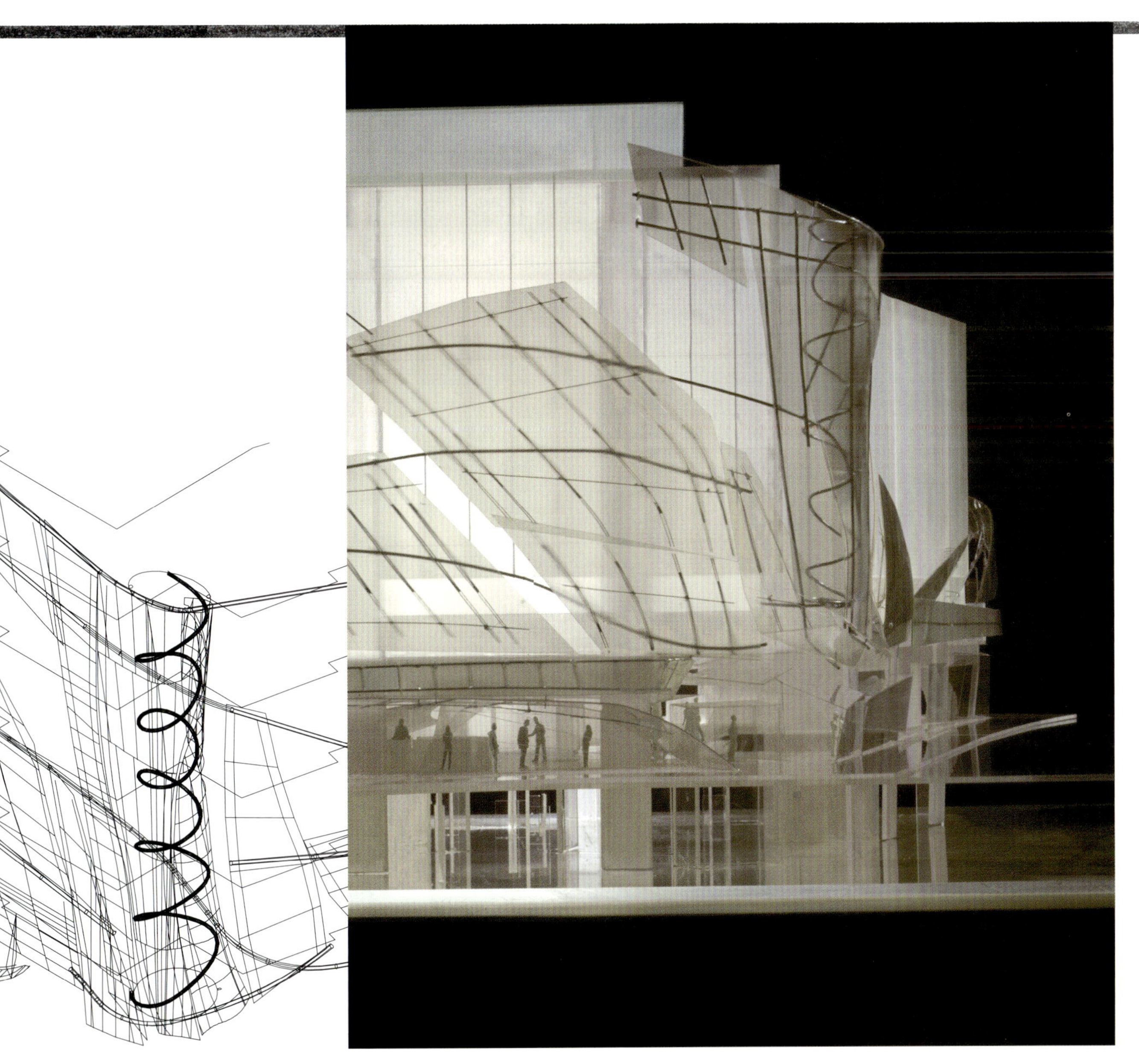

Finding Hugh

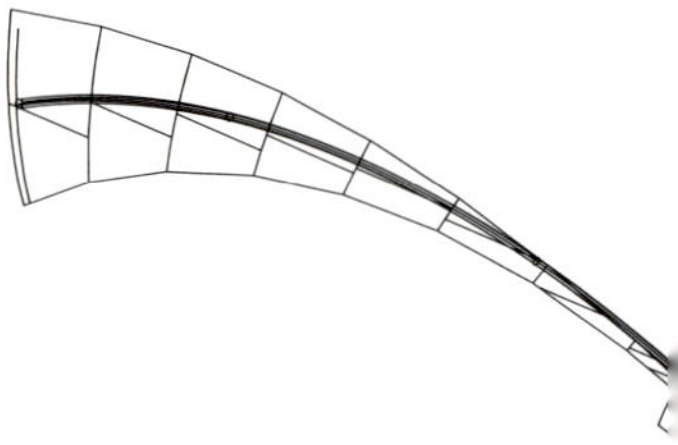

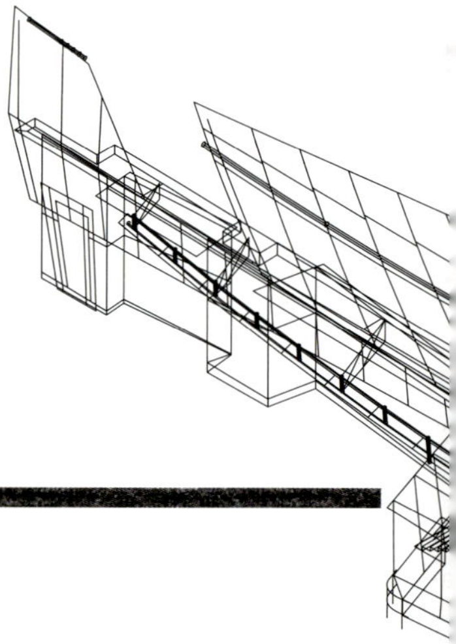

Bringing the new Publicis Drugstore to fruition took four years and changed my life forever. It felt like I was being tested. By God? I don't know, but I accepted each challenge as an opportunity to grow. This was my first time developing in France and I knew from the beginning that I needed a team of architects, designers, engineers, and other experts to help actualize my vision.

First, it was essential to have a French architect who could assist me in the planning and building codes for the city, legal matters, and the construction process for the project. It was not an easy task since anyone I asked would have wanted to take creative control themselves. Meanwhile the design process had already begun. I was running against the clock searching for the technical expertise to make sure my proposals were not just fantasies. I tried seek people with similar sensibilities and an architectural background complementary to mine in order to avoid

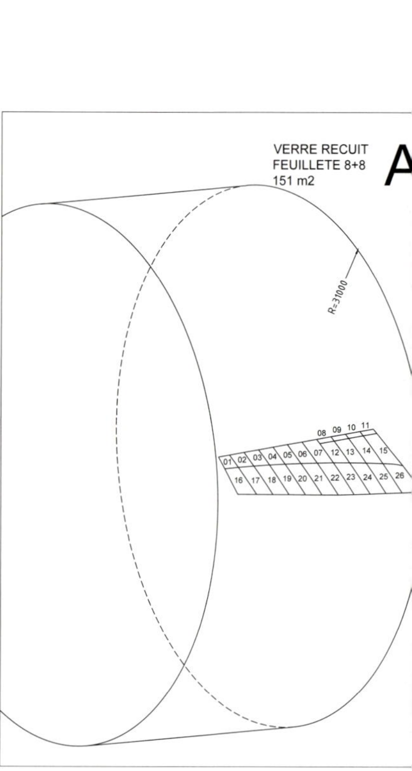

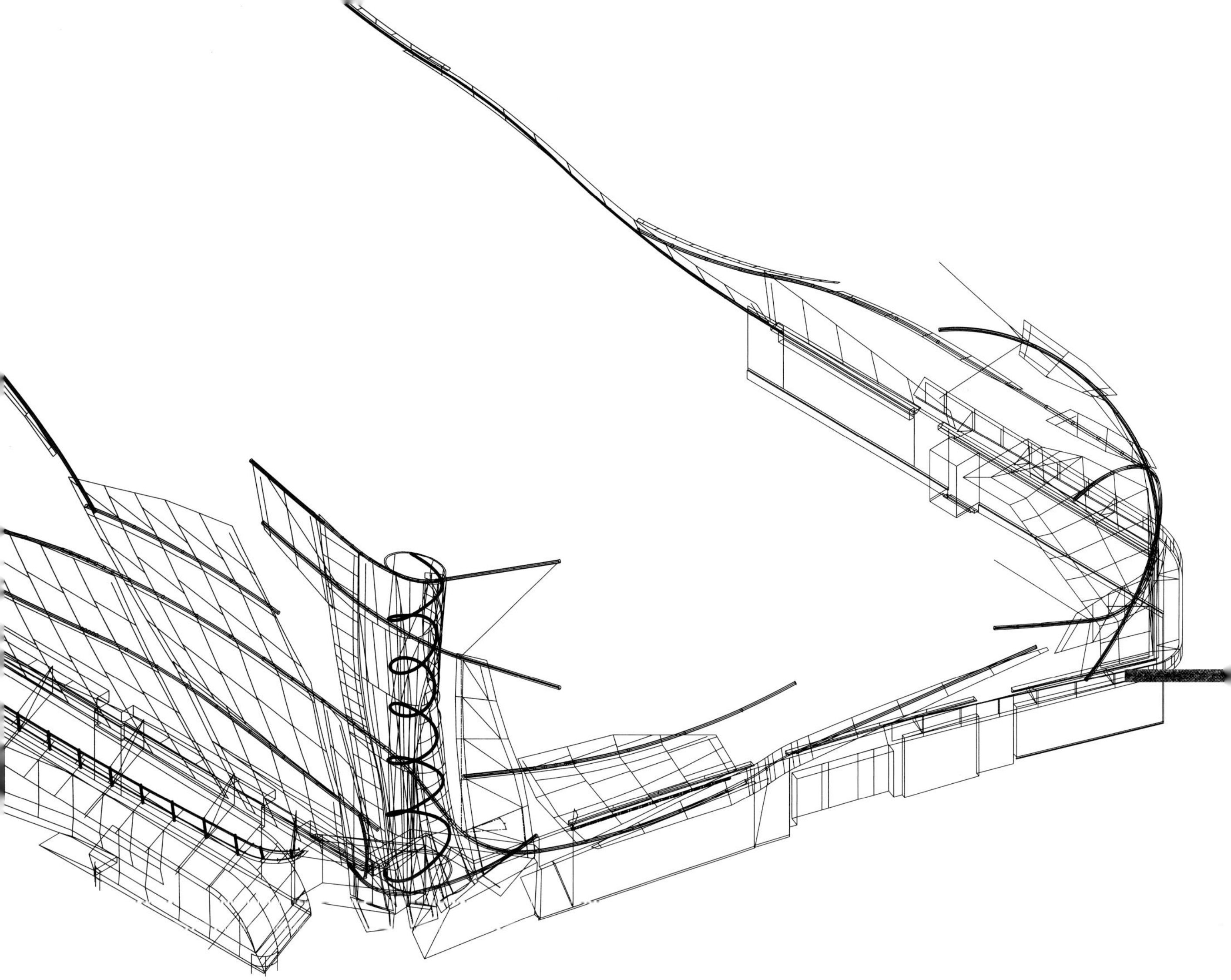

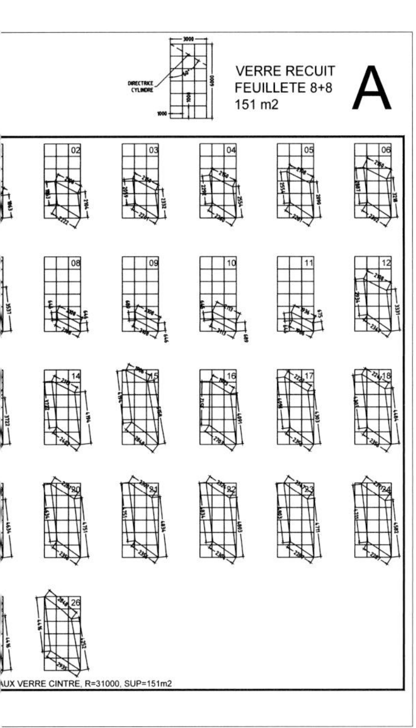
VERRE RECUIT
FEUILLETE 8+8
151 m2
A
DIRECTRICE CYLINDRE
AUX VERRE CINTRE, R=31000, SUP=151m2

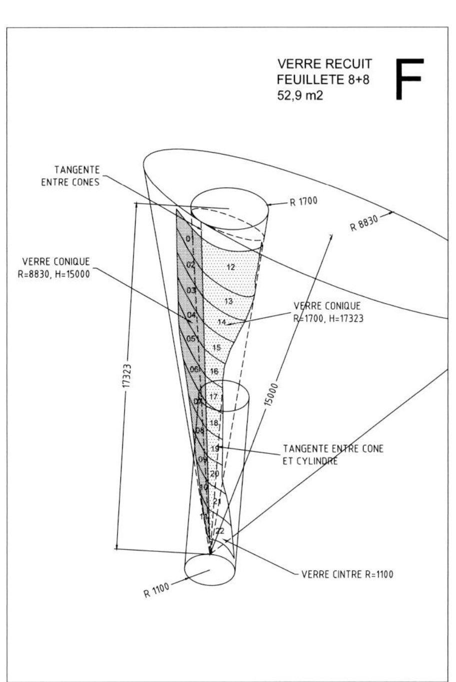
VERRE RECUIT
FEUILLETE 8+8
52,9 m2
F
TANGENTE ENTRE CONES
R 1700
R 8830
VERRE CONIQUE R=8830, H=15000
VERRE CONIQUE R=1700, H=17323
17323
15000
TANGENTE ENTRE CONE ET CYLINDRE
VERRE CINTRE R=1100
R 1100

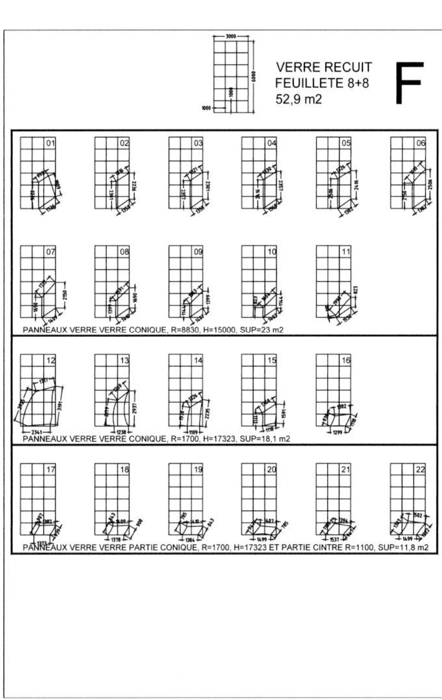
VERRE RECUIT
FEUILLETE 8+8
52,9 m2
F
PANNEAUX VERRE VERRE CONIQUE, R=8830, H=15000, SUP=23 m2
PANNEAUX VERRE VERRE CONIQUE, R=1700, H=17323, SUP=18,1 m2
PANNEAUX VERRE VERRE PARTIE CONIQUE, R=1700, H=17323 ET PARTIE CINTRE R=1100, SUP=11,8 m2

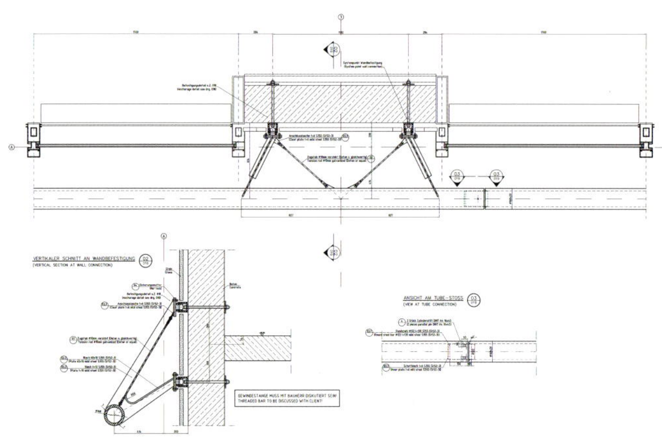

conflict and repetition. My Paris team had be independent enough that they could handle clients and authorities without much oversight.

The search for project consultants wasn't easy. I interviewed numerous structural, mechanical, electrical, plumbing, and acoustical engineers for the position. The main consultant critical in the development of the project would be structural since the façade required somebody experienced in glass technology. There weren't many engineering offices qualified to take on such a feat, and not many believed it possible. I started with the Ove Arup in Los Angeles and our meeting was constructive. Their office seemed competent and interested, but the fact that they weren't based in Paris was discomforting. I needed a local office since I was going to be away for most of the time myself. Then, one night I had dinner with a friend, Francis

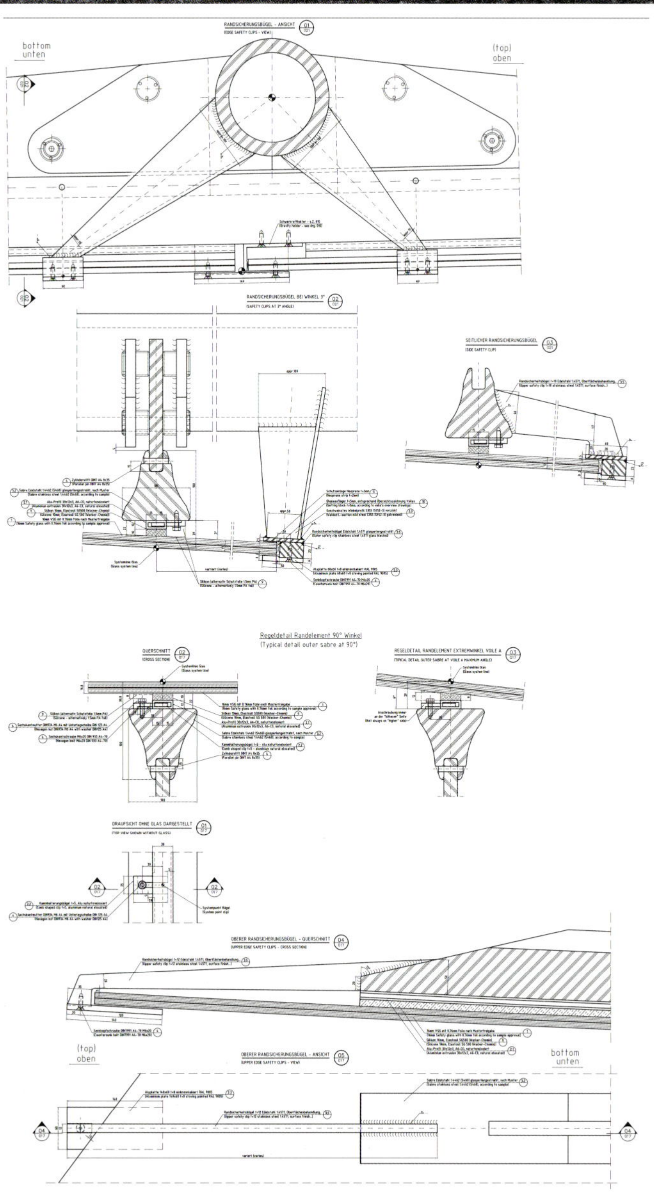

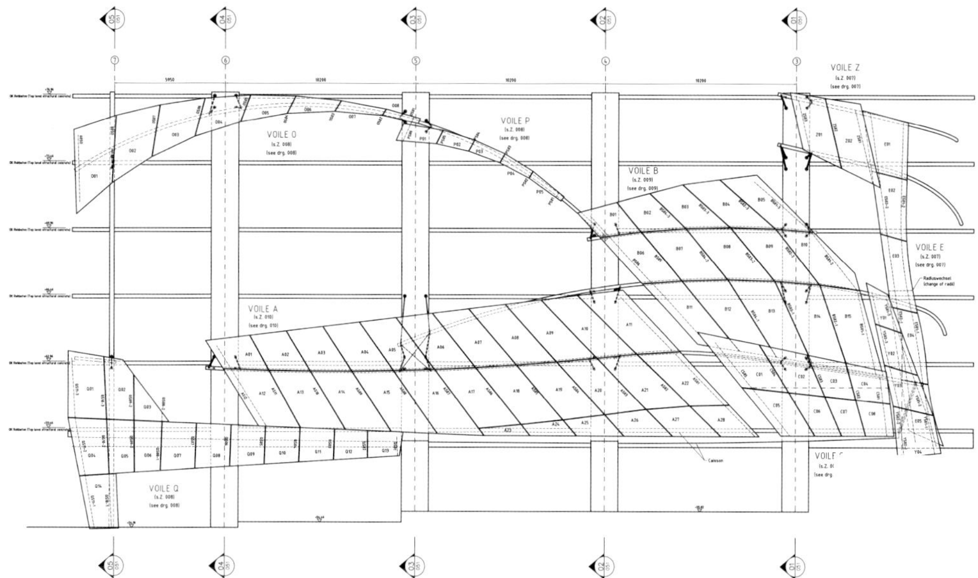

Rambert, who told me about an engineer. Hugh Dutton, the protégé of Peter Rice, had started his own office in Paris after Peter Rice passed away. This interested me to broaden my search to RFR as well.

RFR was founded in 1981 by structural engineer Peter Rice, industrial and yacht designer Martin Francis, and architect Ian Richie. They were considered one of the most creative teams in structural design, largely thanks to Peter Rice was an innovative guy in the glass technology, which was my area of interest and the integral part of the Publicis's façade.

My meetings with RFR and Hugh Dutton were captivating and intense. Both were intrigued by the design challenges of the project and its location near the Arc de Triomphe. In both meetings, each showed me some overlapping projects because Hugh Dutton used to be a part of the RFR office and I was able to hear about their experiences working together from different perspectives. At RFR, I had the pleasure of meeting Henry Barsley. I found it especially easy to talk to him and share my thoughts about my design. My first meeting with Hugh Dutton was at Publicis Drugstore's restaurant the day before I left Paris. I felt his enthusiasm and desire to step up and deal with the upcoming challenges. His soft, modest manners intrigued me. It felt as if we were in a similar place with our professional lives. He didn't hide his excitement, giving resemblance to when I first came to visit Publicis. After the meetings I spoke to Thierry, explaining in detail how I felt about them and asking that he meet with both teams when I was gone. He did and we followed up, asking both teams to submit their proposals.

Then one day I get a phone call from Hugh asking if the project has been already awarded to someone. Hugh's drive surprised me. My heart was telling me one thing, but my logic was dictating something else. If I followed my heart then I would have chosen Hugh, but logically I was leaning toward RFR. Thierry and I agreed that I needed to arrange another meeting with both groups, confident that our answer lay in that final encounter. I prepared myself to ask very confrontational questions and to test their commitment to the project. I would ask how far are they were willing to go to make this vision a reality. Were they ready to do something that had never structurally been done before? These discussions were projections and aspirations, but it was enough for me to understand their real intentions for the collaboration—a true test of commitment that only the labor of love could bring out.

I think back to this time almost every day. The endless hours I spent planning the steps I needed to take for the design, development, and consultation. How I'd refine and develop consensus to get this done.

Standing in front of the half-built project, with all signs pointing to something monumental, I thought back to all the steps and stages I had gone through to get there. The challenges of the job would wake me up at night thinking and worrying about how it's coming together. "How will we clean the back of the glass at the corner of the building?" As time passes, as we grow and develop, so do the magnitude of our problems, worries, and the satisfactions we feel with our accomplishments.

The final meetings were set with Hugh and RFR before I arrived in Paris. I was ecstatic because we were one step closer to making the project a reality. I went to RFR's office first and to my surprise I didn't see Henry until just before I left. Our meeting was conducted by one of the associates. I sensed that they were not sure about the project and their reaction was nothing more than last minute hesitations. It was unexpected, but I left the meeting sure that Hugh was the final choice. I felt good as if the course of the events helped me reach the conclusions I expected. I was worried nevertheless since I had never worked with Hugh before. We had a long and difficult path in front of us.

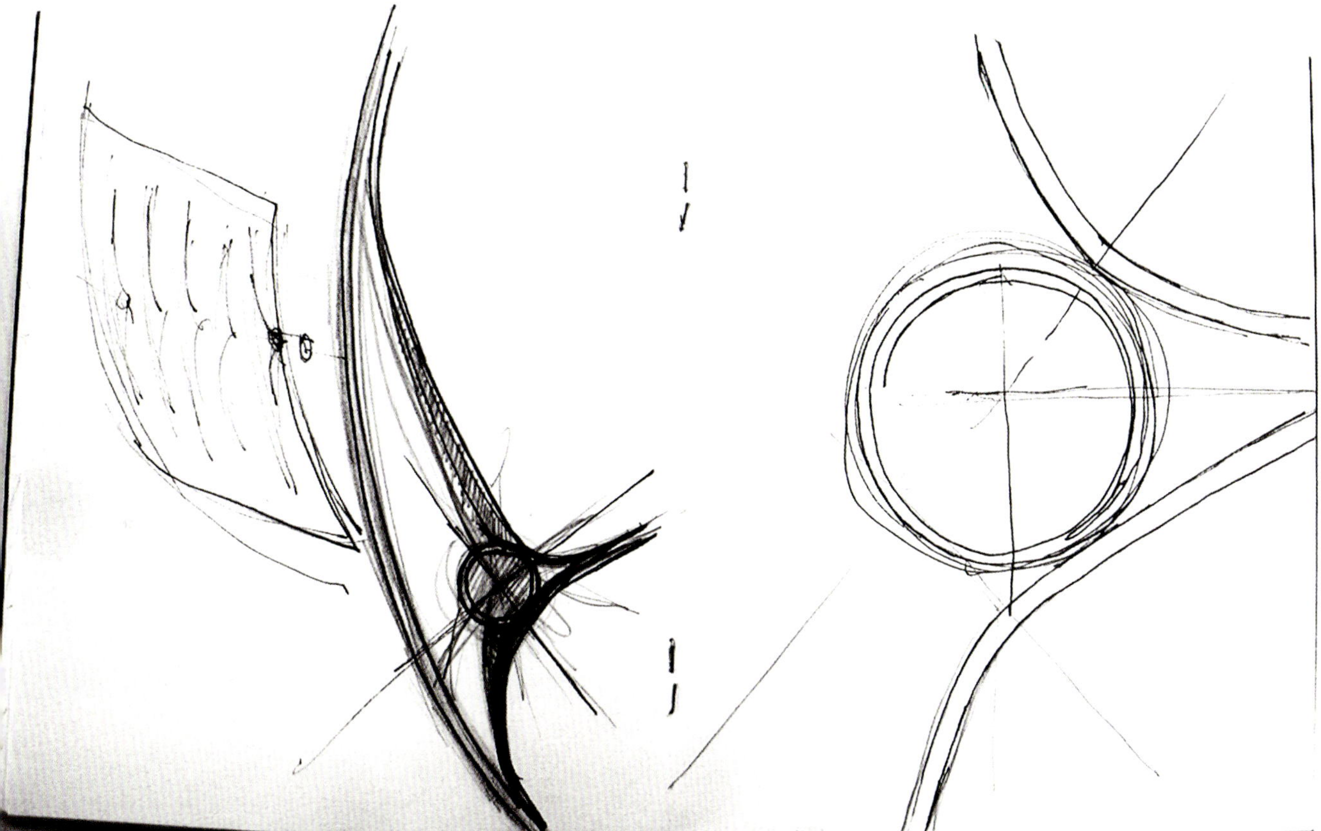

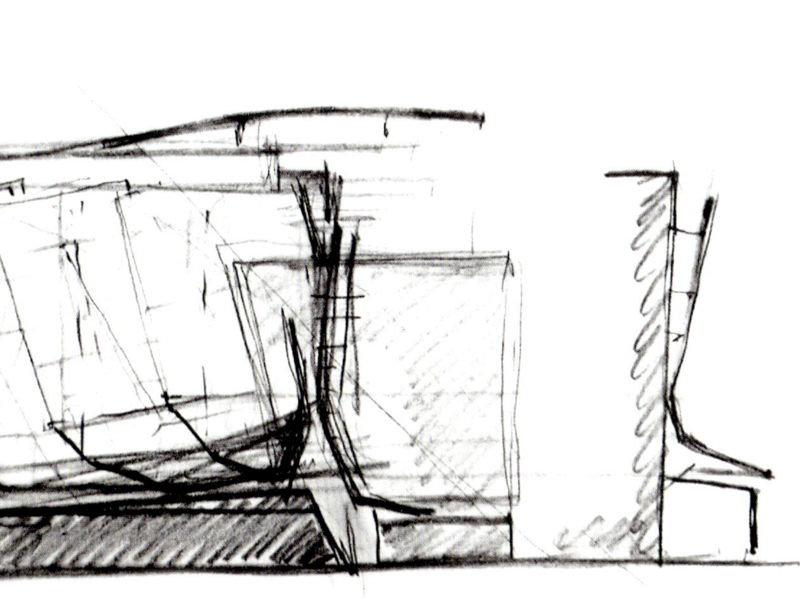

Lesson seven: **When you love what you do there's hope.**

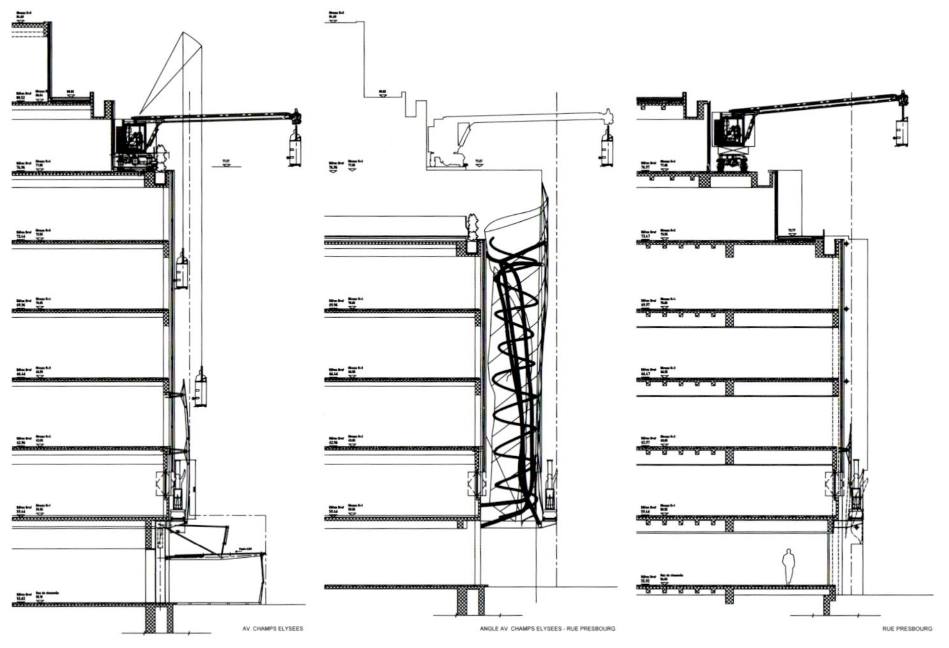
AV. CHAMPS ELYSEES
ANGLE AV. CHAMPS ELYSEES - RUE PRESBOURG
RUE PRESBOURG

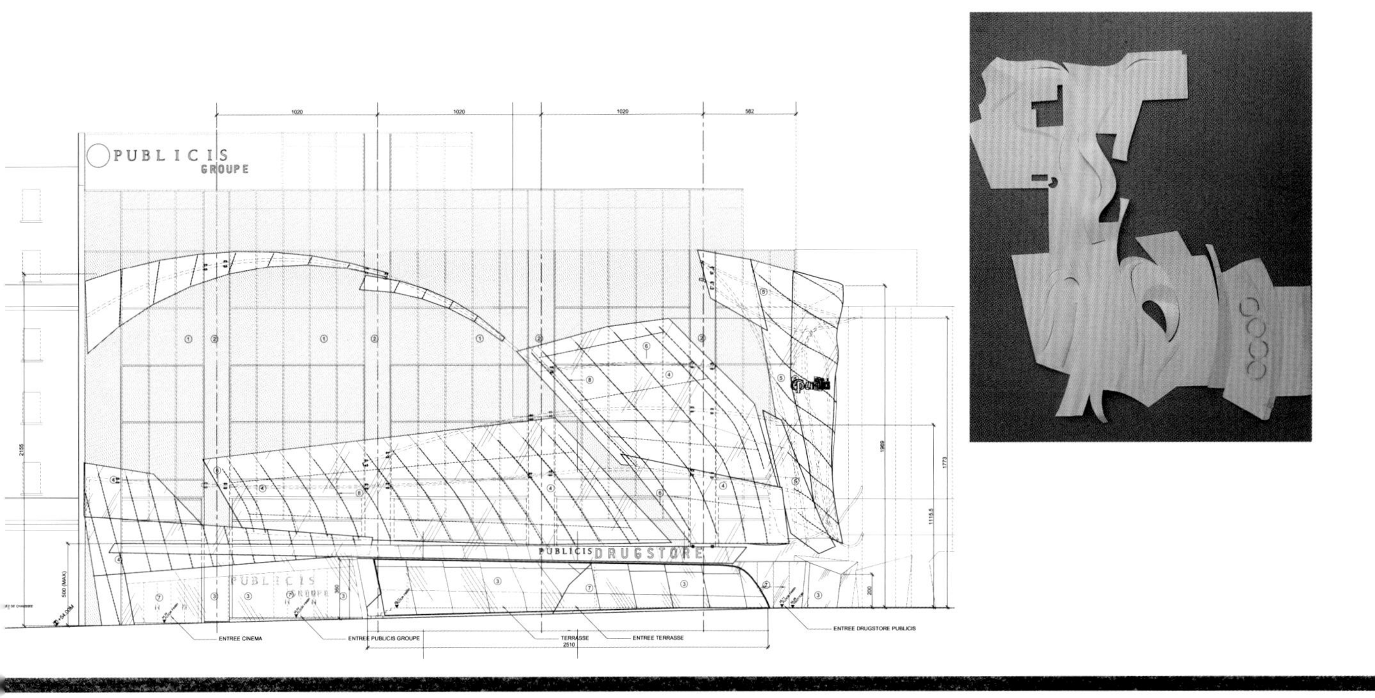

1020
1020
1020
582
PUBLICIS
GROUPE
PUBLICIS DRUGSTORE
PUBLICIS
GROUPE
ENTREE CINEMA
ENTREE PUBLICIS GROUPE
TERRASSE
2510
ENTREE TERRASSE
ENTREE DRUGSTORE PUBLICIS

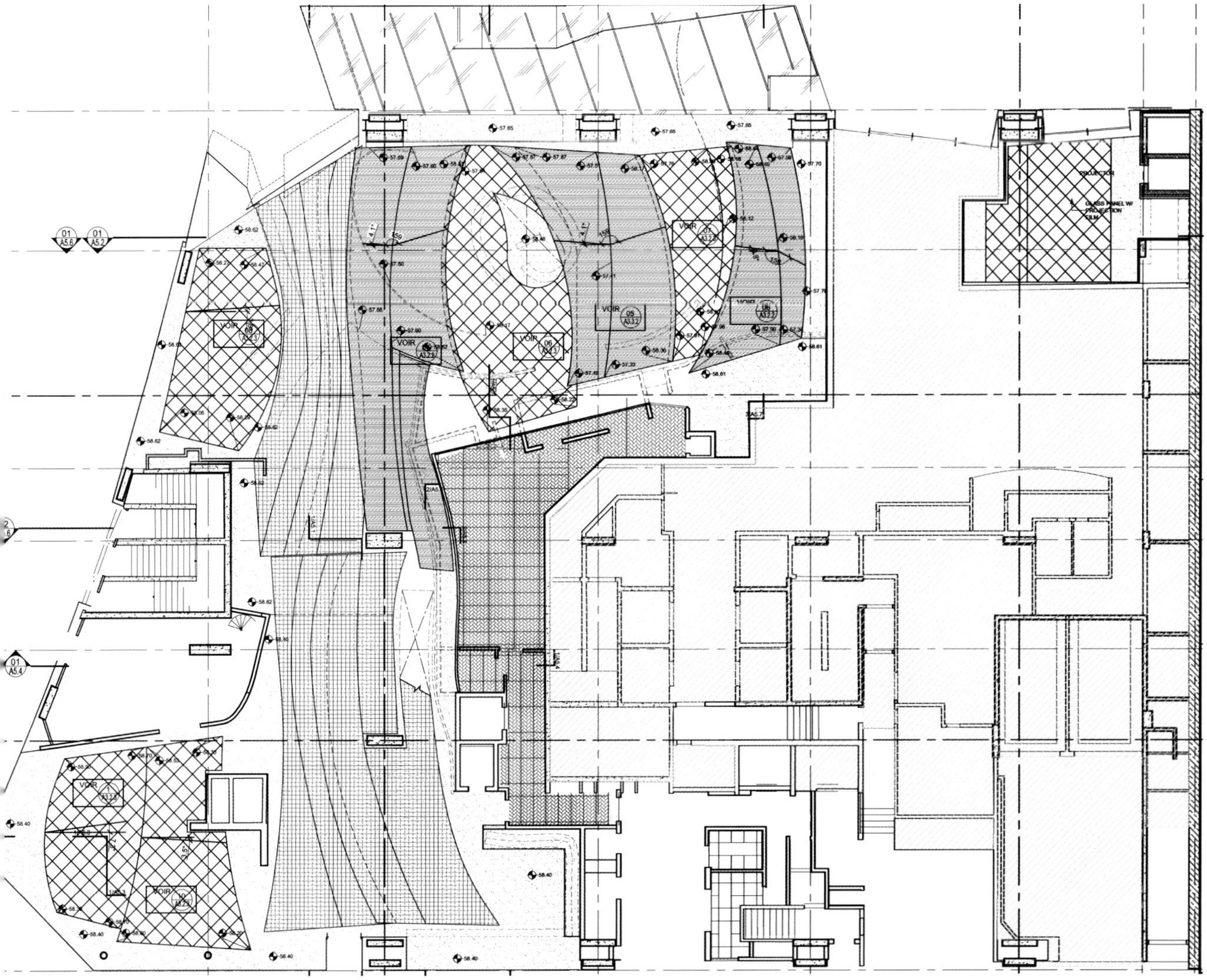

PLAFOND EN PLAQUE DE PLATRE
VERRE TREMPE VOIR ELEVATIONS POUR DIMENSIONS
VERRE TREMPE VOIR ELEVATIONS POUR DIMENSIONS
SUPPORT APPLIQUE
SUPPORT EN ACIER
SUPPORT EN ACIER
SUPPORT EN ACIER
SUPPORT EN ACIER
COUSSIN D'ASSISE EN CUIR
VERRE TREMPE VOIR ELEVATIONS POUR DIMENSIONS
APPAREIL D'ECLAIRAGE
NIVEAU SOL FINI DALLE DE BETON
VARIES
55.02

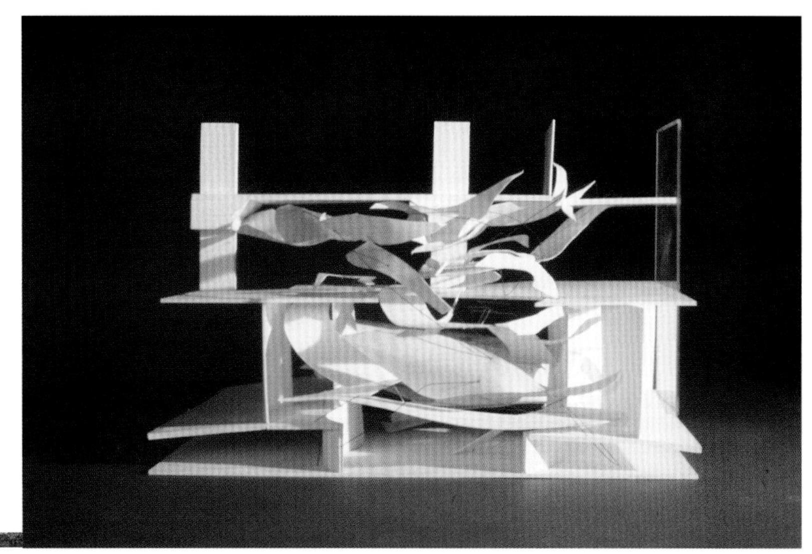

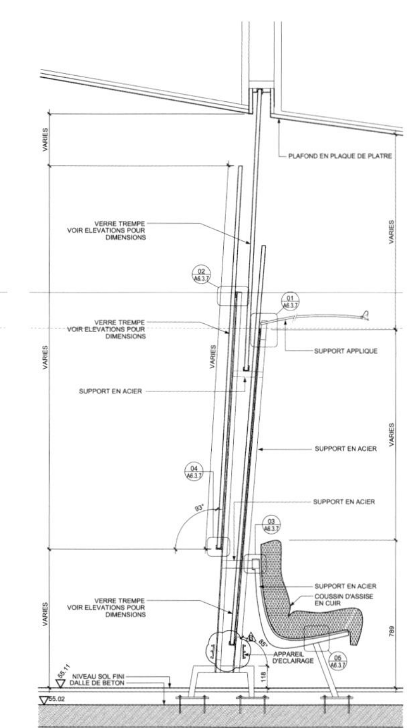

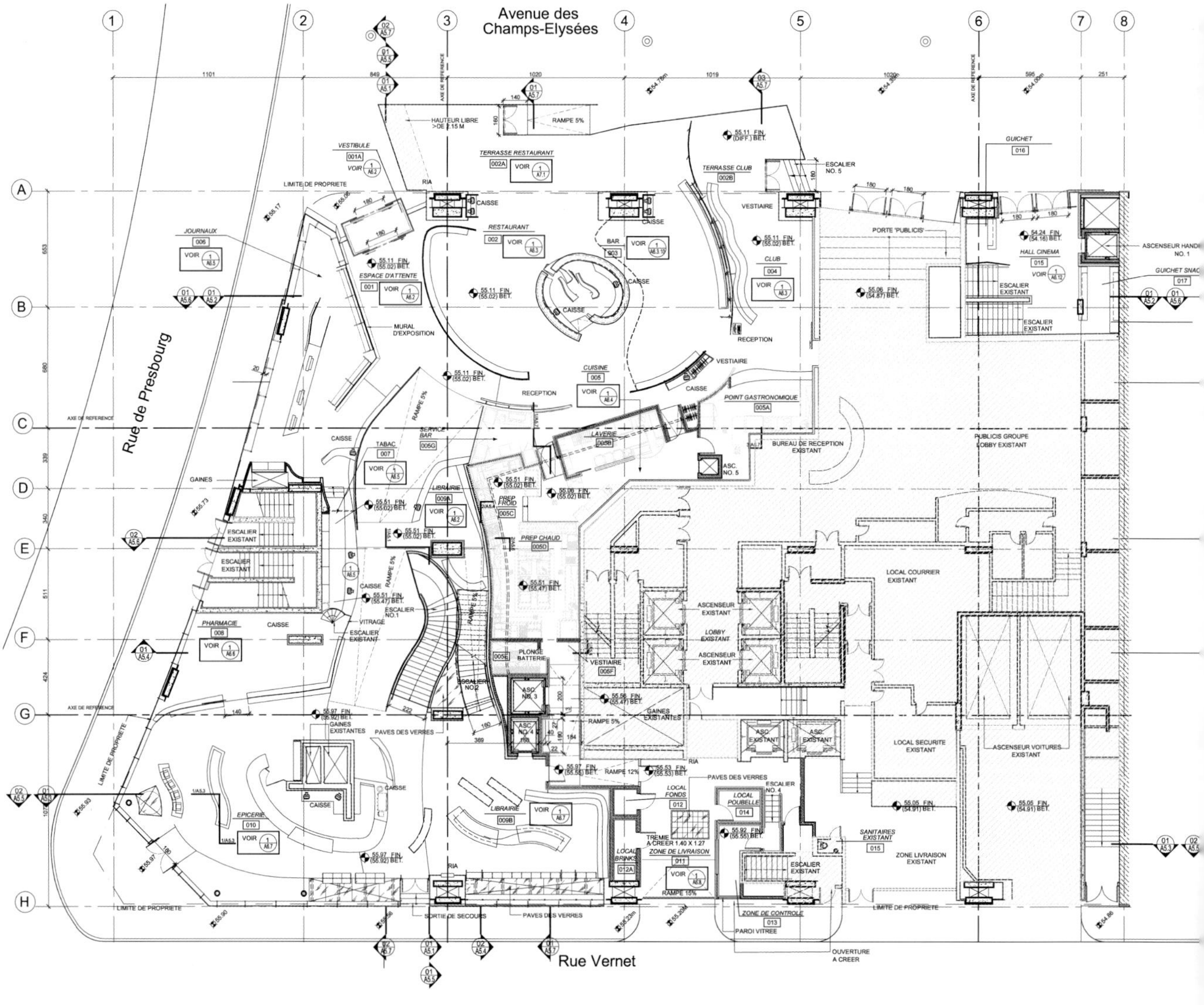

Avenue des Champs-Elysées
Rue de Presbourg
Rue Vernet
TERRASSE RESTAURANT
RESTAURANT
VESTIBULE
JOURNAUX
ESPACE D'ATTENTE
MURAL D'EXPOSITION
BAR
TERRASSE CLUB
CLUB
VESTIAIRE
RECEPTION
CUISINE
POINT GASTRONOMIQUE
LAVERIE
TABAC
SERVICE BAR
LIBRAIRIE
PREP FROID
PREP CHAUD
PHARMACIE
EPICERIE
GUICHET
HALL CINEMA
PORTE 'PUBLICIS'
PUBLICIS GROUPE LOBBY EXISTANT
BUREAU DE RECEPTION EXISTANT
LOCAL COURRIER EXISTANT
LOCAL SECURITE EXISTANT
ASCENSEUR VOITURES EXISTANT
SANITAIRES EXISTANT
ZONE LIVRAISON EXISTANT
ZONE DE CONTROLE
LOCAL FONDS
LOCAL POUBELLE
LOCAL BRINKS
ZONE DE LIVRAISON
LIMITE DE PROPRIETE
PAVES DES VERRES
SORTIE DE SECOURS
OUVERTURE A CREER
ESCALIER EXISTANT
ASCENSEUR EXISTANT
LOBBY EXISTANT
RAMPE 5%
RAMPE 12%
RAMPE 15%

Publicis Drugstore Interior

The gestural vocabulary of the Publicis fabric can also be understood as an analogical reflection of the Parisian metropolis and its streetscape. Underscoring the project's reflective tendencies with project activates a city within and mirrors the city without. Entering beneath of spiral of the façade, the visitor's gaze is trained skyward toward the fusion of the old Publicis drugstore with the new. As the ramp ascends skyward the new Publicis landscape is revealed as it unfolds into various zones of commercial activity evoking the lost Parisian shopping arcades of the last century, so famously lamented by Walter Benjamin.

In keeping with the spirit of the building's exterior, central themes of the interior spaces are also openness and transparency. Inspired by Parisian garden design principals, the public spaces are delineated with a series of transparent and translucent glass partitions deployed to maintain a comfortable level of privacy and intimacy while maintaining a sense of visual continuity throughout the space. Viewing the social and programmatic interactions metaphorically the space again reinforces values of Publicis. The removal of visual barriers, for instance, reinforces a core principal where the company's relationship with their customers is strengthened with corporate transparency.

As one enters through the glass doors of Publicis, the exterior's predominantly vertical geometry is reoriented toward the horizontal. A newsstand and tobacconist to the right are balanced on the opposite side by the curved-glass wall at the perimeter of the restaurant. A little flower stand punctuates the ramp as it continues upward toward a large window offering a view of the pharmacy. From here, stairways lead both up to bathrooms, administrative offices, and the Publicis conference room and down to a well-stocked cigar shop boasting private boxes, a wine corner with an international selection, a radio studio, casting

studio, bathrooms for handicapped patrons, and a prep kitchen and storage area. Continuing toward a library and grocery store and a small Café Nescafe the ramp traces a parallel path along the Avenue des Champs-Elysees and the Rue Presburg, all the way to the Rue Vernet. As it does, the story of the Publicis legacy unfolds through a series of illustrations demonstrating the company's concerns and values.

A second entrance from the Avenue des Champs-Elysees leads both to the Publicis Group offices and to the below-grade cinema complex. Accessed directly from the street the new space of Publicis Drugstore opens outward and eagerly embraces the city and its patrons. As a nexus for a diverse group of clientele to satisfy their need for commerce and congregation the drugstore represents the deeply held principles of Publicis and its foundation. As a social center; people fill their prescriptions, get the news, share ideas, stay informed, have a generous meal, watch a movie or, just meet new people from around the world.

Throughout this journey sculpted floors and ceilings of specific zones interacted with one another in complex harmonies creating sequences of commercial spaces that are both modern and useful. Like a leisurely conversation on a quiet afternoon, the building's various programs flow seamlessly into one another; like surfing the web, one thing leads to the next. As a microcosm of the larger city outside, a visit to Publicis reinforces that the Publicis Drugstore is the heart of Publicis, and an understanding that this place is the heart of Paris.

The new building has become a vehicle of cultural identity where the joie de vies of both Paris and Publicis are communicated to and by the people. Initially, the architecture provokes a curiosity that attracts you inside. Drawn back again and again by a calendar of special activities, seasonal attractions, and special events, the patrons of Publicis also find many habit-forming reasons to return: whether to purchase a favorite cigar, enjoy the atmosphere of the cafe, or to recapture the quality of light across the façade while dining with an old friend. The building engages all currents of life. From the foundations of the village drugstore upon which it was constructed the building has spawned a burgeoning legacy of association in which Publicis has becomes ingrained in public experience. Through modifying its genetic blueprint this drugstore has been recoded to embrace tradition within the age of information.

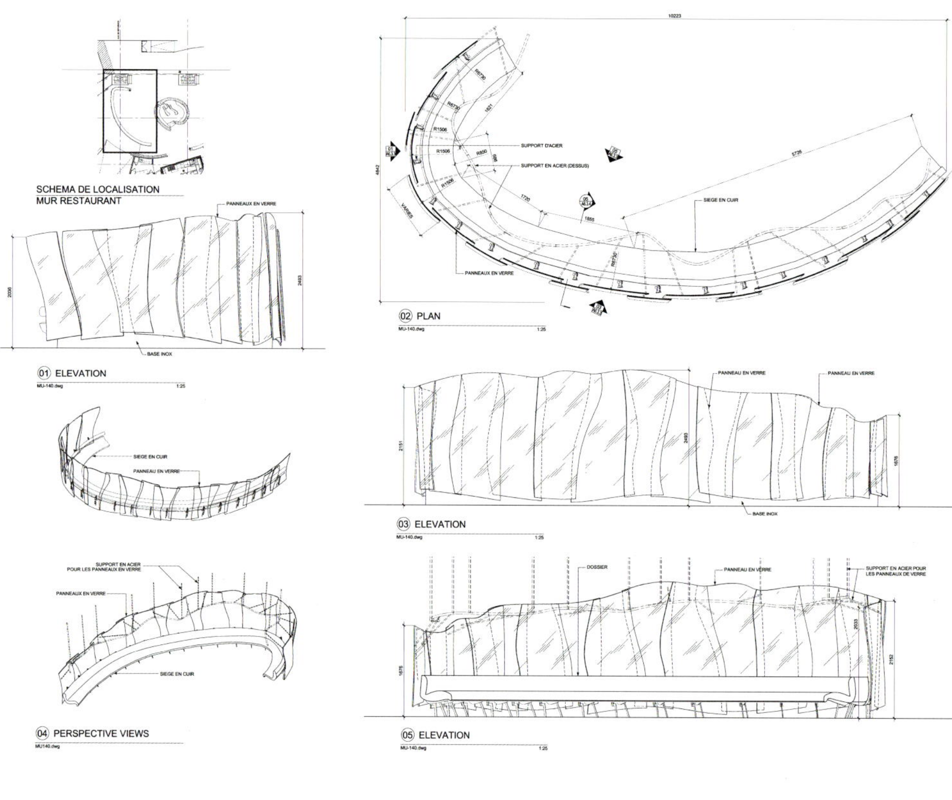

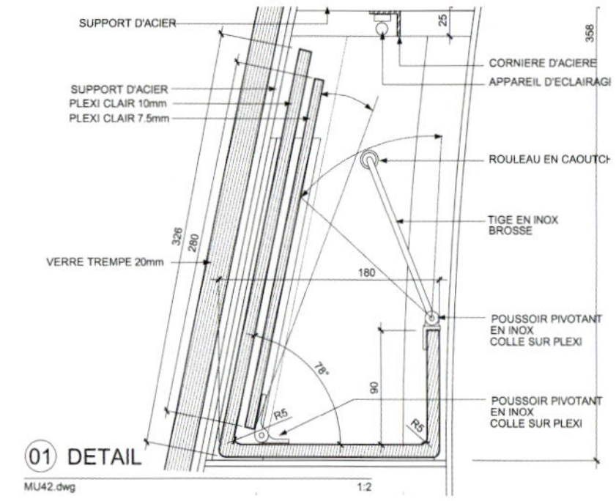

SUPPORT D'ACIER
SUPPORT D'ACIER
PLEXI CLAIR 10mm
PLEXI CLAIR 7.5mm
VERRE TREMPE 20mm
CORNIERE D'ACIERE
APPAREIL D'ECLAIRAGI
ROULEAU EN CAOUTCH
TIGE EN INOX BROSSE
POUSSOIR PIVOTANT EN INOX COLLE SUR PLEXI
POUSSOIR PIVOTANT EN INOX COLLE SUR PLEXI

01 DETAIL
MU42.dwg 1:2

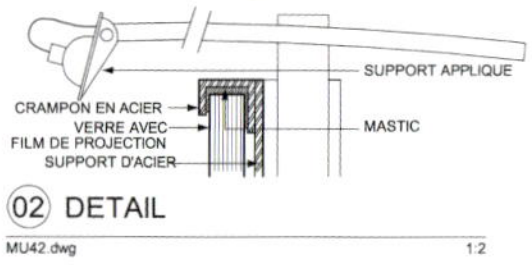

SUPPORT APPLIQUE
CRAMPON EN ACIER
VERRE AVEC FILM DE PROJECTION
SUPPORT D'ACIER
MASTIC

02 DETAIL
MU42.dwg 1:2

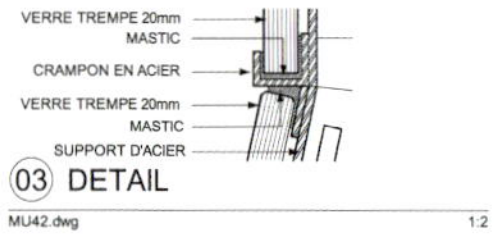

VERRE TREMPE 20mm
MASTIC
CRAMPON EN ACIER
VERRE TREMPE 20mm
MASTIC
SUPPORT D'ACIER

03 DETAIL
MU42.dwg 1:2

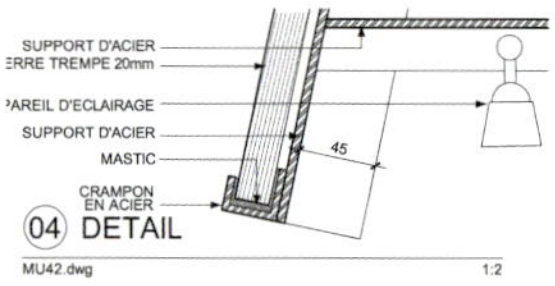

SUPPORT D'ACIER
VERRE TREMPE 20mm
APPAREIL D'ECLAIRAGE
SUPPORT D'ACIER
MASTIC
CRAMPON EN ACIER

04 DETAIL
MU42.dwg 1:2

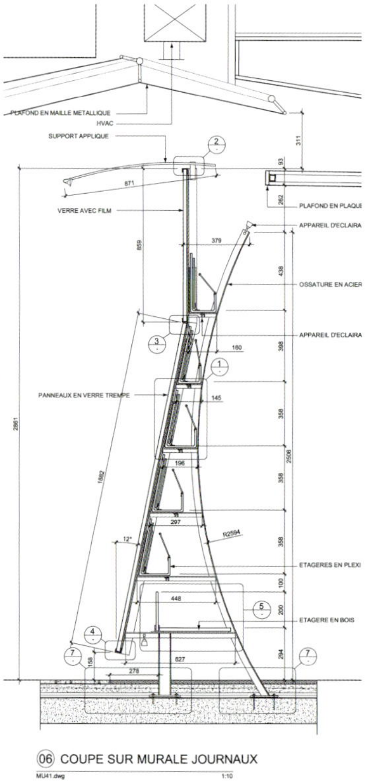

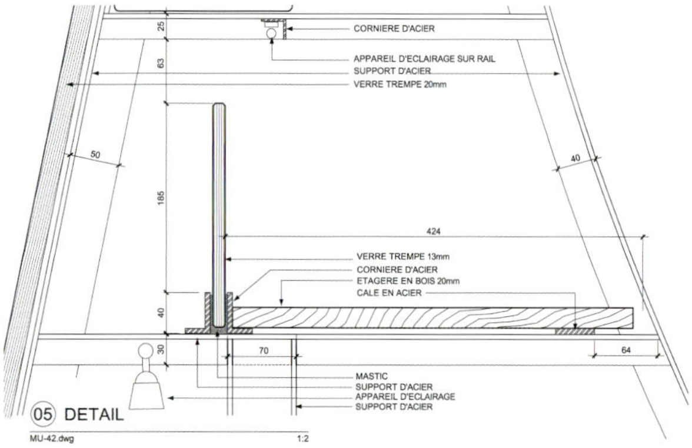

CORNIERE D'ACIER
APPAREIL D'ECLAIRAGE SUR RAIL
SUPPORT D'ACIER
VERRE TREMPE 20mm
VERRE TREMPE 13mm
CORNIERE D'ACIER
ETAGERE EN BOIS 20mm
CALE EN ACIER
MASTIC
SUPPORT D'ACIER
APPAREIL D'ECLAIRAGE
SUPPORT D'ACIER

05 DETAIL
MU-42.dwg 1:2

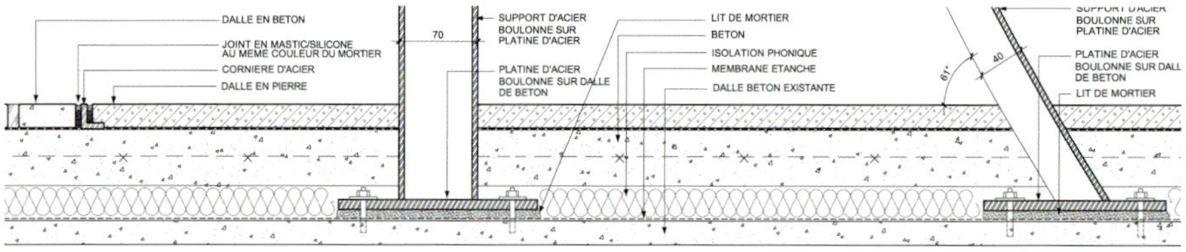

PLAFOND EN MAILLE METALLIQUE
HVAC
SUPPORT APPLIQUE
VERRE AVEC FILM
PLAFOND EN PLAQUE
APPAREIL D'ECLAIRA
OSSATURE EN ACIER
APPAREIL D'ECLAIRA
PANNEAUX EN VERRE TREMPE
ETAGERES EN PLEXI
ETAGERE EN BOIS

06 COUPE SUR MURALE JOURNAUX
MU41.dwg 1:10

DALLE EN BETON
JOINT EN MASTIC/SILICONE AU MEME COULEUR DU MORTIER
CORNIERE D'ACIER
DALLE EN PIERRE
SUPPORT D'ACIER BOULONNE SUR PLATINE D'ACIER
PLATINE D'ACIER BOULONNE SUR DALLE DE BETON
LIT DE MORTIER
BETON
ISOLATION PHONIQUE
MEMBRANE ETANCHE
DALLE BETON EXISTANTE
SUPPORT D'ACIER BOULONNE SUR PLATINE D'ACIER
PLATINE D'ACIER BOULONNE SUR DALLE DE BETON
LIT DE MORTIER

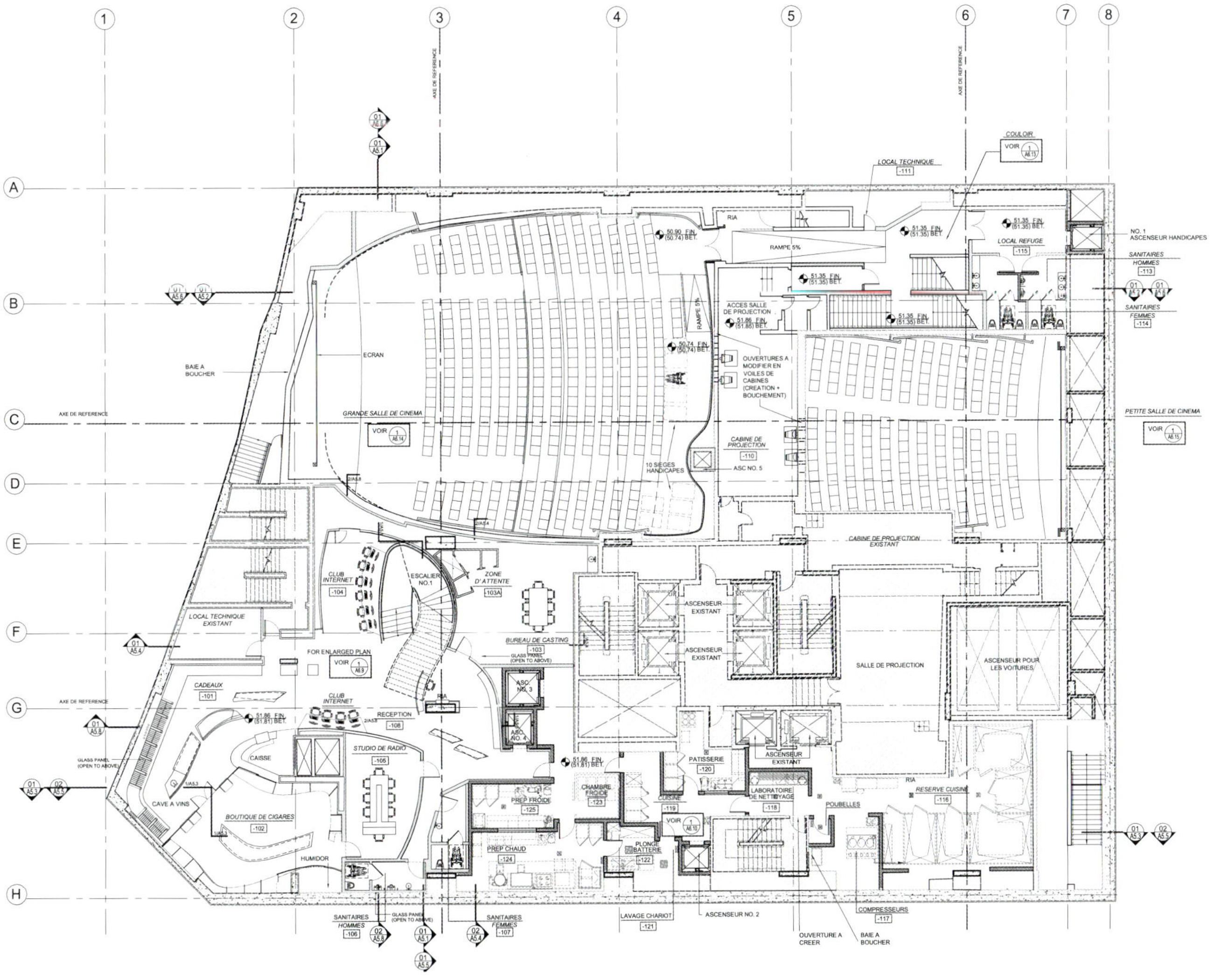

AXE DE REFERENCE
COULOIR
LOCAL TECHNIQUE
-111
NO. 1 ASCENSEUR HANDICAPES
RAMPE 5%
LOCAL REFUGE
-115
SANITAIRES HOMMES
-113
SANITAIRES FEMMES
-114
ACCES SALLE DE PROJECTION
RAMPE 5%
BAIE A BOUCHER
ECRAN
OUVERTURES A MODIFIER EN VOILES DE CABINES (CREATION + BOUCHEMENT)
GRANDE SALLE DE CINEMA
PETITE SALLE DE CINEMA
CABINE DE PROJECTION
-110
ASC NO. 5
10 SIEGES HANDICAPES
CABINE DE PROJECTION EXISTANT
CLUB INTERNET
-104
ESCALIER NO.1
ZONE D'ATTENTE
-103A
LOCAL TECHNIQUE EXISTANT
ASCENSEUR EXISTANT
SALLE DE PROJECTION
ASCENSEUR POUR LES VOITURES
FOR ENLARGED PLAN
BUREAU DE CASTING
-103
GLASS PANEL (OPEN TO ABOVE)
CADEAUX
-101
CLUB INTERNET
RECEPTION
-108
ASC NO. 3
ASC NO. 4
STUDIO DE RADIO
-105
CAISSE
PATISSERIE
-120
ASCENSEUR EXISTANT
RIA
RESERVE CUISINE
-116
CAVE A VINS
BOUTIQUE DE CIGARES
-102
PREP FROIDE
-125
CHAMBRE FROIDE
-123
CUISINE
-119
LABORATOIRE DE NETTOYAGE
-118
POUBELLES
PREP CHAUD
-124
PLONGE BATTERIE
-122
HUMIDOR
SANITAIRES HOMMES
-106
GLASS PANEL (OPEN TO ABOVE)
SANITAIRES FEMMES
-107
LAVAGE CHARIOT
-121
ASCENSEUR NO. 2
OUVERTURE A CREER
BAIE A BOUCHER
COMPRESSEURS
-117

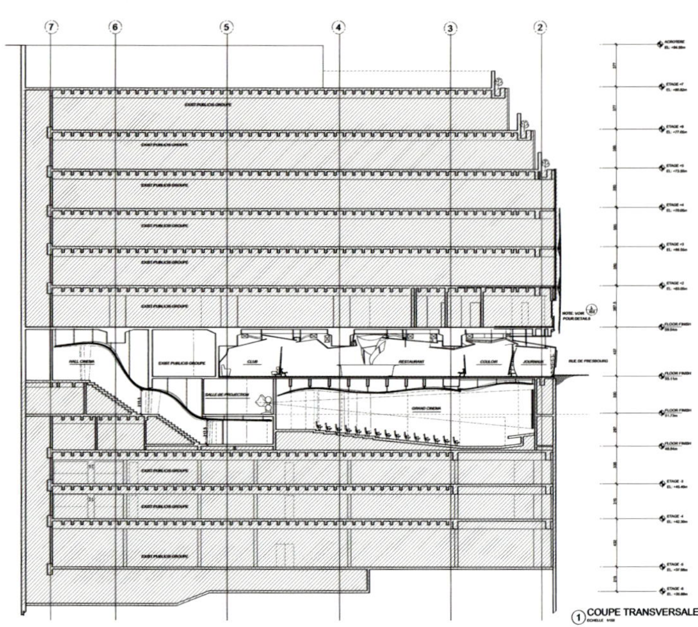
COUPE TRANSVERSALE

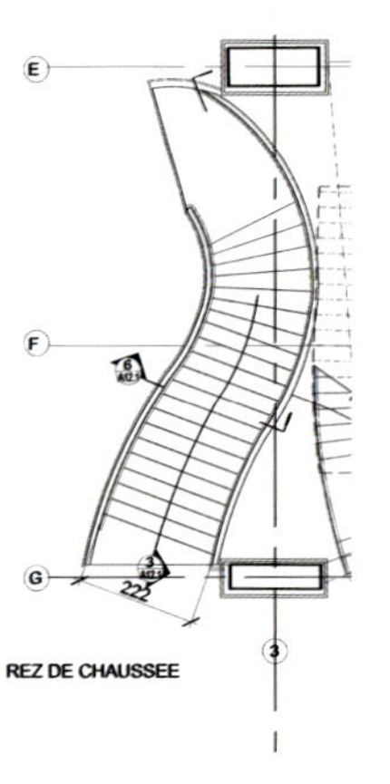
REZ DE CHAUSSEE

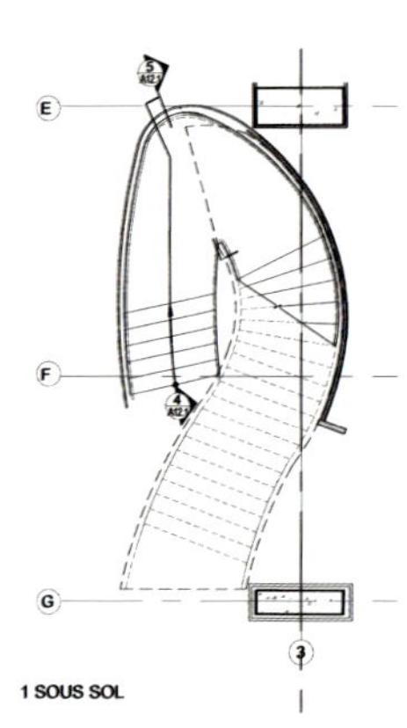
1 SOUS SOL

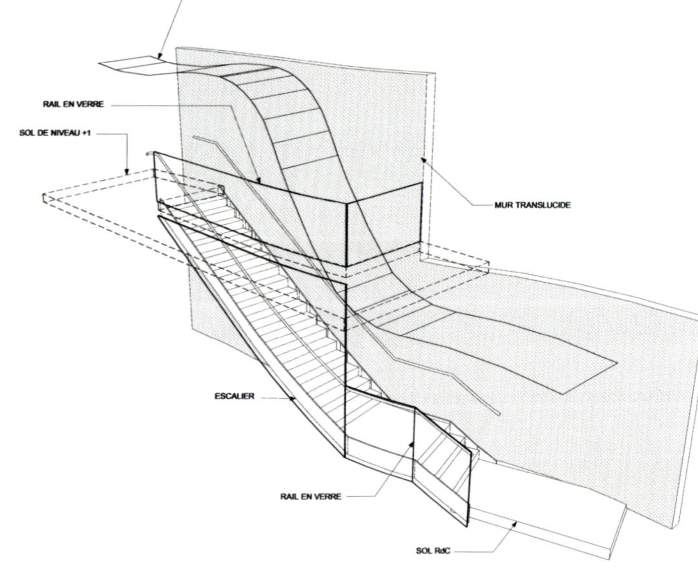
PLAFOND MAILLE METALLIQUE
RAIL EN VERRE
SOL DE NIVEAU +1
MUR TRANSLUCIDE
ESCALIER
RAIL EN VERRE
SOL RdC

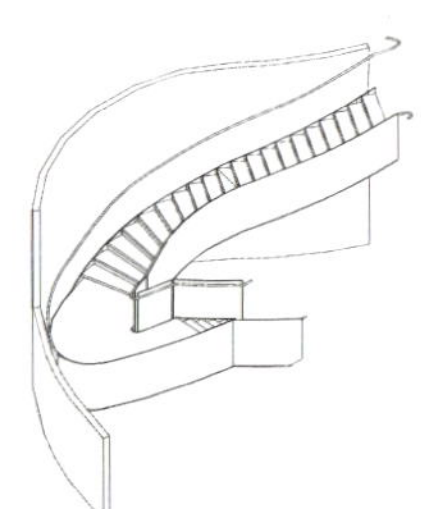

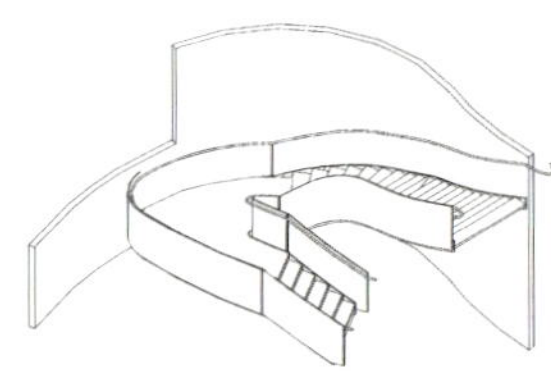

A poetic escape from the hum-drum routine of modern life.

Café Nescafe

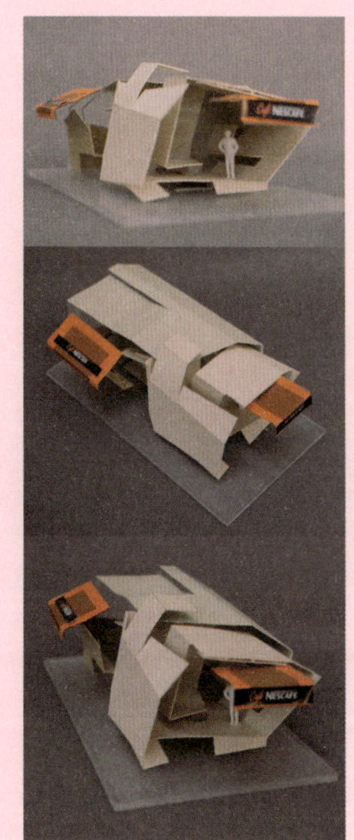

The likes of Simone de Beauvoir and Jean Paul Sartre altered the course of modern thought from sidewalk tables in the 6th Arrondissement. For many, Paris's outdoor cafes are the quintessence of the poetic escape from the hum-drum routine of modern life. The goal of the Nescafe design was to capture this lyrical history while still creating a fully functional and adaptable commercial space.

Requiring a clear brand image that could freshly compete with and distinguish itself from its existing global competitors this project addresses the question of how architecture can fashion corporate identity. Eye-catching, but ultimately bland and cheap, fast-food culture rarely fosters and encourages inventive design. Commercial chain operators are best known for their "rubber stamp" approach to architecture with cookie-cutter compositions of faux-terra cotta roofs, colored Formica counters, and plastic booths. Faced with these prevailing economies the question we were faced with was how could the design of a retail environment transcend a system where architecture is generally secondary in importance to the logo on the drink cup.

Challenged by the requirement for adaptability without resorting to rubberstamping, Saee developed a flexible system composed of three variable elements: a wrapping skin,

a coffee bar interface, and a graphic ribbon. The characteristics of variable components were selected for their potencies for reaction, fluctuation, and engagement with the body, site conditions, geographical forces, and commercial considerations.

The wrapping skin element was co-developed in both wood and glass to encircle space enveloping the customers in a warm and inviting environment. Extenuating the café spaces with an architectural finesse the skin was conceived of and developed to function as an interactive device. Capable of fluctuating and accommodating evolving circumstances, the skin is in continuous flux transforming and redefining itself to accommodate the intricate variabilties of the café experience. Engaging the body as it folds to the form of a bench, or unfolding to become countertop, the spatial grammar of this element takes its cues from the movement of the body. Never straight, it bends and curves channel activity while simultaneously reflecting light.

The graphic ribbon undulates dancing with the skin to create a graphic superstructure as a backdrop for the required product branding images. Rather than resorting to picture frames and posters placed on a wall, Saee used the ribbon structure to create an architectural element capable of both functioning graphically and spatially in the definition of areas and micro-zones. In the same manner as the skin element, the ribbon follows and redirects the currents of the café experience. Architecture and graphics collapse into a malleable fluid.

Café Nescafe

Location:

Paris, France

Year:

2000 – 2002 (built)

Program:

Café prototype for Nestle, France

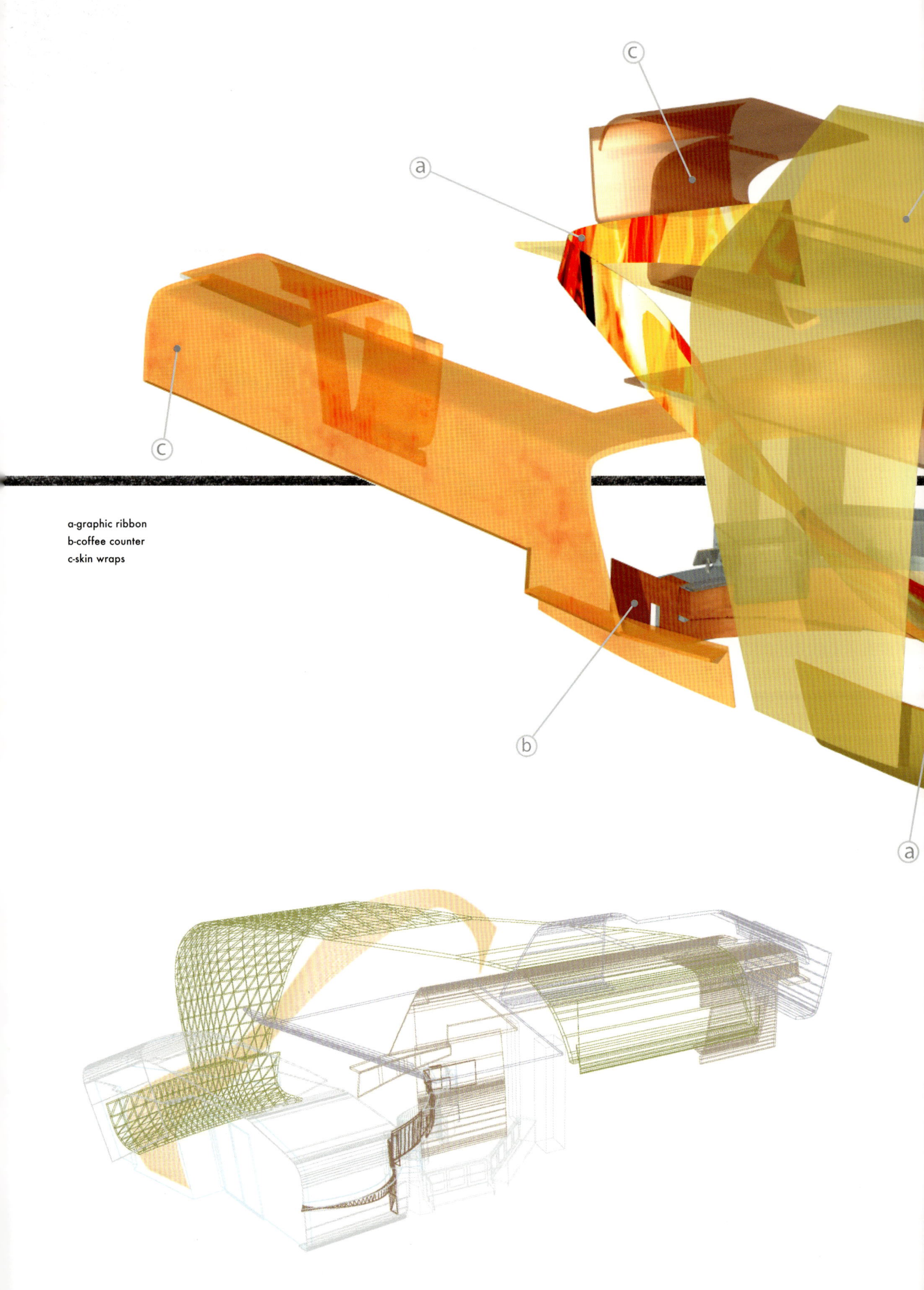

a-graphic ribbon
b-coffee counter
c-skin wraps

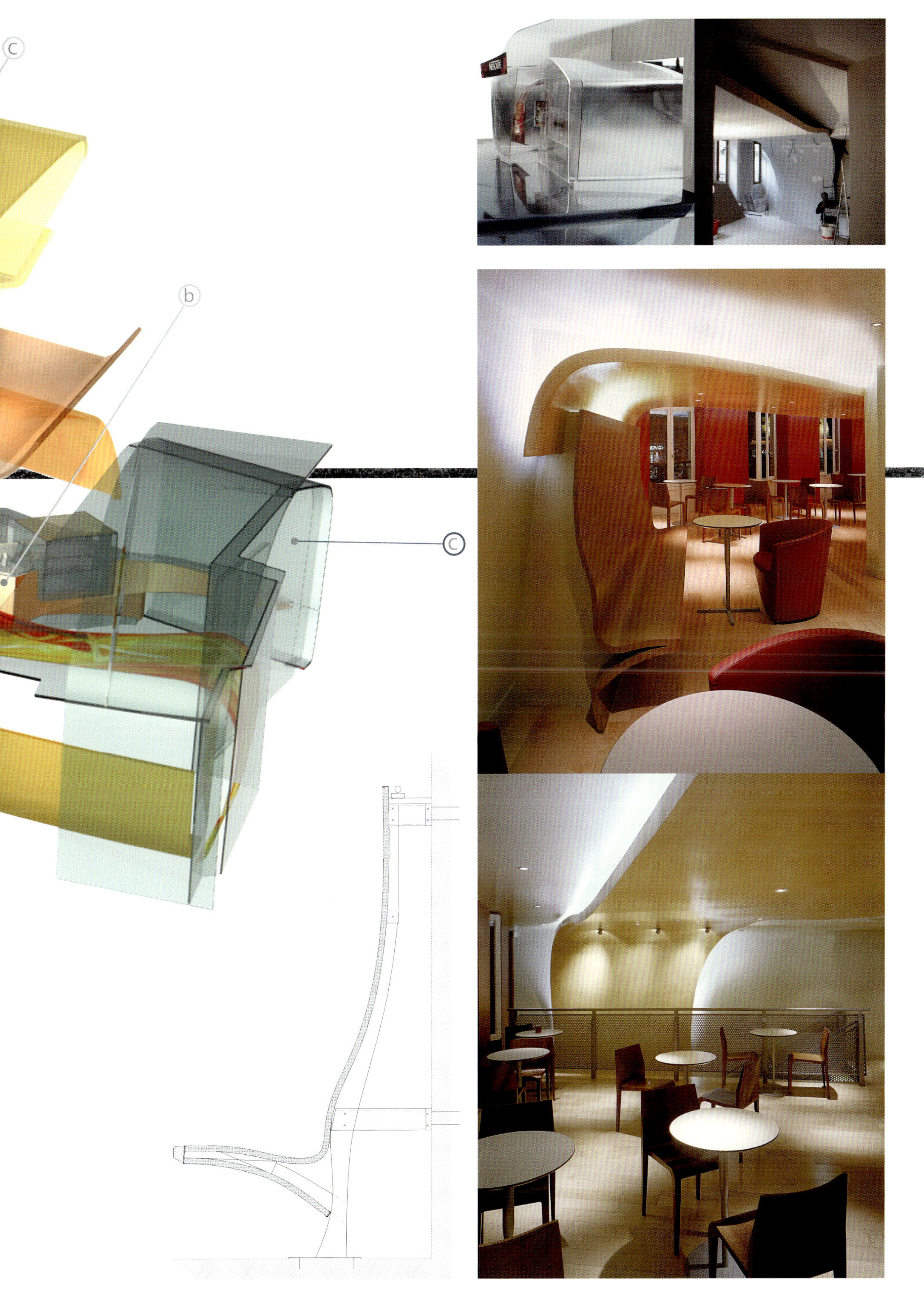

c
b
c

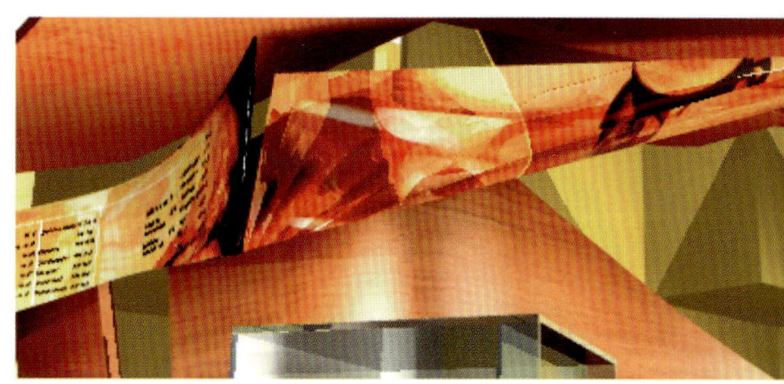

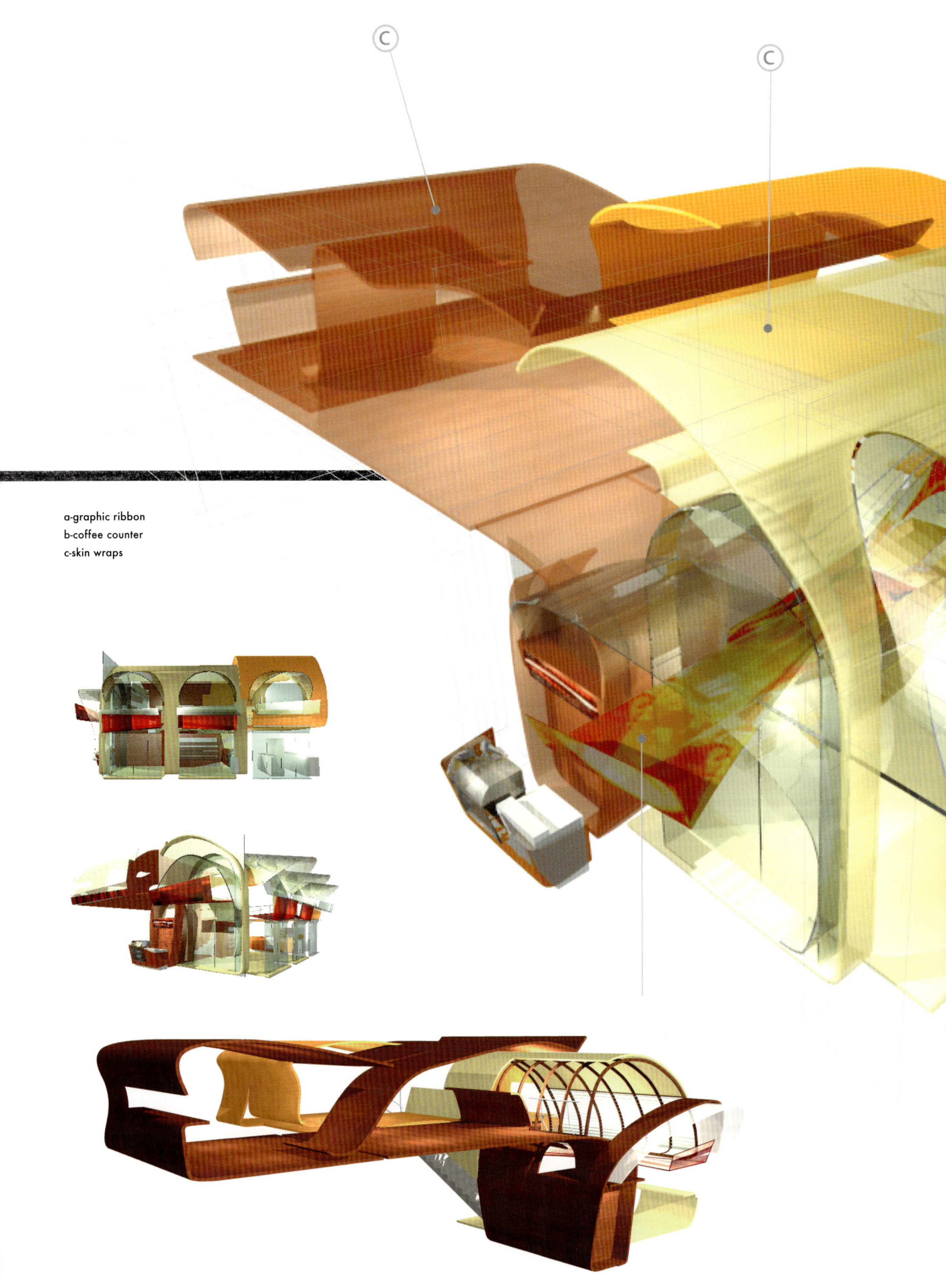

a-graphic ribbon
b-coffee counter
c-skin wraps

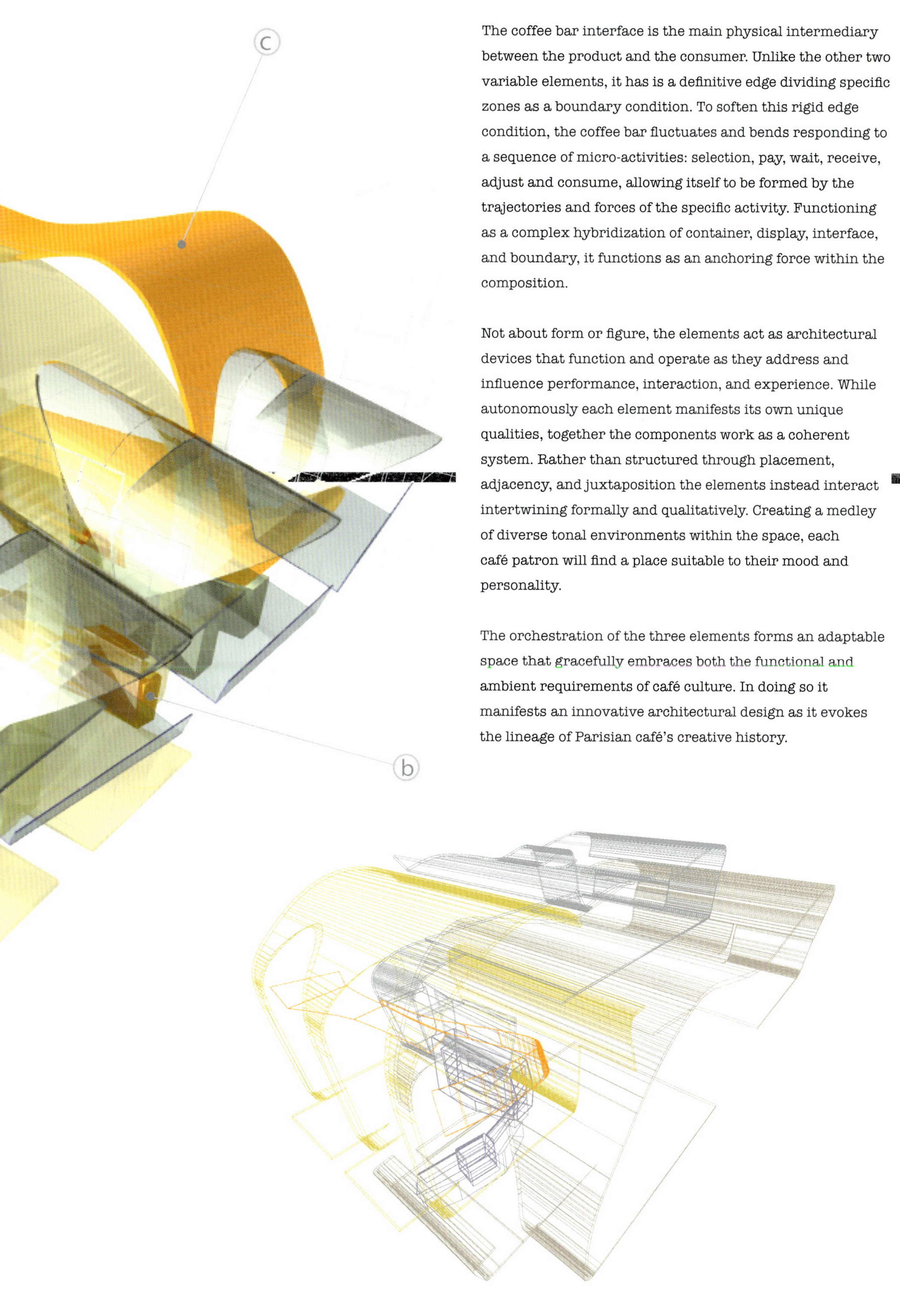

The coffee bar interface is the main physical intermediary between the product and the consumer. Unlike the other two variable elements, it has is a definitive edge dividing specific zones as a boundary condition. To soften this rigid edge condition, the coffee bar fluctuates and bends responding to a sequence of micro-activities: selection, pay, wait, receive, adjust and consume, allowing itself to be formed by the trajectories and forces of the specific activity. Functioning as a complex hybridization of container, display, interface, and boundary, it functions as an anchoring force within the composition.

Not about form or figure, the elements act as architectural devices that function and operate as they address and influence performance, interaction, and experience. While autonomously each element manifests its own unique qualities, together the components work as a coherent system. Rather than structured through placement, adjacency, and juxtaposition the elements instead interact intertwining formally and qualitatively. Creating a medley of diverse tonal environments within the space, each café patron will find a place suitable to their mood and personality.

The orchestration of the three elements forms an adaptable space that gracefully embraces both the functional and ambient requirements of café culture. In doing so it manifests an innovative architectural design as it evokes the lineage of Parisian café's creative history.

a-graphic ribbon
b-coffee counter
c-skin wraps

c
a
a

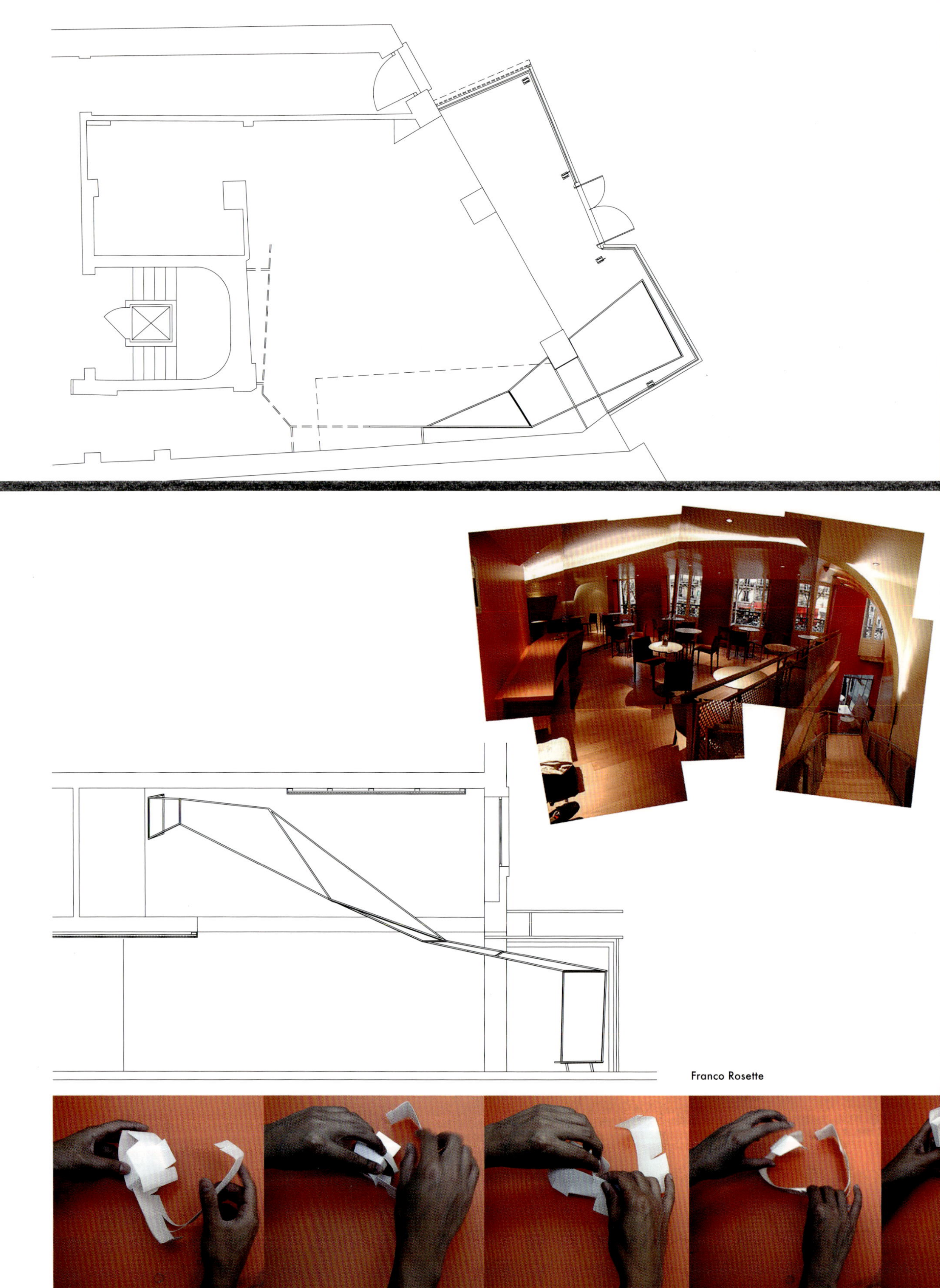

Franco Rosette

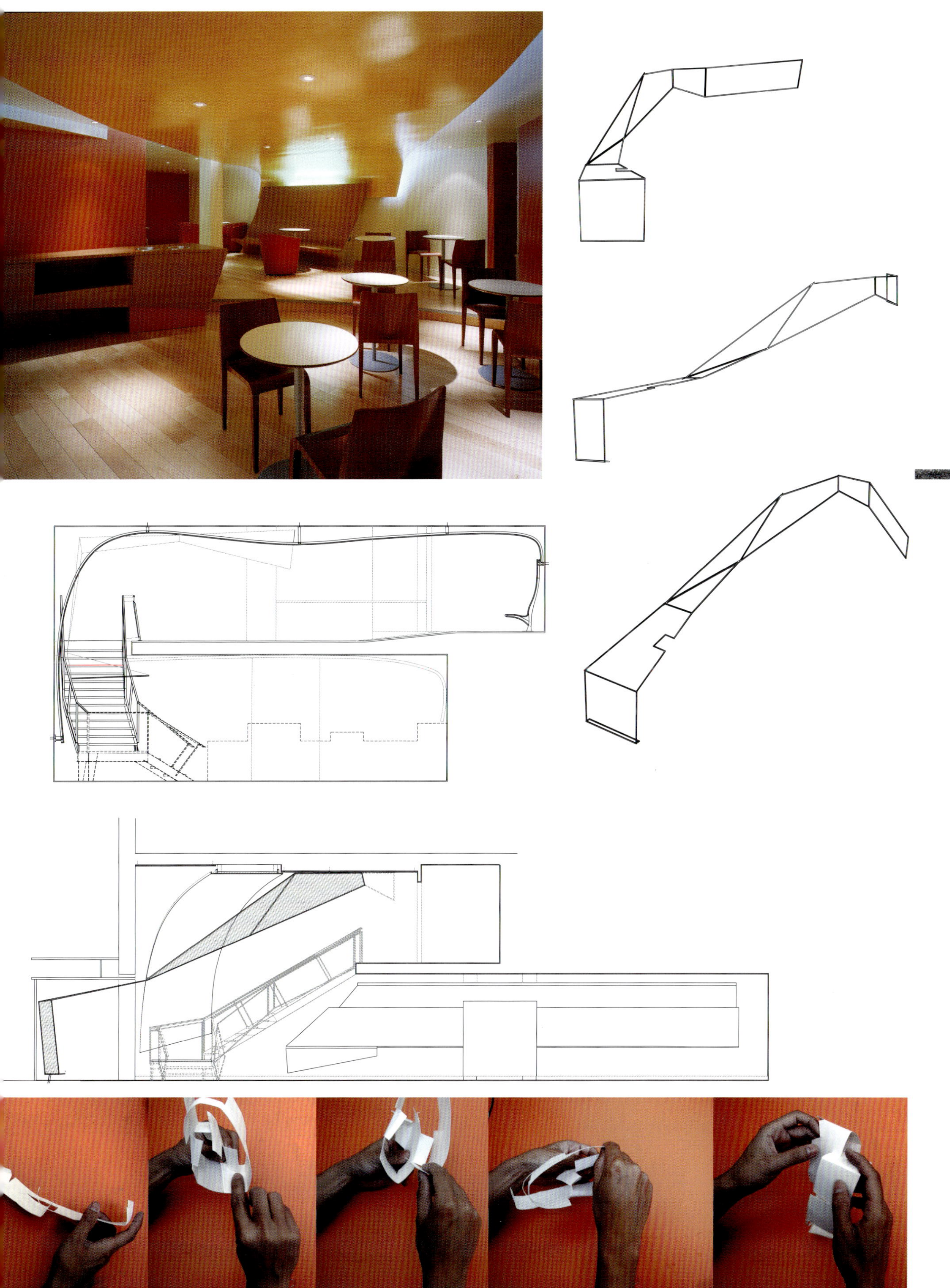

STYLOS
WAGRAM
Café
NESCAFÉ
WAGRAM
WAGRAM
BRIQUETS - CADEAUX

Café NESCAFÉ
15
17
17
Kronenbourg
CAMBRIDGE

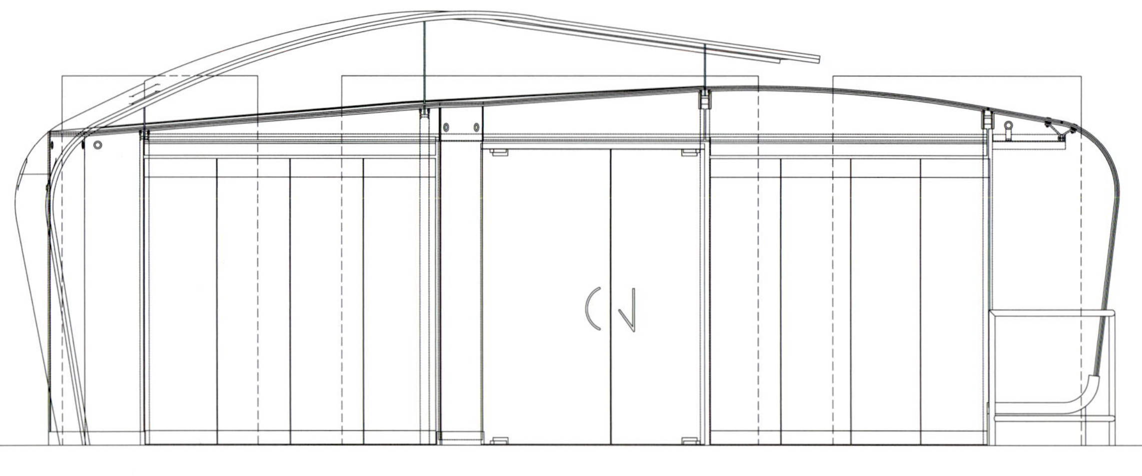

CAMBRIDGE
HOTEL
ELYSEES
PARIS
TUBORG
LE CAMBRIDGE
Café NESCAFÉ

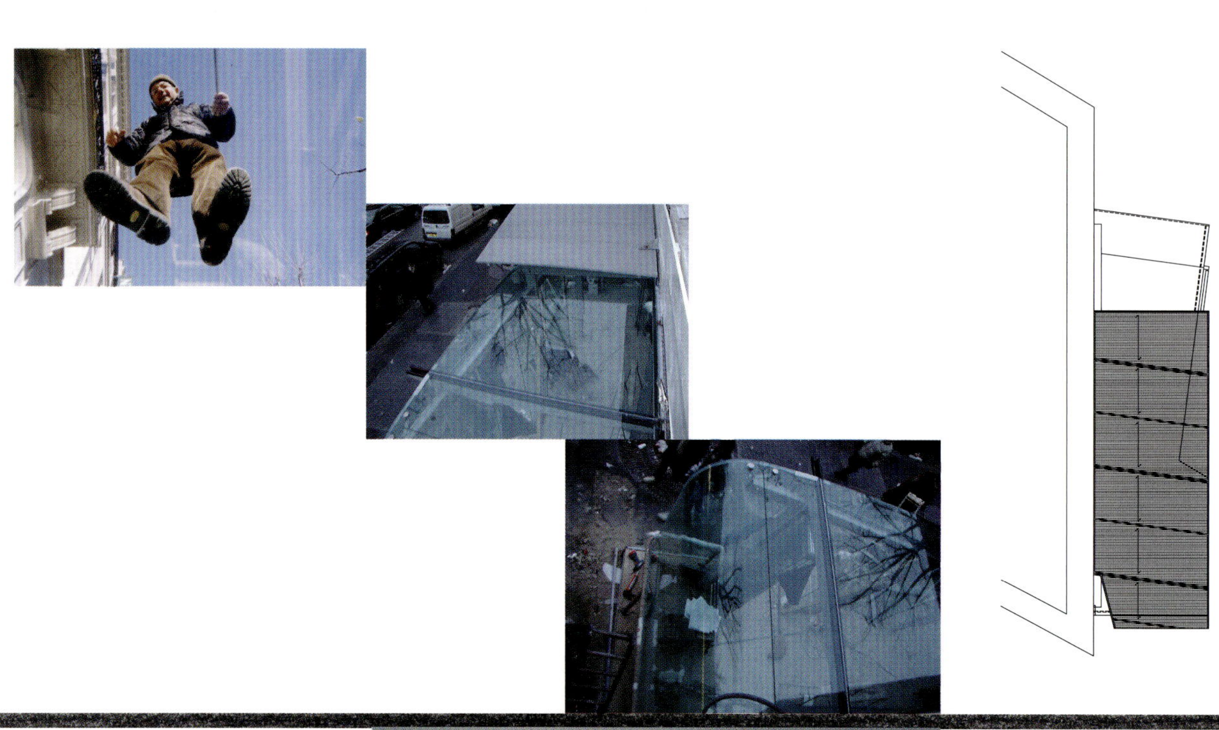

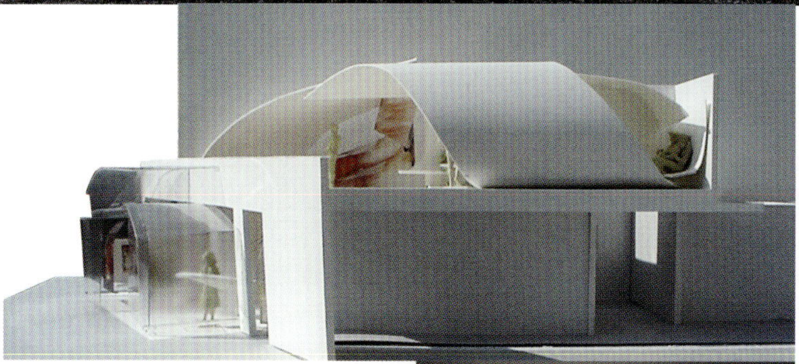

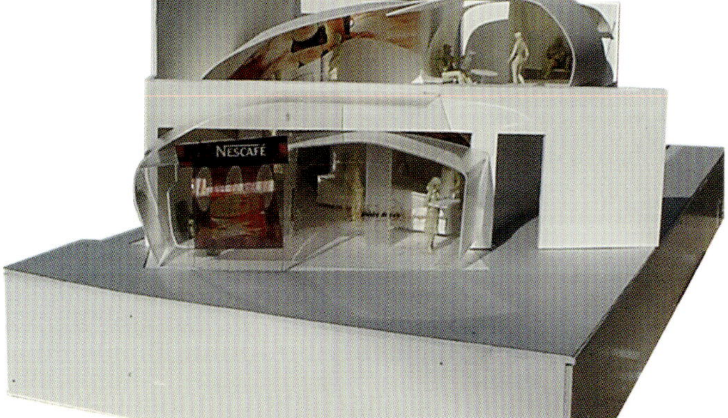

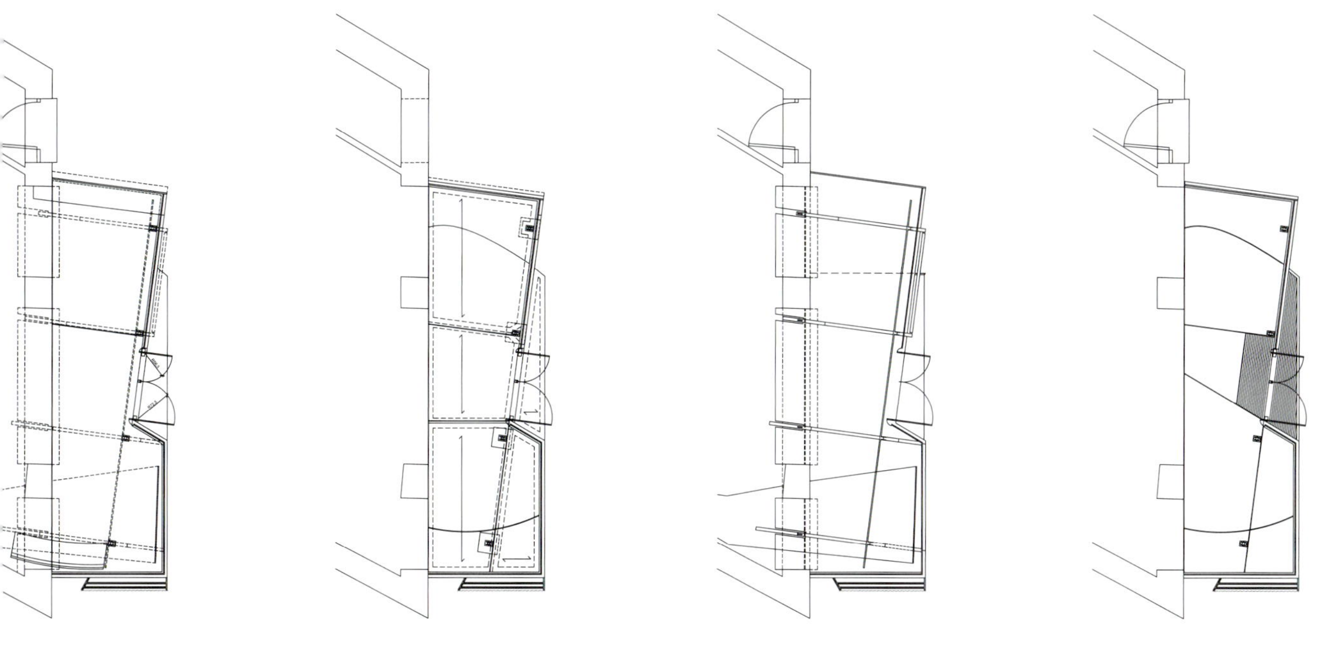

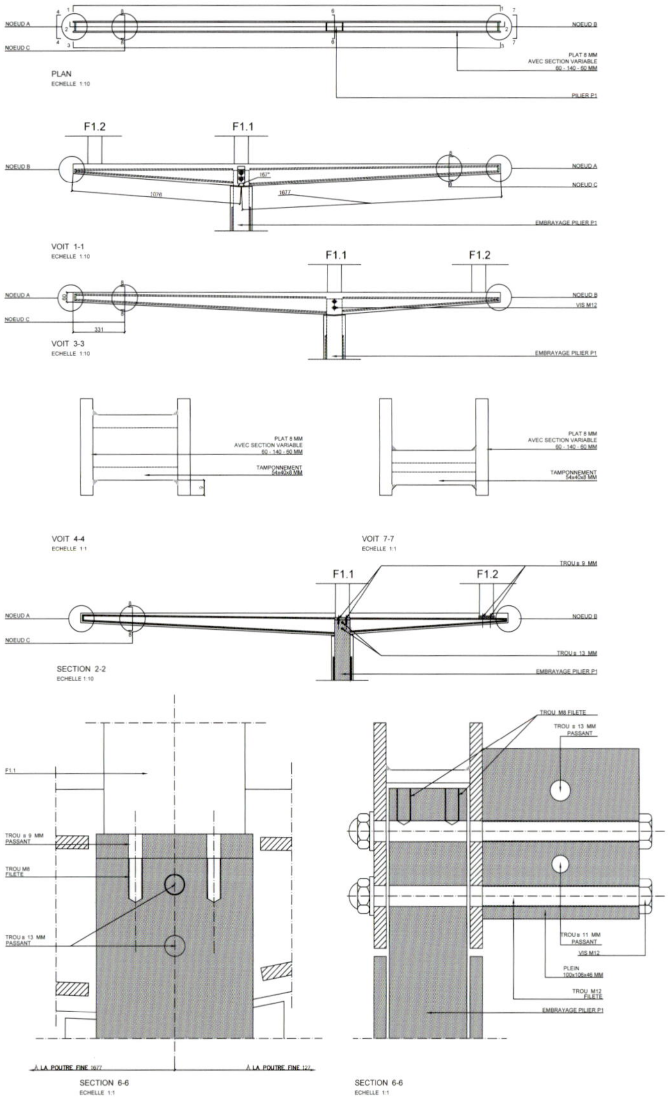

NOEUD A
NOEUD C
NOEUD B
PLAT 8 MM AVEC SECTION VARIABLE 60 - 140 - 60 MM
PILIER P1
PLAN
ECHELLE 1:10

F1.2
F1.1
NOEUD B
NOEUD A
NOEUD C
EMBRAYAGE PILIER P1
VOIT 1-1
ECHELLE 1:10

F1.1
F1.2
NOEUD A
NOEUD C
NOEUD B
VIS M12
EMBRAYAGE PILIER P1
VOIT 3-3
ECHELLE 1:10

PLAT 8 MM AVEC SECTION VARIABLE 60 - 140 - 60 MM
TAMPONNEMENT 54x40x8 MM
VOIT 4-4
ECHELLE 1:1

PLAT 8 MM AVEC SECTION VARIABLE 60 - 140 - 60 MM
TAMPONNEMENT 54x40x8 MM
VOIT 7-7
ECHELLE 1:1

F1.1
F1.2
TROU ø 9 MM
NOEUD A
NOEUD C
NOEUD B
TROU ø 13 MM
EMBRAYAGE PILIER P1
SECTION 2-2
ECHELLE 1:10

F1.1
TROU ø 9 MM PASSANT
TROU M8 FILETE
TROU ø 13 MM PASSANT
À LA POUTRE FINE
À LA POUTRE FINE
SECTION 6-6
ECHELLE 1:1

TROU M8 FILETE
TROU ø 13 MM PASSANT
TROU ø 11 MM PASSANT
VIS M12
PLEIN 100x106x46 MM
TROU M12 FILETE
EMBRAYAGE PILIER P1
SECTION 6-6
ECHELLE 1:1

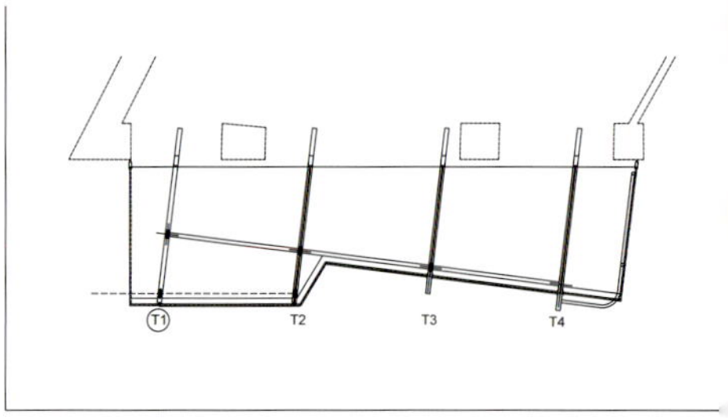

T1
T2
T3
T4

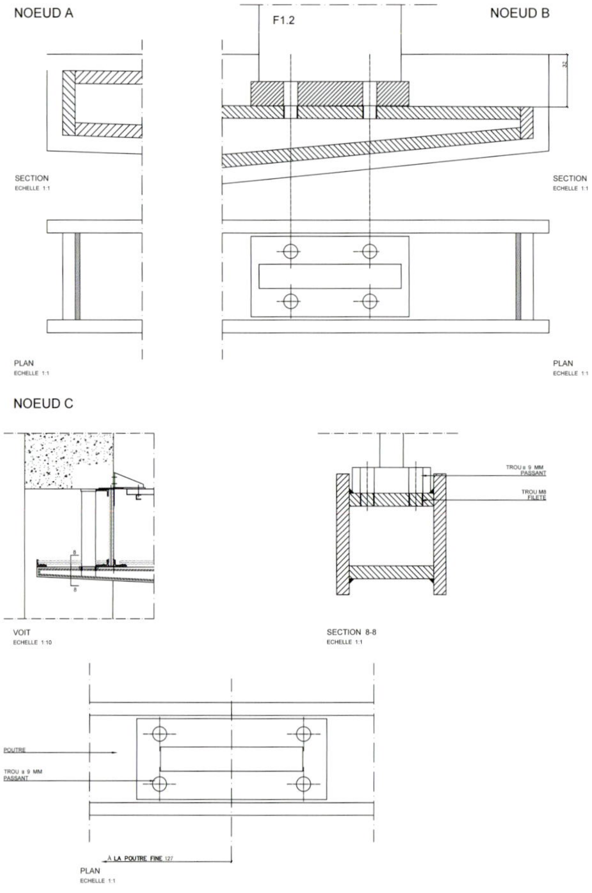

NOEUD A
SECTION
ECHELLE 1:1
PLAN
ECHELLE 1:1

F1.2
NOEUD B
SECTION
ECHELLE 1:1
PLAN
ECHELLE 1:1

NOEUD C
VOIT
ECHELLE 1:10

TROU ø 9 MM PASSANT
TROU M8 FILETE
SECTION 8-8
ECHELLE 1:1

POUTRE
TROU ø 9 MM PASSANT
À LA POUTRE FINE
PLAN
ECHELLE 1:1

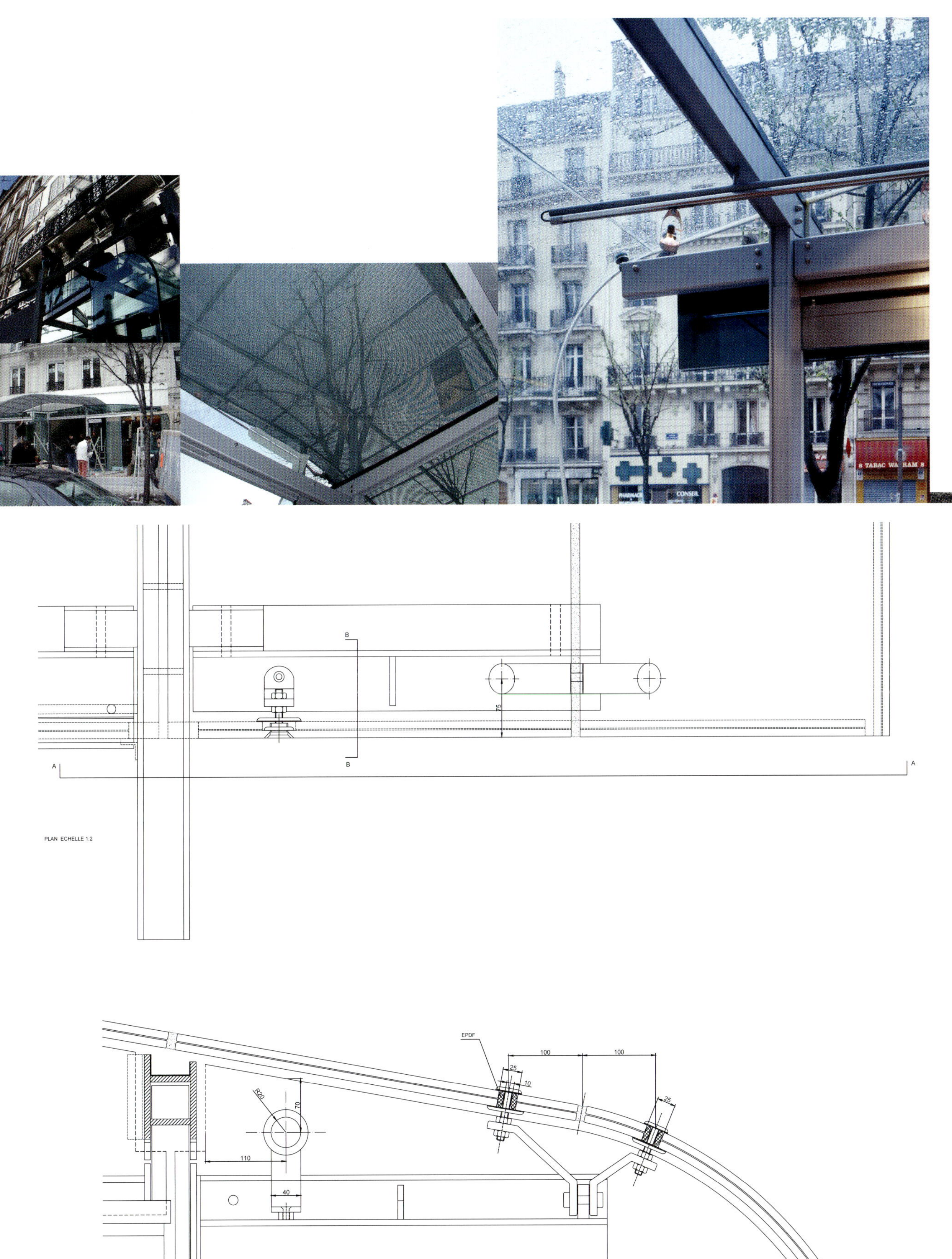

PHARMACIE
CONSEIL
B
75
B
A
A
PLAN ECHELLE 1:2
EPDF
100
100
25
10
25
R20
70
110
40
SECTION A-A ECHELLE 1:2

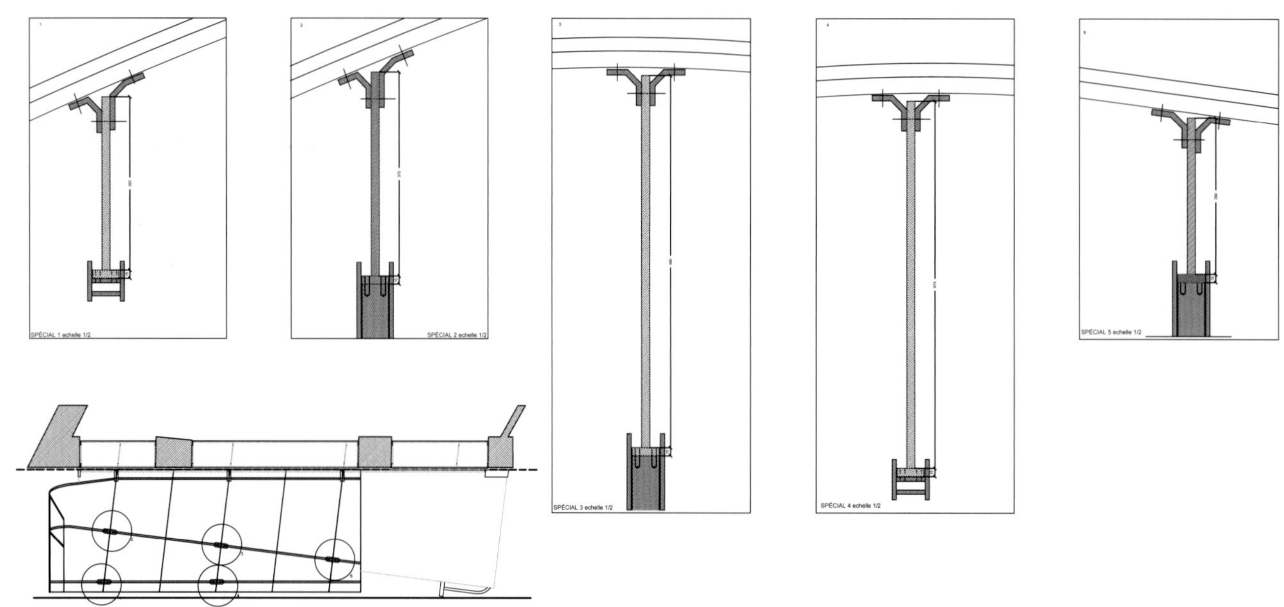

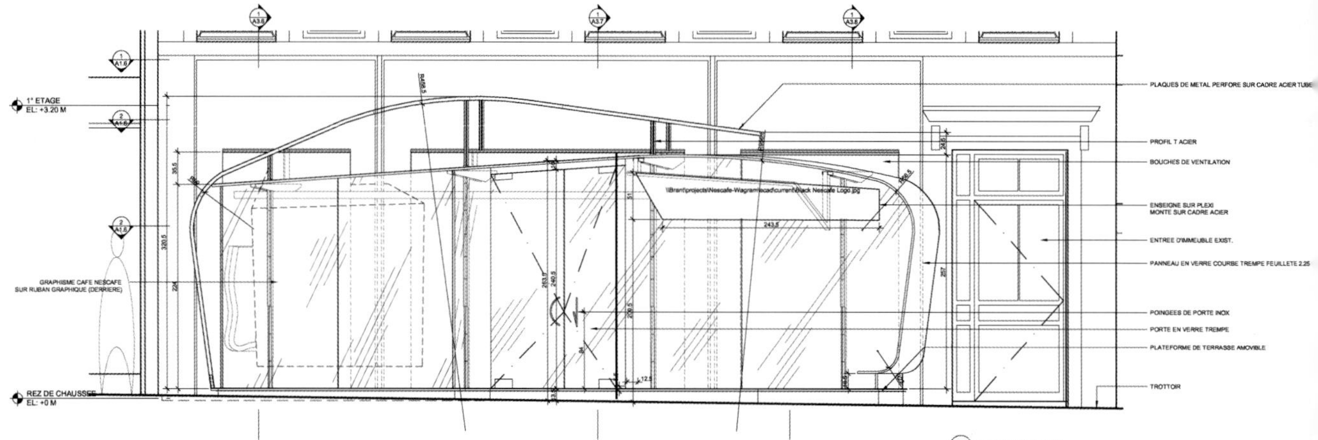

SPÉCIAL 1 echelle 1/2
SPÉCIAL 2 echelle 1/2
SPÉCIAL 3 echelle 1/2
SPÉCIAL 4 echelle 1/2
SPÉCIAL 5 echelle 1/2

1° ETAGE
EL: +3.20 M
REZ DE CHAUSSEE
EL: +0 M
GRAPHISME CAFE NESCAFE
SUR RUBAN GRAPHIQUE (DERRIERE)
PLAQUES DE METAL PERFORE SUR CADRE ACIER TUBE
PROFIL T ACIER
BOUCHES DE VENTILATION
ENSEIGNE SUR PLEXI
MONTE SUR CADRE ACIER
ENTREE D'IMMEUBLE EXIST.
PANNEAU EN VERRE COURBE TREMPE FEUILLETE 2.25
POINGEES DE PORTE INOX
PORTE EN VERRE TREMPE
PLATEFORME DE TERRASSE AMOVIBLE
TROTTOIR

3 ELEVATION

WAGELEV.DWG 1:25

NU DE BÂTIMENT EXIST.
1° ETAGE
EL: +3.20 M
PLAQUES DE METAL PERFORE SUR CADRE ACIER TUBE
PANNEAU DE VERRE TREMPE FEUILLETE 1CM
PLATEFORME DE TERRASSE AMOVIBLE
TROTTOIR
REZ DE CHAUSSEE
EL: +0 M

NU DE BÂTIMENT EXIST.
PERF. METAL SHEATHING ON STL. TUBE FRAMING
1° ETAGE
EL: +3.20 M
PERFORATED METAL SHEATHING
ON STL. TUBE FRAMING
SUPPORT AUVENT EN ACIER
PANNEAU COURBE EN VERRE
TREMPE FEUILLETE 2.25 CM
PLATEFORME DE TERRASSE AMOVIBLE
TROTTOIR
REZ DE CHAUSSEE
EL: +0 M

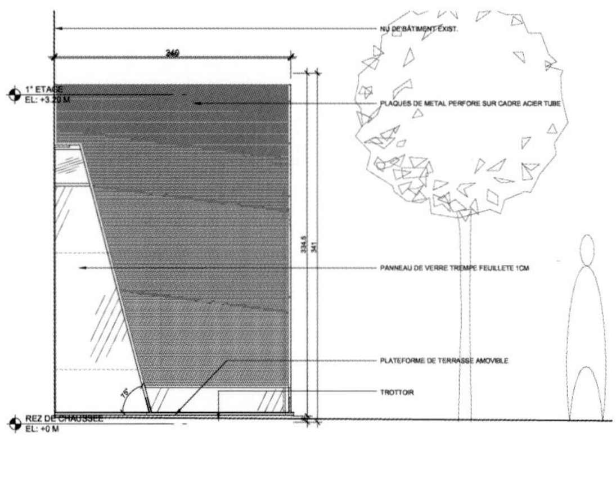

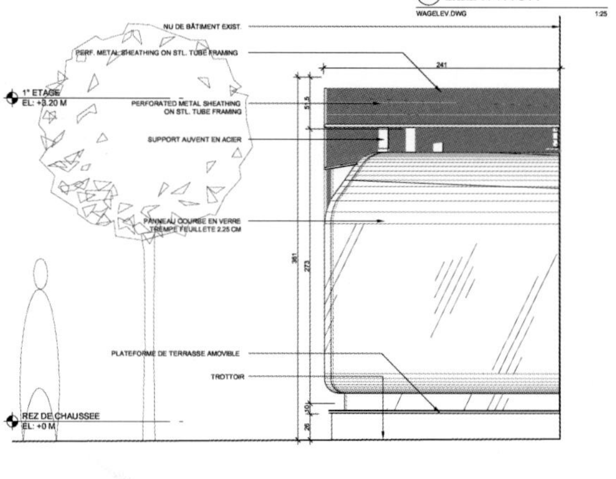

2 ELEVATION

WAGELEV.DWG 1:25

1 ELEVATION

WAGELEV.DWG 1:25

The process of making fascinates me and archi-tecture affords me this pursuit along with challenges of facing the unknown.

While submerged in the design for Publicis Drugstore in Paris, I found the SCI-Arc exhibition to be a perfect opportunity to test my concepts. The renovated façade and five floors of Publicis Drugstore on the Avenue des Champs-Elysees aim to meld idea with structure. The façade is wrapped in curved-glass screens that contrast with the grid of the existing building. Inside, a circulation ramp and stair connect the various programs. Smaller "island" elements create a series of vortices where movement flows and generates territories of activity that are in the state of endless transformation.

In the SCI-Arc installation, as well as in the Publicis building, the steel structure is a force of momentum, rising toward the sky with a kinetic spiral structure, which supports the glass skin and ties the main structure together. Partially veiled with the shifting and overlap of the curved laminated glass panels, the entire surface achieves a quality of both depth and lightness reflecting the cinematic collage of the space and viewers around it. By inserting a room of glass suspended by a random set of metal tubes into a white-cube container at SCI-Arc, we create a structural space that ignores the surrounding box, rendering it as a backdrop to the viewer's attention. The tubes are like the subconscious lines, zigzagging off the building and supporting the interior glass container.

I wanted to go beyond the self-consciousness that our culture exhibits toward technology. The process of making is something that has fascinated me for most of my life,

SCI-Arc Exhibition

Location:

Los Angeles, California, USA

Year:

2003 (built)

Program:

Sculpture

Steel fabrication by Tom Farrage, glass fabrication and installation by Cteck

and architecture affords me this pursuit along with the challenge of facing the unknown. Passion is not described by words alone, but by a connection to its acts. The SCI-Arc Gallery is a place where the traces of my thoughts can be marked in time. When I think about architecture and materials, I think about the body with its amazing construct. I am constantly in search of new materials and new techniques of construction. It sometimes appears unstable, almost in a state of continual becoming, an assembly of fluctuating sculptural forms, of materials that interact with light and with their context. This is the result of reacting or responding to a context that is increasingly more complex and challenging as it affects every aspect of our lives.

The project will enable the people to develop their city into the future with a cognizance of their past heritage.

Santa Marinella City Hall

This project for a new City Hall in Santa Marinella, Italy explores social and structural layering, historical layering, layering of the land, and contextual layering as ingredients of design. The historic preservation regulations in Italy are strongly rooted and easily identified in the culture, art, and architecture, which spans from the Ancient Period to the modern era. I admired how I was able to see the layers of Italy's architectural past preserved and respected.

Sprinkled with pines, palms, and fragrant oleander, Santa Marinella is often cited as one the most beautiful cities on Italy’s Tyrrhenian coast. Possessing good climate all year round, laden with the wealth of its ancient Etruscan past, and within driving distance of Rome, the city has always attracted a large influx of tourists and is now increasingly having success in transforming its visitors into permanent residents. Seeking to accelerate this trajectory into the future, we developed an architecturally bold proposal for Santa Marinella’s new City Hall.

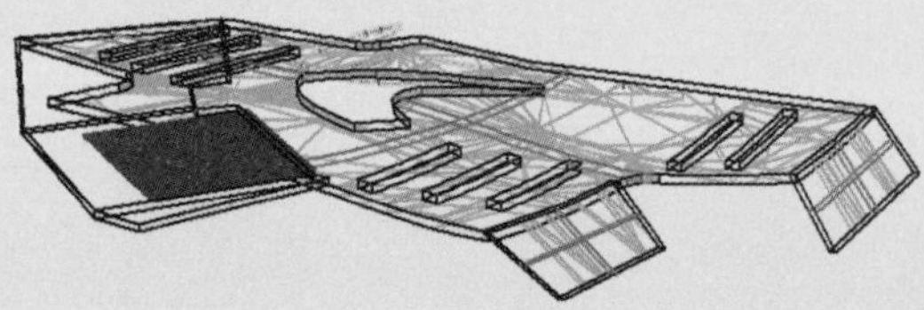

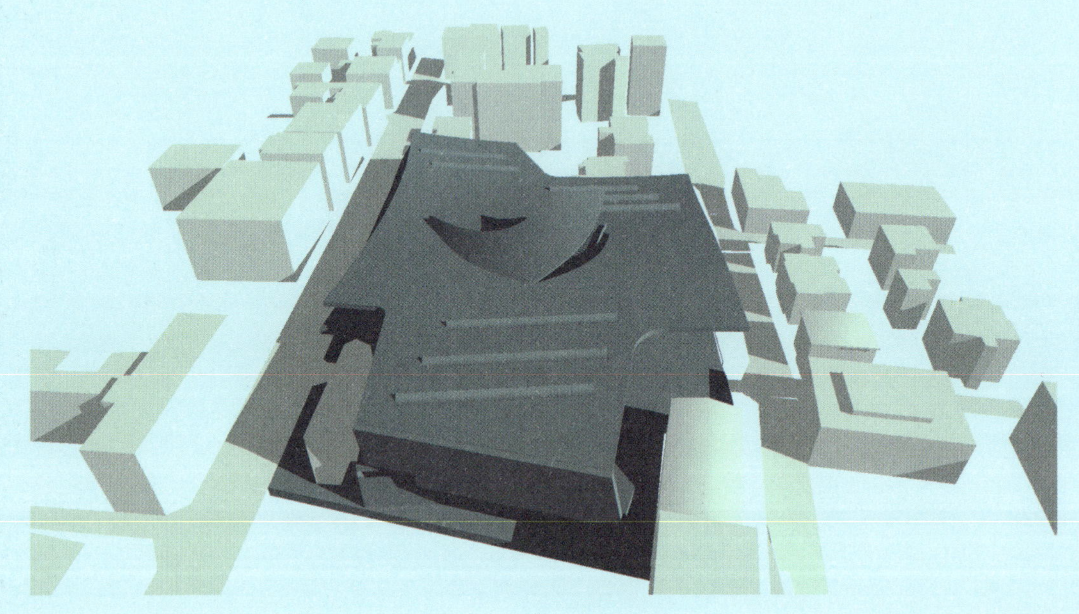

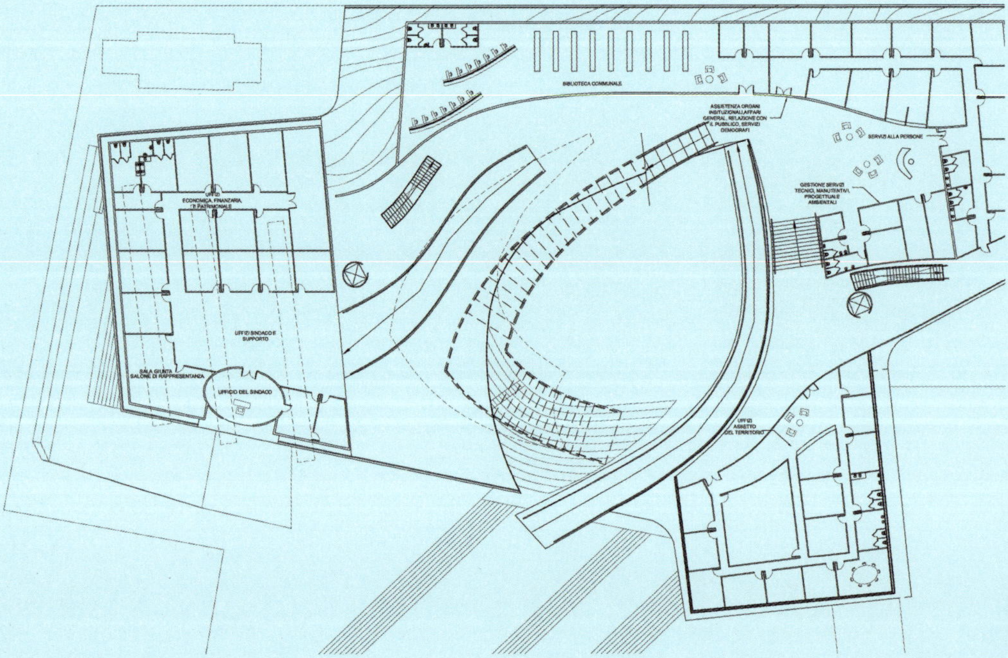

BIBLIOTECA COMMUNALE
ASSISTENZA ORGANI INSITUZIONALI AFFARI GENERAL, RELAZIONE CON IL PUBBLICO, SERVIZI DEMOGRAFI
SERVIZI ALLA PERSONE
GESTIONE SERVIZI TECNICI, MANUTENTIVI, PROGETTUALE AMBIENTALI
UFFIZI ECONOMICA, FINANZARIA, E PATRIMONIALE
UFFIZI SINDACO E SUPPORTO
SALA GIUNTA
SALONE DI RAPPRESENTANZA
UFFICIO DEL SINDACO
UFFIZI ASSETTO DEL TERRITORIO

Santa Marinella City Hall

Location:

Santa Marinella, Italy

Year:

2004 competition (not built)

Program:

City Hall, Offices, and Social Center

Contrary to most assumptions about the homogeneity of the Italian culture and people, there are more layers to Italian ethnicity than we think. Italy had its share of internal and external struggles with foreign powers until it's unification in the mid-19th century, which has influenced every aspect of its art, architecture, and culture from north to south. While Italians are usually identified by their region, their pride in a cultural and ethnic unity came long before the political borders of Italy itself.

With several historic structures and active archeological excavations nearby, the site is saturated with history. Seeking to acknowledge the plot's historical past, I used it's topography to generate the form for the architectural design. Treating the surface of the site as though it were a rigid and movable shell, the roof is lifted above the site to reflect the topography of the land. It hovers above its original location, echoing the sloped shape of the land. To reinforce the clarity of this fictive displacement, the building's elevated

floor and roof perimeters are precisely aligned with their corresponding position on the site below. This radical realignment represents a novelty, revised approach that, rather than responding to the extant physical context of the city, instead reacts to the epistemology of the land and its potentialities for the city's burgeoning future.

In an environment of older buildings and their dominant rectilinear massing, the contemporary design of the Santa Marinella building establishes a progressive precedent. As an injection of contemporary consciousness into the traditional fabric of Santa Marinella, the project attempts to position itself as a catalyst for transformation, pushing the city toward possible futures and away from a stolid architectural monotony.

The program seeks to accommodate an energetic mix of public, civic, and bureaucratic functions creating a center for the city's collective life within the project's boundaries. The ground level includes an amphitheater, which serves as a space for public events, lectures, discussions, forums, public arcades, eateries, impromptu markets, gatherings, and street fairs. This approach toward reclaiming public space reflects a recurring ambition in the work of my office to create architectural responses capable of amplifying the urban intensities of cities. This is particularly appropriate here given the Italian peoples' longstanding propensity to seek out public space as an anchoring element of

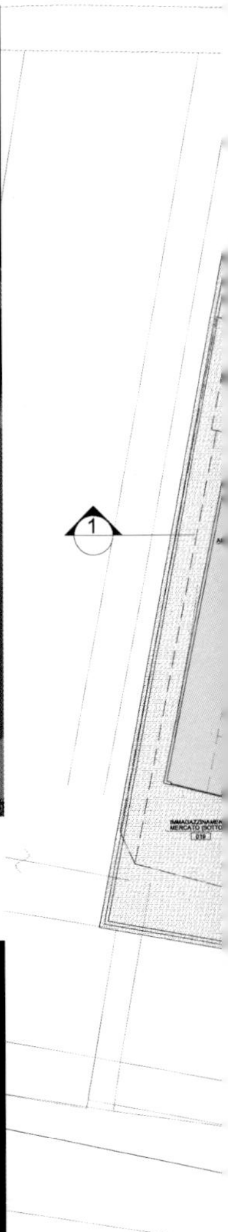

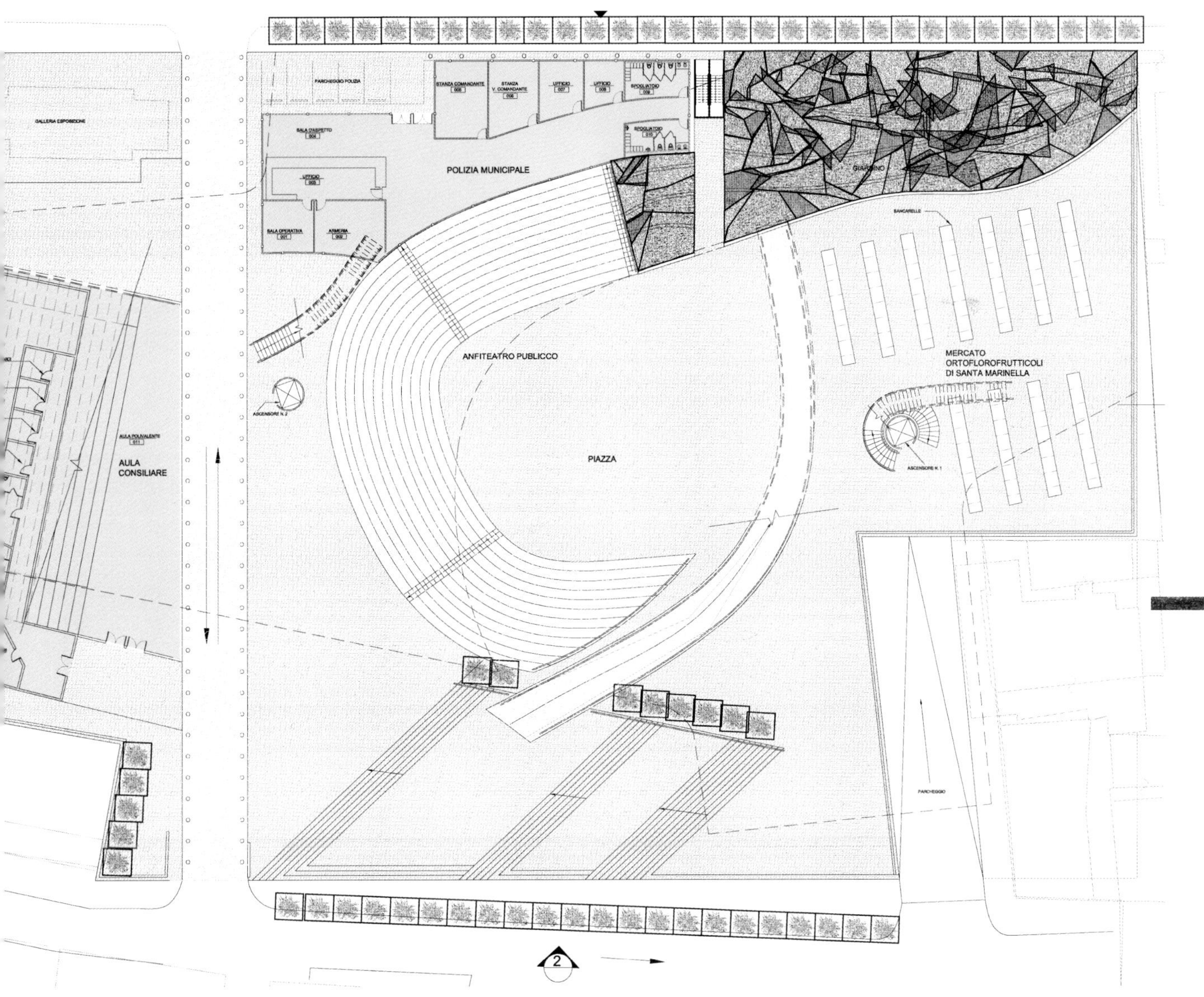

their cultural development. Interacting with the city's pedestrian traffic, the project's intervention at the ground level creates a dynamic spatial interchange for diverse intersections of public movement. Acting as a second stage for urban interactions, the roof of the building provides additional public space where people can stroll or enjoy a picnic while taking in panoramic views of Santa Marinella.

Sandwiched between these two civic arenas, a ramp on the far side of the amphitheater rises up from the ground level granting access to the city's government offices. Here, a raised concrete platform is positioned to face a reflecting pool wrapped entirely in glass, offering a dramatic and inspiring view of the water below. Throughout the project, visual connections such as these are created around important locations of civic discourse, imbuing these activities with connections to the ground and the historical roots, which lie buried there.

Not merely a novelty or prominent attraction within the fabric of Santa Marinella, the New City Hall building is permeated with the perceptual strength and formal structures required for it to actively resonate with the spirit of its location. Blossoming from the city's roots and evoking lineages that lie buried in the earth itself, the project sanctifies the ground as a living repository of information. In this building, the greatness of history and the potentialities of transformation become harmonized at the active center of civic life. As a foundation for the growth of the city, the project enables the people to develop their city into the future with a cognizance of their past heritage.

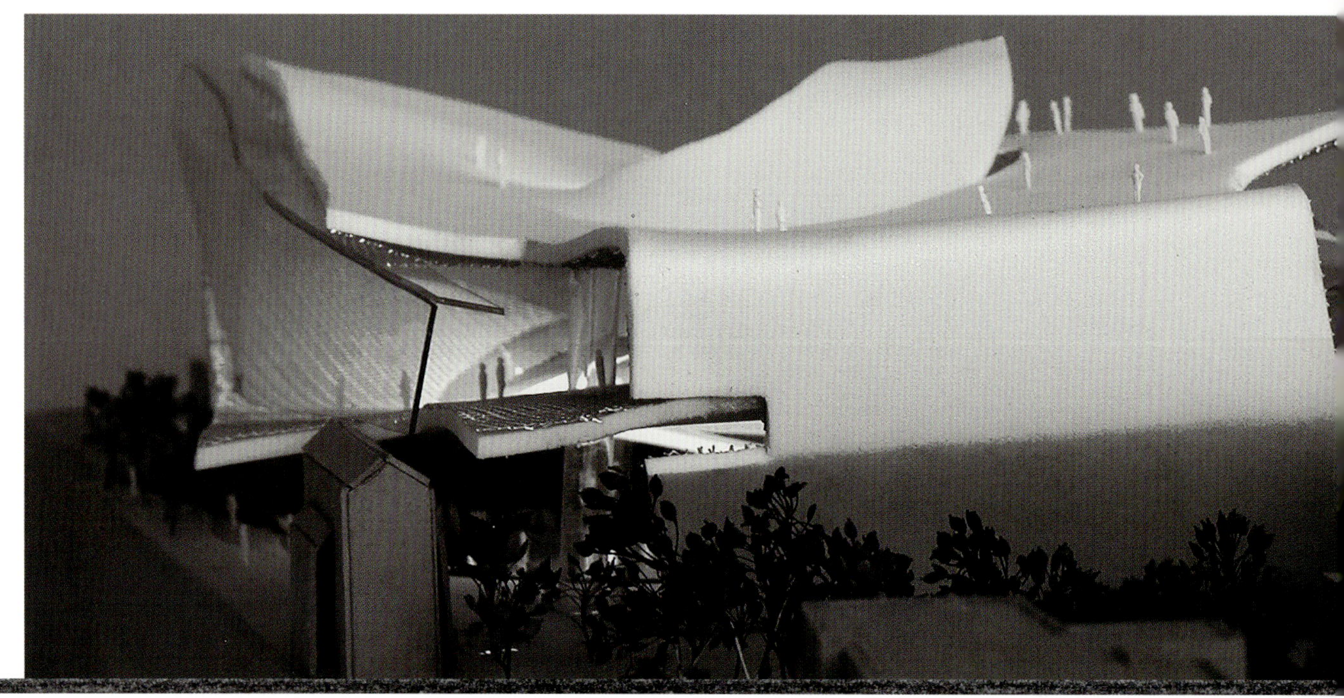

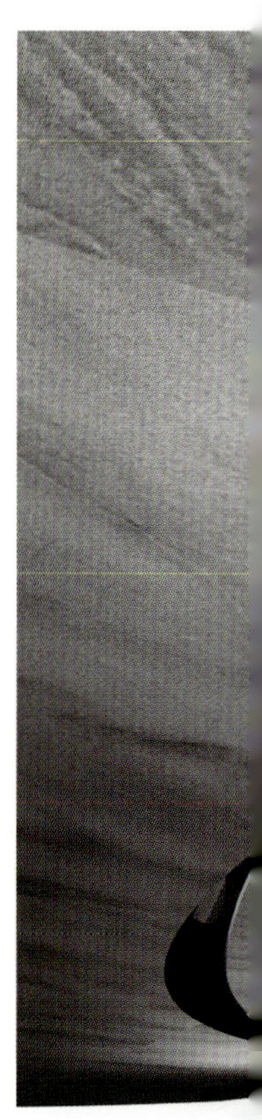

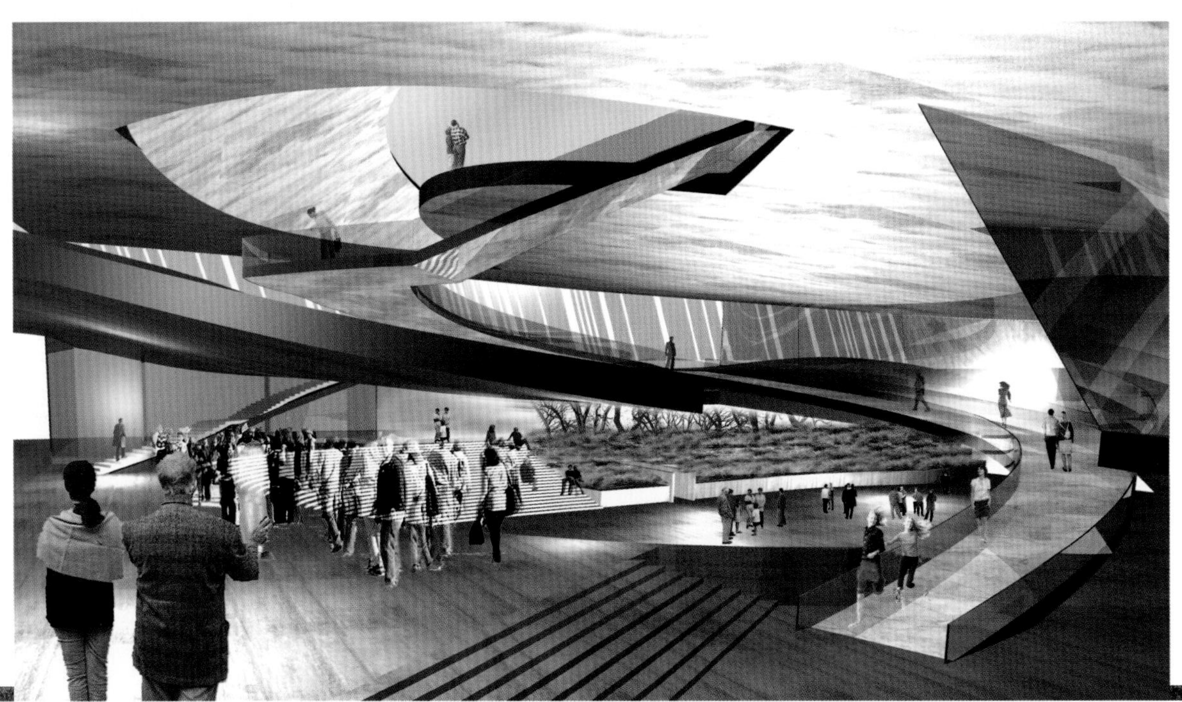

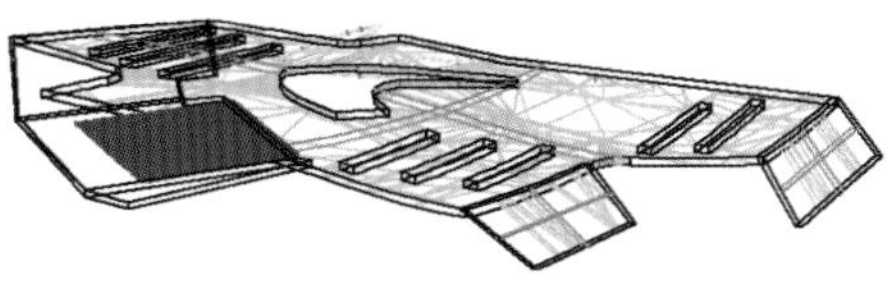

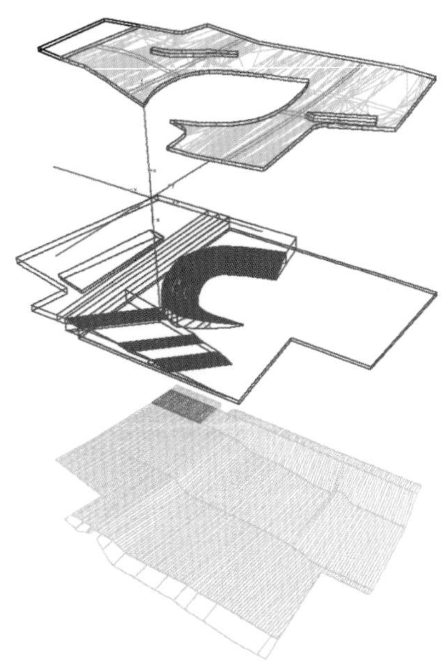

The future of the movie house lies in its ability to dazzle with a fantastic experience and service unmatched elsewhere.

Pathé Cinemas

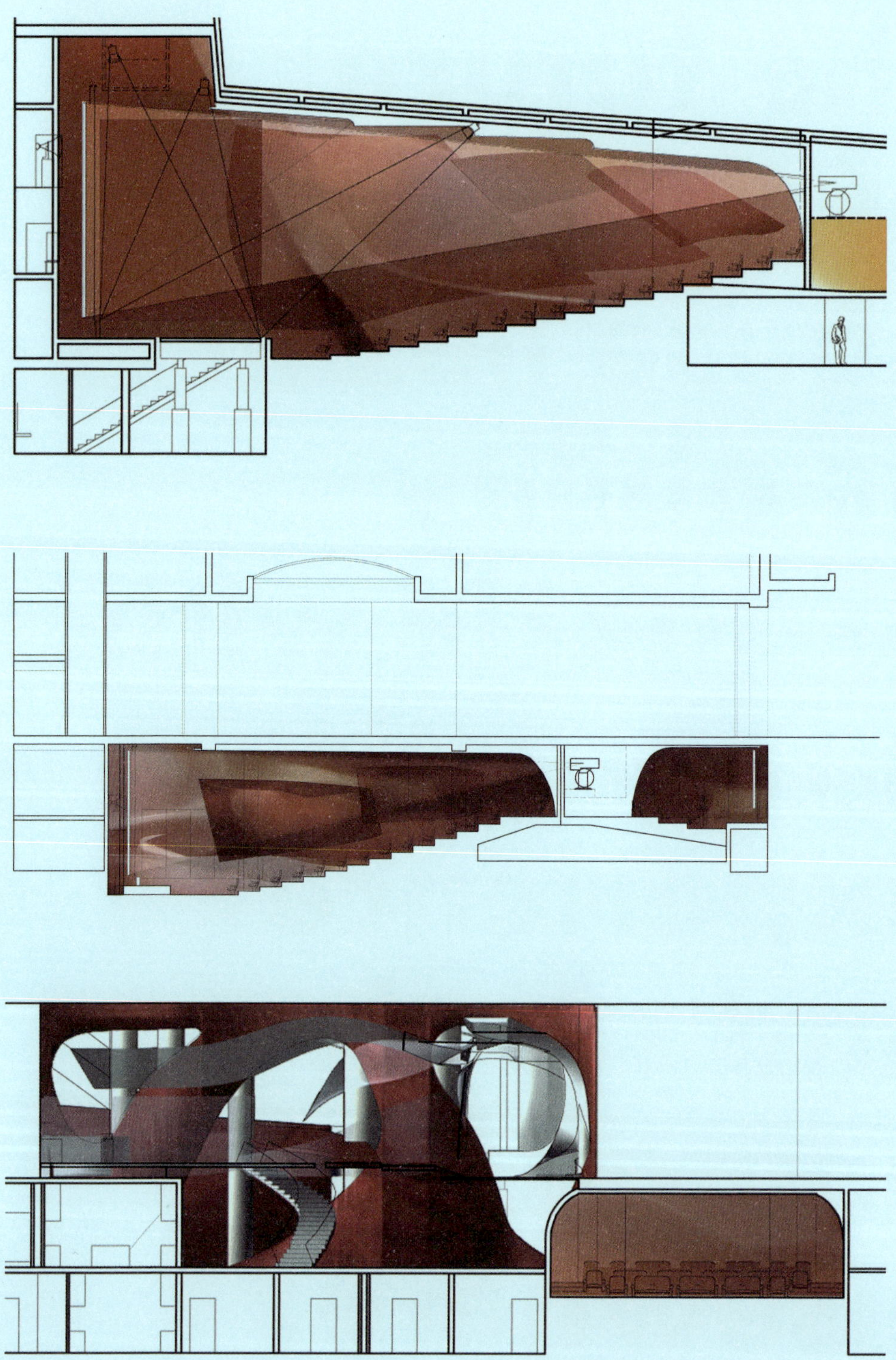

For many, a visit to cinema has an intoxicating draw. Watching a film can transport us to a transcendent state where the boundary between reality and fiction blur. In the darkness of the theater, moviegoers can escape their own lives and enter worlds of luxurious glamour, hearty adventure, or even horrifying fear. Charles Pathé, the founder of the first French cinema empire understood the chemistry between cinema's powerful metamorphic ability and the human need for escape. He was a visionary of epic proportions, again and again proving his acumen in anticipating the future evolution of the cinema industry.

The Pathé-Natan Marignan cinema opened its doors in 1933, in a beautiful building designed by the architect Eugene Bruyneel, at the crossroads of the Avenue des Champs-Elysées and the Rue Marignan. After nearly seven decades of cinematic evolution it was time for one of the first movie palaces of the thirties to adapt to the new movie trends.

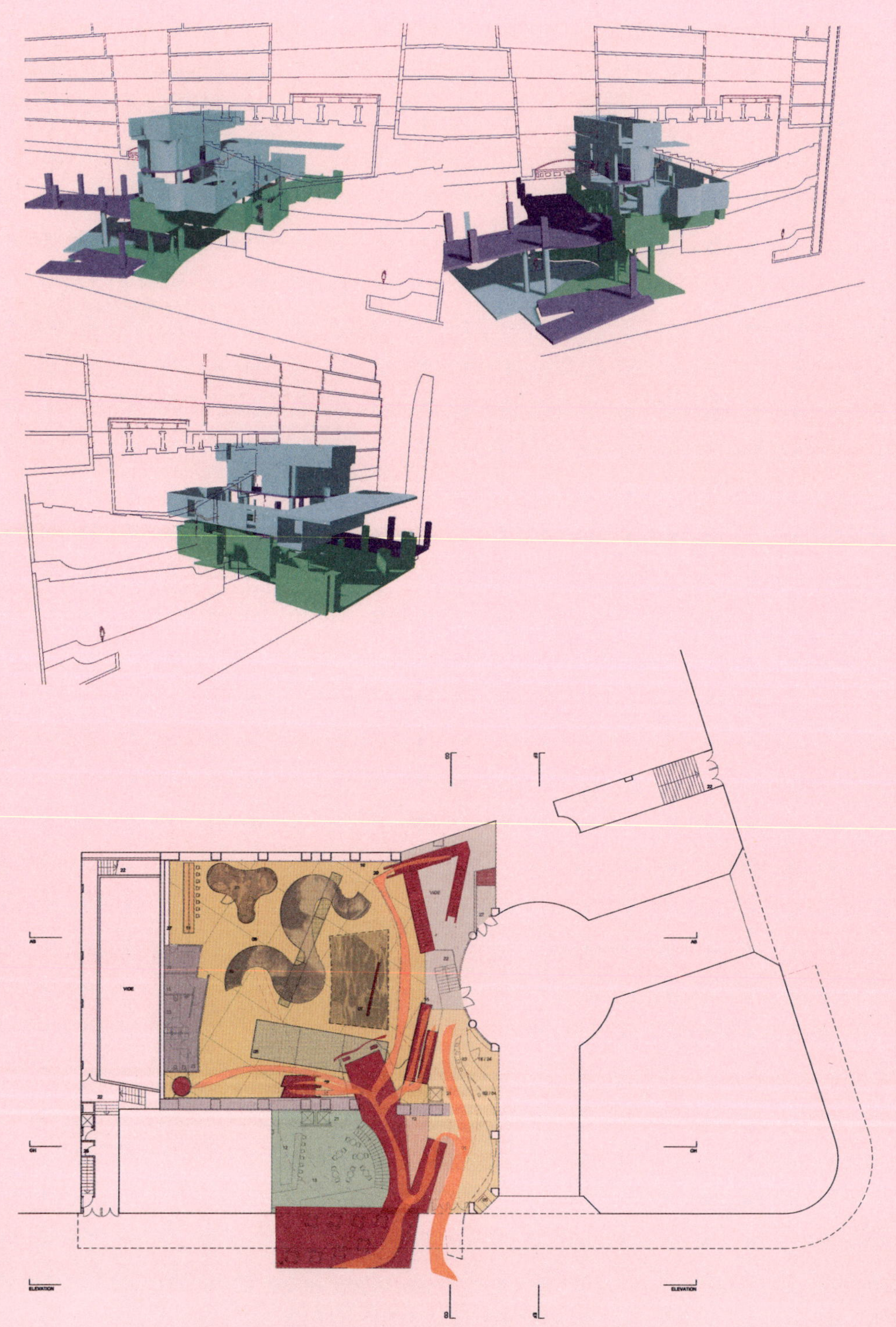

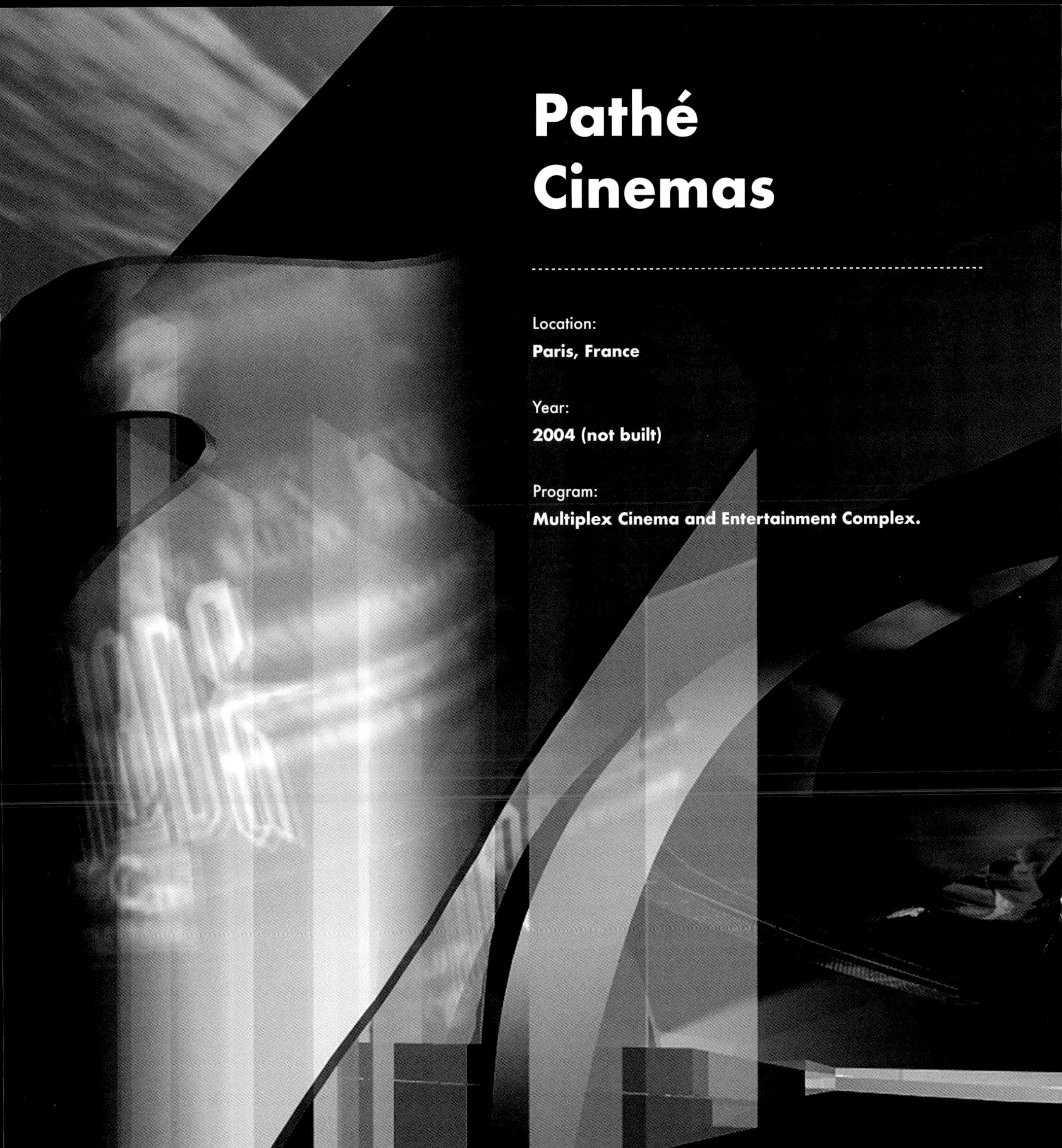

Pathé Cinemas

Location:

Paris, France

Year:

2004 (not built)

Program:

Multiplex Cinema and Entertainment Complex.

Pathé's innovative spirit, as well as the transcendent spirit of cinema, are the acknowledged inspirations behind this project for a new architectural space for Pathé Cinema. Our goal was to accentuate the excitement of the cinema by creating an environment scripted to give each guest their own "star treatment." Visiting the new Pathé Cinemas Marignan involves a choreographed procession through a sequence of fantasy-inspired experiences derived from the mystique of the entertainment industry. Ultimately, we wanted patrons to seek out Pathé Cinemas knowing that their visit would entail much more than just a night at the movies.

Our design necessitated placing five separate theaters into an existing building that had housed one. This required a process of analyzing the existing building to figure out how we could best carve out five theaters and create interactive space that could make the experience more glamorous and seductive. Upon being greeted in your car by the curb-side valet, the Pathé red carpet experience begins. Friendly hosts and hostesses accompany patrons up a ceremonial ramp rising from the Champs-Elysees to "Cinescape," the interior landscape forming the heart of the Pathé Marignan entertainment complex. More than a mere lobby, the Cinescape is a large flexible space that can accommodate any variety of events such as film premieres, awards ceremonies or a party in the honor of Brigitte Bardot while broadcasting the latest gossip of the movie industry. Able to be transformed into a stage for pre-show or aftershow performances, the Cinescape is also a place to purchase tickets and stock up on a wide array of gourmet food and drink.

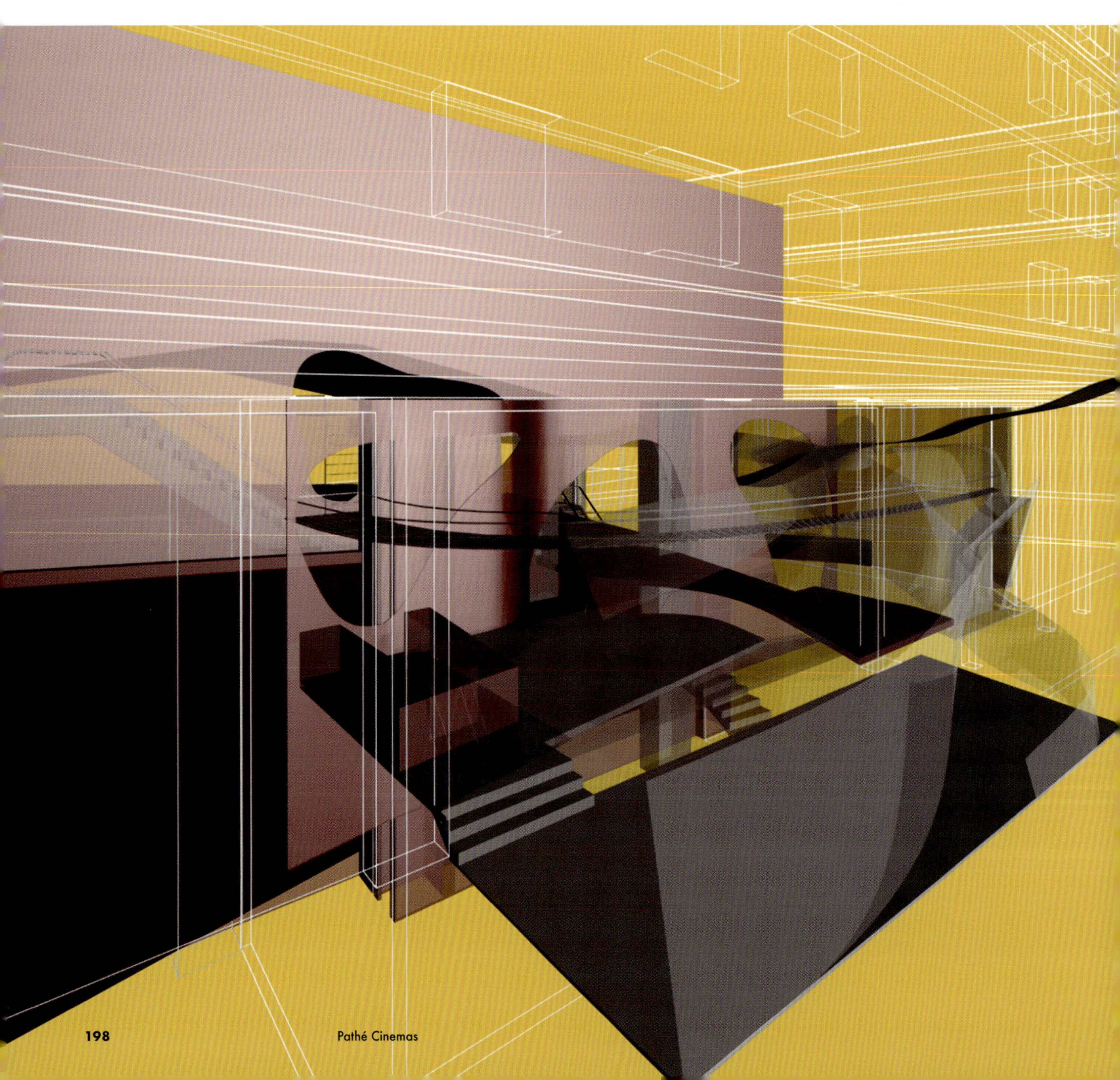

Moving from the Cinescape ticket counter to a seat in a cinema space is a transformation acknowledged by the design of the architectural procession. The patron leaves the known world behind and enters into the world of the film. A gradual constriction of the passages leading to the cinema space lends the feeling that one is about to enter a sacred space. This sense of drama and anticipation gives way to a theater chamber space that is calming. The light level is low and cool, the texture of the seats soft, and the walls recede; it is a quiet architectural space that echoes the power of the stories residing within our collective unconscious. In this space where darkness thrives, with membrane-like wall surfaces flowing with delicacy. Linear patterns of low-level LED lighting reinforce the edges of the aisles leading down to the seats. The space, curving to echo-cupped hands, is surrounded black walls that translucently veil the structure behind. Completed with the sensual lightness of a floating screen the space is both a cavern and a canvas poised for voyages of imaginative exploration.

As the closing credits roll and the theatrical experience is complete the movie patrons move through an exiting sequence structured to gradually ease them back into the public environment. Designed as an intentionally intimate space, closely spaced walls and a lowered ceiling create a quiet passage that naturally channels the body and mind to a place of reflection and recovery. Windows consciously "fade up" to allow a gradually expanding view of the outside. Greeted again by the Pathé hosts, the guests find tea, coffee, and spaces conducive to contemplation. Allowing a return from the world of the cinema to reality,

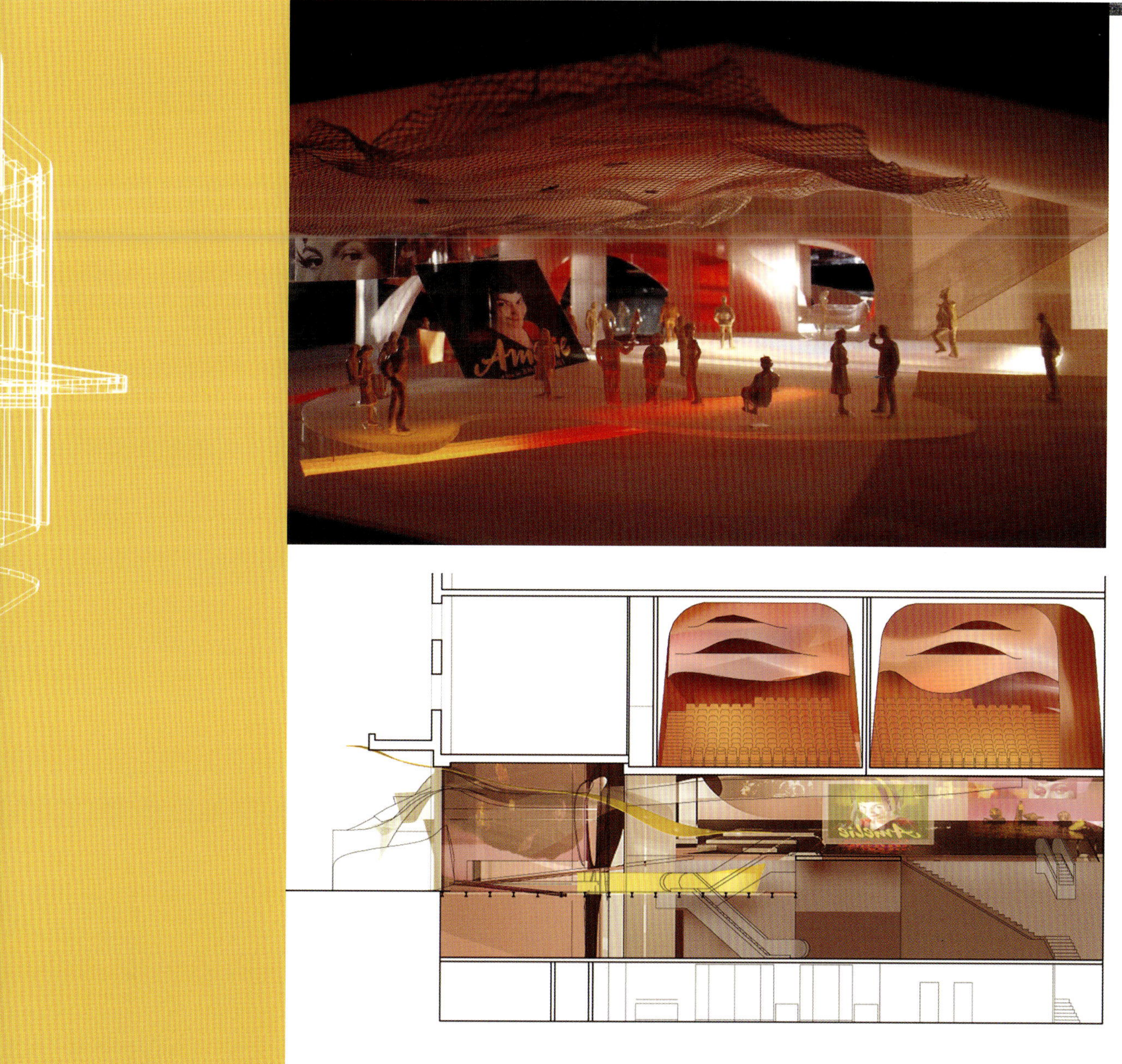

this reentry space maintains a connection to the cinema's aura of collective awareness and otherworldliness.

Nearly a century after it began, Pathe Cinema continues its founder's vision of a company poised at the leading edge of innovation and creativity. The Pathé Marignon Cinema extends this vision to new heights of service and theatricality. Responding to advancements in digital imaging and sound technologies now available to the home theater audience, this new space for cinema demonstrates that in order to survive, the future of the movie house lies in its ability to dazzle with a fantastic experience and service unmatched elsewhere. The design for Pathé glamorizes the cinema experience with a unique architectural environment bringing life into cinema and cinema into life.

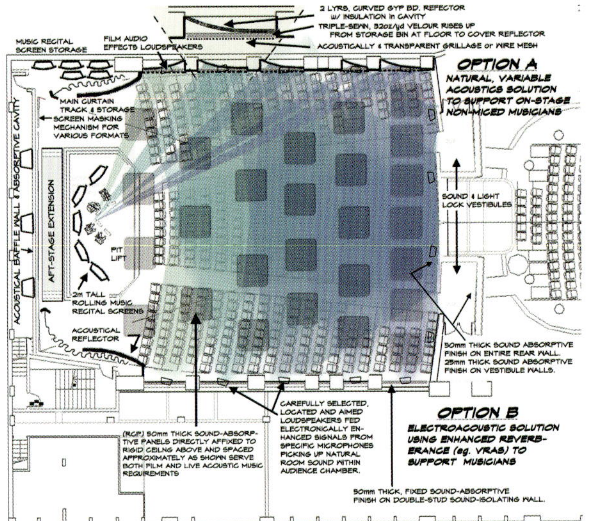

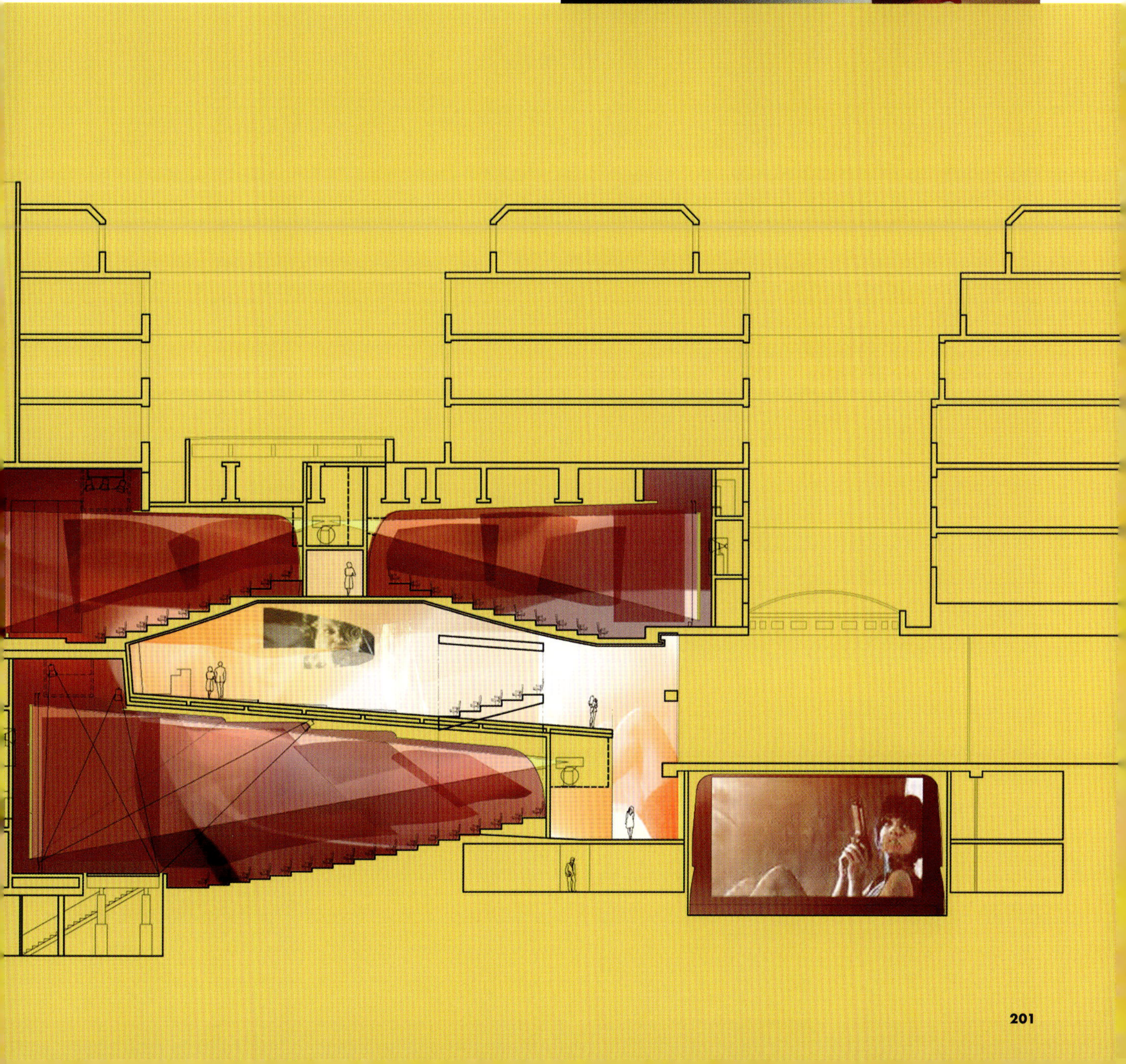

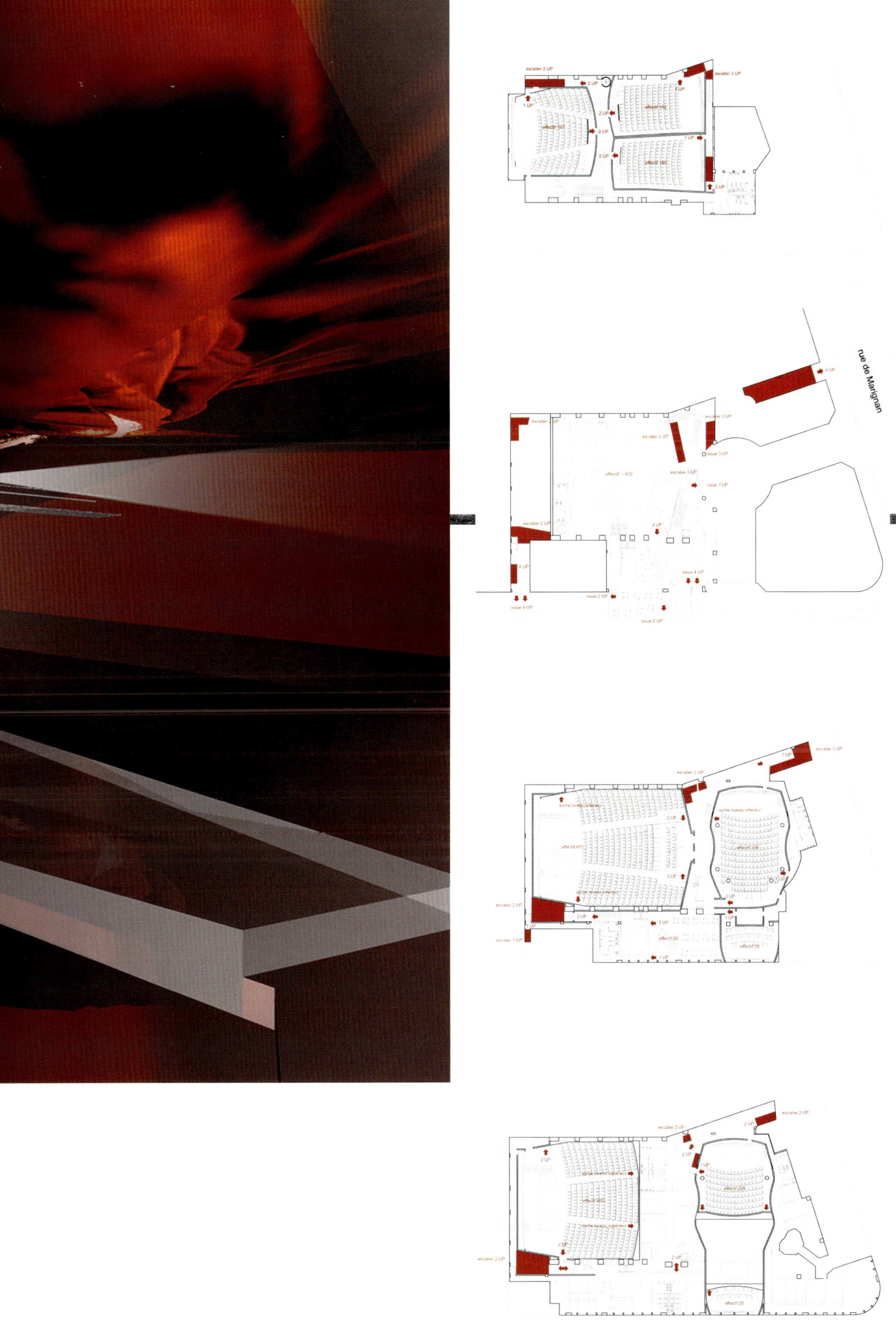
rue de Marignan

PATHÉ !

One container within another; the secondary skin embodies the idea of vessel.

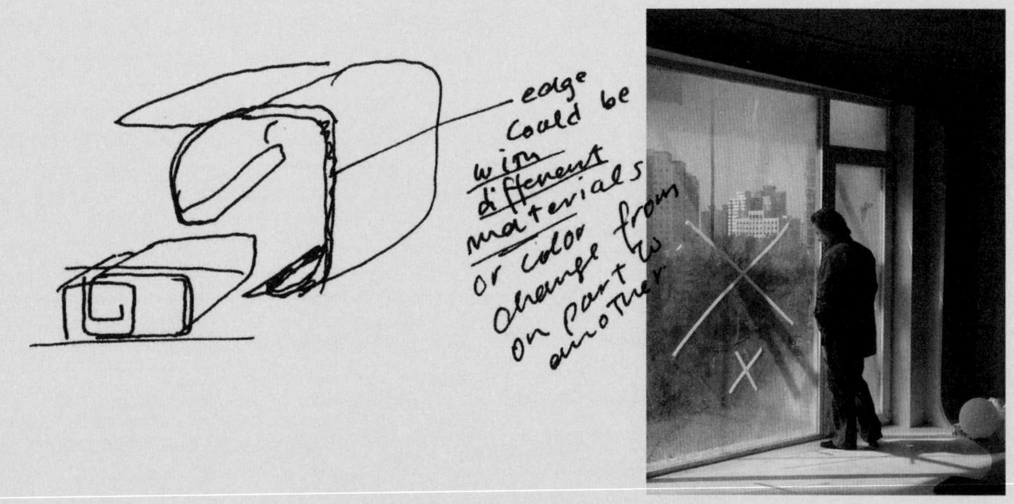

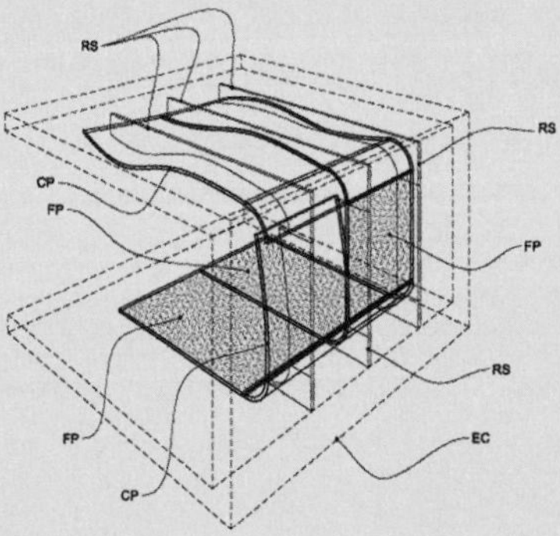

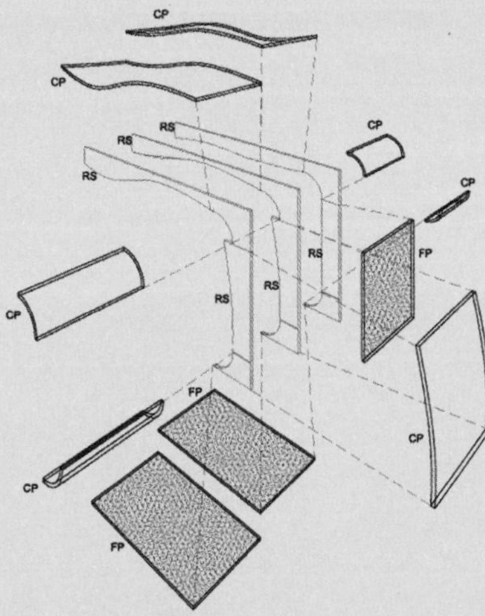

LEGEND

EC EXISTING CONCRETE
FP FLAT PLYWOOD PANEL
CP CURVED PLYWOOD PANEL
RS PLYWOOD RIB STRUCTURE
SB STEEL BRACKET
LB LATERAL BRACING SUPPORTS

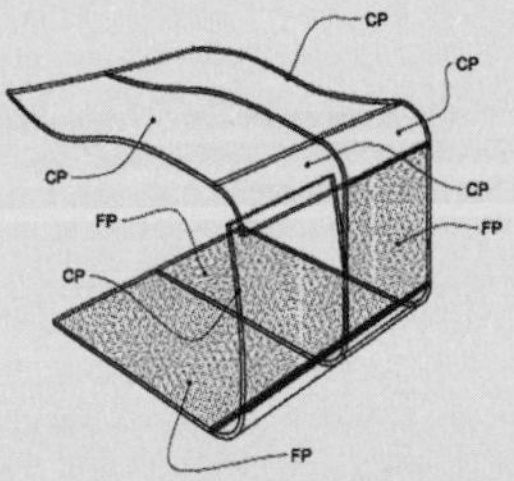

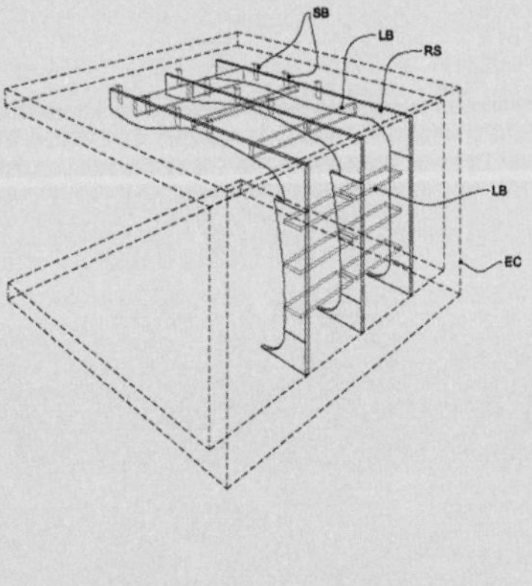

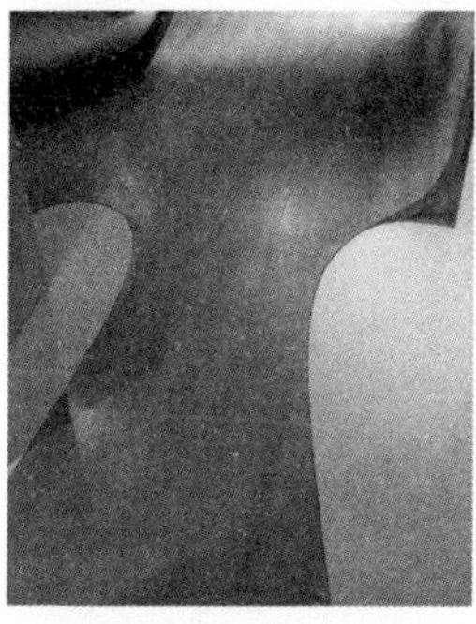
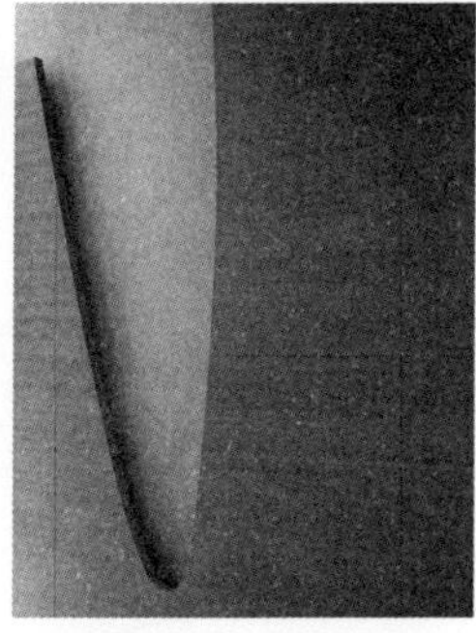

Template House was one of ten interiors designed for an exhibition called Infinite Interiors and constructed within at a high-rise condominium building in Phoenix City for China's First Architectural Biennial. My goal was to create a living environment that served as place of escape; a quiet, contemplative oasis in the midst of Beijing's tumultuous racing modern growth.

As an architect from the United States, having the opportunity to design and build in the People's Republic of China was a great and exciting challenge. Working within any foreign culture I have always tried to situate myself within the daily lives of my clients, using my heart to ground myself while establishing a respect and understanding for the local culture and customs.

For this project I harnessed the principals of the ancient practice of Feng Shui to guide the process of design. Feng Shui is a discipline focused on achieving harmony and balance through the orchestration and arrangement of spaces. Acting as a natural filter to arbitrary or impulsive decisions its precepts function to divide all things into complementary dualities linking humans to heaven and earth. The Chinese believe that the Ch'i, the life force or spiritual energy pervading all matter, determines each individual's movements and actions. Intrigued by these mystical principals I submerged myself in this belief system with the hope of creating a space that would be suitable to the Chinese nature.

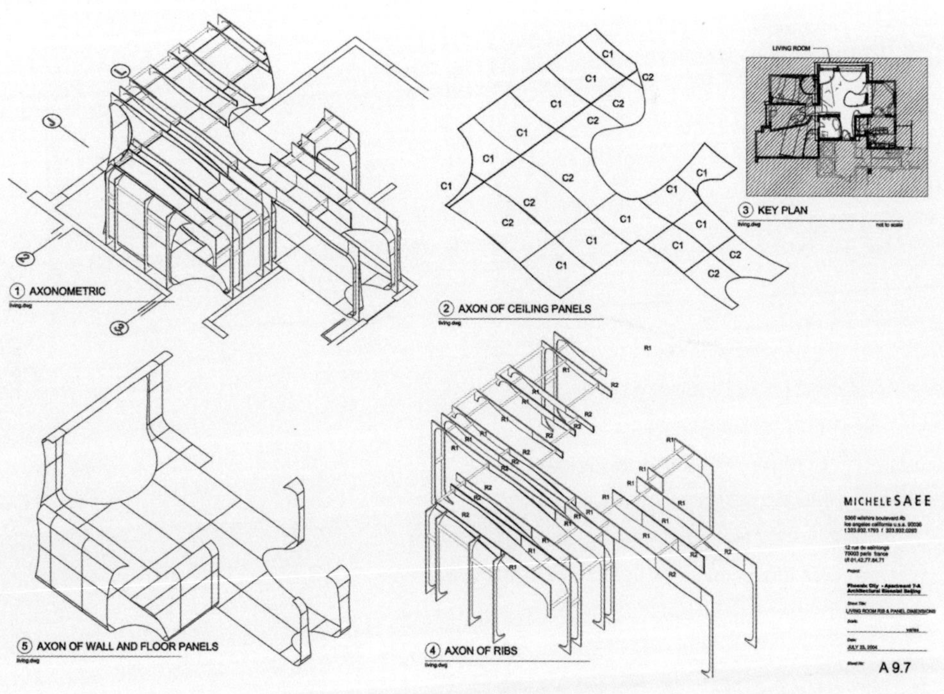
1 AXONOMETRIC
living.dwg
2 AXON OF CEILING PANELS
living.dwg
C1
C2
3 KEY PLAN
LIVING ROOM
living.dwg
not to scale
5 AXON OF WALL AND FLOOR PANELS
living.dwg
4 AXON OF RIBS
living.dwg
R1
R2
MICHELE SAEE
5366 wilshire boulevard #b
los angeles california u.s.a. 90036
t 323.932.1793 f 323.932.0293
12 rue de saintonge
75003 paris france
t/f 01.42.77.84.71
Project:
Phoenix City - Apartment 7-A
Architectural Biennial Beijing
Sheet Title:
LIVING ROOM RIB & PANEL DIMENSIONS
Scale:
Date:
JULY 23, 2004
Sheet No:
A 9.7

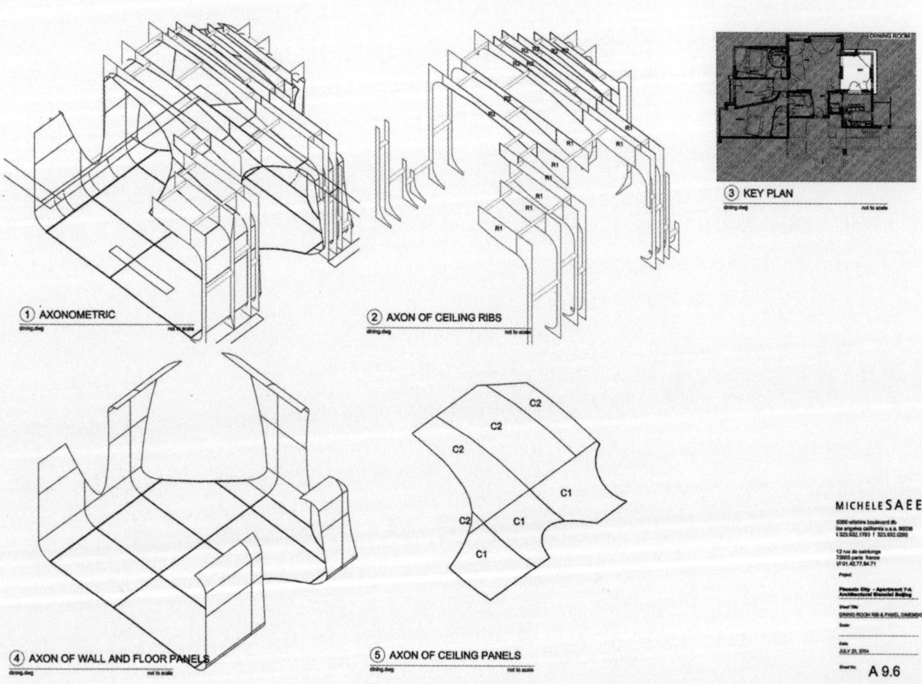
1 AXONOMETRIC
dining.dwg
not to scale
2 AXON OF CEILING RIBS
dining.dwg
not to scale
R1
R2
3 KEY PLAN
DINING ROOM
dining.dwg
not to scale
4 AXON OF WALL AND FLOOR PANELS
dining.dwg
not to scale
5 AXON OF CEILING PANELS
dining.dwg
not to scale
C1
C2
MICHELE SAEE
5366 wilshire boulevard #b
los angeles california u.s.a. 90036
t 323.932.1793 f 323.932.0293
12 rue de saintonge
75003 paris france
t/f 01.42.77.84.71
Project:
Phoenix City - Apartment 7-A
Architectural Biennial Beijing
Sheet Title:
DINING ROOM RIB & PANEL DIMENSIONS
Scale:
Date:
JULY 23, 2004
Sheet No:
A 9.6

The Template house

Location:
Beijing, P.R. China

Year:
2004 (built)

Program:
Model Apartment

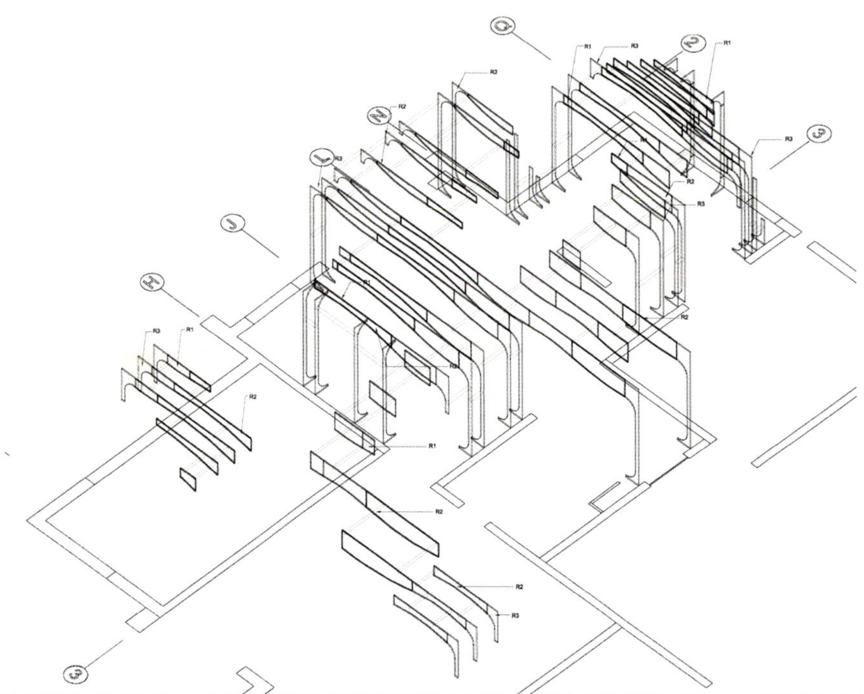

The design for the house was developed in two parts: the outer container, which was the existing concrete building and the inner container which was the Template House. Like the body, both spaces were composed of many parts. The individual elements had to work together to ensure the balance and health of the organism.

Our initial presentation of non-accurate line drawings to the carpenter initiated our exploration of the template. Involving more about the nature of the lines than what they were describing, the manner in which a line was drawn, its thickness, its errors, and so on, became determinate factors in the generation of shapes, guiding the process rather than defining.

As a result of the construction documents inherit limitations, templates developed as a crucial tool in our ability to move the construction process forward. Prepared by the Chinese carpenters with a basic bendable wood spline and a pencil, the templates were simple site-fabricated translations of the designer's drawings. These prototypes were then given to the other carpenters and while they were cutting the complex shapes of the formwork more templates were constructed. Once the formwork frame was complete, the process of installing the cladding began. The sheets of plywood were formed to the frame created by the templates, and sheet by sheet the form took shape with each successful panel informing the profile of the next.

In its final form the Template House challenges our expectations regarding structure and the process of construction producing a fluid space where everyday activities can occur with a minimum of resistance and clutter. Unifying the floor, walls, and ceiling with the flowing wood "skin." the design result was in continuous space able to accommodate all the functions and technical necessities of the living organism. The template is not fixed. Flexibility is introduced into the design through suitable materials and movable partitions allowing an infinite variety of spatial reconfigurations and permitting the rooms to be divided and modified according to the evolving needs of the inhabitants.

A continuous secondary skin, interrupted only at certain points where panels of white and pale green Venetian plaster are allowed to peek through, is constructed from clear-finished cherry plywood flows throughout unifying the living spaces. The only counterpoints to this treatment were the kitchen and the bathroom, which is enclosed on one side by a glass wall with a floor tiled with deeply colored glass pebbles.

Like one container nested within another, the secondary skin embodies the idea of the vessel. The shape of the container influences the activities of life that form its contents. Gathering distinctly separate architectural elements with a sense of unity the experimental design of the Template House results is an open, spacious layout within a warm protective atmosphere.

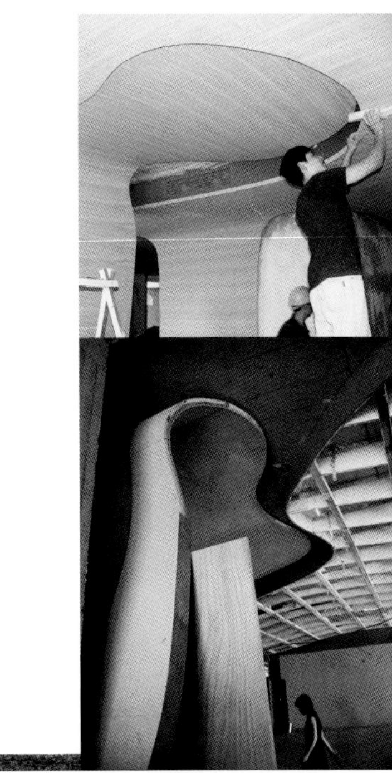

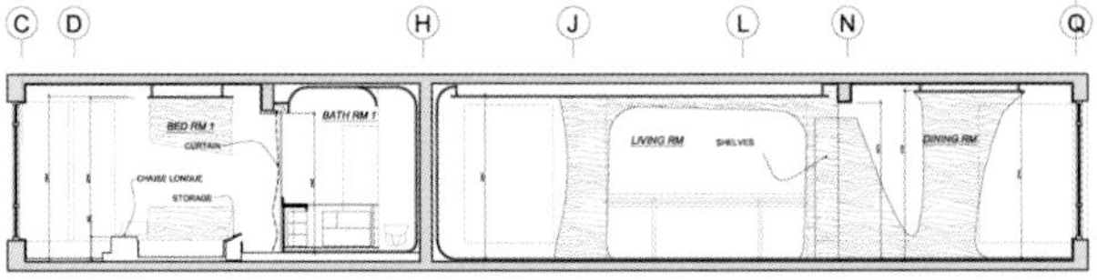

A LONGITUDINAL SECTION
Plan.dwg 1:50

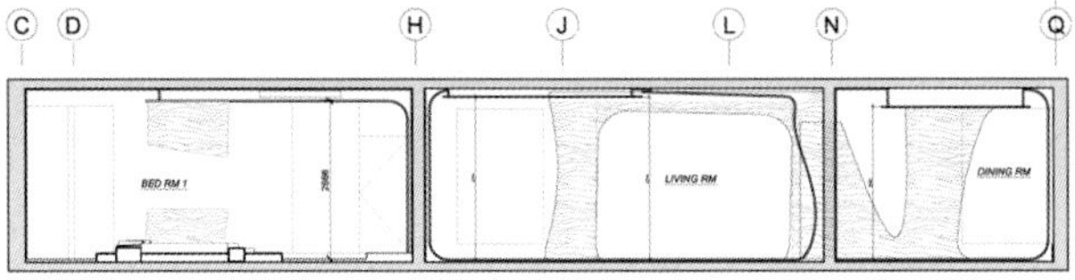

B LONGITUDINAL SECTION
Plan.dwg 1:50

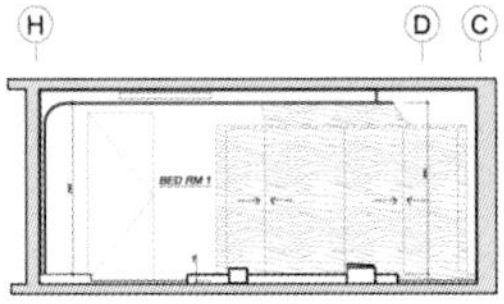

B2 LONGITUDINAL SECTION
Plan.dwg 1:50

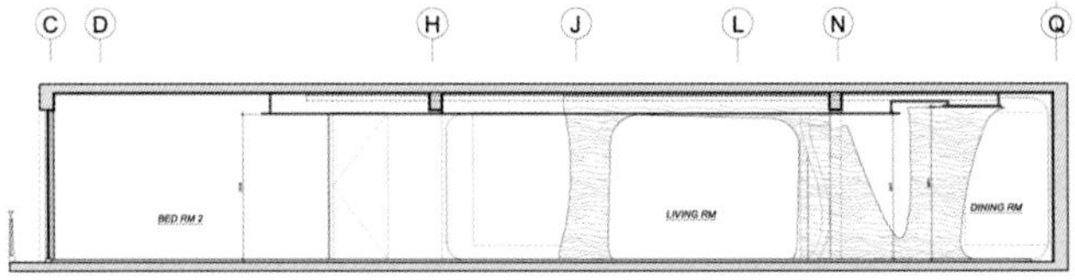

C LONGITUDINAL SECTION
Plan.dwg 1:50

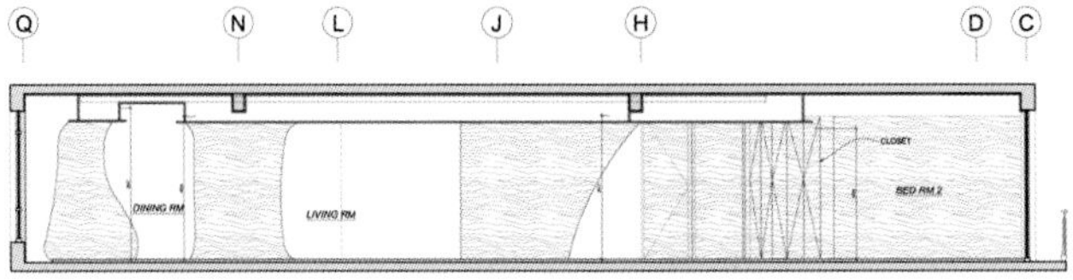

C2 LONGITUDINAL SECTION
Plan.dwg 1:50

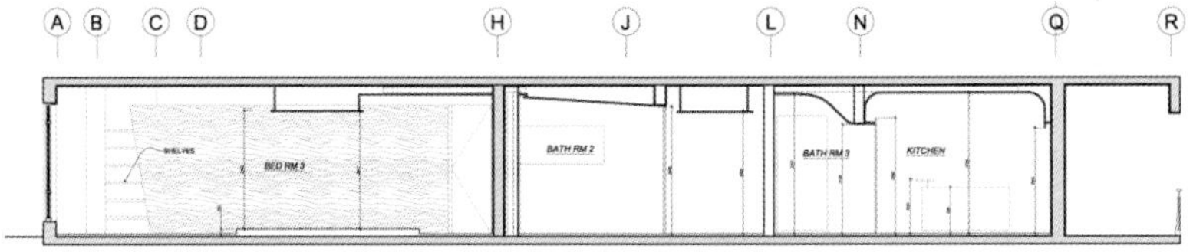

D LONGITUDINAL SECTION
Plan.dwg 1:50

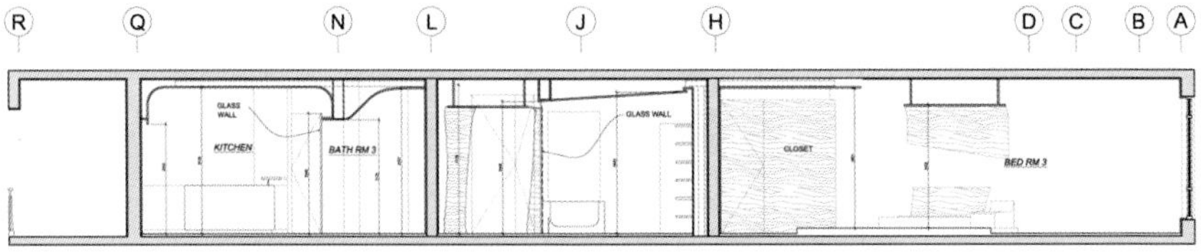

D2 LONGITUNDINAL SECTION
Plan.dwg 1:50

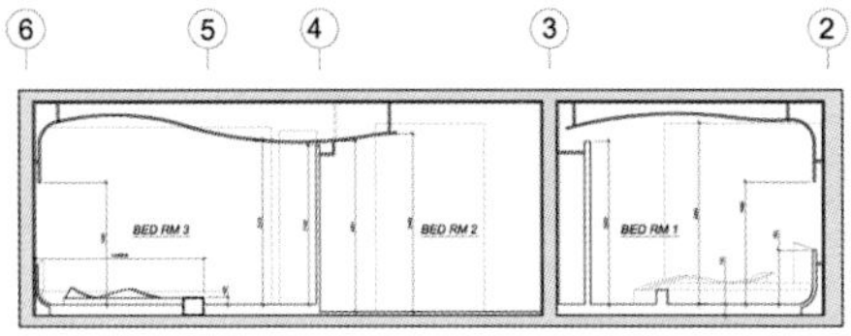

1 TRANSVERSE SECTION
Plan.dwg 1:50

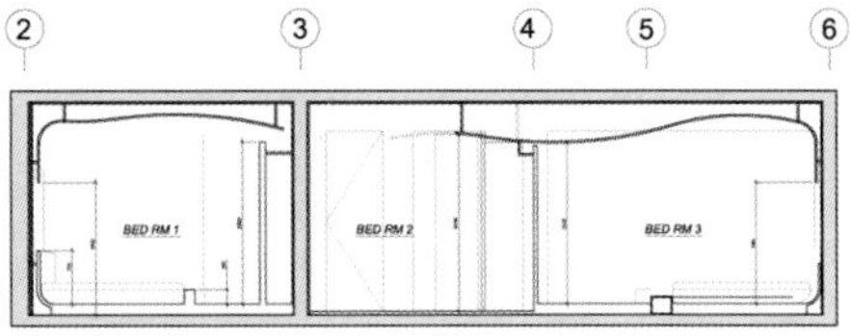

1A TRANSVERSE SECTION
Plan.dwg 1:50

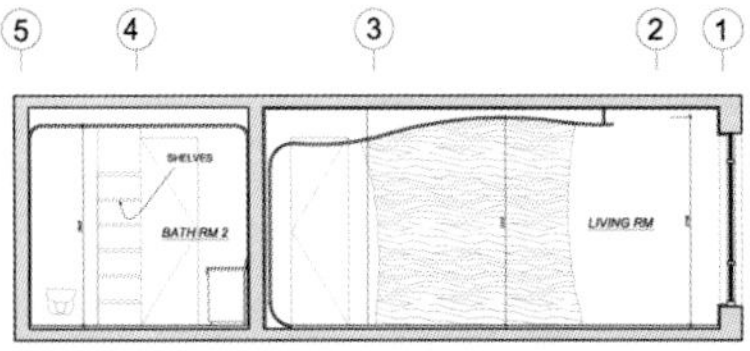

2 TRANSVERSE SECTION
Plan.dwg 1:50

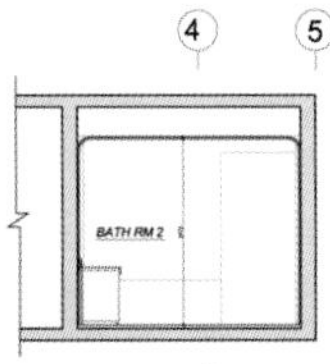

2A TRANSVERSE SECTION
Plan.dwg 1:50

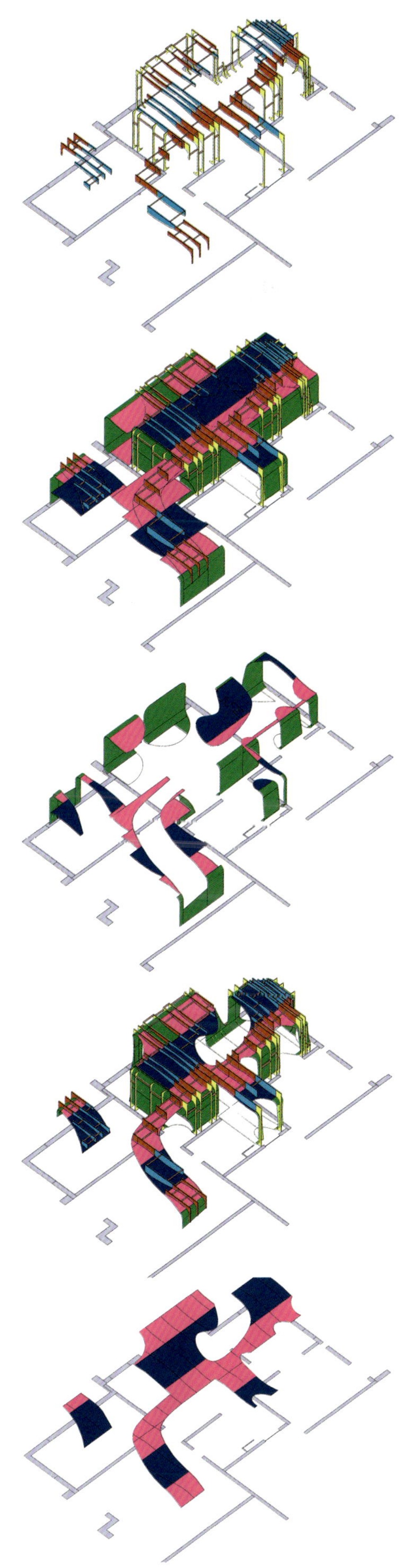

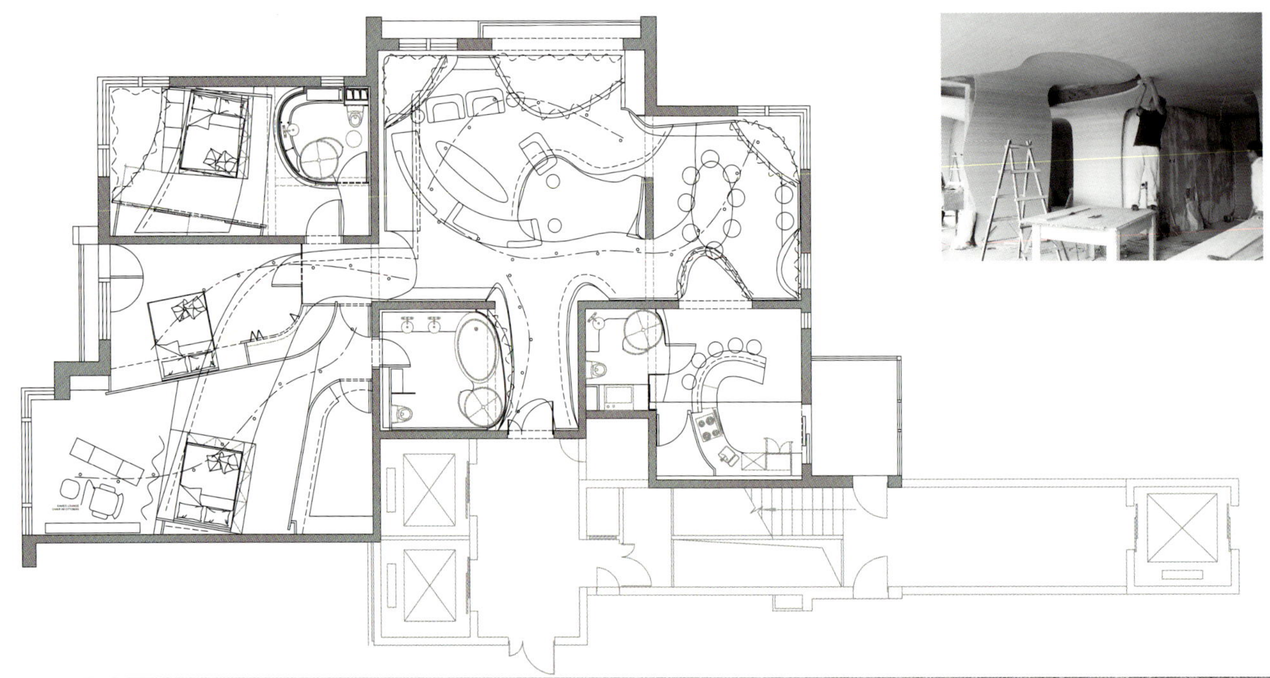

The Template House (Story)

My father used to tell me, "no thinking, if thinking, think nothing." Therefore, in 1995 I taught a design studio at SCI-Arc with that notion in mind, calling it "No Thinking Tank" (NTT). The premise of the NTT was to propel ourselves into a fictional future (2013). To release our thoughts from a prior, self-imposed knowledge and invite reflections on who we are, what we think, and how we live. NTT existed as a conversation. A re-examination and a re-imagining of our methods to making architecture. Aware of the breach between our conceptual and perceptual tools, we invented new tools as well as new ways of using the ones we knew. The following text is from NTT pamphlet:

Los Angeles, 2013: back in 1995, it seemed as if the drift of life and work into the computer was so widespread that all that could be left would be for our bodies to become binary code, for our physical world to be sucked into the screen leaving us to hover, as diffused as mist. This proved to be temporary phase in the advance of our civilization: we know now that the computer became as simple to use and as pervasive as the telephone (while swallowing all of the capabilities of the telephone and television.) It became a common and utilitarian as pencil and paper.

It began—if there can ever a beginning to something which has no end—with a kind of sadness mixed with hope. A sadness that the world we live in is less and less human. Where words like love, passion, and friendship have lost their true meanings in the "glamorous" world of computer chat rooms, instant phone messaging, and (not so) reality TV shows. The new dazzling social, cultural, and technological revolution, similar to an explosion, has only de-sensitized us to the world. The new technological tools of communication and interaction demonstrate movement away from direct bodily interaction. This becomes more apparent because these devices are in the service of seeking and expanding markets for consumer goods rather than what they're pretending to be: communication tools for the masses. I do think these tools raise our awareness about each other, but don't we lose something in this process?

It is important to be aware of the self-consciousness we tend to exhibit toward technology. The sophistication with which we create patterns and systems in our consumption of products, especially information products, tricks us into thinking these are creative endeavors. A generic character begins to evolve in many of the objects and relationships which surround us. We can become seduced by the market culture as if it were a human being.

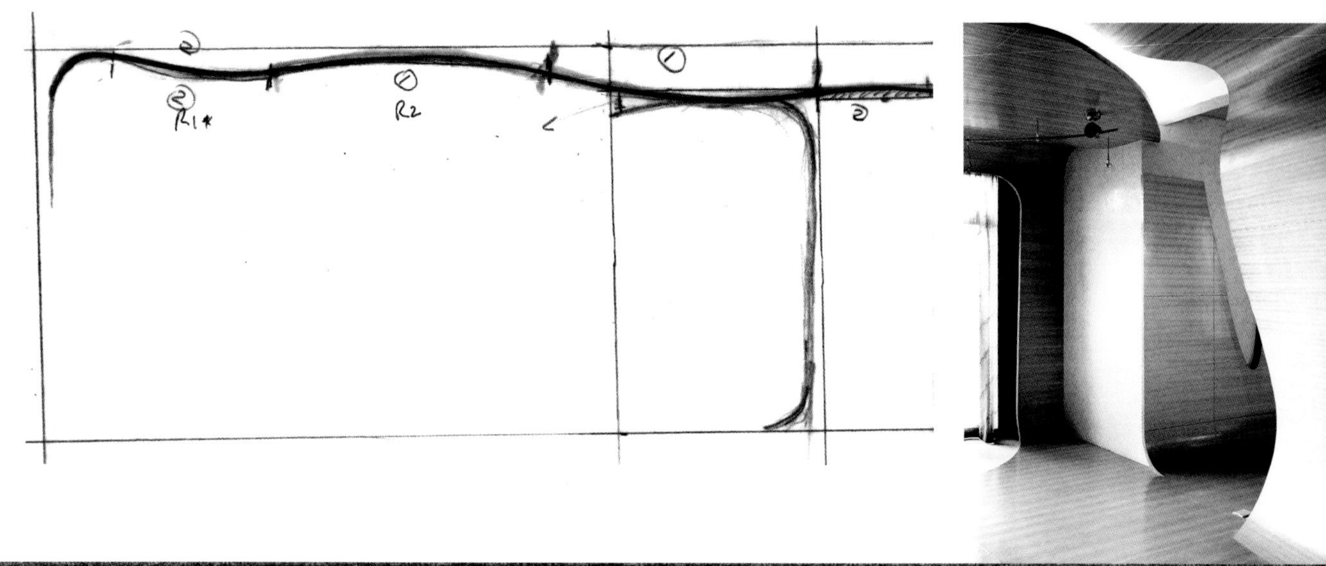

War, hunger, genocide, and poverty have been reduced to repetitive images on the computer screen like Exxon Mobile, Coca Cola, Nike, or Microsoft. The system of communications and technology is filled with machines so ugly and banal that the culture establishing itself around computing reflects this avarice.

Our culture's fascination with technology, evident in the developments of the last few decades, seems to be more a fascination with the object of the technology rather than how our lives are affected by it. In the creative process there is a battle with murky boundaries and complex adversaries. Because of the production capabilities and sophistication of the tools, it is not easy to separate the fakers from the makers. The new tools are in their infancy as far as architecture is concerned and most of what is used for architectural design was designed for use elsewhere. Programs like Rhinoceros was intended to be used for computer-aided manufacturing (CAM), rapid prototyping, 3D printing, and reverse engineering in product manufacturing industries like aircraft, automotive, multimedia, and graphic design. Another popular software used in architectural design or production is 3D Studio Max, which was developed for animation, models, games, and images. Modo Creative software is for modeling, texturing, and movie animation. CATIA's 3D platform originated in other industries, being used in aircraft manufacturing and engineering. CATIA was adopted by Frank Gehry and was developed to facilitate construction of buildings with volume complexities for lower prices that encourage developers to invest.

Unfortunately these programs and "tools" can be very seductive, giving the user the illusion that they are engaged in making architecture. The image is important in the creation of architecture, but there are issues far more critical: the environment the architecture has to interact

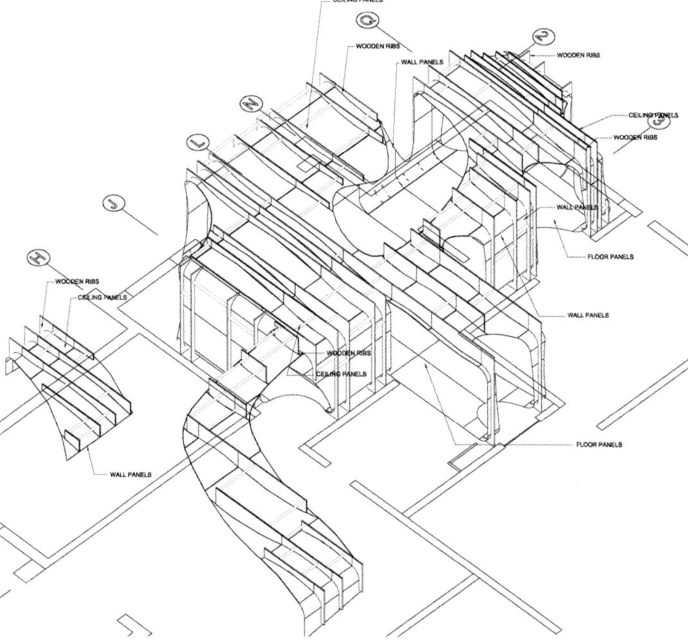

with or respond to, the socio-political context, the economic implications, functionality and use, interaction between the space and participant, and more.

My experiences in China from 2004 to 2007 were an awakening. I had the opportunity to see, firsthand, China's transformation on a small scale, which forced me to reexamine my encounters with France and the US during the technological revolution of the early '80s or '90s.

The Chinese transformation through new urban developments has been mainly influenced by Chairman Mao's successor, Deng Xiaoping, who led China with market economy reform, which began in the late seventies and continues to this day. The opening of China meant it was ready to play an important role on the world stage and it was physically visible being there. I never forget watching construction workers across my hotel in Beijing. On a high-rise building, they would work 24 hours around the clock, finishing a floor every week.

In 2004 when I arrived at my first construction site in Beijing, I was confronted with a new reality. I still couldn't quite believe it when I saw the construction crew walk into the space with their small, trivial boxes of hand tools. I thought, "The rest of the crew must arrive later with the real tools," but soon learned that they were it. They were carrying all they need to build my "sophisticated" project.

There were a group of men—two young, two old—being led by a middle-aged man carrying my drawings. I stood in the raw concrete space on the 7th floor, my jaw hanging in

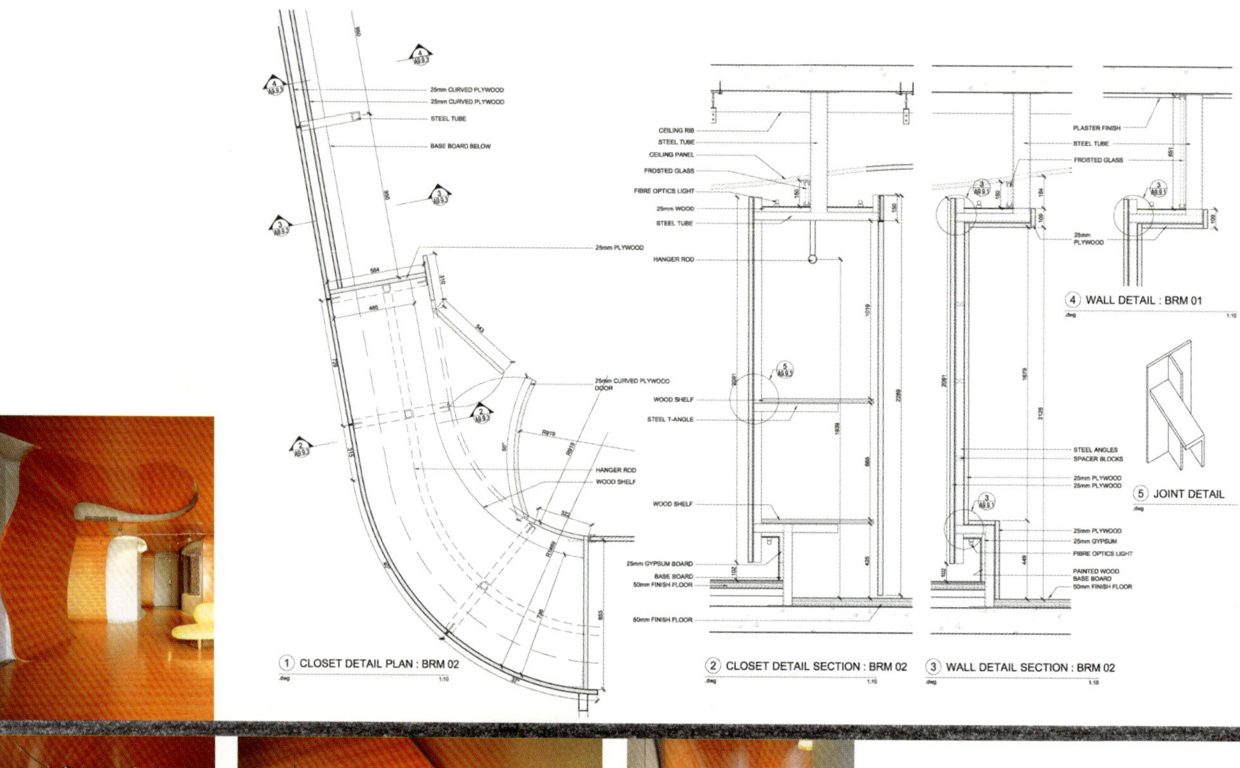

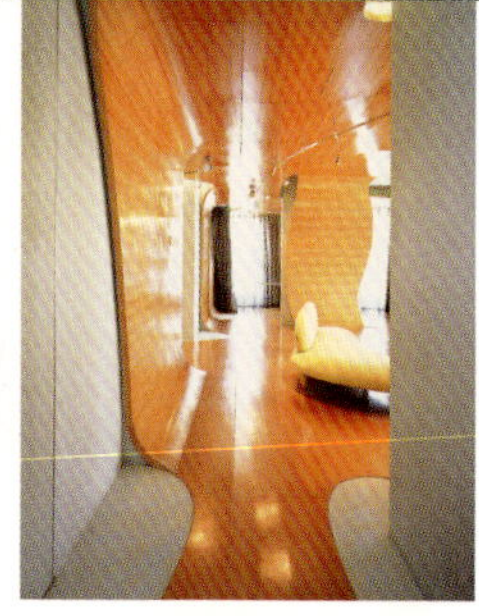

disbelief as they unpacked their modest hand tools one by one. I was nervous and unsettled thinking to myself, "This is not going to work!" They were confident and calm as they prepared their tools and space. One or two carpenters began to look through a pile of uneven pieces of wood and began to plane them with a compact machine no bigger than a microwave. The wood dust and smell coming from the bench-top planer filled up the room and before I knew it everyone was engaged in different activities.

I aim to think creatively and live a creative life, but like everybody else I sometimes lose track of what is real and what is a product of my imagination. My desires sometimes supersede reality and I create an image of something or someone to fit my expectation regardless of the true nature of the subject I am observing or the person I am interacting with. I began to realize that I was judging them because of my unfamiliarity with the conditions and circumstances. I can get so involved that I lose myself, and as a result, see what I want to see instead of what is really there in front of my eyes. Internally, I turn blind and begin visualizing with my eyes closed. I invent my environment and build it with fictional materials that don't exist in the physical world. I use structural systems that in the real world would not be sustainable.

Because of my western cultural biases, I assumed Beijing, China to be unsophisticated. My experience working in the US and Europe influenced me to expect a certain type of experience resembling Euro-centric stereotypes. When I didn't see the signs and symbols I was familiar with—stereotypical construction workers with hard hats and a plethora of tools which took up to a week to set up—I didn't see the true quality nor ability of the people in front of me. I was judgmental, but after a day I started to question my narrow perception.

Here I was blinded by the "technology"—its gadgets and communication systems. This was a great test of faith for me to get back in touch with my human side and having to let go; to abandon my preconceived notions about technology, process, product, and people. I had to accept that the human's mind and hands are capable of creating wonders. I was thinking about the pyramids of Egypt, the Great Wall of China, the Forbidden City, and many other great creations in history. As I was wandering

in my thoughts the construction crew built everything they needed on the site; ladders, tables saws, chairs, and shelves. Everything was flowing with ease, so I decided to participate instead of resisting.

As soon as they got set up my, Chinese assistant, Zhang Haitong and I were asked to join them to discuss the project. She helped me communicate my ideas with the construction team. Up until then, I was not sure how I was going to be received by them. It was simple and clear from the beginning. They were asking me to trust them, to believe they would build my project to the best of their ability. I thought about my faults, my desire to find clarity in a world that has its own set of rules and describable outcome. For a moment I was trying to understand something without knowing what it was. I was unable to trust or understand their proposed way of building my design. They suggested to build a piece of it to portray their method and to see if I liked it. After that we would discuss the entire project.

This was a brilliant approach since we were dealing with the real thing now. No more discussions and assumptions. I decided to hang out at the site and see the process for myself, which made everyone a little nervous at the beginning. By the end of the day we we'd created our own language with our eyes and body movements. At the end of the day we had another meeting and I was told that they can't build the project the way I designed it and the way I wanted it or intended to be built. I reached a sensitive moment, characteristic of any collaboration, where I needed to delegate and step back for the benefit of the project. I had to relinquish full control of my work, my child. I had to rely on my faith and logic to direct me to make the best decision, each reliant on the other with the power and momentum of water. It is in that moment when one opens themselves to discoveries and a vast plethora of possibilities come to life.

So instead of asking why, I asked, "How do you think we can build it?" I opened a new vantage point from which to move forward. I became reasonable in my search for a vision of architecture that is meaningful to everyone involved in the process of its making.

That night, from my room's window on the fourteenth floor of Kunlun Hotel I looked out for hours. I was excited about what the next day would be like at the construction site. It was past midnight and I could see the welding sparks of steelworkers in the high-rise buildings across the street. So I thought, "Do my faults define me or the passion I put into them? I am my faults and I am fearful that I might lose myself if I abandon them."

Having things run entirely contrary to our desires, being frustrated in our wishes...

Via De La Paz house

Pacific Palisades is another unique neighborhood in the midst of the sprawling city of Los Angeles, only a few minutes from the Pacific Ocean, with its variety of houses styles on the typical 50x150-foot lots. This house was designed for a family: a couple, their two sons and the mother-In-law.

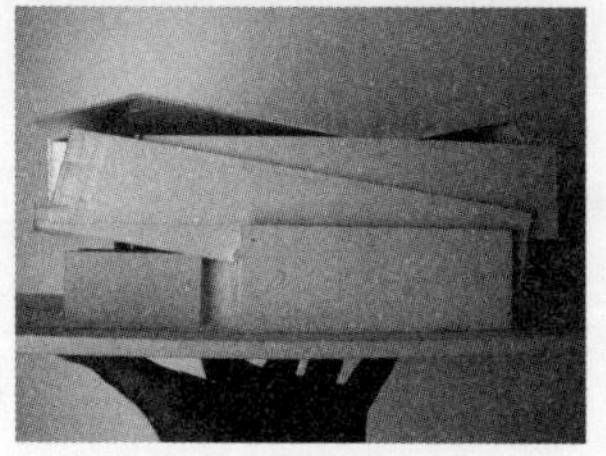

In designing of the Via De La Paz House, (AKA Via House), I was interested to study whether the distinctly separate formal, functional, and structural elements of a house could be independent and yet interact to create a sense of compositional unity. The architectural forms are simple while their juxtaposition and their interaction exposes a rich quality of details and discovery of newfound unpredictable spaces.

The basic organization of this building consists of four masses; two rectangular volumes floating over a rectangular base and one volume that break away from it. The two almost parallel volumes are slightly sloped toward the front and back of the site to accentuate their separation and as the result they create the space where the main entrance and the central staircase are positioned.

The interior spaces and the exterior are distinctly contained and clearly represented in the composition of the building. As one approaches the building the parking garage block is positioned next to the main entrance/living/dining/kitchen, and services. Right above it on the second floor, the self-contained master bedroom suite is located facing the front yard with its glass façade and a private balcony to the back giving the living area below a higher ceiling. Two bedrooms and study cantilever above the garage, which is skinned with wood paneling.

My compositional and formal studies led me to a series of interesting ideas to bring natural light and views into each space and I was able to create a sense of individuality and privacy for each member of the family. The curved central staircase is the heart of the house, leading toward the second

floor. On the right a curved-glass window gives a glimpse of the study, which is flooded with light entering through the floor-to-ceiling windows and skylight. At the top of the landing there is the entrance to the younger son's bedroom. Another four steps leads to the master bedroom suite, and a ramp that leads to the mother-in-law bedroom. All the rooms are independent and have private balconies.

The parking garage location and its relationship to the house, especially on this typical Los Angeles lot where there is only one front entrance, has been one of my greatest design challenges. In most cases I find the garage volume intrusive and disproportionate to the scale of the house itself. In this case I designed the house with the intention to minimize the importance of the garage volume by separating it from the rest of the house and placing the cantilevered mass on top of it.

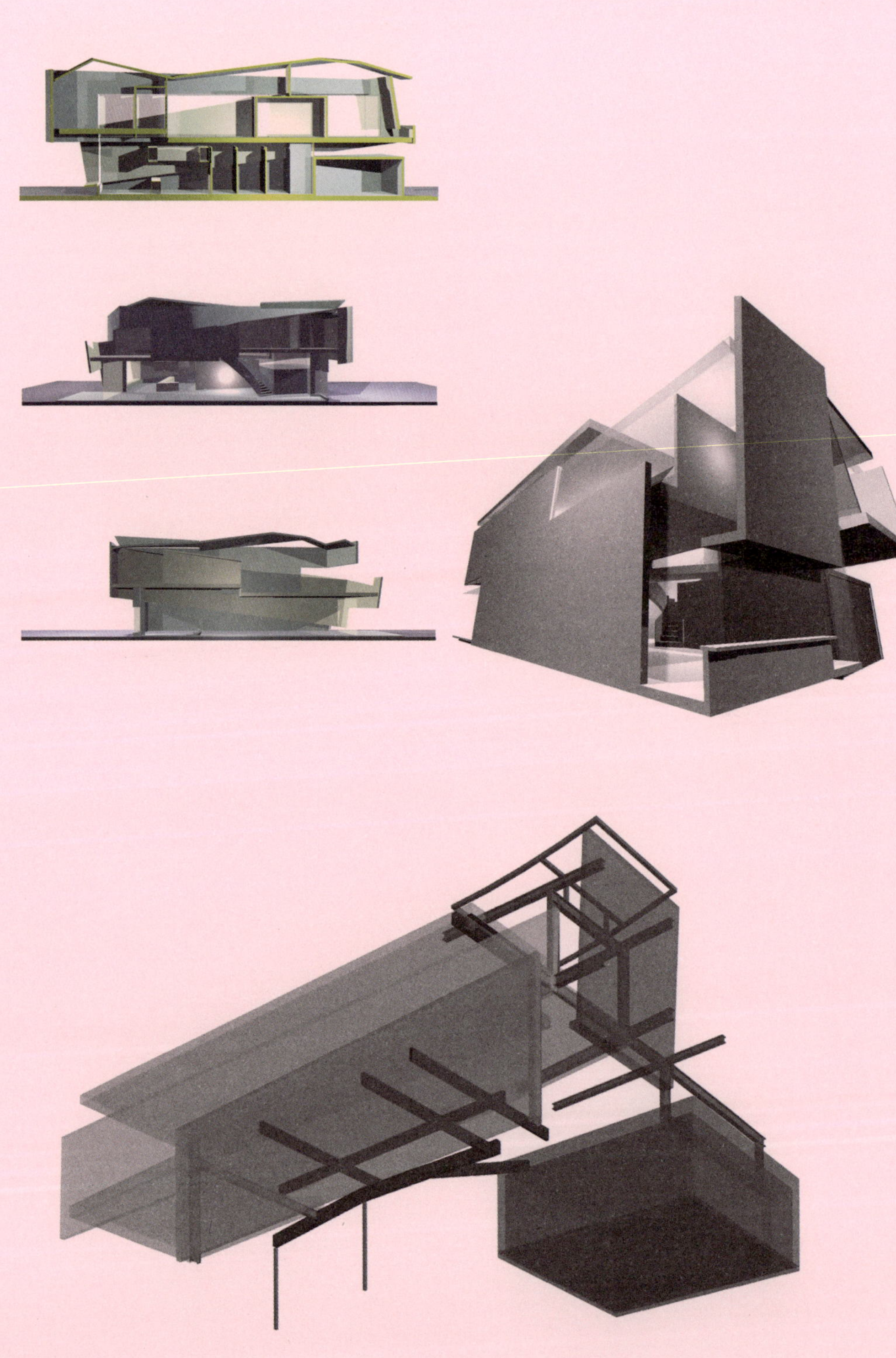

Via De La Paz house

Location:

Pacific Palisades, California, USA

Year:

2005 (built)

Program:

Single family House

For the Via House construction the process was longer than our original estimation because the client changed their mind about the program almost half way through the framing of the house. At the beginning the client wanted to build the house as an investment project but six month into the construction, when they could see and feel the quality of spaces, they decided to move into it themselves when finished.

This decision drastically changed the course of the construction and brought us back to the design stage, and required the revision of the entire construction document and new permits. The re-design and re-structuring to accommodate their new requirements had a chain reaction, sometimes in the areas we didn't even considered in our original design. Other than the obvious physical, form, and material changes, we were now dealing with the concerns of an actual client with very specific needs and emotional specificities. This was a very interesting investigation because I realized how much of the Interactions and process of development is missing from when someone moves into an existing house or apartment, which they simply must and adapt to. The design process for each project or project type is different and when it is a single-family house it becomes more personal since we have to understand the client at a more personal level. We need to know some of the more intimate aspects of their lives and so on.

The physical changes, just to list a few examples, included the front two story wall, which was a solid wall, but which was changed to glass wall to allow light into the living room below and the master bath on the floor above. The study on the second floor used to be a balcony space and it was transformed into the study with a large skylight.

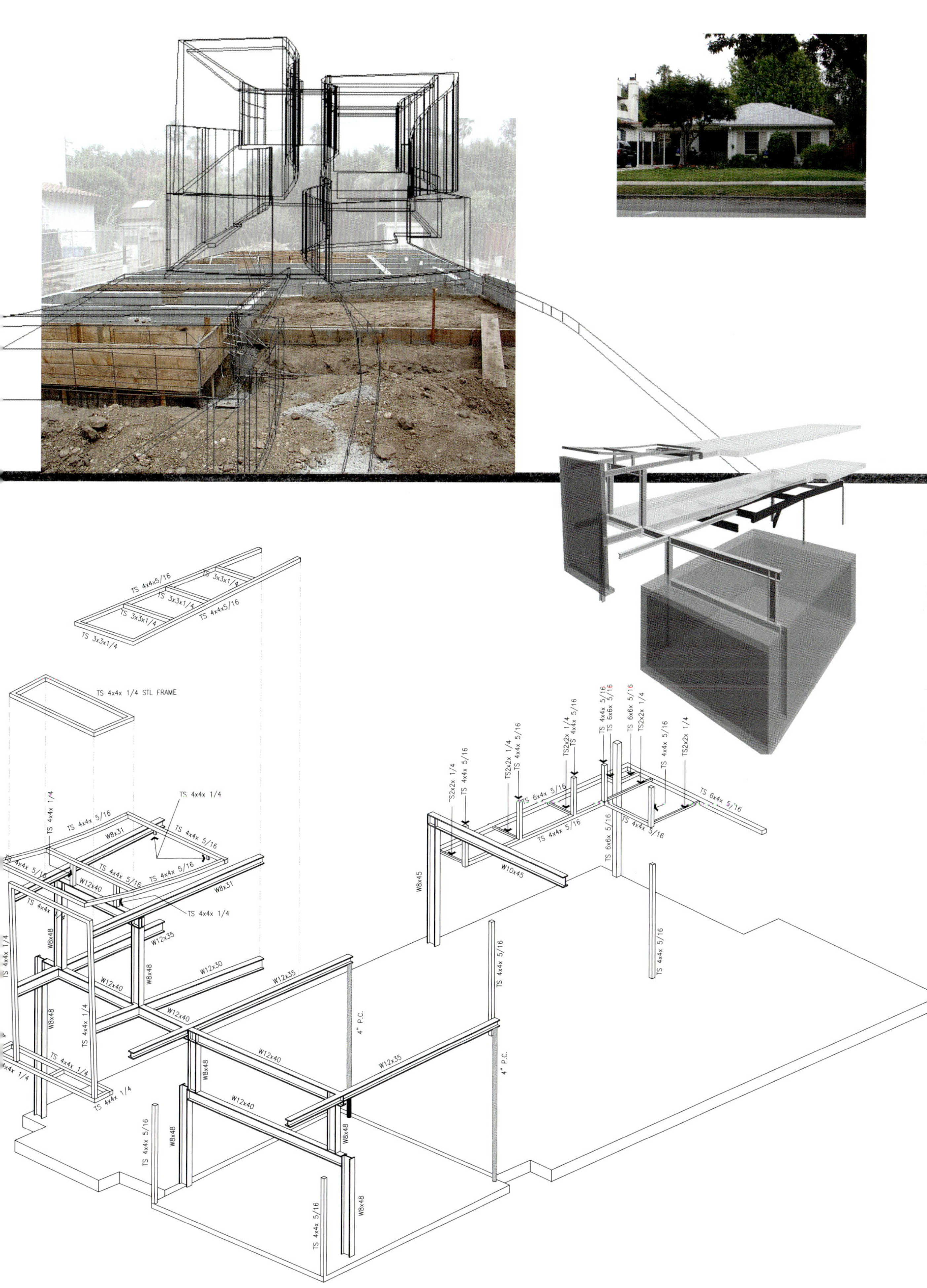

TS 4x4x5/16
TS 3x3x1/4
TS 3x3x1/4
TS 3x3x1/4
TS 4x4x5/16
TS 3x3x1/4
TS 4x4x 1/4 STL FRAME
TS 4x4x 1/4
TS 4x4x 5/16
W8x31
TS 4x4x 5/16
TS 4x4x 5/16
TS 4x4x 5/16
W12x40
W8x31
TS 4x4x 1/4
W8x48
W12x35
W8x48
W12x40
W12x30
W12x35
W12x40
W8x48
TS 4x4x 1/4
TS 4x4x 1/4
W8x48
W12x40
W12x40
4" P.C.
W12x35
4" P.C.
W8x48
TS 4x4x 5/16
W8x48
TS 4x4x 5/16
W8x48
W8x45
W10x45
TS 4x4x 5/16
TS 4x4x 5/16
TS 6x4x 5/16
TS 4x4x 5/16
TS 6x6x 5/16
TS 4x4x 5/16
TS 6x4x 5/16
TS2x2x 1/4
TS 4x4x 5/16
TS2x2x 1/4
TS 4x4x 5/16
TS2x2x 1/4
TS 4x4x 5/16
TS 4x4x 5/16
TS 6x6x 5/16
TS 6x6x 5/16
TS2x2x 1/4
TS 4x4x 5/16
TS2x2x 1/4

The curving-glass walls that enclosed the master suite were solid, and surfaces were highly improved with stone, tiles, windows, and door of high quality. In addition, all the spaces Including bedrooms, bathrooms, closets, etc. needed to be designed with very specific needs for each member of the family. It took about two and half years which based on our estimations took about a year longer than we expected.

I believe to make any meaningful work here in Los Angeles there is resistance and it is extremely difficult. My design process for every project is different. I look at everything that has any relation to the site, program, client, life, etc., and I value the nature of the site—its history and memories and like to use their influences in my design.

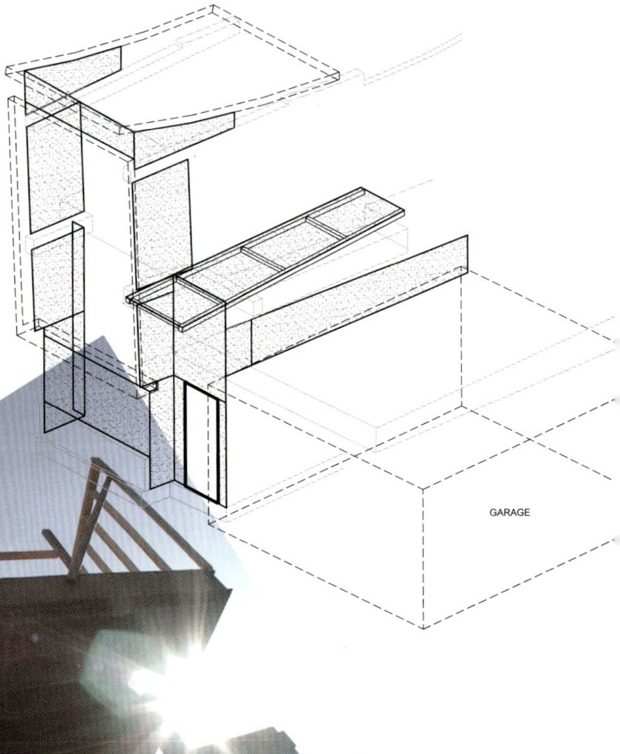

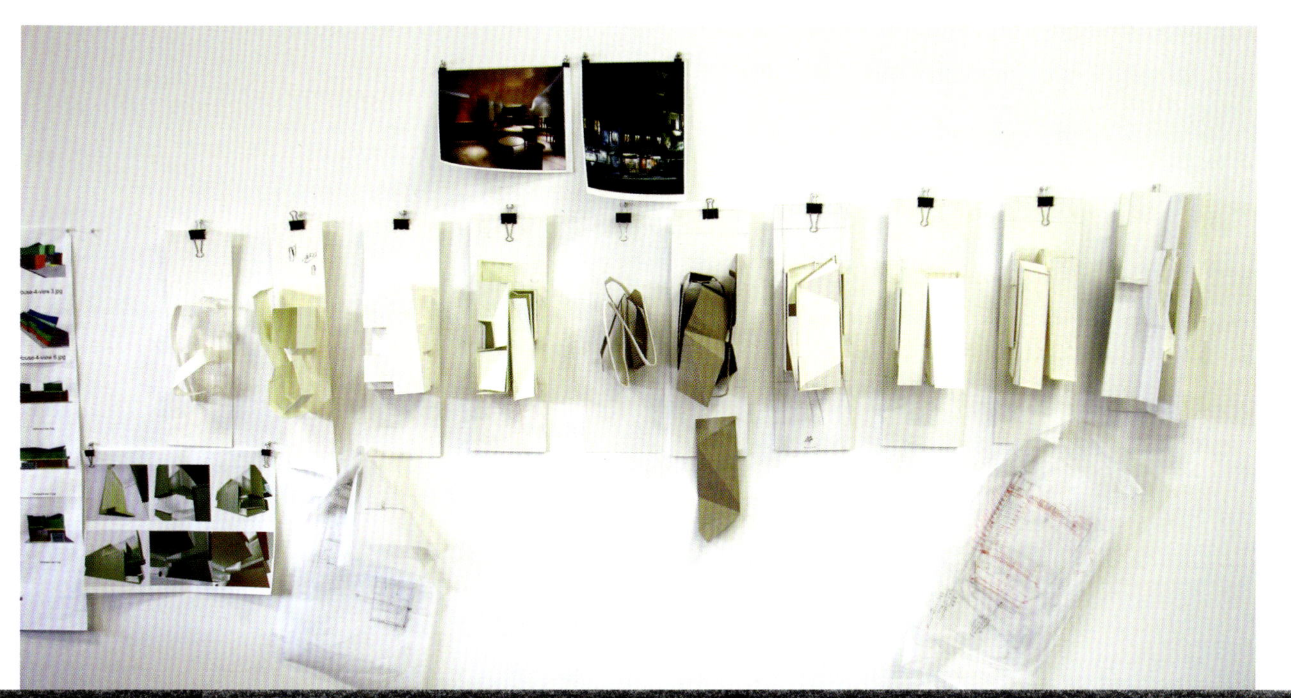

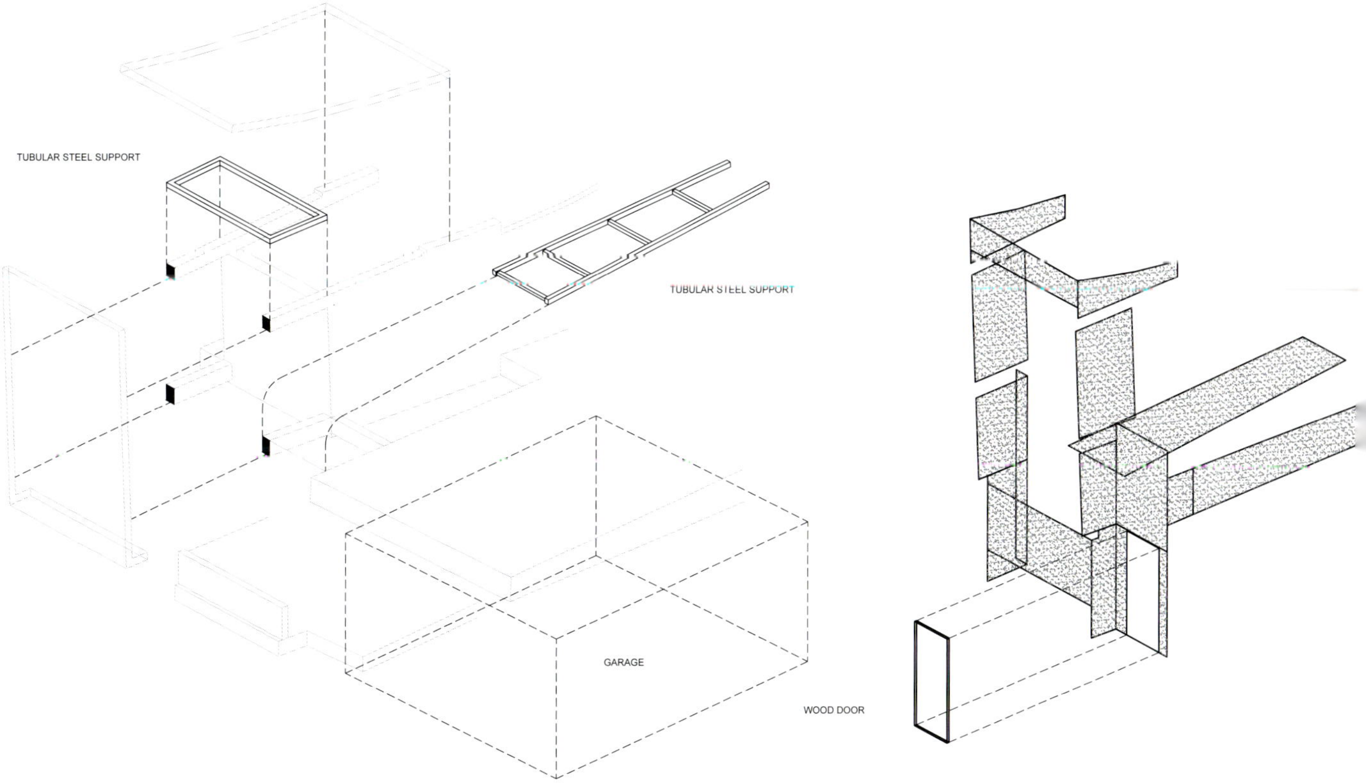

TUBULAR STEEL SUPPORT

TUBULAR STEEL SUPPORT

GARAGE

WOOD DOOR

7
8
8
5
12
8
12
5
7
6
7
5
12
12

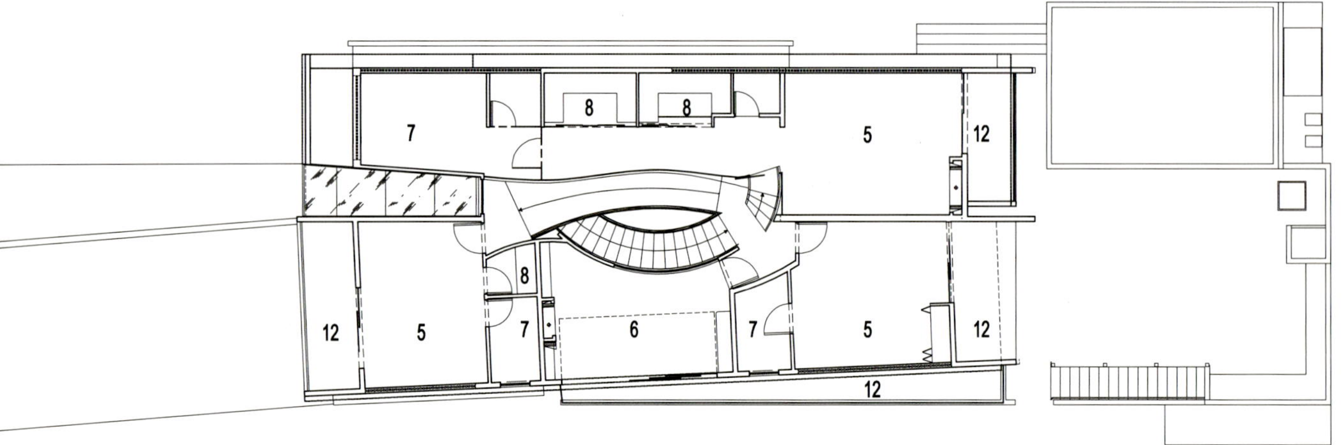

I resist following styles or trends and I don't want my work to be categorized since I believe the work of architecture is rooted in its place with its cultural connections and inspirations.

I am not concerned about styles or trends in design or architecture in my work. In designing in the most highly populated urban settings in the world, especially in Los Angeles, the style is dictated by economics and laws and an architect has to deal with many standardized sets of rules and regulations before being free to creatively reflect on the project: the planning department, building and safety,

SECOND FLOOR PLAN
5 Bed Room
6 Study
7 Bathroom
8 Closet
12 Balcony

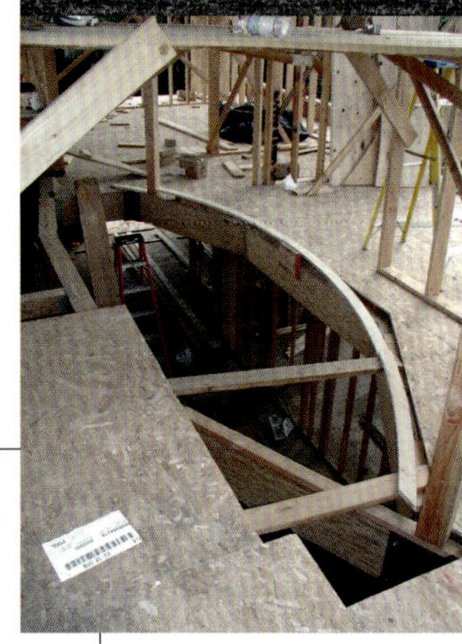

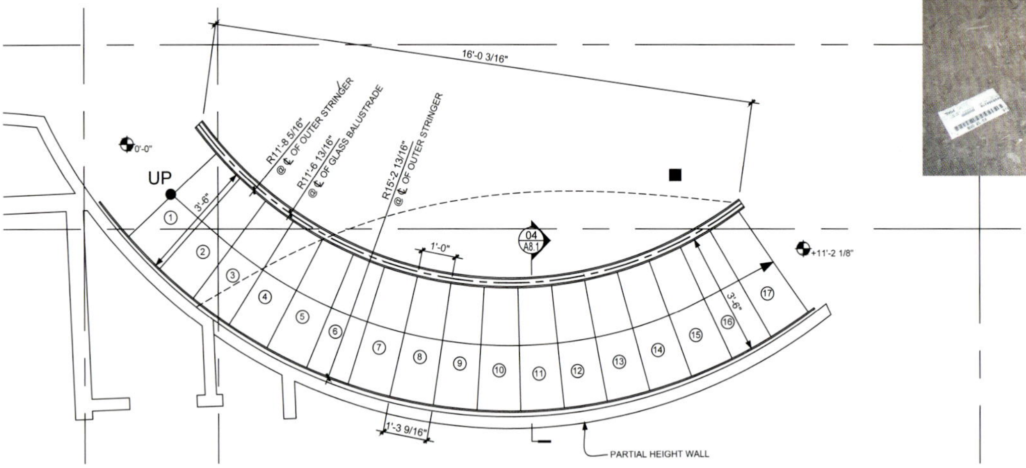

16'-0 3/16"
R11'-8 5/16" @ ℄ OF OUTER STRINGER
R11'-6 13/16" @ ℄ OF GLASS BALUSTRADE
R15'-2 13/16" @ ℄ OF OUTER STRINGER
0'-0"
UP
3'-6"
1'-0"
04
A8.1
+11'-2 1/8"
3'-6"
1'-3 9/16"
PARTIAL HEIGHT WALL

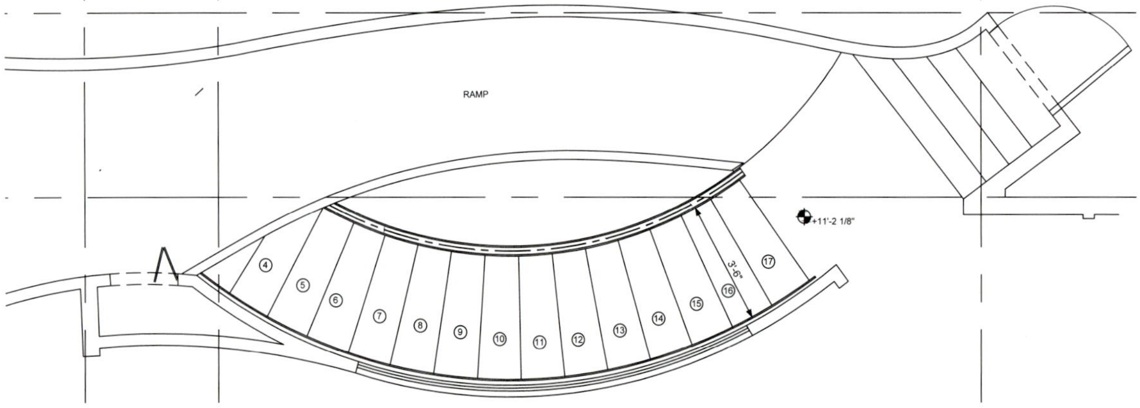

RAMP
+11'-2 1/8"
3'-6"

public works, engineering (Los Angeles is in an earthquake zone), and neighborhood association are just a few examples. This is the reason for the monotonous urban environment here in Los Angeles that shocks most visitors when they visit for the first time.

As the architect of a house I feel it is my responsibility to translate the owner's needs and personality into the design while expressing my ideas and how to interpret theirs into architecture. The client's knowledge of architecture or their artistic sensibility definitely can help in the communication process.

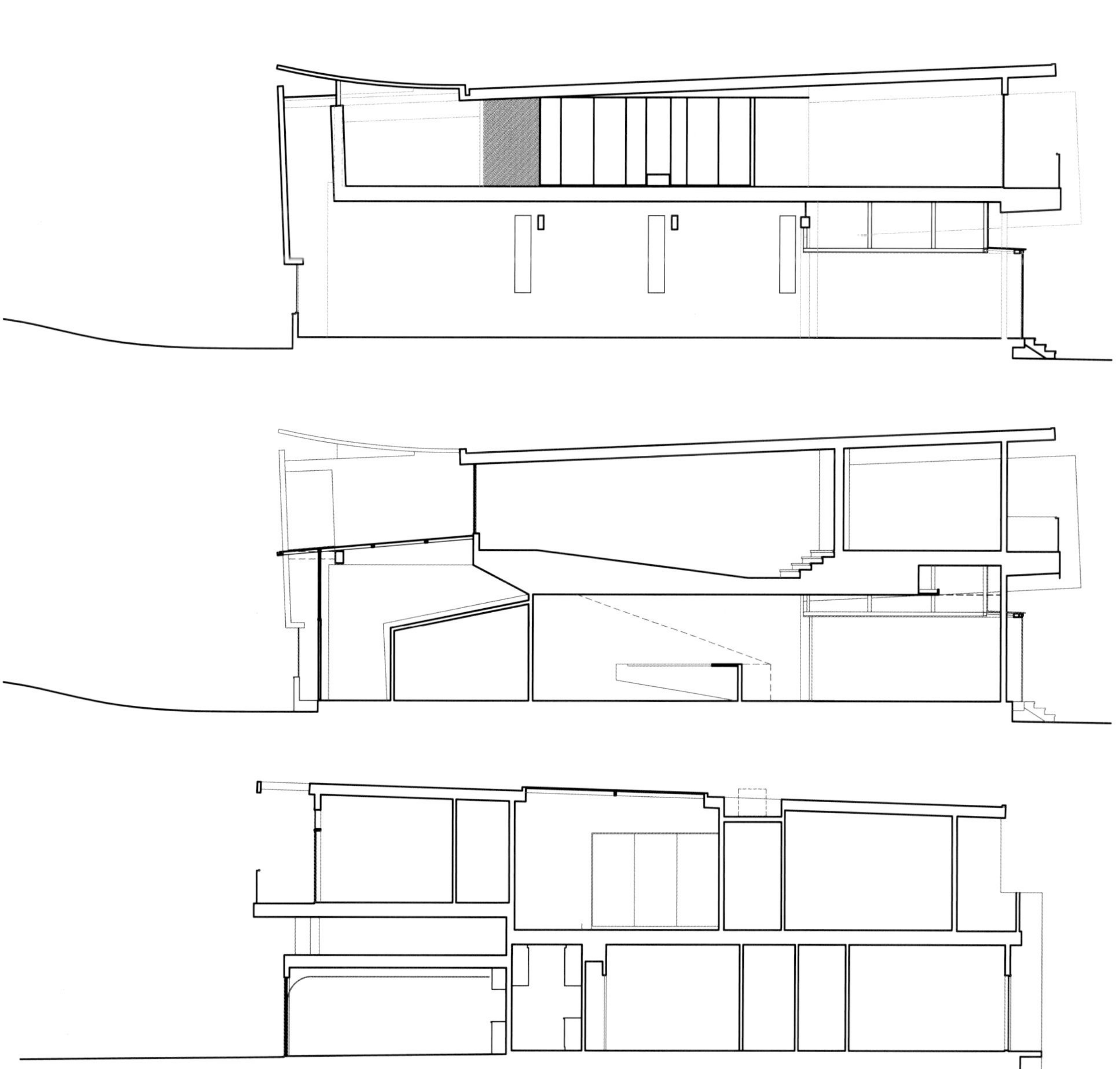

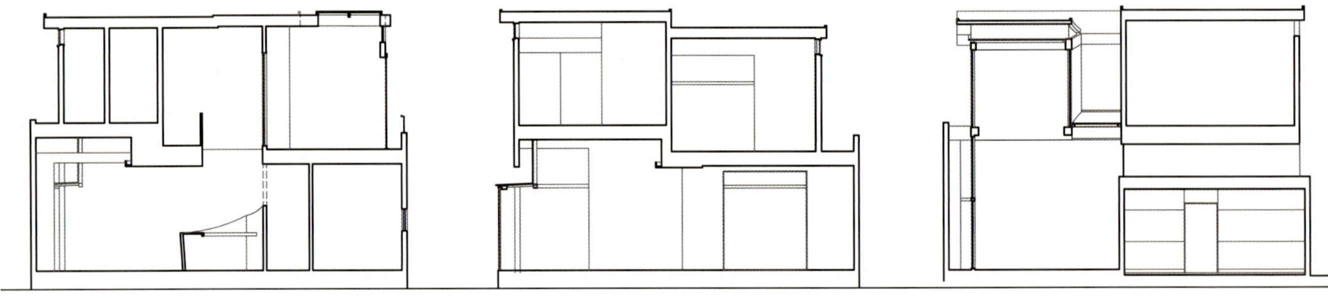

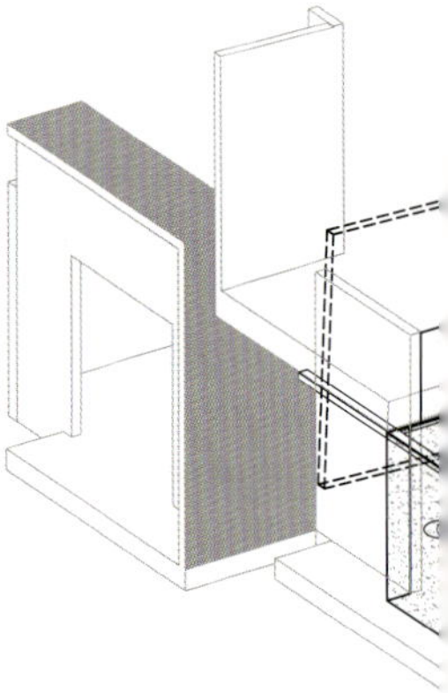

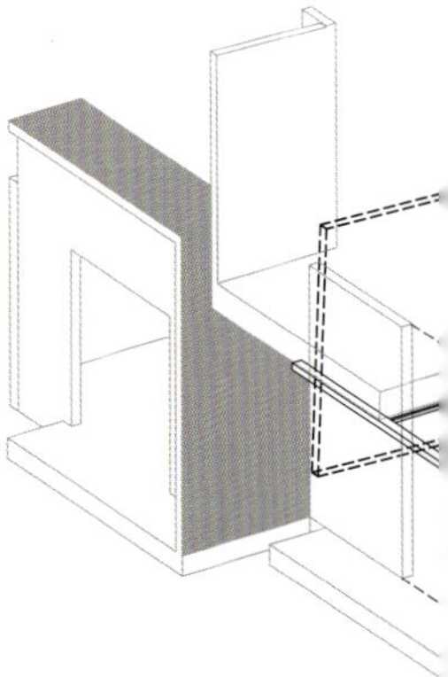

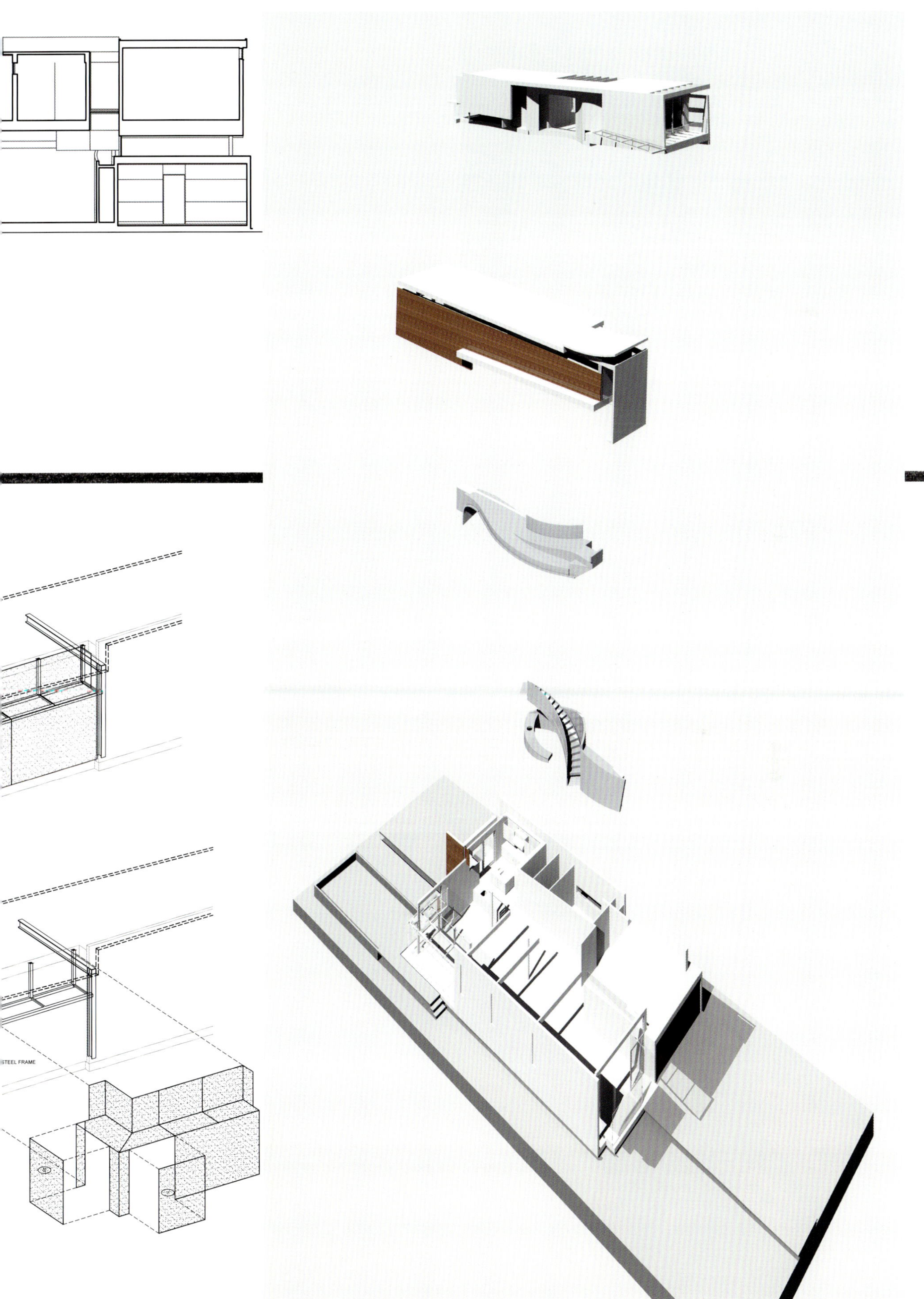
STEEL FRAME

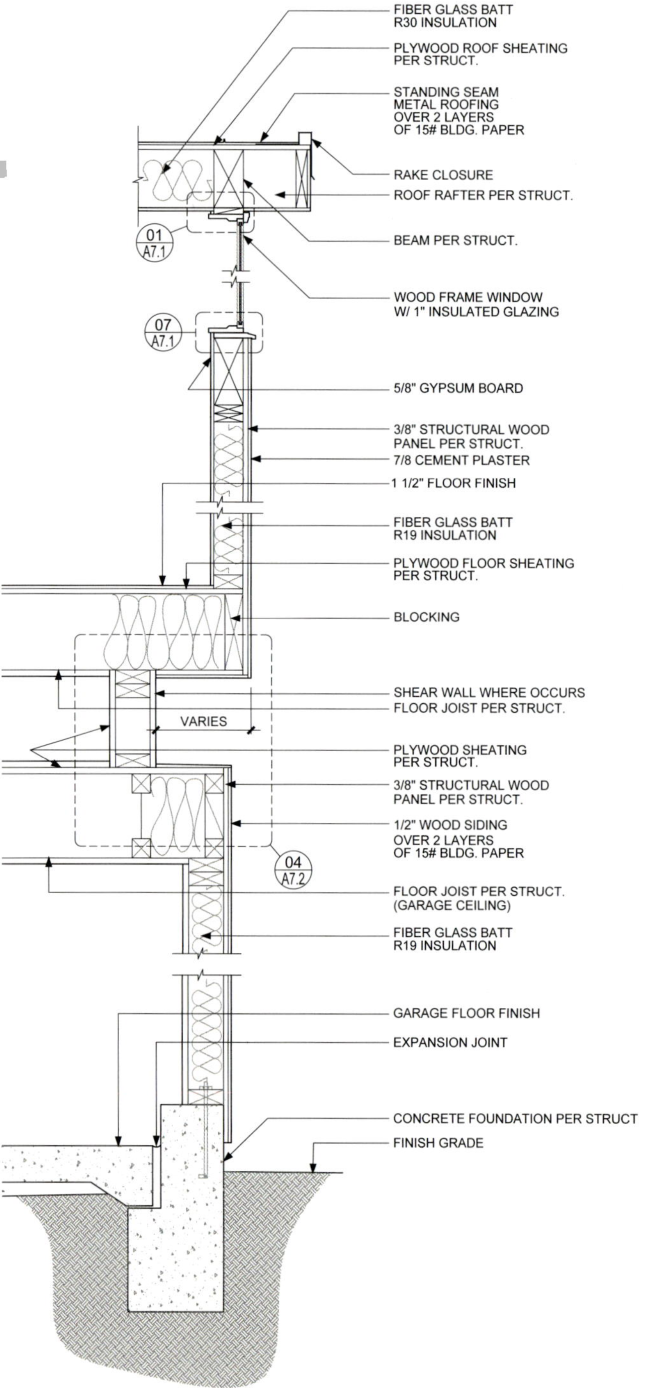
FIBER GLASS BATT
R30 INSULATION
PLYWOOD ROOF SHEATING
PER STRUCT.
STANDING SEAM
METAL ROOFING
OVER 2 LAYERS
OF 15# BLDG. PAPER
RAKE CLOSURE
ROOF RAFTER PER STRUCT.
01
A7.1
BEAM PER STRUCT.
WOOD FRAME WINDOW
W/ 1" INSULATED GLAZING
07
A7.1
5/8" GYPSUM BOARD
3/8" STRUCTURAL WOOD
PANEL PER STRUCT.
7/8 CEMENT PLASTER
1 1/2" FLOOR FINISH
FIBER GLASS BATT
R19 INSULATION
PLYWOOD FLOOR SHEATING
PER STRUCT.
BLOCKING
SHEAR WALL WHERE OCCURS
FLOOR JOIST PER STRUCT.
VARIES
PLYWOOD SHEATING
PER STRUCT.
3/8" STRUCTURAL WOOD
PANEL PER STRUCT.
1/2" WOOD SIDING
OVER 2 LAYERS
OF 15# BLDG. PAPER
04
A7.2
FLOOR JOIST PER STRUCT.
(GARAGE CEILING)
FIBER GLASS BATT
R19 INSULATION
GARAGE FLOOR FINISH
EXPANSION JOINT
CONCRETE FOUNDATION PER STRUCT
FINISH GRADE

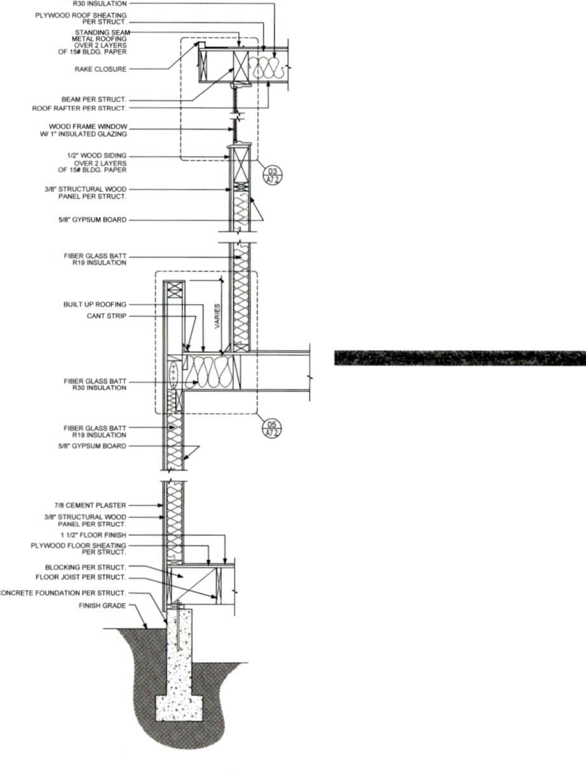
FIBER GLASS BATT
R30 INSULATION
PLYWOOD ROOF SHEATING
PER STRUCT.
STANDING SEAM
METAL ROOFING
OVER 2 LAYERS
OF 15# BLDG. PAPER
RAKE CLOSURE
BEAM PER STRUCT.
ROOF RAFTER PER STRUCT.
WOOD FRAME WINDOW
W/ 1" INSULATED GLAZING
1/2" WOOD SIDING
OVER 2 LAYERS
OF 15# BLDG. PAPER
03
A7.2
3/8" STRUCTURAL WOOD
PANEL PER STRUCT.
5/8" GYPSUM BOARD
FIBER GLASS BATT
R19 INSULATION
BUILT UP ROOFING
CANT STRIP
VARIES
FIBER GLASS BATT
R30 INSULATION
05
A7.2
FIBER GLASS BATT
R19 INSULATION
5/8" GYPSUM BOARD
7/8 CEMENT PLASTER
3/8" STRUCTURAL WOOD
PANEL PER STRUCT.
1 1/2" FLOOR FINISH
PLYWOOD FLOOR SHEATING
PER STRUCT.
BLOCKING PER STRUCT.
FLOOR JOIST PER STRUCT.
CONCRETE FOUNDATION PER STRUCT.
FINISH GRADE

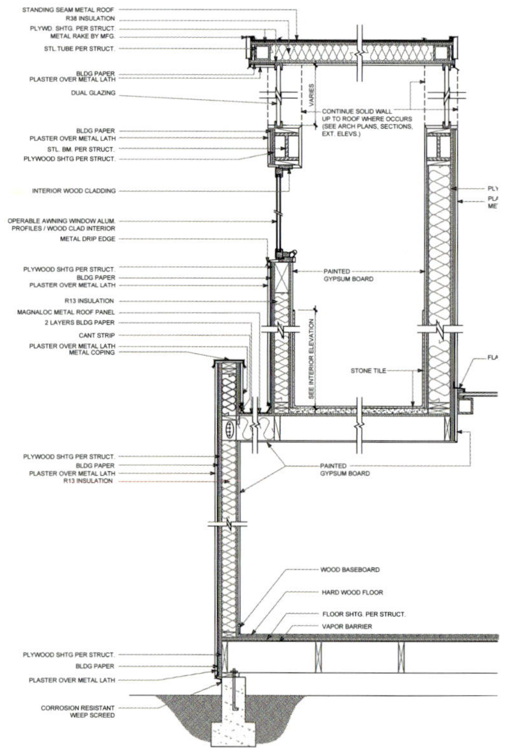
STANDING SEAM METAL ROOF
R38 INSULATION
PLYWD. SHTG. PER STRUCT.
METAL RAKE BY MFG.
STL.TUBE PER STRUCT.
BLDG PAPER
PLASTER OVER METAL LATH
DUAL GLAZING
VARIES
CONTINUE SOLID WALL
UP TO ROOF WHERE OCCURS
(SEE ARCH PLANS, SECTIONS,
EXT. ELEVS.)
BLDG PAPER
PLASTER OVER METAL LATH
STL. BM. PER STRUCT.
PLYWOOD SHTG PER STRUCT.
INTERIOR WOOD CLADDING
OPERABLE AWNING WINDOW ALUM.
PROFILES / WOOD CLAD INTERIOR
METAL DRIP EDGE
PLYWOOD SHTG PER STRUCT.
BLDG PAPER
PLASTER OVER METAL LATH
PAINTED
GYPSUM BOARD
R13 INSULATION
MAGNALOC METAL ROOF PANEL
2 LAYERS BLDG PAPER
CANT STRIP
PLASTER OVER METAL LATH
METAL COPING
SEE INTERIOR ELEVATION
STONE TILE
PLYWOOD SHTG PER STRUCT.
BLDG PAPER
PLASTER OVER METAL LATH
R13 INSULATION
PAINTED
GYPSUM BOARD
WOOD BASEBOARD
HARD WOOD FLOOR
FLOOR SHTG. PER STRUCT.
VAPOR BARRIER
PLYWOOD SHTG PER STRUCT.
BLDG PAPER
PLASTER OVER METAL LATH
CORROSION RESISTANT
WEEP SCREED

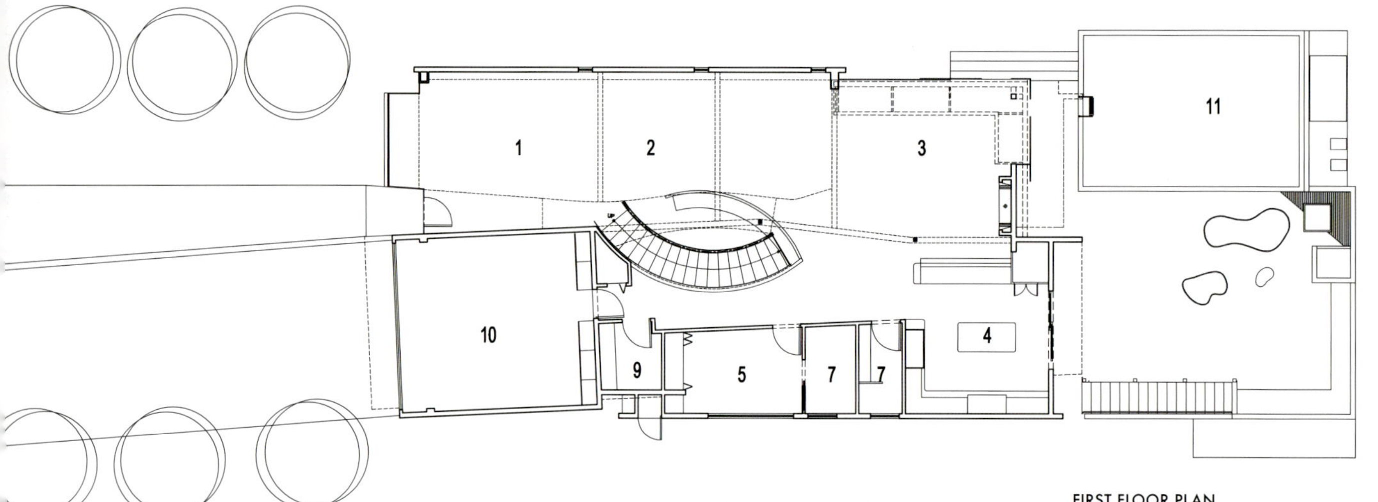

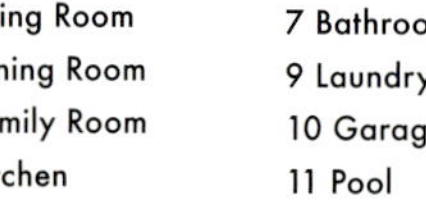

FIRST FLOOR PLAN

1. Living Room
2. Dining Room
3. Family Room
4. Kitchen
5 Bed Room
7 Bathroom
9 Laundry
10 Garage
11 Pool

We must always stick to the difficulties. In our view, the outermost things will be the things we want most and find most easily.

Banda Ache

If only we arrange our life according to that principle which counsels us that we must always hold to the difficult, then that which now still seems to us the most alien will become what we most trust and find most faithful.
— Rilke

Cultures that lose their sense for the right balance between the individual and the community, and for the balance between the natural environment and human habitat, are turning the greatest gift of Nature into its opposite. They destroy the complexity and diversity in Nature and Culture, causing so much disruption that it threatens humans and nature alike.
— Fons Elders

In 2004, I finished Publicis in Paris and had the opportunity to exhibit my work in Venice. It was a dream come true, but soon none of that mattered. All understanding of my security, and therefore freedom, began to crumble once the hopeful images I associated with the world were confronted by destruction of an unimaginable scale. The Indian Ocean tsunami that year massively impacted the the Indonesian province of Aceh and its capital city, Banda Aceh. Reports estimated that over 200,000 people died and one million were affected, attesting to the need for and difficulty of disaster response and relief in Southeast Asia as a whole. I was in my studio when I saw the devastating pictures of the tsunami's aftermath and it hit me in a way that I didn't know was possible. I'd wake up from nightmares of drowning, and re-evaluated my work and my motives as an architect. I was proud of my accomplishments, but something was missing.

Banda Ache

Location:
Banda Ache, Indonesia

Year:
2006 (not built)

Program:
Prefabricated Housing

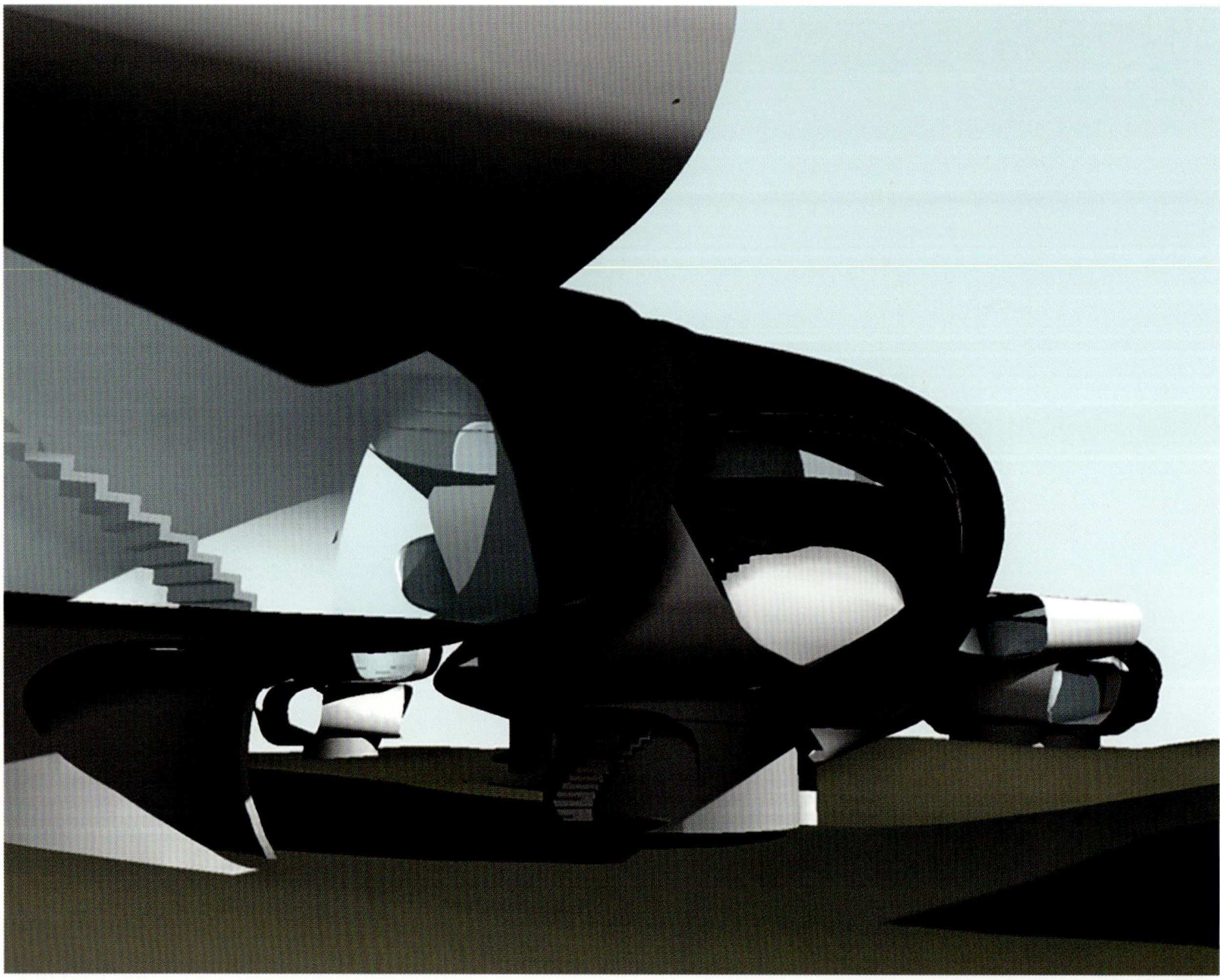

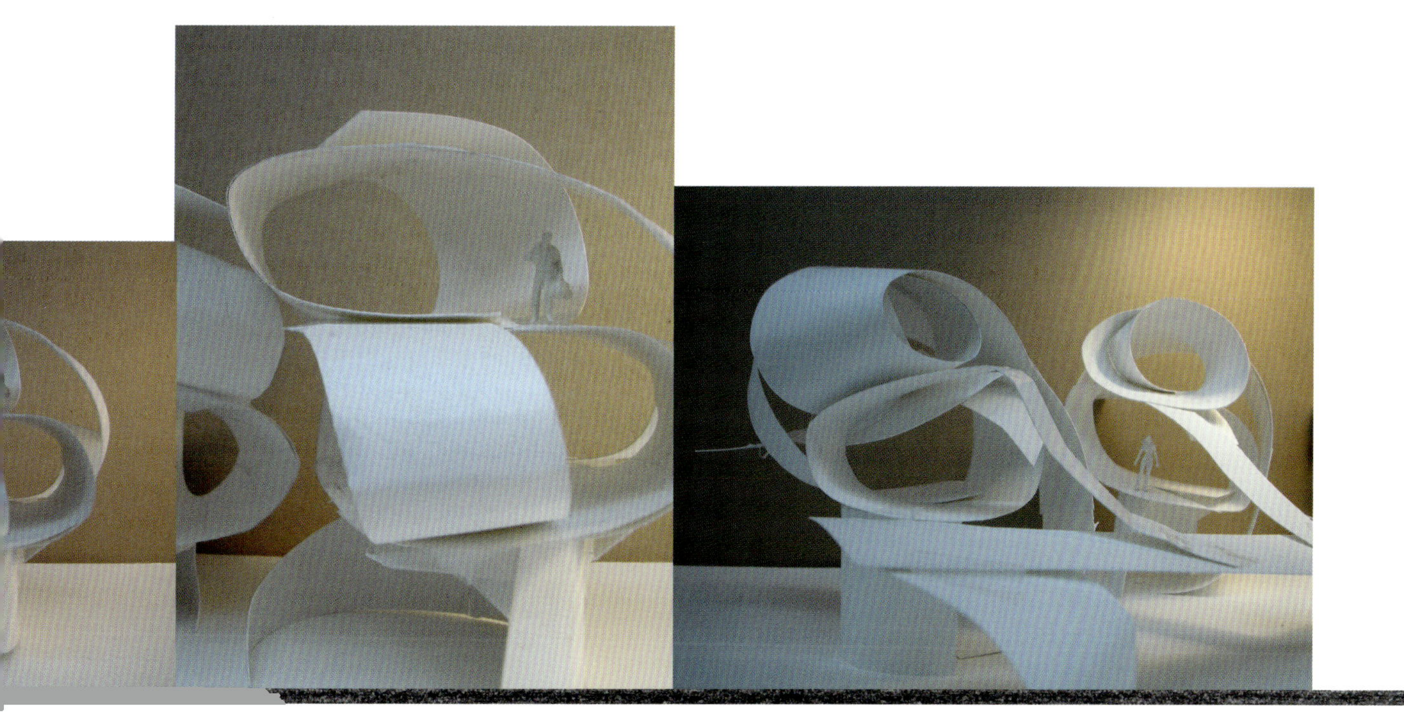

I was well aware of my limited abilities as an architect, especially when so much work needed to be done before architecture could begin, but I wanted to get involved in the only way I knew how. I wanted to help people become more aware of how we can propose a new relationship between architecture and the environment in the time of crisis. Most people weren't aware of the meaningful effects architectural design could have on their lives. That being said, the profession is also to blame for this ignorance. It has been a historic problem, both in terms of architectural culture and professional practice, that needs to be addressed with education and action in order to resolve these fundamental issues. As architects it is our ethical duty to educate the public about the importance of healthy space in our daily lives because this was not the first tsunami and I knew it wouldn't be the last. I was overwhelmed with the urgency for expression. I needed to act, to face the issues concerning our changing environment.

Rebuilding helps healing

Our harmonious interaction with our living environment is like a dance between body and space. A continuous dialogue is created between the building's habitants and the buildings themselves. The energy of this interaction can develop a contemporary landscape of hope for a community of world citizens coming together.

For the proposed design and construction in Banda Ache, I looked at the natural environment and indigenous methods of architecture. The past was my teacher as I found how the local Indonesian culture was able to make the most complex structures with the simplest materials, but I'd ask myself, "Would I want to return to a bamboo and fiber hut after witnessing destruction?" I decided to take what I thought was useful from the traditional architecture and design and to use it to react to the current conditions.

Our proposed architectural solution took the shape of river pebbles to form a village-like environment. The dynamic shapes of the units were made of prefabricated, light concrete components that could be erected quickly to be used and occupied. All units were constructed on stilts, which reduced the building's carbon footprint, protected it from moisture, and allowed it to absorb shock waves.

All the parts would be fabricated off site and delivered to be installed. The simplicity of the construction system would be an asset in the circumstances. The buildings could be quickly erected in any weather. The prefabricated building components include the foundation system of stilts, floors, walls, and roof elements with a compact shared core system component for utilities. The buildings use of passive systems for ventilation, lighting, and heating reduces the negative environmental impact. The interior space is flexible and gives the owners the ability to modify their unit with movable, lightweight partitions, while using locally fabricated furniture and materials. A number of templates are proposed, so each owner can customize their homes.

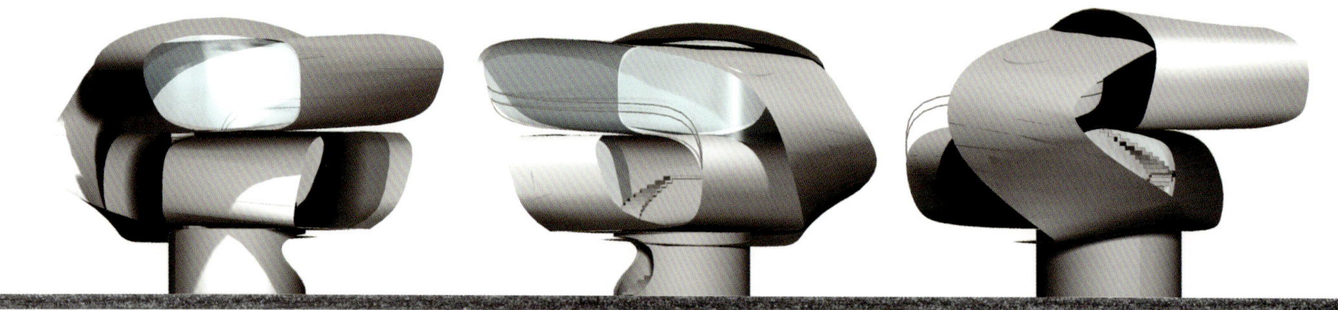

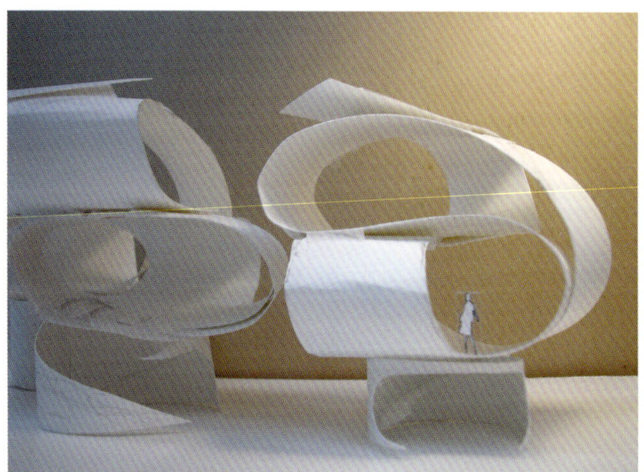

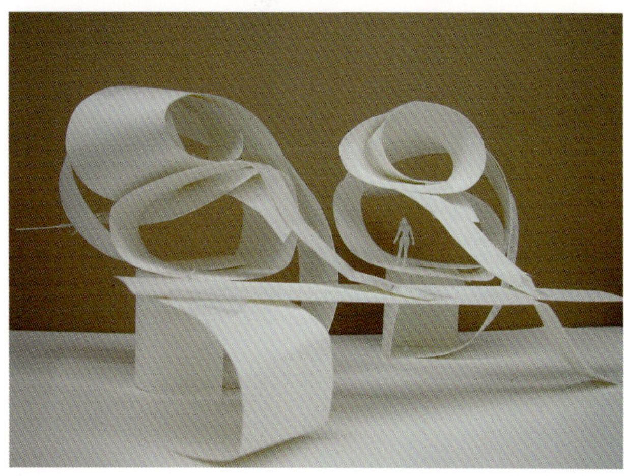

It is our intention to express both symbolically and experientially the coming together of the world in peace and harmony.

Paris Landmark

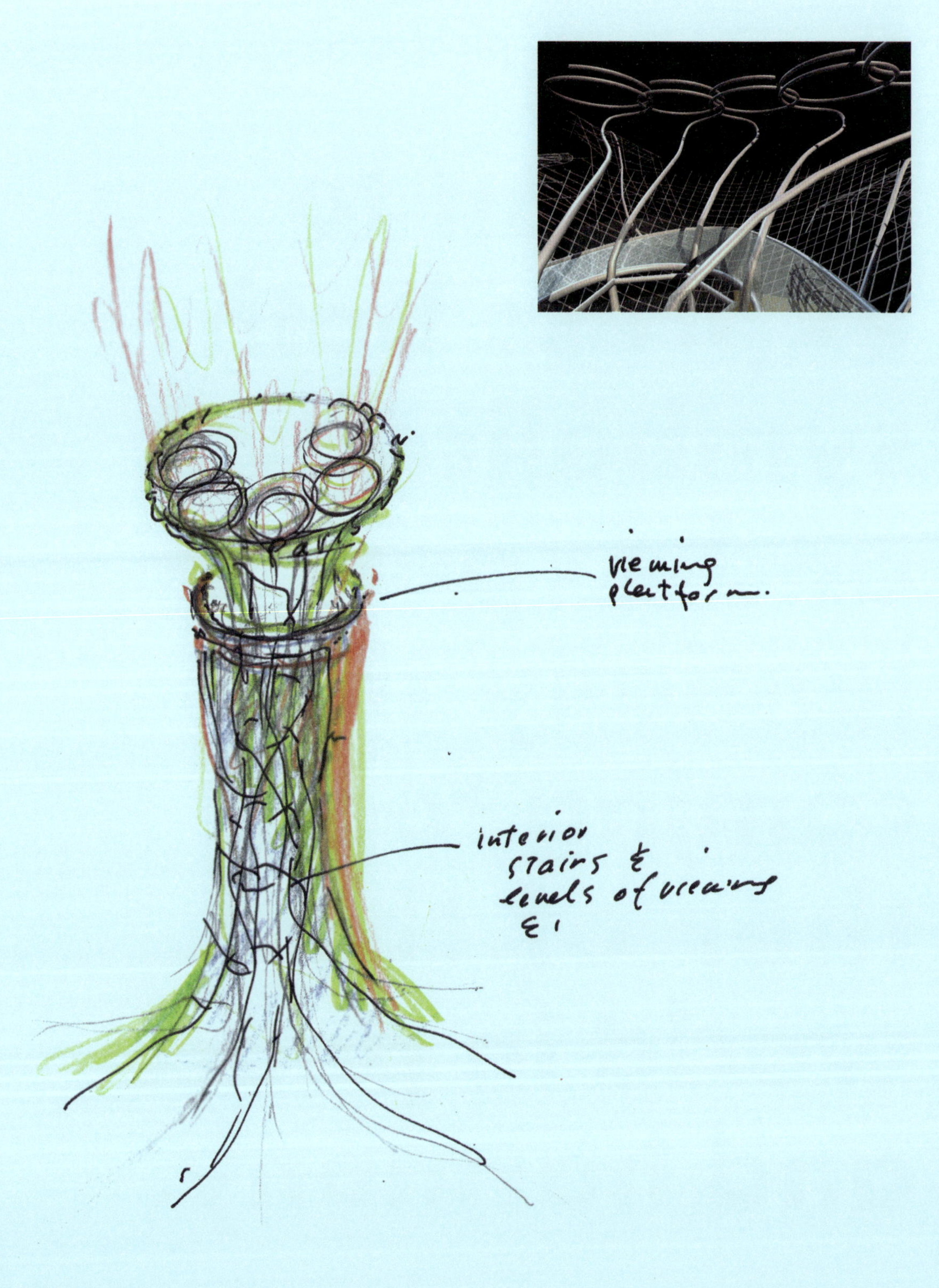
viewing platform.
interior stairs & levels of viewing

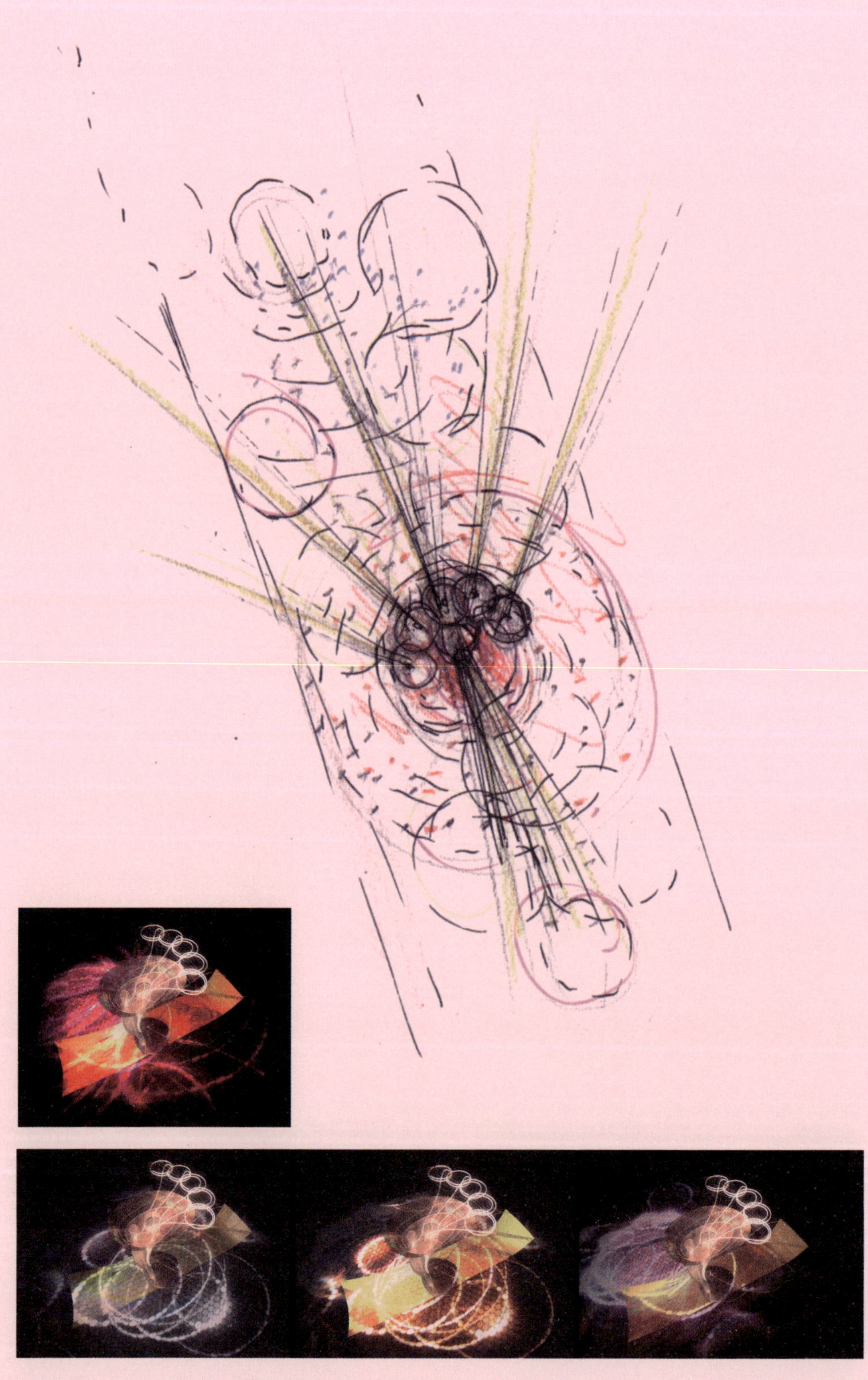

Paris Landmark

Location:
Paris, France

Year:
2005 (not built)

Program:
Olympic Landmark, and Event Space

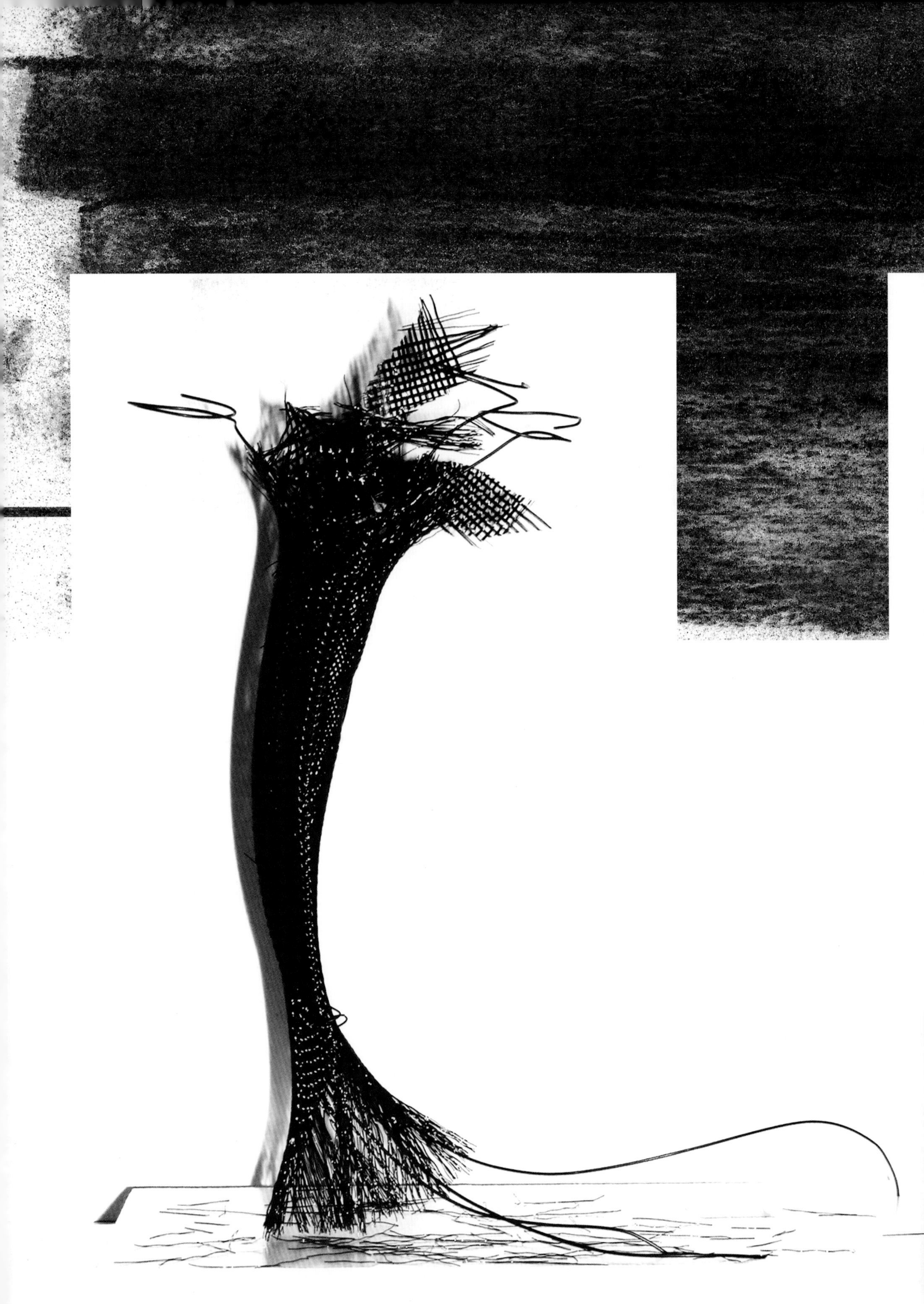

The Olympic Landmark proposal draws its inspiration from the ubiquitous Olympic rings, representing the union of the five continents and the meeting of athletes from throughout the world. The project was intended to express both symbolically and experientially the coming together of the world in peace and harmony. The structure is composed of five independent spines of steel that intertwine and spiral up from the ground into a viewing platform 27 meters high, allowing panoramic views of the Olympic village and the city of Paris. The five spines terminate at the top, forming the five Olympic rings. Attached within the rings are automated light fixtures that beam a spectrum of colors and provide for an array of light shows. The spiraling structure is wrapped in a metal mesh functioning as a translucent screen for projecting images. At the base of the landmark is the Olympic Plaza, an elevated landscape providing a clear zone for gathering. The rectangular plaza tilts upwards at both ends, celebrating the entrance to the Olympic village and announcing the gateway to the venue.

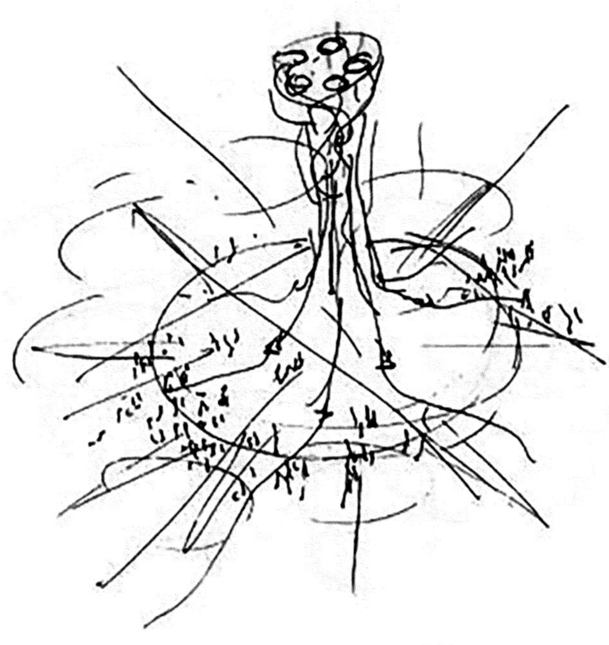

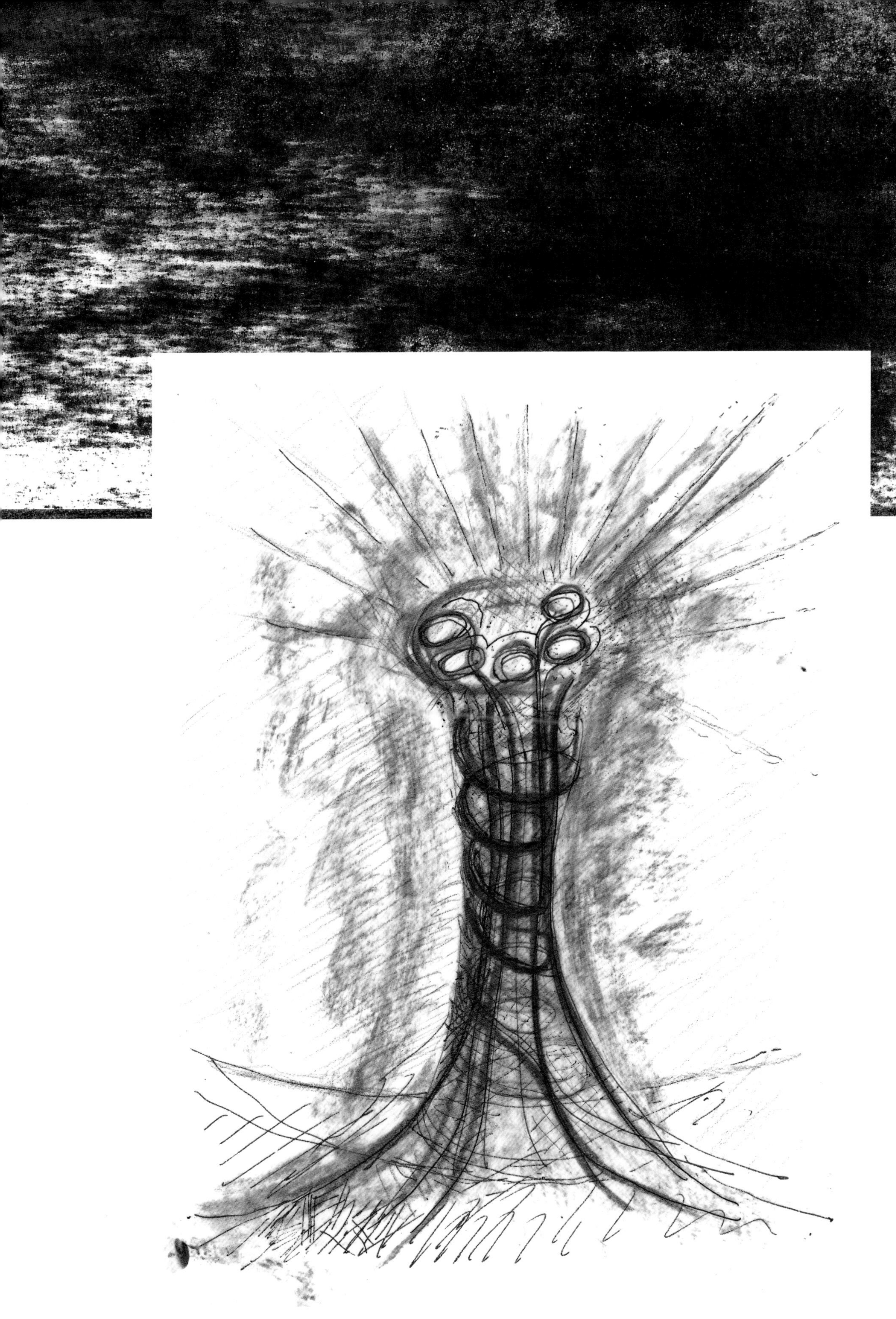

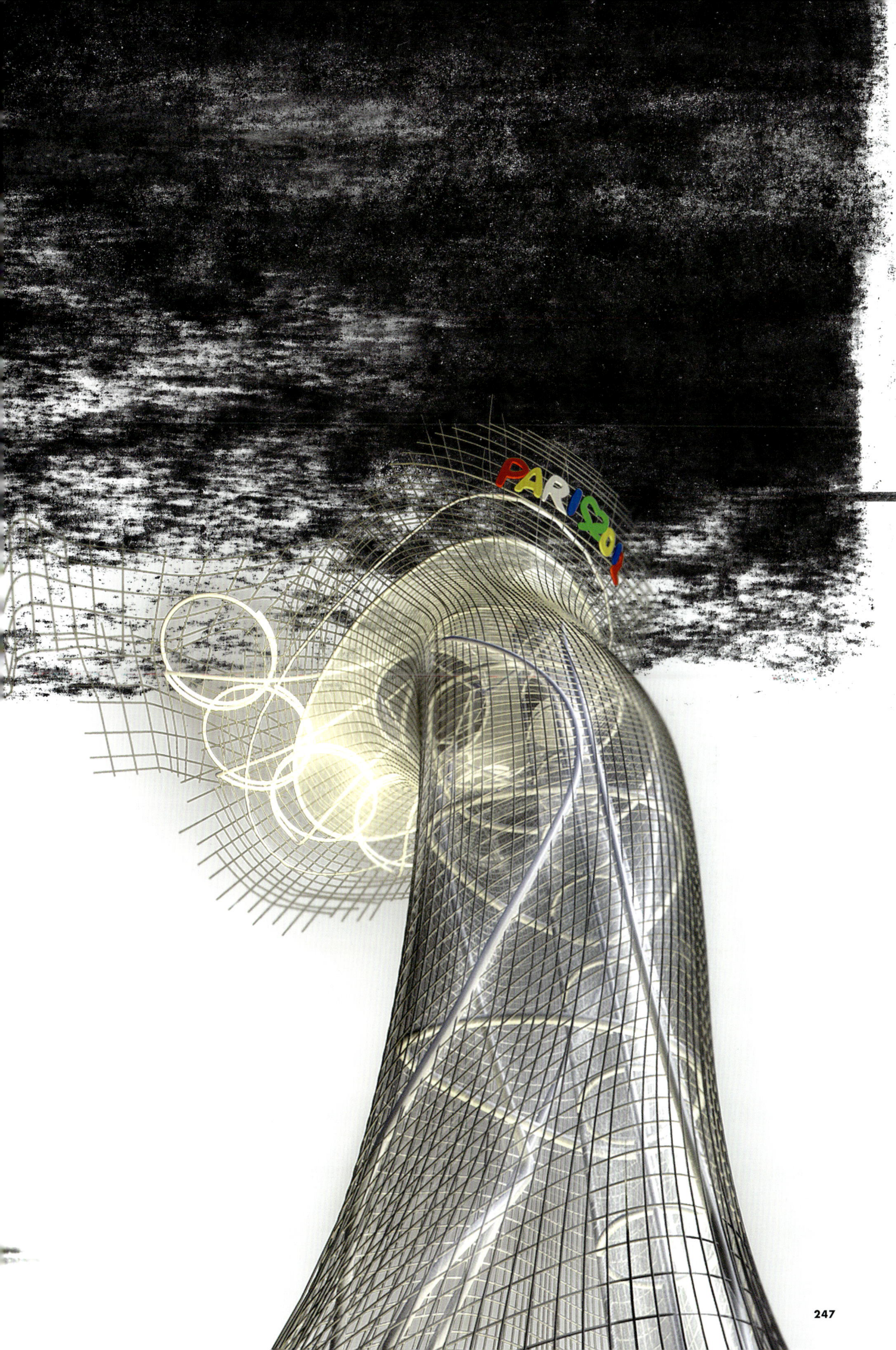
PARIS2012

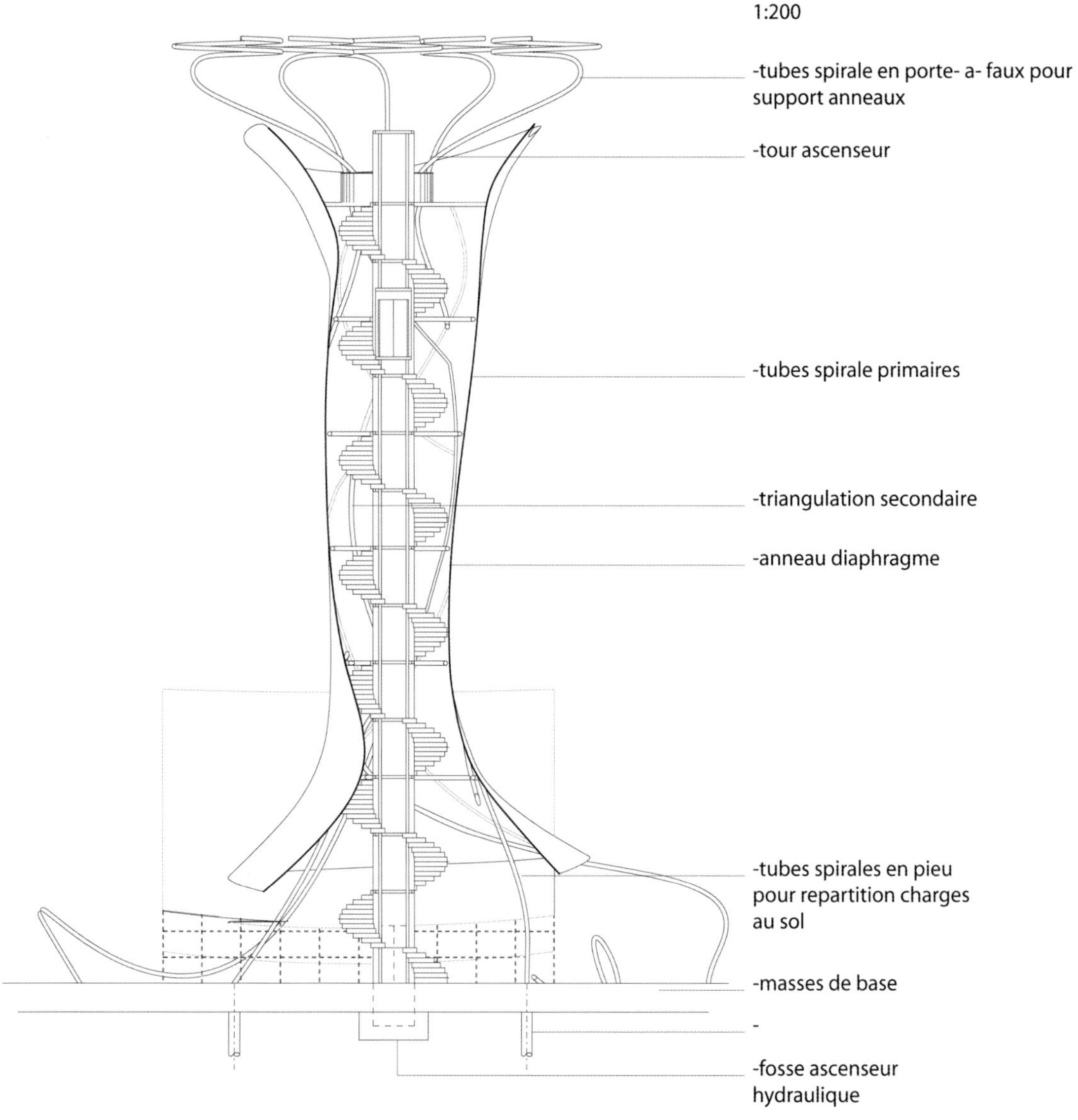

1:200

-tubes spirale en porte- a- faux pour support anneaux

-tour ascenseur

-tubes spirale primaires

-triangulation secondaire

-anneau diaphragme

-tubes spirales en pieu pour repartition charges au sol

-masses de base

-

-fosse ascenseur hydraulique

Our memory is our coherence, our reason, our feeling, even our action. Without it, we are nothing...

by Luis Bunuel

Museum of Antiquity

Michele Saee's drawing inspired by Marc Antoine Laugier "The Primitive Hut."

Museum of Antiquity

Location:
Beijing, P.R. China

Year:
2006 (built)

Program:
Exhibition of Antique Buildings, Furniture, and Objects

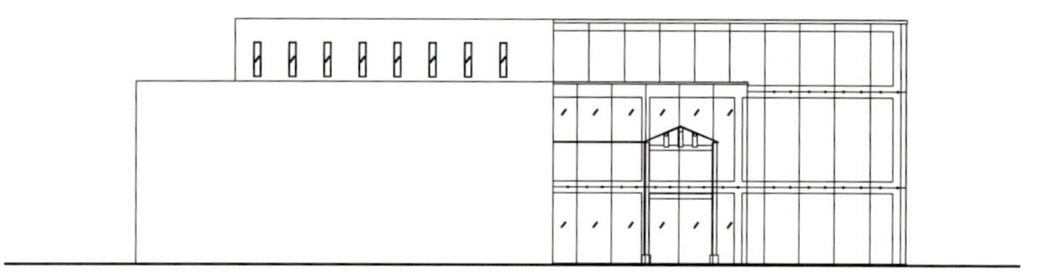

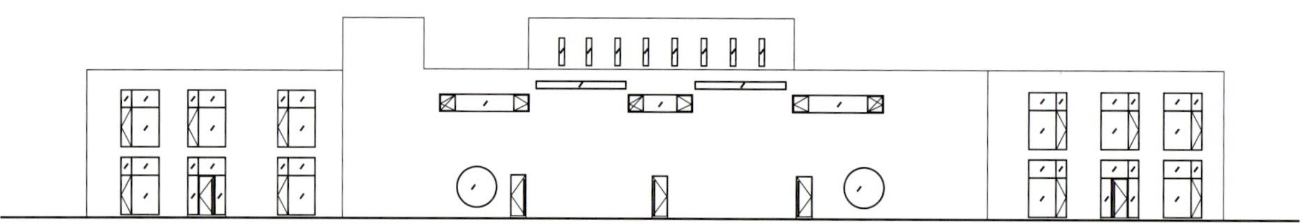

There have been moments in my life where I've visited certain buildings and could hear them breathe. They would listen to me and in return tell me their stories. It has led me to believe that buildings possess the ability to participate in their design and in the selection of their materials. In the mid-seventies I was in Barcelona where I met the Sagrada Familia by the master Spanish architect Gaudi. Before visiting, I knew of Gaudi's work mainly from publications. It was a surreal experience for a variety of reasons.

The main facade of the building was featured with its monumental towers and their sculptural organic shapes and material. The images were intentionally showing what was built and not telling the whole story. The nave or the crossing of the church was not built. The surrounding neighborhood appeared much smaller because of the grand scale of the front façade. It was quiet and desolate. A few kids where playing in the front area and a group of old men were sitting around chatting and smoking. I was surprised because there was no one there to guard or tour the premises. So, like every other curious architecture student, I went in and started to wander around. The building was floating in time. It felt like a building that was in the state of destruction due to its architectural style. It seemed to be decaying because it was abandoned, but in reality it was in the process of completion.

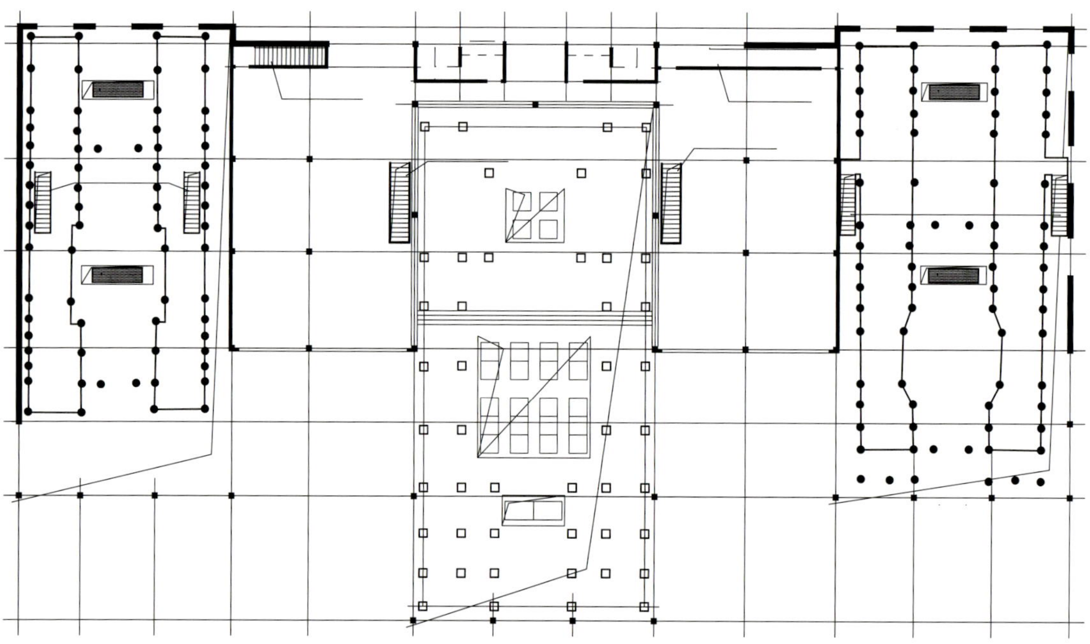

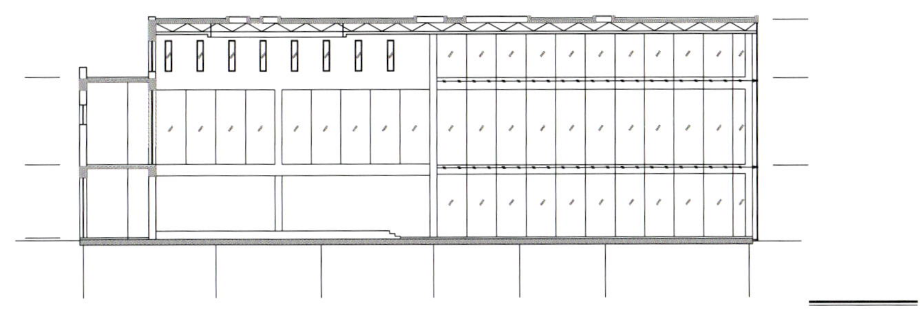

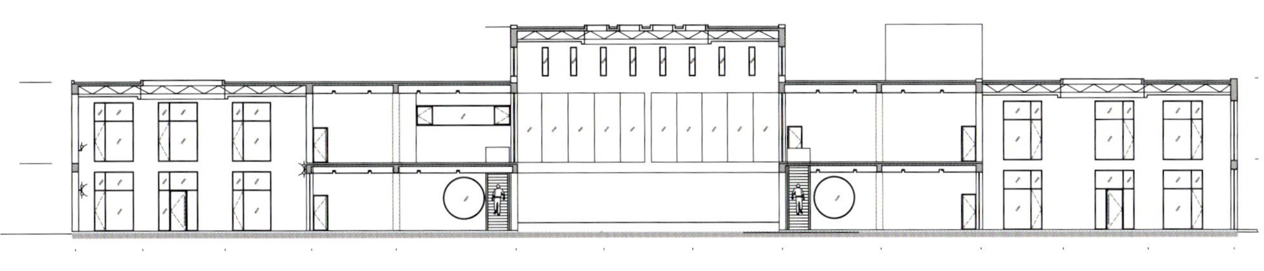

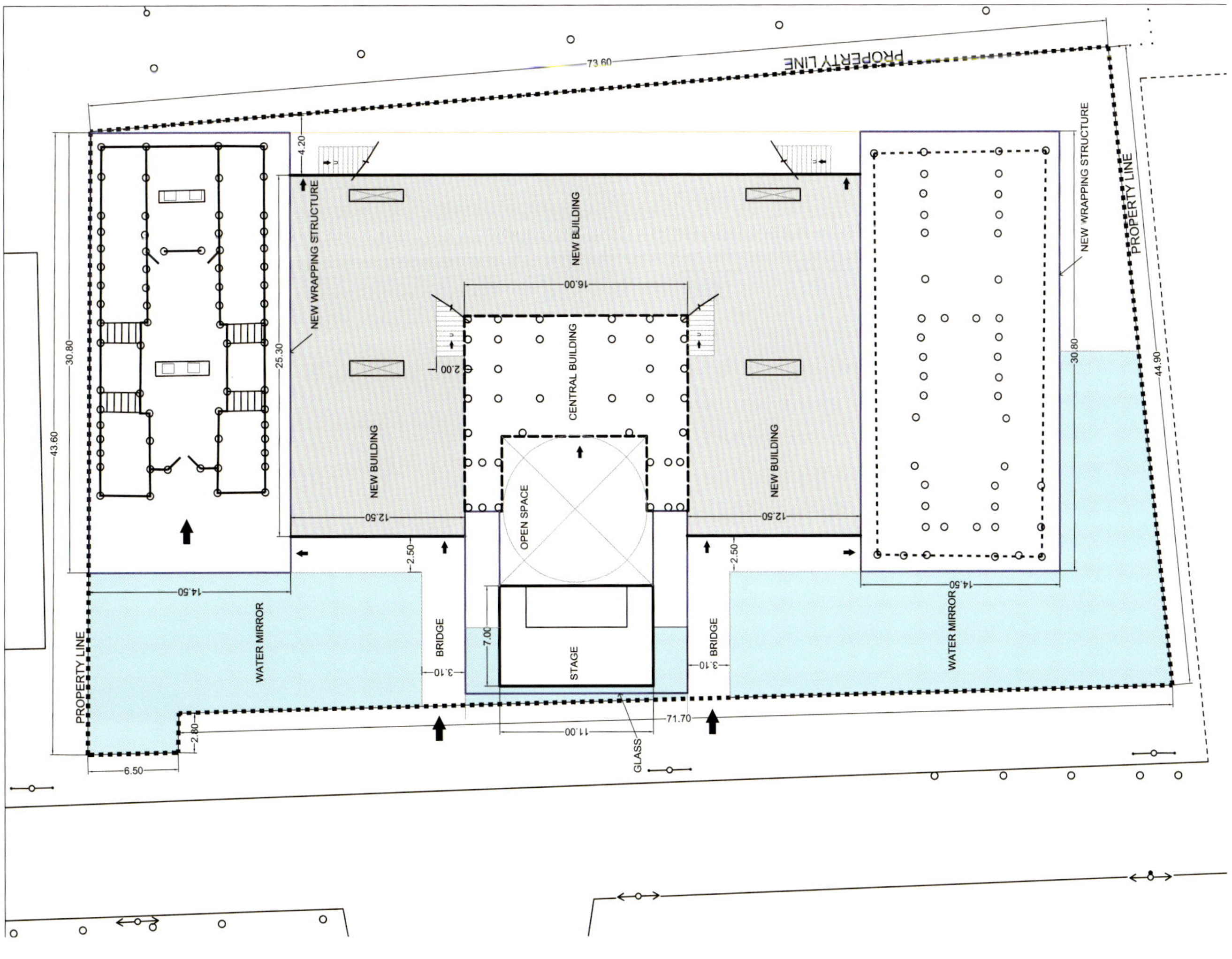

PROPERTY LINE
73.60
NEW WRAPPING STRUCTURE
NEW BUILDING
16.00
CENTRAL BUILDING
2.00
NEW BUILDING
NEW BUILDING
12.50
12.50
OPEN SPACE
4.20
25.30
30.80
43.60
2.50
2.50
14.50
WATER MIRROR
BRIDGE
3.10
7.00
STAGE
BRIDGE
3.10
WATER MIRROR
14.50
30.80
44.90
NEW WRAPPING STRUCTURE
PROPERTY LINE
PROPERTY LINE
2.80
6.50
71.70
11.00
GLASS

When I think about architecture and materials, I visualize the multiplex construct of the body. The bones, muscles, nerves, and skin with their very precise shapes, their interlocking joints and functions reminds me of the building's organization. Columns and beams act as structural elements that balance the body and give it stability. The functions of the electrical, mechanical, plumbing, and informative systems spaces serve the body similarly to how muscles and the nervous system create a sense of comfort and ability. Finally, the skin, which like the building's façade, surfaces, finishes, and materials, covers our bodies and protects us in our environment.

In my own work, I am constantly in search of new materials and different approaches to construction. It sometimes appears unstable, almost in a state of continual becoming, an assembly of fluctuating sculptural forms of materials, which interact with light and with their context. This is the result of reacting or responding to the context, which is becoming more and more complicated, and continues to challenge architects in every aspect of our lives and creativity.

Therefore, when my client Mr. Wang, an antique dealer passionate about the antique buildings in Anhui Province, China, asked me to design a building using two houses and a theater from the Qing dynasty, I accepted without any hesitation. I was on a path similar to the one in Barcelona. I was given buildings that were detached from their sites and no longer had any specific purpose. Their original use was in a state of becoming based on the best possible proposal.

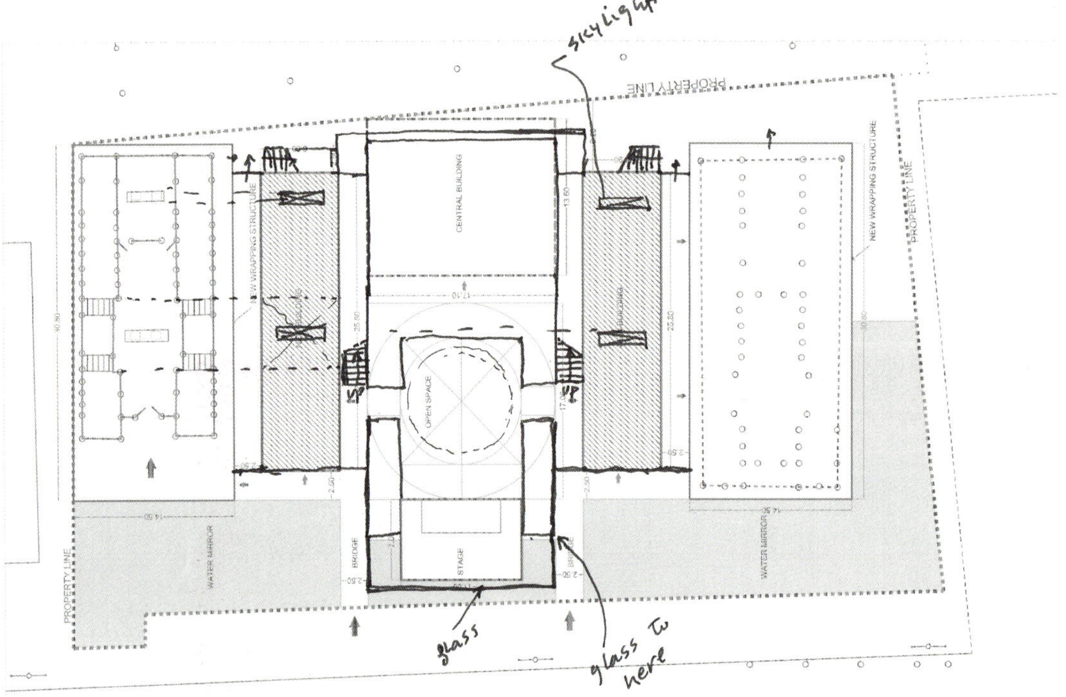

Silent in their appearance they were loud in exerting their will through their materials and structural order. They felt damaged and exhausted by the natural elements—their use and abuse of time. It was a hot summer day when we first visited the location. The old wooden building parts, columns, and beams were resting on the ground. At the first glance one could see clearly from their intricate carvings and details that they could have been homes of nobility. And now their pride and glory was dismantled in pieces. The buildings looked weak and humble, dusty, ravaged by the elements of nature and human (ab)use. This was just another stage in their growth since, after a few months, they were erected to their original positions. With their beautiful carvings and flying roves they began to reveal the passage of time and share the stories hidden in them for hundreds of years. I had many interactions with those buildings as they were being restored and discovered new thoughts when I was at the site. They were once beaten and misplaced, but their spirit was always alive.

In the design of the Museum of Antiquity, memory becomes the indication of synthesis for architectural space. One person's memory becomes another person's dream or "reality." I believe the space of the future does not exist without the memory of the present or the past.

It was a fascinating experience when I was first approached to design a building using some of the oldest standing structures in China. I had to reassemble the pieces from Anhui Province and place them on a new 3,000-square-meter site in Beijing while adapting them to be used for their new function. From tea houses to a museum for antique objects and furniture.

The roughly 400-year-old wooden buildings measured 400 to 700 square meters. They had pitched roofs and were carved with ancient Chinese stories much older than themselves. An unending layering of time, memories, and history. I began dreaming about their lives and the people who lived in them wondering what these buildings might have witnessed. The buildings were crumpled and on the verge of being demolished before the client bought them and transported them to Beijing.

When I first saw them, piled up at their future home, they were tired, damaged, and deprived of their dignity. As a witness I was mournful, but I had hope for their future, which began to unfold within the context of my work and life. I challenged myself to do the project for free because I felt a strong connection that needed to be explored. I made a commitment to the future of discovering something

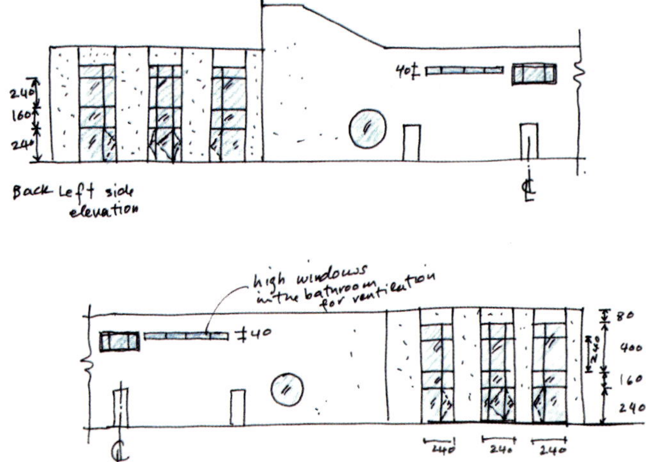

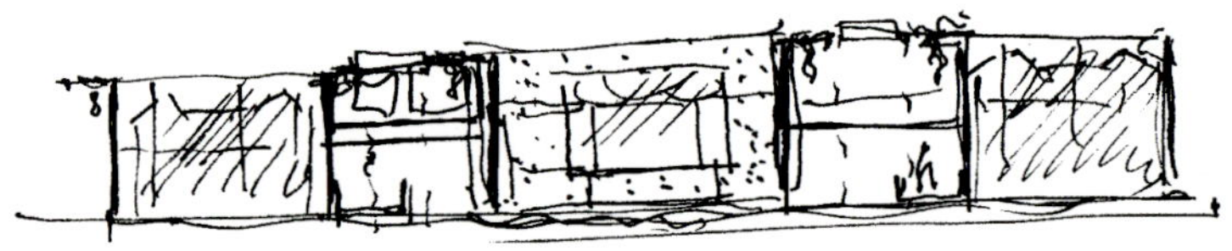

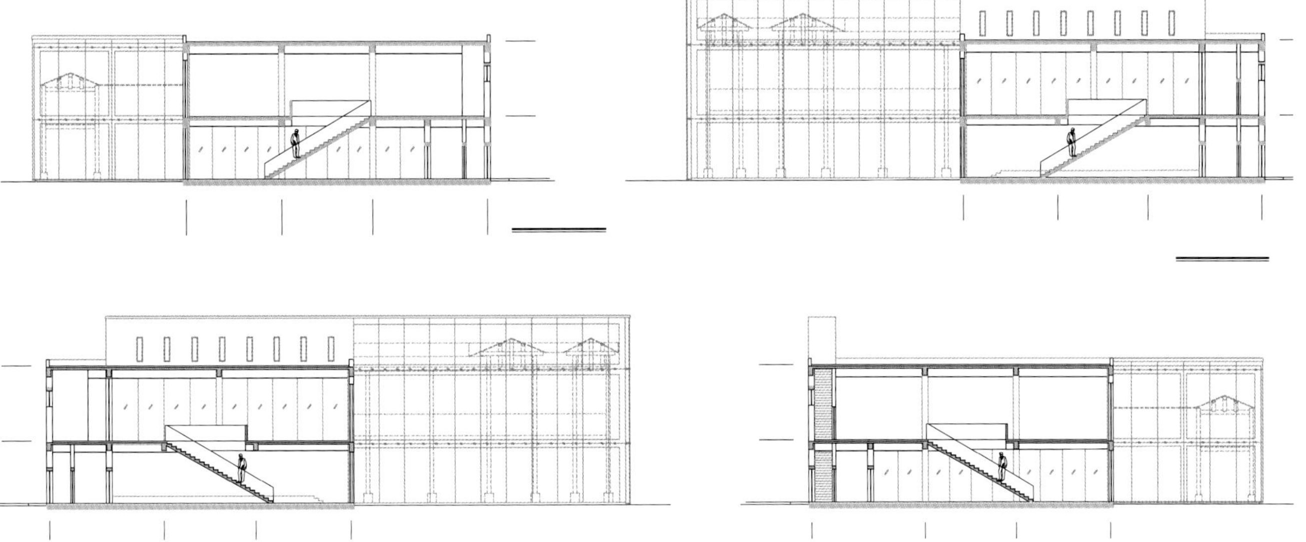

new about architecture and life. Passion is not described by words alone, but by a connection to its acts. I had to be honest with myself and those around me. It was at this point that some of the concepts began to reveal themselves to me.

I looked to these antique buildings as time capsules of stories, an expression of their time, place, and the life of the people they served. Therefore, I based my reading not on the purported functions, but on the lived experience of the architectural space which no longer existed. They were detached from a site that gave them their roots, context, relationships, and sense of belonging, but now they were floating in timelessness without a site, identity, or future. Their lives seemed miserable and in need of some change.

Like most of the buildings comparable to them, at best their parts would have ended up decorating an entrance to a building, a fireplace mantle, or maybe a lobby or conference room for a new development faking a sense of history or respect.

In "The Poetics of Space," Gaston Bachelard applies the method of phenomenology to architecture basing his analysis not on purported origins (as was the trend in enlightenment thinking about architecture), but on lived experience in architectural places and their contexts in nature. He focuses especially on the personal, emotional response to buildings both in life and in literary works, both in prose and in poetry. Bachelard writes,

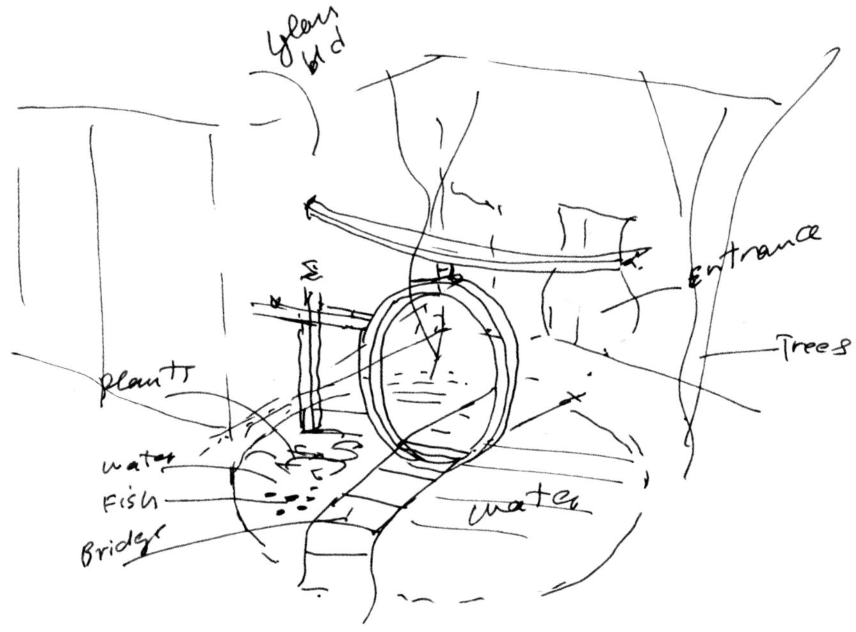

"Thus the house is not only experienced from day to day, on the thread of a narrative, or in the telling of our own story. Through dreams, the various dwelling-places in our lives co-penetrate and retain the treasures of former days. And after we are in the new house, when memories of the other places we have lived come back to us, we travel to the land of Motionless Childhood, motioning away all immemorial things are. We live fixations, fixations of happiness.

Sometimes the house of the future is better built, lighter and larger than all the houses of the past, so that the image of the dream house is opposed to that of the childhood home... Maybe it is a good thing for us to keep a few dreams of a house that we shall live in later, always later, so much later, in fact, that we shall not have time to achieve it. For a house that was final, one that stood in symmetrical relation to the house we were born in, would lead to thoughts—serious, sad thoughts—and not to dreams. It is better to live in a state of impermanence than in one of finality."

He is thus led to consider spatial types such as the attic, the cellar, drawers, and the like. Bachelard implicitly urges architects to base their work on the experiences it will engender rather than on abstract rationales that may or may not affect viewers and users of architecture.

The antique buildings were already detached from their site and had to be reconstructed in their new home. Now they were placed in a different time to serve a completely different purpose, therefore, I chose to treat them with

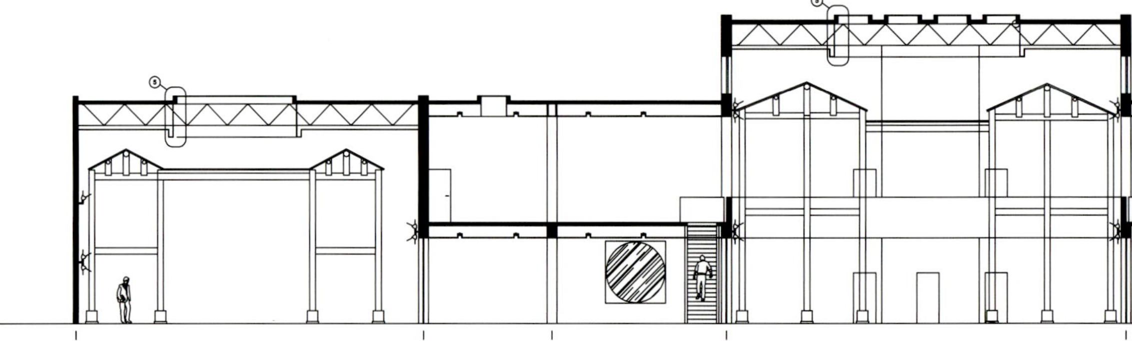

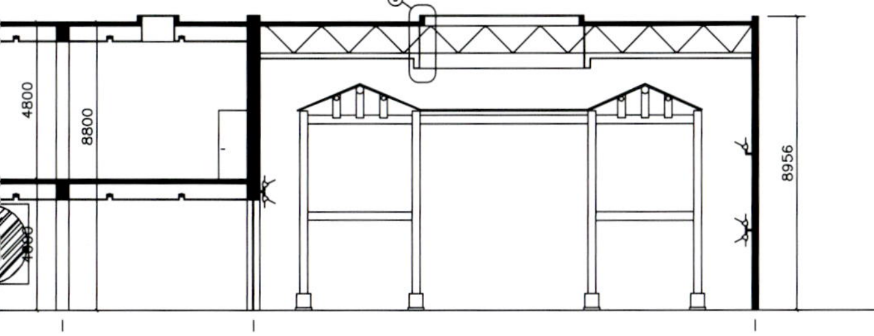

5
4800
8800
8956

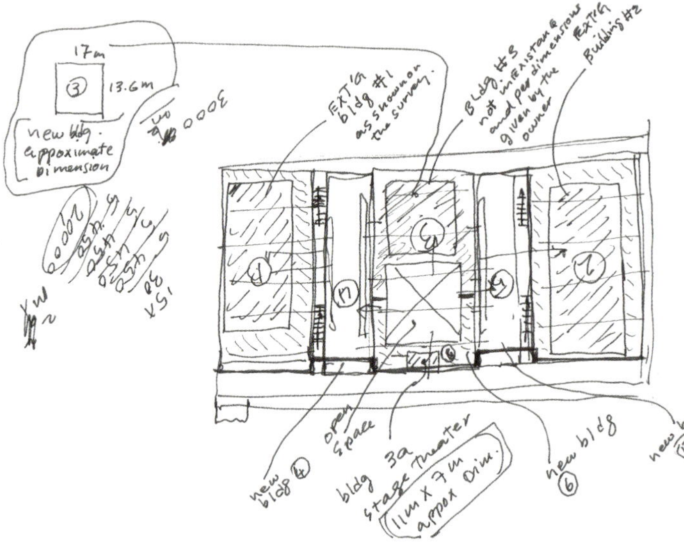

honesty and dignity. I knew from the beginning that the new site would only be their place and never their true site. I wanted to restore them in the best possible way and protect them as symbols of their time by placing them inside a series of modern, largely glass cubes. The historical buildings of the past become the containers of time and history that project themselves into the future.

In the museum, the antique buildings also become objects on display. In this project I am recycling some of the oldest standing structures in China to design a contemporary museum that becomes a bridge to connect the past, present, and the future. Individual experience, knowledge, and memories guide our perception to the poetic and transformative qualities of our environment. Through seeing, making begins. The way of seeing invariably shapes the invention even though our capability to see is in direct relationship to our awareness of what we are seeing, which is our mental model of the world. The improved architecture of the Museum of Antiquity strongly exerts it's new character while engaging the antique buildings with a mutual respect while crafting a dynamic connection with the city. Encompassing the work with a fragile character of light and transparency that is at the same time strong and old, (the glass) embraces the city and its history. Far from ignoring the past, the old and new collide in a gesture of celebration and regeneration, collectively contributing more as a cohesive whole than they ever would have individually.

The work began with the restoration by local craftsmen, which included replacing decaying parts, replacing damaged carvings, and hoisting up the frames by hand. As the antique buildings were coming to life the construction of the new buildings began. The new building was surrounded by concrete columns and a beam system with brick infills, each being two stories tall. The new buildings have external steel structures supporting the glass curtain wall. The glass is low E double layered glass to improve insulation and to reduce the sun exposure. The plan was to make the museum look like the Chinese figure for mountain, since the original houses were in the mountains of Anhui Province. The museums landscaping, a stone and pebble rock garden, was to be punctuated with four circular water ponds (circle is the Chinese symbol for sky), with bamboo plants, and with zigzagging bridges (such entrances are a necessary function of feng shui) which one must cross to enter the building.

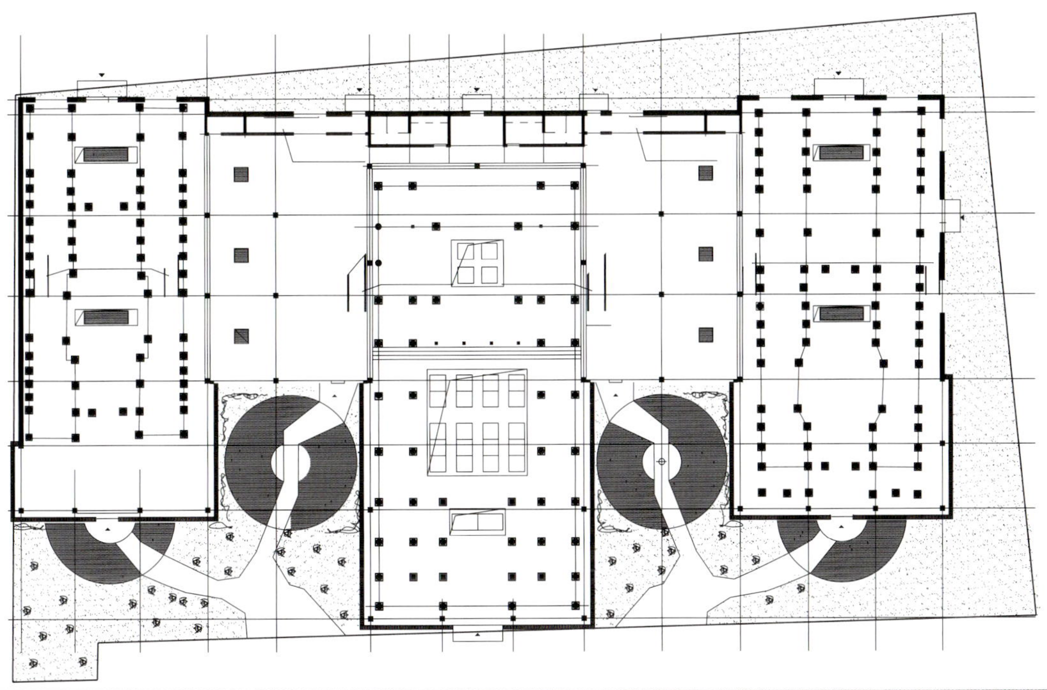

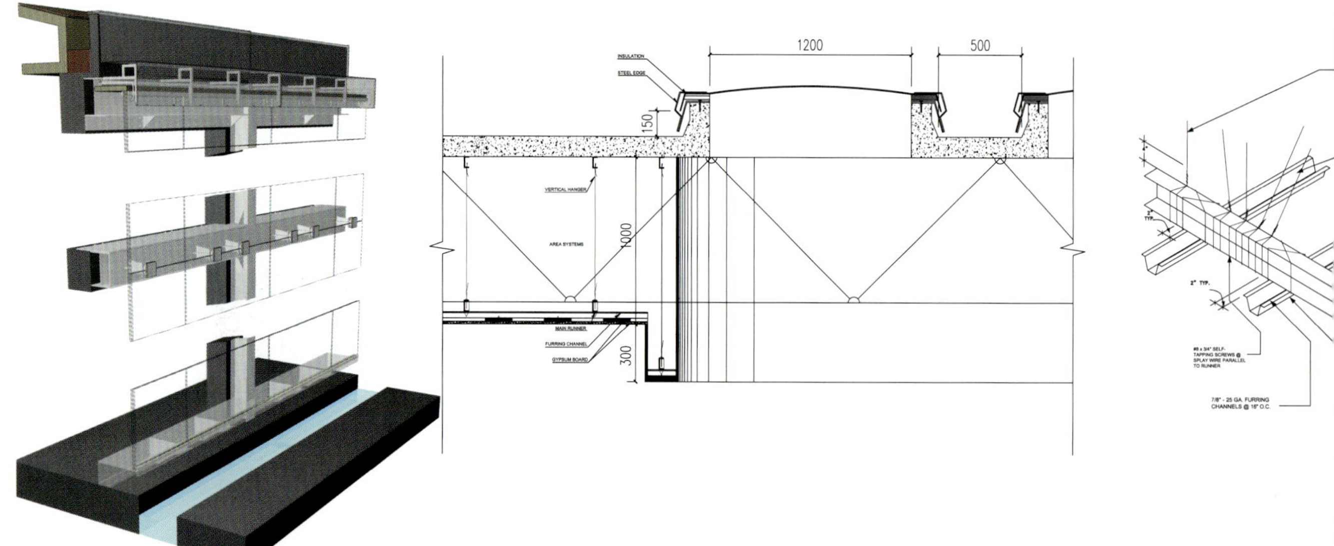

Now the antique buildings from Anhui Province are back to life in their new site serving their new patrons. They are the largest objects to be displayed in the Museum of Antiquity, but they are not only displays, but the means to display other historical objects. I have experienced many great things during the time I have worked on this building and learned many lessons about architecture and more about life. As they say in China, this life is Yin and Yang. I've learned that architecture becomes a place in which we organize our point of view in order to see reality in different ways. It is my belief that without passion and the power of conviction, nothing meaningful ever happens in life. Sometimes it takes long periods of conscious or unconscious preparation to find the right projects or opportunity. We go through life's process longing for them not realizing what is in store for us until we are fully engaged and involved. Just how the antique buildings float through time, we experience a similar existence and before we know it we're both grounded. I wonder what will be their next transformation, as well as mine.

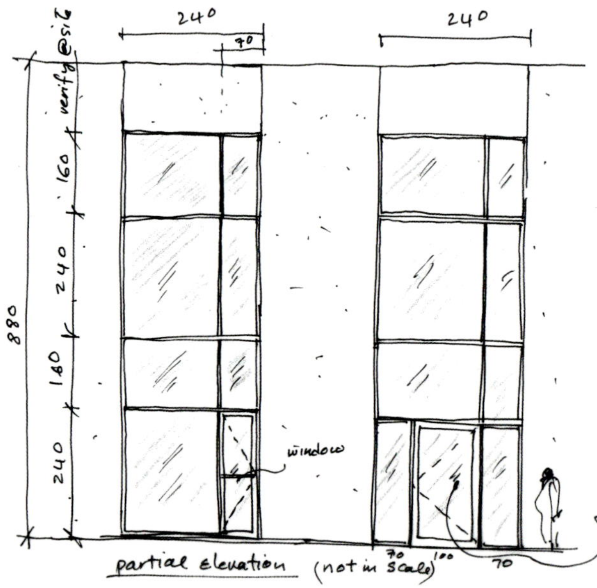

For the first time visitors can occupy the piazza freely and comfortably framed by the spirits of Brunelleschi and Michelucci.

Piazza Brunelleschi

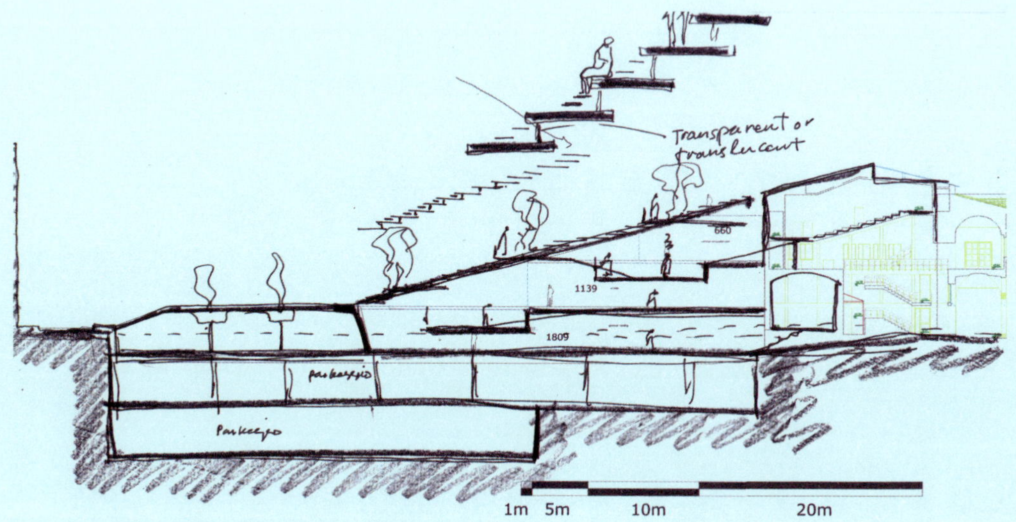

The piazza Brunelleschi, the site of the University of Florence's new Humanities Library, is surrounded by colossal buildings and inundated with the buzz of cars, motorcycles, and bicycles. Functioning as a chaotic ad-hoc parking lot, the city's flowing traffic conspires to completely obscure the buildings designed by Fillippo Brunelleschi (1377-1446) and Giovanni Michelucci (1891-1990), the most important architects in Italy's history.

The Brunelleschi Rotunda, as it is known, is the nucleus of what should have become the Rotunda of the Santa Maria degli Angeli, a rotunda constellated with several chapels, which could have become one of the most innovative buildings in Renaissance Florence. Unfortunately, it was abandoned because of a lack of funds. Situated at the corner of Via degli Alfani and Via del Castellaccio, the Rotunda guides the pedestrian into the piazza. The building used to be an Italian language school for many years. Now with the current proposal for the Piazza Brunelleschi and the Humanities Library in progress, this would be a good time for the restoration and projection of new possibilities for this important and interesting historical building.

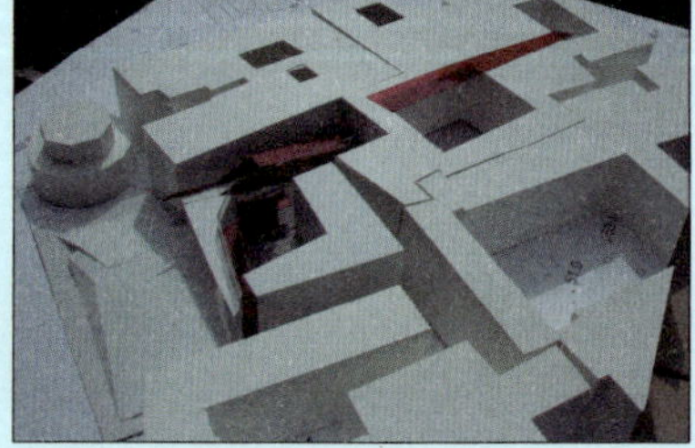

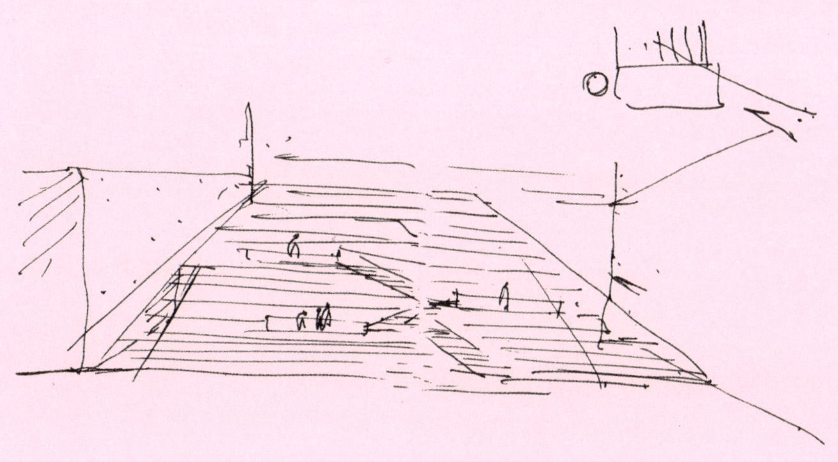

In 2005, two of my classmates from the University of Florence, Stefano Matteoni and Domenico La Gioia, reached out regarding a competition for the Humanities Library. The project for the new library would functionally replace the old one, while the old library's space would be used for other functions of the university. They invited me to join them and I accepted without any hesitation.

The program for the library would relieve the congestion of the piazza by eliminating one of the existing office buildings onsite. The elimination of the offices would permit unobstructed, centralized views of both the Piazza's natural boundaries and how the piazza is book-ended to the east and west by the Brunelleschi and Michelucci structures. Yet, by Florentine principles, the removal of any building would be considered revolutionary. Having a history of careful preservation that dates back centuries, any proposal, even those creating a small window of change within the city, can trigger a city-wide debate.

However, at the conclusion of a spirited debate between Stefano, Domenico, and I, we agreed that the price of losing one undistinguished building will be more than made up for by the new project's ultimate goal of creating a gateway to Italian culture that is both useful and architecturally pleasing.

Piazza Brunelleschi

Location:
Florence, Italy

Year:
2005 (not built)

Program:
Humanities Library at the University of Florence, Italy

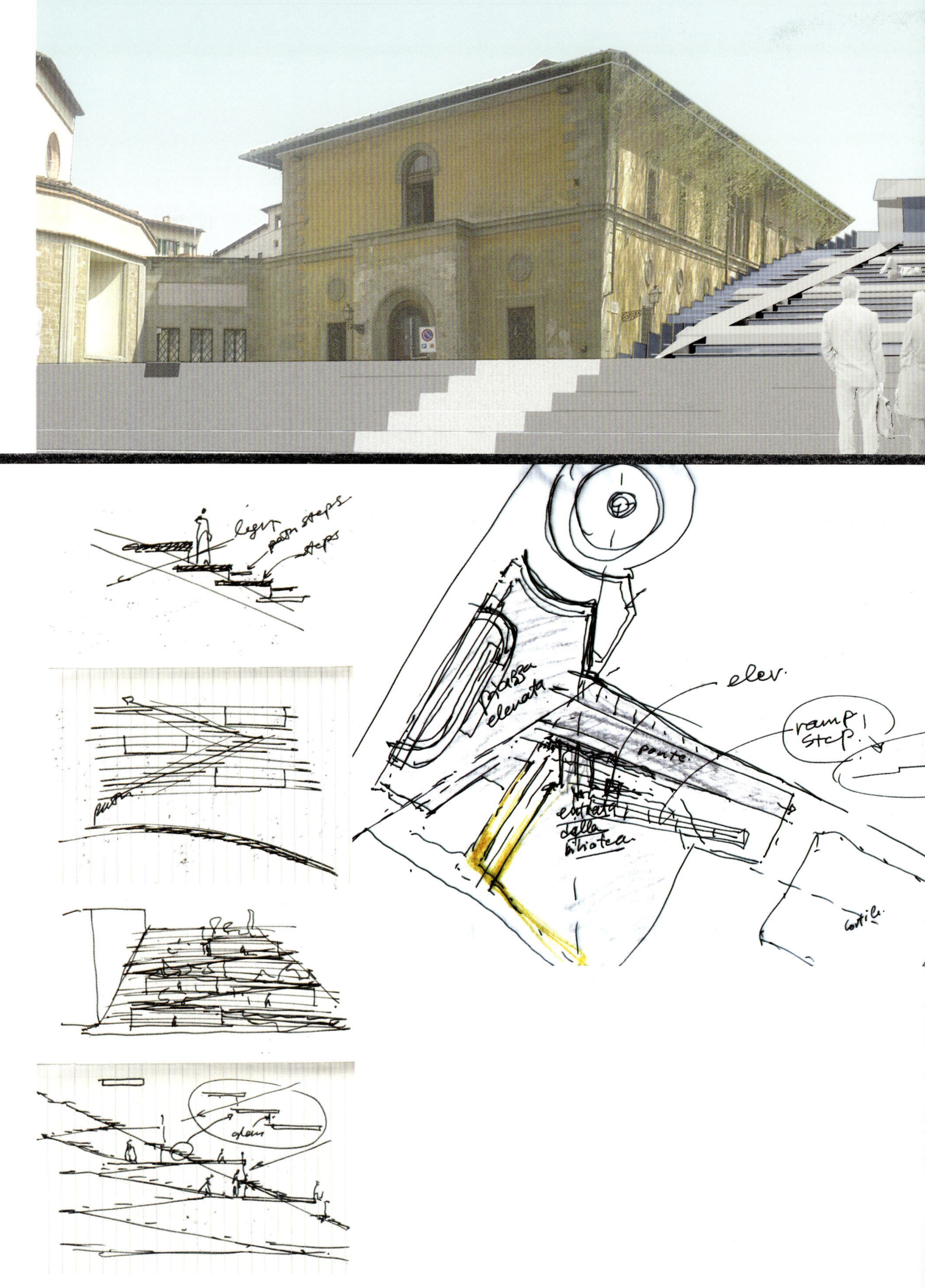
legno
passo steps
steps
piazza elevata
elev.
ramp/step
ponte
entrata dalla biblioteca
cortile

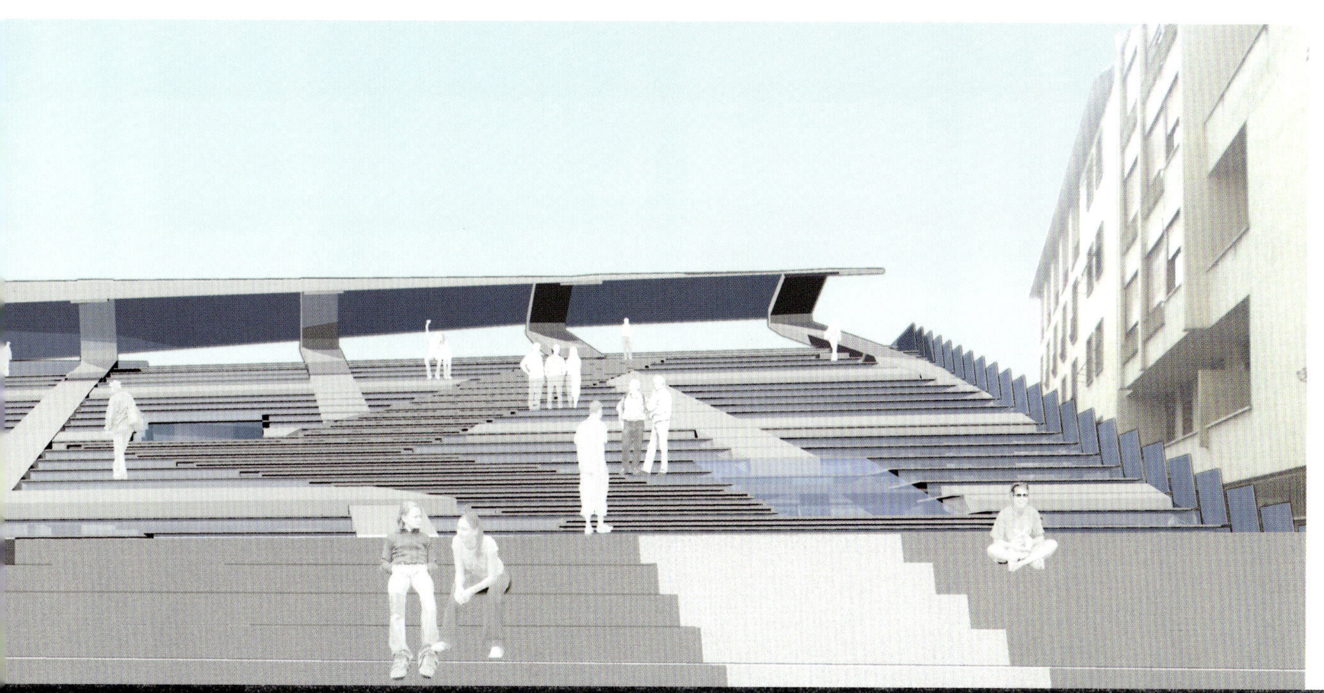

To enhance and showcase this new vista within the urban fabric, we proposed to construct a public space elevated above the piazza. Taking the form of an occupiable terrace, the elevated structure resembles classical Greek architecture in the Italian style. The amphitheater serves as the roof for the new library, with steps that lead to the Humanities department, opening up the Piazza as never seen before. The new civic square lends itself to a variety of public activities including theater, concerts, or outdoor markets.

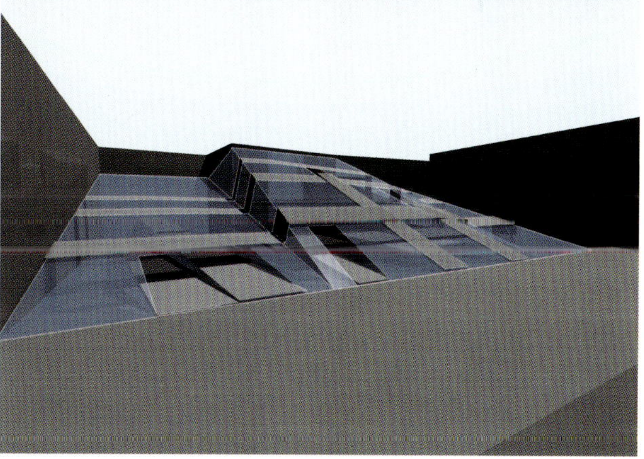

The structure is an open amphitheater for the city. The steps of the amphitheater, which also form the roof of the Library, are covered with a local stone called Pietra Serena whereas the risers in between the steps are enclosed with insulated, clear laminated glass. During the day, the glass would provide daylight to the library space below and at night would glow with the interior's artificial light.

Taking full advantage of the spectacular view, a café restaurant is placed on top of the broad glass steps. The space emotes feelings of comfort by creating an open and fluid space with delicate articulations accommodating diverse activities.

The library's design is structured to create separate entrances for the university population and the general public. The public will enter from the mezzanine level containing an exhibition area, conference rooms, and the bookstore. Crossing a bridge through the lobby, the upper entrance grants views of both the level below and the two levels above. University students who will use the humanities library can enter through the first level entrance located in the connection core and connective space of the courtyard. Beneath the piazza is the new three-story parking structure. We decided to expand the space to be five times larger than the original capacity with three levels for 296 cars.

The design for the Piazza Brunelleschi and the new Humanities Library of the University of Florence illustrates a key element of our philosophical approach to architecture. Architecture should create meaning and in doing so create purposeful opportunities for the occupation of space. To achieve this balance we aim for an architecture that is strong, but not imposing. Avoiding the temptation to make statements at the expense of space, our goal is to use space as a vehicle for human interaction. The building's use and occupation should inspire its banal physicality with the charge and celebration of life.

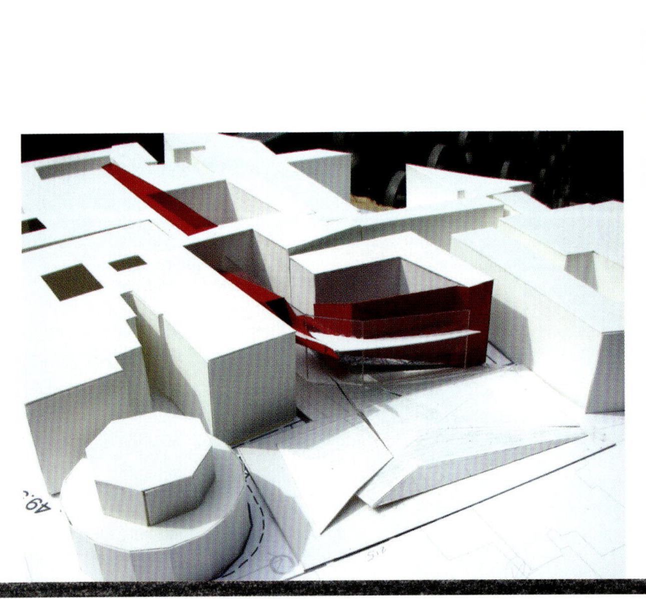

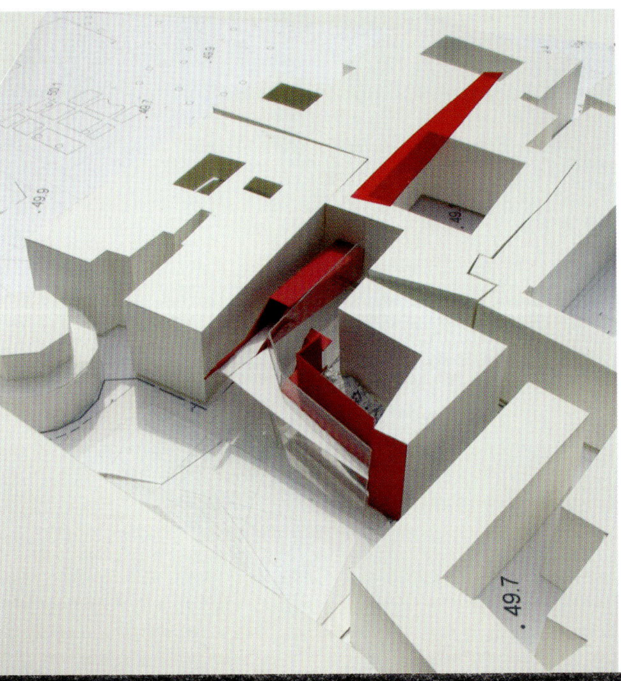

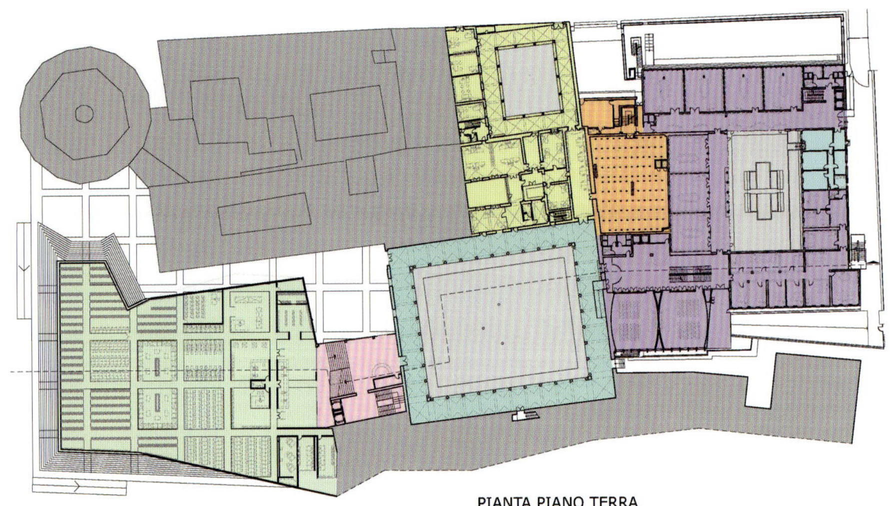

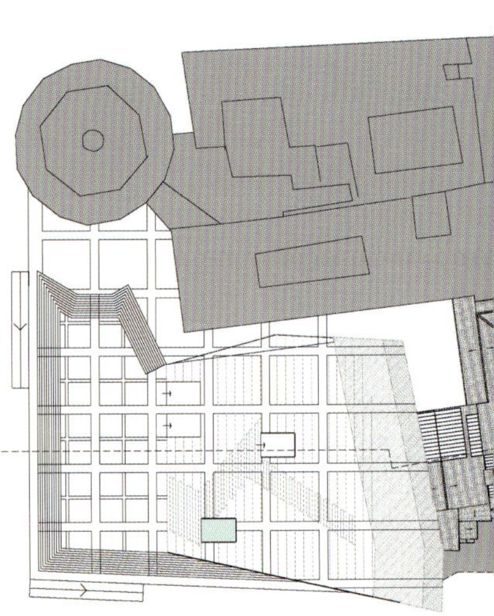

PIANTA PIANO TERRA

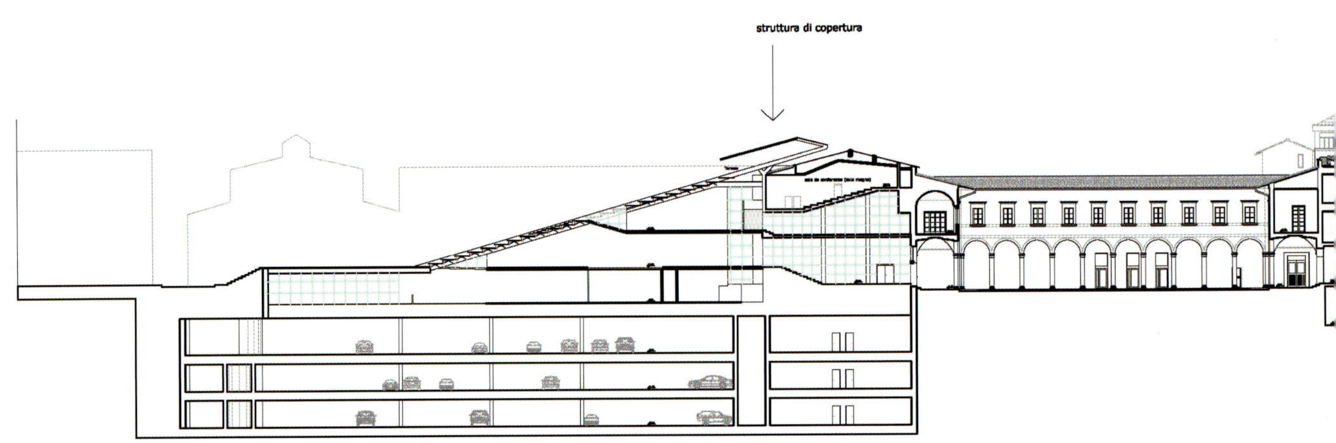

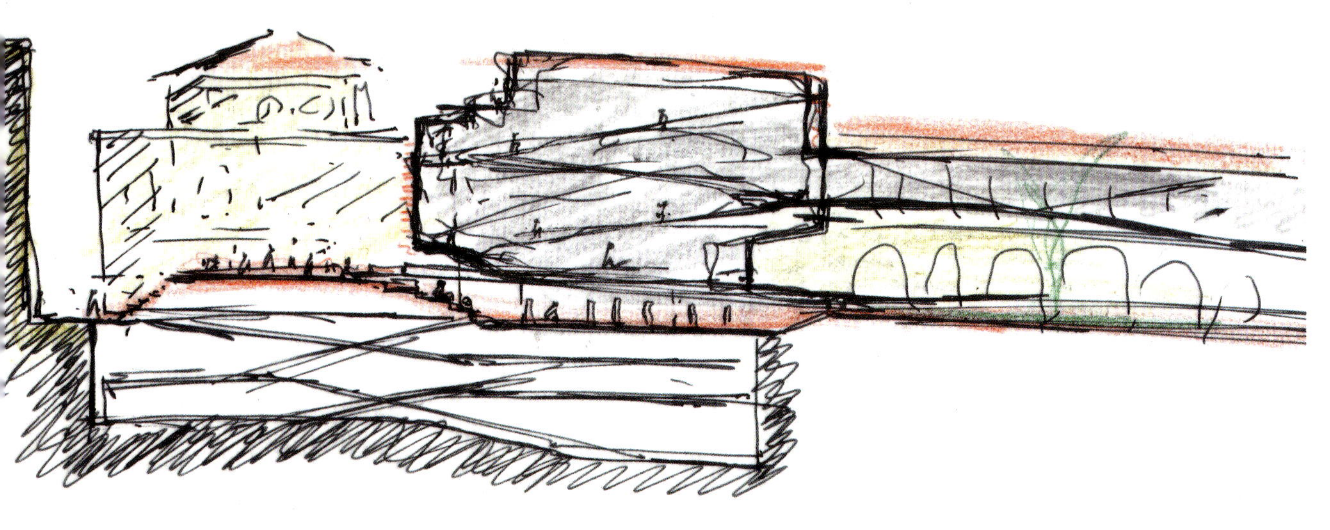

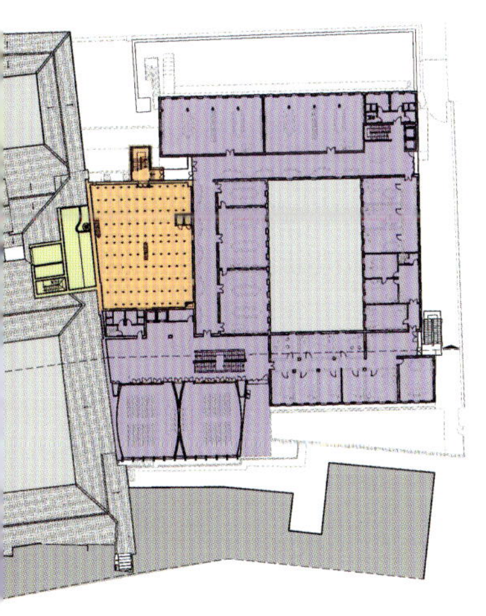

PIANTA PIANO SECONDO

PIANTA PIANO PRIMO

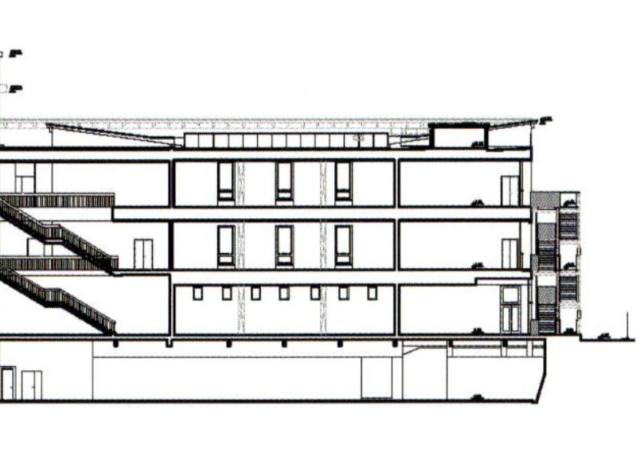

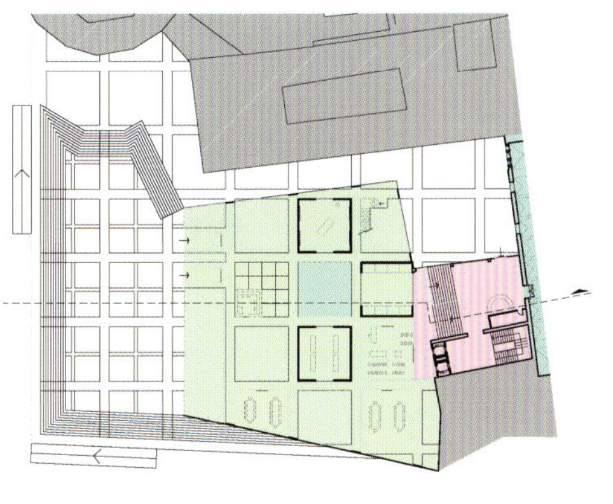

PIANTA PIANO AMMEZZATO

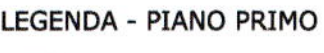

LEGENDA - PIANO TERRA

NUOVO EDIFICIO D'ACCESSO MQ 2153
NUCLEO DI CONNESSIONE MQ 309
SPAZI CONNETTIVI MQ 732
AREA DI SERVIZI INTERNI E TECNICI MQ 966
POZZO LIBRARIO MQ 453
DIPARTIMENTO DI STUDI SUL MEDIOEVO E RINASCIMENTO MQ 1918
CASA DEL CUSTODE MQ 125

LEGENDA - PIANO PRIMO

NUOVO EDIFICIO D'ACCESSO MQ 566
NUCLEO DI CONNESSIONE MQ 230
SPAZI CONNETTIVI MQ 822
AREA DI SERVIZI INTERNI E TECNICI MQ 877
POZZO LIBRARIO MQ 375
DIPARTIMENTO DI LINGUISTICA MQ 2053

LEGENDA - AMMEZZATO

NUOVO EDIFICIO D'ACCESSO MQ 1460

LEGENDA - PIANO SECONDO

AREA DI SERVIZI INTERNI E TECNICI MQ 118
POZZO LIBRARIO MQ 375
DIPARTIMENTO DI SCIENZE DELL'ANTICHITA' MQ 2025

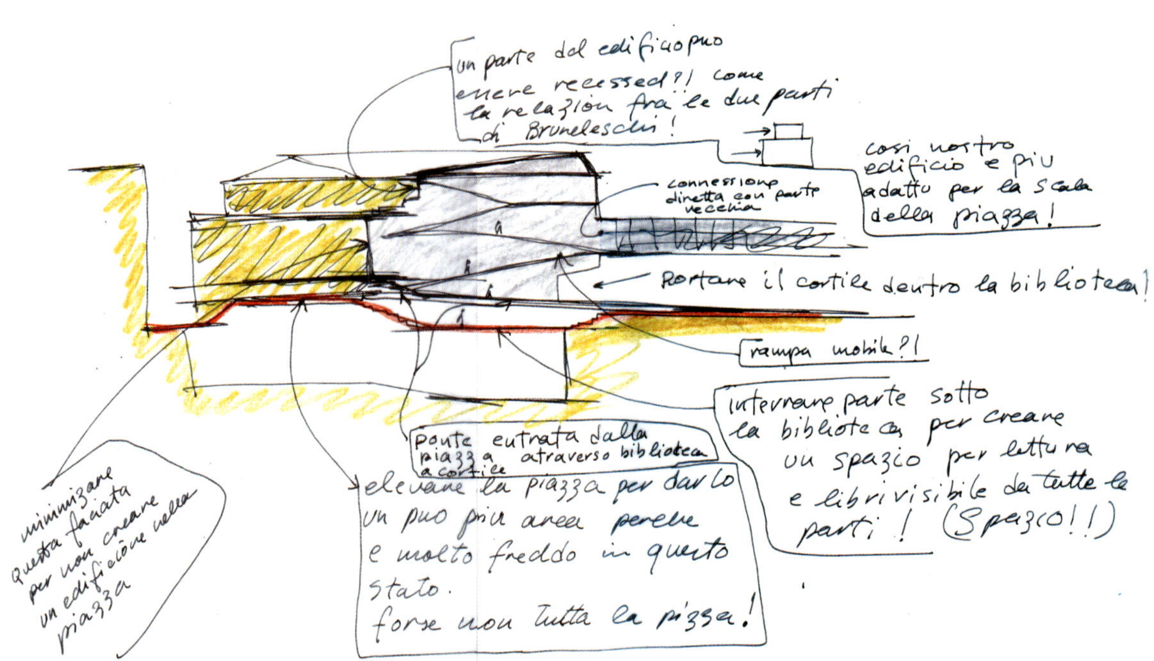
un parte del edificio puo essere recessed?! come la relazion fra le due parti di Brunelleschi!
cosi nostro edificio e piu adatto per la scala della piazza!
connessione diretta con parte vecchia
Portare il cortile dentro la biblioteca!
rampa mobile?!
intervenire parte sotto la biblioteca per creare un spazio per lettura e libri visibile da tutte le parti! (Spazio!!)
ponte entrata dalla piazza a cortile atraverso biblioteca
elevare la piazza per darlo un puo piu area perche e molto freddo in questo stato. forse non tutta la pizza!
minimizare questa facciata per non creare un edificione nella piazza

Skinned entirely in double-glazed glass, the structure's transparency blends the perception of nature and form.

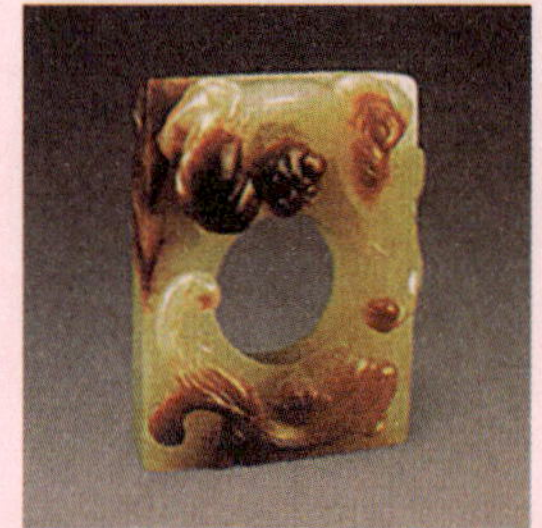

I met the client, a development company, through a friend at the Chinese Architecture Biennale in 2004. I was in Beijing interviewing for potential projects and a few days before I returned to the US, I got a call to meet Director Wang. After he briefly described the project I was hooked. He wanted to develop a building on a 25-acre plot, but only a small portion of the structure could touch the ground. I suggested that he give me a chance to show him a few sketches of my ideas, hoping I could convince him of our collaboration. He agreed and that day I was driven to the site. The plot, like most other development land in Beijing, used to be for agricultural production. The most noticeable quality of the site was it's vast, limitless sky. As I walked along the plot, I'd search for the right place to position the structure where it would be integrated with the least effort possible. As if it was always there, but never noticed.

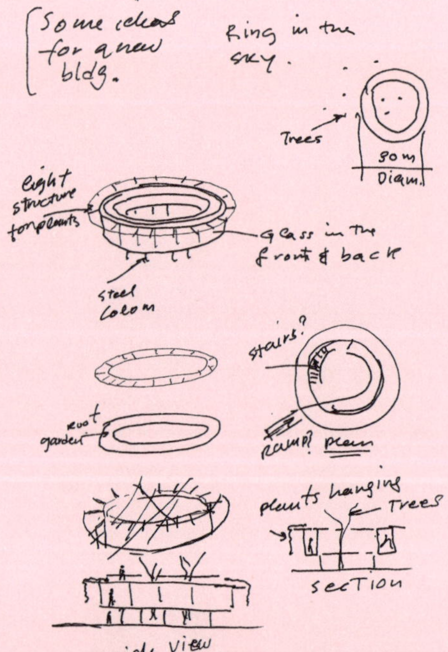

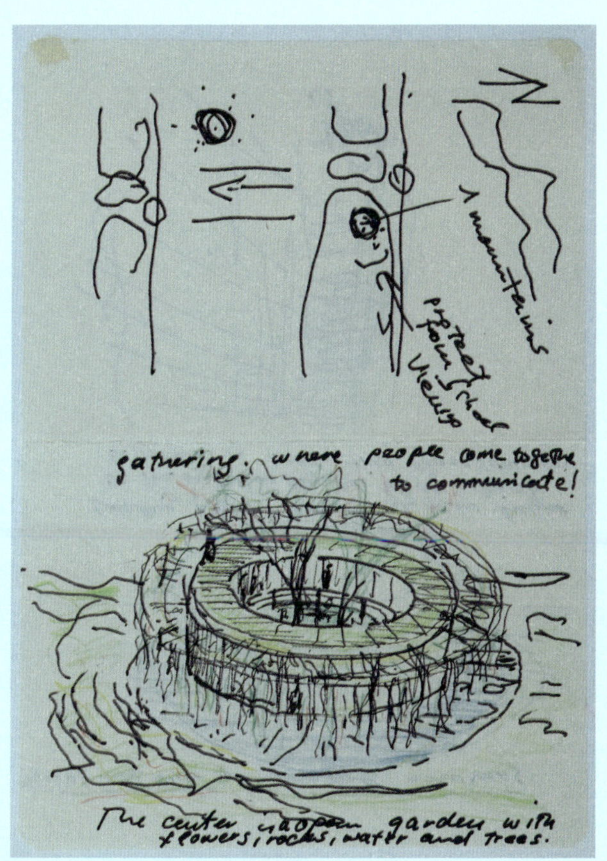
mountains
gathering, where people come togethe
to communicate!
The center is a open garden with
flowers, rocks, water and trees.

After a few hours the site revealed itself. I noticed a groove in the natural plain of the land. It was instinctively suitable. I took a few pictures, marked the spot on the survey I was given, and we drove back through the brutal Beijing traffic to their office. When we arrived, Mr. Wang was waiting for me to discuss my ideas and I expressed my enthusiasm to work on the project. He suggested that we meet again on Monday, but I was leaving on Monday afternoon. He prompted me that our meeting would only be for an hour and that he'll have their car take me to the airport after. Therefore, I assumed that we were going to talk mainly about the program, our collaboration, and to start the design ideas when I got back to LA.

I drew ideas in my sketchbook all weekend. I wanted to maximize the building presence on the site even though I was minimizing its contact with the site. On the other hand, the sky's impression and Mr. Wang's strong personality led me to define the shape of the building and from there everything else took shape. I went to their office on Monday with my suitcase, only to find Mr. Wang and a team of their employees and consultants waiting for me. It was unexpected. They were anticipating me to arrive with presentation boards, but I pulled out my sketchbook instead. I then tore out the drawing and passed them out around the conference table, while explaining the concept. Mr. Wang's eyes lit up as he saw the 2x3-inch sketches. After, he grabbed the phone and started dialing.

At this time everyone started talking to each other in Mandarin, asking me questions in between. All of a sudden, Mr. Wang turned to me and asked, "What is the circumference of the circle? What is the height of the glass? What type of glass?" That's when I realized he was talking to a glass company. I had some basic ideas about the project so, to the best of my knowledge, I provided him with the information. After, he hung up the phone and said, "Can we meet in three weeks to review the schematic design drawings here?"

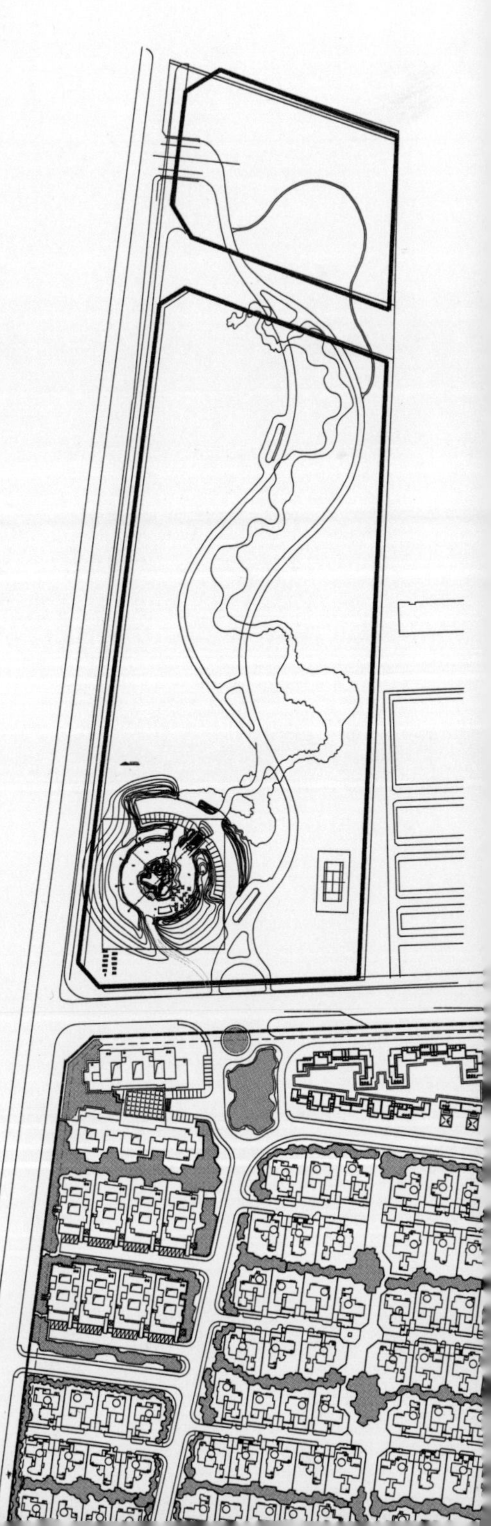

Sky

Location:
Beijing, P.R. China

Year:
2006 (built)

Program:
Exhibition and Multifunctional Space

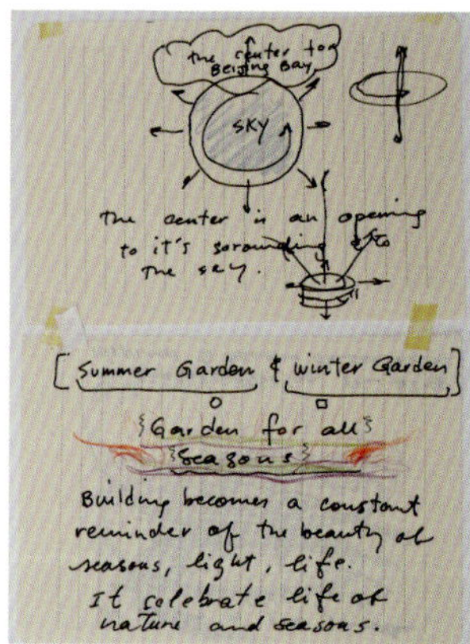

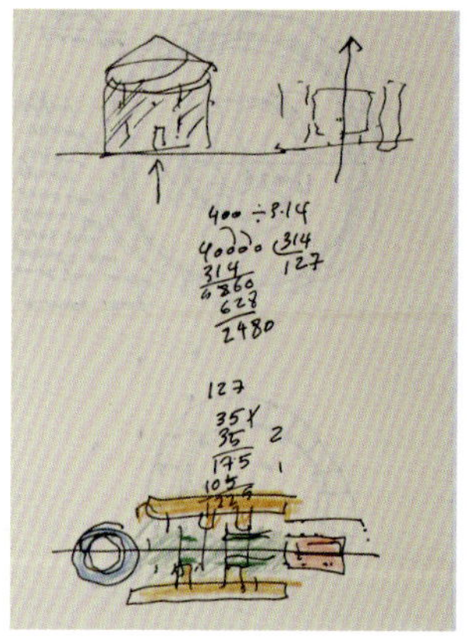

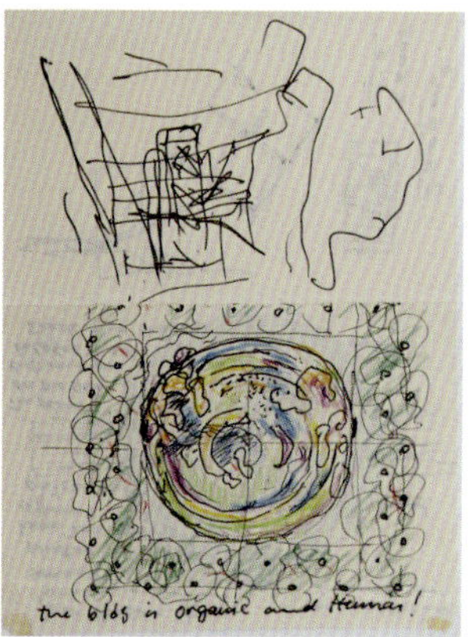

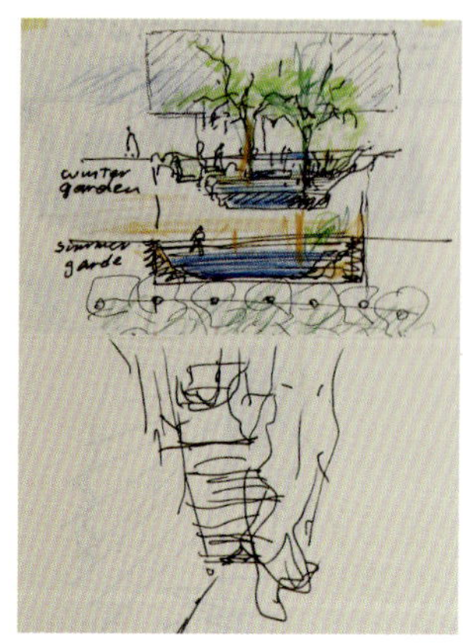

The concept for the Beijing Bay Center was greatly influenced by both current and historical Chinese culture, reflecting old and new, familiar and foreign. Nestled in 25 acres of landscaped woods, a perfect glass ring hovers above a lake and gardens, creating a new window onto the sky. According to ancient Chinese culture, the earth takes the shape of the square and the sky is in the form of a circle. Symbolically, the circle represents unity and family, and the Beijing Bay Center, an exhibition and sales venue for the new Zhongguancun Technological Park development, is a perfect circle. Cradled by the earth, which serves as its container and protector, the building takes the form of a glass ring standing as a solitary figure in the landscape. Awaiting further development of the property, the structure is to be used as the park's exhibition and event center.

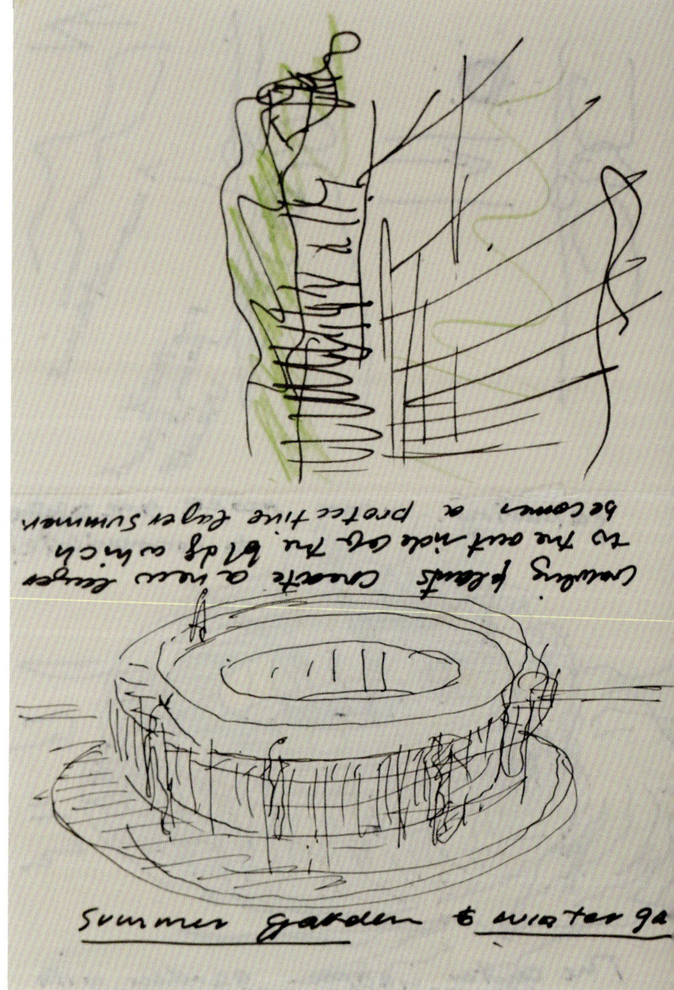

Prevalent throughout Chinese culture, signature stamps, in the form of seals, uniquely identify an individual's elevated status. A Han Dynasty legend states that the Yellow Emperor was given the first seal by a yellow dragon. Receiving it signified the bestowal of the emperor's heavenly mandate and established his power to rule the Chinese empire. I envisioned the Beijing Bay Center taking the form of the client's seal, situated in the midst of a rolling landscape.

The design was inspired by elements that are normally found in traditional Chinese gardens. Practiced as an art form of subtle elegance, Chinese garden designs historically included one or more sections composed of plants, rocks, coy ponds, streams, and small buildings. Interconnected to form an active matrix of nature and social spaces, they commonly included a stream and, following the order of Feng Shui, a crooked bridge across the water. Gracefully commingling grand and human dimensions, Chinese gardens depart from their western counterparts by integrating nature within the built environment. Utilizing a composition of landscape elements, a building's gardens are harmonized with its architecture as an irreplaceable part of the overall conceptual and decorative structure.

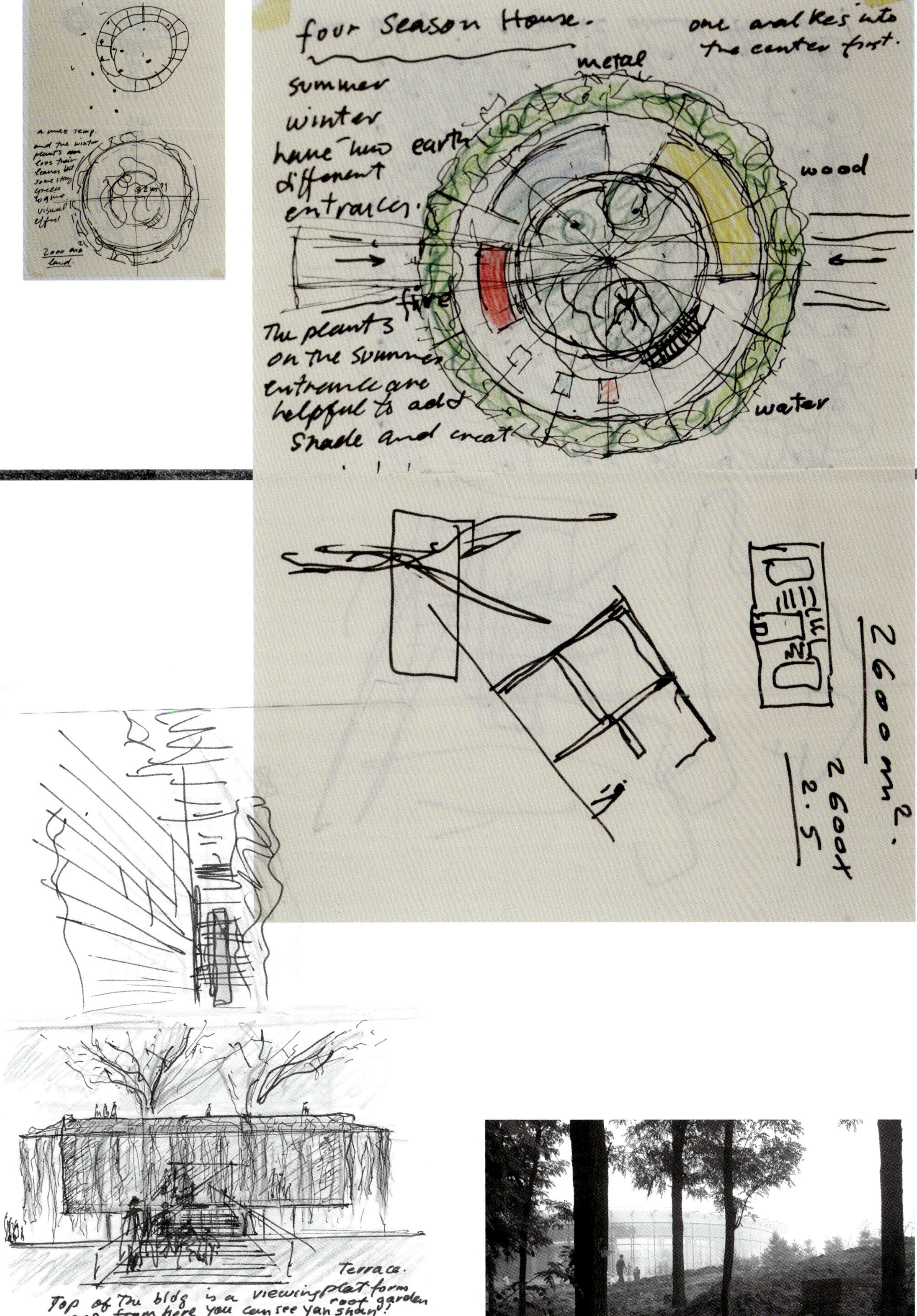
four Season House.
one walks into the center first.
metal
summer
winter
have two different entrances.
wood
fire
water
The plants on the summer entrance are helpful to add shade and creat
2600 m2.
2600 x
2.5
Terrace.
Top of The bldg is a viewing platform roof garden
360° from here you can see Yan Shan!

The process of design and development of the project was exceptionally fast. After the schematic design meeting I was introduced to the "design institute" who was going to assist me and prepare the technical package of drawings for the construction of the building. Design institutes in China are technical offices licensed and regulated by the government. Due to the short time we had, we prepared the design development and construction document drawing at the same time collaborating with our design institute.

Like the buildings of a classic Chinese garden, the Beijing Bay Center is so well suited to its site that it gives the illusion of being a natural occurrence. The approach from the main road reveals a glowing circular form; a gradually sloping ramp brings guests to the sales center while two other paths descend to the garden plaza below. On the sales center level, visitors are greeted at an information counter and then led through a gallery space containing models, drawings, and descriptions of the development.

Skinned entirely in double-glazed glass, the structure's transparency encourages a perceptual blending of nature and form. An array of trees and plants were carefully selected to unify and shade the interior spaces, making the gardens an integrated part of the overall programmatic structure. As different rooms within the circular center

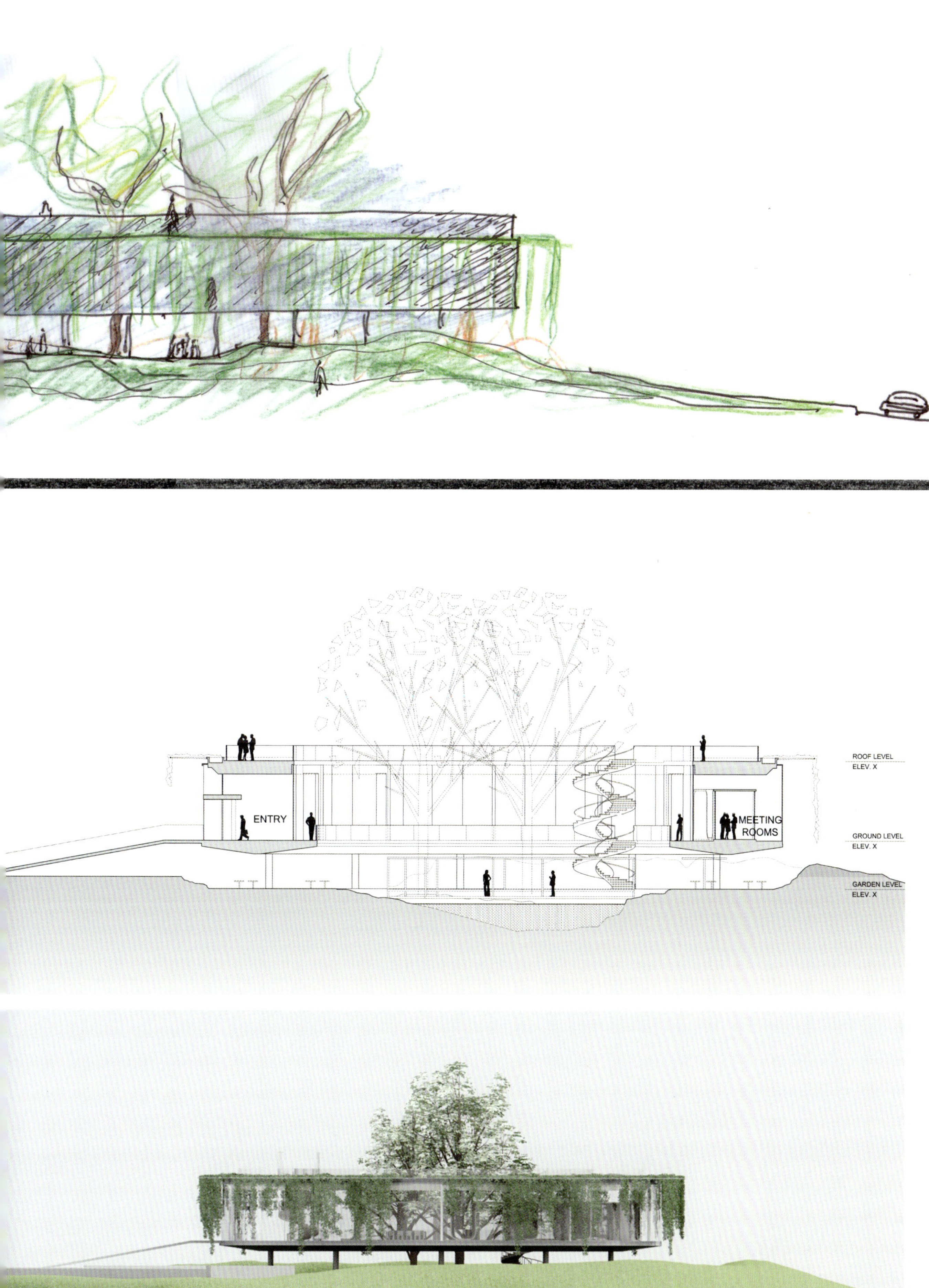
ENTRY
MEETING
ROOMS
ROOF LEVEL
ELEV. X
GROUND LEVEL
ELEV. X
GARDEN LEVEL
ELEV. X

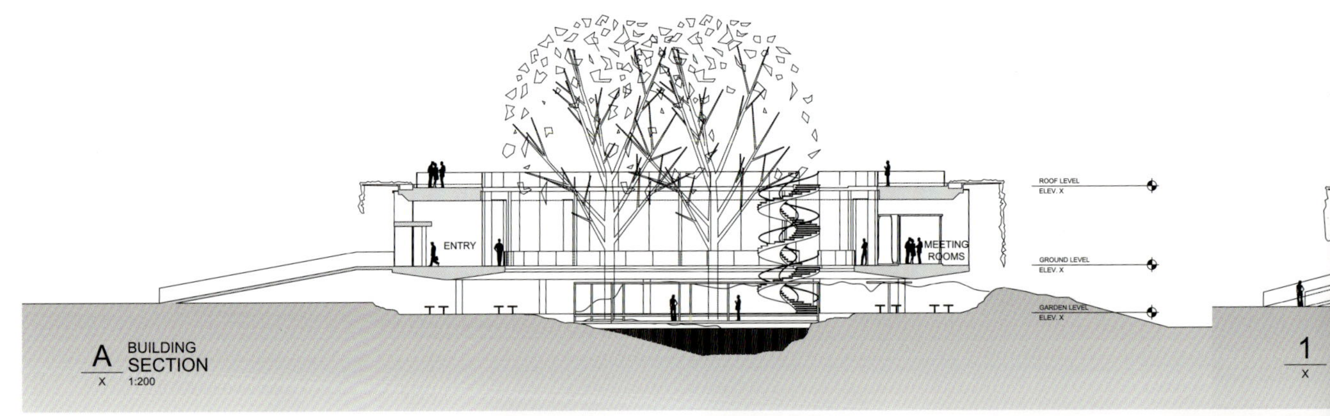
ENTRY
MEETING ROOMS
ROOF LEVEL
ELEV. X
GROUND LEVEL
ELEV. X
GARDEN LEVEL
ELEV. X
A
X
BUILDING SECTION
1:200
1
X

float above the internal patio, nature and building are tightly intertwined as trees and plants circumscribe the glass ring. Separated by the central open space, the meeting rooms and conference area frame unobstructed views of the entire surroundings. A circular staircase leads to the rooftop patio, where a breathtaking, 360-degree view takes in the expanse of the development and yields glimpses of the garden and water sculptures below.

Both grounded by its human scale and elevated by a grander scale, the treatment of the structure and garden in the Beijing Bay Center results in a harmonious and indivisible composition completed by the surrounding landscape's embrace. Offering a solution to the mathematical paradox of squaring the circle, this project succeeds in allowing sky and earth to become one.

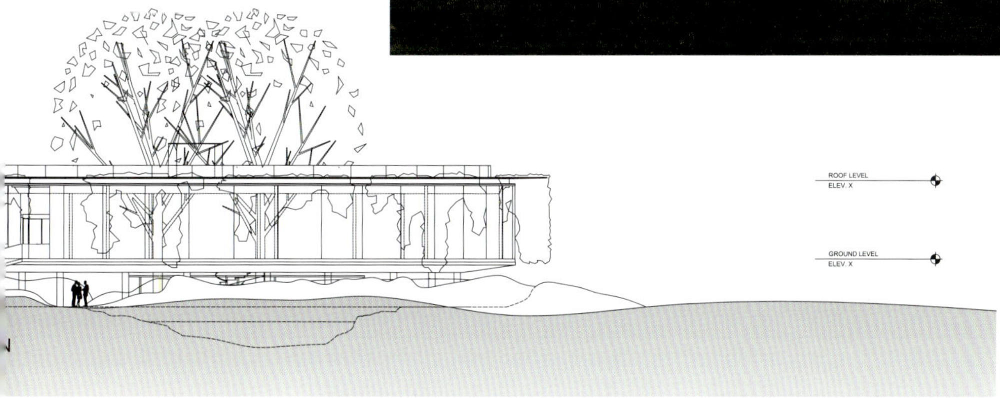

ROOF LEVEL
ELEV. X

GROUND LEVEL
ELEV. X

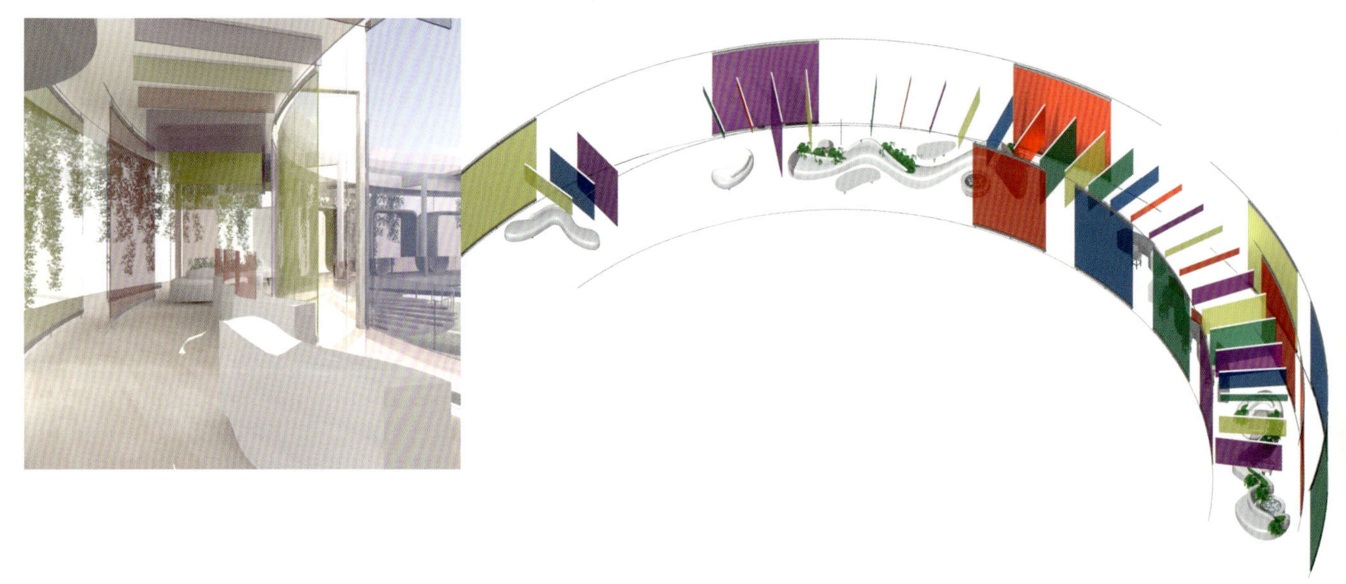

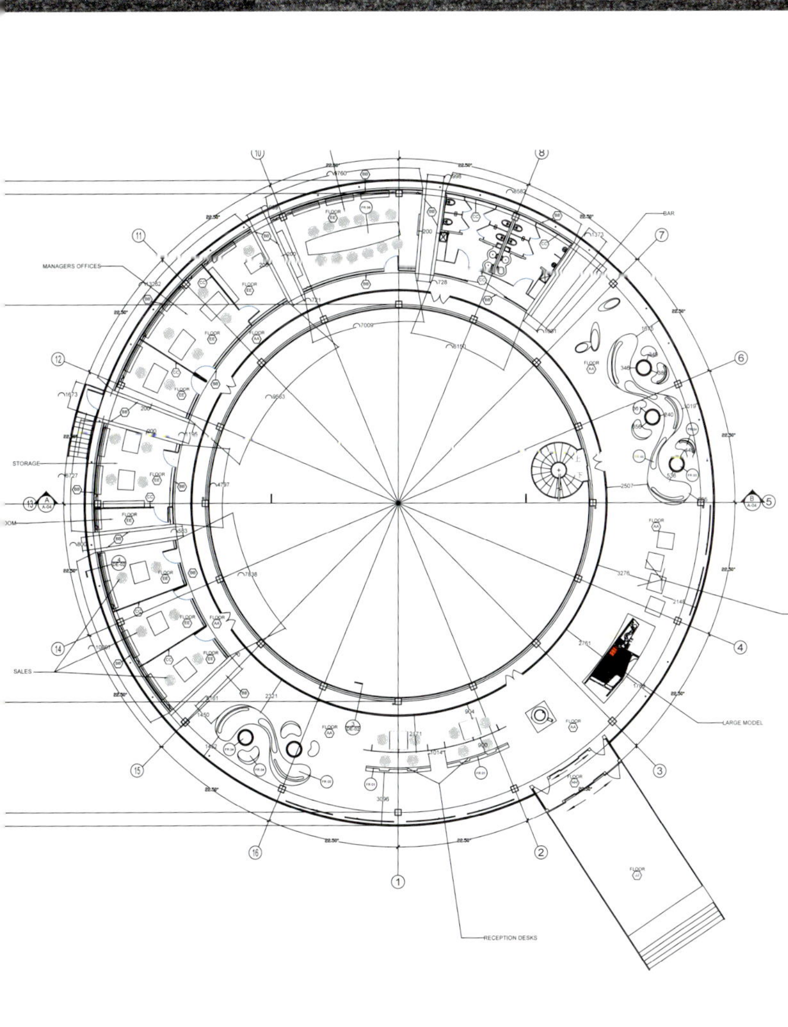
MANAGERS OFFICES
STORAGE
SALES
BAR
LARGE MODEL
RECEPTION DESKS

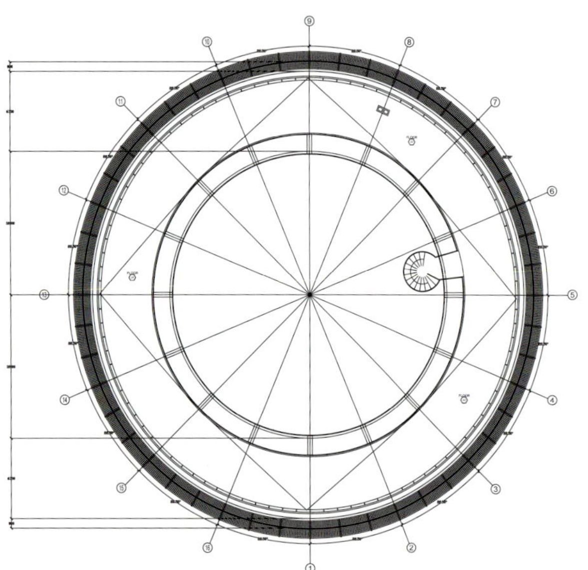

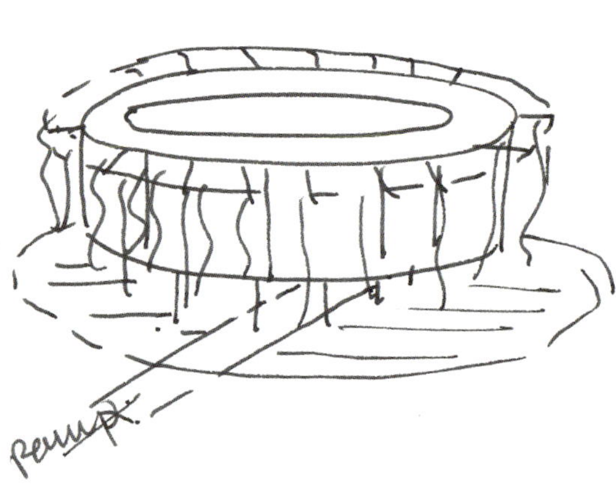

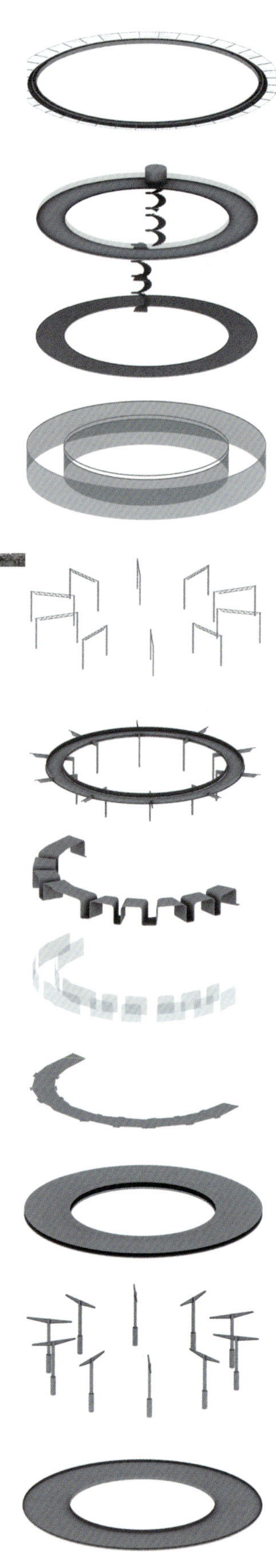

Some ideas for a new bldg.

Ring in the sky.

Trees

30m Diam.

light structure for plants

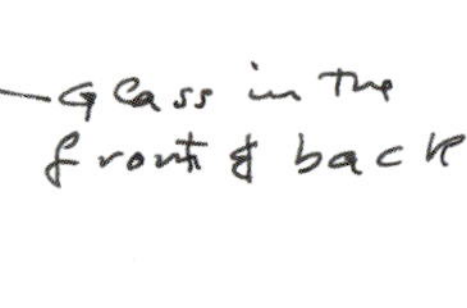

glass in the front & back

steel colom

roof garden

side view

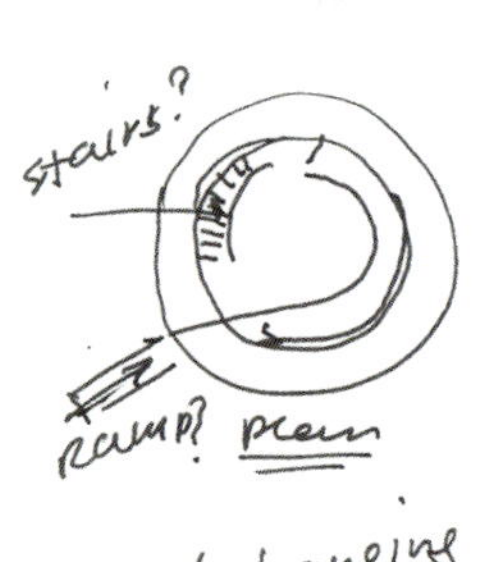

stairs?

ramp? plan

plants hanging

Tree

section

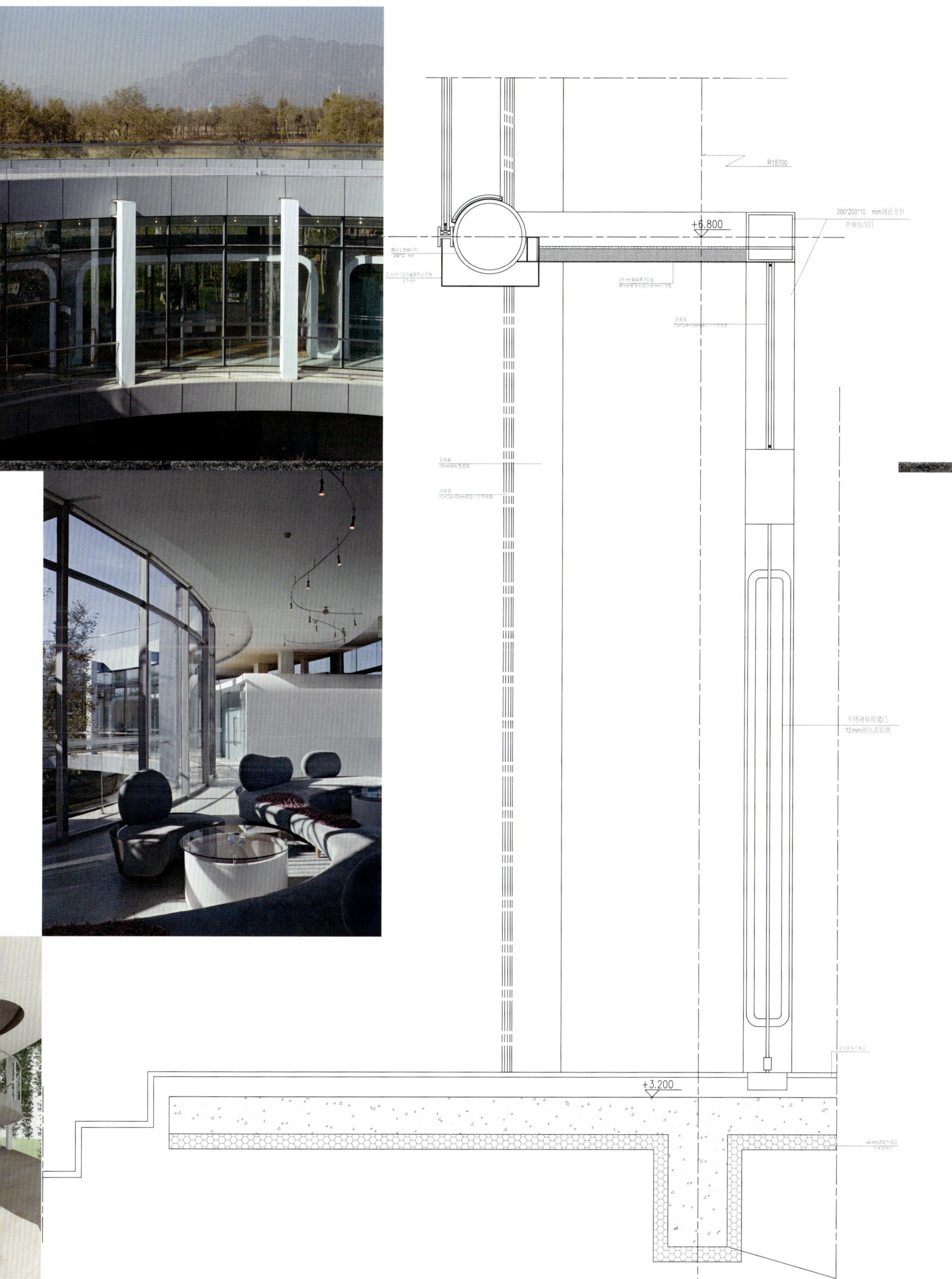

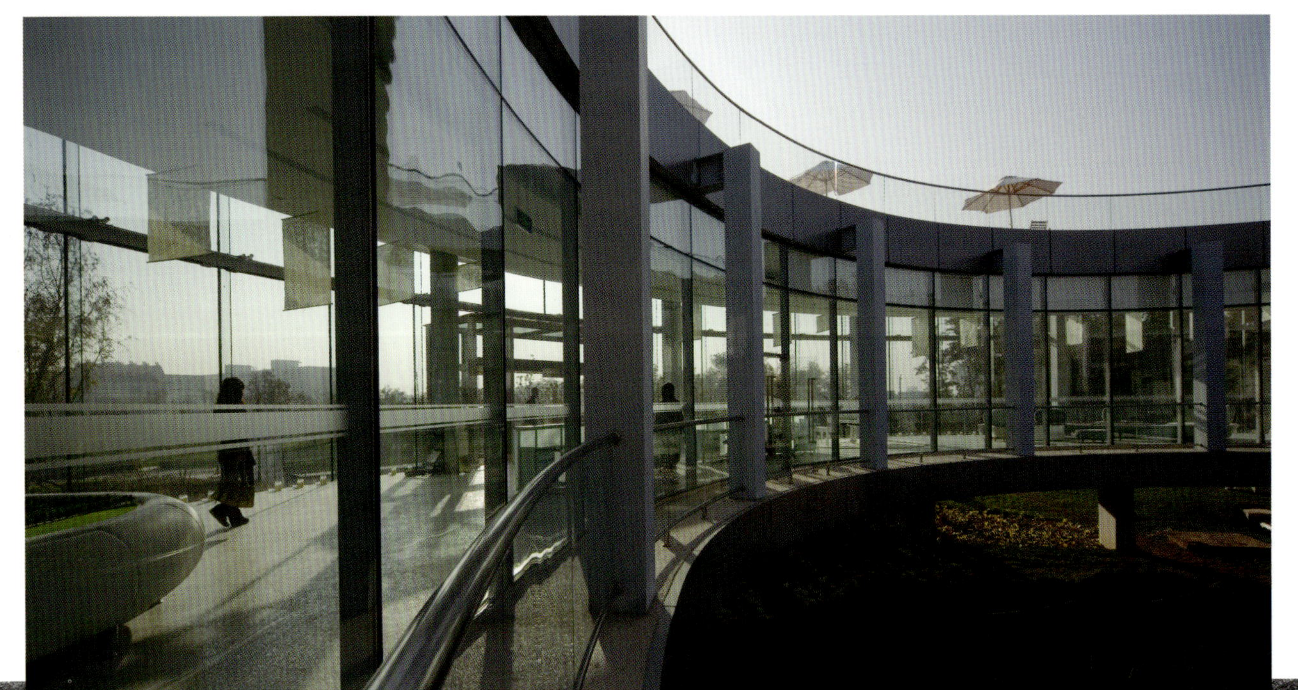

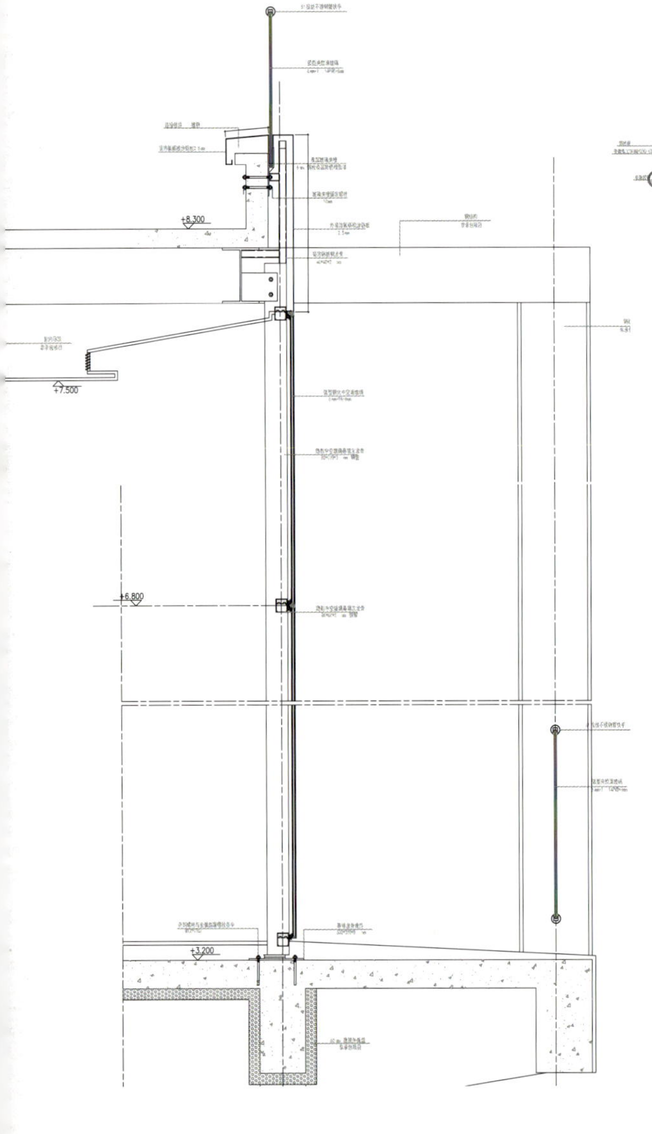
+8,300
+7,500
+6,800
+3,200

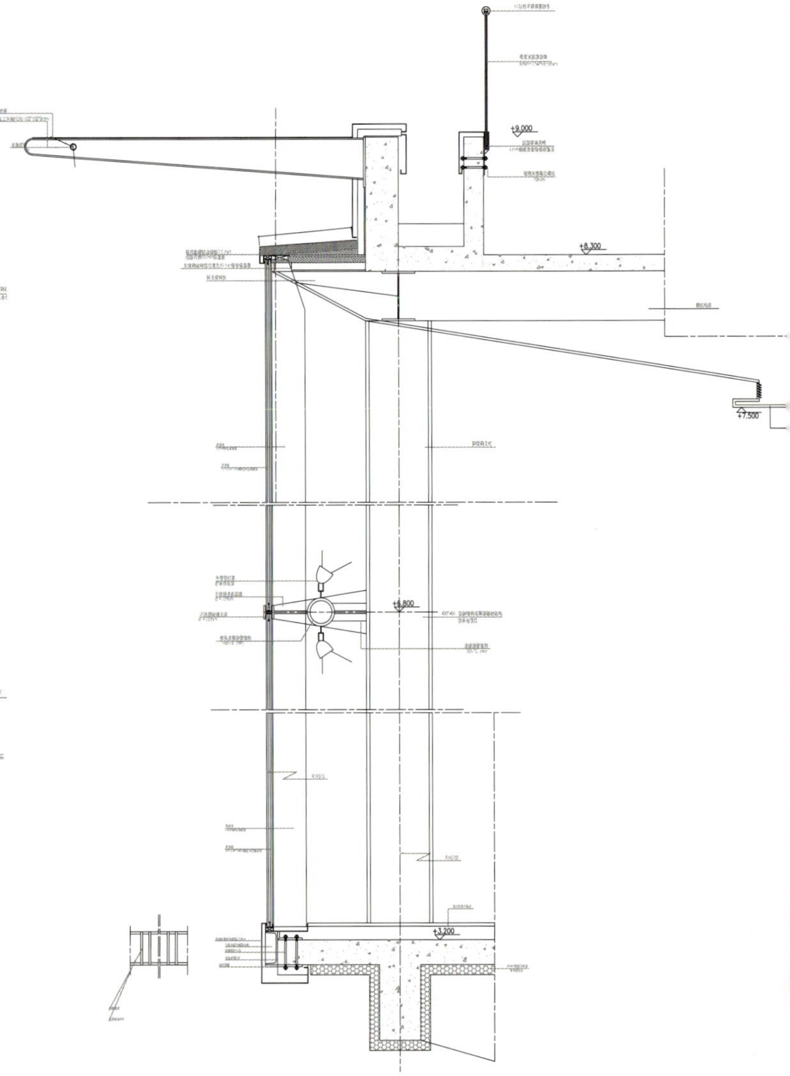
+9,000
+8,300
+7,500
+6,800
+3,200

The vast Gobi Desert rich with history and its poetic mystery calls for creativity.

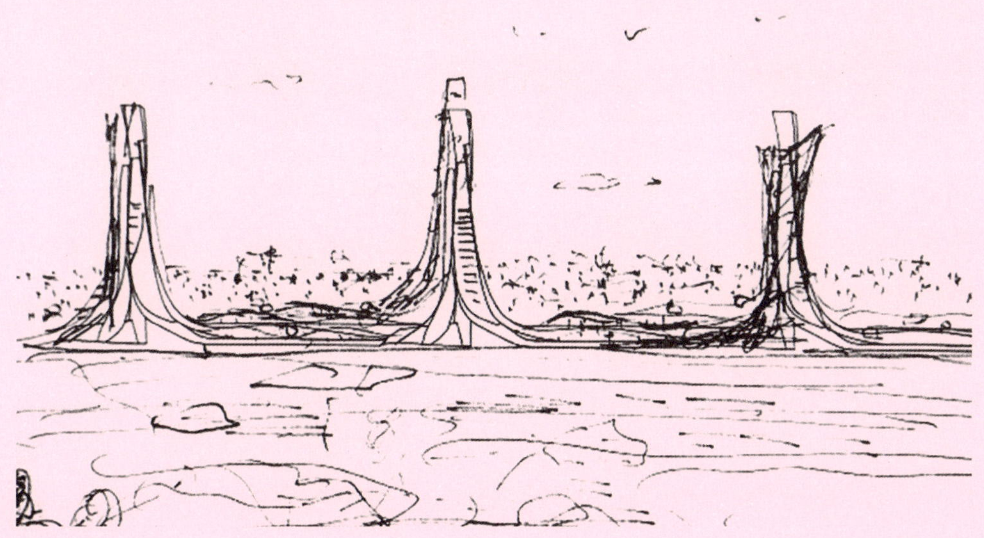

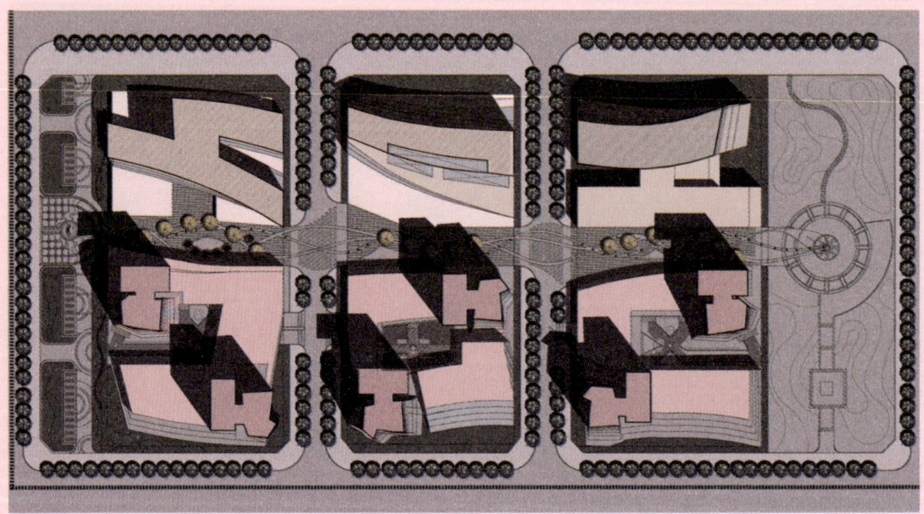

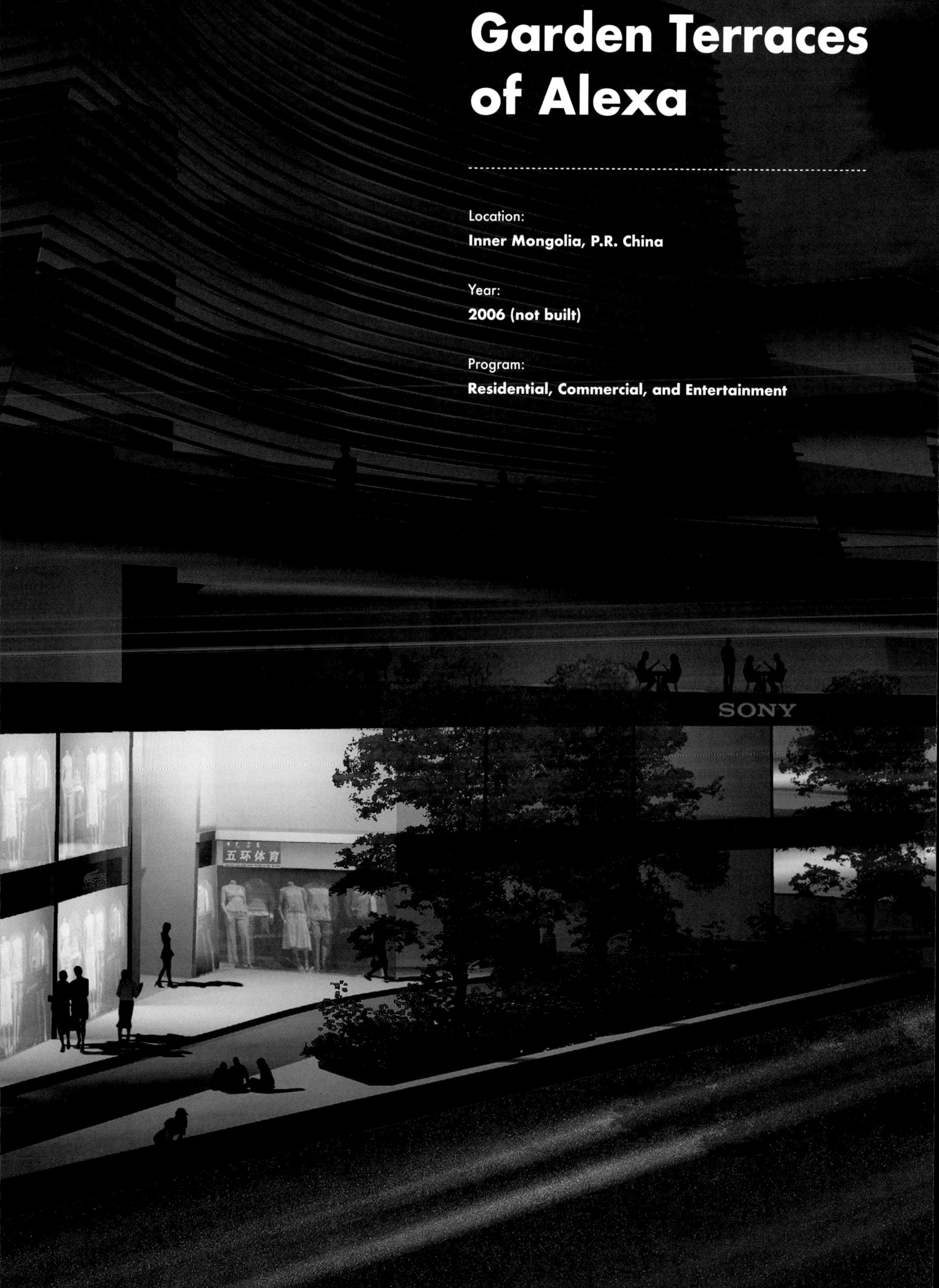

Garden Terraces of Alexa

Location:
Inner Mongolia, P.R. China

Year:
2006 (not built)

Program:
Residential, Commercial, and Entertainment

Inner Mongolia, with the beauty of its landscapes and the extraordinary diversity of its land, inspired our design. The vast Gobi Desert, rich with history and poetry, calls for creativity. In this mysterious region, the natural beauty of the landscape transforms from the undulating sandy desert to the powerful Helan Mountain to the rare mountain forests. In the Garden Terraces of Alexa we find an opportunity to bring these three remarkable ecologies together, illuminating a bright future for this young territory with a past reaching back more than 2,000 years.

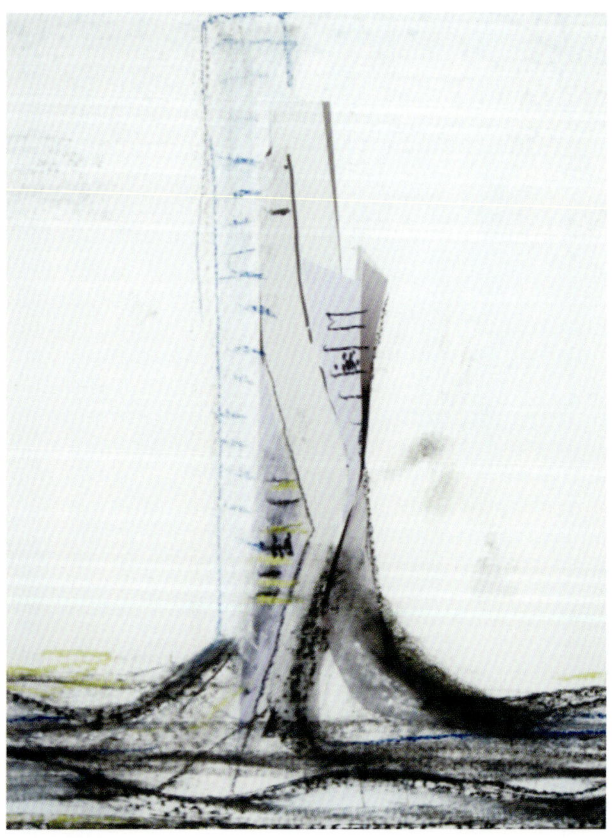

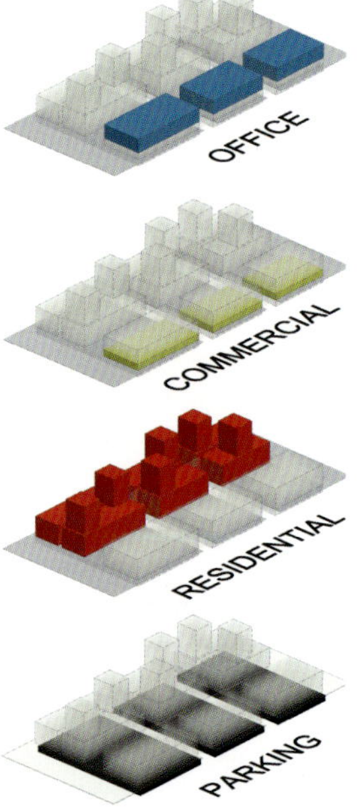

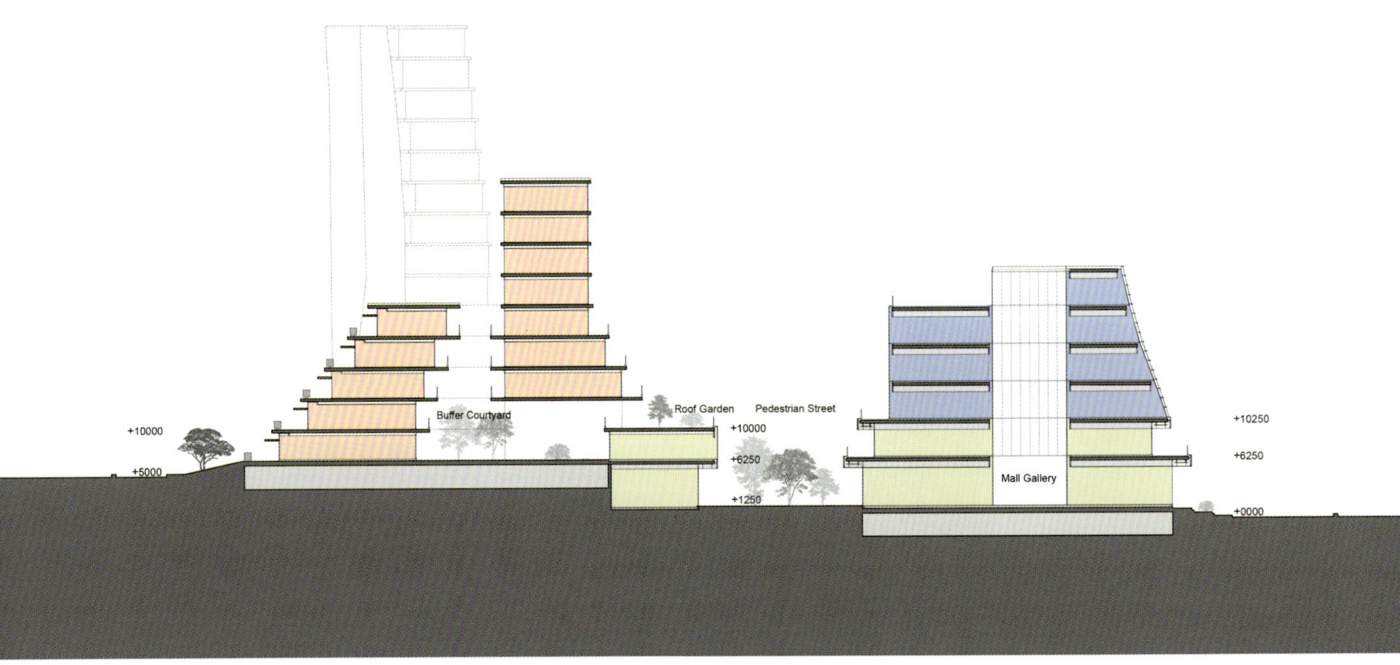

Newly created neighborhoods tie into the life of a future city, where hopes are made. The Garden Terraces of Alexa are positioned on the site according to its natural topography. Undulating sand forms step up and back creating garden roofs, as an organic structure rises to erupt into dynamic Babylon-like garden towers. Each residential housing terrace steps back from the city's central park to give every citizen a beautiful view of the park and personal gardens to enjoy.

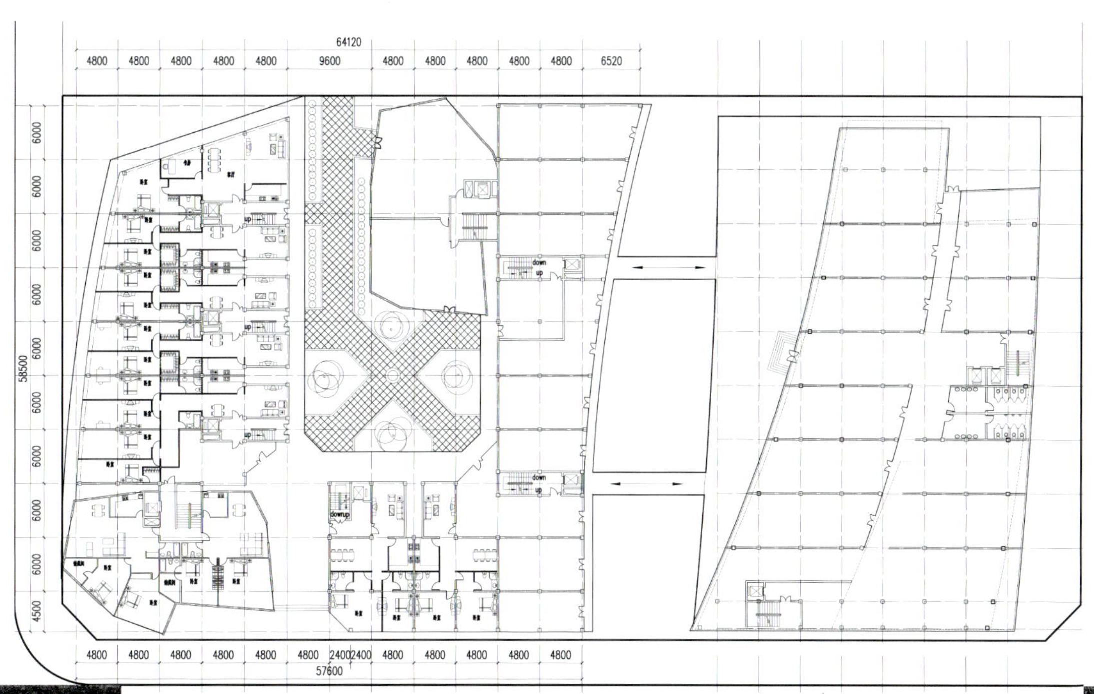

64120
4800 4800 4800 4800 4800 9600 4800 4800 4800 4800 4800 6520
58500
6000 6000 6000 6000 6000 6000 6000 6000 6000 4500
4800 4800 4800 4800 4800 4800 2400 2400 4800 4800 4800 4800 4800
57600
down
up

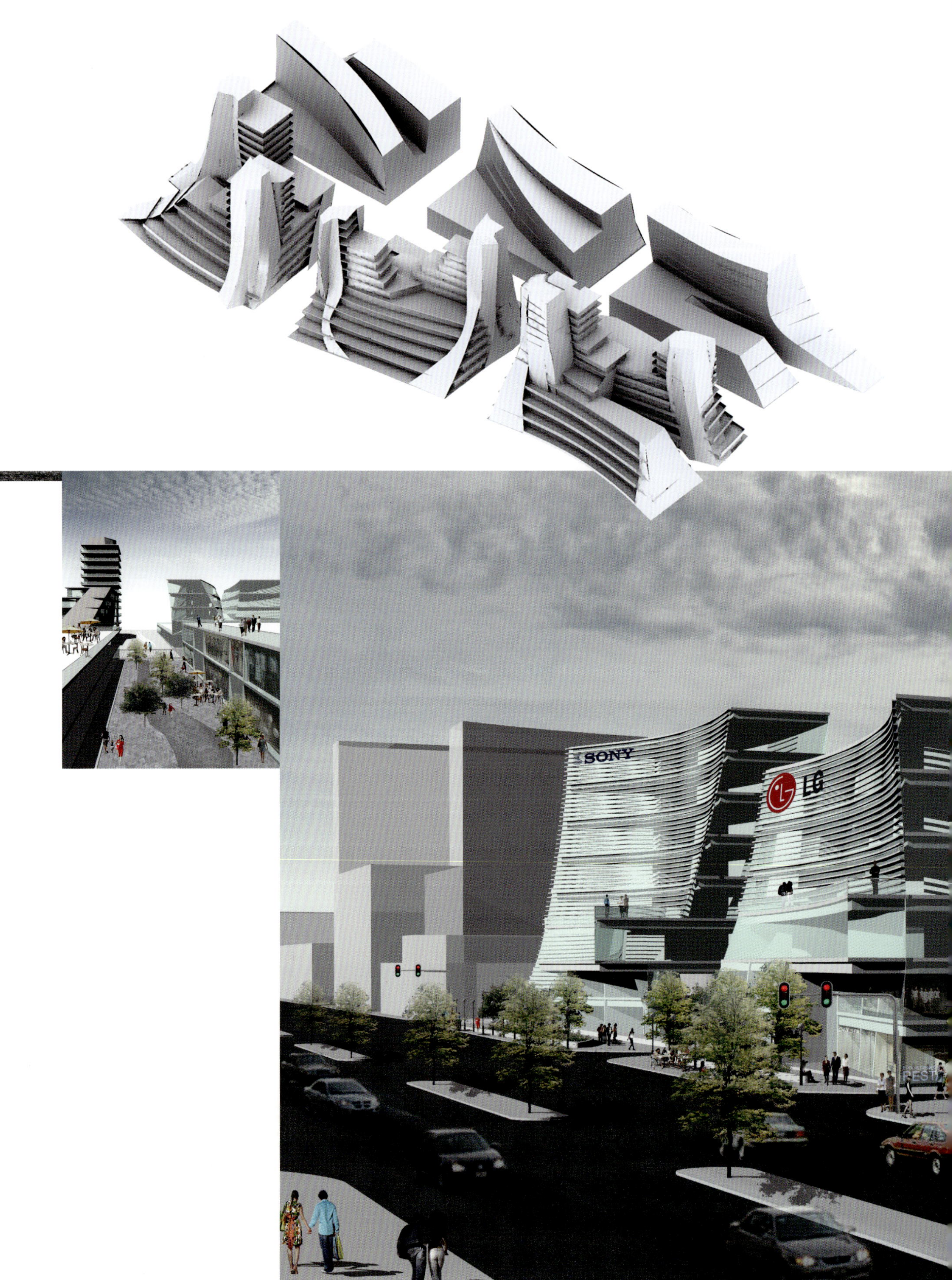
SONY
LG

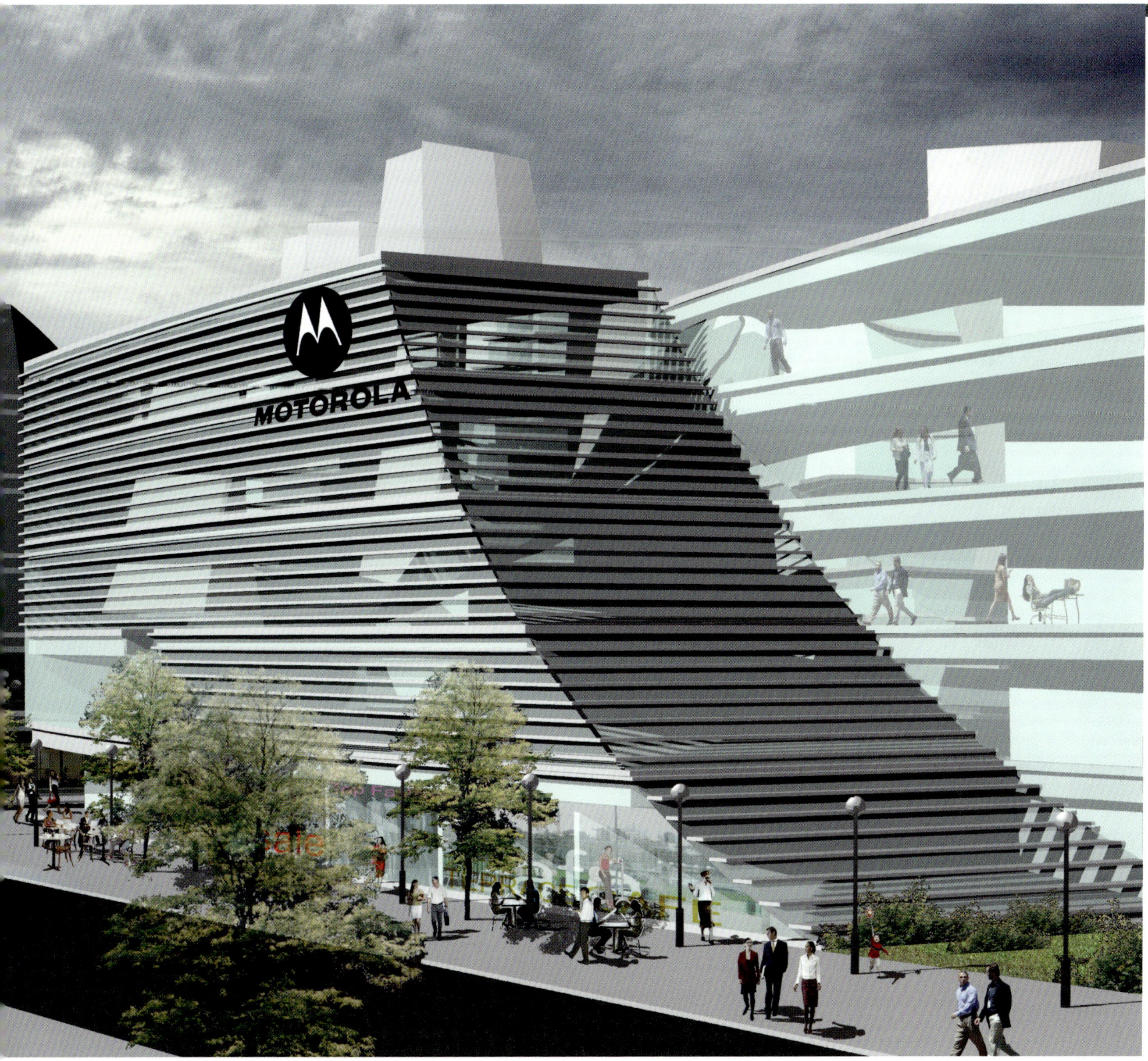

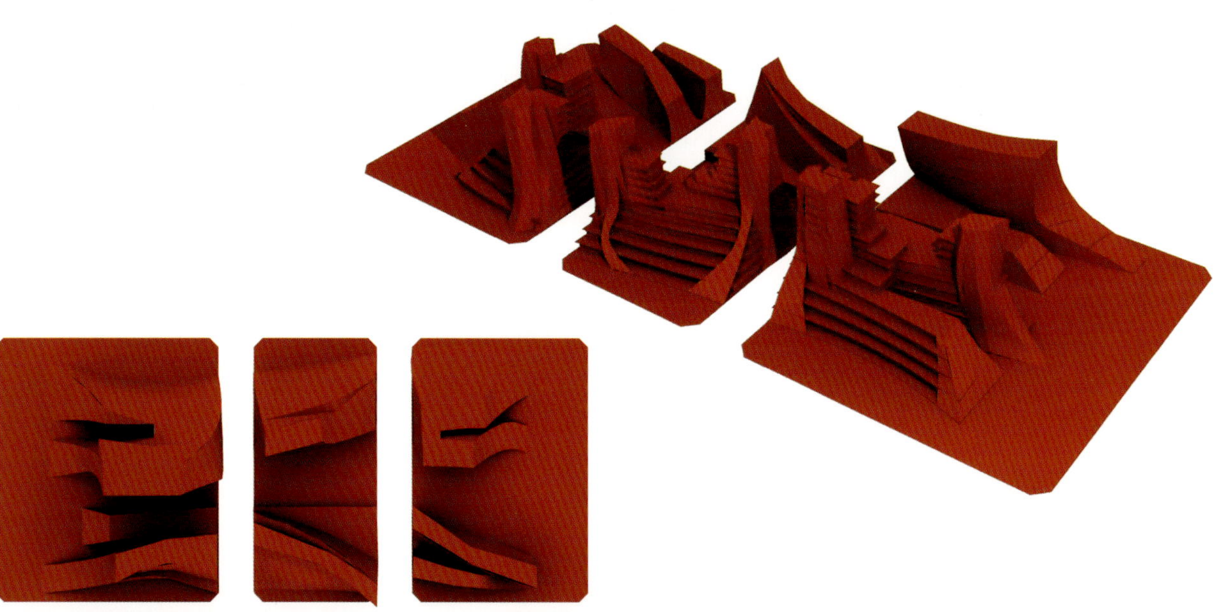

We wanted to see their movements and inter-actions translated into the physical space of the theater.

Shakespearean Theater

Location:

London, England

Year:

2006 (not built)

Program:

Experimental Theater

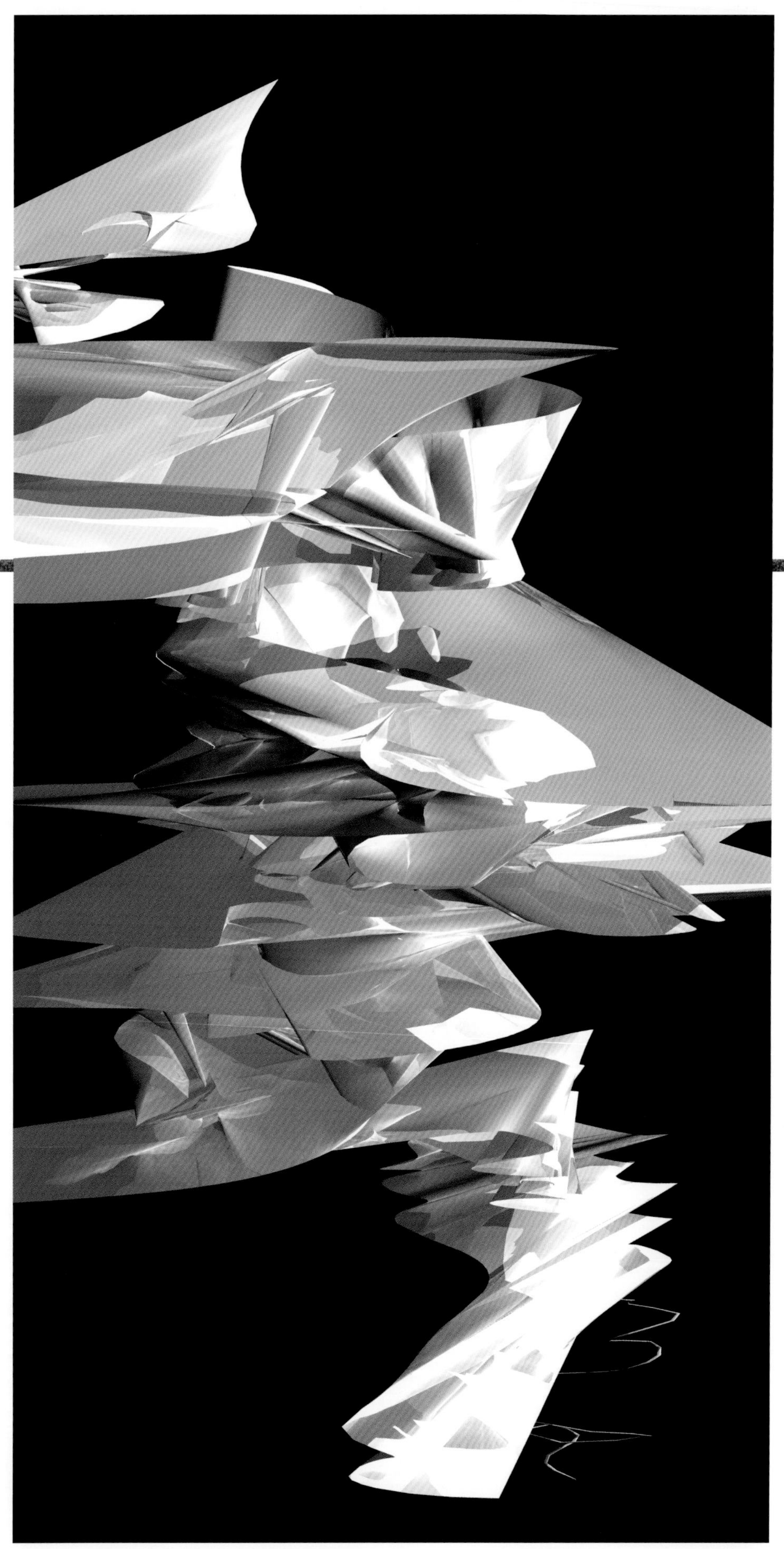

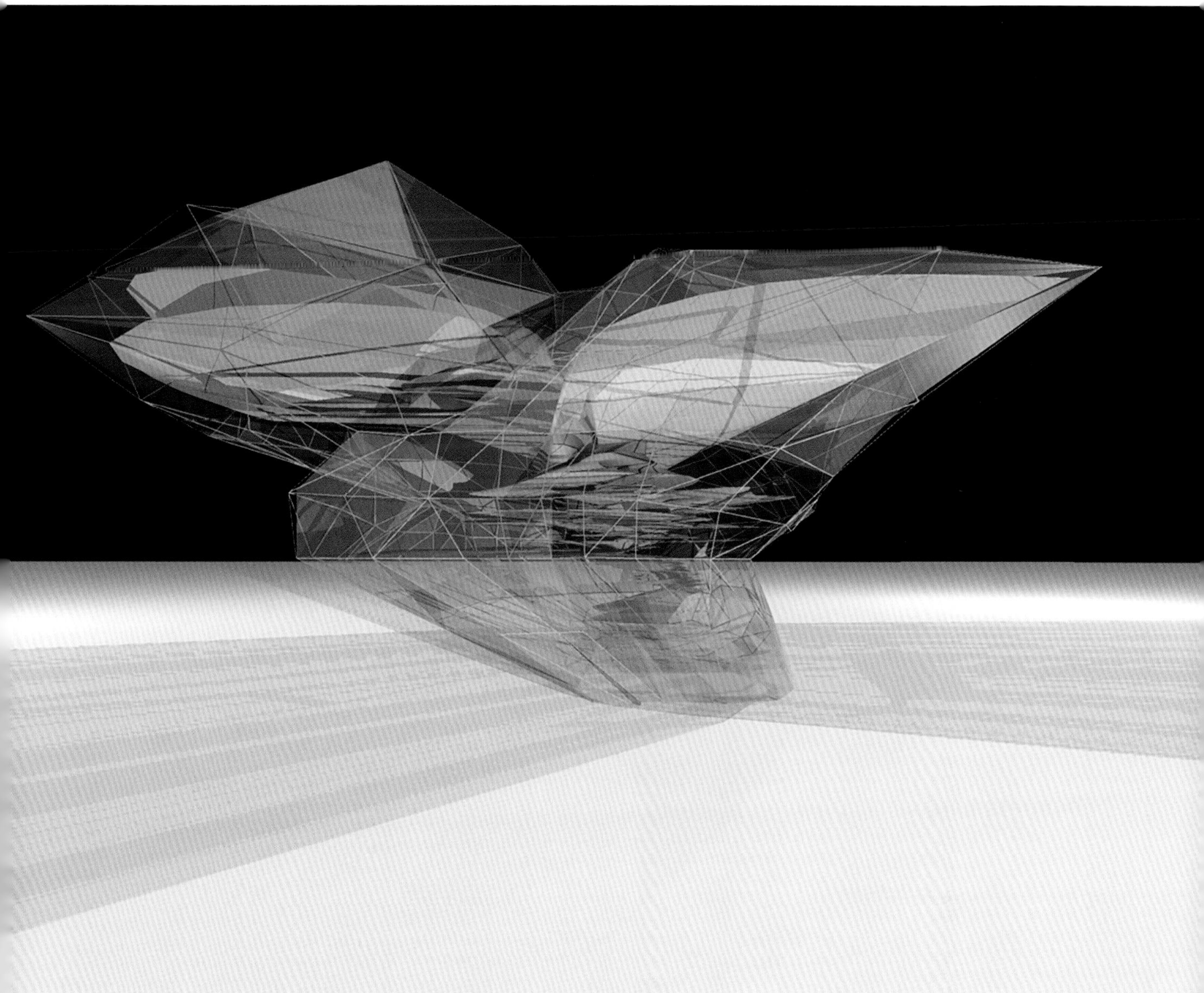

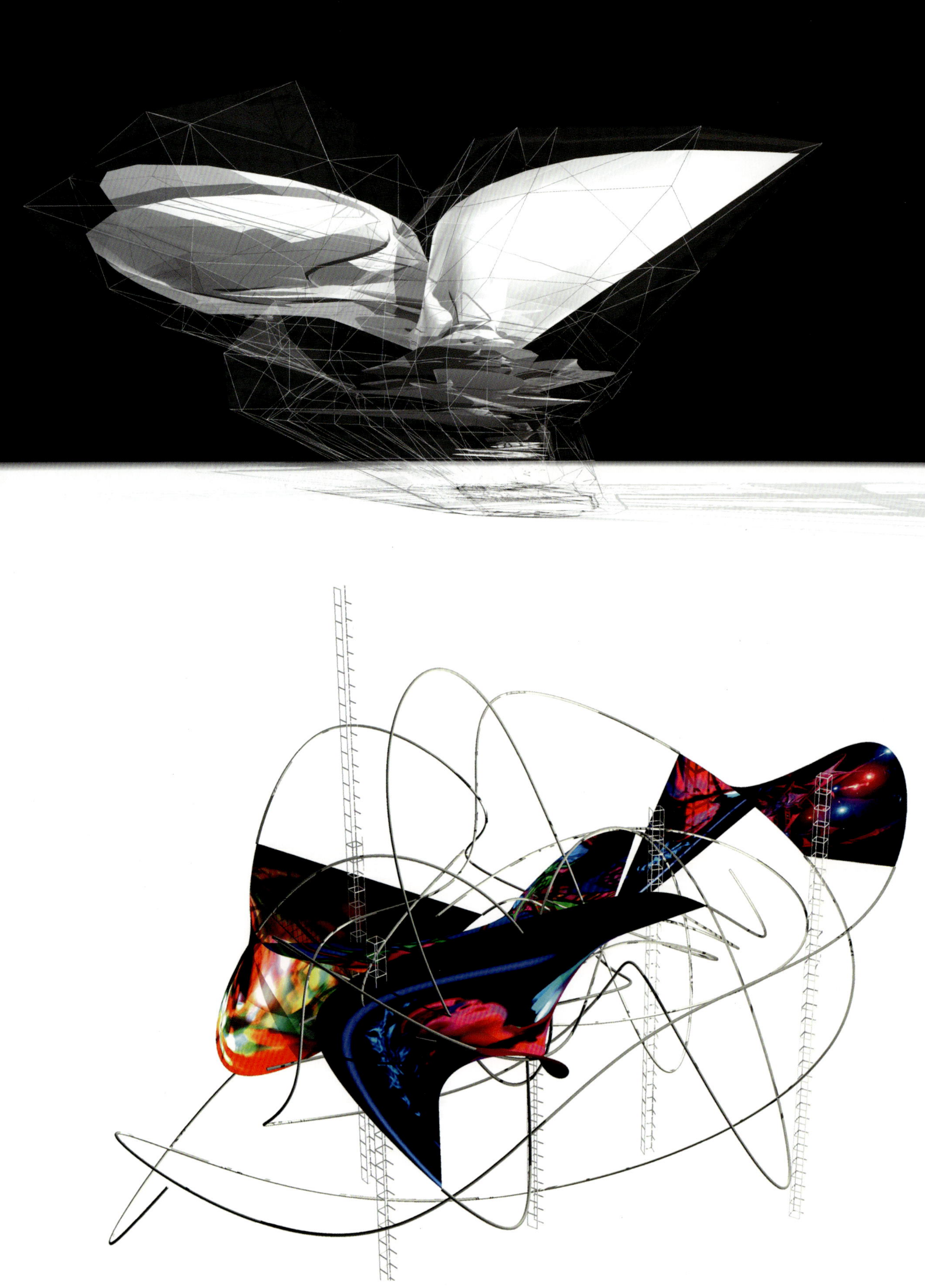

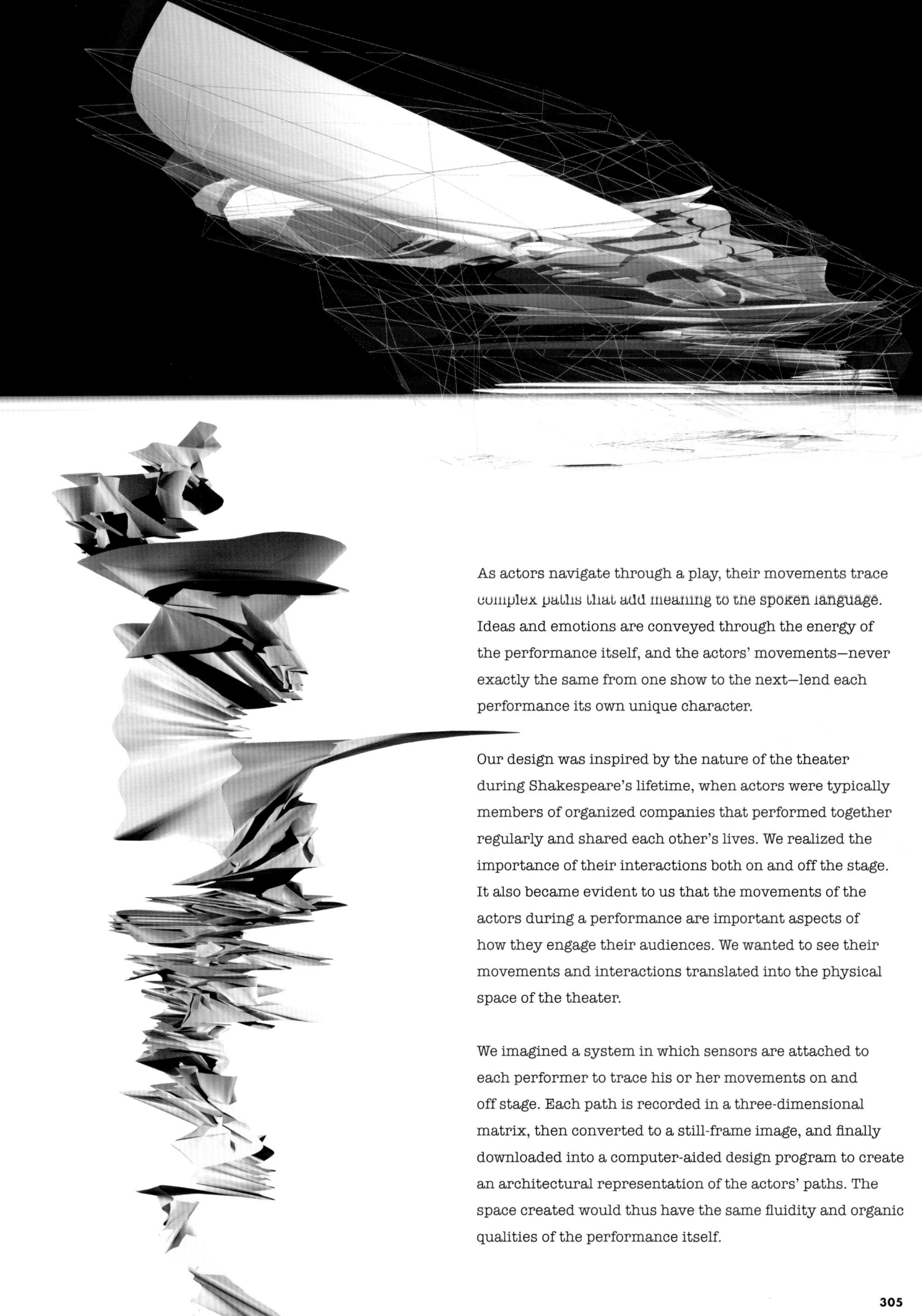

As actors navigate through a play, their movements trace complex paths that add meaning to the spoken language. Ideas and emotions are conveyed through the energy of the performance itself, and the actors' movements—never exactly the same from one show to the next—lend each performance its own unique character.

Our design was inspired by the nature of the theater during Shakespeare's lifetime, when actors were typically members of organized companies that performed together regularly and shared each other's lives. We realized the importance of their interactions both on and off the stage. It also became evident to us that the movements of the actors during a performance are important aspects of how they engage their audiences. We wanted to see their movements and interactions translated into the physical space of the theater.

We imagined a system in which sensors are attached to each performer to trace his or her movements on and off stage. Each path is recorded in a three-dimensional matrix, then converted to a still-frame image, and finally downloaded into a computer-aided design program to create an architectural representation of the actors' paths. The space created would thus have the same fluidity and organic qualities of the performance itself.

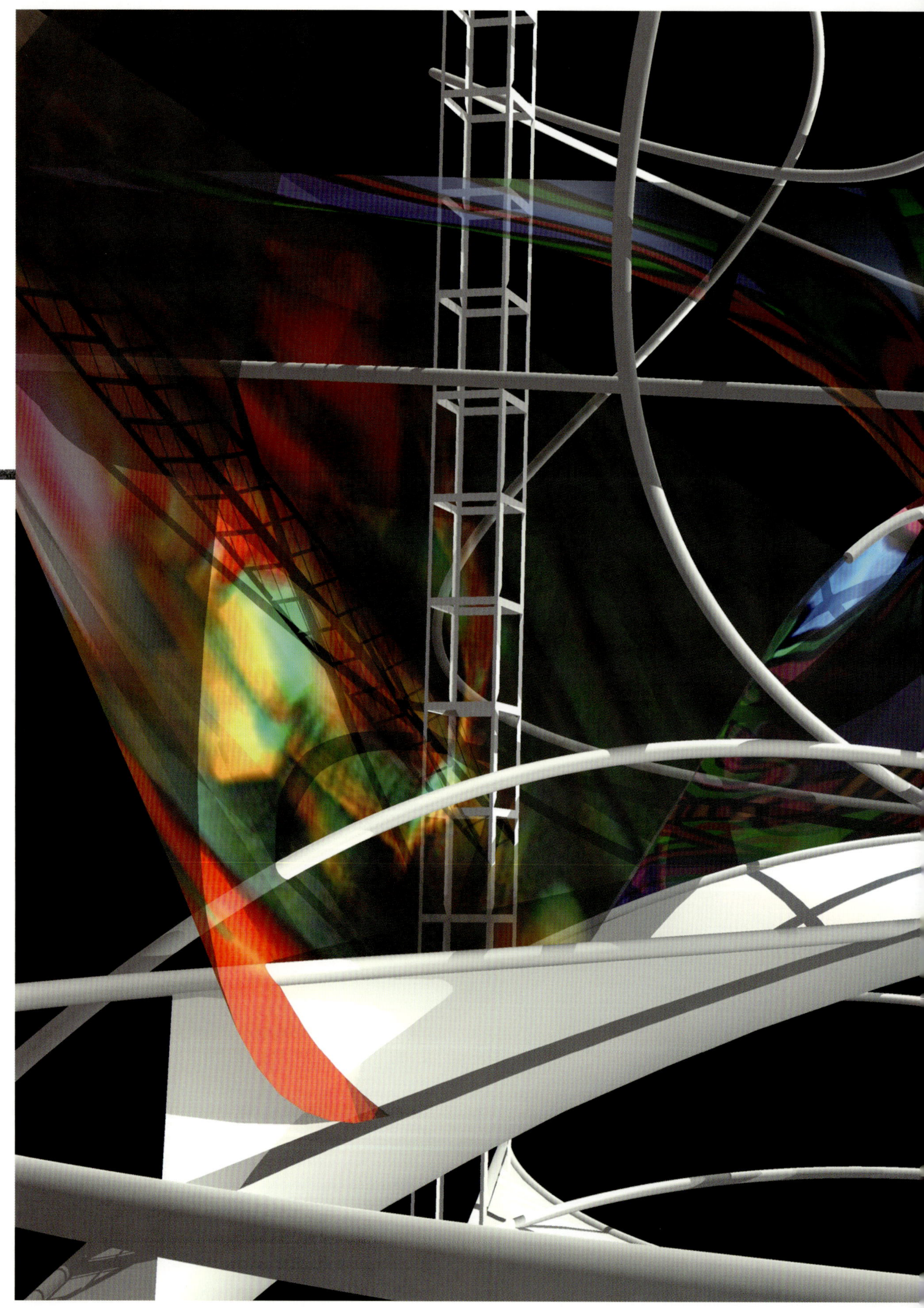

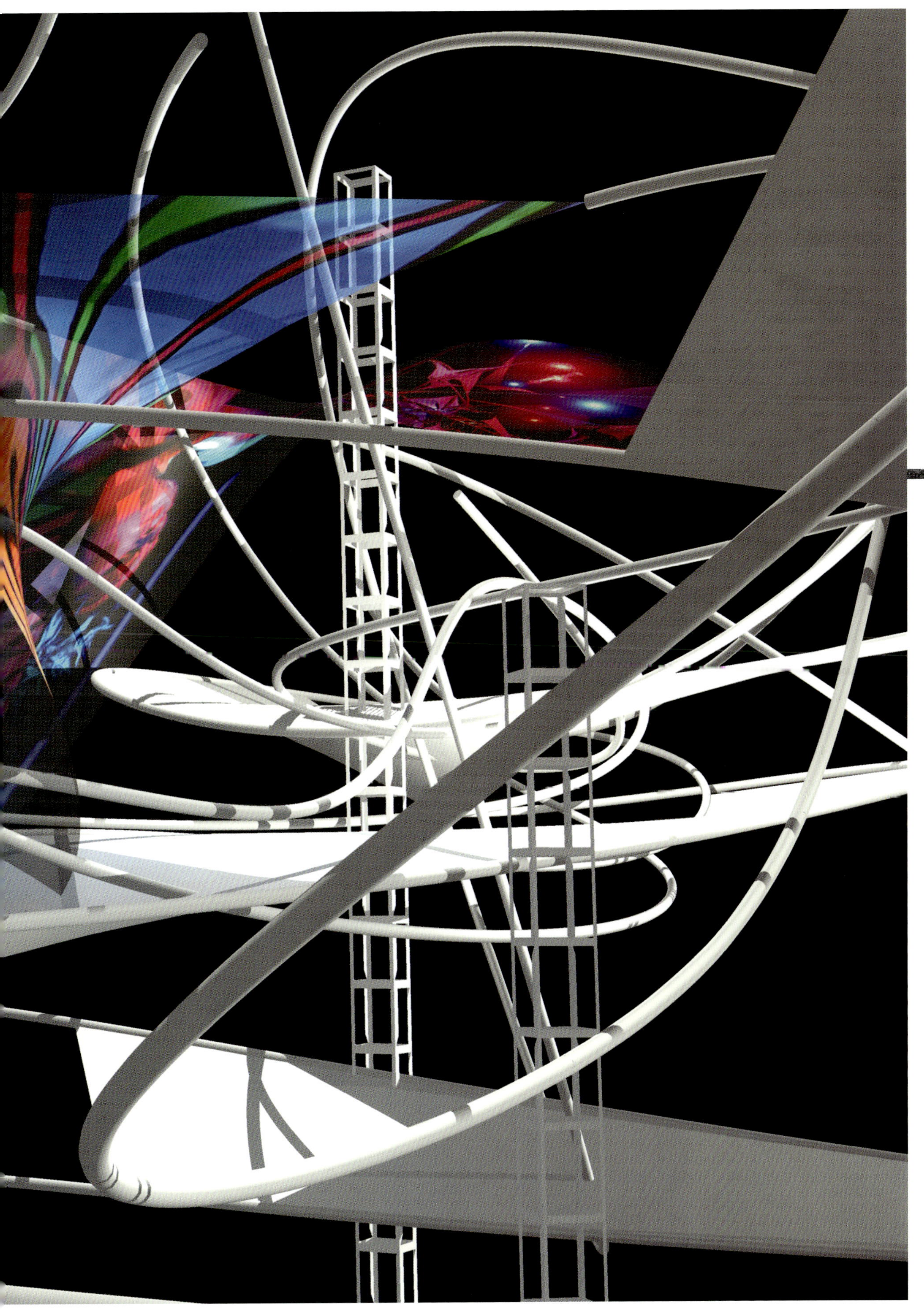

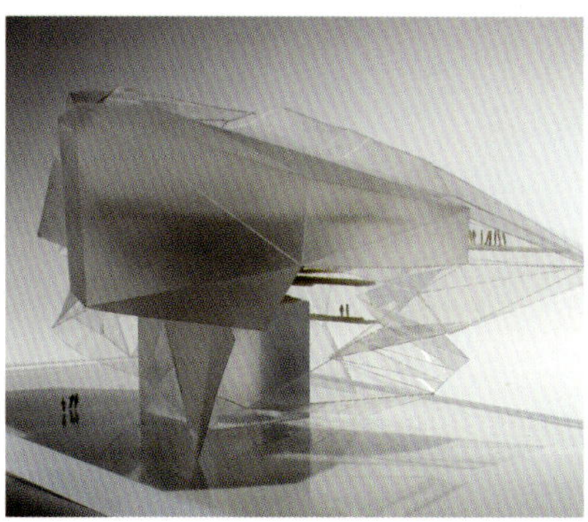

The multifaceted building transforms as the observer changes their vantage point.

FPT Tower

My first visit to Vietnam: I will never forget that morning when Hien, my dear old friend and student from SCI-Arc, picked me up at around 2:00 a.m. from Ho Chi Minh airport. A Vietnamese-American, he had moved to the United States at an early age with his mother and brother and was raised in Southern California. He became a very kind and talented architect and decided to move back to Vietnam in the mid-nineties, when he started a very successful firm of his own. We stayed in touch through the years and in 2007 he invited me to participate a joint venture on a high-rise building competition in Hanoi for FPT, a fast-growing tech company in Vietnam.

I was expecting to be dropped off at the hotel that night but, instead we went for a tour of the city; its energy and lively images are still vivid in my memories. We met Hien's family and friends at an outdoor rooftop restaurant and ate, drank, chatted, and took passport photos before I was dropped off at my hotel around 4:00 a.m. The vibrancy of the city was contagious and left me surprisingly energized after my long trip.

The new FPT is Vietnam's first information and communication technology company. Like most tech companies, they were seeking a more social and interactive workplace to reflect their brand. The cities in Vietnam are changing rapidly and the high-rise building typology needs to change in response to these different contexts and cultural conditions. In the FPT model the people actually work together and interact, they talk to each other to exchange ideas; therefore the spatial organization is less restrictive.

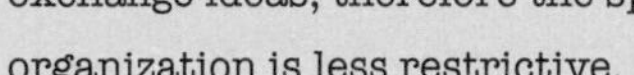

FPT Tower

Location:
Hanoi, Vietnam

Year:
2007 (not built)

Program:
Office Building

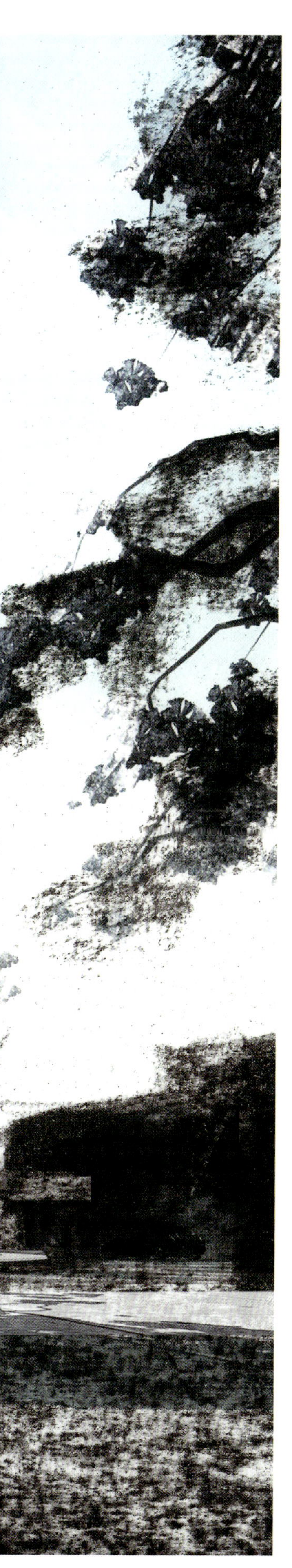

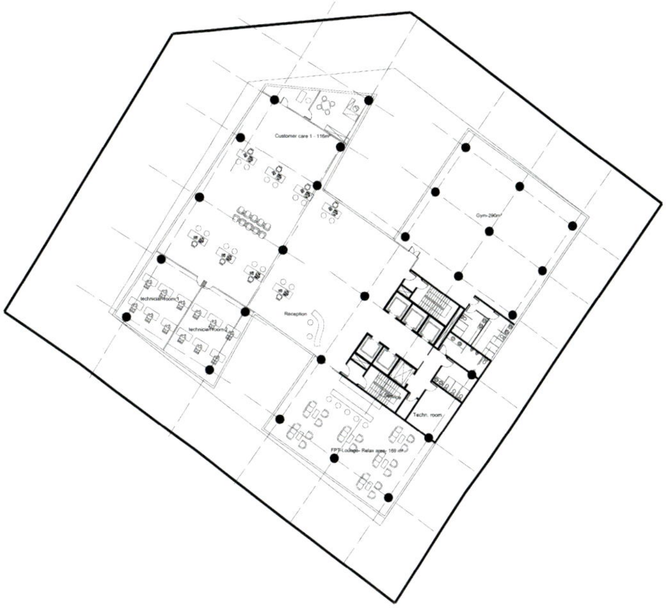
Reception
Techn. room

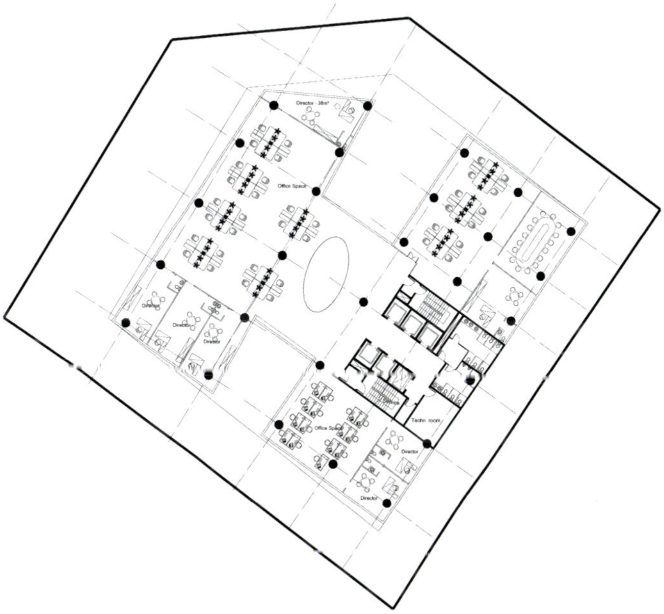
Office Space
Director
Techn. room

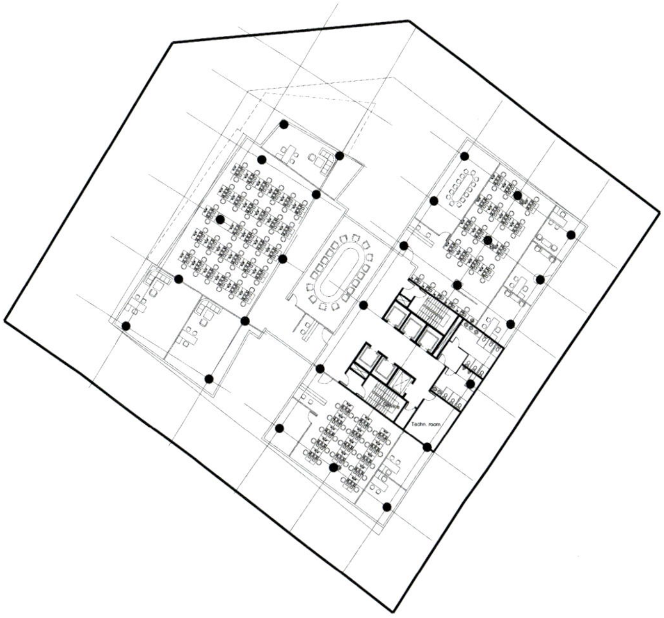
Techn. room

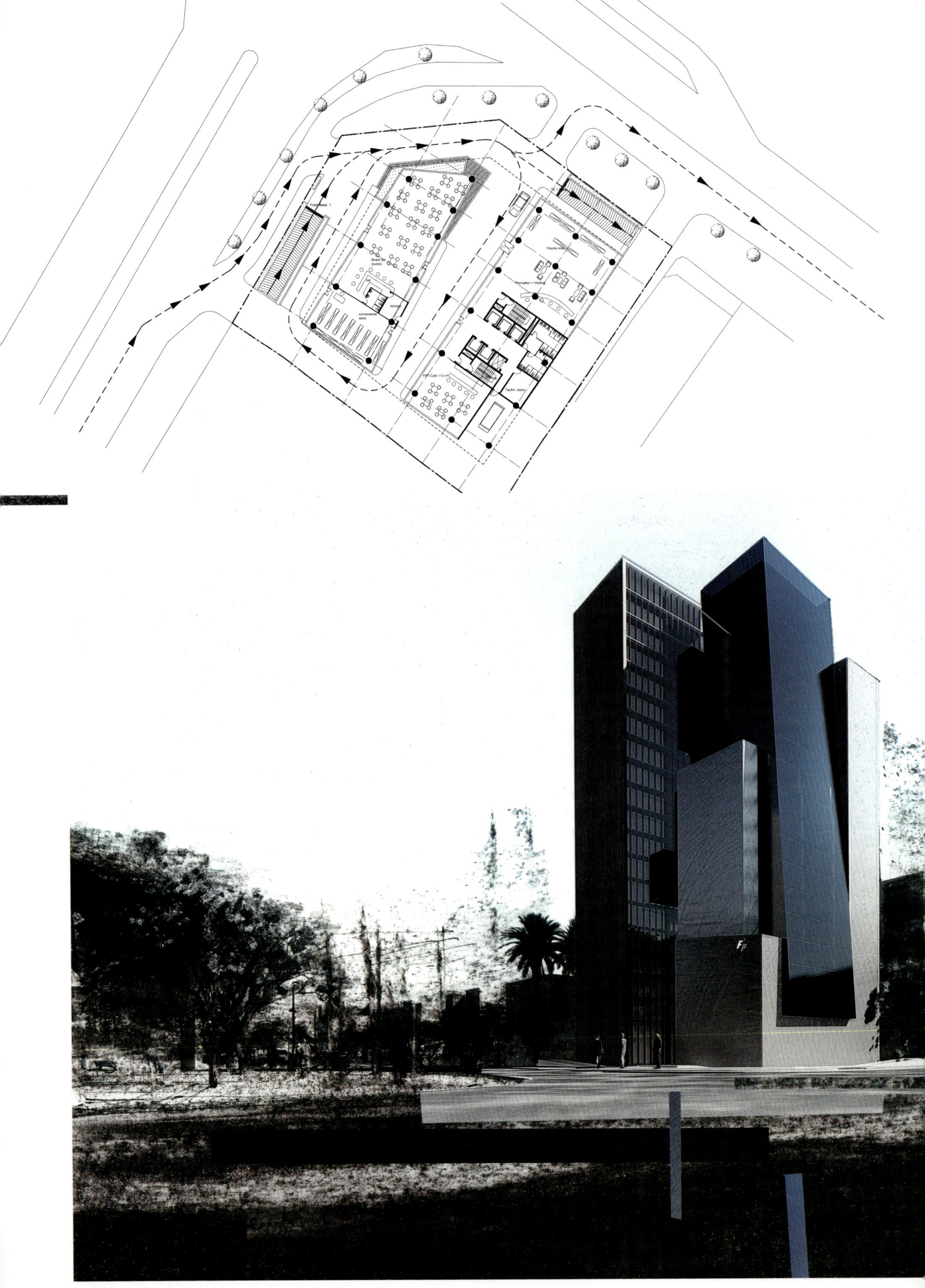
From Base. 1
Snack bar
(public)
bar
storage
convenience
store
Display area
Reception + Waiting
FPT-Cafe 113 m²
Techn. room

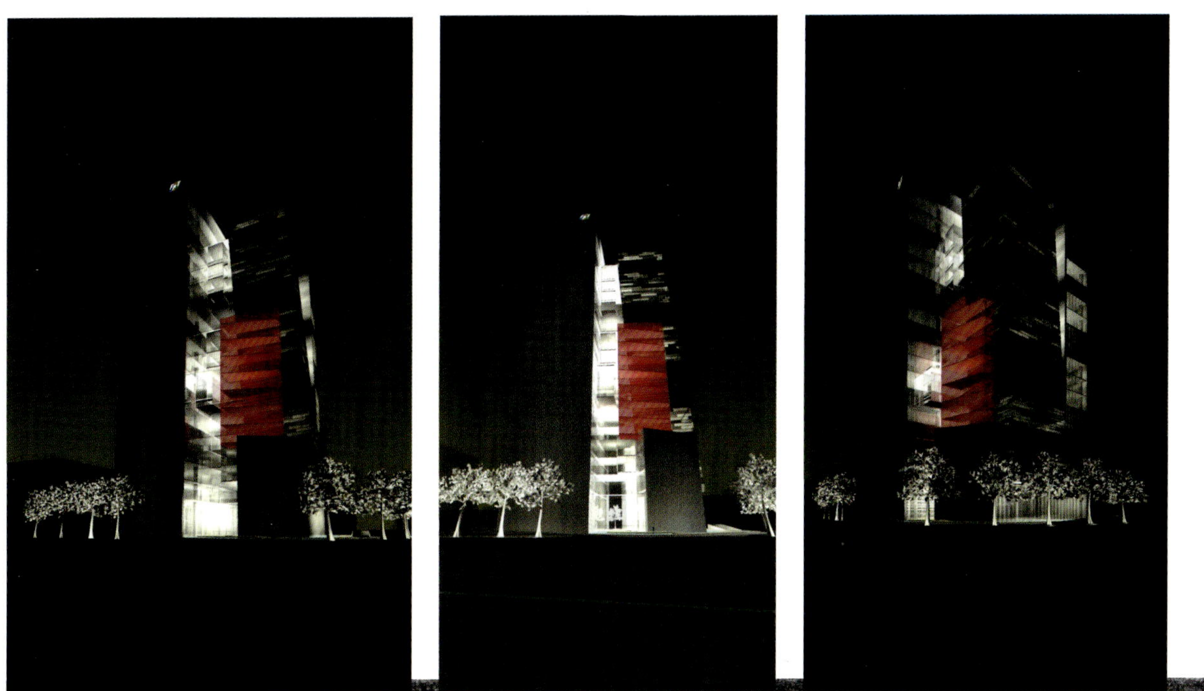

The way we achieved this objective was to divide the different entities of the company into four different building elements. For example, the "main building" houses the administration offices, financial department and services. The "Tower," which leans on the main building is where the technical departments are located, including research and development, laboratories, and presentation areas. The third "space of interaction" is the area between the main building and the tower. This is the social workplace where communication takes place internally and with the outside world. The conference rooms, presentation rooms, and meeting rooms are in this area. In the space of interaction we saw the opportunity to bring daylight down into the center of the space using passive technologies and local materials.

And, finally, the "base" is the entrance, where the building's public space accommodates social events, galleries, and gathering space. This space also includes a fitness and health center, child care center, open garden for relaxation, and a gym and pool area. Our design optimizes the use of the property to maximize the allowable buildable area in a very delicate and strategic way while maintaining a meaningful and dynamic architectural composition.

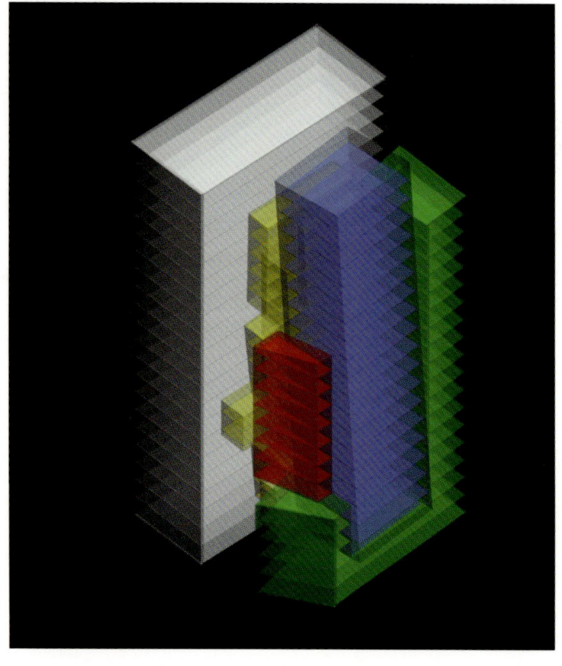

The four elements converge to create the architecture of the building. Situated at the corner of a busy intersection the building changes depending on the viewer's point of approach. The multifaceted building transforms as the observer changes their vantage point. This dynamic interaction was carefully studied to make sure that the building interacts with its surroundings and immediate context in order to connect people and makes the life of the city more enjoyable.

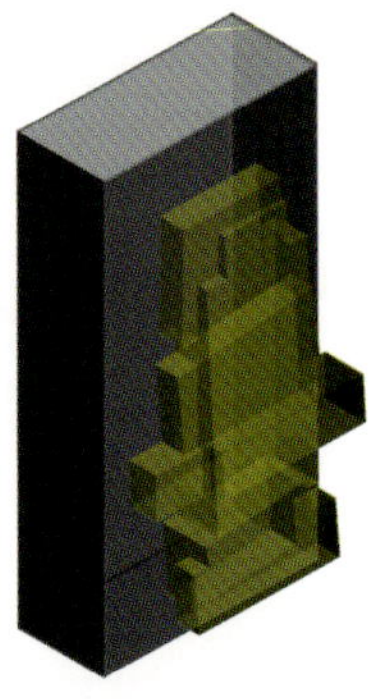

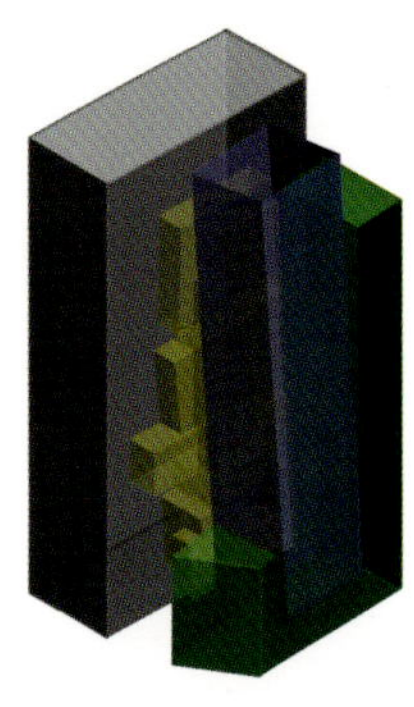

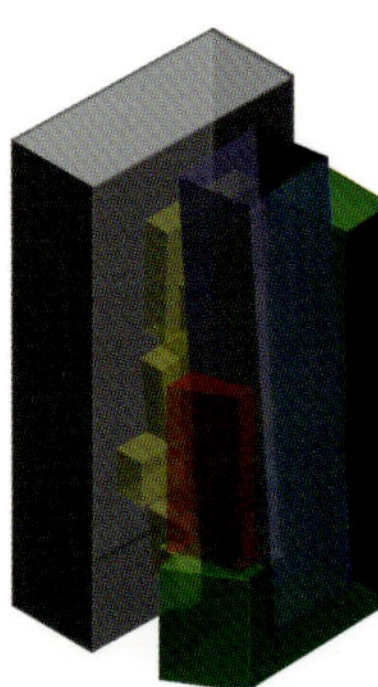

...an architectural diversity which lends itself to an architectural language that is local but it is also global.

BIDV Tower

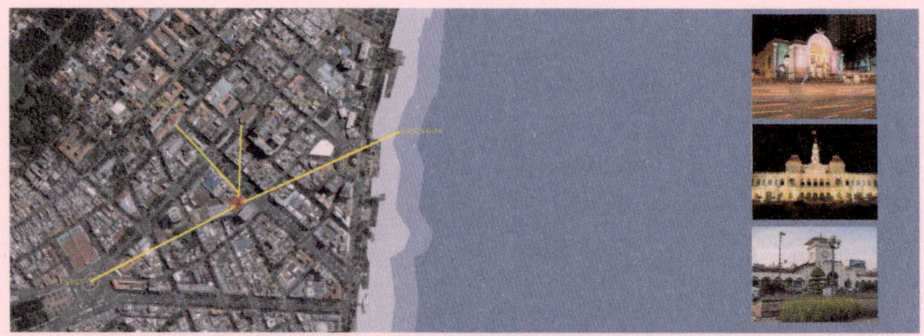

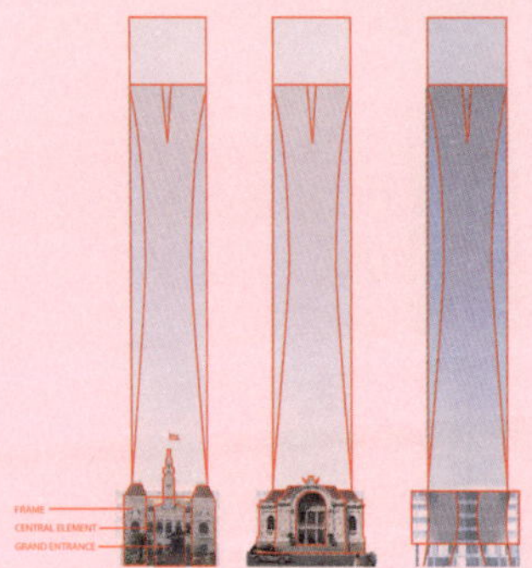

The history of Vietnam dates back more than 4,000 years. For most of the period, from 111 BCE to 1975, Vietnam fought the invasion of the Chinese, Mongols, French, Japanese, and Americans for its independence and freedom. Vietnam's history for its independence through the ages has created an architectural diversity that lends itself to a design language that is both local and global.

In navigating Ho Chi Minh City we discovered the architectural diversity that represents its rich history. There is a plethora of architectural archetypes represented in this crowded yet romantic place, including traces of the ancient Chinese, the Ly, Tran, Le, and Nguyen, the French Colonial era, and modern and postmodern buildings. There is a delicate balance in play here; we felt we were obligated to use architectural forms that speak to the paradigm shifts that distinguish our current global culture from those that preceded it. The new architecture for the BIDV Tower design is therefore contemporary but with an eye on Vietnam's cultural past.

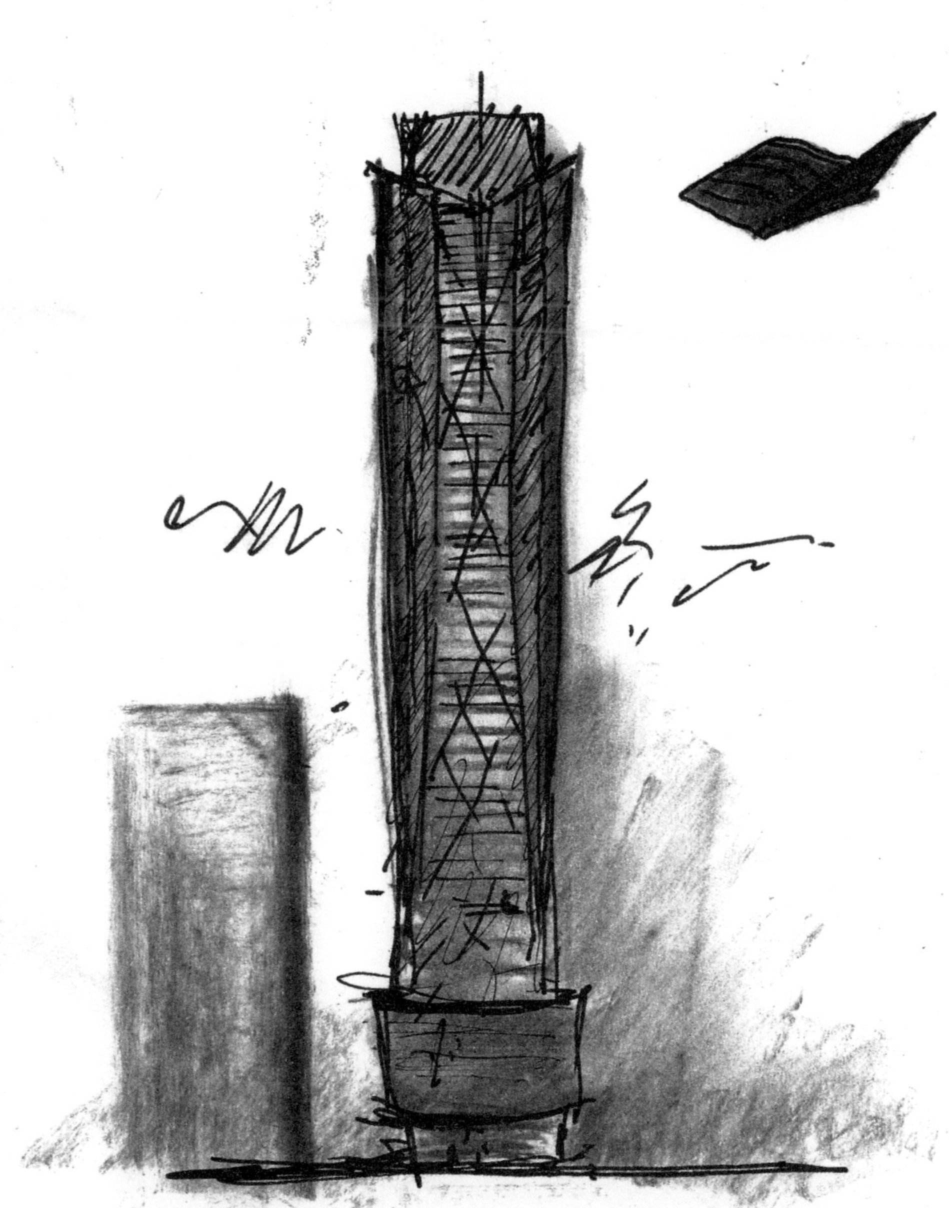

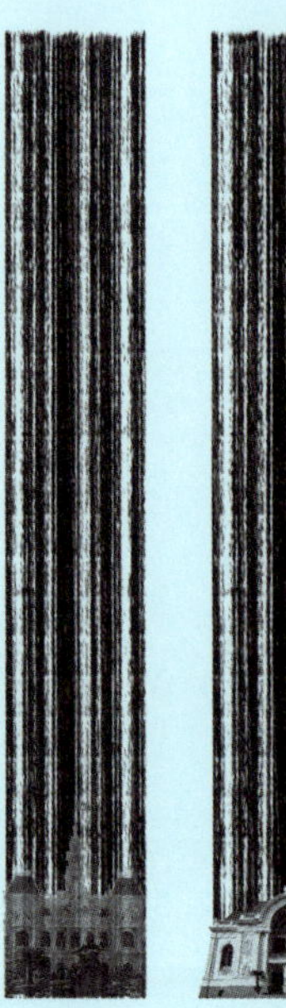

By studying the tower location and the fact that it is between one existing tower to the south and a future one to the north we realized that new BIDV Tower would be set back from the street in relationship to its southern neighbor. We decided that our design should look beyond the immediate context and reach out to the city, resulting in a symmetrical tower that faces the main street.

A new language and geometry was required that takes the observer into account in a fundamental way. The new BIDV Tower would become the symbol of contemporary Vietnam for the new generation of entrepreneurs while also representing Vietnam in the global market. We studied the relationship of the new tower with its surroundings, including its relationship to the opera house, central committee building, and the existing and new towers that were about to be constructed at the time. Our design proposed an elegant geometric organization that acknowledged the very dynamic future development of the existing site, its relationship to its surroundings, and the site's circumscription by strong currents of human, motorcycle, and automobile traffic.

BIDV Tower

Location:
Ho Chi Minh City, Vietnam

Year:
2007 (not built)

Program:
Commercial Office Building

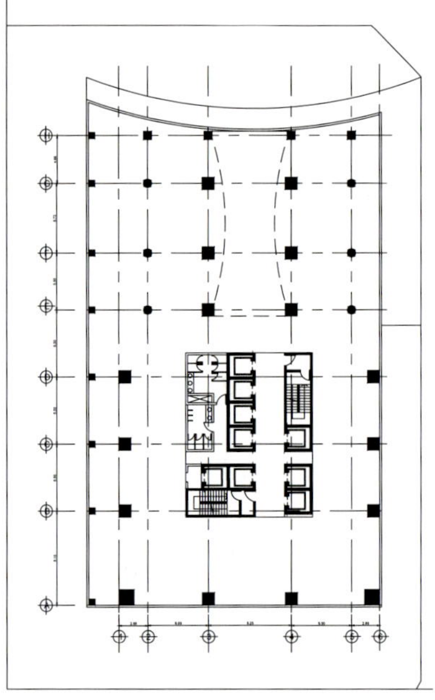

Ground

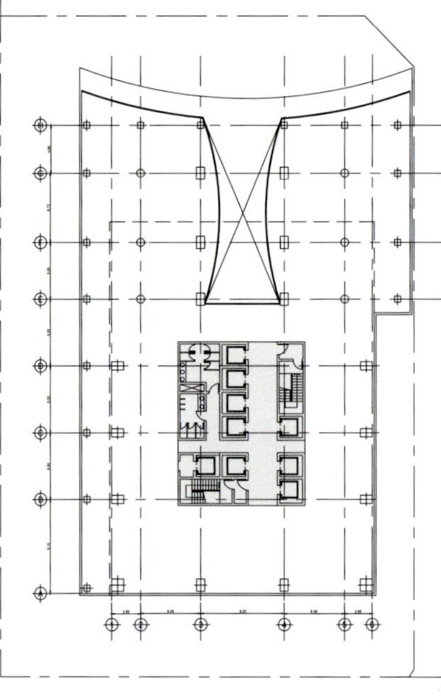

Typical Podium

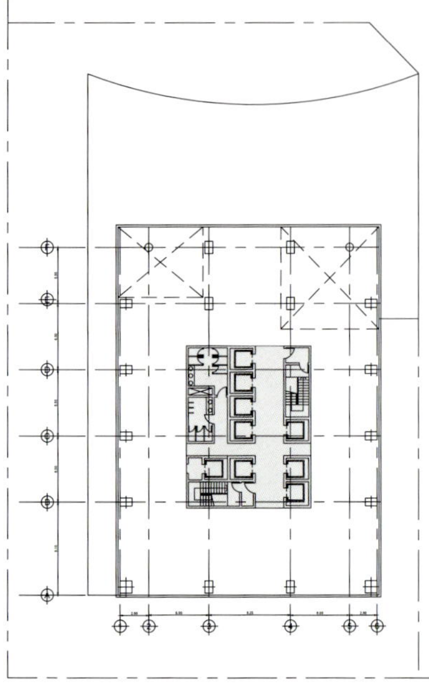

Typical Tower (23rd floor)

The introduction of a bold symmetrical tower integrates the building's interface with its surroundings. Charged with the expansiveness of a daring sculptural form this spatial attractor is further energized by the trajectories of pedestrians and vehicles as they move through and around the building. The two balanced corner openings redefine the strong tower shape and suggest how its footprints reach out to the boundaries of the city. Another narrow and elegant opening in the back reinforces the boundaries of the tower and its connectivity to its surroundings. The lines are carefully calculated to achieve a proportional excellence in shape, size, and style. The façade achieves qualities of both depth and lightness reflecting the activity of the building, the activity of the street, and signage.

The primary arching steel structure of the main entrance orients the center of the building along Nguyen Hue Boulevard. It opens onto a luminous six-story space overlooked by balconies on either side. This dynamic monumental space brings the natural light into the core of the podium portion of the building where the transaction, national and international representative offices, BIDV finance banking, conference area, services office for lease, and lobby areas are situated.

Aspiring to defy the forces of gravity and geometry, we imagined a new face for BIVD tower heading skyward like an angel. Weightless and airborne with its wing stretched outwards toward Ho Chi Minh City, limbs of glass and steel dynamically imply a capacity for flight.

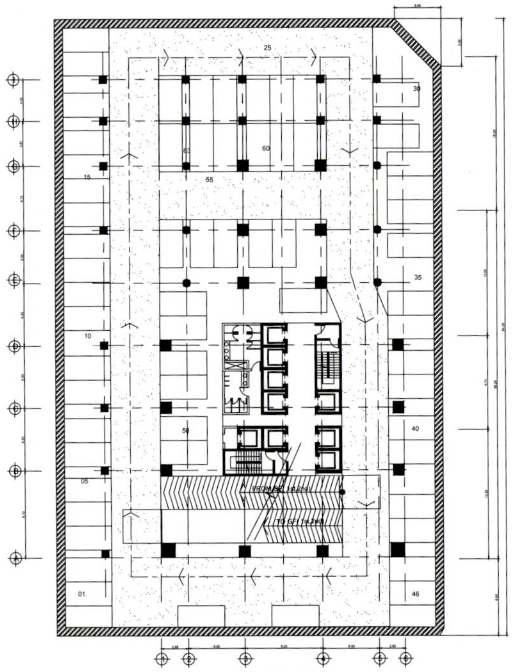

Typical Parking

The gestural vocabulary of the BIDV fabric can also be understood as an analogical reflection of this future international city and its streetscape. The project's reflective tendencies activate the city with a doubling produced by mirroring. Entering beneath the grand arch of the façade, the visitor's gaze is trained skyward toward the fusion of the outside and inside. New zones are revealed as the space unfolds into various activities. In keeping with the spirit of the building's exterior, the central themes of the interior spaces are also openness and transparency. Public spaces are delineated with a series of transparent and translucent glass partitions deployed to maintain a comfortable level of privacy and intimacy while providing a sense of visual continuity throughout. The vertical circulation core—clear, functional, and elegant—speaks to the efficiency and functionality of the design. The elevators, stairs, and public restrooms are carefully positioned like a block puzzle while using the minimum space possible to achieve the best lifestyle and safety requirements. Elevators bring users to the various levels of activities, climaxing at the café restaurant on the top level, where guests are treated to panoramic views of the city and beyond. The new BIDV Tower will embrace tradition within the age of information, communicating to and for the people.

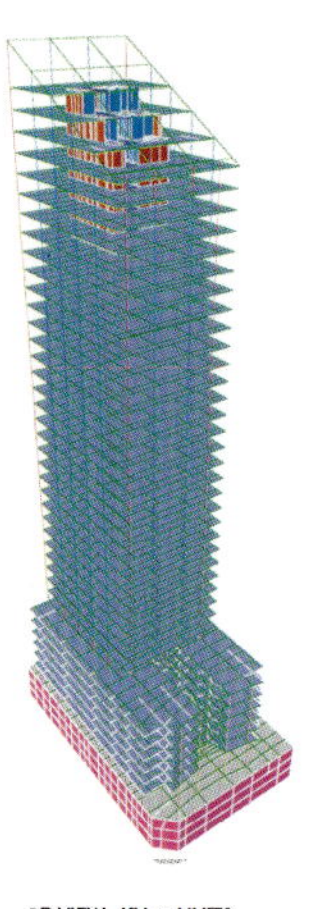

3D VIEW - KN-m UNITS

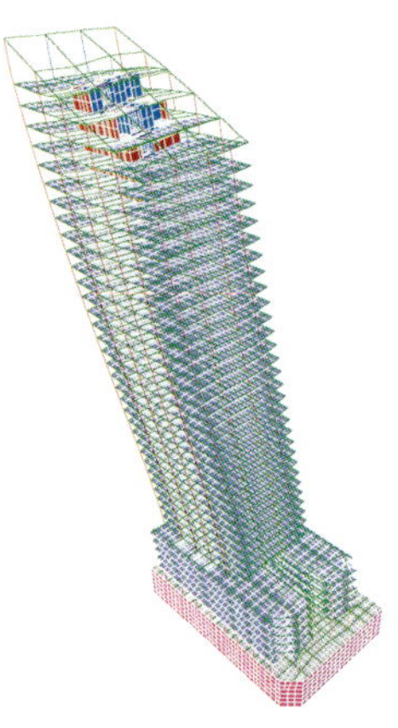

MODE 1 PERIOD 4.3412 seconds

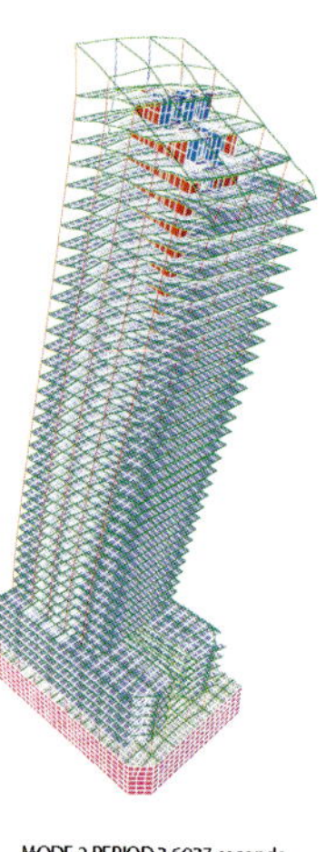

MODE 2 PERIOD 3.6037 seconds

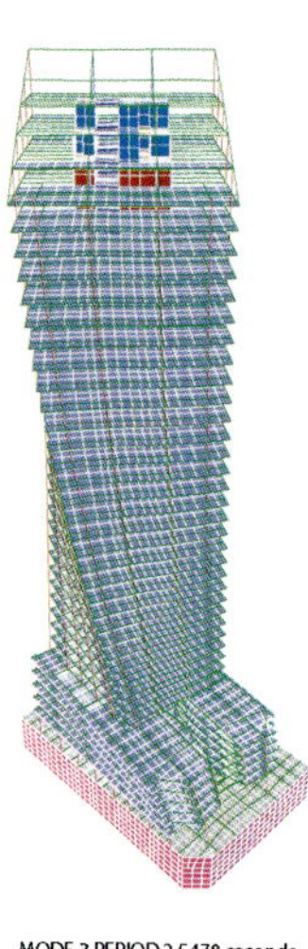

MODE 3 PERIOD 2.5478 seconds

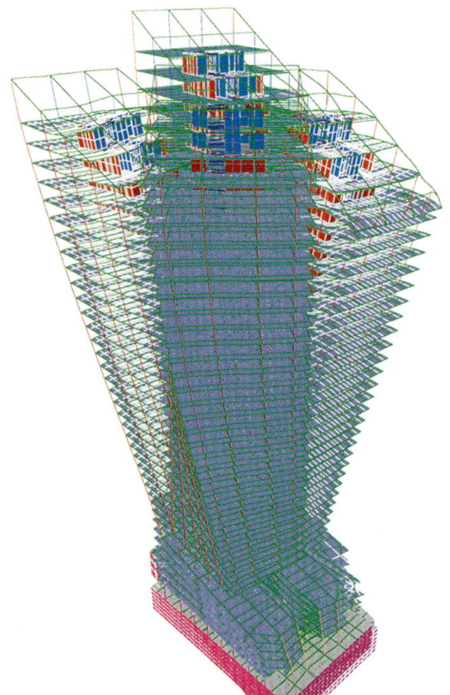

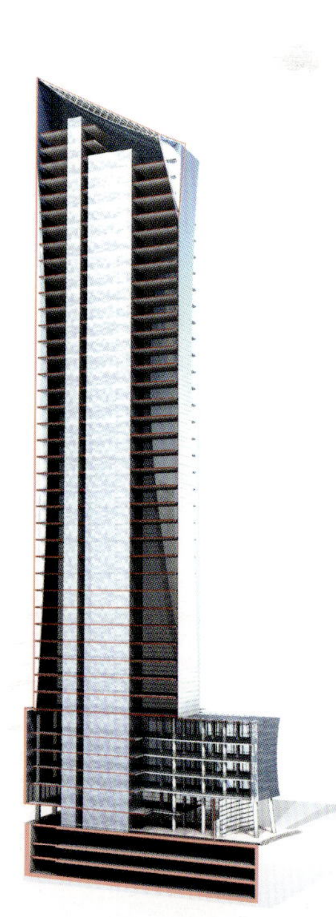

It's an era that is attempting to grapple with irregularity, metamorphic forms, and changing notions about order and disorder.

Shanghai Aquarium

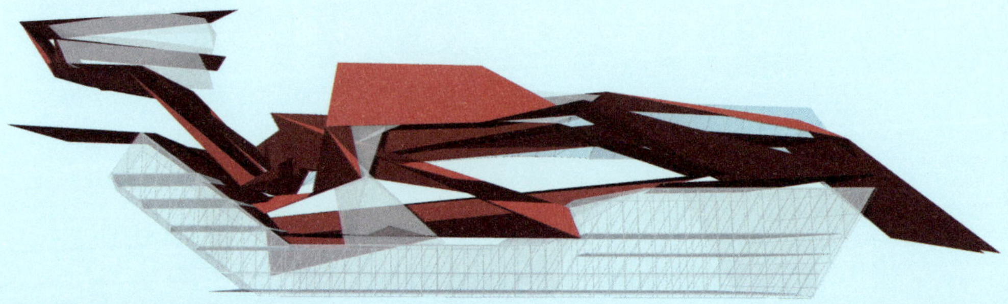

In 2007, I was introduced to Mr. Wu when visiting the construction site for Beijing's Antique Museum. The Straco CEO was looking for my client, Mr. Wang, who was helping him obtain antique furniture and other art pieces for his house. Straco was a public real estate company in Singapore specializing in providing attractions and tourism-related programs, with a focus on cultural and environmental sustainability.

That night we all went for dinner and Mr. Wu seemed interested in my design ideas. A few days later I received an email from Mr. Wu's assistant and was invited to Straco to discuss my involvement in designing an addition to the existing Shanghai Ocean Aquarium project. This was my first time in Shanghai and the gorgeous cosmopolitan megacity took me by surprise. On my way to the hotel, the taxi navigated through the financial district's elevated roads and bridges. All I could see were highrises on either side, hundreds or more, with their special designs, materials, and lighting.

I was picked up from my hotel the following morning and brought to the existing aquarium, where the offices of Straco were also located. I was given a detailed tour of the existing aquarium and the site for the future Shanghai Ocean Aquarium Museum and Theater. North of the site was the majestic Huangpu River, which flows into the Yangtze River. To the west, you could see one of China's contemporary landmarks, the Oriental Pearl TV Tower. South of the offices, you could see the Shanghai World Financial Center piercing the sky and giving the site an incredible scale.

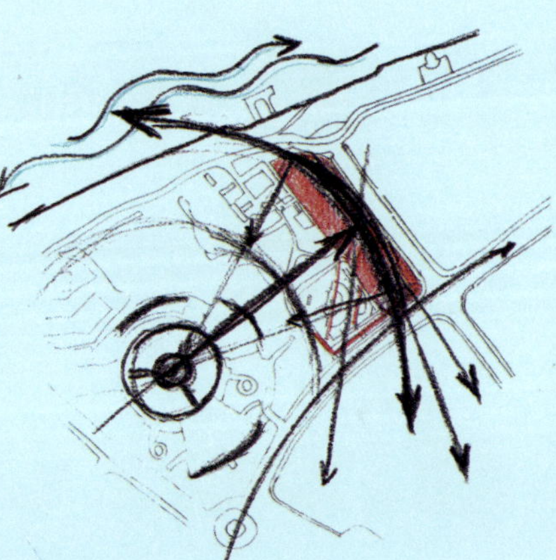

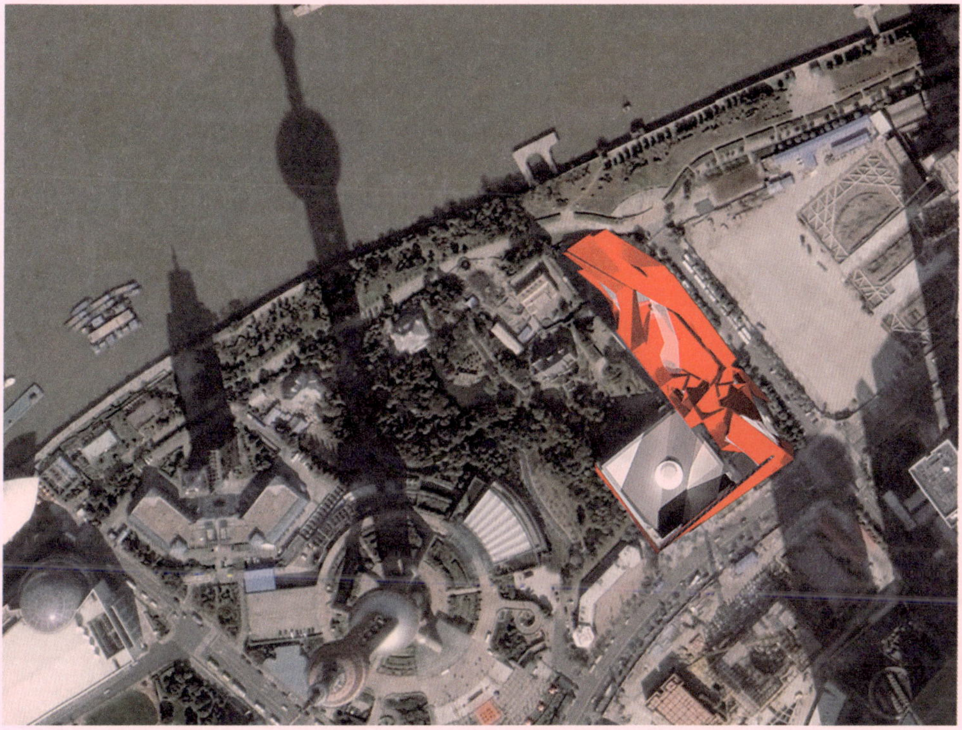

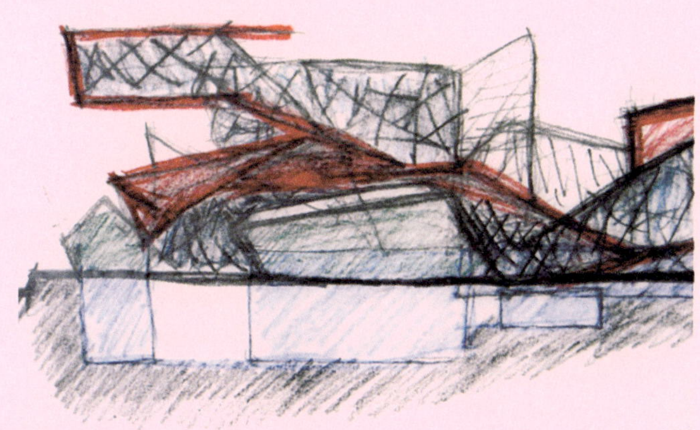

Being there felt familiar, like the first time I visited Publicis. I tried to contain my excitement, yet everything I saw would trigger my imagination; I was glued to my sketchbook. Every building and every city has its own field of energy and movement, but this site was by far the most demanding. It had a powerful architectural presence that contributed to the vibrant urban conditions that surrounded it. It was my intention to use these fields when creating architecture that is responsible and responsive to the needs of the clients and the city. I finally had to force myself to sleep because I was meeting Mr. Wu.

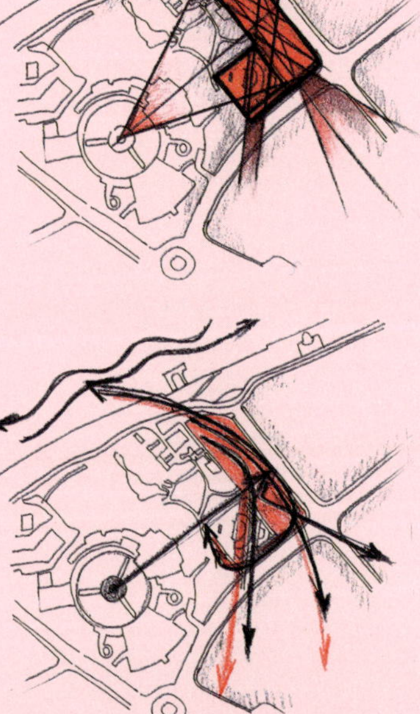

The next morning I walked to Straco to meet Mr. Wu and discuss his vision for the project. We talked about the need to define the aquarium's role as a hub for research and development in protecting the aquatic environment. Aquariums were evolving in their missions, launching initiatives to advance conservation and promoting public programs that increase environmental awareness. We reached a mutual understanding and developed an admiration for each other that led to other collaborations.

Shanghai Aquarium

Location:

Shanghai, P.R. China

Year:

2007 (not built)

Program:

Aquarium and Theater

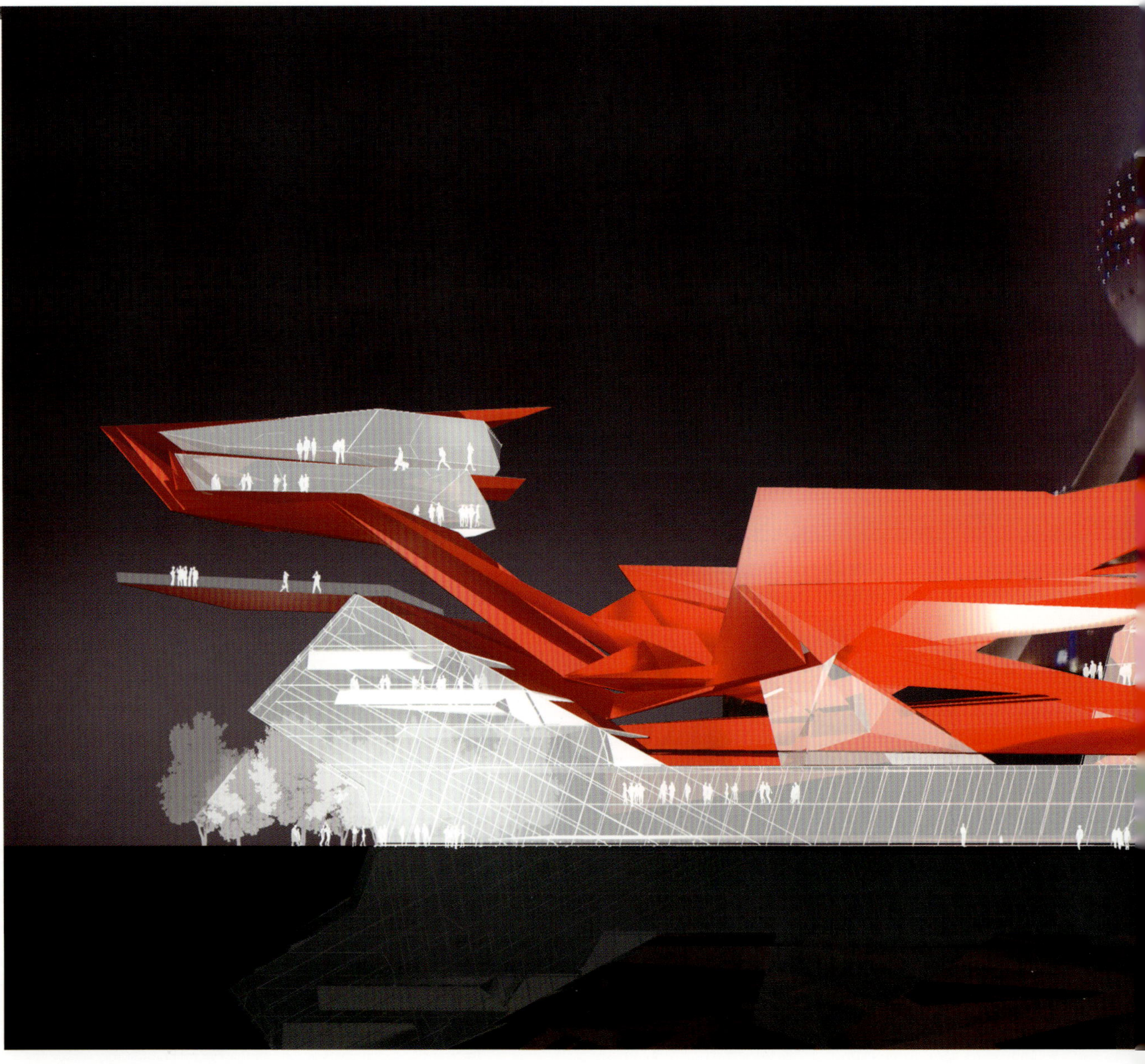

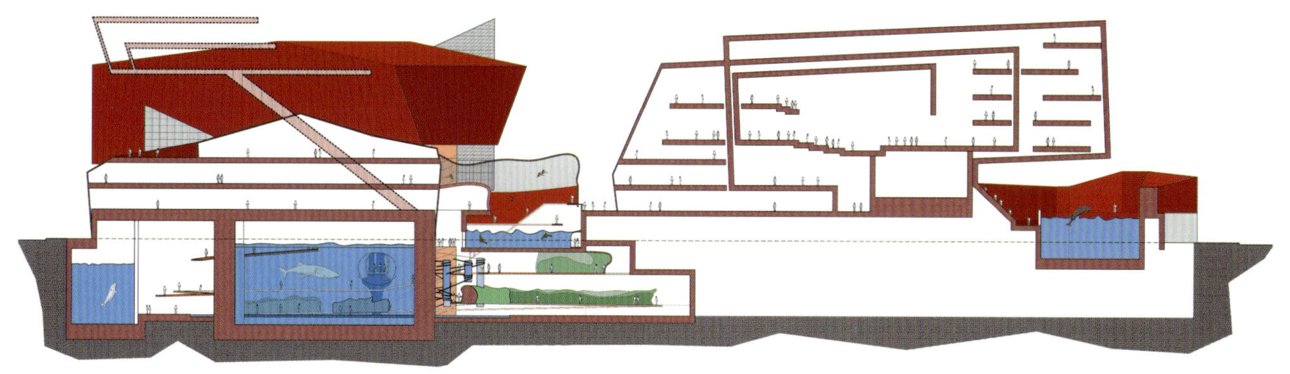

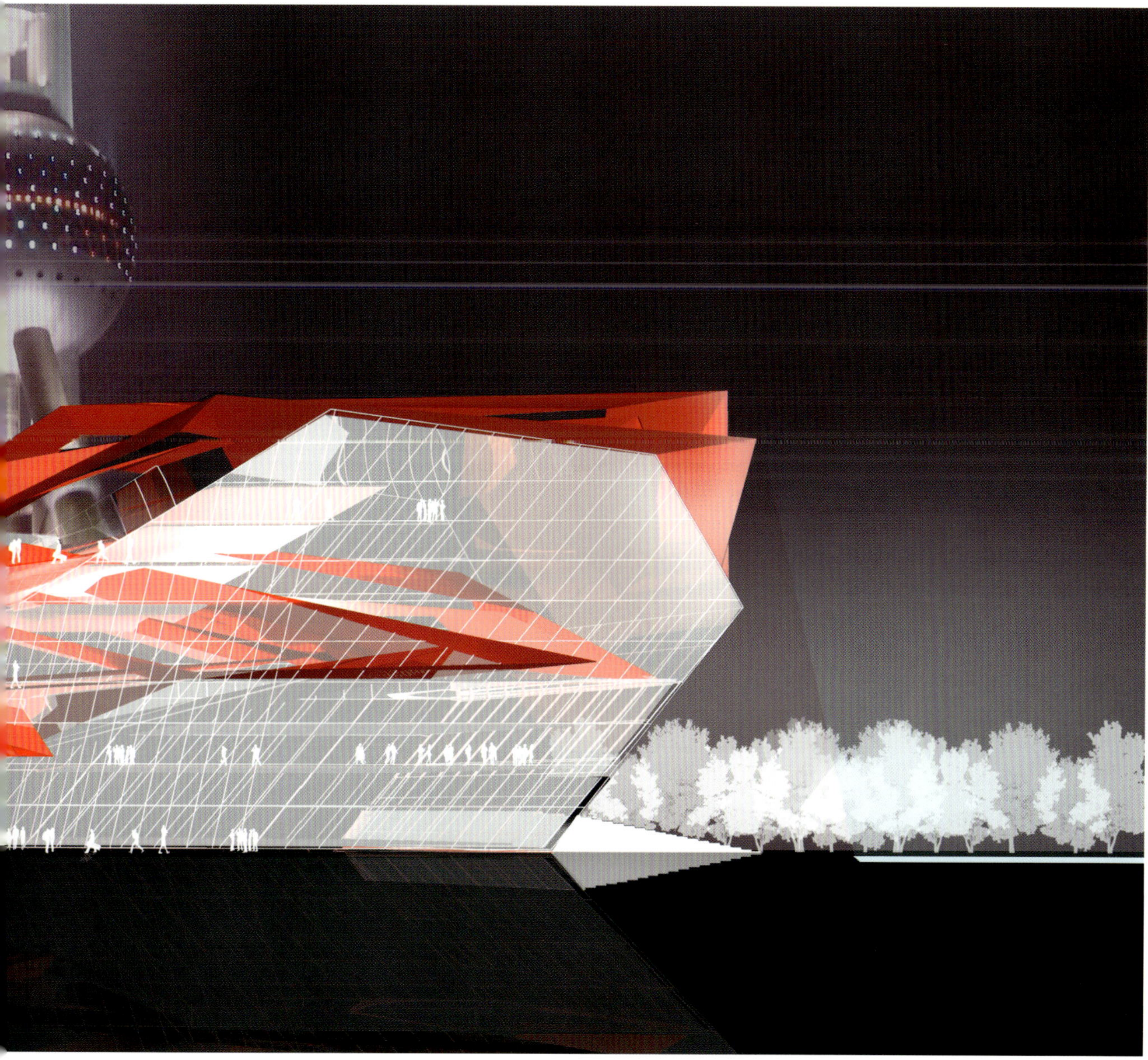

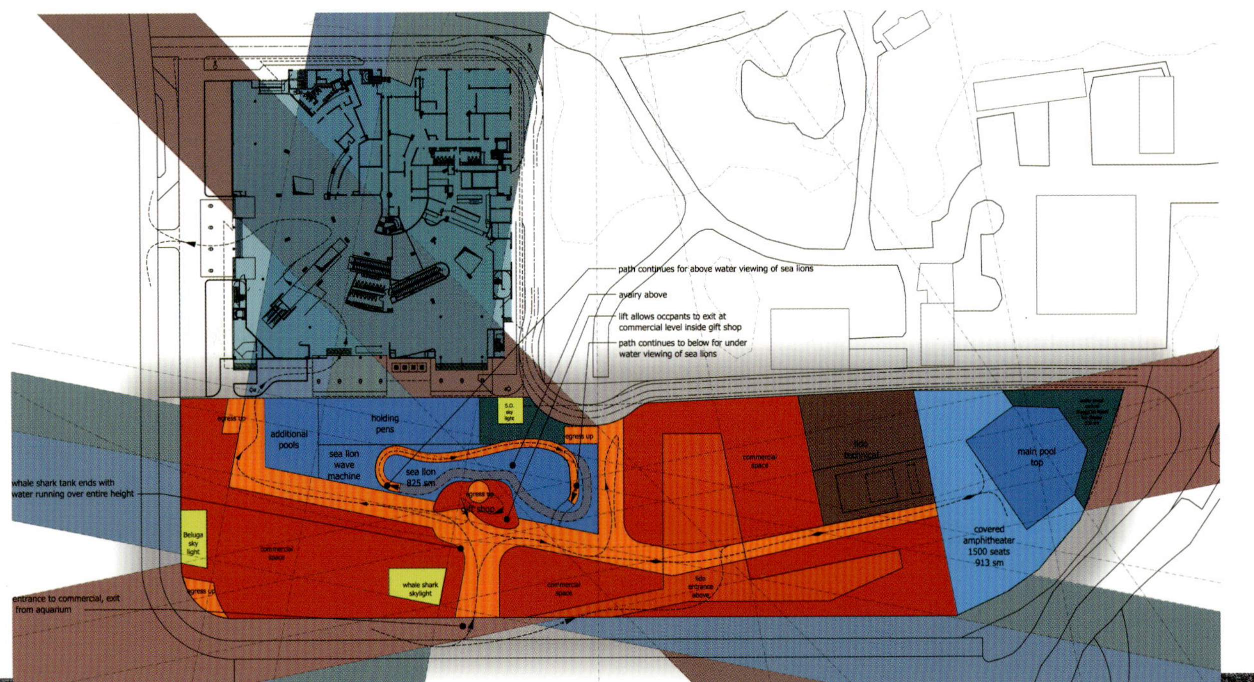

We began working on the project soon after finalizing a collaboration framework with Straco. I needed to familiarize myself with the building type and put a team together to tackle the issues. The client's team that worked in their existing aquarium were very helpful in the process and they were appointed to work with us on different areas of the project as aquarium consultants, biologists, facility management, marketing consultants, construction supervisors, economists, and theater consultants. I realized there were very few technical firms in the world that specialized in aquarium design, so the Australian company who designed the original Shanghai aquarium was our consultant by default. After numerous visits to document the site and meet with the clients and team, we began developing the concept sketches.

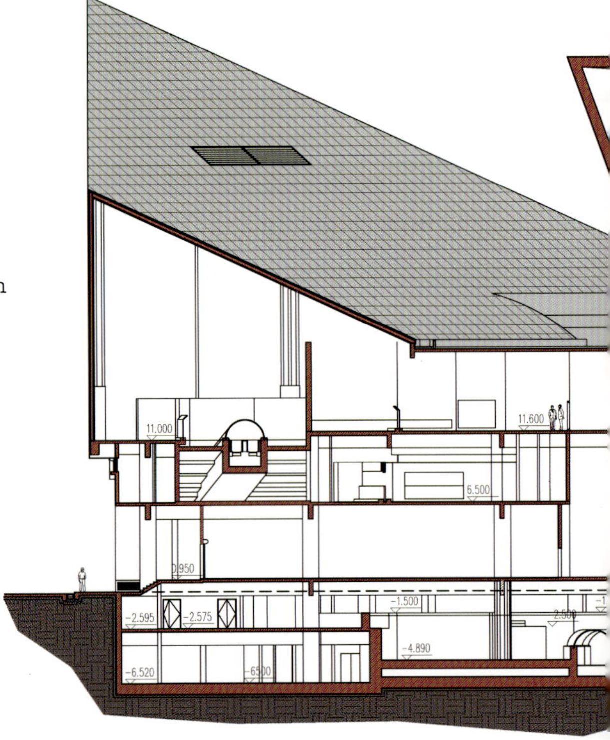

The new Shanghai Aquarium Museum and Theater includes exhibition areas from all continents, research laboratories, collection areas, educational facilities, a state of the art conference center (Shanghai Cabaret Lido) that seats 1,200, and a commercial complex consisting of stores, restaurants, entertainment, and a luxury gathering hall.

I drew my inspiration from the site's surrounding dynamics, notably the Huangpu River, the Oriental Pearl Tower, and the iconic highrises to the south. The building's rising composition gestures away from the river and moves toward the towers, lifting itself with strength and balance into the air, emulating flight.

The new architecture of the aquarium wraps around the preexisting building in an attempt to create a unified contemporary building. Environmentally sensitive materials and energy-efficient building systems/strategies are employed throughout the building. The architecture's contemporary language embraces the city and its energy.

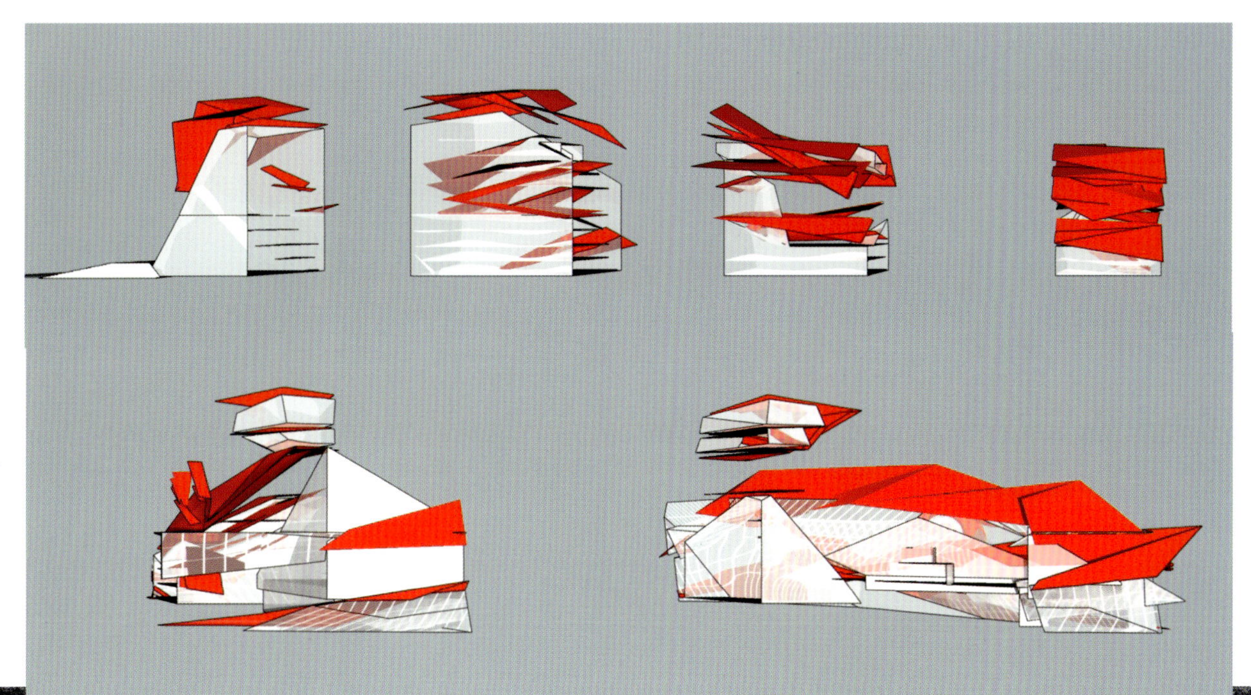

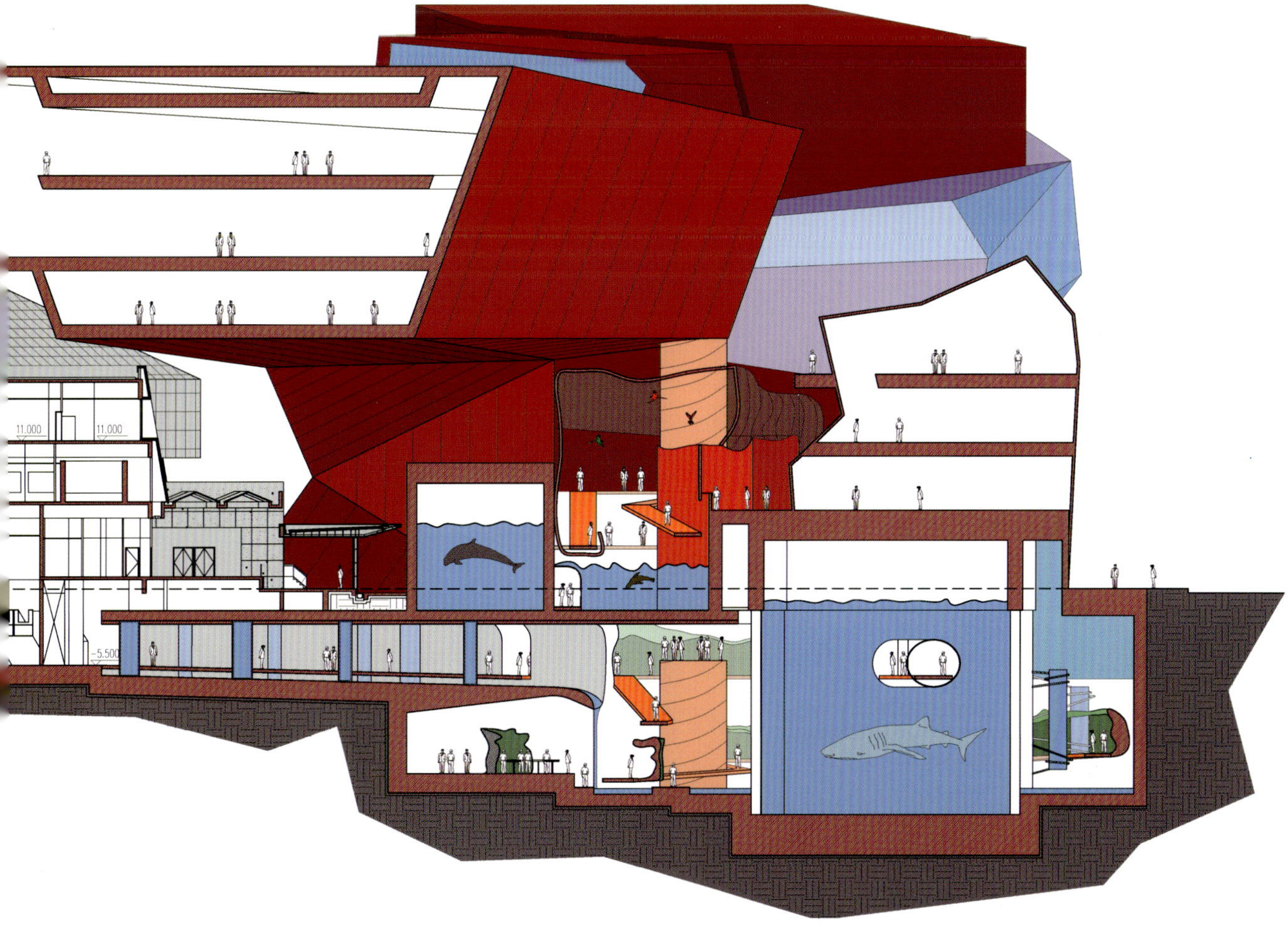

LIDO
shanghai ocean aquarium

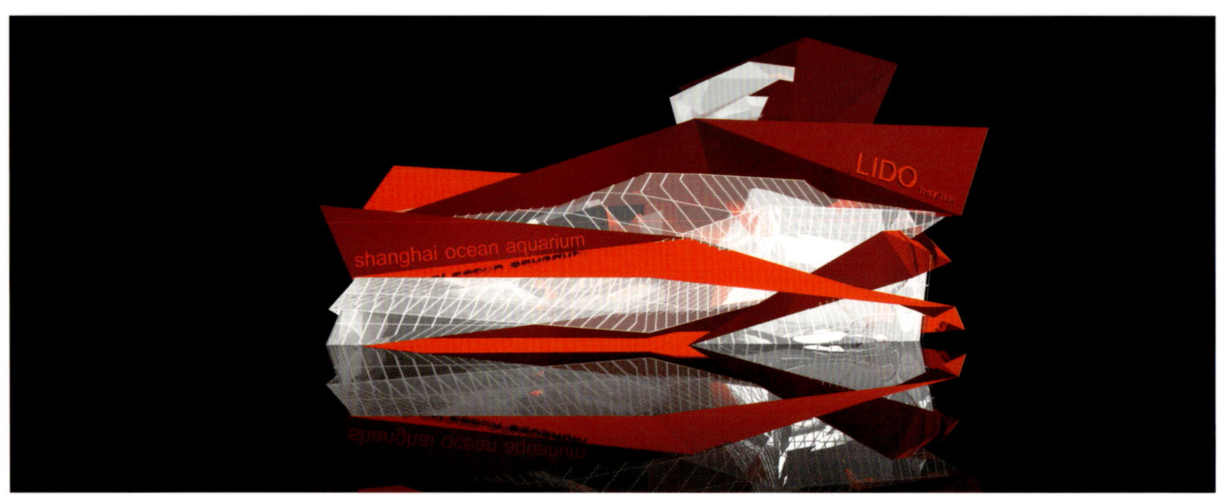

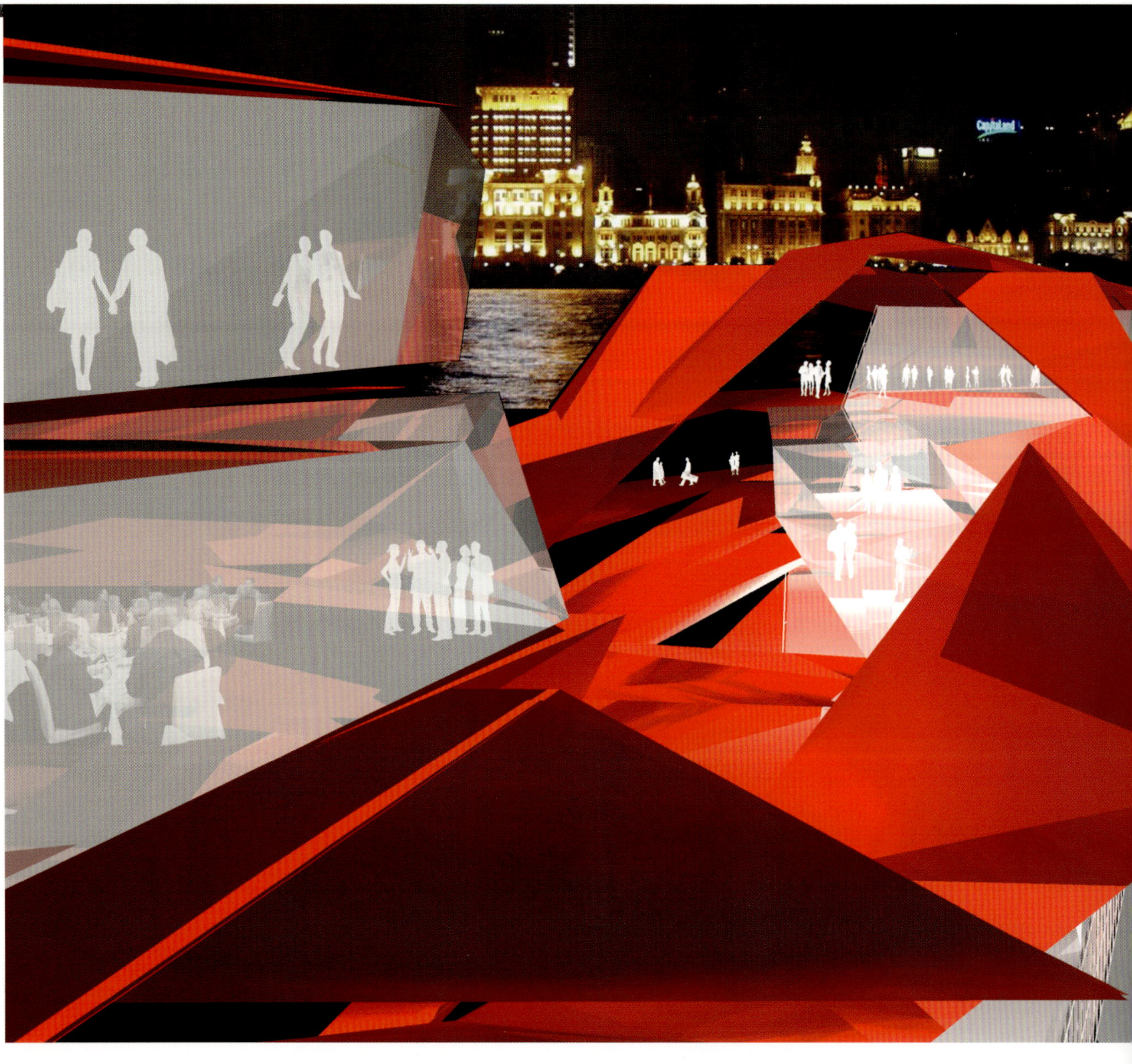
CapitaLand

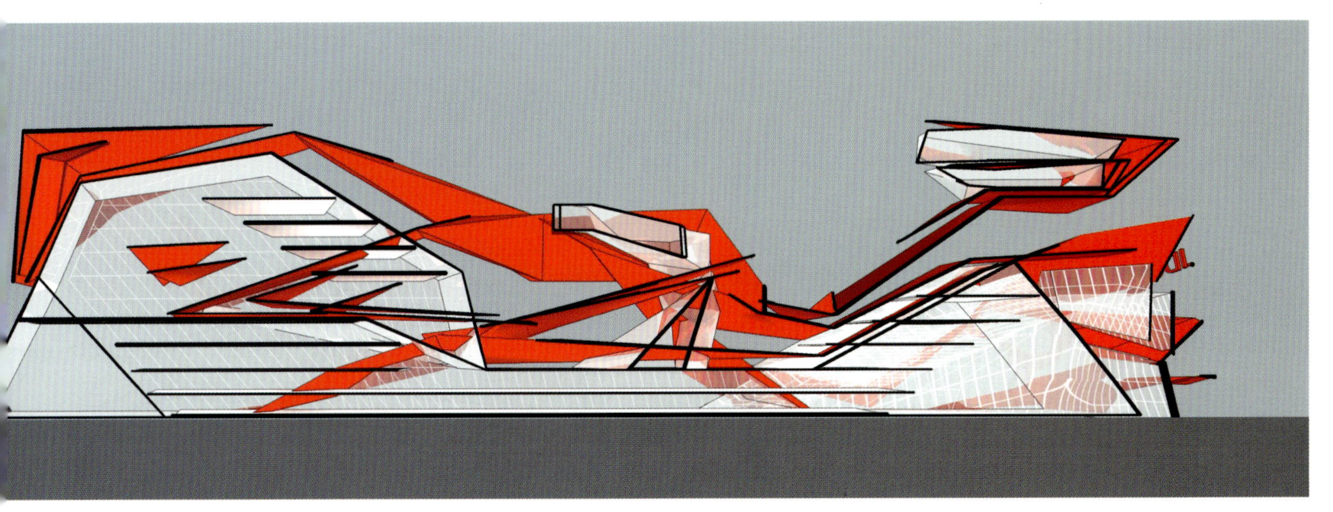

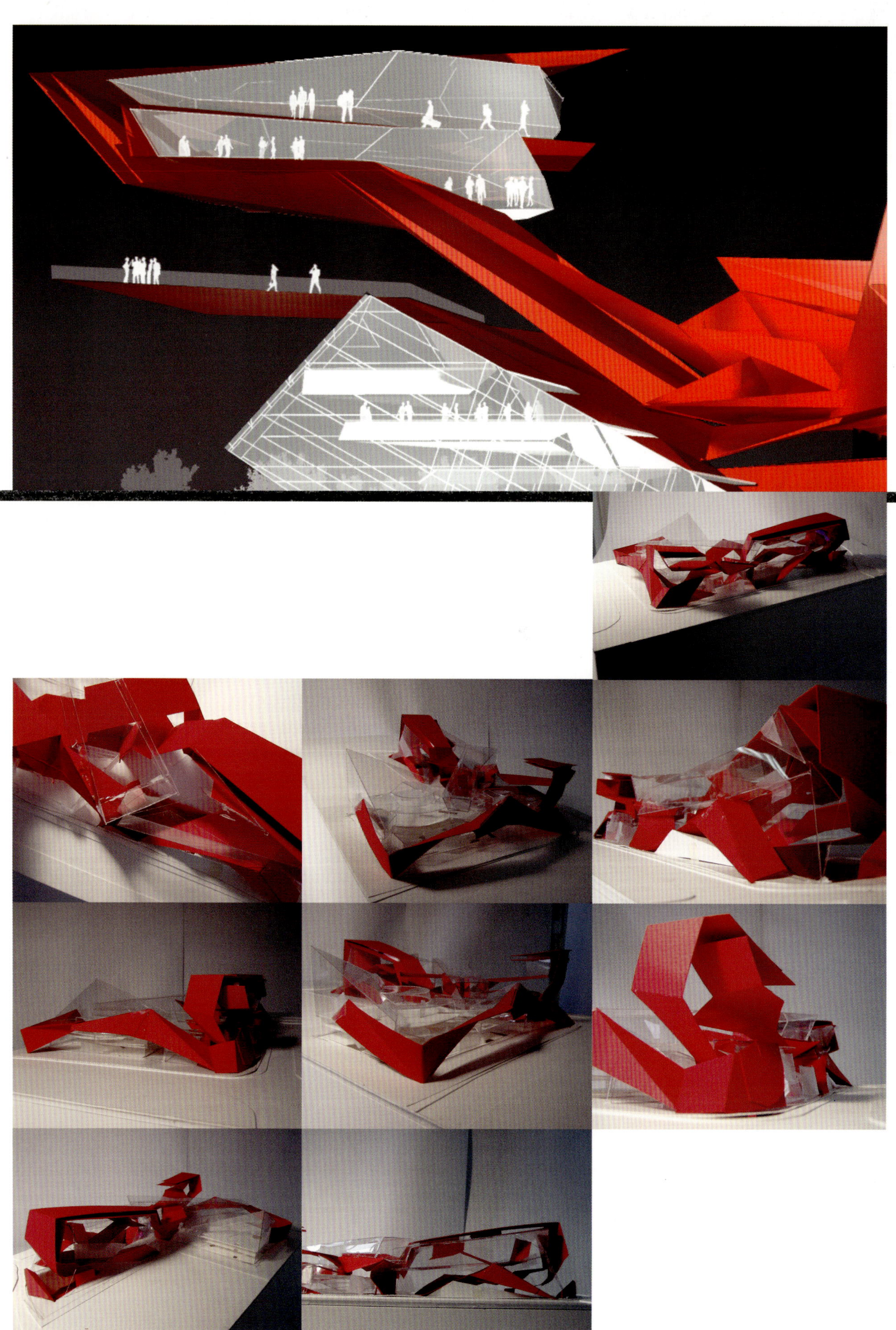

Gulang Island, with its natural beauty, is our main source of inspiration for our design...

Drum Wave Island

The waves come on with an oily sweep,
but plunge with a thunderous blow,
Like a big drum banged by a steady
hand: certain, full, and slow,
And Westward from the Drum Wave
Island the evening sky's aglow.
— Unknown

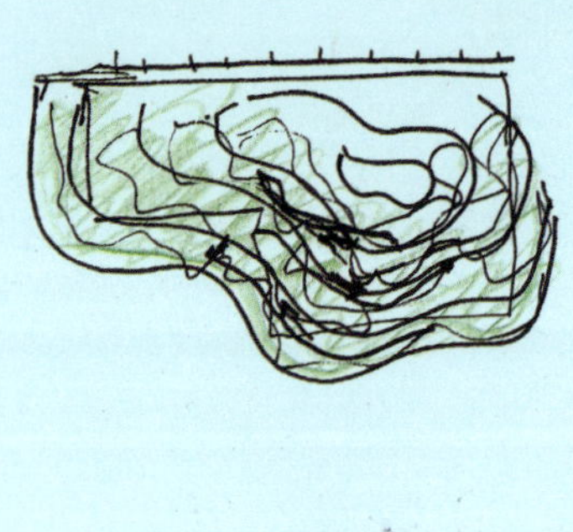

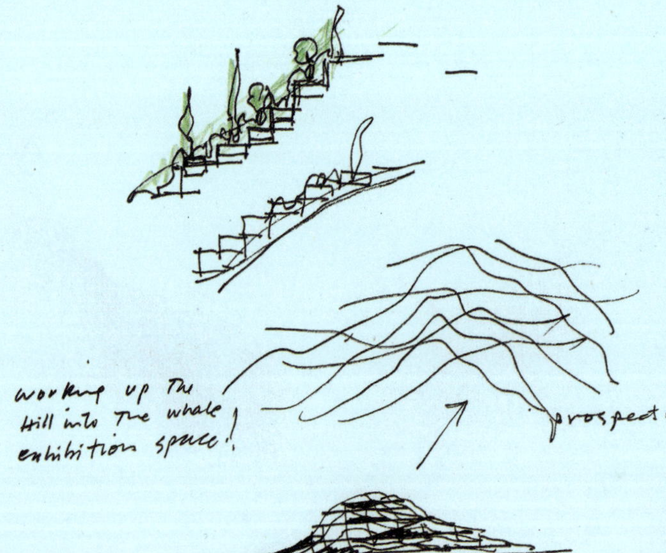
working up The
Hill into The whale
exhibition space!
prospect.

Xiamen Aquarium

Location:

Xiamen, P.R. China

Year:

2009 (not built)

Program:

Aquarium and Park

Is it possible to revise a building's relationship to its site by hiding it, reinvigorating it's context?

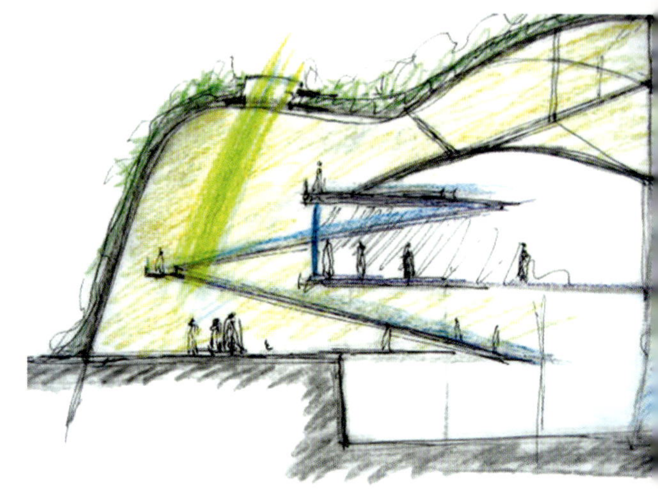

My design for the Xiamen Underwater World embraces the site in every way. It was our intention to create architecture that was harmonious with the site's natural, cultural, and historical setting. Gulang Island, often praised as "Garden on the Sea," is located in Xiamen, at the southeast tip of Fujian Province located at the southeast coast of China. A ferry service links Xiamen with Gulang Island where there are no cars, motorcycles, or other modes of transportation, making their way of life peaceful and relaxing.

The existing architecture of Gulang Island reflects its colonial past, which through the years has established its own charming variety of styles. Gulangyu's soft undulating

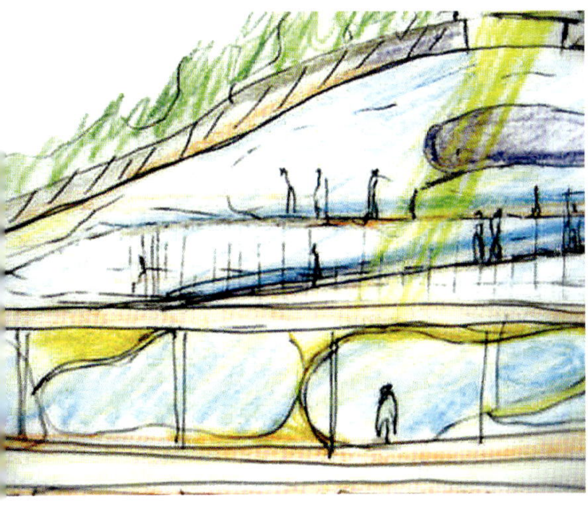

hills, gargantuan rocks, and surrounding beaches became our main source of inspiration for the design. One of the main attractions on Gulang Island is the Xiamen Underwater World, which opened in 1998. Their exhibition areas show visitors glimpses of offshore China and the Indian Ocean, and of Australian aquatic animals. In addition to permanent exhibitions, Xiamen Underwater World regularly launches special exhibitions on different themes every year, which comprehensively display the diversity, fun, and interaction between marine species.

In 2008, Straco purchased Gulang's Xiamen Underwater World with the intention of improving it and developing more. During my first visit I was surprised to find the existing dilapidated 7,000m2 aquarium in such poor condition. I could not believe it was only ten years old, but was told that its unexpected success and fast expansion were the main reasons for its advanced decay. My observations that day led me to believe that it had to be completely remodeled. This included its building systems (electrical, mechanical, plumbing, heating, air conditioning, etc.), building structures, display tanks, and fire safety and circulation systems.

Later that day, Mr. Wu arrived from Singapore and met with me to discuss the project further. I needed to take advantage of this opportunity to report my findings and discuss potential ideas. How could we preserve what was left of Xiamen Underwater World and transform it into a contemporary research center for the next generation?

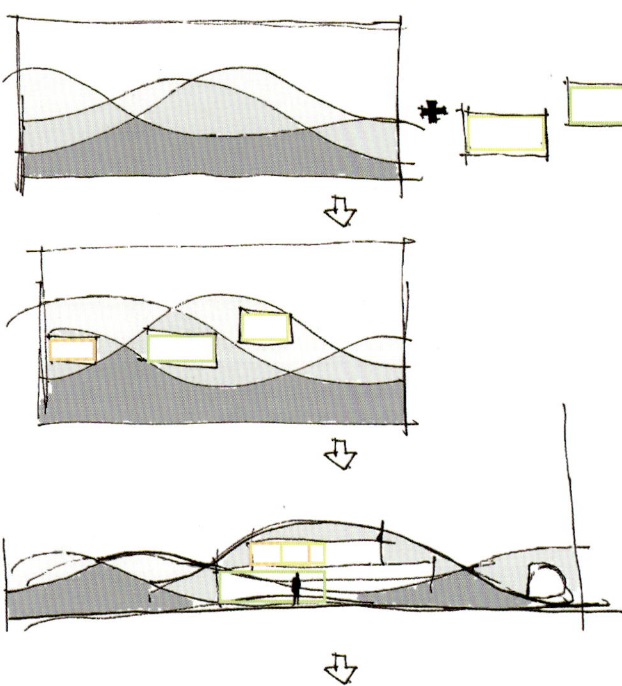

The conversation with Mr. Wu led to a program that was more ambitious than I expected. He knew that the aquarium's existing conditions were counterproductive to its purpose and its potential was wasted. Therefore, our objective was to expand the program and create an exceptional destination place for the region and beyond. The program was to remodel the aquarium by combining the old and new and developing a more sustainable facility for future research in marine biology and applicable sciences.

We performed multiple design studies based on the building's role within the island's context and how we'd respond to its preexisting, diverse architectural influences. The one principal that was never challenged was that the existing building appearance had to change, so all of our proposals began with how to cover the existing building in some way.

Our first designs were based on creating a singular building that served as a landmark. This was not unusual since there were many other period buildings with similar qualifications like the Kulangsu Organ Museum or Tian Zhu Tang. After sketching a few possibilities, we were discouraged, so we abandoned this approach and searched

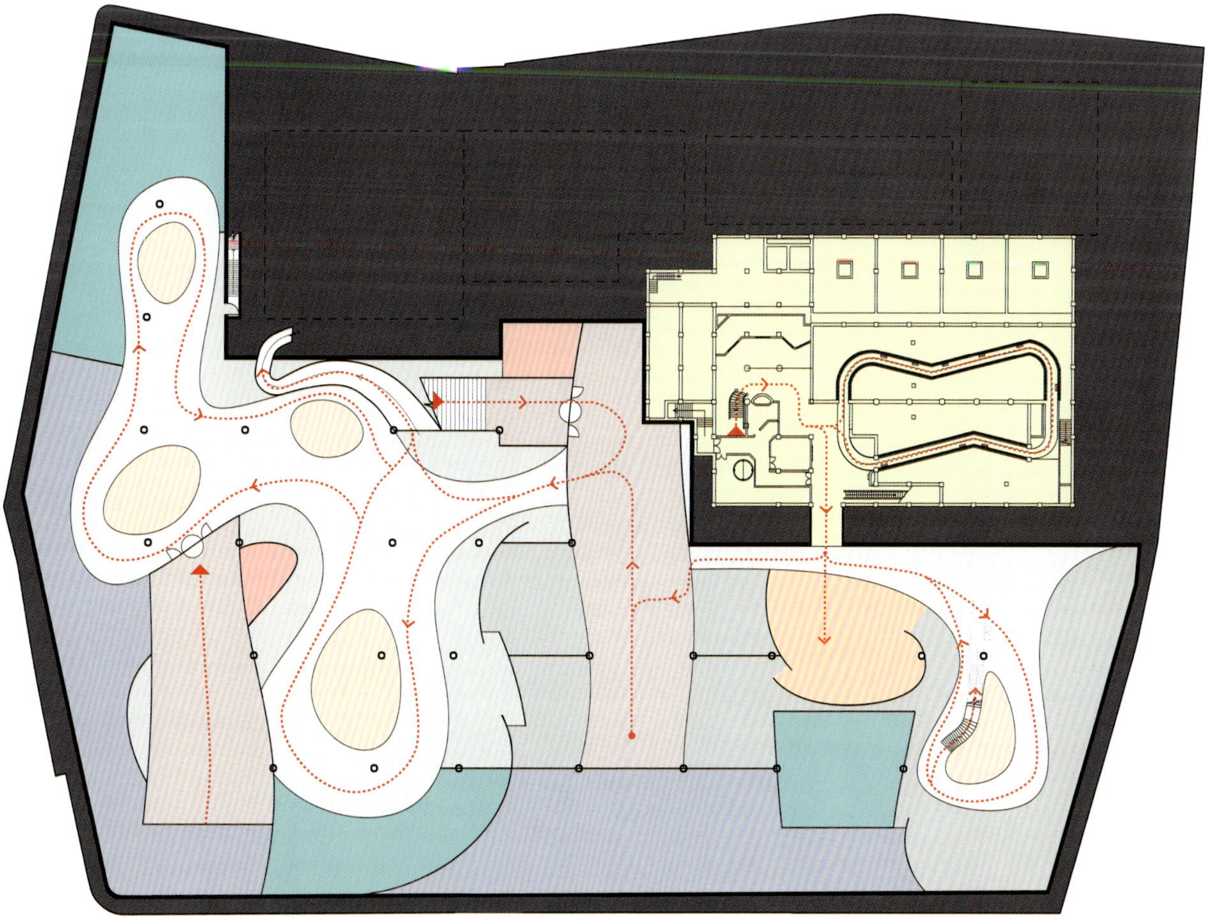

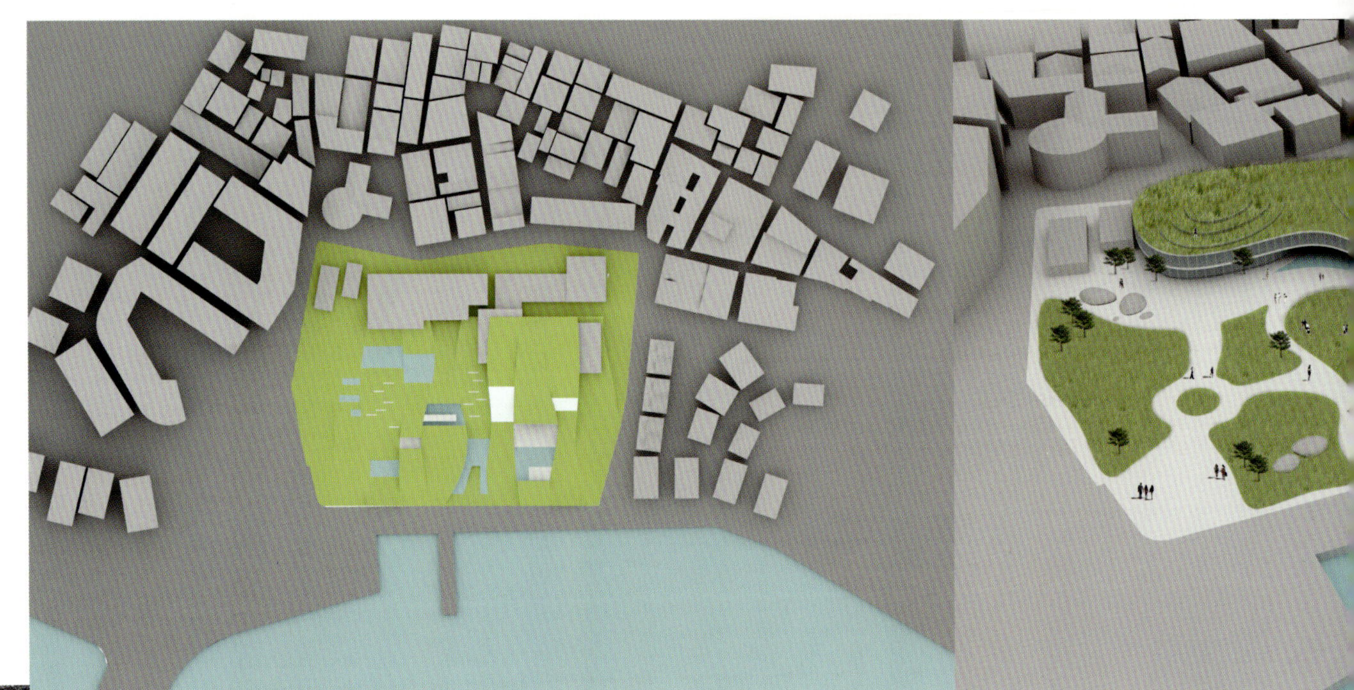

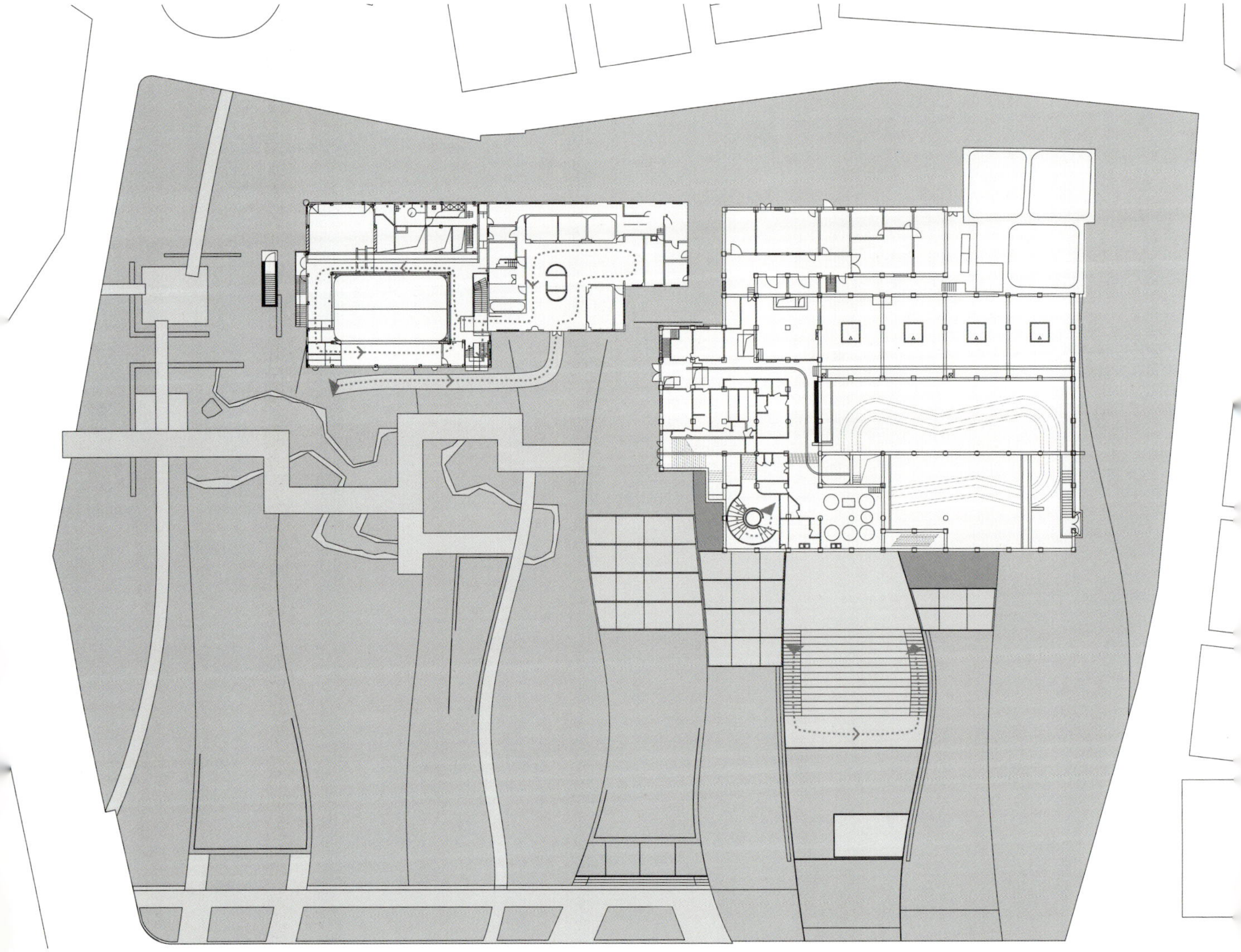

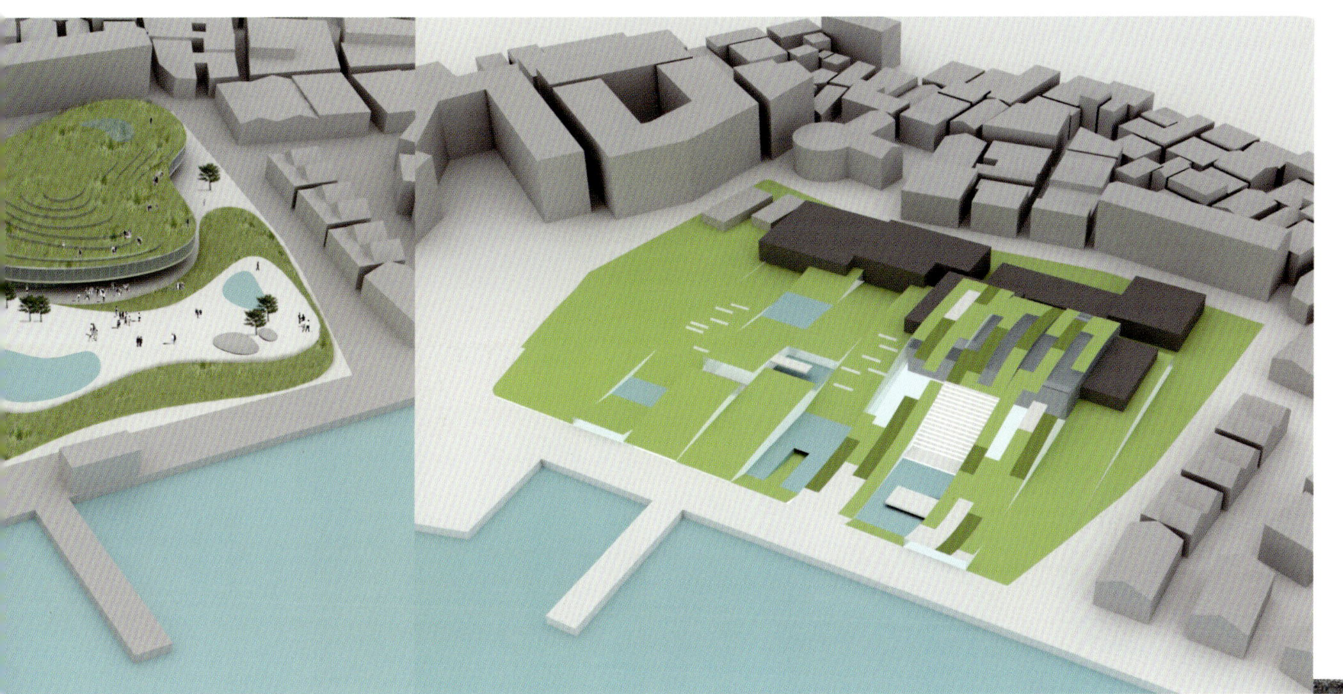

for a more harmonious solution. Straco wanted a more contextual approach, but the context is so diverse that such a concept did not make sense.

Inspired by the Hermes Cultural Center, we started investigating a "non-architectural", landscape proposal for the project. We considered placing the existing aquarium inside a human-made hill by building a large roof, pierced to allow light into the spaces below. The roof and exterior structure were then landscaped and terraced to allow the visitors to climb it, like a hiking ground, and use it as a public space. This client rejected the proposal and the island's authorities. We were at a standstill since many of our ideas were challenged or rejected. After some review and analysis, we realized that we needed to propose an organic solution that would combine our two previous concepts. The third solution attracted everyone's attention and support, but the final decision was put on hold by Gulang's authorities. For a few months we were in the dark, unaware of what was going on. Finally, we received a letter that Gulang Island had been recognized by UNESCO as a World Cultural Heritage Site, which led authorities and the client to believe that one of our rejected proposals may actually be the suitable solution. After a few more meetings and studies, we agreed to cover the preexisting building with a green roof, giving the impression that it is hidden.

The new Xiamen Underwater World covers approximately 10,400m^2 (111,000 sf) of underground space, roofed with

a live garden and park consisting of native plants. The roof structure covers almost 60% of the remodeled building and compatibility ties with the island's natural beauty.

We used more than 90% of the underground site for the new aquariums, conference areas, classrooms, state of the art research laboratories, exhibition spaces, library, performance area, and services. The building's green roofs are covered with locally sustainable plants visually fused into the park through various, dynamic scenes. The view from the boats approaching the island is important to attract guests to the UWX. Visitors will catch glimpses of the building and its landscape as they get closer. Finally, the sign that marks the main entrances to the Xiamen Underwater World reveals itself with celebratory water displays and lights. The new roof not only creates a natural environment for the visitors above, but also keeps the underground building 10 degrees cooler than the standard roof, which would reduce energy usage.

The main entrance pathway is approximately 18m (59 feet) wide and 60m (196 feet) long, which will lead people to the lobby area where the ticket booth is located. We propose a series of small stores and cafés along the pathway to make this main entrance a gathering place. The west-side pathway brings the patrons through the landscaped garden decks, overlooking the ponds and an intimate tea garden deck. This offers guests a moment of rest and contemplation before they're led toward the amphitheater.

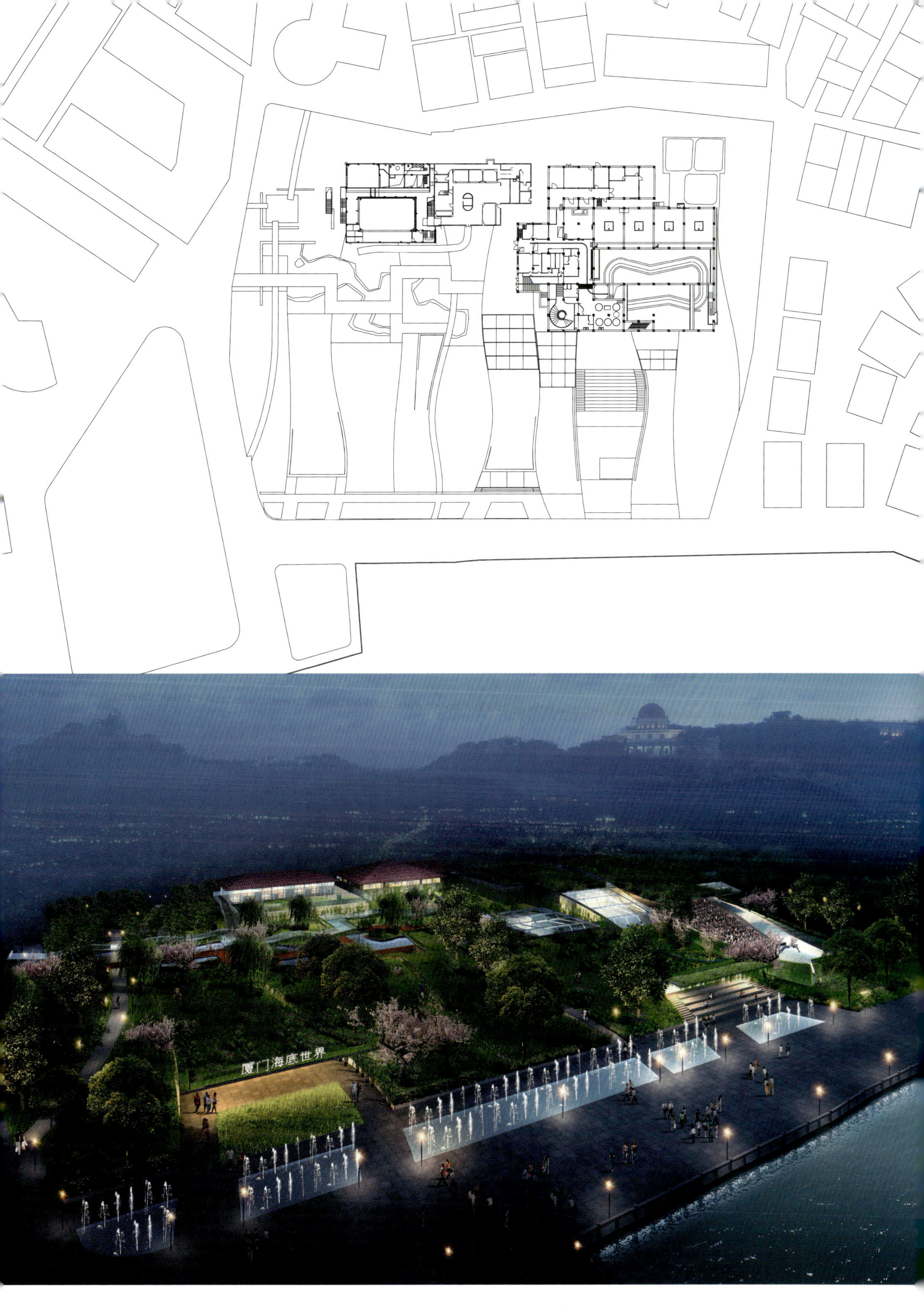
厦门海底世界

The proposed open-air performance pool is situated on the northeast side of the site for approximately 700 spectators. The seats are positioned toward the sea for the audience to see the performance with Xiamen's cityscape in the background.

The new Xiamen Underwater World preserves Gulang Island's natural beauty, while creating a more functional home for the local population and visitors.

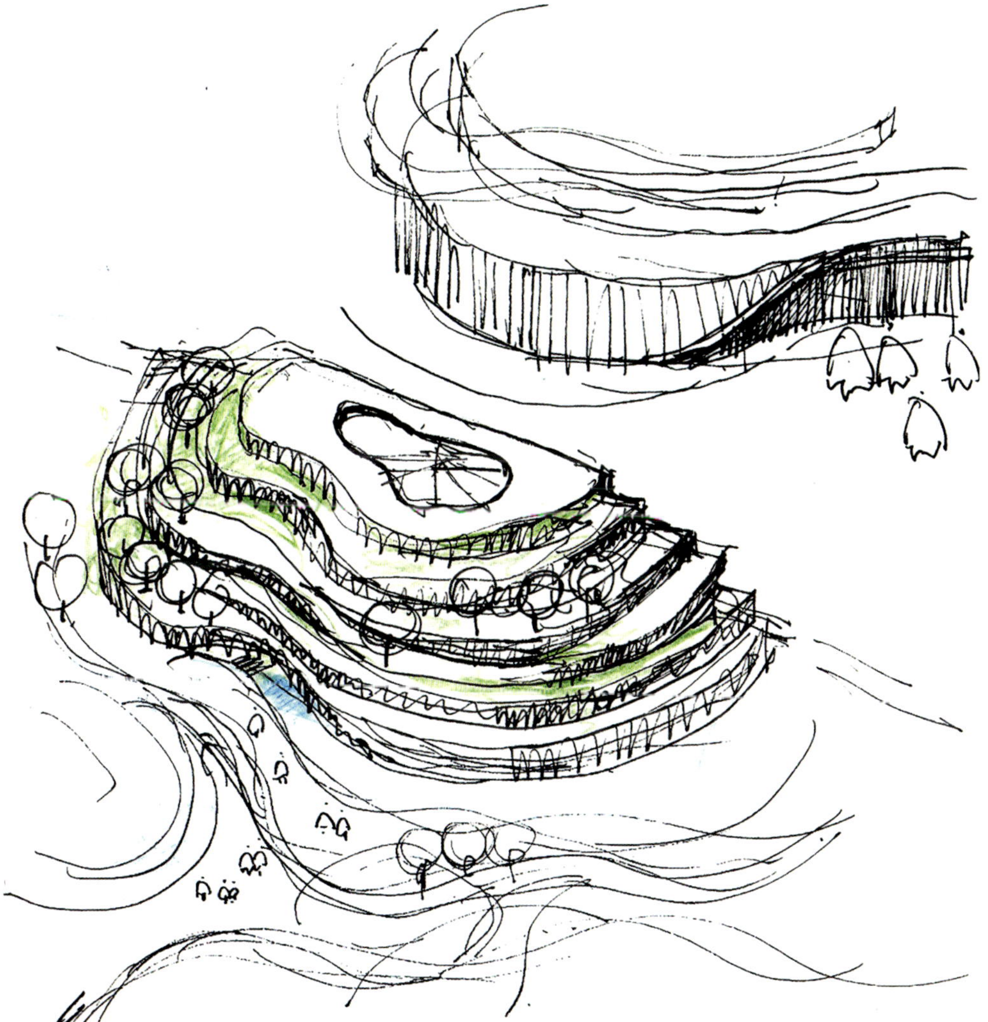

厦门海底世界

Architectural design and artistic design are based on a symbol representing cultural symbols.

VISION

Vision

Location:
Beijing, P.R. China

Year:
2009 (built)

Program:
Vision Magazine Offices, and Studios

Vision is an influential international visual art, fashion, and culture magazine in China. We were commissioned to design the publication's headquarters in Beijing just before the release of its 100th issue. The process of navigating through the magazine's rich work over nearly ten years allowed us to witness the incredible transformation in Chinese graphics and visual language since the Chinese revolution.

Our architectural design was based on the word forming the title that represents this cultural icon. It echoed the production format of the magazine since its conception, when the offices were divided in two separate but connected sections, with the creative studio of artists, graphic artists, writers, and designers on one side and the administrative, financial, and strategy departments on the other. We designed the space using the "V" and in Vision as the graphic, design and programmatic component where the two meet at the middle.

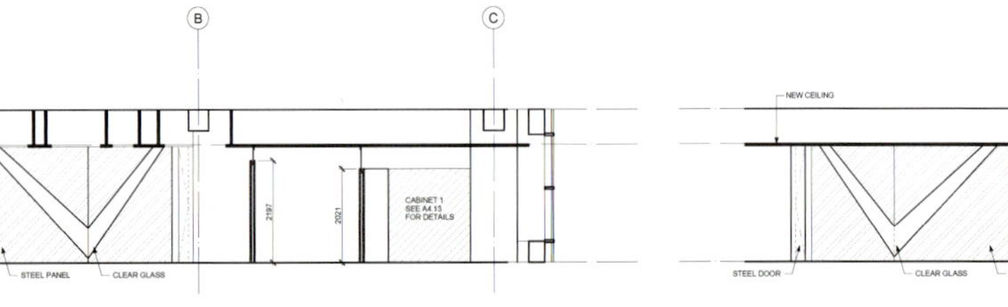

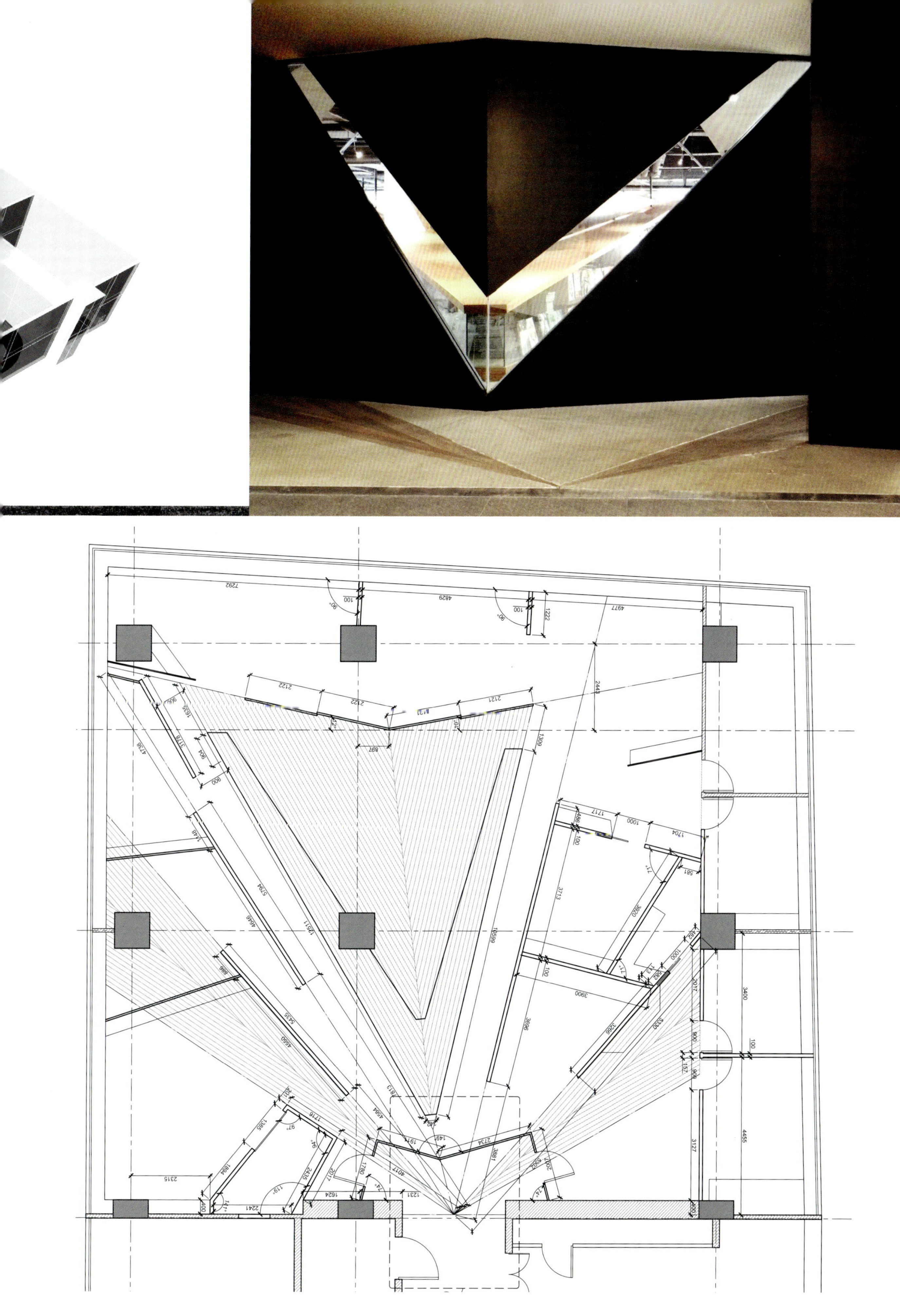

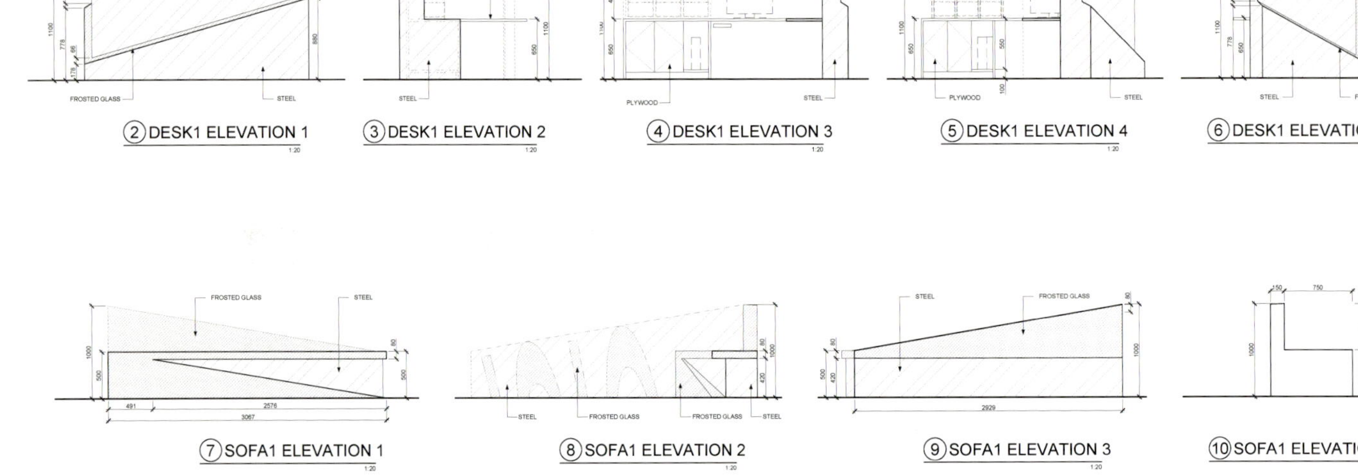

FROSTED GLASS
STEEL

(2) DESK1 ELEVATION 1
1:20

FILE ORGANIZER
SHALL BE PROVIDED
BY OWNER
PLYWOOD
STEEL

(3) DESK1 ELEVATION 2
1:20

FILE ORGANIZER
SHALL BE PROVIDED
BY OWNER
PLYWOOD
STEEL

(4) DESK1 ELEVATION 3
1:20

FILE ORGANIZER
SHALL BE PROVIDED
BY OWNER
PLYWOOD
STEEL

(5) DESK1 ELEVATION 4
1:20

STEEL

(6) DESK1 ELEVATIC

FROSTED GLASS
STEEL

(7) SOFA1 ELEVATION 1
1:20

STEEL
FROSTED GLASS
FROSTED GLASS
STEEL

(8) SOFA1 ELEVATION 2
1:20

STEEL
FROSTED GLASS

(9) SOFA1 ELEVATION 3
1:20

(10) SOFA1 ELEVATIC

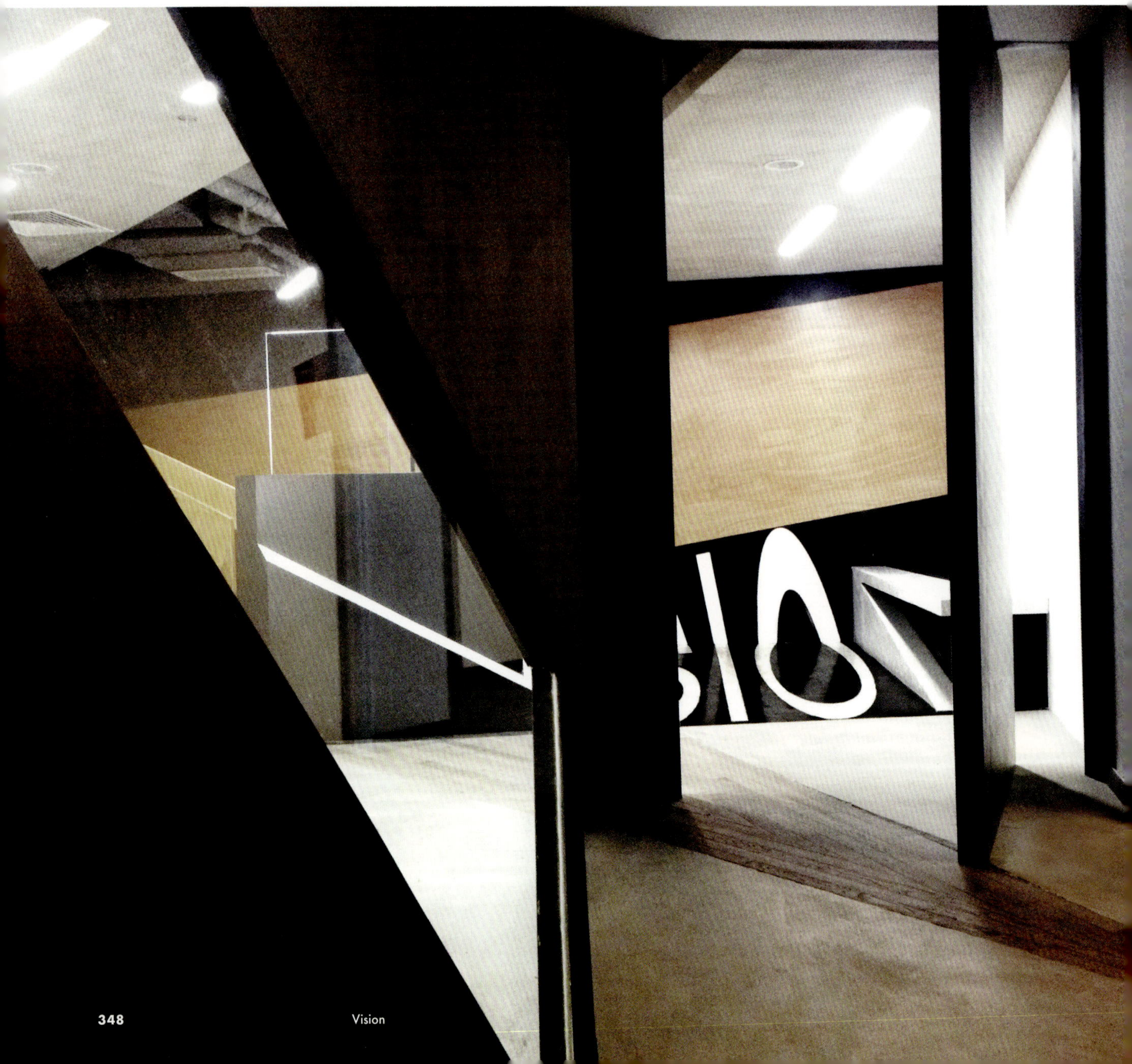

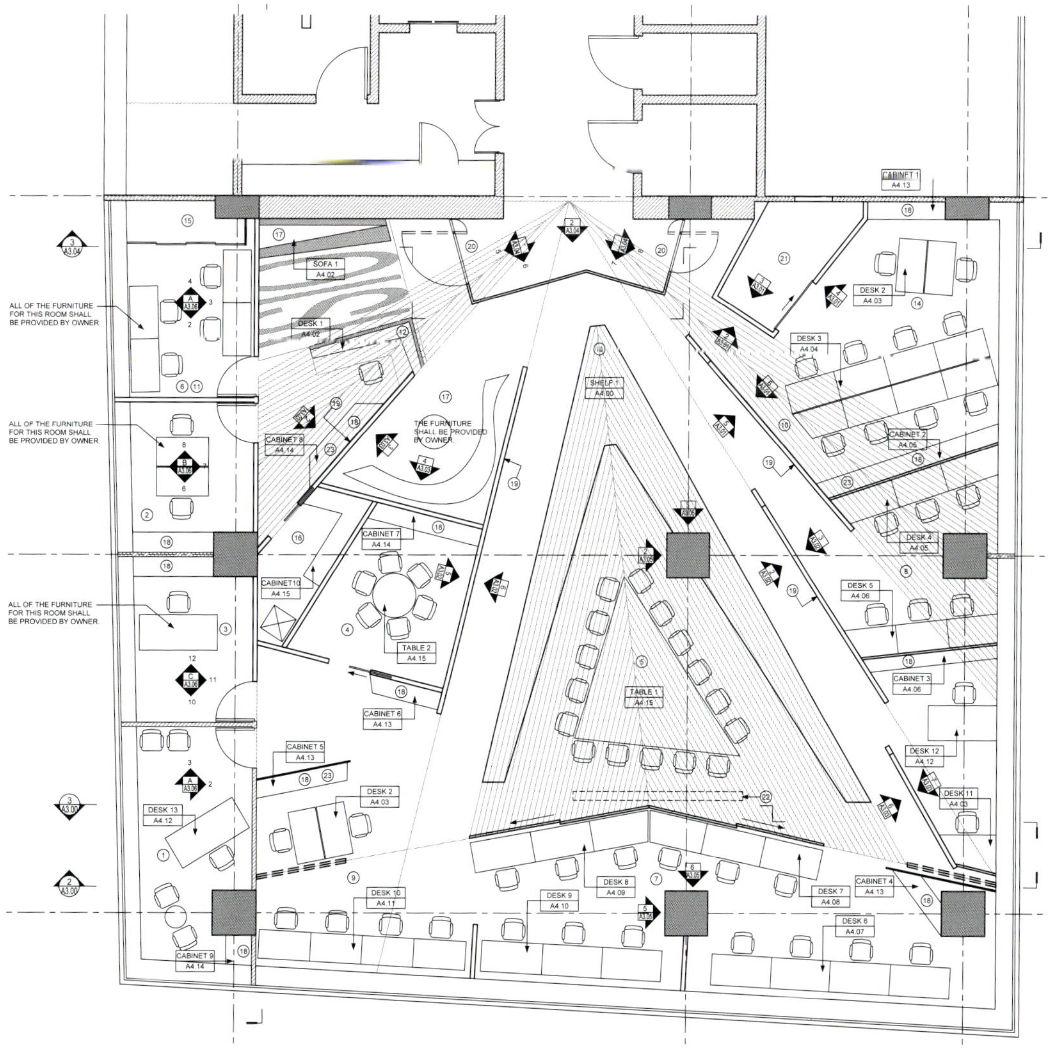

ALL OF THE FURNITURE FOR THIS ROOM SHALL BE PROVIDED BY OWNER.

ALL OF THE FURNITURE FOR THIS ROOM SHALL BE PROVIDED BY OWNER.

ALL OF THE FURNITURE FOR THIS ROOM SHALL BE PROVIDED BY OWNER.

THE FURNITURE SHALL BE PROVIDED BY OWNER.

CABINET 1 A4.13

SOFA 1 A4.02

DESK 1 A4.02

DESK 2 A4.03

DESK 3 A4.04

SHELF 1 A4.00

CABINET 2 A4.05

CABINET 8 A4.14

CABINET 7 A4.14

CABINET10 A4.15

TABLE 2 A4.15

DESK 4 A4.05

DESK 5 A4.06

TABLE 1 A4.15

CABINET 3 A4.06

CABINET 6 A4.13

CABINET 5 A4.13

DESK 12 A4.12

DESK 11 A4.03

DESK 13 A4.12

DESK 2 A4.03

DESK 10 A4.11

DESK 9 A4.10

DESK 8 A4.09

DESK 7 A4.08

CABINET 4 A4.13

DESK 6 A4.07

CABINET 9 A4.14

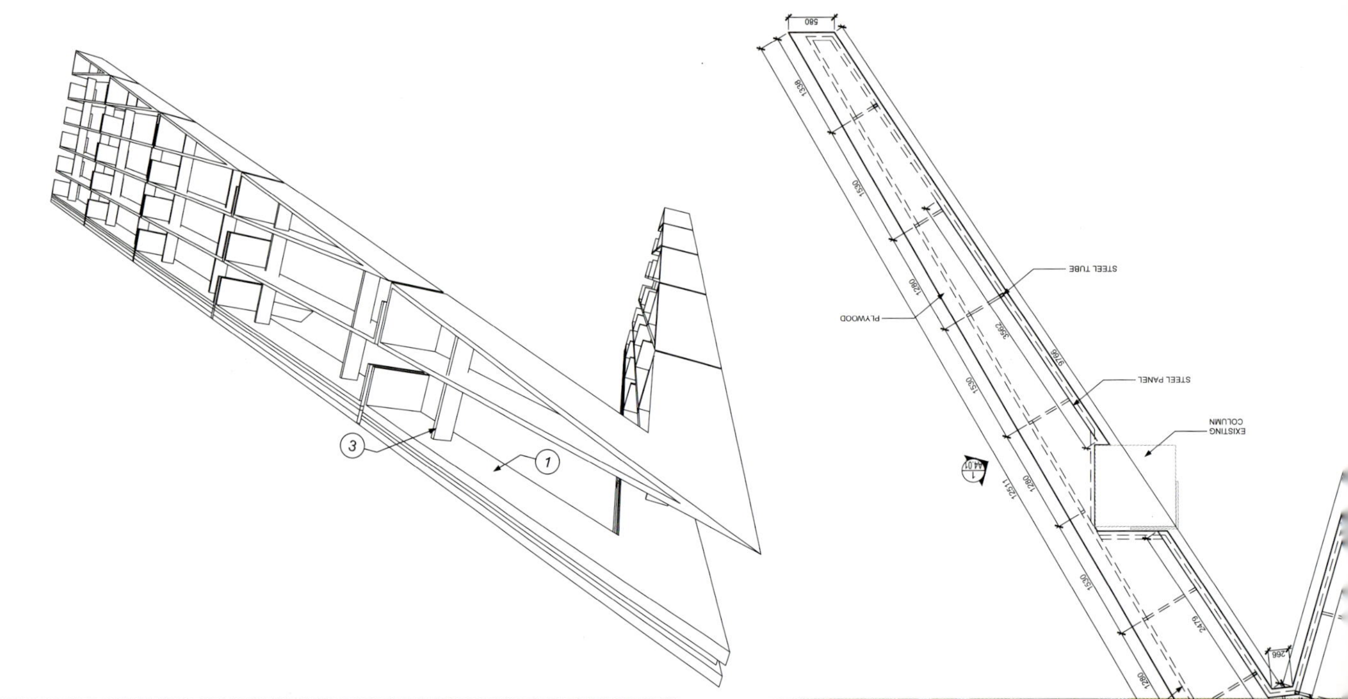

STEEL TUBE
PLYWOOD
STEEL PANEL
EXISTING COLUMN

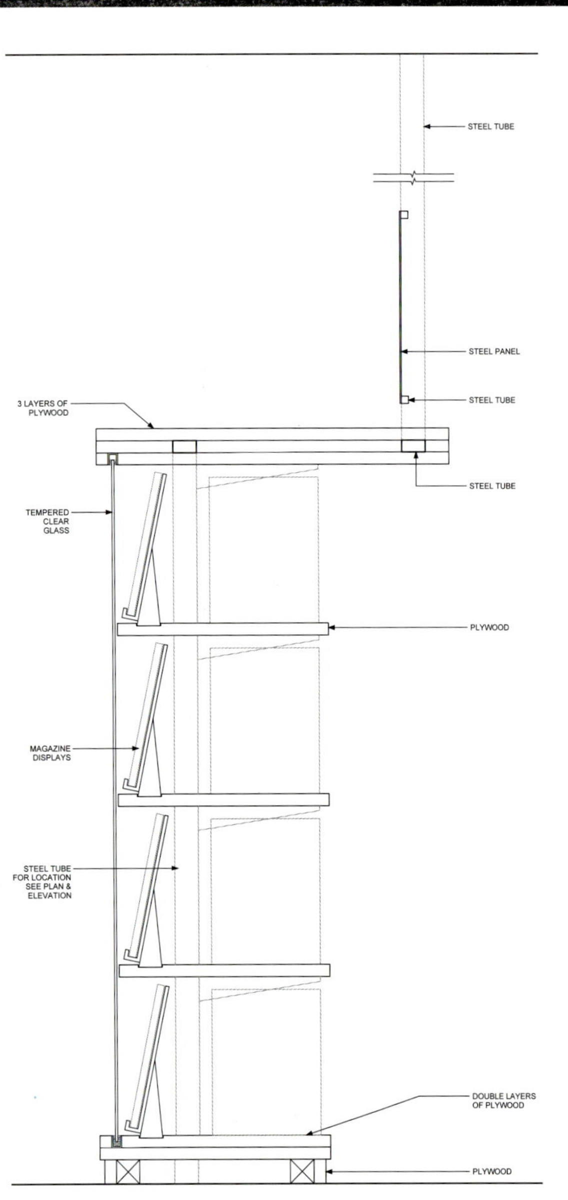

STEEL TUBE
STEEL PANEL
STEEL TUBE
3 LAYERS OF PLYWOOD
STEEL TUBE
TEMPERED CLEAR GLASS
PLYWOOD
MAGAZINE DISPLAYS
STEEL TUBE FOR LOCATION SEE PLAN & ELEVATION
DOUBLE LAYERS OF PLYWOOD
PLYWOOD

VISION
青年视觉
Spend A Little Time With Me....

PLYWOOD
STEEL PANEL
SUPPORT TUBE
TEMPERED CLEAR GLASS
VISION

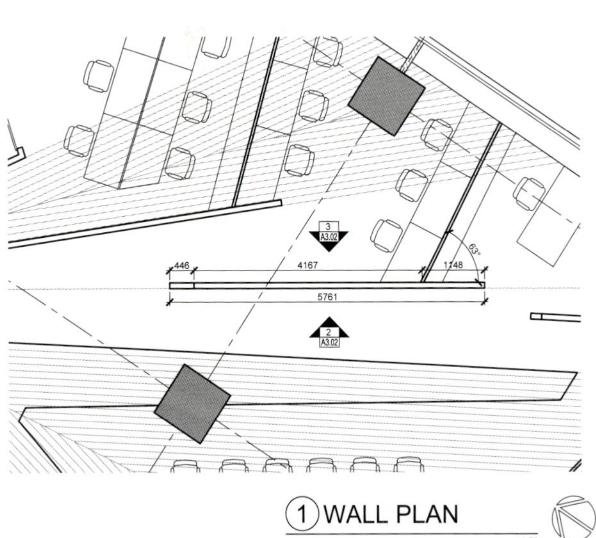
3
A3.02
446
4167
1148
63°
5761
2
A3.02
1 WALL PLAN
1:50

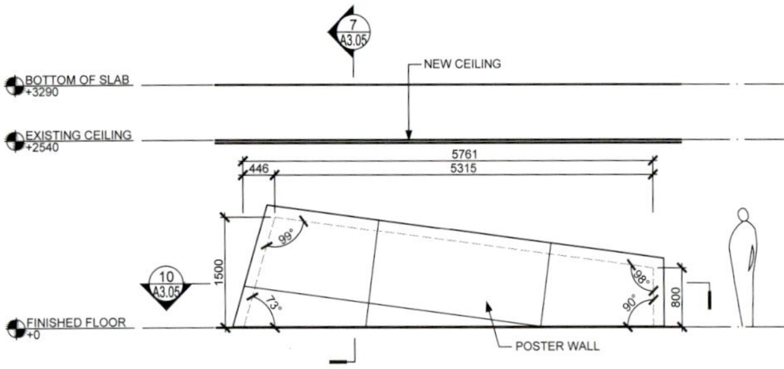
7
A3.05
BOTTOM OF SLAB
+3290
NEW CEILING
EXISTING CEILING
+2540
5761
446
5315
10
A3.05
1500
800
FINISHED FLOOR
+0
POSTER WALL
2 WALL ELEVATION 1
1:50

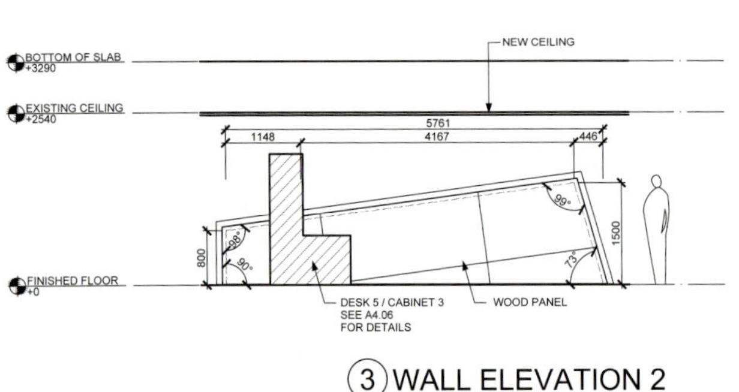
BOTTOM OF SLAB
+3290
NEW CEILING
EXISTING CEILING
+2540
5761
1148
4167
446
800
1500
FINISHED FLOOR
+0
DESK 5 / CABINET 3
SEE A4.06
FOR DETAILS
WOOD PANEL
3 WALL ELEVATION 2
1:50

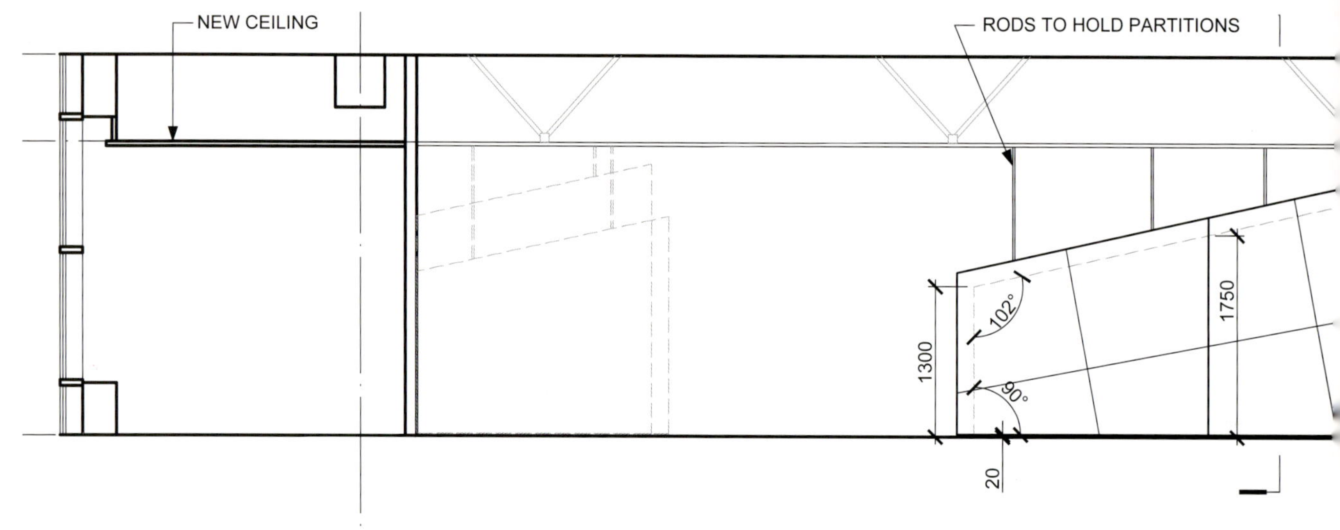
NEW CEILING
RODS TO HOLD PARTITIONS
102°
1300
90°
1750
20

TRACK
1700
104°
90°
1200
MOVING PARTITIONS

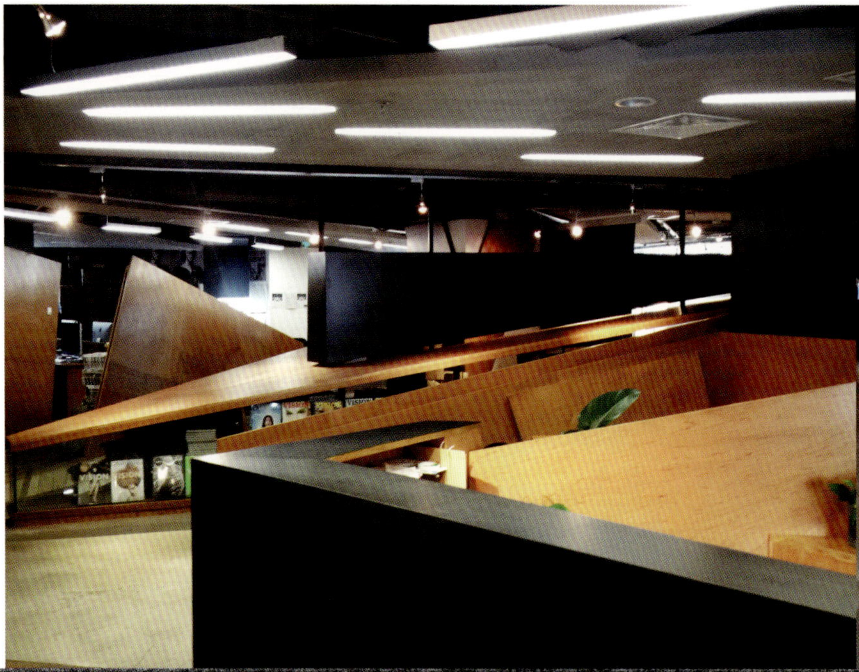

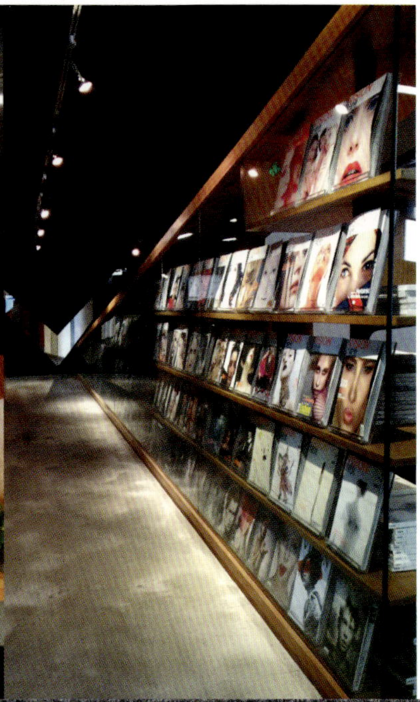

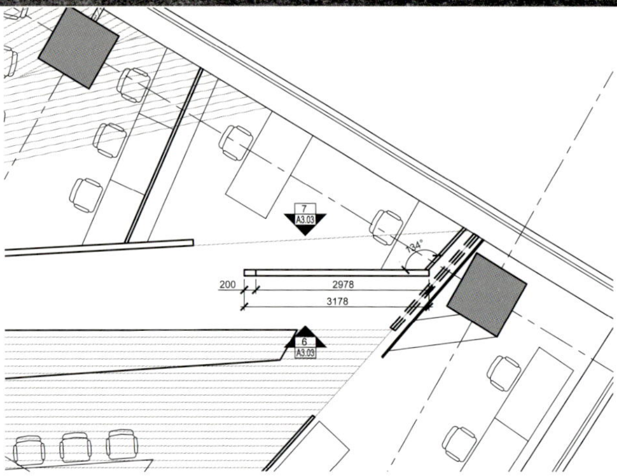
7
A3.03
200
2978
3178
6
A3.05

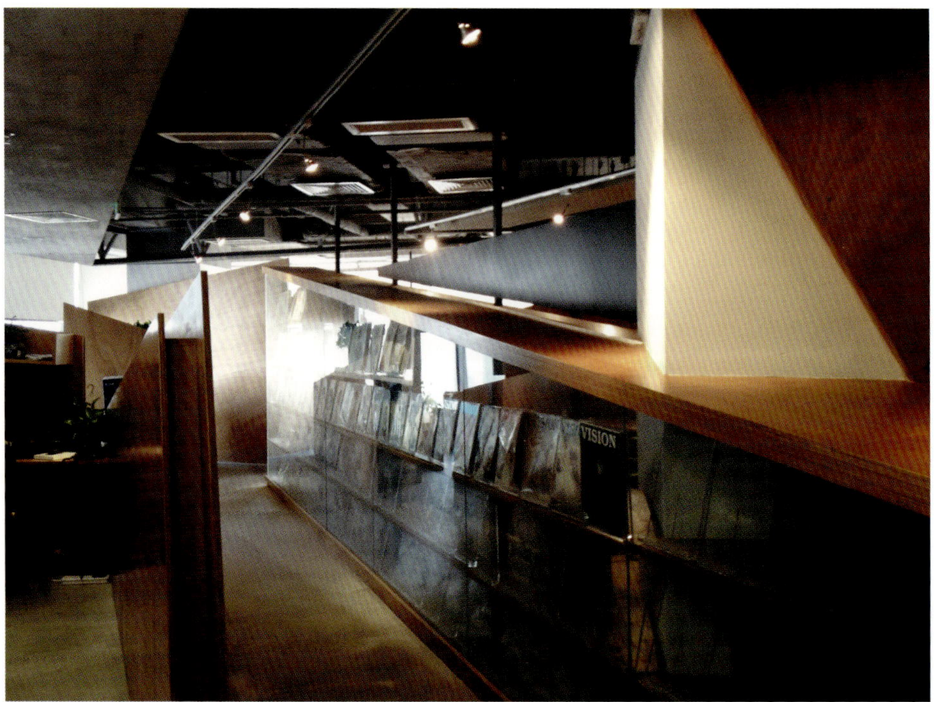

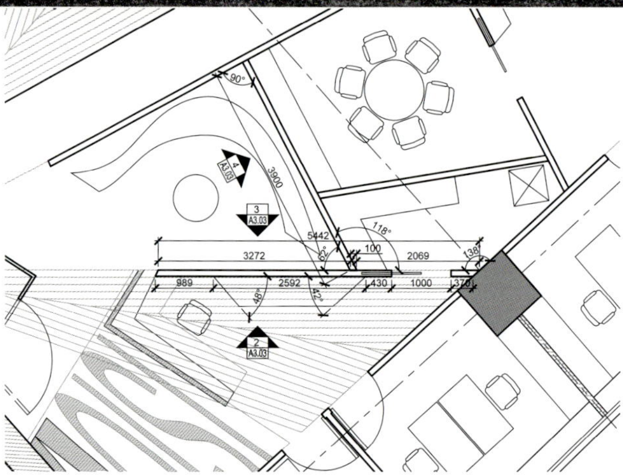
90°
4
A3.03
3900
3
A3.03
5442
118°
3272
100
2069
989
2592
430
1000
2
A3.03

VISION

"The window from which the world enters, the world watches."

by Carlo Truppi

At the corner of Burton Way and Clark sat a box with its brick walls, wood truss roof, and steel-framed windows. Like many other corner buildings in Los Angeles, it was there for 50 years completely unaware of its potential. It was just another container, only identifiable by a number. I sometimes imagined it being dropped off by a storage company with the sole purpose of being filled. While it might have been perfect for a craftsman workshop or office space, the dilapidated building in my client's hands had to be transformed into a showroom for the eclectic combination of classical and contemporary designs of kitchen cabinets and appliances.

One critical problem with the site was location. It sat on a commercial street, but there weren't any other stores in its vicinity. To be successful as a showroom, it needed to become a location, which meant that it had to attract and be visible to passing cars. When designing local projects in the past, I experimented with concepts of treating the buildings as billboards or signs. I was inspired by traditional Los Angeles architecture known as "novelty," mimetic, or "programmatic," which were styles of design popularised in the United States between 1920s and 1950s. During this time, the design of the building would mimic the function of the building, or the product it is associated with. When I first arrived in Los Angeles, I would drive

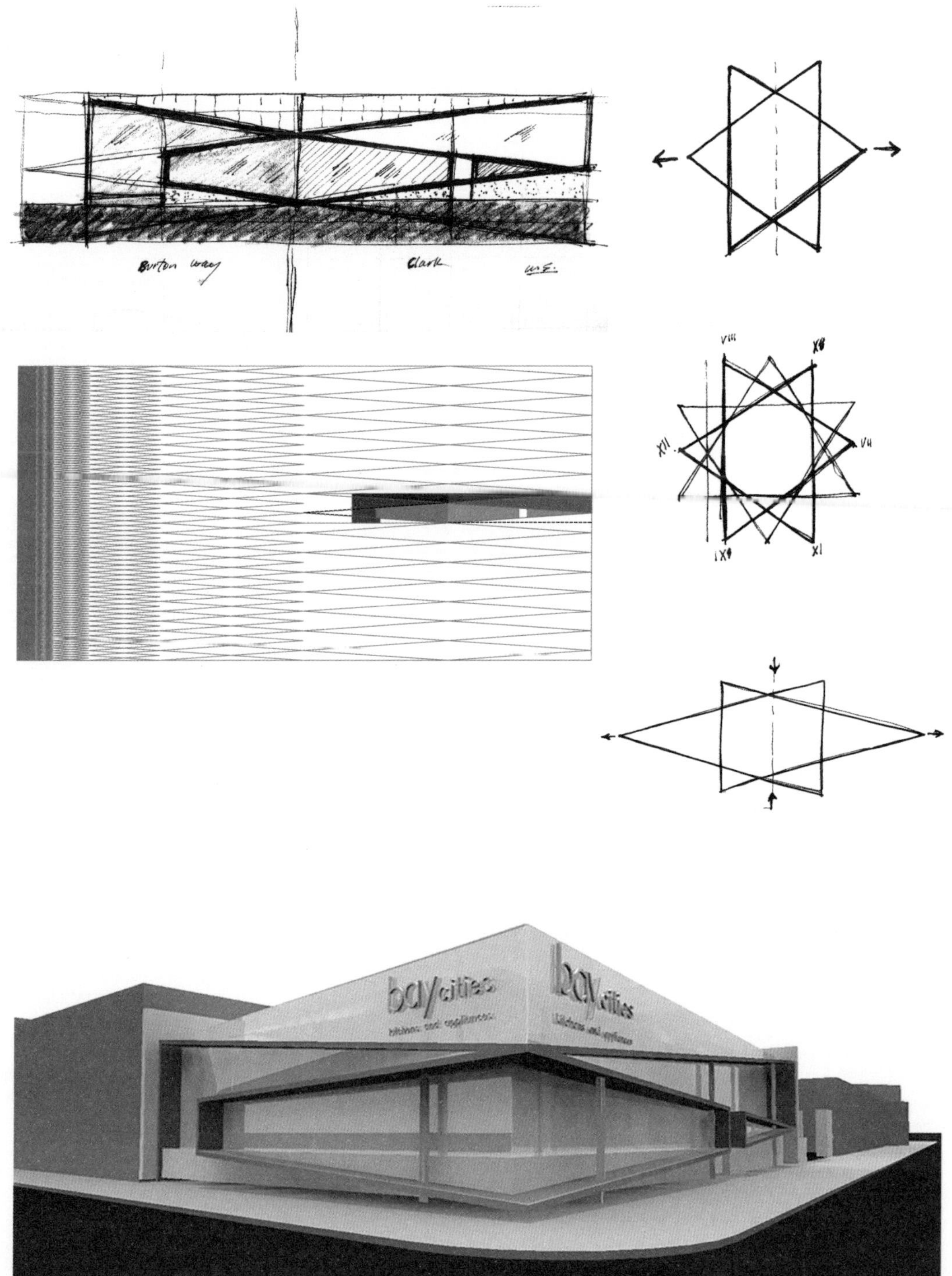
Burton way
Clark
bay cities
kitchens and appliances

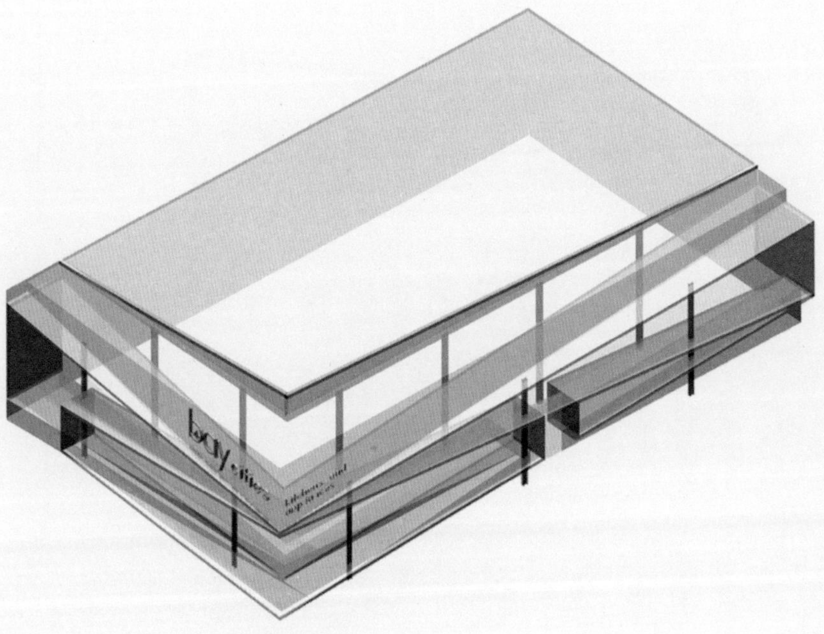

aimlessly, amazed to see the dog-shaped Pup Cafe, hat-shaped Brown Derby, and Randy's Donuts with its iconic donut. I later realized how much Los Angeles has changed and how much it has been desperately trying to become like other American cities.

To respond to my current reading of Los Angeles, I wanted to design a contemporary "programmatic" or "mimetic" type of building that becomes a brand representing it's product. My architectural response to the site would reject the standard planning and building models of twentieth-century New York, which, unlike Los Angeles, has established the corner location with a hierarchy and symbolic importance within the city's context. Los Angeles on the other hand, lacks this context and therefore defies specificity. The main entrances to it's corner buildings are located in the back or through the parking structure, which makes these structures no different than their counterparts in the middle of the block.

Baycities

Location:
Beverly Hills, California, USA

Year:
2009 (built)

Program:
Kitchen Cabinets, and Appliances Store

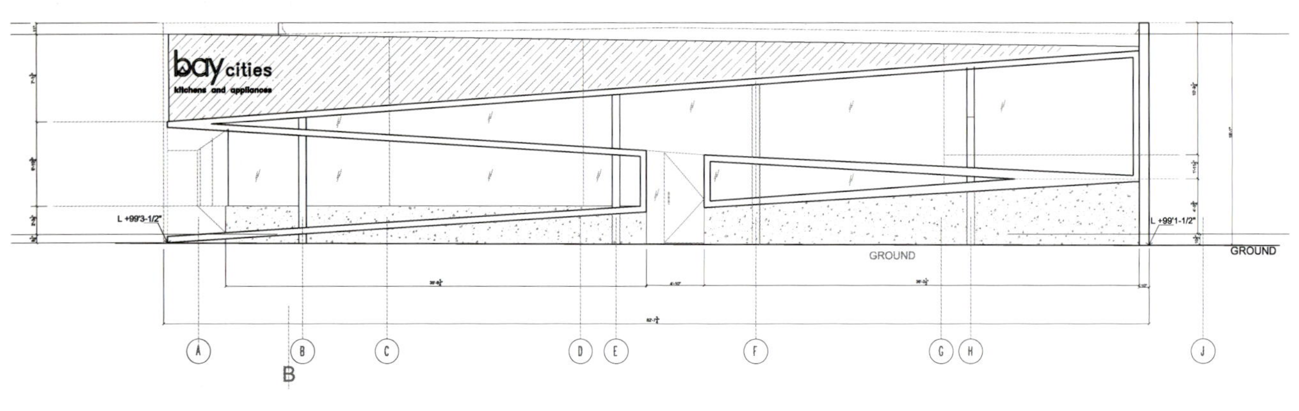

bay cities
kitchens and appliances
L +99'3-1/2"
L +99'1-1/2"
GROUND
GROUND
A
B
C
D
E
F
G
H
J
B

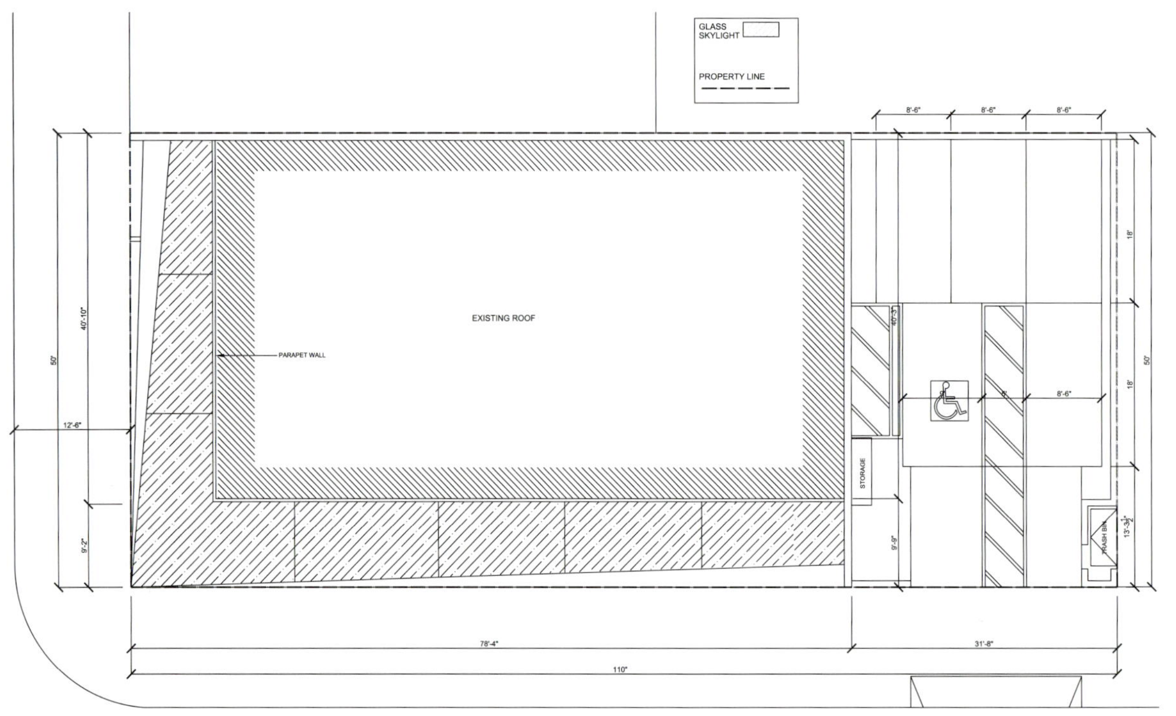

GLASS SKYLIGHT
PROPERTY LINE
8'-6"
8'-6"
8'-6"
EXISTING ROOF
PARAPET WALL
STORAGE
50'
40'-10"
12'-6"
9'-2"
9'-9"
18'
18'
50'
8'-6"
13'-3"
78'-4"
31'-8"
110'

The intention for the design was to go beyond the architectural implication of the site and remove the corner completely, both conceptually and literary. I wanted to treat the box as if it's south and west walls were both unfolded, creating a flat surface.

We first removed the entire front portion of the building. It was then replaced by a ten-foot façade constructed with steel and glass planes that inclined toward the corner and opposite sides of the property. The planes' orientation effect created a different field of vision, which can be experienced from every direction inside and outside the building. The existing and the new are juxtaposed independently and then joined by a skylight, which runs across the entire front portion of the building.

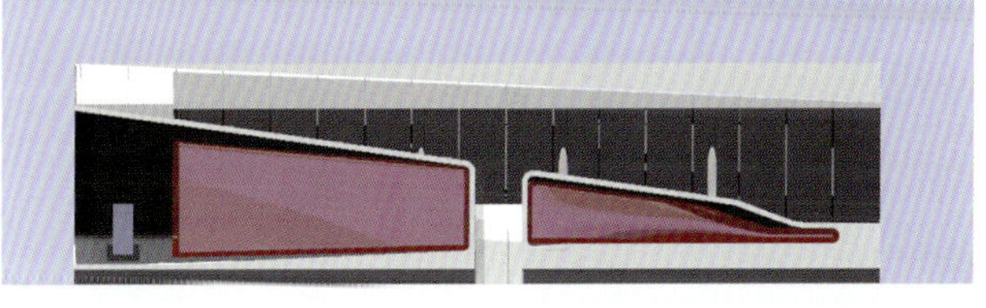

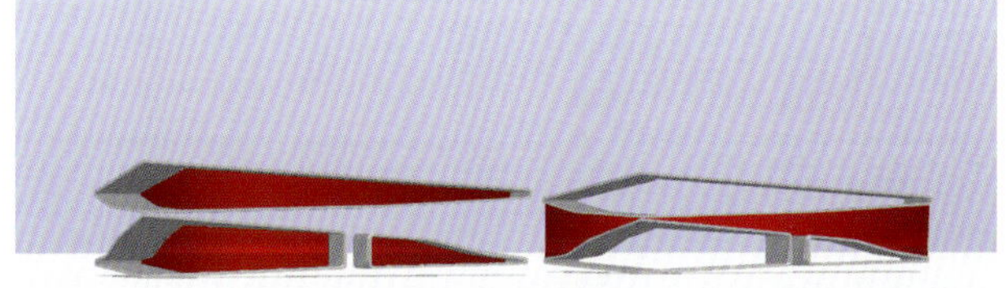

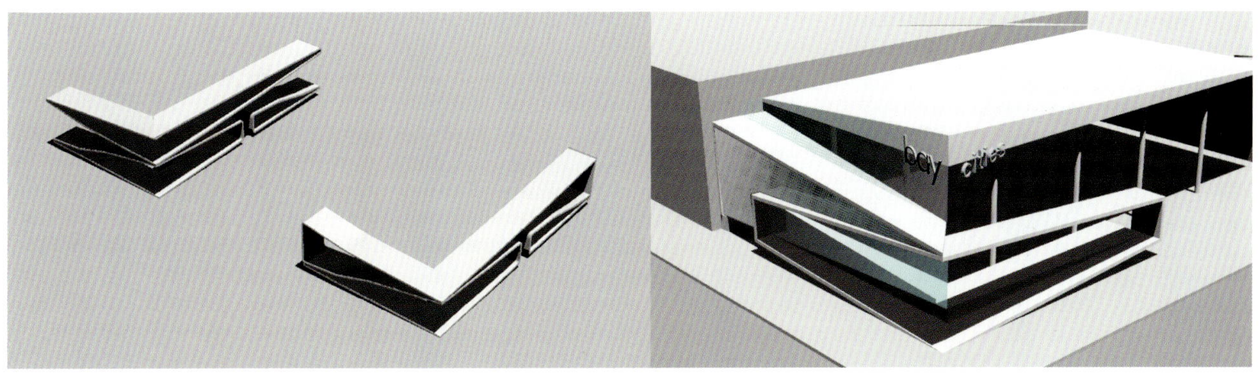

Weight and gravity are key elements in the organization of perception. The notion of up and down linked to the earth's gravity is just one element of perspective.
— Paul Virlio, interview with Enrique Limon

In the design's exploration stage, I realized that the box needed to be upgraded structurally to comply with the city's current life and safety requirements. This would've also affected the new intervention from the façade, which played an important role in advertising the business and it's products. Therefore, we proposed two separate, but interconnected structures. The first would be steel columns, beams, and grade beams. The second would be an independent steel structure to hold the new façade.

The shapes of the facade slanted from the central corner to the east and south edges of the building. The facade's planes changed in direction to alter our perception of the space and how it interacts with its surroundings. This created a visual field of forces that bent the extremities of the building, in which case the body adjusted itself and extended beyond the boundaries of the building site.

The space's steel and low-iron, tempered laminated glass formed angles for the viewing of displays. The view of the space from the outside in and inside out keeps the viewer's gaze moving in every direction. As the facade opens up, the building appears to have part of it erased. In that instant, the viewer can see through the building onto the other side. I removed the walls and replaced them with oriented surfaces whose angles were defined by me. The new geometrical composition has its symbolic intentions to transform an ordinary street corner into an interactive destination.

bay cities
Kitchens & Appliances

Abbas Safii & Armineh Ghariban

John Mccoy

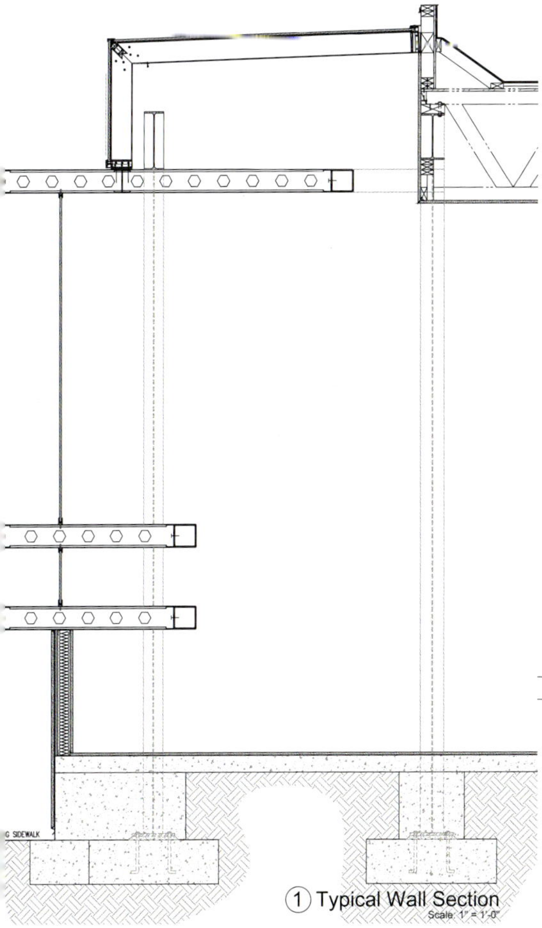

① Typical Wall Section
Scale: 1" = 1'-0"

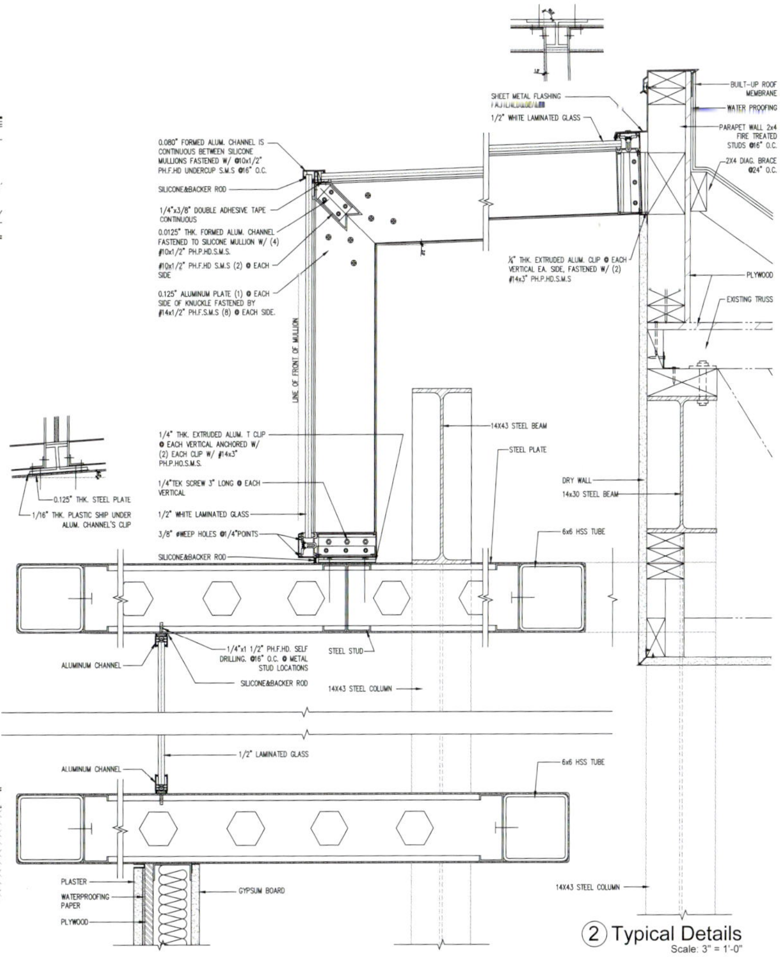

② Typical Details
Scale: 3" = 1'-0"

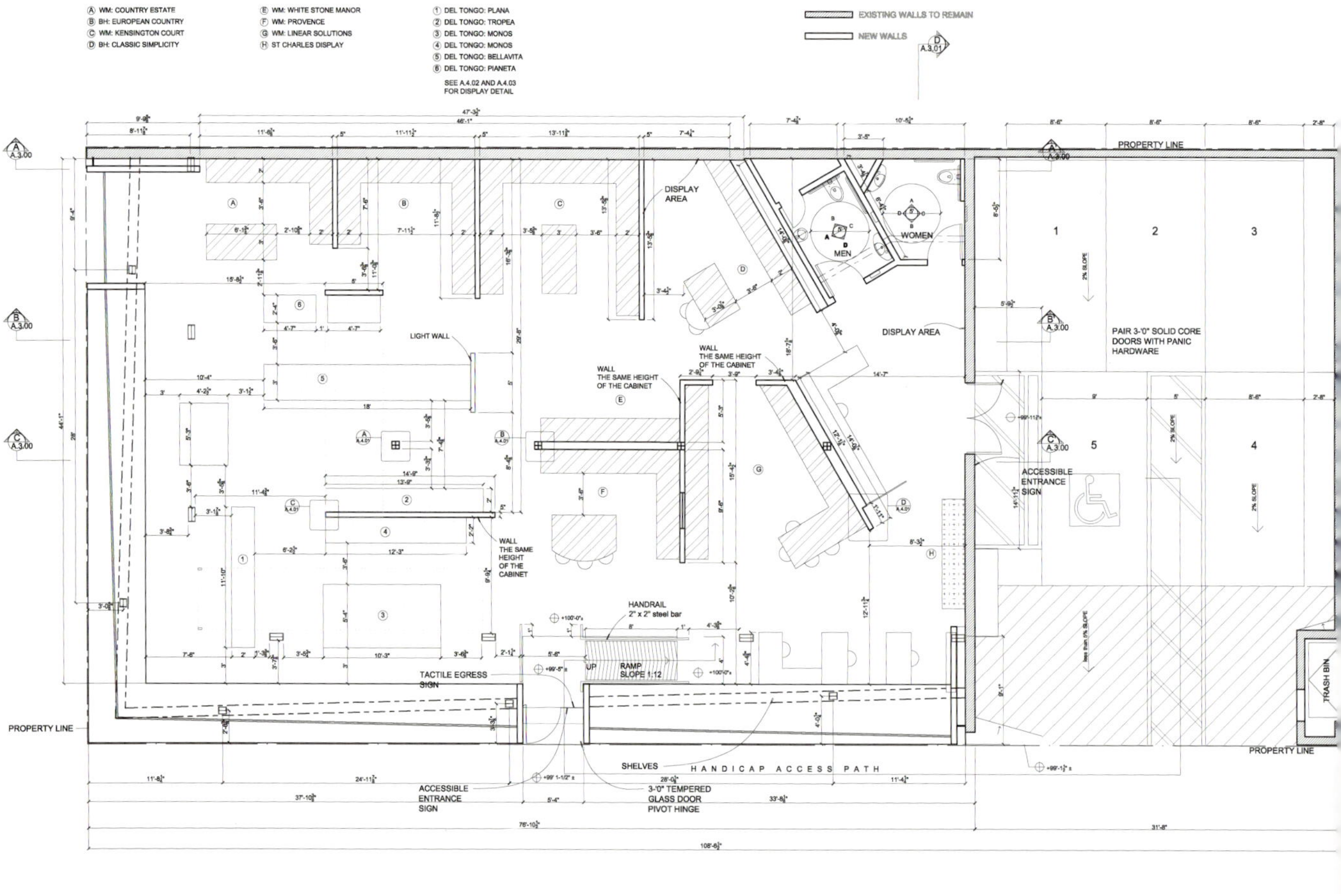

Ⓐ WM: COUNTRY ESTATE
Ⓑ BH: EUROPEAN COUNTRY
Ⓒ WM: KENSINGTON COURT
Ⓓ BH: CLASSIC SIMPLICITY

Ⓔ WM: WHITE STONE MANOR
Ⓕ WM: PROVENCE
Ⓖ WM: LINEAR SOLUTIONS
Ⓗ ST CHARLES DISPLAY

① DEL TONGO: PLANA
② DEL TONGO: TROPEA
③ DEL TONGO: MONOS
④ DEL TONGO: MONOS
⑤ DEL TONGO: BELLAVITA
⑥ DEL TONGO: PIANETA

SEE A.4.02 AND A.4.03
FOR DISPLAY DETAIL

EXISTING WALLS TO REMAIN
NEW WALLS

DISPLAY AREA
WOMEN
MEN
LIGHT WALL
WALL THE SAME HEIGHT OF THE CABINET
DISPLAY AREA
PROPERTY LINE
PAIR 3'-0" SOLID CORE DOORS WITH PANIC HARDWARE
ACCESSIBLE ENTRANCE SIGN
WALL THE SAME HEIGHT OF THE CABINET
HANDRAIL 2" x 2" steel bar
TACTILE EGRESS SIGN
UP
RAMP SLOPE 1:12
TRASH BIN
PROPERTY LINE
SHELVES
HANDICAP ACCESS PATH
ACCESSIBLE ENTRANCE SIGN
3'-0" TEMPERED GLASS DOOR PIVOT HINGE

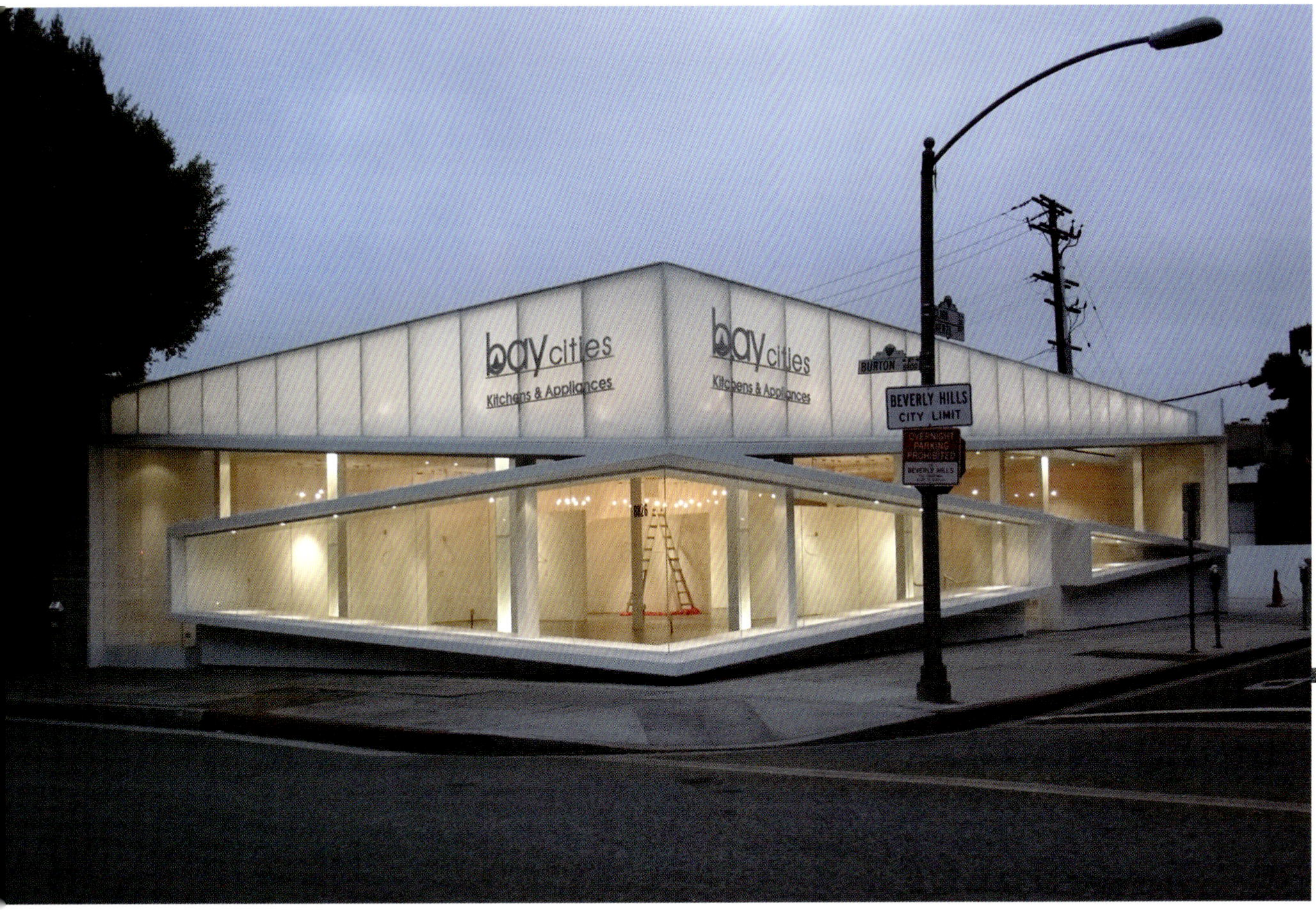
bay cities
Kitchens & Appliances
bay cities
Kitchens & Appliances
BURTON
BEVERLY HILLS
CITY LIMIT
OVERNIGHT
PARKING
PROHIBITED

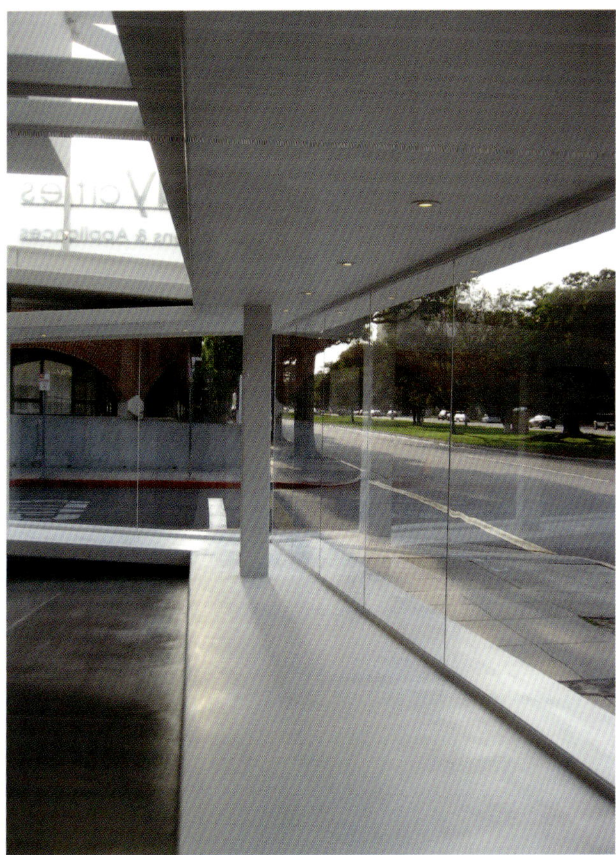

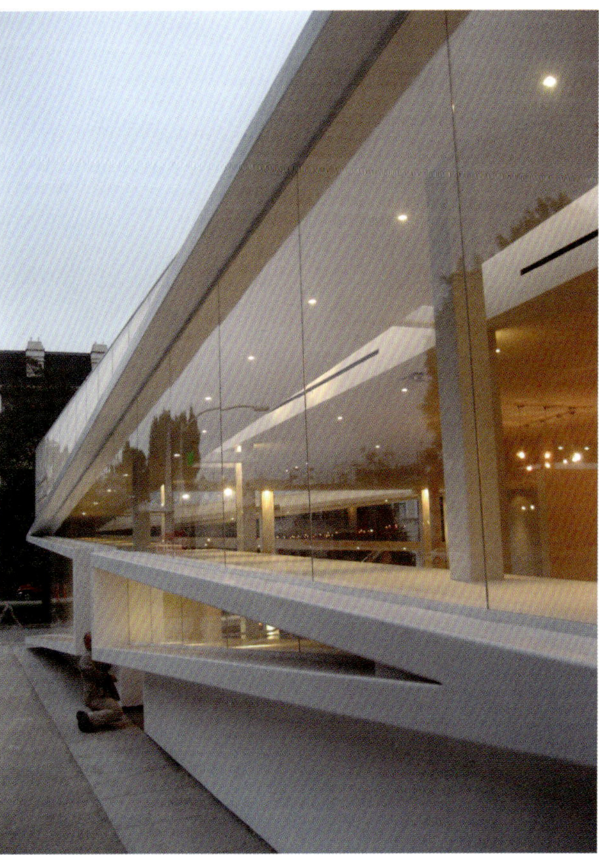

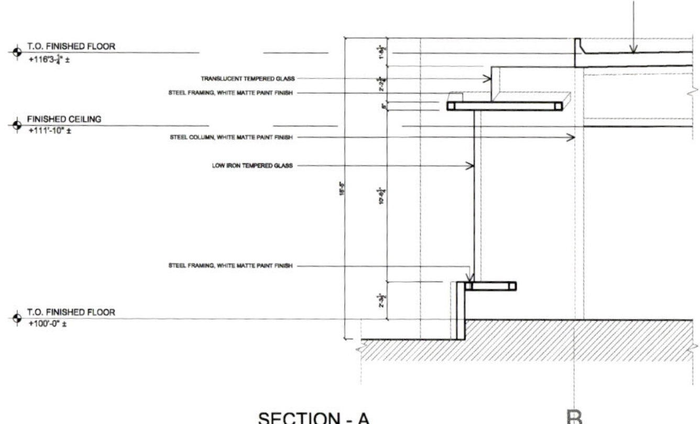

SECTION - A

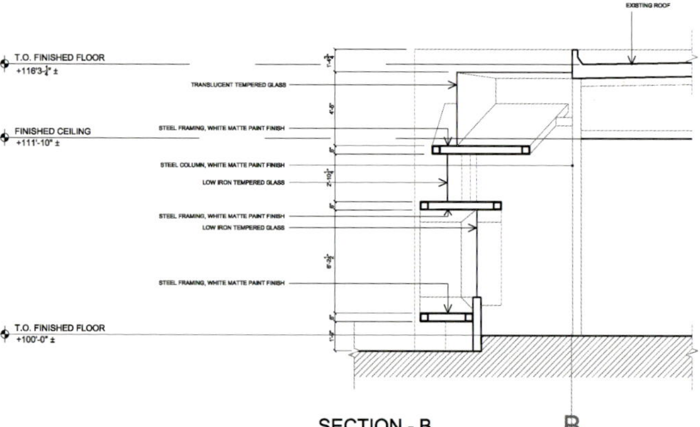

SECTION - B

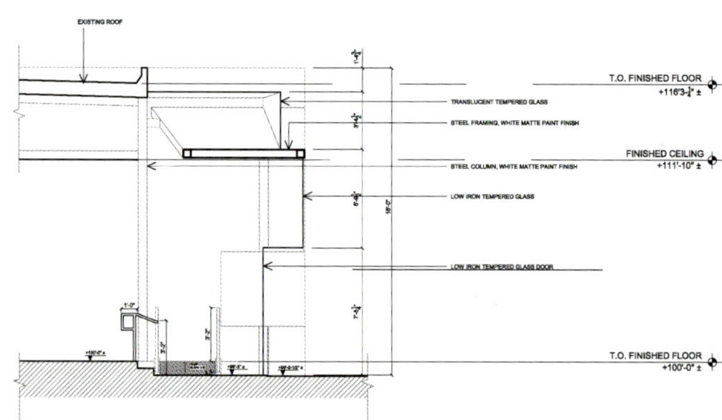

SECTION - D

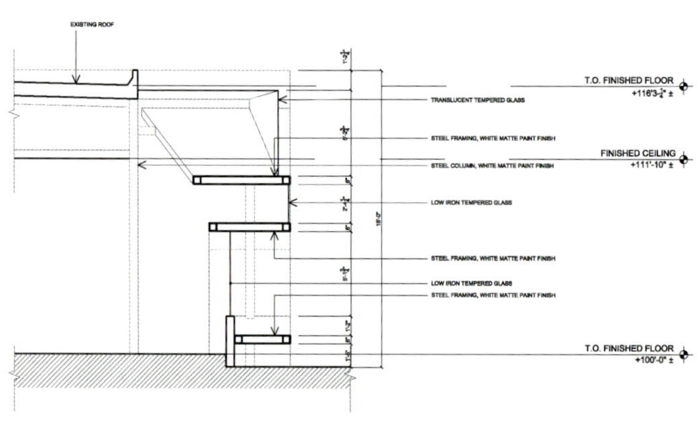

SECTION - E

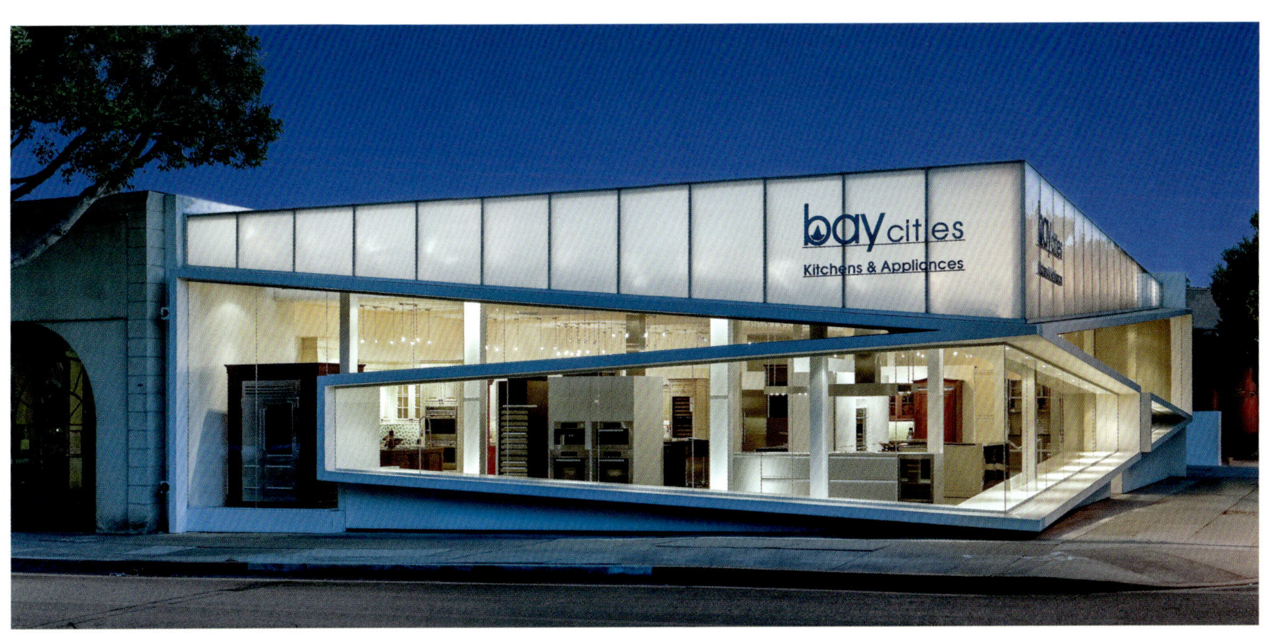

bay cities
Kitchens & Appliances

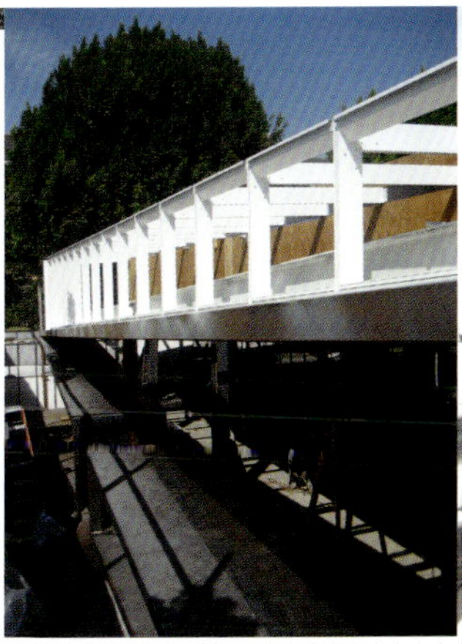

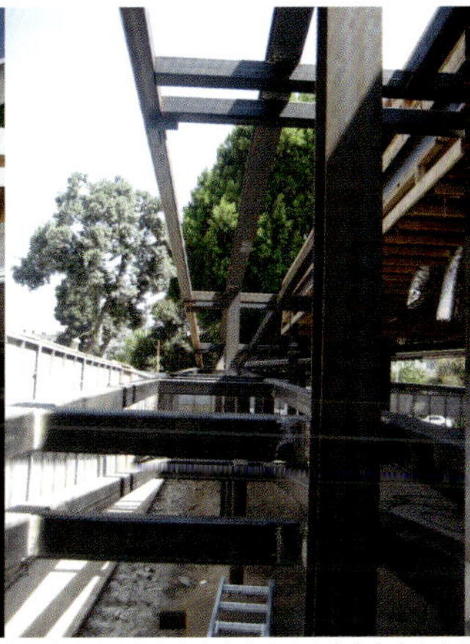

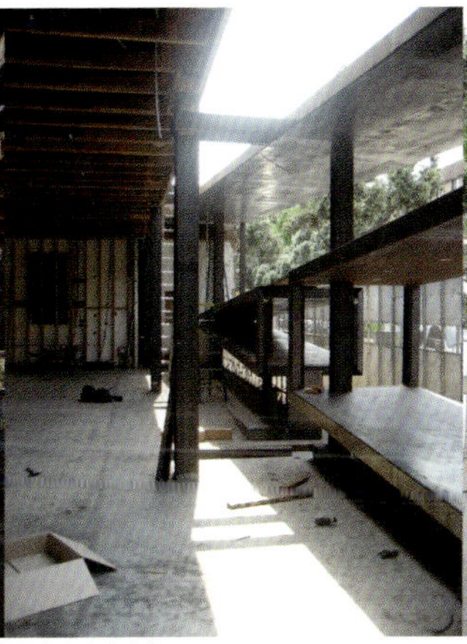

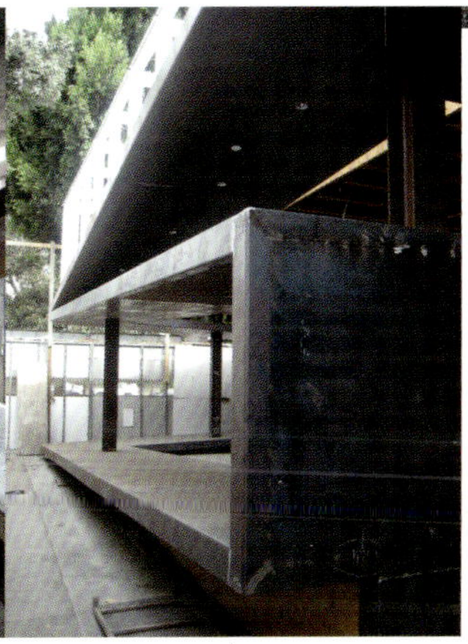

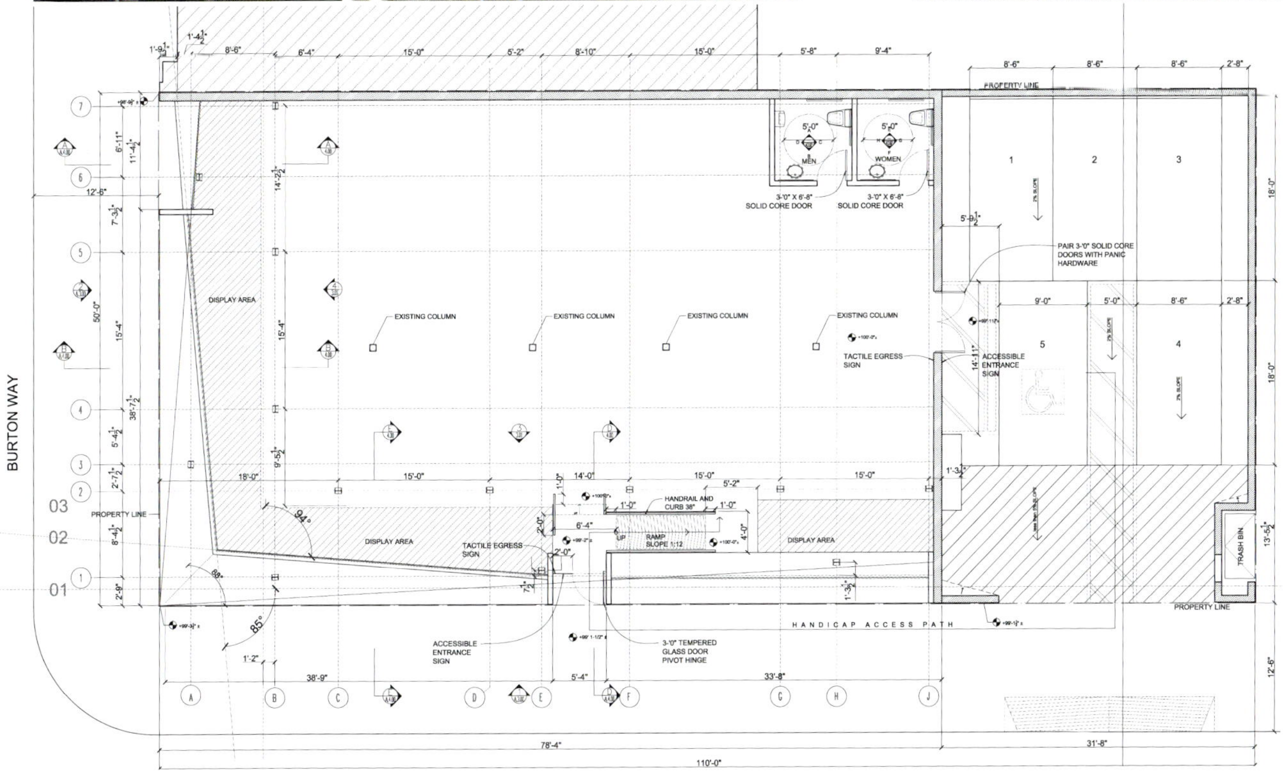
BURTON WAY
PROPERTY LINE
DISPLAY AREA
EXISTING COLUMN
MEN
WOMEN
3'-0" X 6'-8" SOLID CORE DOOR
PAIR 3'-0" SOLID CORE DOORS WITH PANIC HARDWARE
TACTILE EGRESS SIGN
ACCESSIBLE ENTRANCE SIGN
HANDRAIL AND CURB 38"
RAMP SLOPE 1:12
3'-0" TEMPERED GLASS DOOR PIVOT HINGE
HANDICAP ACCESS PATH
TRASH BIN
78'-4"
31'-8"
110'-0"

The concept of landscape and residential buildings are combined together tightly; it works like a parallel movement.

CRLand Mountain

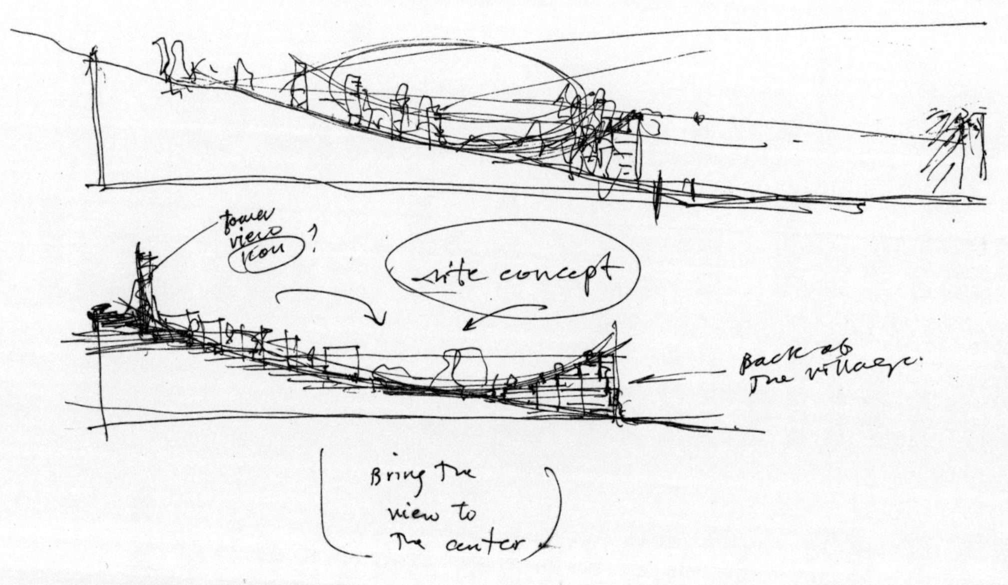

tower
view
?
site concept
Back of
the village.
Bring the
view to
the center

garden
M
2
3
EXT
yard
20'

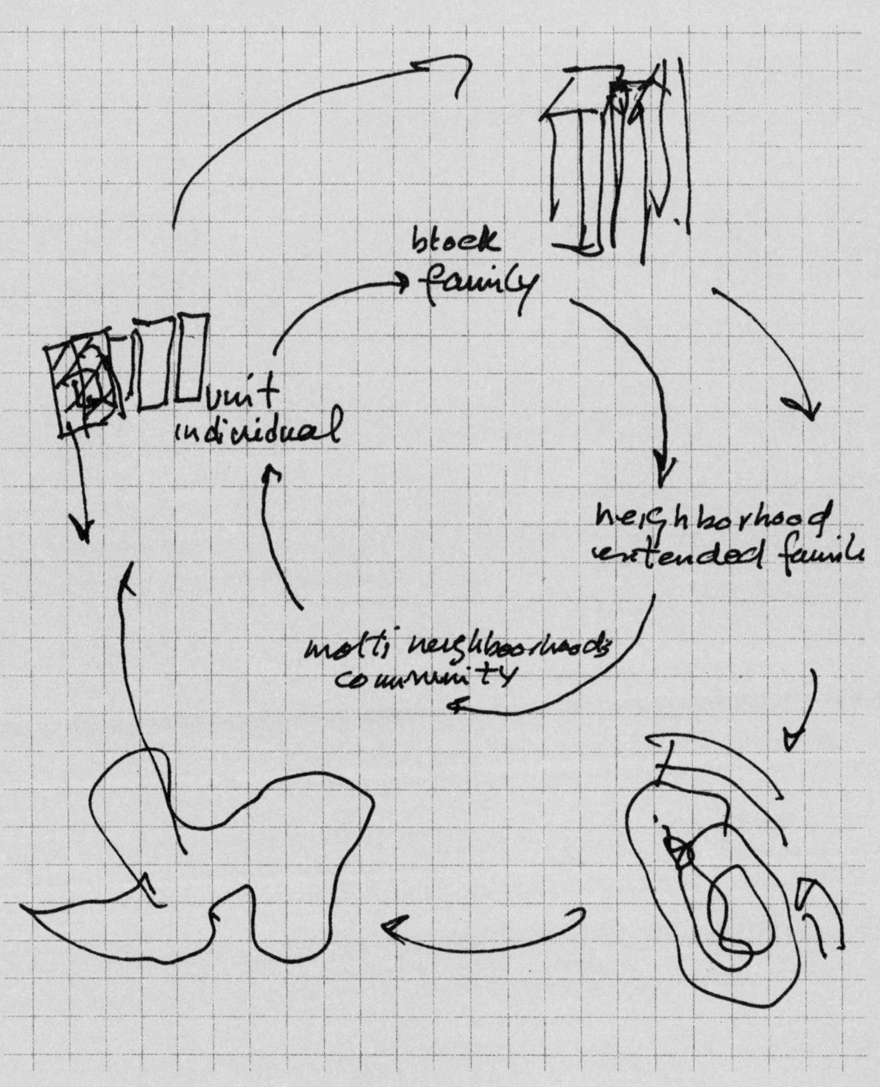

block
family
unit
individual
neighborhood
extended famil
multi neighborhoods
community

CRLand Mountain

Location:
Beijing, P.R. China

Year:
2010 (not built)

Program:
Residential Garden Community

Inspired by the international hillside cities and gardens, this community is situated in western Beijing on a site notable for its two Buddhist temples. The mountainous Mentougou district boasts a height of 2,300 meters and is surrounded with hills and valleys. The site is low density based on zoning requirements and is one of very few large pieces of real estate available for development in Beijing.

The design proposal gathers landscape and residential buildings together tightly, working in parallel. The nature of the site lends itself to a serene human-scale setting, with roads carefully carved into the natural topography to minimize excavation and grading. An inspired variety of gardens has been created. Each garden delineates a small neighborhood with residential buildings and unique characteristics and each features a unique design that creates a joyful, pleasant environment with different types of trees, plants, and water elements.

Taking advantage of the southern exposure was an important design inspiration. In the low-rise building area, 81% of the units have views to the south;

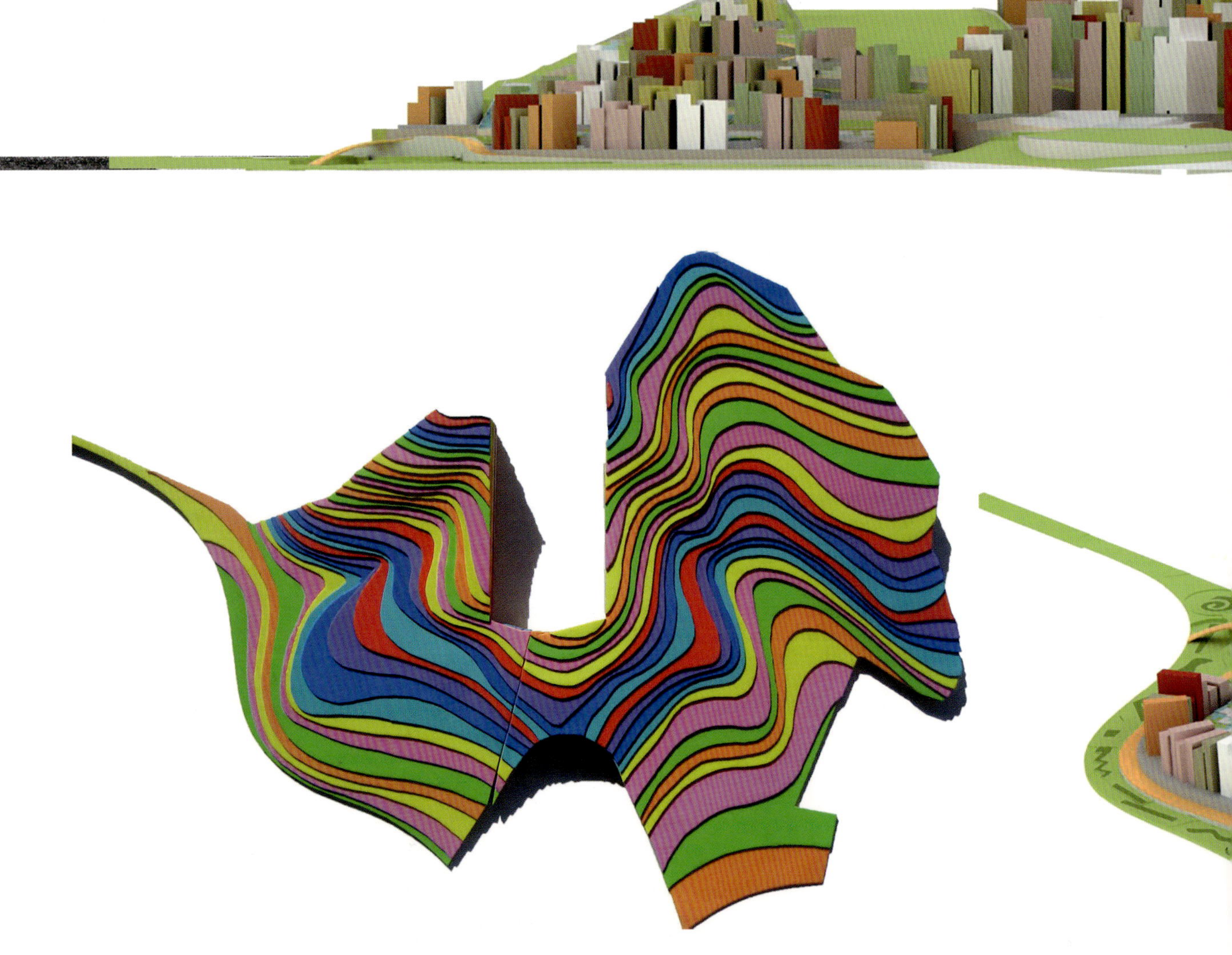

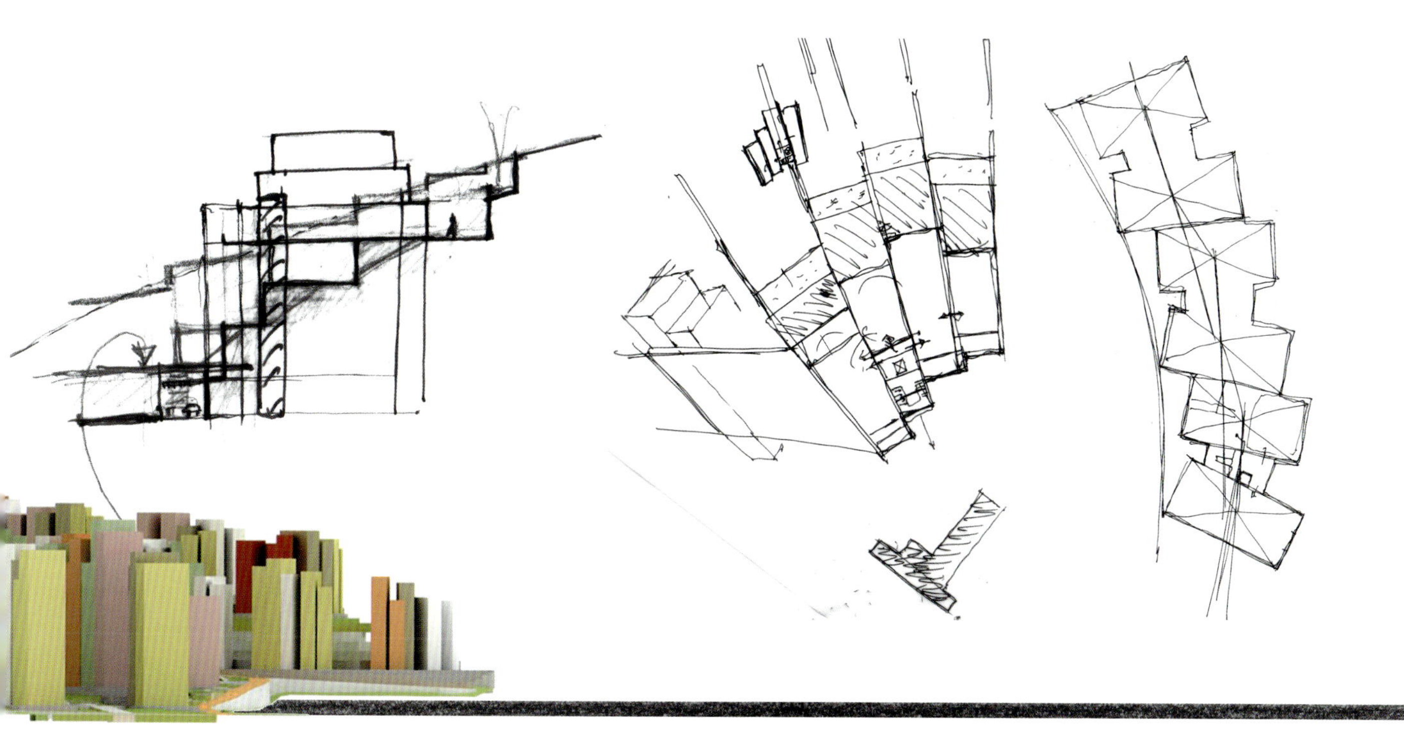

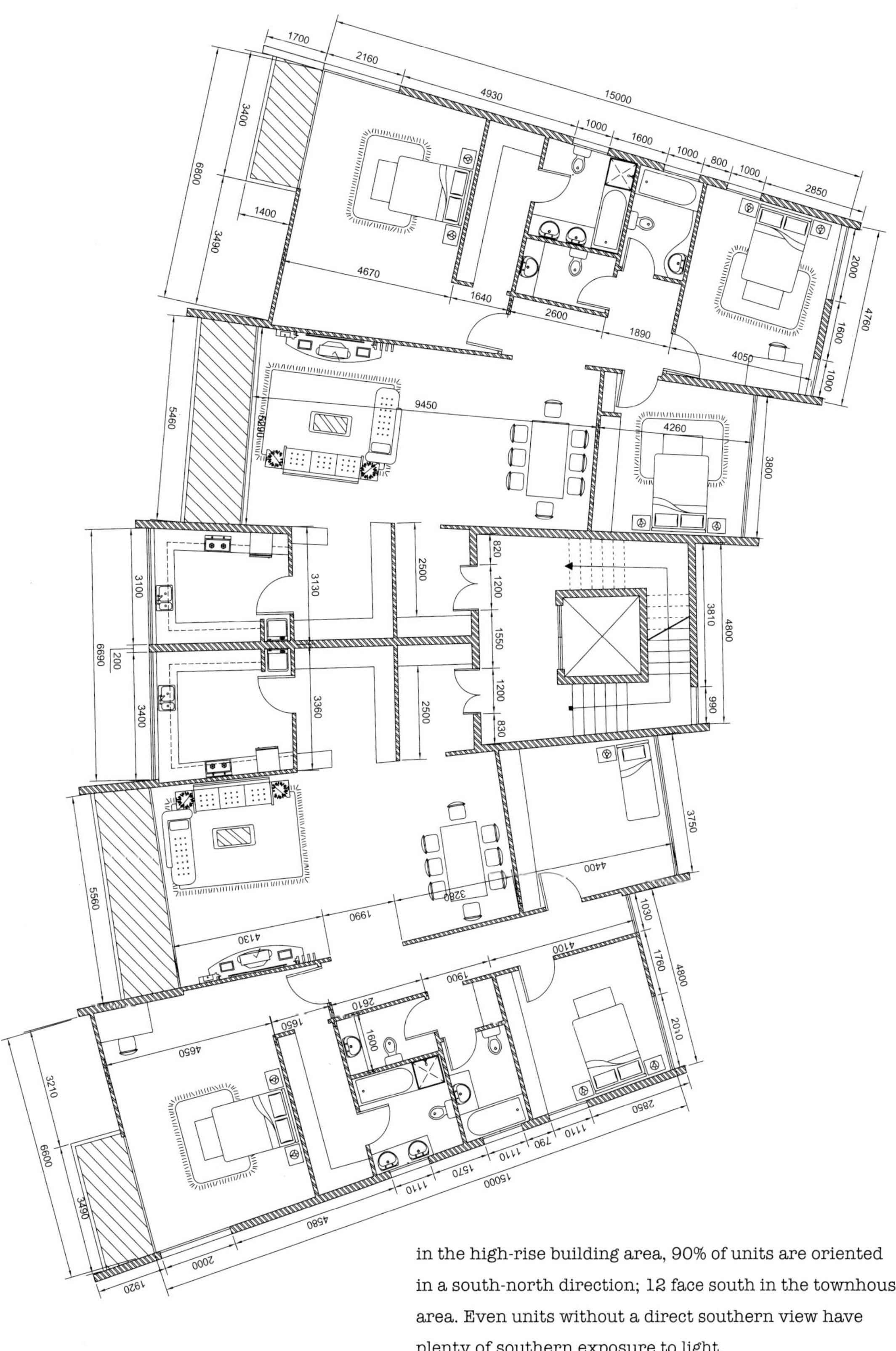

in the high-rise building area, 90% of units are oriented in a south-north direction; 12 face south in the townhouse area. Even units without a direct southern view have plenty of southern exposure to light.

Typical successful building plans in Beijing dictate the following for exterior spaces: low-rise buildings usually have two units sharing one gate, while high-rise buildings feature three units and a smaller gateway. Town houses have standard gate size and every house has its own private courtyard but shares an access staircase with one other house.

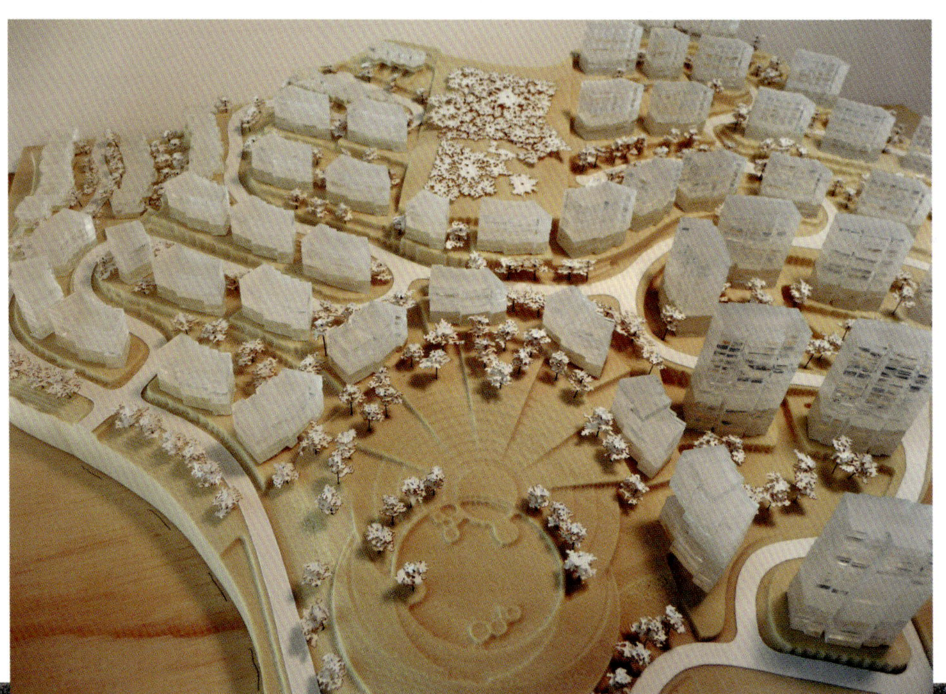

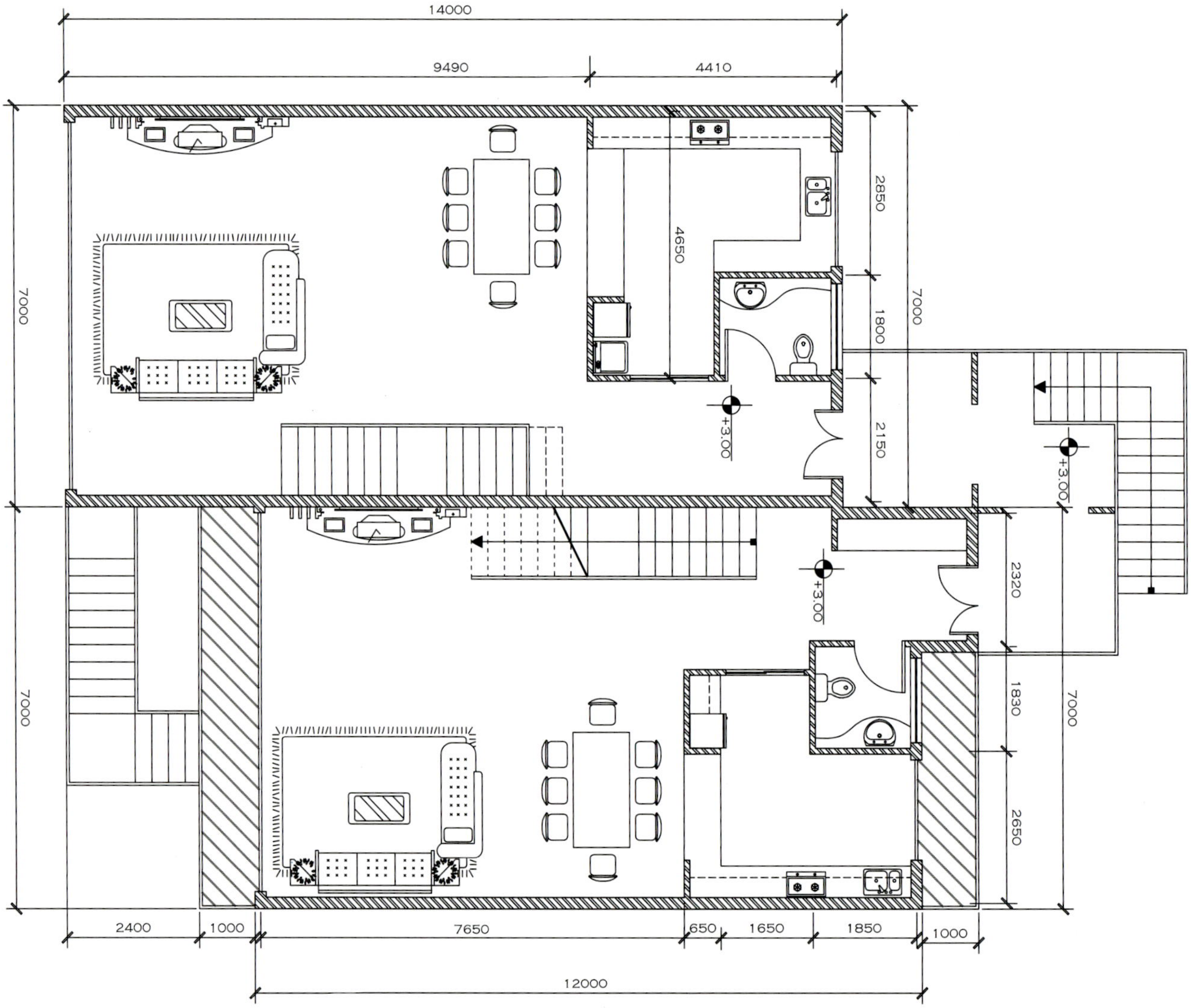

14000
9490
4410
2850
4650
1800
7000
2150
+3.00
+3.00
+3.00
2320
1830
7000
2650
7000
2400
1000
7650
650
1650
1850
1000
12000

Here the passage of time and the new site gives new life to the antique building by upstaging it with respect.

Nanchang Center

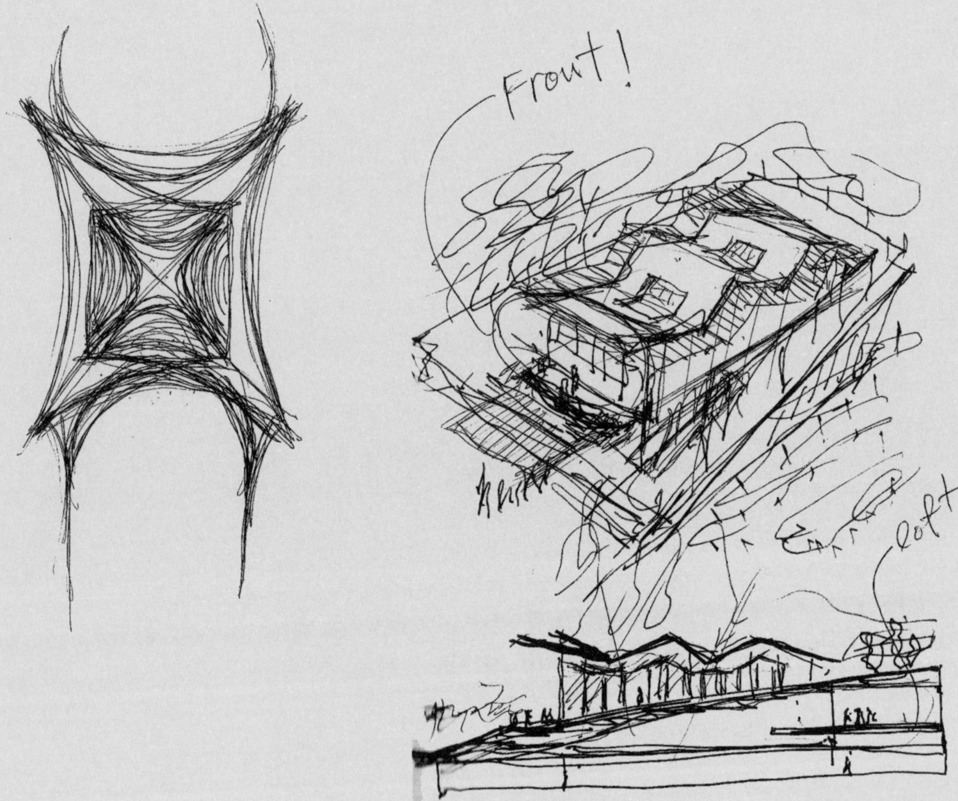
Front!
loft

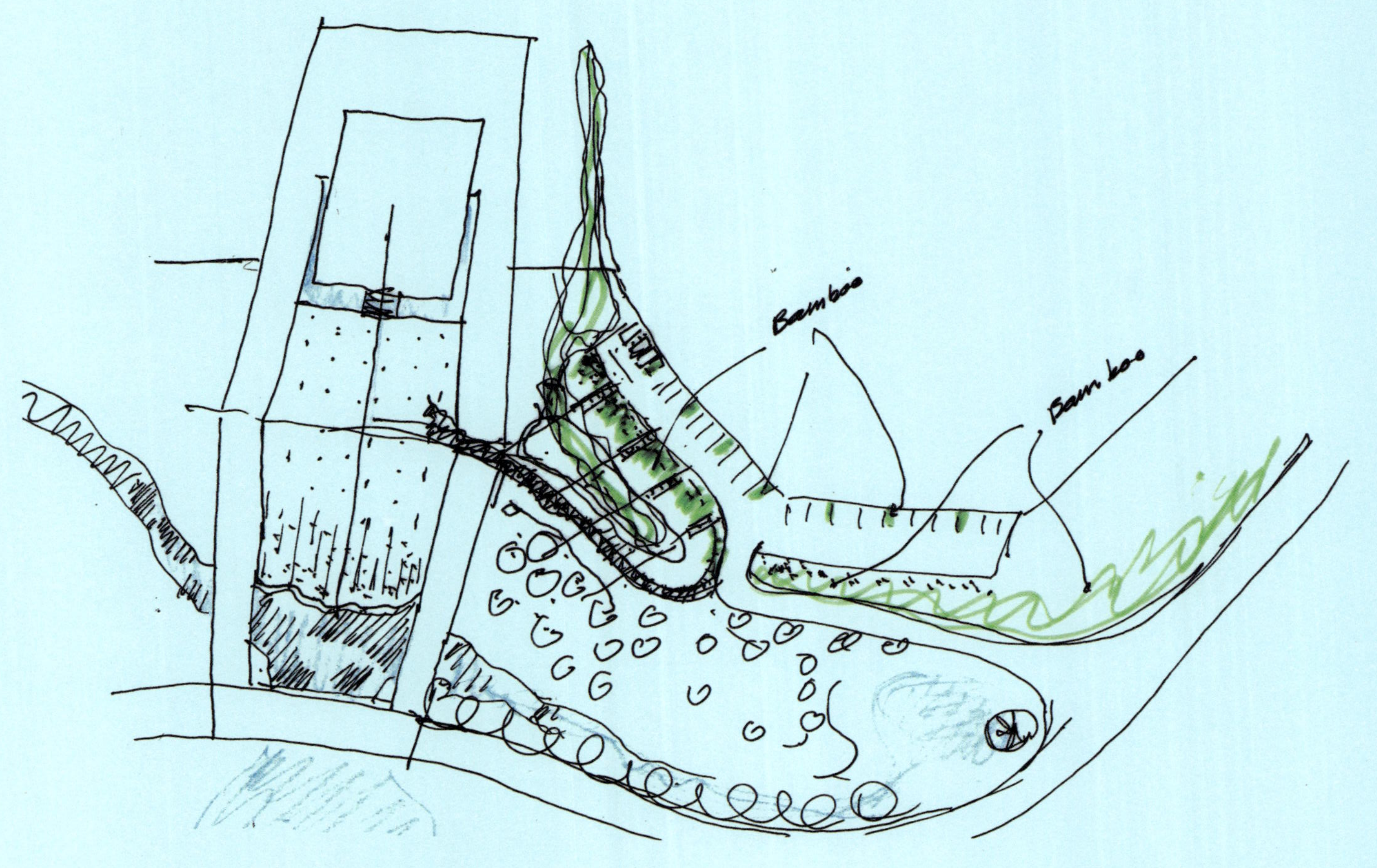
Bamboo
Bam boo

Nanchang Center

Location:
Nanchang, P.R. China

Year:
2010 (not built)

Program:
Community Center

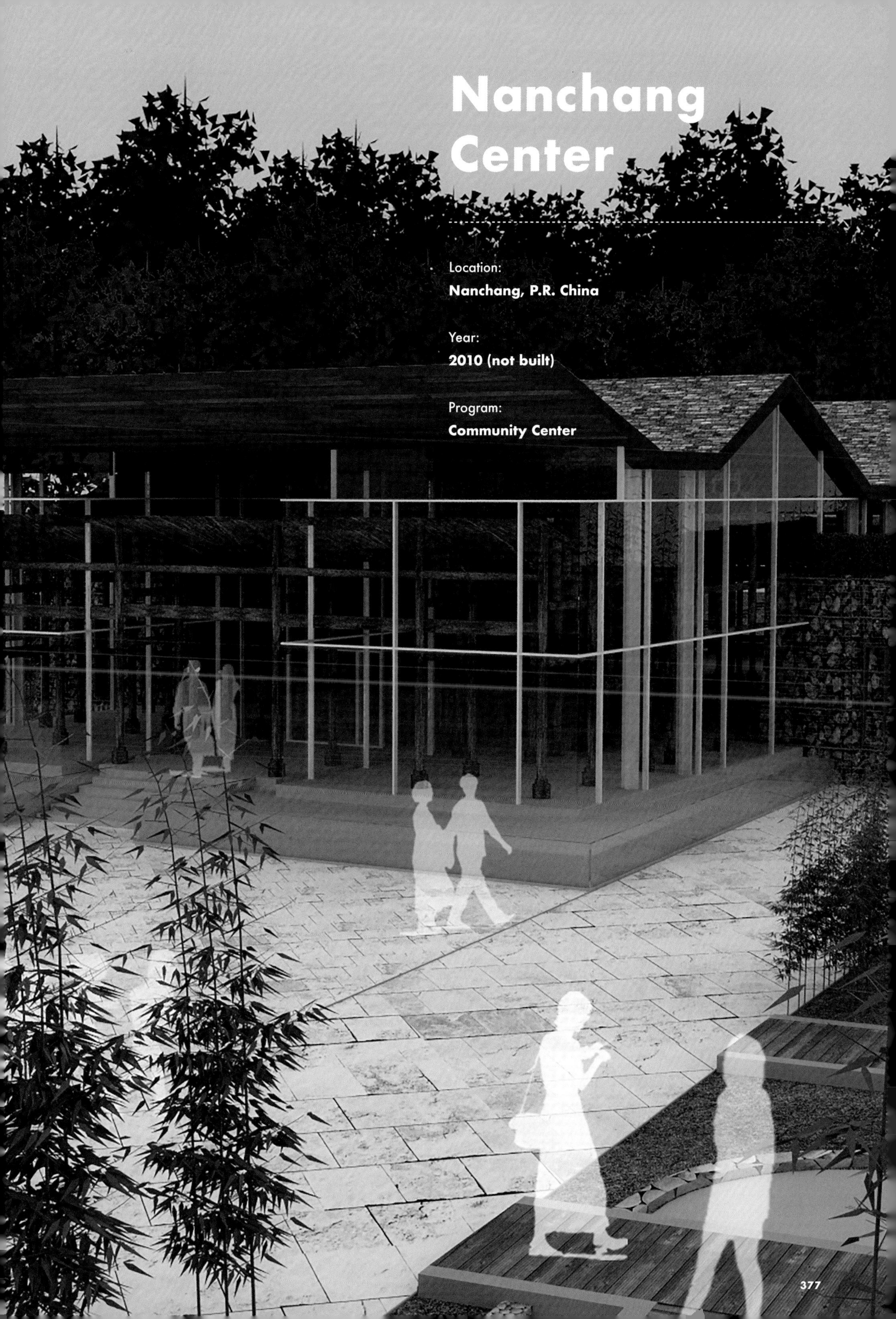

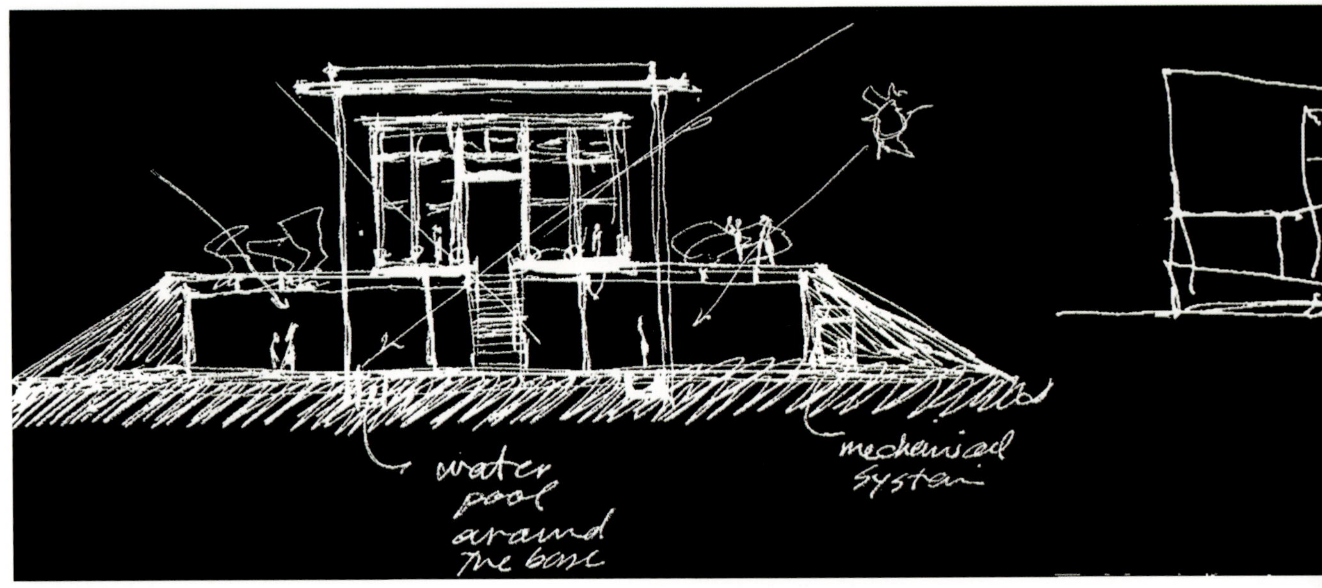

Amidst a lush, hilly landscape the Nanchang Sales Center provides the gateway to a new development represented by architecture that's an organic fusion between old and new. The design respects and values the past while projecting it into contemporary life. Building and landscape are fused together organically.

Visitors are welcomed by a wooden entryway to an antique, pitched-roof building that's been moved to the site. The old building is for exhibition only; highlighted are its powerful tree-trunk columns that have maintained their integrity over time, surviving corrosion, weathering, and human destruction. Their carvings tell stories of their past and the people who made them, lived with them and admired them. They are messengers from an era that is long gone but their traces guide us into the future.

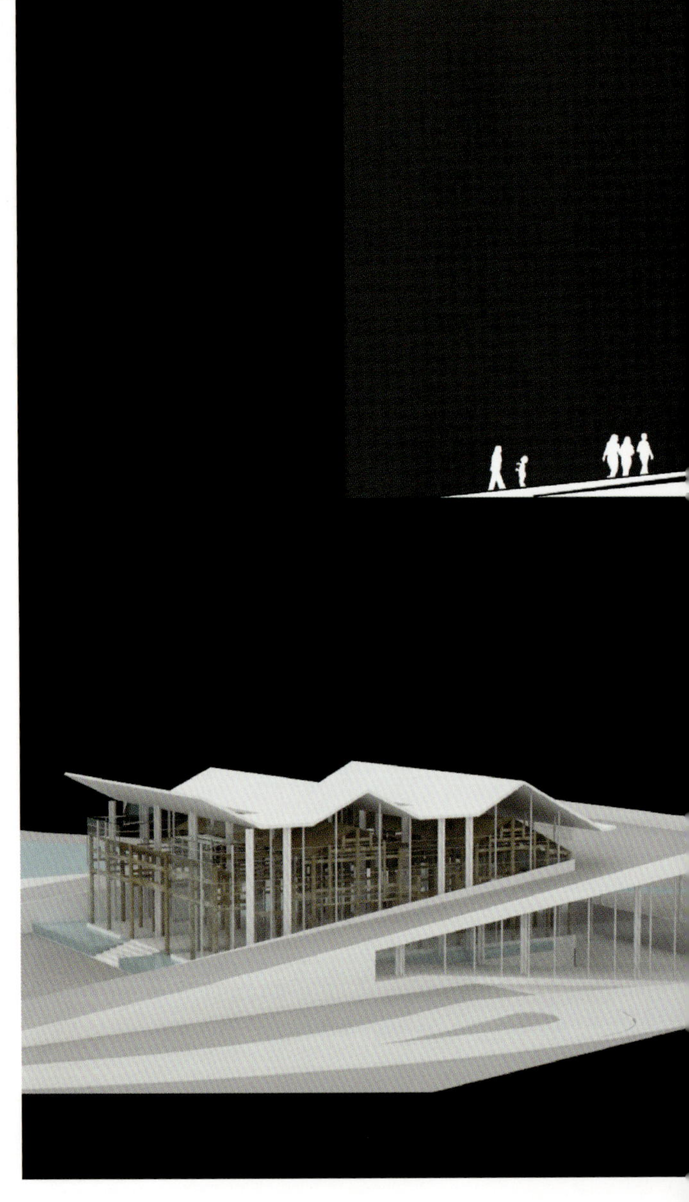

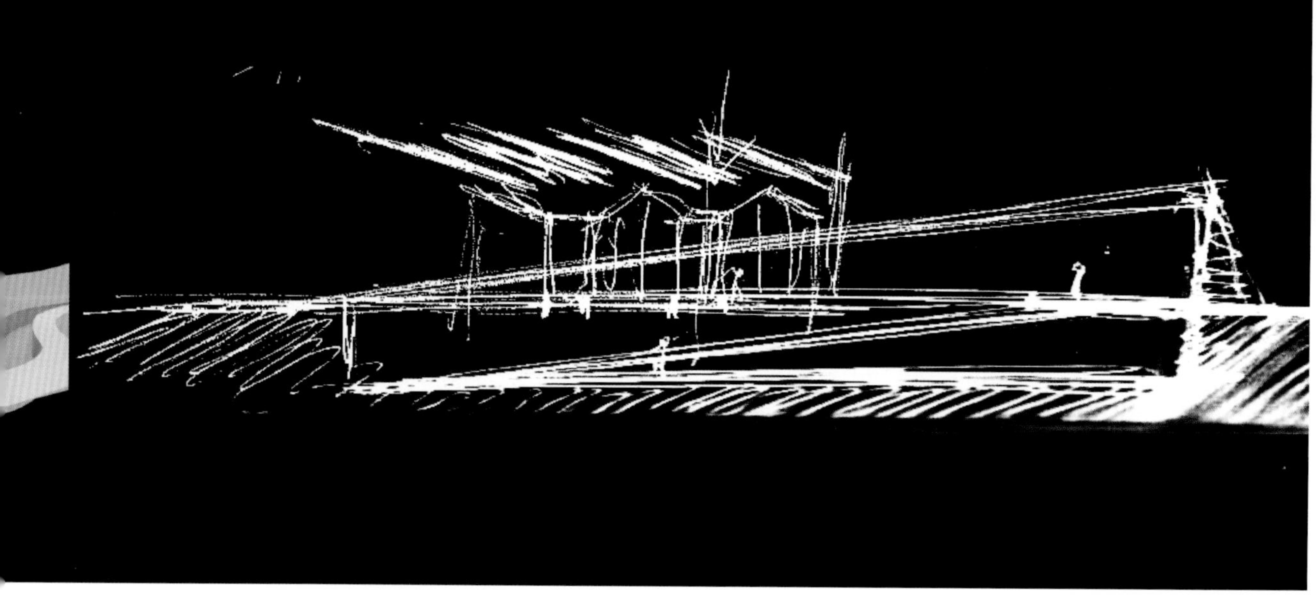

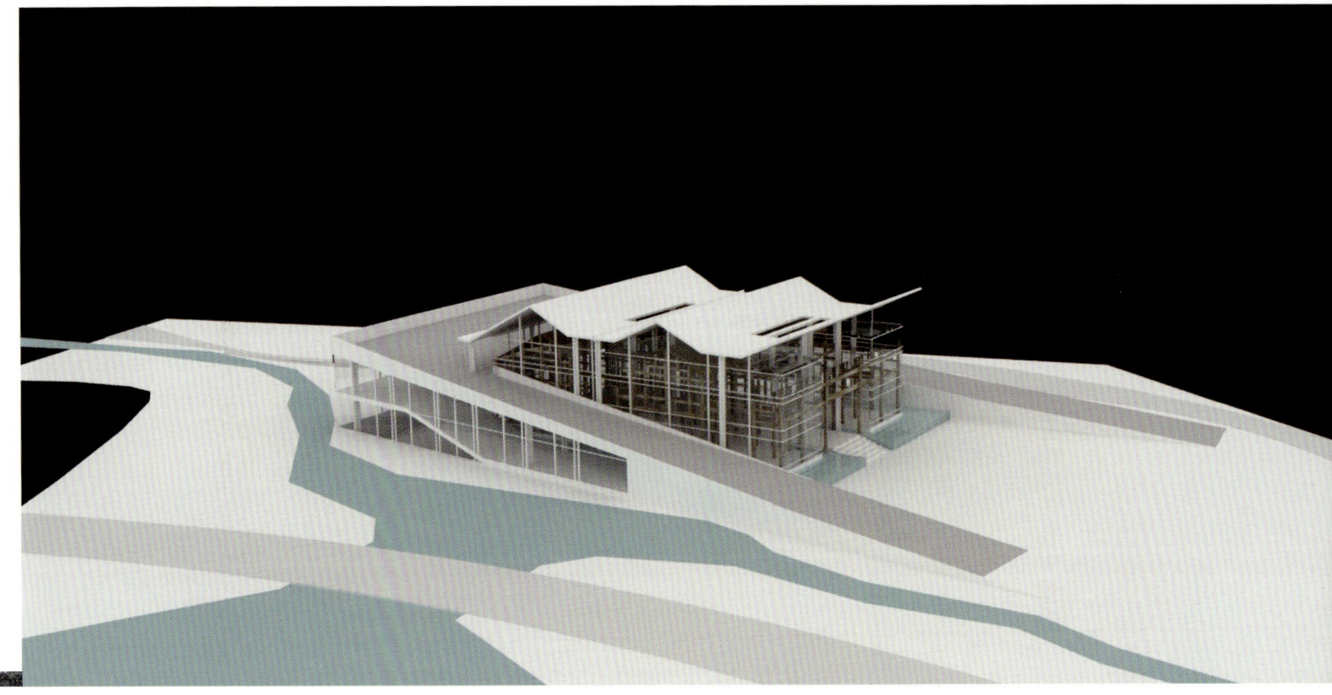

Because the antique building does not have any structural value, it needed to be placed inside another container building. The new container is a simple steel-frame structure whose lines follow the antique building's footprint and roof structure. It's surrounded by another pitched-roof building and provides two functions: additional floor area for the program of the Sales Center and a landscaped area around the antique building. Visitors may walk on the landscaped roof and enjoy the gardens there while glimpsing the antique building from outside. The building's entrance is elevated to create a platform, with the antique building displayed prominently in the background. A water fountain in front captures the reflection of the antique building and heightens its prominence on the site. The total interior floor area of the antique building is 420m^2; the floor area of the additional building surrounding it is 670m^2.

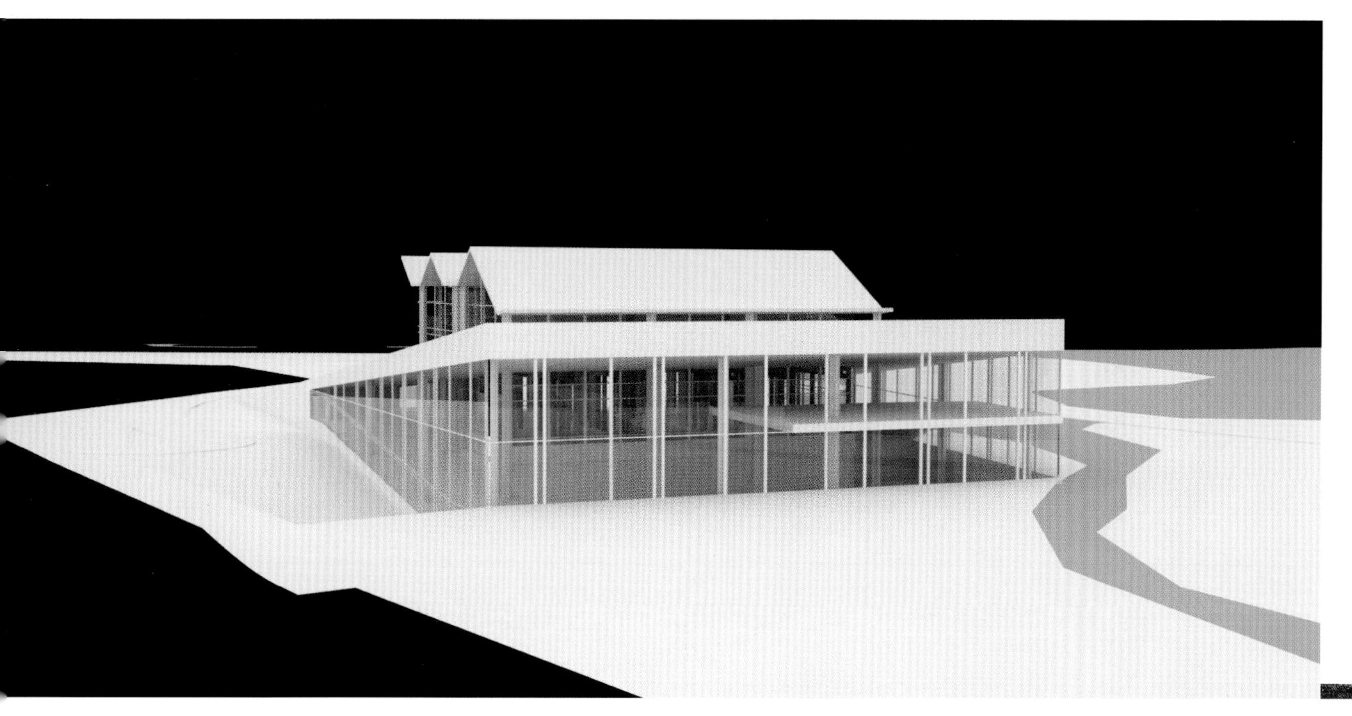

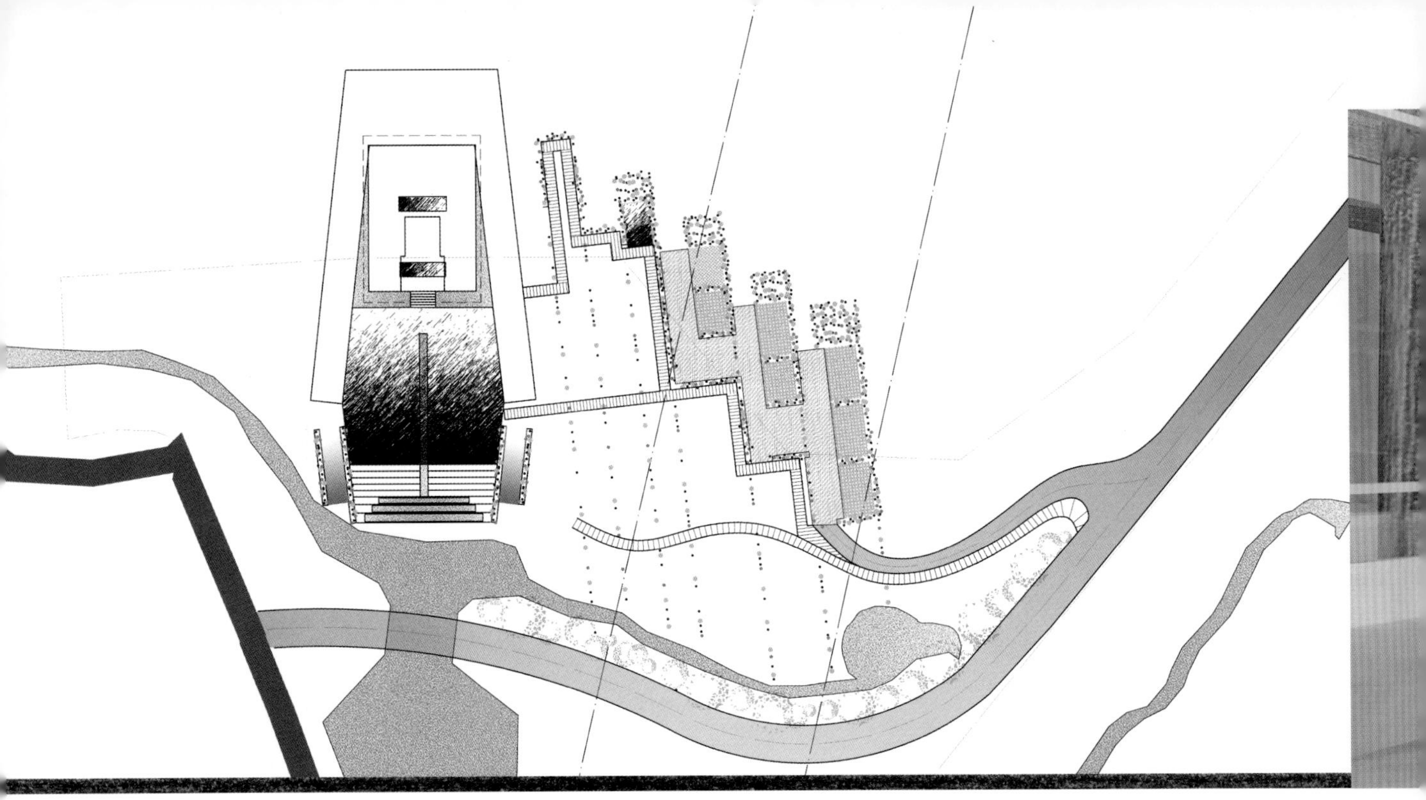

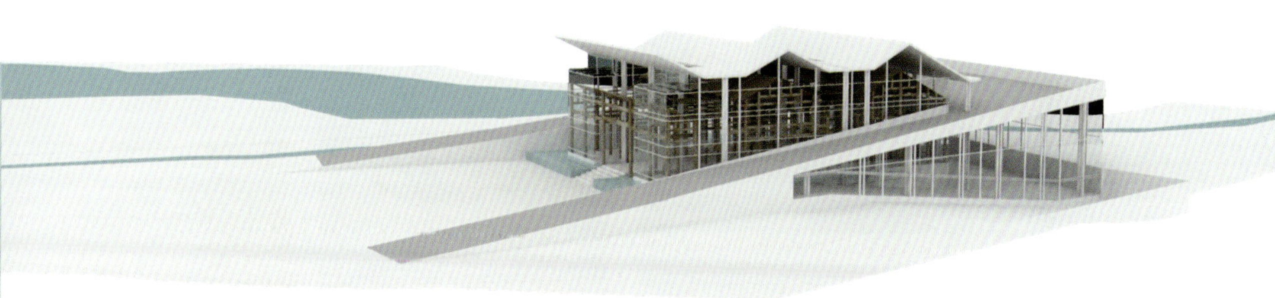

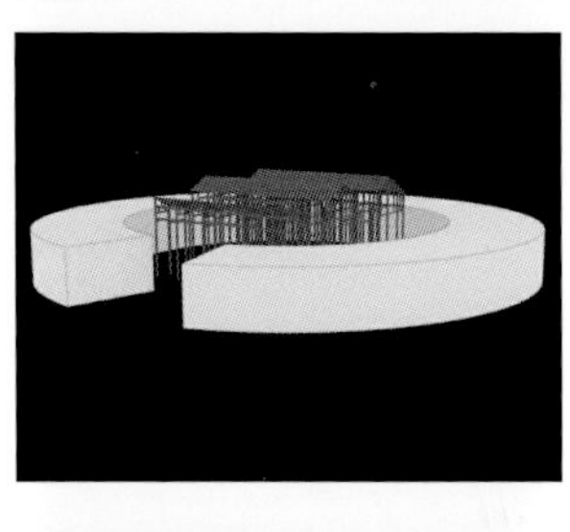

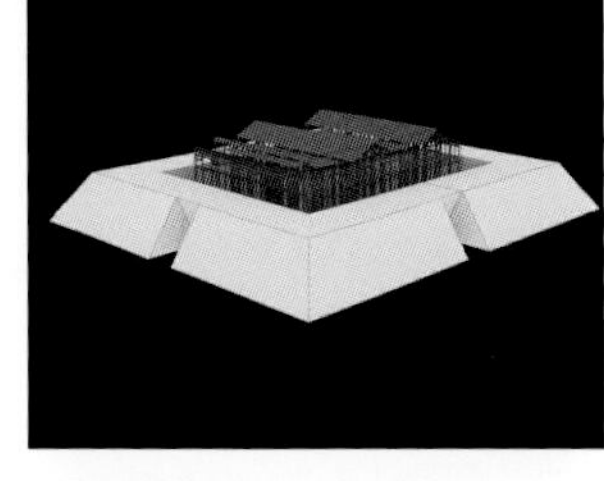

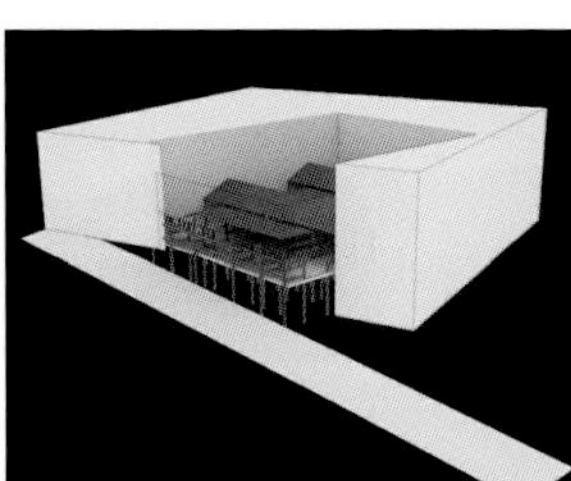

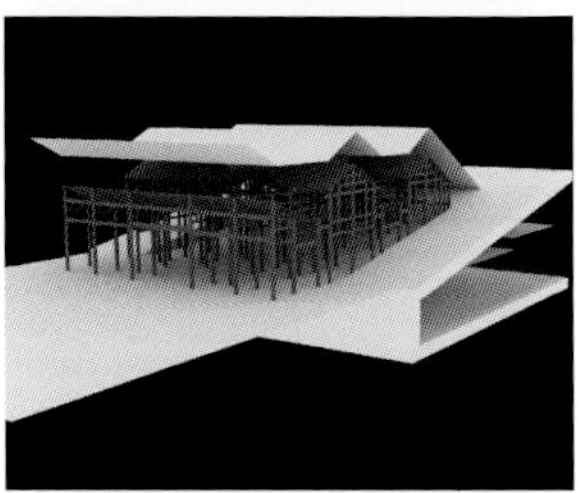

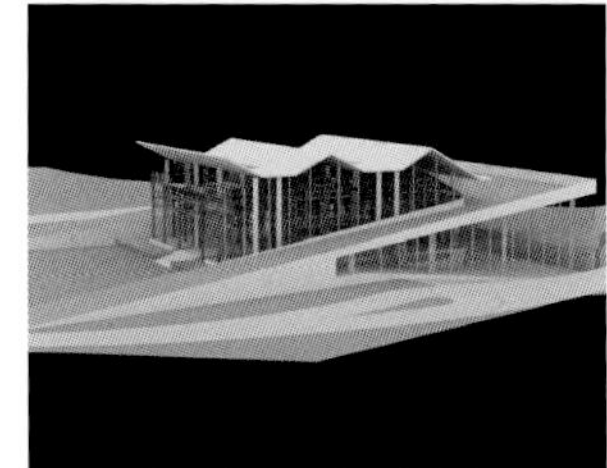

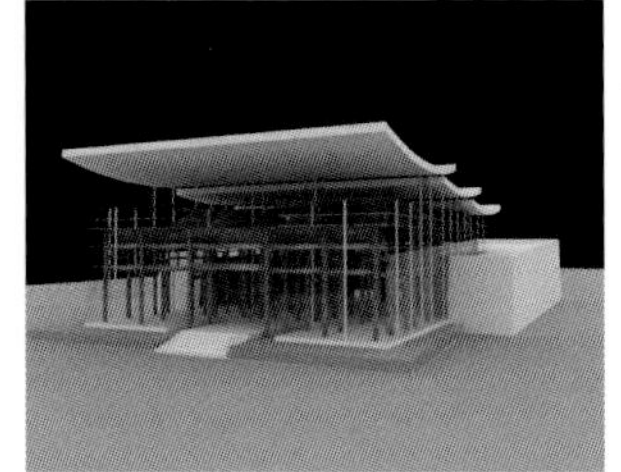

Body of water and body of user cross one another.

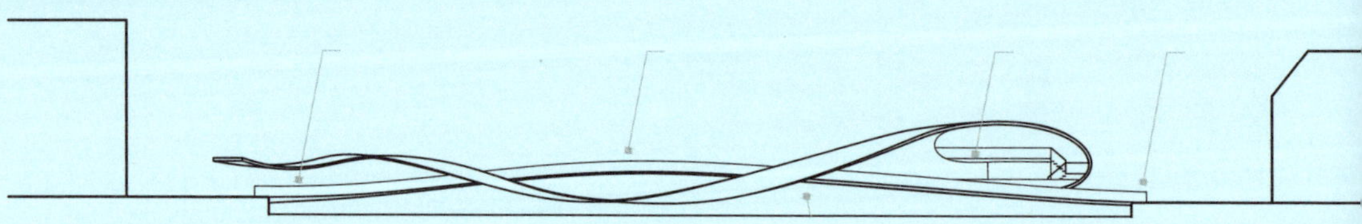

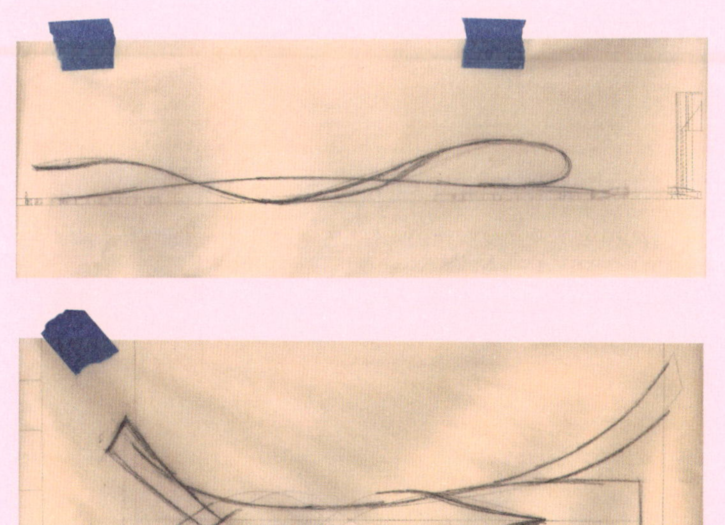

What if crossing a bridge is its least important function?

This pedestrian bridge in Amsterdam is designed to enhance the landscape and be used as a functional sculpture to complement the city. The new pedestrian bridge is located in front of the Hermitage Amsterdam Museum on the east bank of the Amstel River. The bridge's piers are located at each end because of the length of the bridge. The 300-foot-long footbridge will serve the existing community and visitors and form a gateway to the museum while creating a space for gathering or interaction. The latter case would require the bridge structure to be designed to support a working load of thousands of people on the bridge at one time. There are different paths for crossing the bridge with special moments for the user to discover his or her surroundings. The suspension design has supporting members forming cross bracings above and below the bridge to make a truss through which the pathways weave into each other, creating a dynamic voyeuristic space of interaction by which the body of water and the bodies of the users cross one another.

Pedestrian Bridge

Location:

Amsterdam, The Netherlands

Year:

2011 (not built)

Program:

Pedestrian Bridge

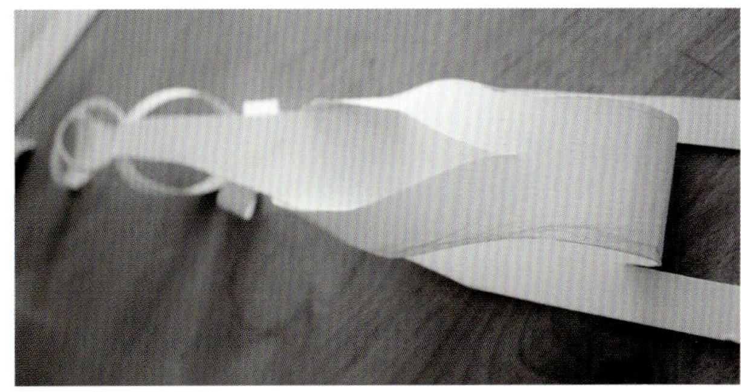

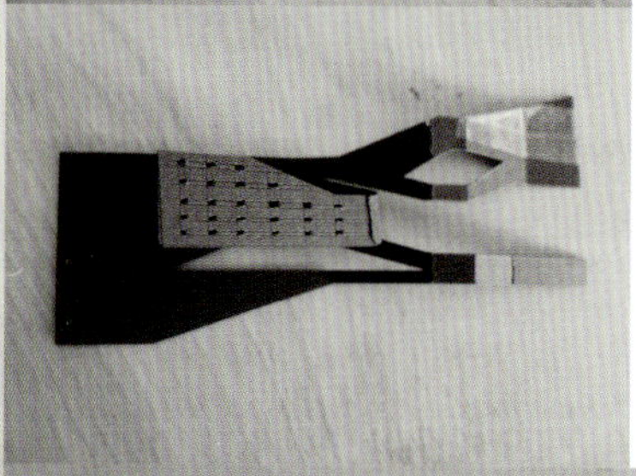

"How does one building affect the meaning of another when their expressions are combined and interact?"

Paul Spencer Byard,
The Architecture of Addition

Glenroy House

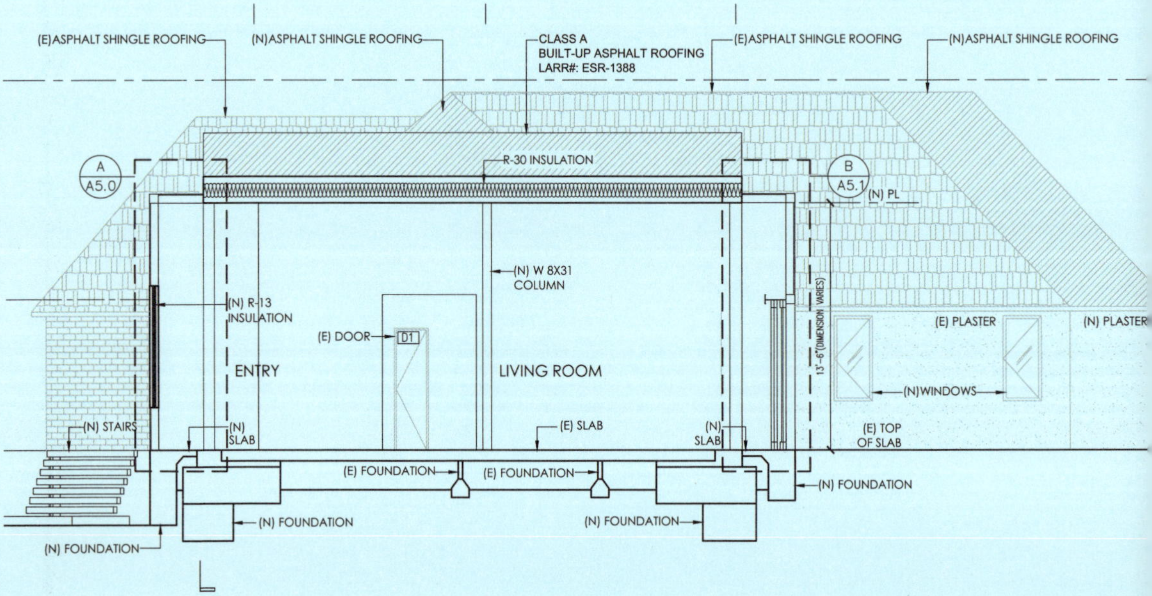

(E)ASPHALT SHINGLE ROOFING
(N)ASPHALT SHINGLE ROOFING
CLASS A
BUILT-UP ASPHALT ROOFING
LARR#: ESR-1388
(E)ASPHALT SHINGLE ROOFING
(N)ASPHALT SHINGLE ROOFING
A
A5.0
R-30 INSULATION
B
A5.1
(N) PL
(N) W 8X31
COLUMN
(N) R-13
INSULATION
(E) DOOR
D1
ENTRY
LIVING ROOM
13'-6" (DIMENSION VARIES)
(E) PLASTER
(N) PLASTER
(N)WINDOWS
(N) STAIRS
(N)
SLAB
(E) SLAB
(N)
SLAB
(E) TOP
OF SLAB
(E) FOUNDATION
(E) FOUNDATION
(N) FOUNDATION
(N) FOUNDATION
(N) FOUNDATION
(N) FOUNDATION

Glenroy House

Location:
Bel Air, California, USA

Year:
2012 (built)

Program:
Single family House

North of Sunset Boulevard and not far from the 405 freeway in Los Angeles there is an area called Bel Air where a house, like many others near it, is backed into the hills in a seemingly quite neighborhood.

We were asked by the client to transform their 1940s bungalow into a contemporary house and keep as much of the existing building as possible. We needed to examine the existing house and evaluate its architectural value before we could propose a design strategy. My overall impression, after numerous meetings with the clients and site visits, was that every space seemed to be small and limiting in terms of what could be done and how the house and the site lacked breathing space at every turn.

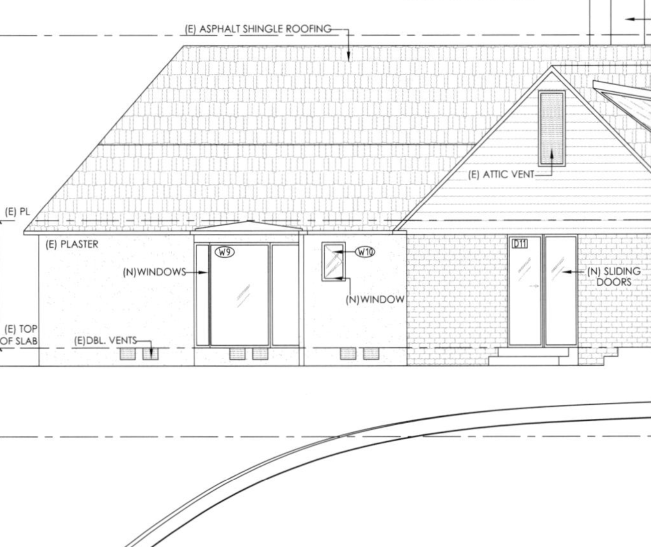

The hillside rising on the west side of the house limited its exposure to sunlight while the large row of trees on the east were protecting it from the street traffic disturbances of cars that were rushing to access the freeway. The bungalow appeared to be built about the same time, and by the same builder, as others like it on the street, since the floor plan and architectural features were very similar. The hillside restriction and lack of meaningful architectural qualities

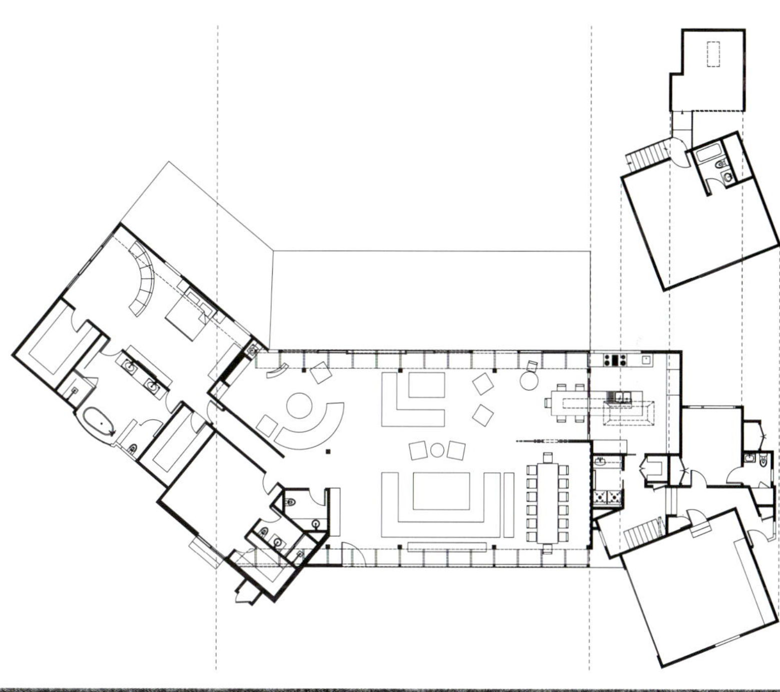

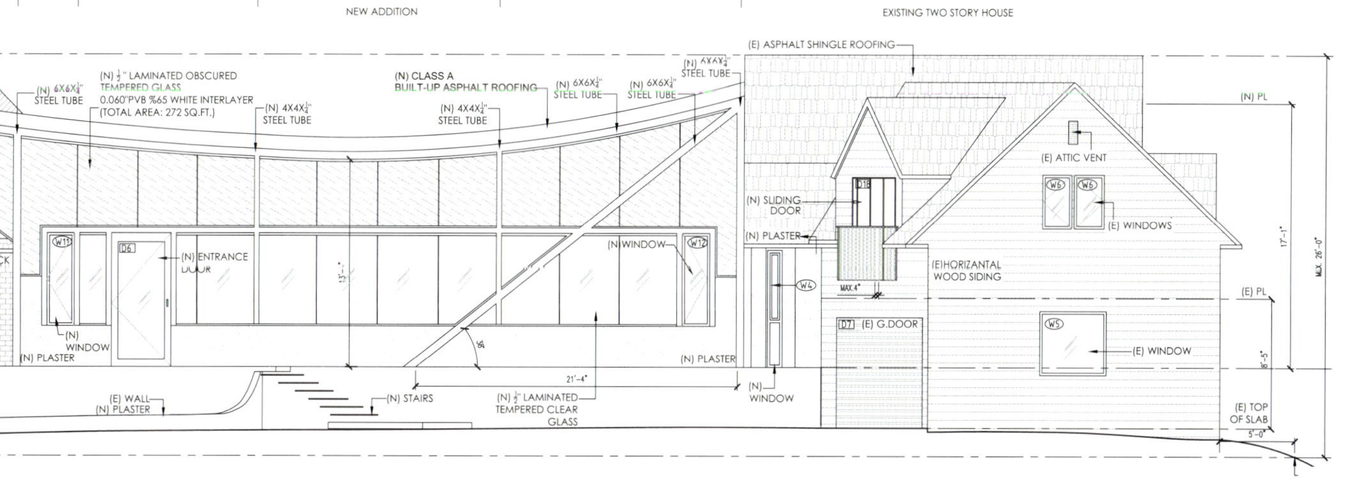

NEW ADDITION
EXISTING TWO STORY HOUSE
(E) ASPHALT SHINGLE ROOFING
(N) 6X6X¼" STEEL TUBE
(N) ½" LAMINATED OBSCURED
TEMPERED GLASS
0.060"PVB %65 WHITE INTERLAYER
(TOTAL AREA: 272 SQ.FT.)
(N) CLASS A
BUILT-UP ASPHALT ROOFING
(N) 4X4X¼" STEEL TUBE
(N) 4X4X¼" STEEL TUBE
(N) 6X6X¼" STEEL TUBE
(N) 6X6X¼" STEEL TUBE
(N) PL
(E) ATTIC VENT
(N) SLIDING DOOR
(N) PLASTER
(E) WINDOWS
(N) ENTRANCE DOOR
(N) WINDOW
(E)HORIZANTAL WOOD SIDING
MAX 4"
(E) PL
(E) G.DOOR
(E) WINDOW
(N) WINDOW
(N) PLASTER
(N) PLASTER
(E) WALL
(N) PLASTER
(N) STAIRS
(N) ½" LAMINATED TEMPERED CLEAR GLASS
21'-4"
(N) WINDOW
(E) TOP OF SLAB
5'-0"
17'-1"
MAX. 26'-0"
8'-5"

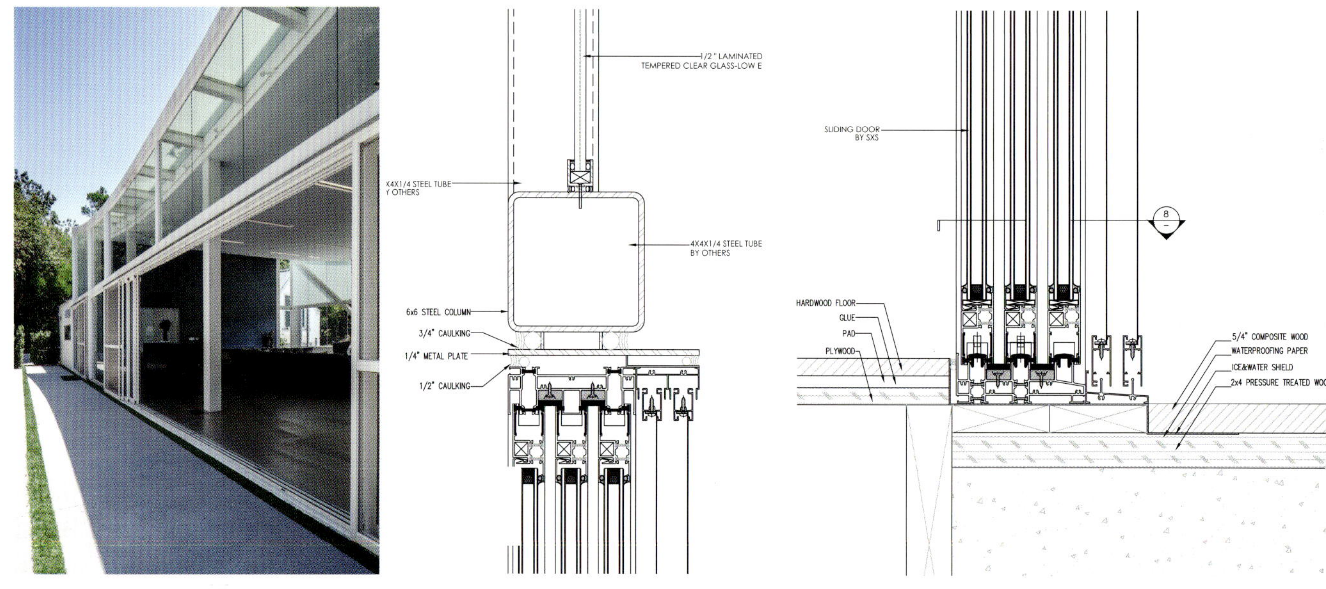

1/2" LAMINATED TEMPERED CLEAR GLASS-LOW E
X4X1/4 STEEL TUBE Y OTHERS
4X4X1/4 STEEL TUBE BY OTHERS
6x6 STEEL COLUMN
3/4" CAULKING
1/4" METAL PLATE
1/2" CAULKING
SLIDING DOOR BY SXS
8
HARDWOOD FLOOR
GLUE
PAD
PLYWOOD
5/4" COMPOSITE WOOD
WATERPROOFING PAPER
ICE&WATER SHIELD
2x4 PRESSURE TREATED WOO

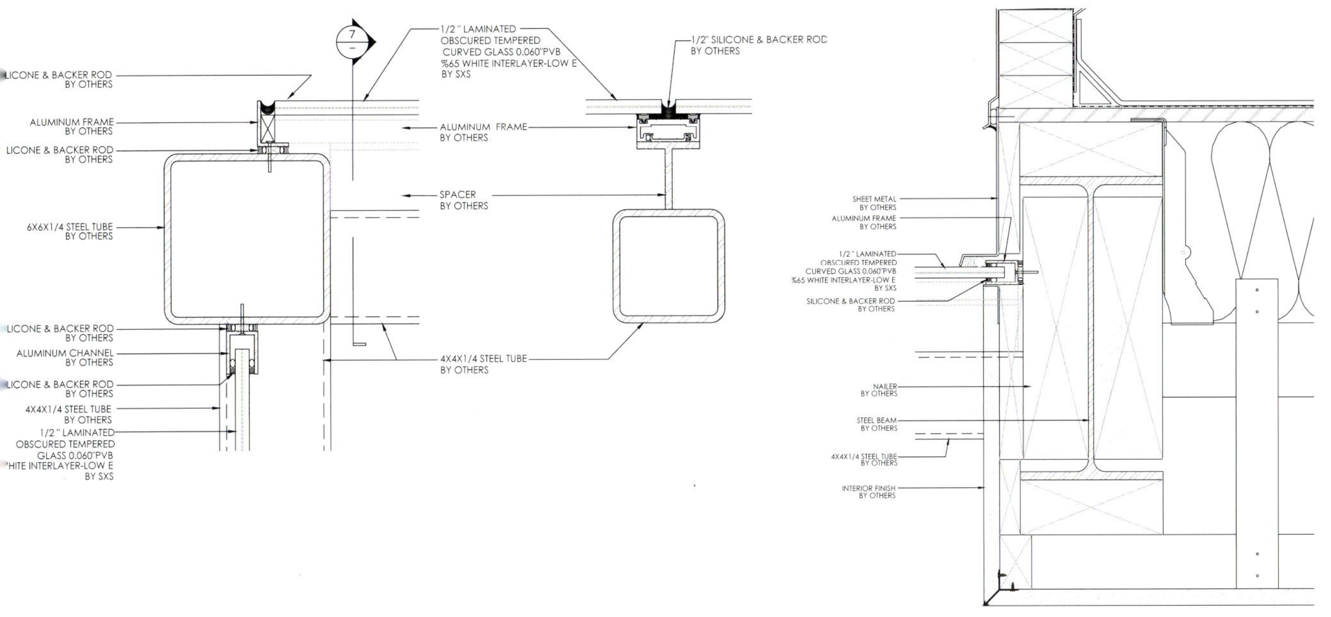
LICONE & BACKER ROD BY OTHERS
ALUMINUM FRAME BY OTHERS
LICONE & BACKER ROD BY OTHERS
6X6X1/4 STEEL TUBE BY OTHERS
LICONE & BACKER ROD BY OTHERS
ALUMINUM CHANNEL BY OTHERS
LICONE & BACKER ROD BY OTHERS
4X4X1/4 STEEL TUBE BY OTHERS
1/2" LAMINATED OBSCURED TEMPERED GLASS 0.060"PVB HITE INTERLAYER-LOW E BY SXS
7
1/2" LAMINATED OBSCURED TEMPERED CURVED GLASS 0.060"PVB %65 WHITE INTERLAYER-LOW E BY SXS
ALUMINUM FRAME BY OTHERS
SPACER BY OTHERS
4X4X1/4 STEEL TUBE BY OTHERS
1/2" SILICONE & BACKER ROD BY OTHERS
SHEET METAL BY OTHERS
ALUMINUM FRAME BY OTHERS
1/2" LAMINATED OBSCURED TEMPERED CURVED GLASS 0.060"PVB %65 WHITE INTERLAYER-LOW E BY SXS
SILICONE & BACKER ROD BY OTHERS
NAILER BY OTHERS
STEEL BEAM BY OTHERS
4X4X1/4 STEEL TUBE BY OTHERS
INTERIOR FINISH BY OTHERS

of the existing house led me to believe that the client's needs for expansion or transformation of the house could not be met unless we did something drastic, but with sensitivity.

After evaluating our options, we proposed to remove the central part of the house that included the living, dining, and family areas and in its place erect a new steel and glass structure that could transform the house and accommodate the owners' needs. The proposed design looked like a "tent" that draped between the two remaining parts of the house. The new element improved the relationship of the house to the site and increased the size of the living area by 40% and its volume by 100%: the central space ranges from 14 to 18 feet. The steel structure covered with insulated glass panels and sliding doors opened the house completely to the front and back yard creating a comfortable and functional inside-outside relationship.

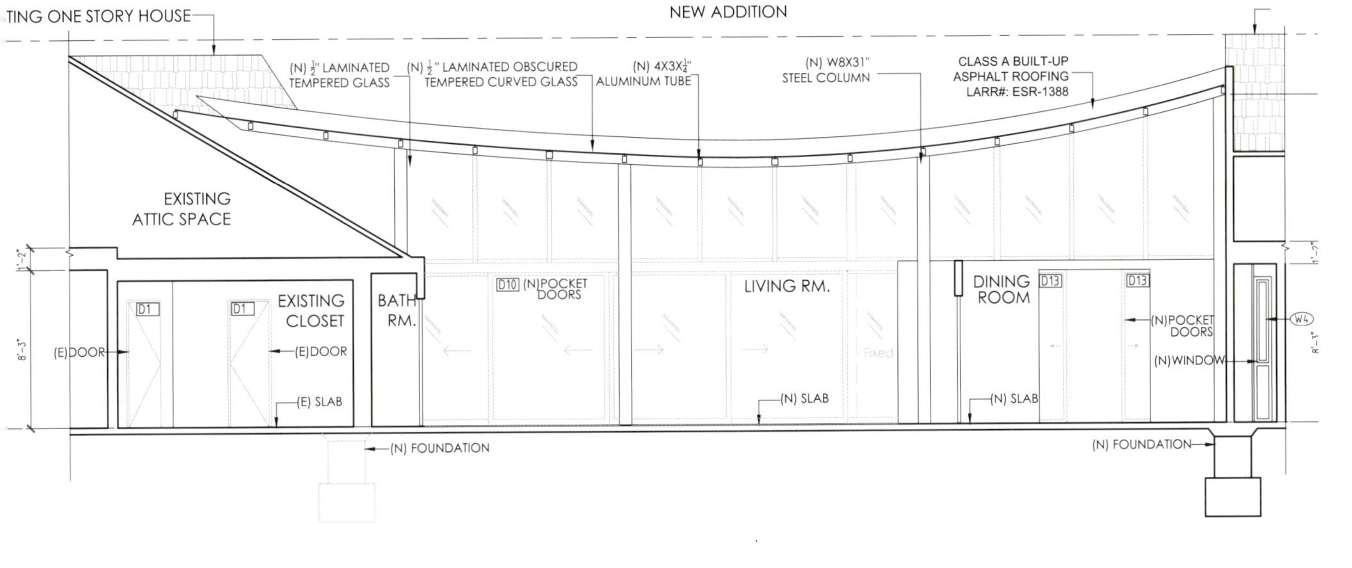
TING ONE STORY HOUSE
NEW ADDITION
(N) $\frac{1}{2}$" LAMINATED TEMPERED GLASS
(N) $\frac{1}{2}$" LAMINATED OBSCURED TEMPERED CURVED GLASS
(N) 4X3X$\frac{1}{4}$" ALUMINUM TUBE
(N) W8X31" STEEL COLUMN
CLASS A BUILT-UP ASPHALT ROOFING LARR#: ESR-1388
EXISTING ATTIC SPACE
EXISTING CLOSET
BATH RM.
LIVING RM.
DINING ROOM
D1
D1
D10
(N)POCKET DOORS
D13
D13
(N)POCKET DOORS
W4
(E)DOOR
(E)DOOR
(E) SLAB
(N) SLAB
(N) SLAB
(N)WINDOW
(N) FOUNDATION
(N) FOUNDATION
1'-2"
8'-3"
1'-2"
8'-1"
Fixed

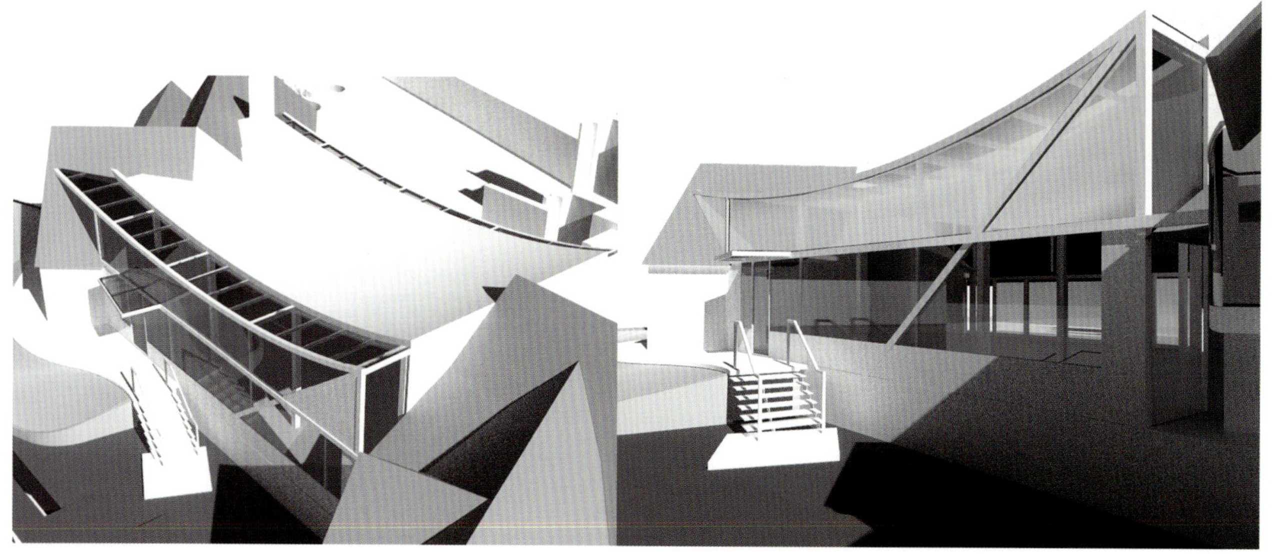

It's light and airy with its organic language as if it is made by nature itself; it feels as part of the landscape of the site.

Pedestrian Bridge

Literally, a bridge takes us from one point to the next. It is constructed to span physical obstacles like rivers, valleys, or roads. In the contemporary urban context it allows us to cross highways and railroad tracks and gives us the opportunity to connect our homes to public spaces, parks, and places of social gathering. The idea of a bridge is something else; it has rich cultural and historical implications in our lives. We all have relationships with bridges we know or use. Some may be purely utilitarian while others provoke certain emotions in our subconscious about a special experience we had, or views we got the chance to see while crossing them.

In our bridge design for CRLand Residential and Commercial Center we proposed the concept of a sculptural bridge that could become a point of reference for residents and visitors to the Center. The concept was developed with programs that could attract the residents to use the bridge not only for its function as a connector but also as a place to gather, to meet a friend for a coffee, for children to play, a place to see an exhibition, or just simply hang out during the day or at night.

Our research and studies resulted in two potential design schemes, each with three bridges. All are used to connect the public spaces surrounding the residential area to the commercial area.

Scheme A was inspired by organic shapes and the movements of body in space. This scheme contrasts with the architecture of the buildings around it and is more in harmony with nature. The forms and shapes of the bridge suggest a sense of flying across the space from one point to the next. The imagery evokes flowing water and plants moving in the wind. This flow creates spaces within the composition for programs nested within. It's light and airy and feels like part of the landscape. Bridges 1 and 2 in this scheme fuse together with the point of their connection marked by a café or a gathering place.

Pedestrian Bridge

Location:
Qingdao, P.R. China

Year:
2011 (not built)

Program:
Pedestrian Bridge

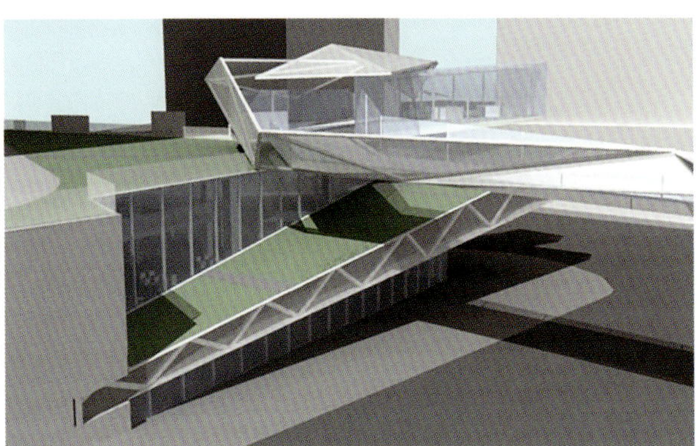

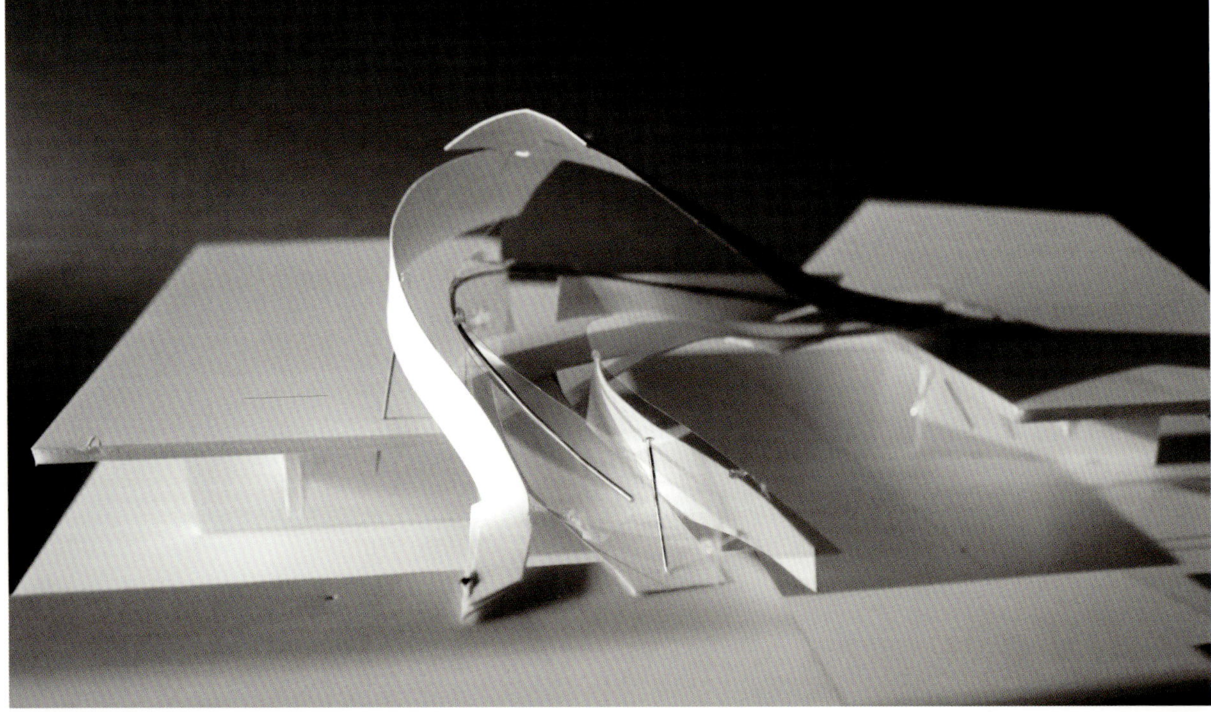

Bridge 3 uses the same organic language but flows out of the building like a waterfall. In this scheme the movement of the bridges and the surfaces that construct its composition transform the intersections and the views, which vary according to the pedestrian's location.

Scheme B is the opposite of Scheme A. It harmonizes with the architecture of the surrounding buildings. The concept was inspired by the way the first bridges were made by nature itself—as simple as a log fallen across a stream or stones in a river. It is a geometrical composition of similar elements such that their juxtaposition creates the bridge and the space within. It is simple but complex in its composition. This bridge is composed of three different interconnected bridges that lead to a variety of points while creating an experience of unconventional space. People can cross using different routes and on their way be exposed to the fantastic spatial experience and programs that can make them stop and take notice of their environment, see an exhibition, light show, video display, meet friends, sit and play, or get a coffee and relax.

Both schemes propose not only a physical connection between two spaces but a living element to enrich the life of the residents and to bring them together in an environment where they can connect.

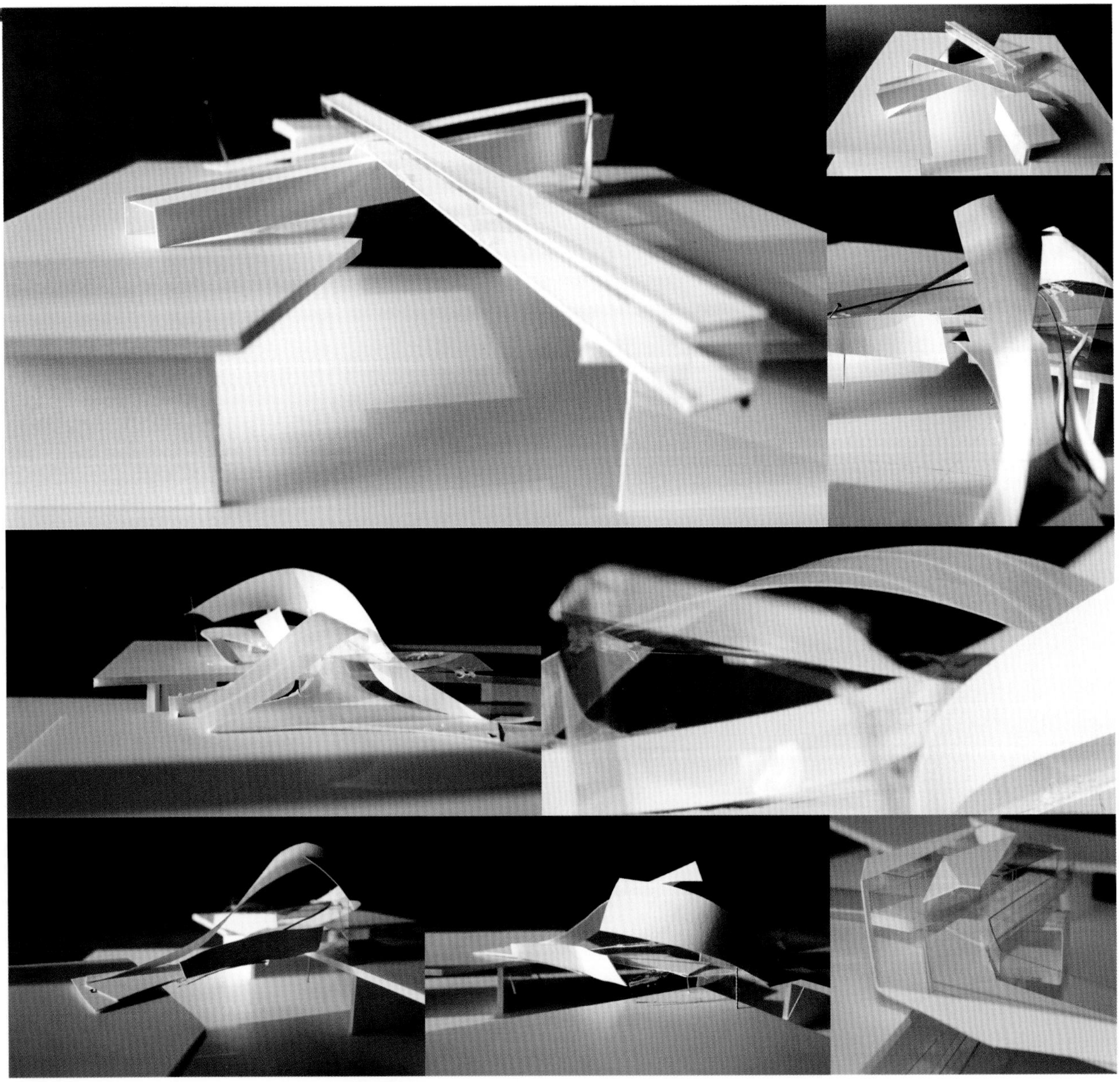

They come afar to pay tribute to the symbol of com-passionate inspiration.

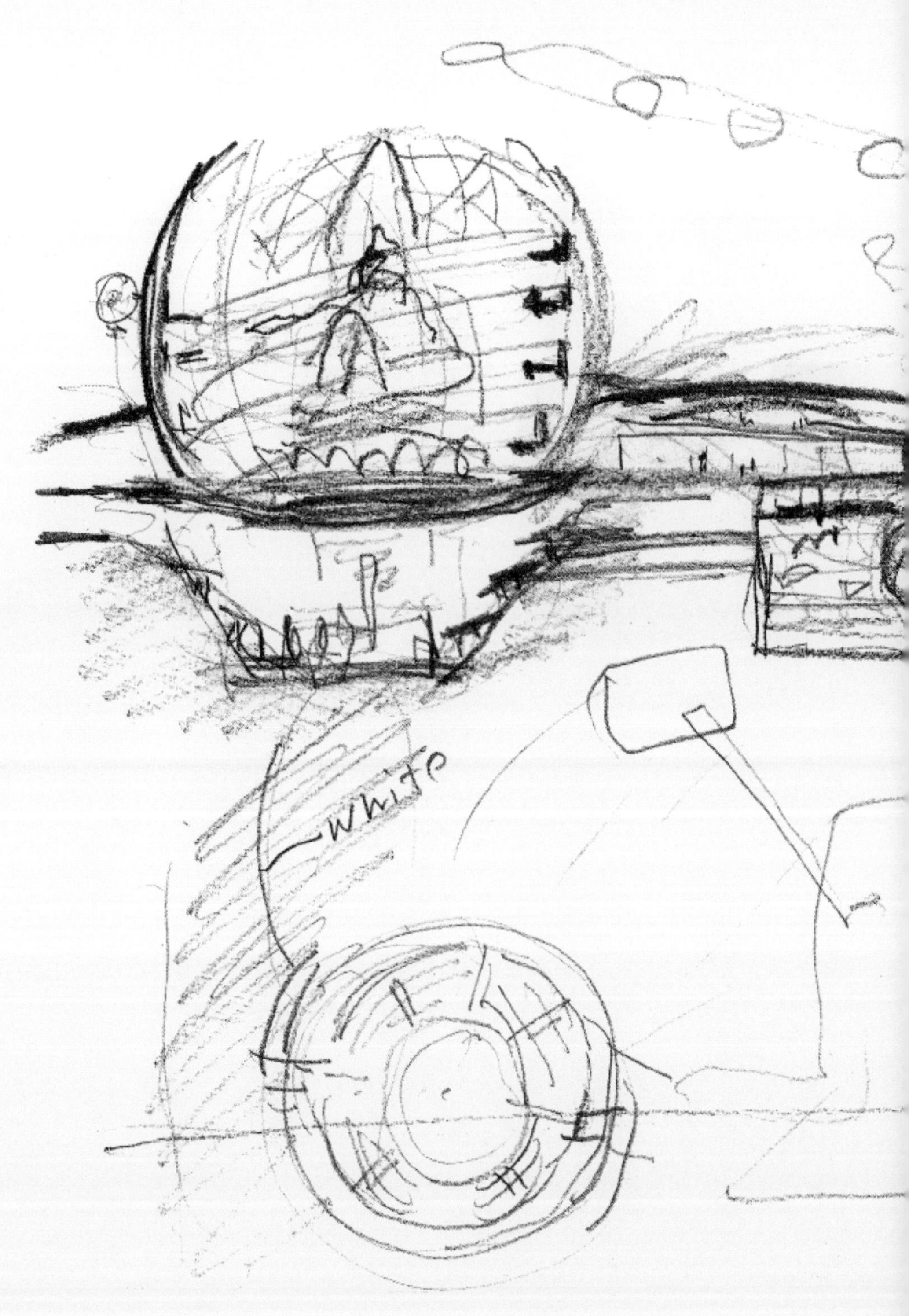
white

Guanyin Center

Location:
Shanghai, P.R. China

Year:
2013 (not built)

Program:
Cultural, Entertainment, and Commercial Center

Guanyin's place in the heart of the lotus is what the visitors will remember for the rest of their lives. They come from afar to pay tribute to this symbol of compassionate inspiration.

The site for Guanyin Center is a unique opportunity to create a world-class spiritual mixed-use entertainment project. Our concept divides the center into five thematic zones with each featuring distinct characteristics and offering a unique experience to all ages.

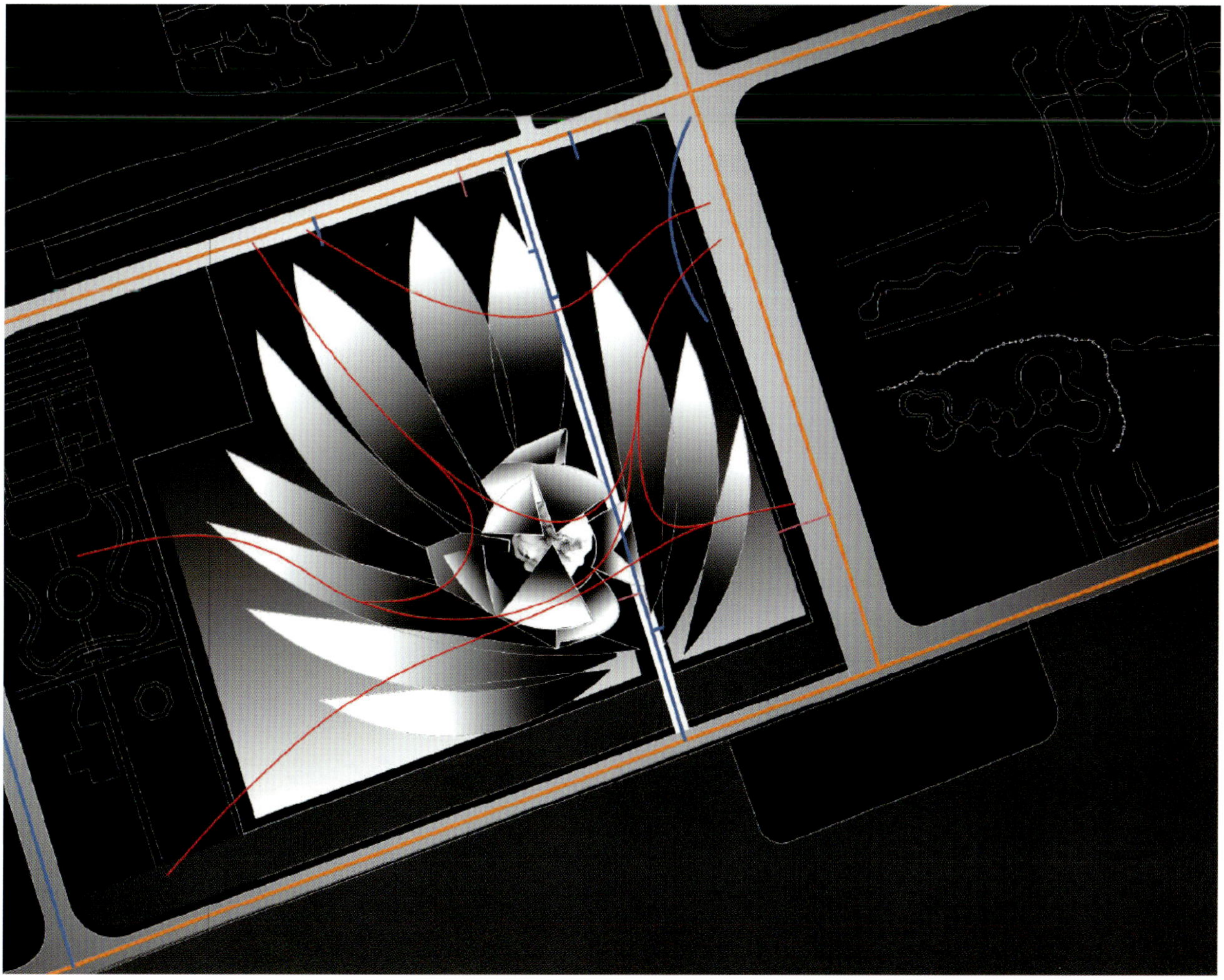

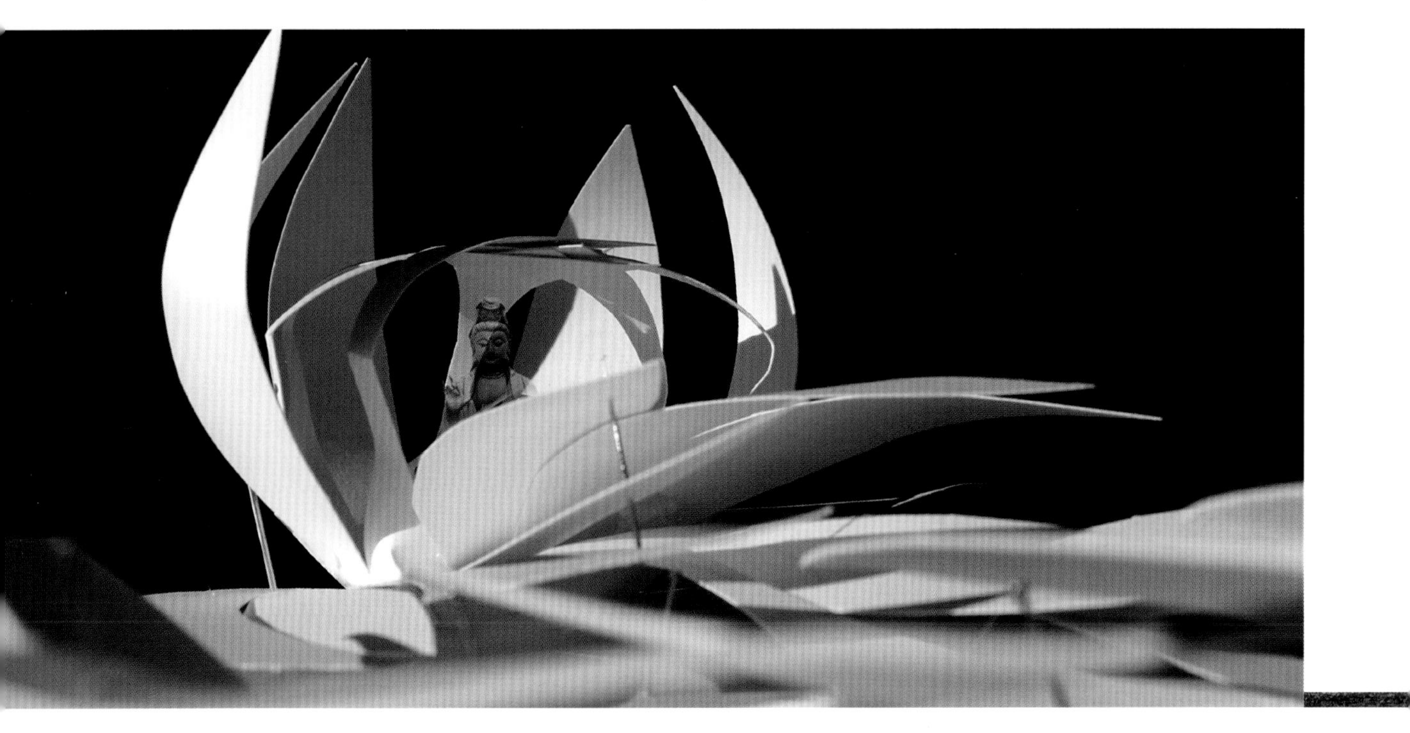

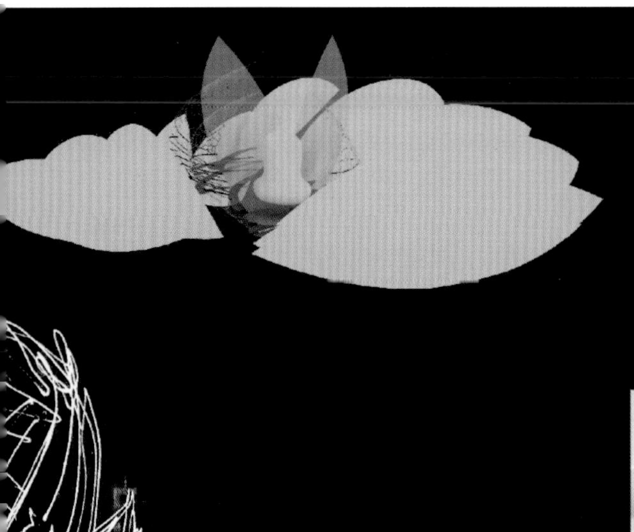

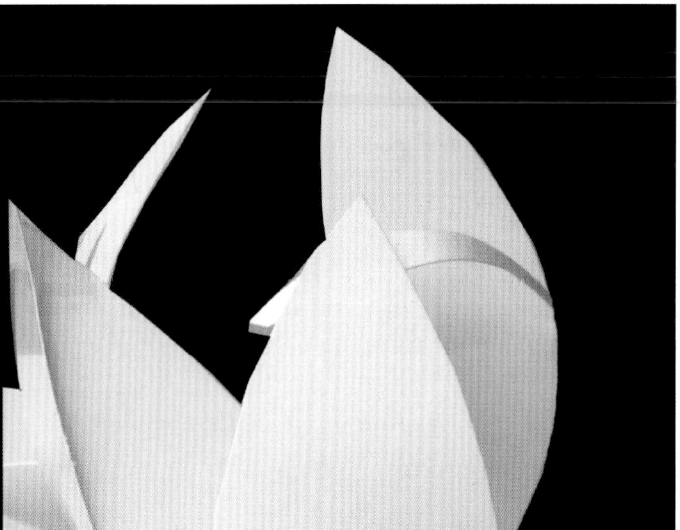

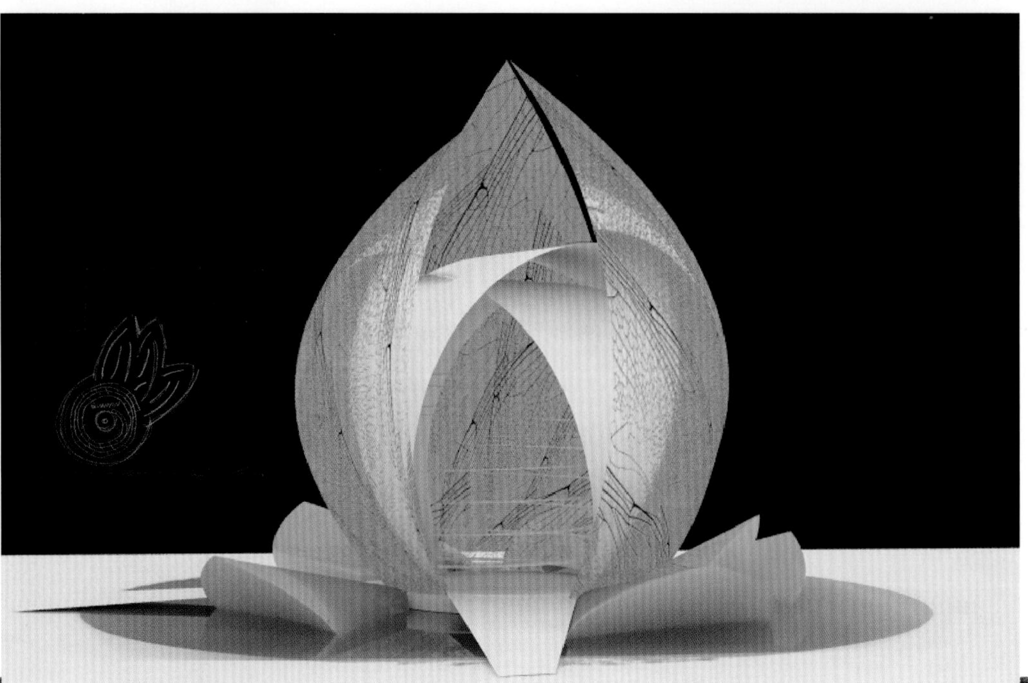

The theory of five elements based on Chinese philosophy and medicine explains how Qi (the vital substances) cycle through various stages of transformation. As Yin and Yang continuously adjust to one another and transform into one another in a never-ending dance of harmonization, they tend to do so in a predictable pattern.

Zone 1 – Fire: Spiritual and Educational
Zone 2 – Wood: Discovery Park
Zone 3 – Water: Fun Park
Zone 4 – Earth: Tourism World
Zone 5 – Metal: Retail and Entertainment

The Guanyin Center would be a pedestrian-oriented environment with each zone flowing naturally into the next. All zones would have a dedicated entertainment street with a diverse offering of restaurants and rest spaces. Guests leave their cars in the parking structure outside of the center where the experience begins. Service vehicles access the site with minimal visual impact from separate entrances.

3
2
4
1
1
5

We are exploring how to improve the visibility of buildings and how to interact with the rich environment adjacent to the Pacific Ocean.

The wetlands or, as it was referred to, mud flats are where the five acres of land known as "Marina del Rey" reside. It was the vision of a 19th-century real estate speculator that had endured bankruptcy, two world wars, and mother nature in order to become an unincorporated, relatively quiet residential, and commercial area of Los Angeles County. Marina del Rey was developed based on the Land Use Plan to address future land use and needed improvement of existing facilities. The land lease agreements between the county of Los Angeles and private lessees began in 1963, which would last 60 years. As the renew date was approaching, the county seized the opportunity to ask for a renovation as a condition for its renewal and that's how we got involved in the project.

The three-story 149-unit apartment building over an open-air parking garage needed to be renovated in three phases. We were getting familiar with the site, zoning and building codes, and design review board requirements while exploring how to increase the building's visibility and interaction with its rich surroundings and the Pacific Ocean.

I met Isaac Hakim, the owner's nephew and representative, through a friend/client. We connected at our first meeting and talked more about our personal lives, our kids, and then work, which I believe we both appreciated. We both were in a sensitive phase in our lives, dealing with the loss of our marriages in search of ourselves. Going through the divorce, my family life was difficult. I was at my lowest point, and having trouble communicating with my wife and my teenage kids. Staying productive and creative was challenging, but focusing on an interesting project like this was therapeutic and alleviated financial stress. I kept in touch and called Isaac every few weeks to ask what was going on. After a few months passed I thought they had decided to work with someone else.

The project's location and scale intrigued me. I'd catch myself thinking what I would do if I had the opportunity to work on it. I was conflicted, questioning if I could make something meaningful considering the budget, scale, updated building codes, fire codes, and accessibility codes. I'd need the approval from the Design Control Board (DCB), Coastal Commission, possibly the Environmental Impact Report (EIR), and the list continues. After 30 years of experience, it was impossible to ignore the invisible (plumbing, electrical, mechanical, water proofing, roofing, etc.) cost of remodeling a 50-year-old building sitting on reclaimed wetland. Every single additional dollar per square foot multiplied by the area of the building, which meant hundreds of thousands of dollars. I reached out to my friend Eric Rosen to discuss the project with the idea of a collaboration.

I met Eric in the early nineties when he came to LA to work with me during my transitional period. It only lasted a short time since he left to start his own firm, but we've remained good friends.

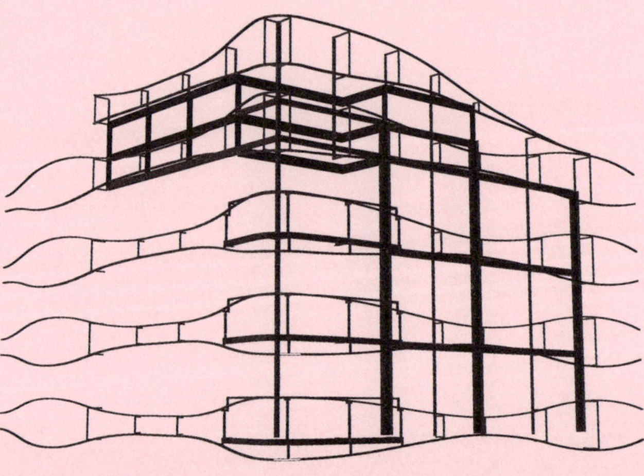

Tahiti Marina Apartments

Location:

Marina Del Ray, California, USA

Year:

2011 – 2014 (built)

Program:

Apartment Building

Isaac finally called one day to have a meeting with Eric and I to discuss the scope of the project, fees, and time frames. After our meeting he asked us to join him to go to a Beaches and Harbor meeting of the DCB. As we arrived I recognized a few old friends serving as board members. Peter Phinney, architect, and Susan Lewin, public relations, were surprised to see me there since I wasn't on the agenda. Both showed positive reactions to the prospects of me doing a project in Marina, which I felt was advantageous for Isaac to witness.

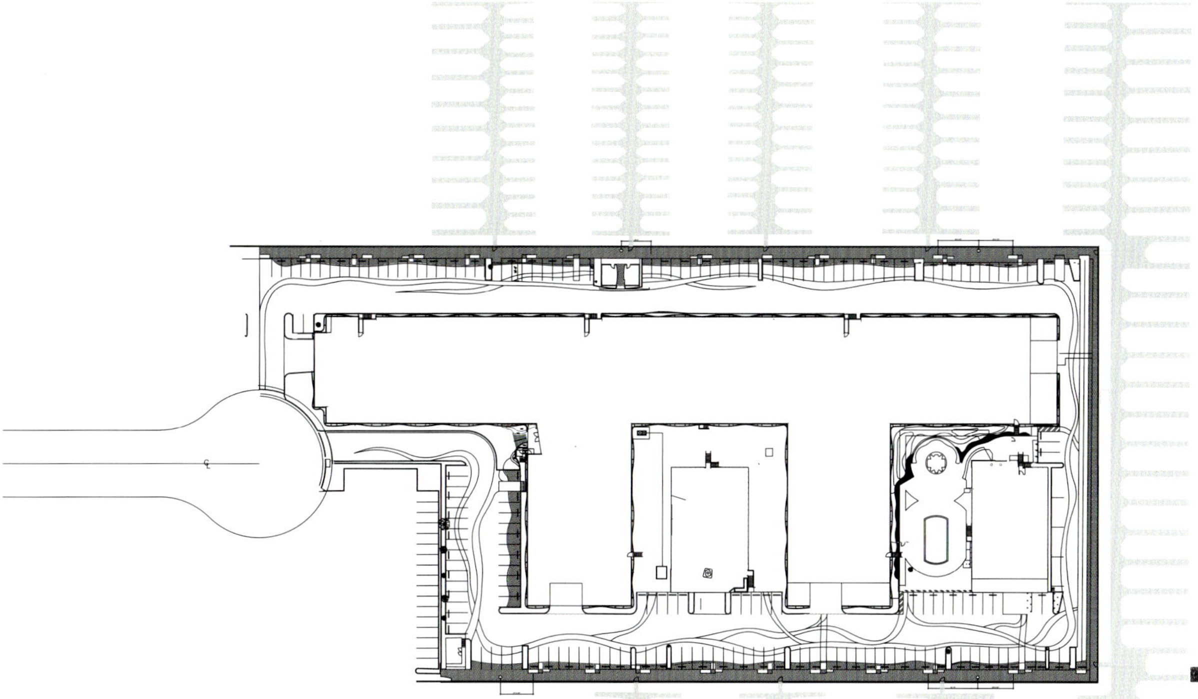

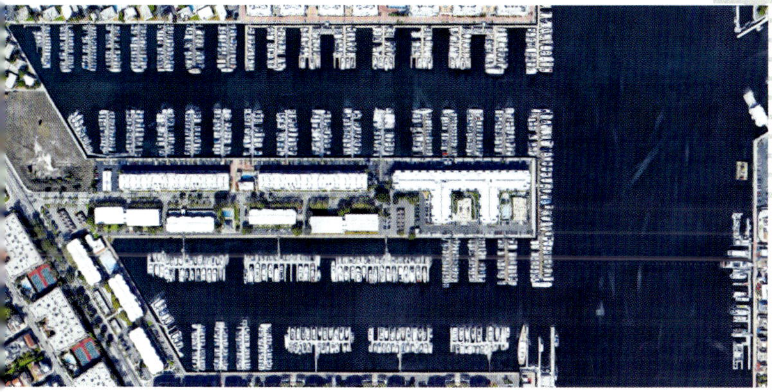

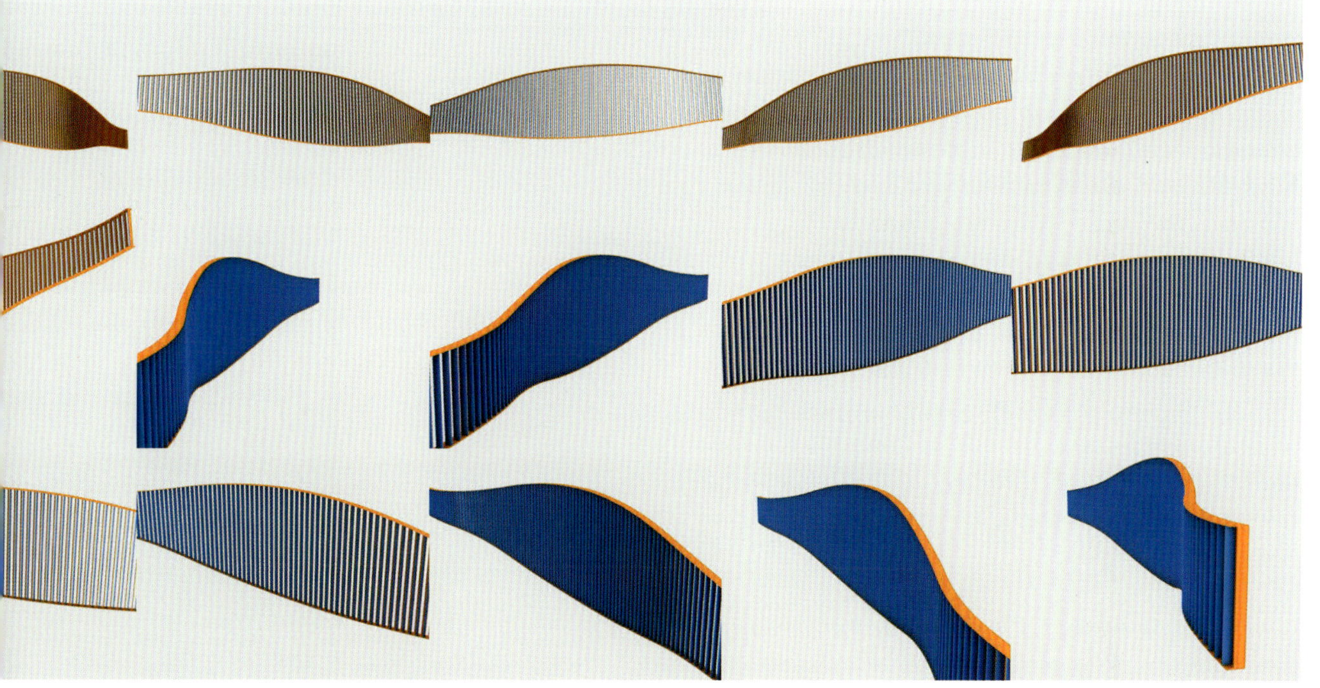

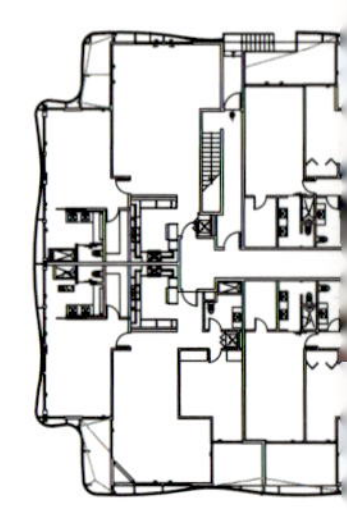

At the break Isaac asked to speak to me privately and we left the meeting room. My intuition was right. He had been working with another team that was present at the meeting. Our invitation to the Beaches and Harbor meeting was an attempt to introduce us to this team and collaborate on the project. Mr. Hakim planned for us to meet that night, but I was apprehensive, needing time to think about it.

I was very disappointed, but I tried to mask it for the rest of the evening. I could not imagine working with someone else, let alone a team, that I didn't know or select. I'd also put myself in their shoes, imagining that they wouldn't want someone else (me) stepping on their toes. I explained my predicament to Isaac a few days later and told him that it is not in the project's interests to have two designers involved. He was on the contrary, convinced that this was the best solution and told me the other team, Grace Partnership, supported my involvement and wanted me to take lead on design. At this point there was only one thing we had to do—meet.

The first meeting with Leo Cho, Stephen Kim, and the rest of GP team was great. I got a good feeling with them especially with Leo, as if we knew each other from another life. But unfortunately one of Mr. Hakim's consultants, for unknown reasons (to me), detested my involvement and her behavior toward me made everyone, including Isaac, very uncomfortable while testing my patience, integrity, and my desire to move forward.

These conferences triggered many doubtful thoughts. I would question myself, my career, and whether or not this kind of

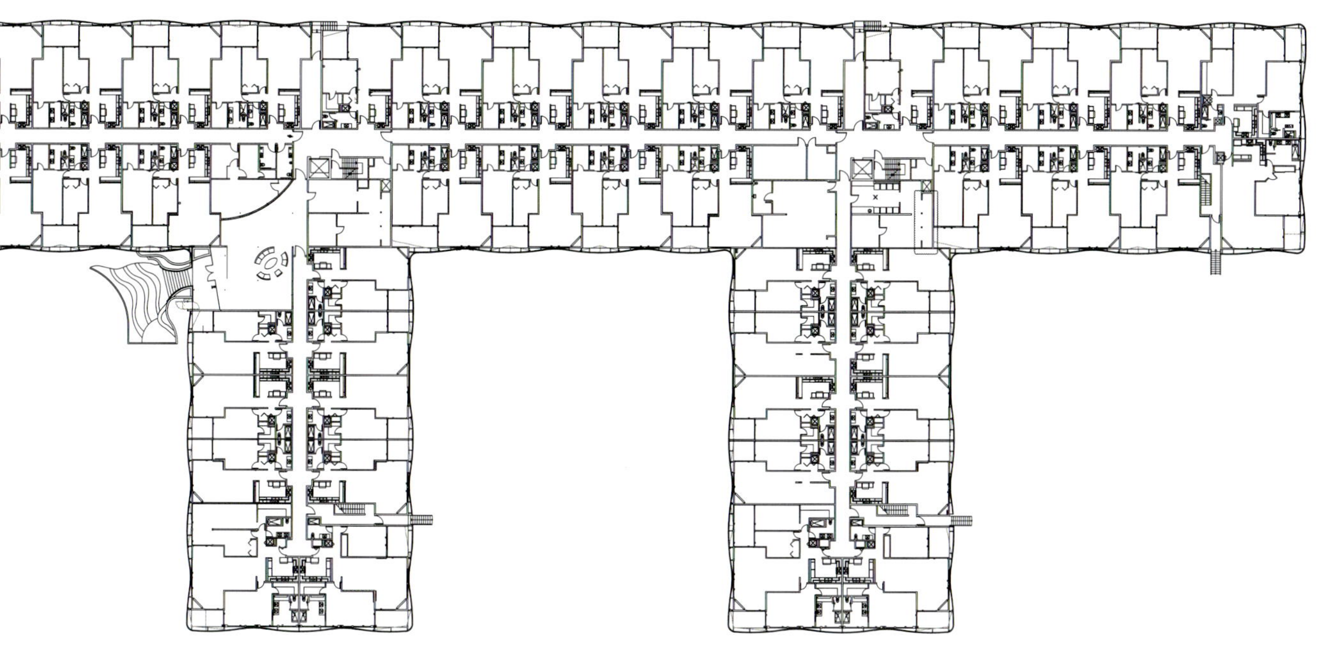

behavior should be tolerated or is even professional. The truth is, if you love the vision you have to love it in its entirety. You can't pick and choose between the exciting, creative times and the boring, disappointing moments. Also, it is fair to mention that I needed the work.

Both in practice and teaching I have always noticed a disconnection in the way architecture is perceived in the society at large. In the United States, architecture (not building) or the practice of architecture doesn't appear to be integrated in the daily life of people, but rather seen as more of a luxury or element of privilege for a small social group. Therefore, to most, it is unappreciated and irrelevant when it should be ingrained in their way of life. The awareness of architecture's importance in everyday life is felt, for example, in Italy and France. During my first year at the University of Florence, approximately ten thousand students registered at its school of architecture in 1974, which is the same amount of degrees awarded to all US architecture students in 2016. The majority of my graduating class were interested in the culture of architecture because they saw it as an integral part of their environment. Their involvement was seen to influence society and their surroundings. Architecture is buildings, cars, shops, cloth, food, etc. Architecture is a part of life like any other and its presence is not announced with pretentious gestures, but ingrained in the way things are.

In the late nineties I ran for the director position at SCI-Arc and it bothered me how socially isolated the school was. With the introduction of new advancements in digital technology and new processes of architectural design and production, it was a critical time for architectural education and practice. This was the beginning of a new era. The Guggenheim Bilbao by Gehry was inaugurated in 1997, which, in my opinion, was and still is the symbol of this beginning. Technology, like CATIA, could facilitate buildings, but for perceiving an architectural space, it isn't

developed to the point of evaluating experience, perception, human interaction, etc. In an interview with B. Diamond Stern, Frank Gehry talks about this balance:

"It would be much better, I think, to go into the field, and build hands on. It's a more positive and optimistic kind of attitude about work. When the artist and sculptors I know work, there's sort of a free play idea. You try things; you experiment; It's kind of naive and childish; It' is like a playpen. Scientists work that way too—for example, genetic scientists that I have been involved with, through a genetic foundation that I work with, seem to work similarly. It's kind of like throwing things out, and then following the ideas, rather than predicting where you're going to go."

"On another front there were people like Boyer and Mitgang alarming us about the disconnect between architecture and society, which has been inherently part of the education and practice of architecture in the US. *In Building Community: A New Future for Architecture Education and Practice*, Boyer and Mitgang write,

"Architectural community's long history of failure to connect itself firmly to the larger concerns confronting families, businesses, schools, communities and society, ...too many Americans will spend their lives as architectural illiterates unless those connections can be more clearly established in schools and in public discourse, architecture will remain omnipresent yet underappreciated and shrouded in mystery. Even on college campuses where most architectural programs are located, the potential of design education to enrich learning and life has been inadequately explored. We discovered that architecture students and faculty are too often disconnected from other disciplines, and distant from the social and cultural mainstream of campus life."

We could identify with both concurrent positions, but we know which school of thought dominated the last two decades. As a result, architecture continues to be disconnected from everyday life and schools become less involved in the communities they claim to be a part of.

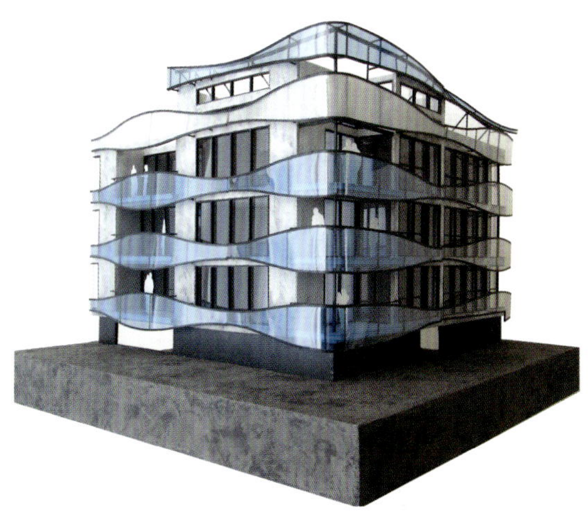

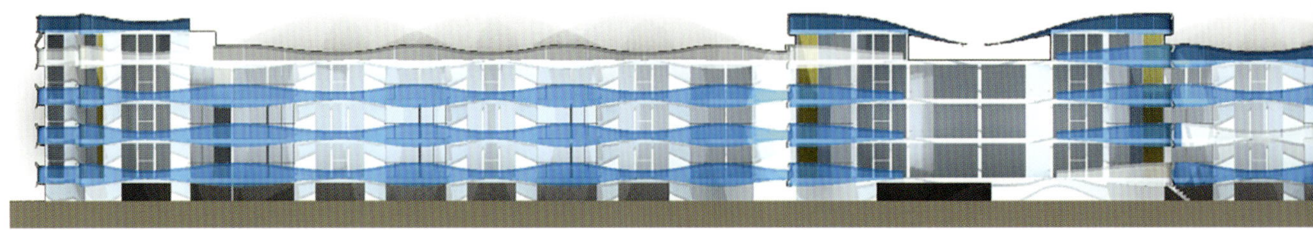

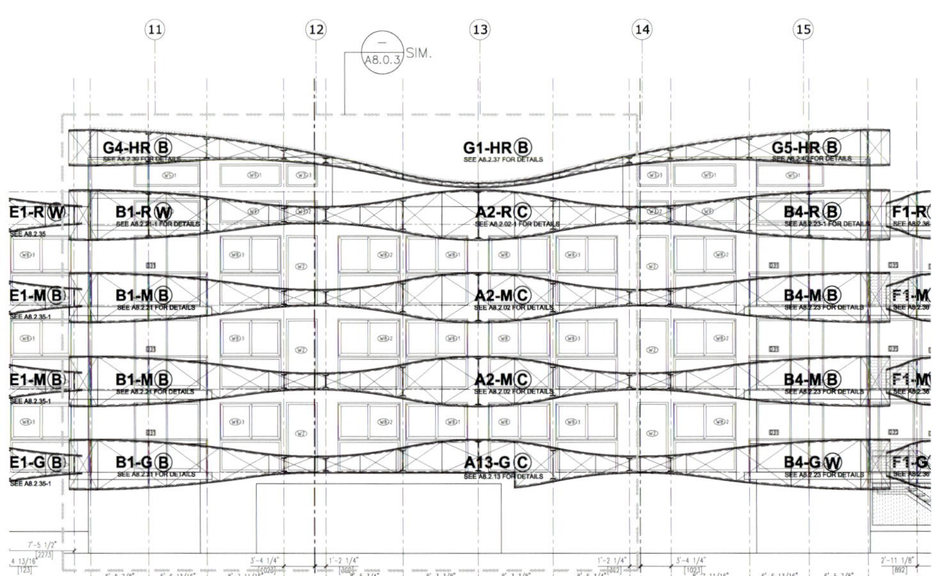
11
12
13
14
15
A8.0.3
SIM.
G4-HR B
G1-HR B
SEE A8.2.37 FOR DETAILS
G5-HR B
E1-R W
B1-R W
A2-R C
B4-R B
E1-M B
B1-M B
A2-M C
B4-M B
E1-M B
B1-M B
A2-M C
B4-M B
E1-G B
B1-G B
A13-G C
B4-G W

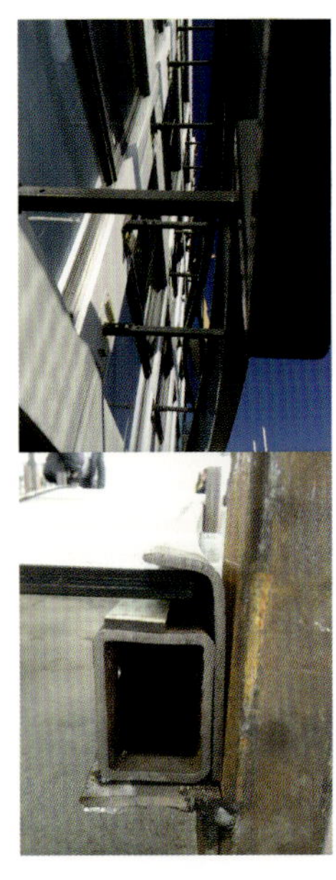

RUBBER GASKETS
1/2" LAMINATED GLASS
1/2" LAMINATED GLASS
RUBBER GASKETS
SIM.

1-1/2"X1-1/2"X3/16" STEEL TUBE
BENT STEEL TUBE
3/8" STEEL PLATE W/ 2-1/2"ϕ TREADED BOLTS IN 5/8"x 1 1/2" SLOTTED HOLE
1/2" LAMINATED GLASS
1/4" BENT PLATE
1-1/2"X1-1/2"X3/16" STEEL TUBE
3/8" STEEL PLATE W/ 2-1/2"ϕ TREADED BOLTS IN 5/8"x 1 1/2" SLOTTED HOLE
1/2" STEEL PLATE
3/8" SHAPED STEEL
1/4" BENT PLATE W/ SCREWS
STEEL TUBE
10"X4"X3/8" PLATE W/ 2-5/8"X1 1/2" SLOTTED HOLES
1/4" STIFF PLATE
SEE 15/A8.3.11 FOR PHASE 1 & 2
2-1/2"ϕ WELDED STUDS (FEILD WELDED)
1 1/2" SLOTTED HOLE

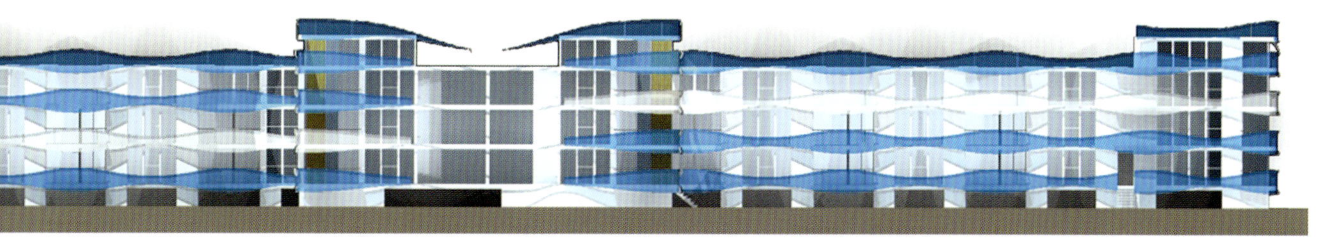

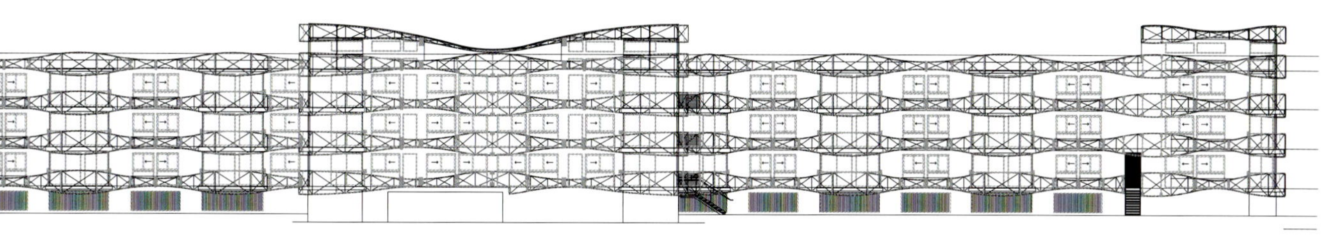

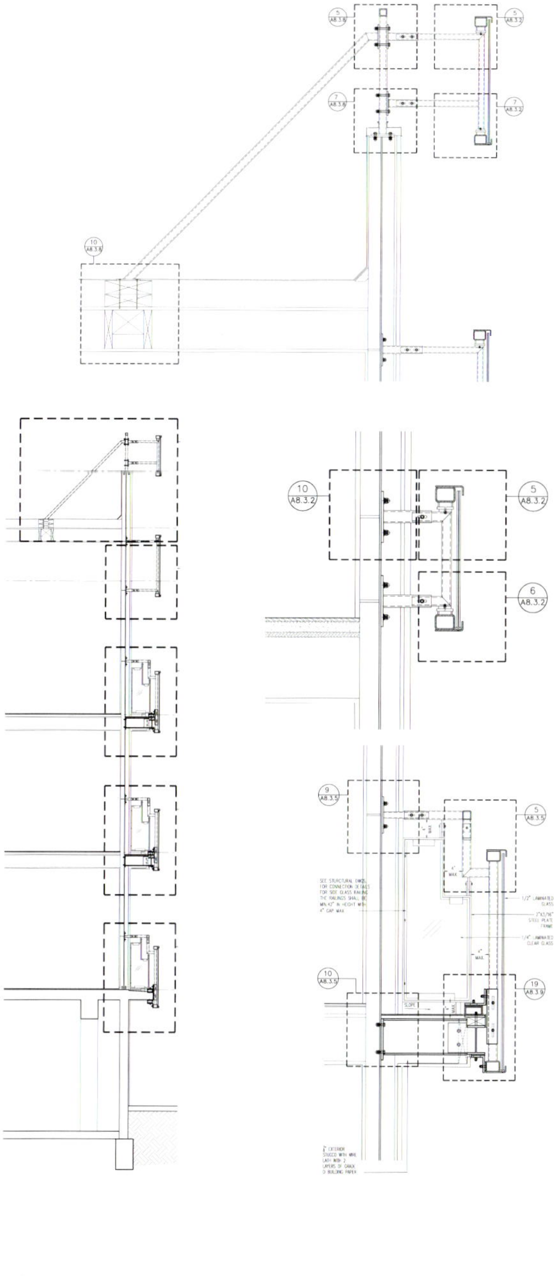

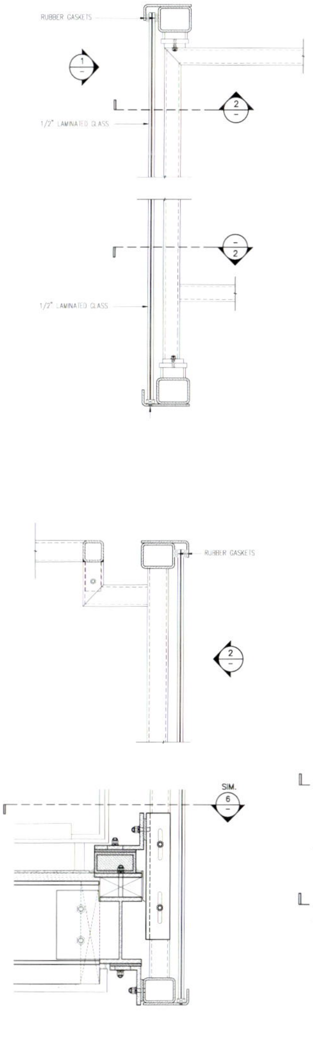

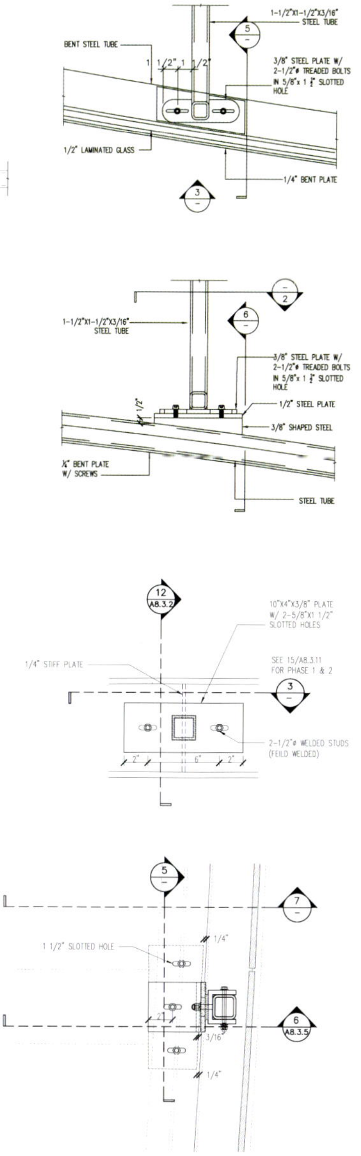

What I see in Gehry's approach to technology and in his use of technology in architectural production differs from many others. Gehry uses CATIA as a tool to facilitate the construction of his vision; it is to simplify the building's complexity for the builders, which as a result lowers the cost, making it easier to build. In a way his use of technology is demystifying the work that, from the outside, seams complex and inaccessible. He is aware that these programs can aid him in his process to develop his concepts and ideas and ultimately build it using the tools as the means, not the end.

In contrast to this approach, Andrea Branzi of Archizoom sees the model or as he calls it, the "plastic model," as the most synthetic tool for communicating the architectural project. In most cases this plastic model becomes the final building.

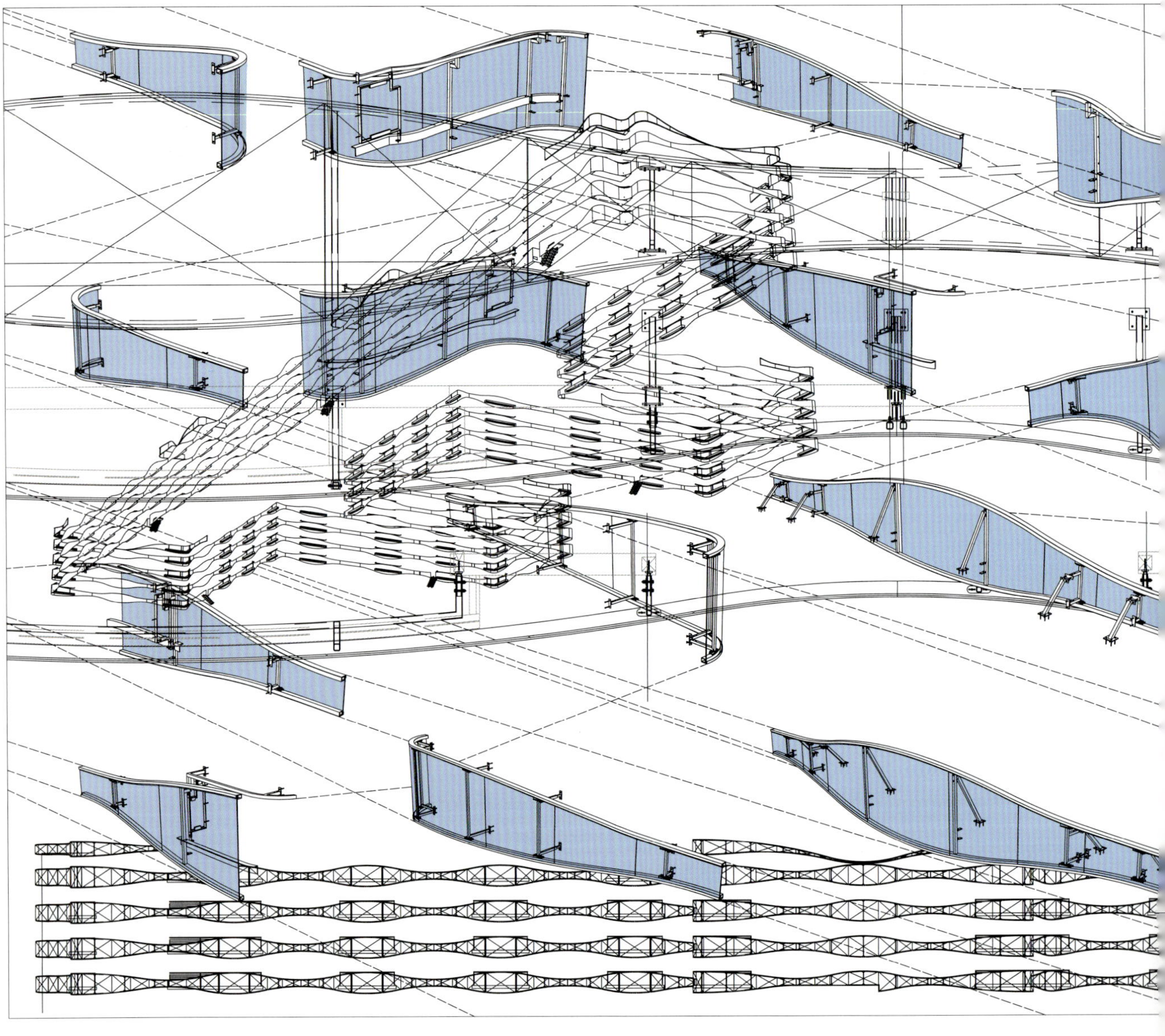

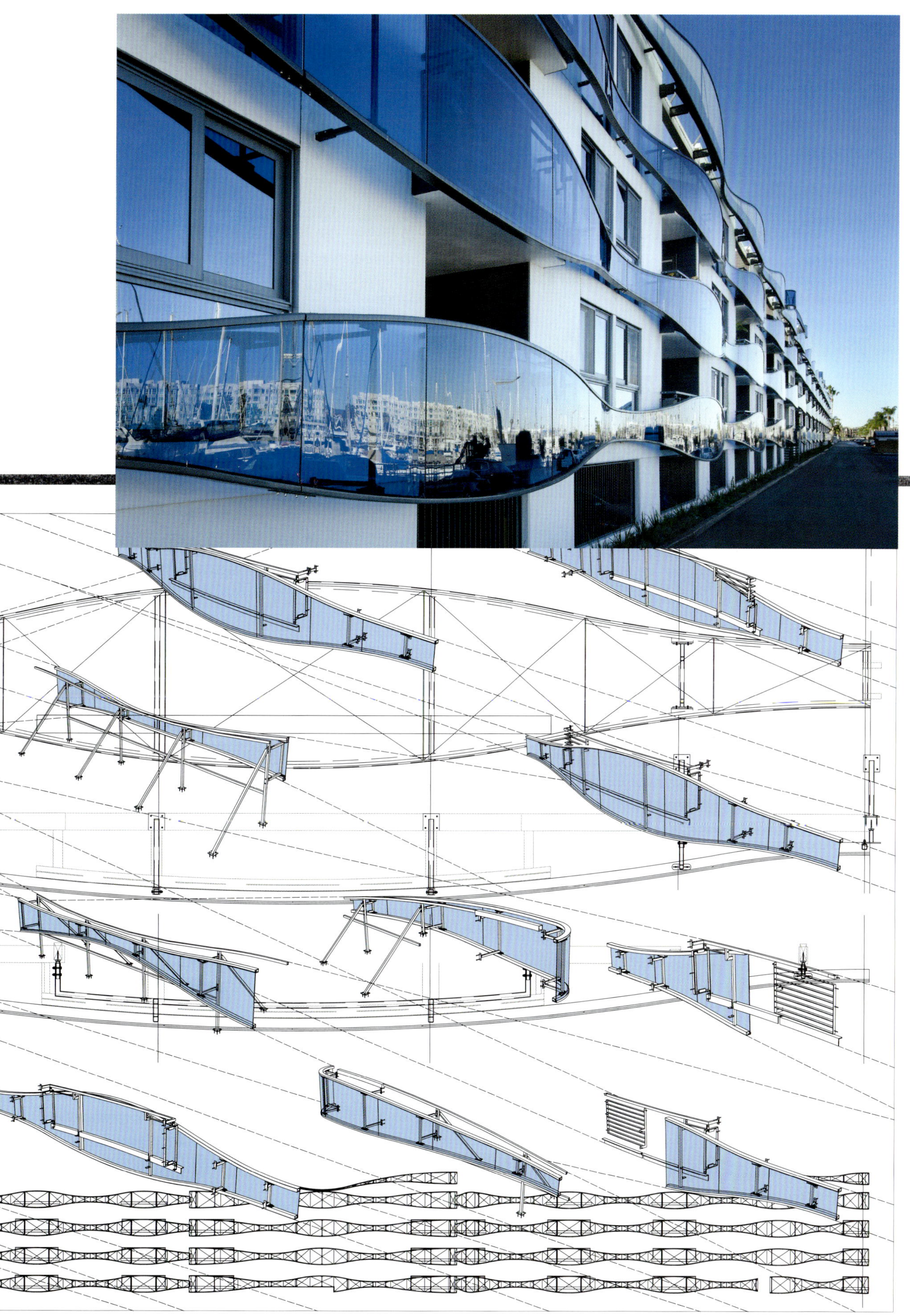

"The plastic model is the most synthetic tool for communicating the project, and became the project itself. In its absurd perfection it calms the neurosis and exorcises the sure failure. The plastic effects it represents will be perceived in reality if viewed from 1,000 meters high. In fact, the yacht has not restored the instruments of representation; it is still linked to the simulation and the miniaturization of reality... These limits mean that architecture tends to renew itself only on the linguistic level... The city before a tool of use is a grand figurative system of representation of society. The difficulty in overcoming one's figurative limits is the serious handicap of all modern architecture."

This claim resonates in the architectural production of the last two decades where architects rely on the effects, which will be perceived in reality from a bird's-eye-view using instruments to replace their instinctive capabilities to understand and integrate user needs into their design. Instruments that are linked to the simulation and miniaturization of reality. This means that architecture tends to renew itself only on the linguistic level. This is not an argument against the use of tools (models) in the process of developing architectural projects but rather is more about the understanding of the process of architectural production and the need for awareness in utilizing the tools in the service of developing the projects to reflect their social contexts and needs.

Ultimately, the tools are seductive and sometimes gives the inexperienced user the illusion that they are engaged in a creative process, but it is the program that is doing the work and it is the program's creativity that allows the product to appear amazing. It is like an iPhone that is only fascinating until the next model comes out.

The Santa Monica School, at one point in its conception, was professing to balance the practice and education of architecture by teaching a new generation to be involved hands on in the field, showing by example the need for being involved. Yet it ended up imitating East Coast institutional models like Colombia's, getting consumed by generating sophisticated images of an architectural utopia in the fictional environment of a specific future.

This so called experimental architecture has become a cliché and it is designed by software programmers that originally made these tools for Hollywood productions. The software creates the illusion of authorship and creativity in the way a game does for which success is measured by who comes up with the next cool gadget to produce the most seductive image. The self-indulging practice of the last 20 years has further reduced the number of dismal projects that the so called "contemporary" "experimental," "avant-gard" architects were interested in dedicating their lives to.

"The truth is simple, very simple. Centered. But people crave other nourishment besides the truth. Its privileged distortions, in philosophy and literature. For example."
– Susan Sontag

I craved this nourishment, and without it I didn't know how I could tolerate the humiliation and abuse of those meetings. How could I compete for a speculative project having to deal with code restrictions that would restrict me to make airless, lightless boxes deprived of human needs based on autocratic laws generated by insurance companies and banks?

Contemporary architecture is not in demand because it is not understood, appreciated, or accepted in our society. It is for this reason that there is a large group of architects competing for less than one percent of work in the market. The problem is complex and rooted in the overall economic, political, and cultural system. Unless we embrace architectural education, starting at the elementary level, and teach the general public about the importance of architecture as part of daily life, then we will be contributing more to segregated cities and inhumane living conditions dictated by zoning and building codes.

The Tahiti Marina project took off fast after the initial hiccups and, like Isaac said, I found it easier than previously thought to collaborate smoothly with GP. The pressure was on from the beginning and we needed to submit a concept design to the DCB in a month.

As I started sketching I was timid and overly limiting myself because of the size, cost, time, and schedule. On the other hand, the site was encouraging and liberating. It's hard to miss the Pacific Ocean when it is at your doorstep.

I visited the site frequently during this time. It helped to improve my mood, calming me down and leaving me refreshed. The work process calms me generally. I can think, make, create, and imagine until restlessness crawls up my back and suddenly I am worried, missing my children.

The financial crisis of 2008 was historically devastating not just for the US, but all over the world. According to some accounts it was worse than the Great Depression. With banks and other financial institutions collapsing, corporations were laying off thousands of people every day. I began my days with strong emotional uncertainties and all I could do was try to concentrate on issues at hand. Who are people I need to contact? Where do I need to go? What are my priorities? I tried to accept my vulnerability and weaknesses with open arms. I ignored my unrealistic expectations before they entangled me in a web of sorrows. This was when I discovered who my true friends were, the people that I could count on. "This is it," I kept repeating to myself. "I am here. I have what I need with my faults and imperfections; I am..." (Feb. 3, 2009)

"Not until we are lost do we begin to understand ourselves."
– H.D. Thoreau

The apartment building, like many others in the Marina, was more like a speculative box, disinterested in its amazing site. Surprisingly, in some of the well positioned units there were windowless closets facing the ocean view instead of a better positioned living room or bedroom. Our hands were tied as to the degree of changes we could make.

The apartment's layout and long corridors, which ran the entire length of the building, unfortunately had to stay. We turned our attention to developing the façade.

The architecture of the new façade exerted new character and engaged the existing building to celebrate the unique site's most important elements: boating and the water. A curving, horizontal, laminated, blue-color glass surface wrapped around the entire building creating balcony enclosures, changing the dynamic of the static building into a more fluid and organic vessel. The new elements of the façade created a variety of textures and forms, which made the building seem lighter.

The pool area, club house, toilet facilities, landscaping, lighting, promenade, and bulkhead railing were all renovated as part of this project. The existing pool area was improved with a new glass/metal pool area enclosure, renovated spa, paving enhancement, water feature, and wood decks with updated landscaping to enhance the quality of the space. The construction of a new gym below the deck on the east side of the building was improved with new equipment, lockers, showers, and toilet facilities.

The existing concrete curb edge between the driveway and waterfront walk were removed to visually treat the entire perimeter of the building as the Marina Promenade. In lieu of the concrete curb and drains, a portion of the parking stalls were paved with drivable grass treated with bio-swale to satisfy the project's storm water management requirements and create a park-like promenade. A seamless edge of vehicular parking and the waterfront walk was delineated with a line of concrete ball bumper stops and punctuated with flowering trees and benches. Ultimately, the Tahiti Marina Promenade successfully interacted with its participants and engaged its surroundings.

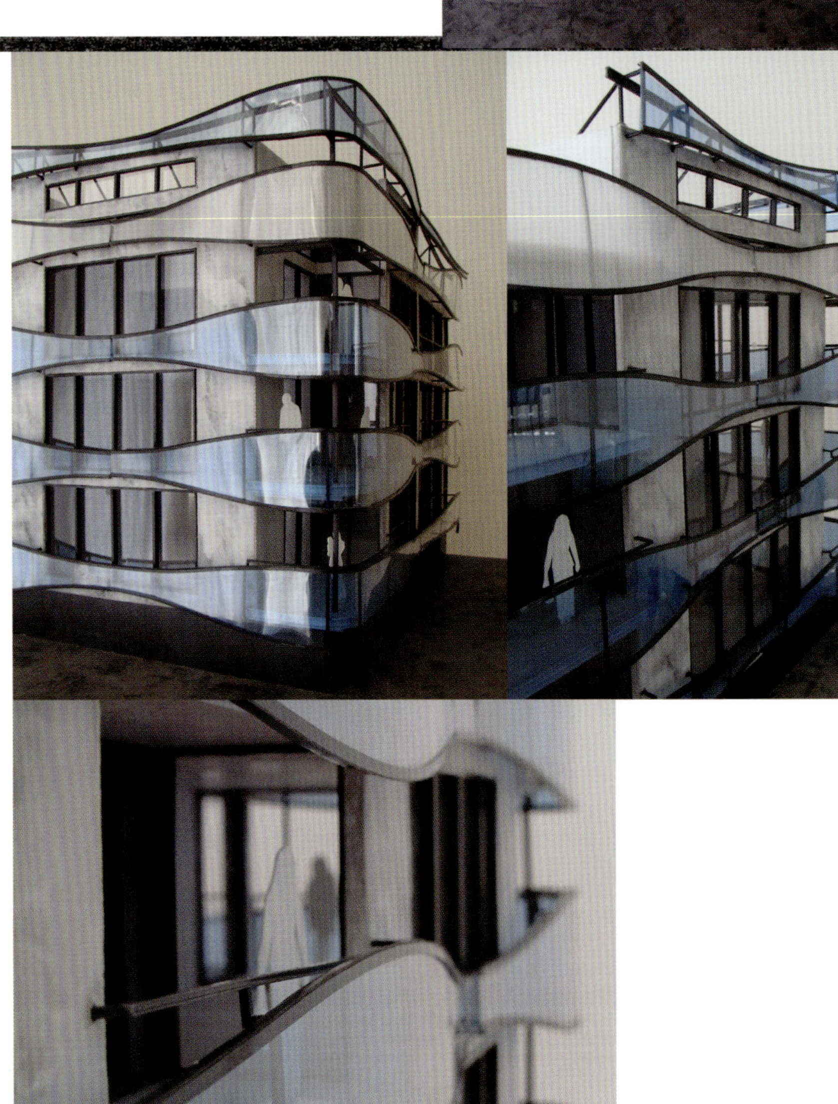

How can we translate the lively horizontal, high density urban envi-ronment into a cosmopo-litan vertical tower?

Ho Chi Minh City is named after the revolutionary leader who united his country and is the father of modern Vietnam. In 1976, Saigon was merged with surrounding provinces to form what is now the financial center of Vietnam and headquarters to many national and international companies. Ho Chi Min City is located in the south with a population of about nine million.

With the unprecedented growth of Asian cities over the last few decades, the demand for alternative living spaces has been greater than ever. Mixed-use development, the combination of commercial, hospitality, residential, and services could consolidate activities within a structure in a neighborhood, and has become a necessary typology in most cities in the world due to population growth.

I will never forget my first night in Ho Chi Minh City eight years ago. The aroma of the foods and spices in the air, the sounds of music, interactions and laughter in the city had their distinct qualities. There was a rush of energy and I was curious to identify it. The streets full of people of all ages, shops, lights, and trees created a background which guided my experience. By contrast with Los Angeles, the introverted city that is my home, what I witnessed surprised me.

These memories colored our design for the Vietnam Tower. Could we somehow translate the high-density, horizontal urban environment into a cosmopolitan vertical tower? Could we respect the existing city, its culture and values, and also create architectural elements for its future?

The site was located in the Central Business District, fronted by the historic Le Duan Boulevard, Hai Bai Trung Avenue, and Nguyen Van Chiem Street and is easily accessible and in close proximity to other central city districts.

The Vietnam Tower was developed as a mixed-use building on a site measuring 4,900 m^2 (52,000 sq.ft.). The six-story podium and 30-story tower above cover 65% of the site. The total gross area is approximately 66,400 m^2 (715,000 sq.ft.) and the height 160 m (1,720 feet).

The podium included hotel and apartment services, a fitness center, pool, children's playground, restaurants, meeting facilities, a dividable ballroom accommodating 800 to 1,000 people, retail, and offices. The tower featured 220-300 hotel rooms and suites with entertainment on the top floor, including a sky bar, restaurant, etc.

Vietnam Tower

Location:
Ho Chi Minh City, Vietnam

Year:
2016 (not built)

Program:
Mixed-use Commercial, Hotel, and residential

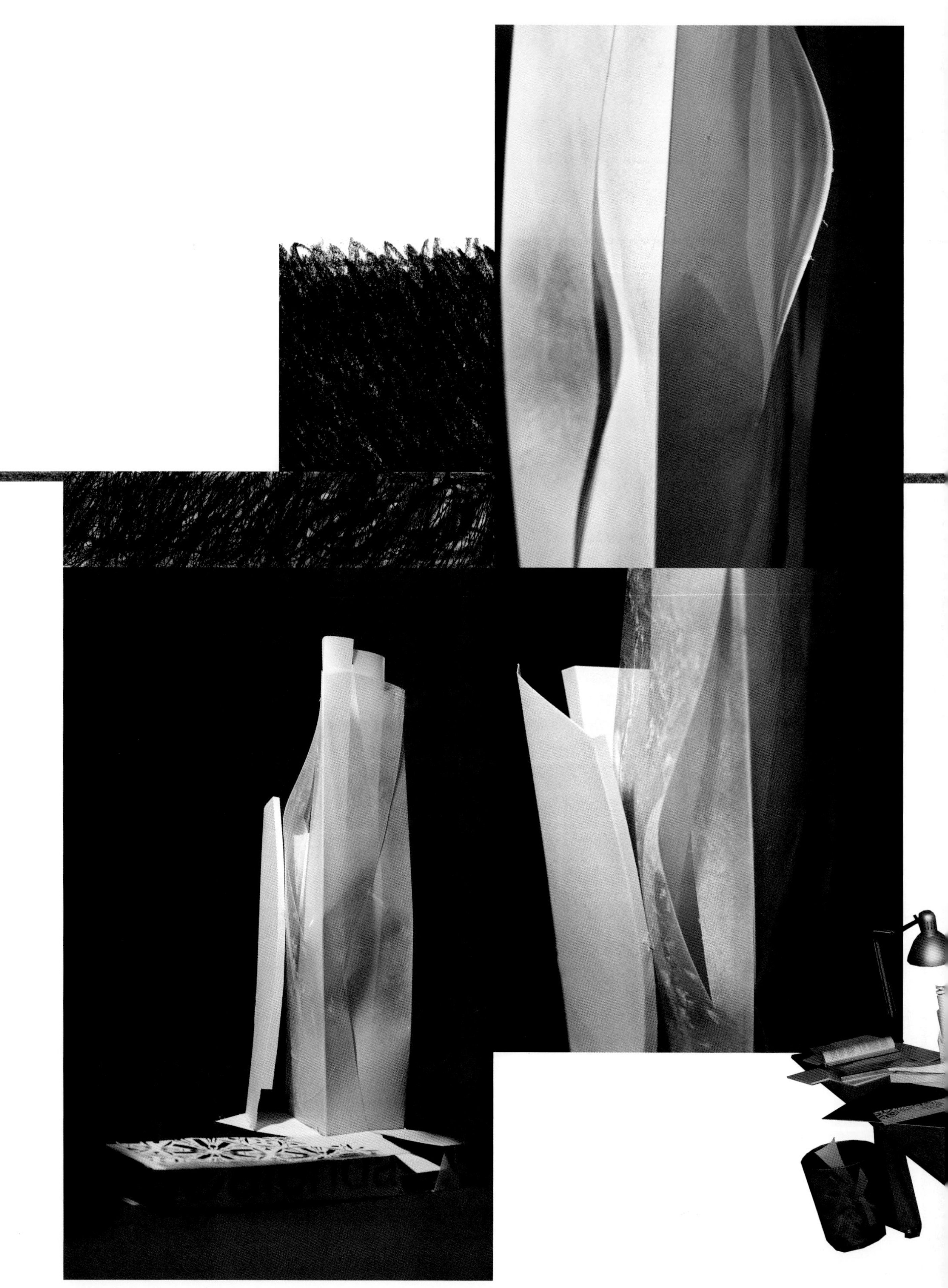

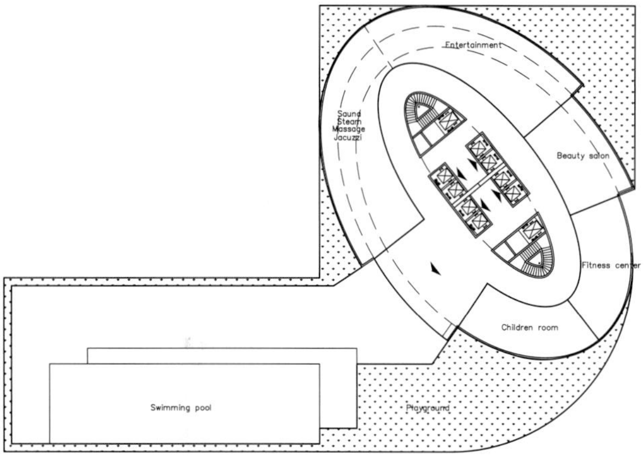

Entertainment
Sauna
Steam
Massage
Jacuzzi
Beauty salon
Fitness center
Children room
Swimming pool
Playground

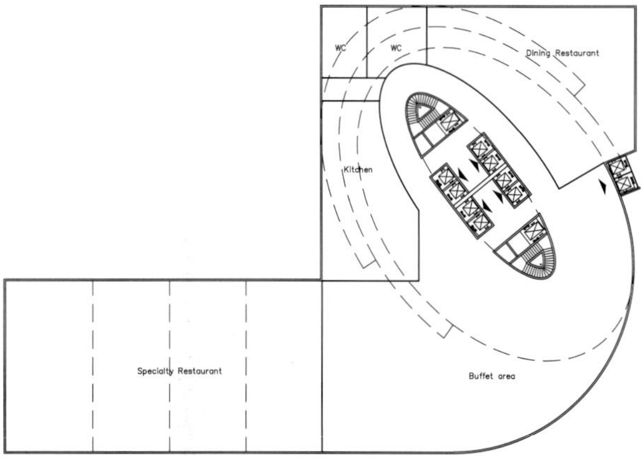

WC
WC
Dining Restaurant
Kitchen
Specialty Restaurant
Buffet area

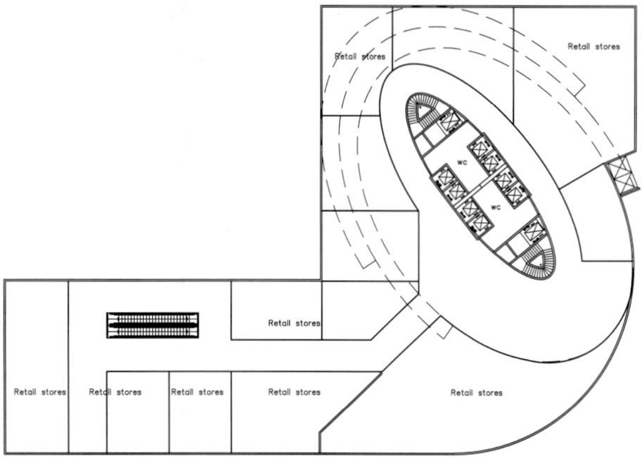

Retail stores
Retail stores
WC
WC
Retail stores
Retail stores
Retail stores
Retail stores
Retail stores
Retail stores

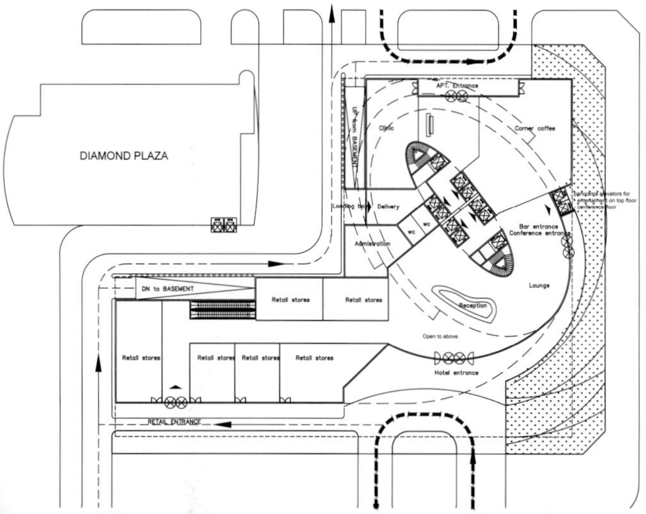

DIAMOND PLAZA
APT. Entrance
Clinic
Corner coffee
Loading bay
Delivery
Administration
Bar entrance
Conference entrance
Lounge
Reception
Open to above
Hotel entrance
DN to BASEMENT
Retail stores
Retail stores
Retail stores
Retail stores
Retail stores
Retail stores
RETAIL ENTRANCE

In Vietnam, the building envelope for a structure of this size, scale, and location is typically predetermined by the city's planning and architectural authorities with the possibility of proposing minor changes. As architects, we can at best propose an architectural composition that deals with restrictions and other requirements fulfilling the developer's financial analysis and requirements.

After studying the building envelope and roughly locating the program within the shell we sketched a few possibilities for the building's tectonics and form in relationship to its site and the dynamic of its interaction with the surrounding area. One was a rectangular building and the other cylindrical. The two options were developed further with consultants and the client's representatives simultaneously. We decided to continue with the cylindrical geometry because the building had a better interaction with its surroundings and more viewing options for the individual units all around.

The building podium interacts with the activities of the streets surrounding the site, creating a grand entrance to a five-star international luxury hotel and a plaza along the commercial strip, which invites patrons inside for a new and exciting experience.

The primary architectural surfaces of the podium façade orients the corner of the building along Le Duan Boulevard. A powerful force rises from the corner with a kinetic spiral structure reinforcing the architecture of the building and its relation to the site, where the historic citadel was once. The dynamic tower gains momentum as it rises twenty-two floors, becoming lighter and more transparent and diminishing in diameter to comply with the planning and zoning requirements. Its three distinct sections are woven together to create a unified composition that seems to defy gravity.

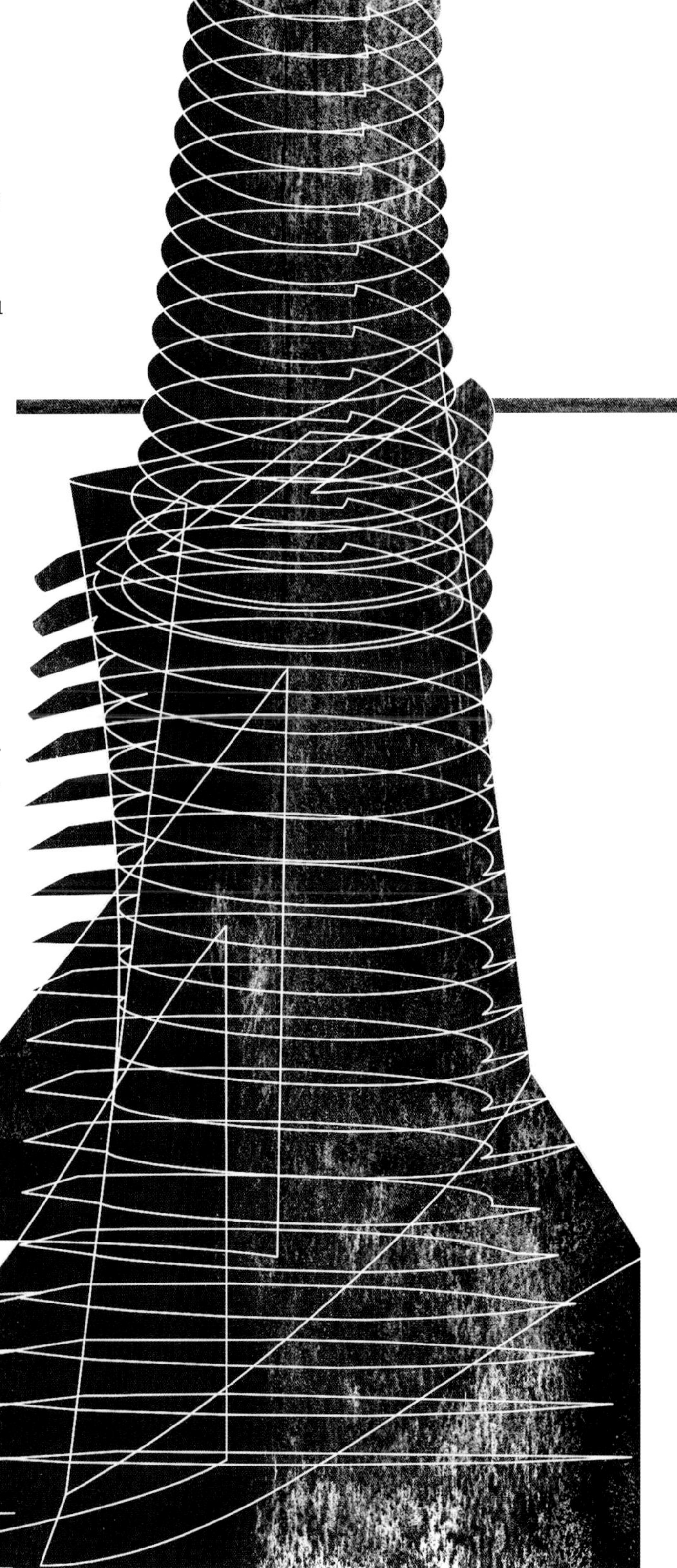

The lines are carefully calculated and studied to achieve a proportional shape and size. A grand opening with a skylight marks the main entrance, creating an open, luminous space which balconies on either side look onto. This dynamic monumental space brings the natural light into the core of the podium, where the hotel lobby, offices, conference area, services offices are situated. The podium opens as it reaches the corner creating a grand open

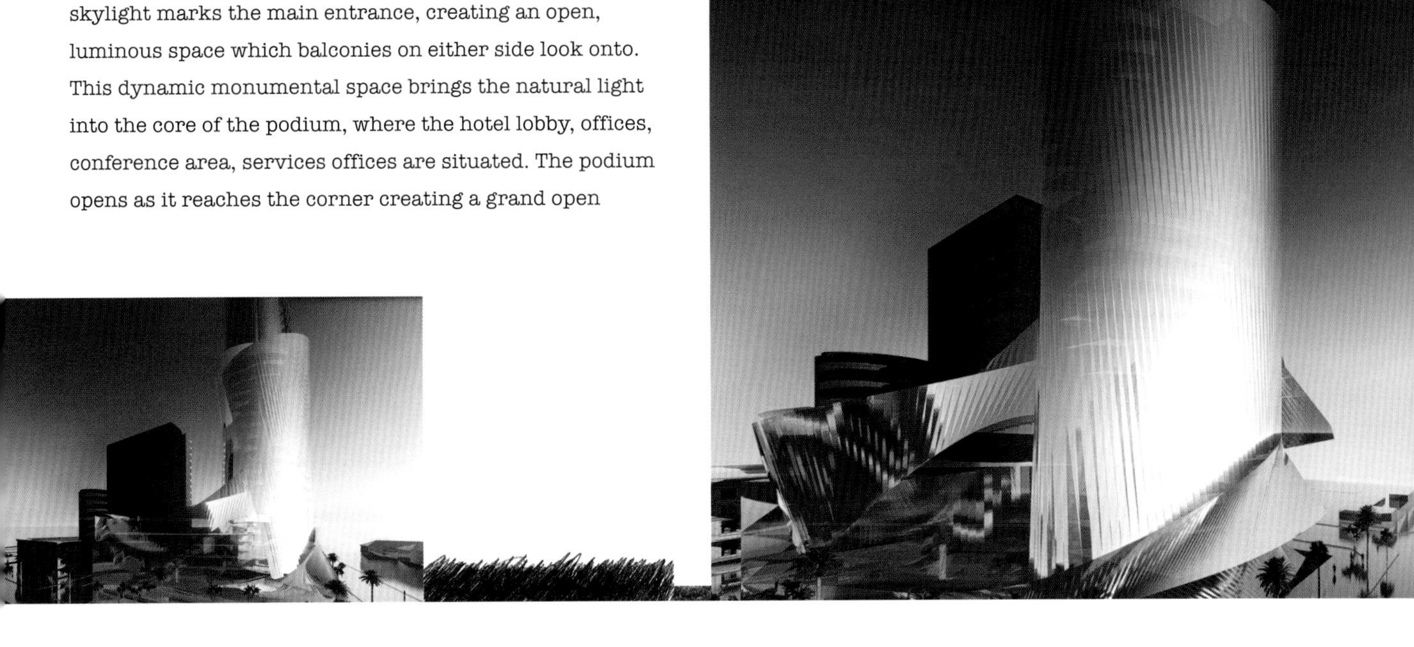

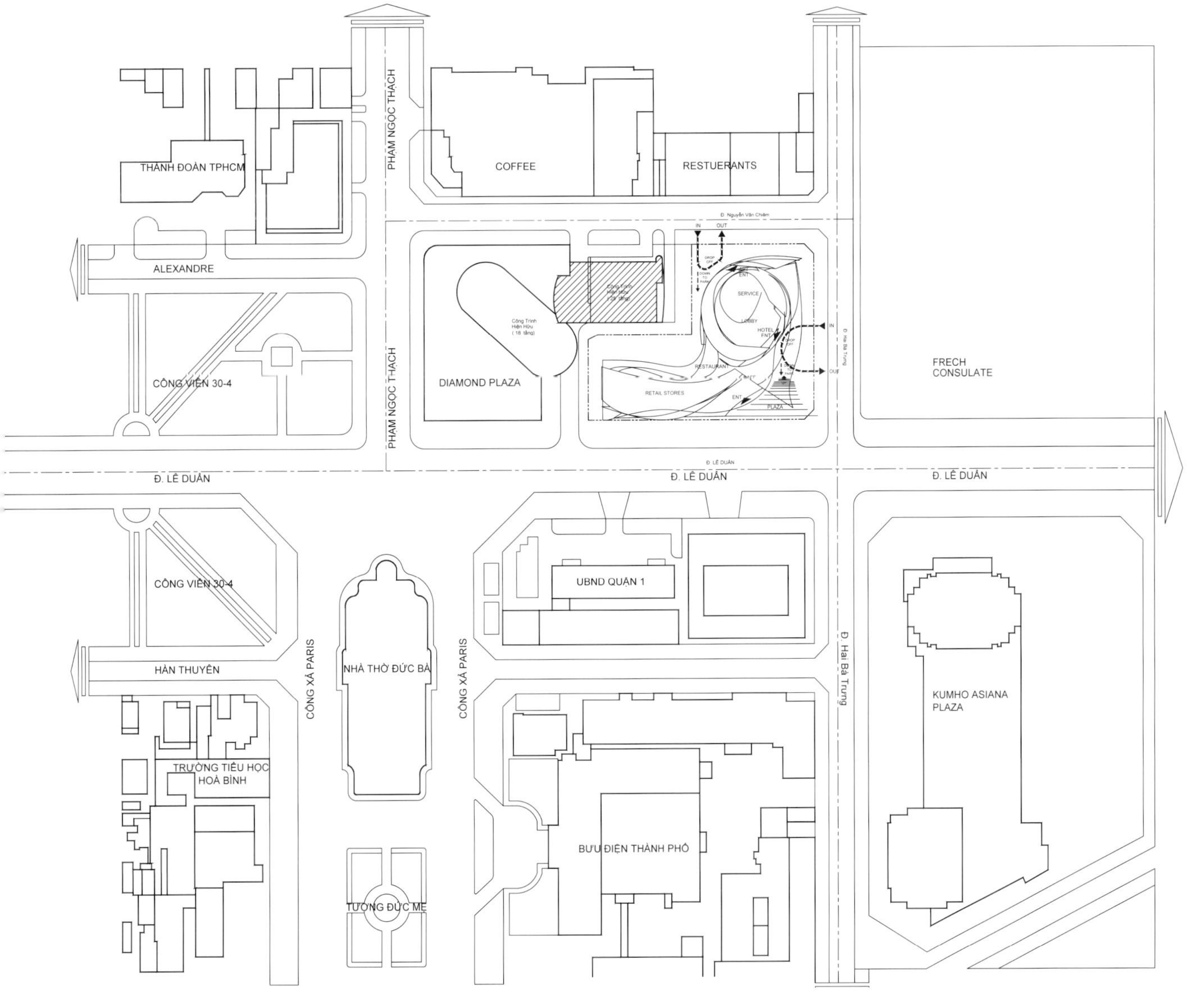

THÀNH ĐOÀN TPHCM
PHẠM NGỌC THẠCH
COFFEE
RESTUERANTS
ALEXANDRE
CÔNG VIÊN 30-4
PHẠM NGỌC THẠCH
DIAMOND PLAZA
RETAIL STORES
FRECH CONSULATE
Đ. LÊ DUẨN
Đ. LÊ DUẨN
Đ. LÊ DUẨN
CÔNG VIÊN 30-4
UBND QUẬN 1
HÀN THUYÊN
CÔNG XÃ PARIS
NHÀ THỜ ĐỨC BÀ
CÔNG XÃ PARIS
Đ. Hai Bà Trưng
KUMHO ASIANA PLAZA
TRƯỜNG TIỂU HỌC HOÀ BÌNH
BƯU ĐIỆN THÀNH PHỐ
TƯỢNG ĐỨC MẸ

space where the entrance to the hotel and commercial strip is created. In keeping with the Vietnamese social spirit, the space welcomes the city in.

The overall effect is of an object in the landscape whose real estate value increases as it rises into the sky. It's veiled with shifting surfaces and overlapping glass panels so that the entire surface achieves various qualities of depth and lightness, reflecting a cinematic collage of building elements and their interaction with the city near and far. It's a visual marker in the landscape of a historic place that will soon not be recognizable.

I was conflicted from the beginning of the project, which poses an inevitable formalistic contradiction. Apart from economics, an important factor, there is very little we could say in defense of such a tower in a city like Saigon. On the other hand, observing the growth and development of cities like Beijing, Shanghai, Singapore, and Tokyo we also couldn't ignore the potential for Ho Chi Minh City to become a very different place than the one I first visited. What if we can integrate the humanity and inclusiveness we witnessed in the city into a tower? The city of the future is already here and the current urban and social crisis we are witnessing is only the beginning.

...like the old city in the spirit of the con-temporary new territory that we can call "Not City"!

Ghaleh Morghi

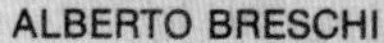

ALBERTO BRESCHI

FORMA URBANA E PROGETTAZIONE ARCHITETTONICA

APPUNTI PER UNA TEORIA ED ESPERIENZE DIDATTICHE

Presentazione di Marco Dezzi Bardeschi

Lino Bellia, Gino Boccabella, Flaviano M. Lorusso
Tommaso Manco, Reza Masud Ansari

CLUSF
Cooperativa Editrice Universitaria Firenze

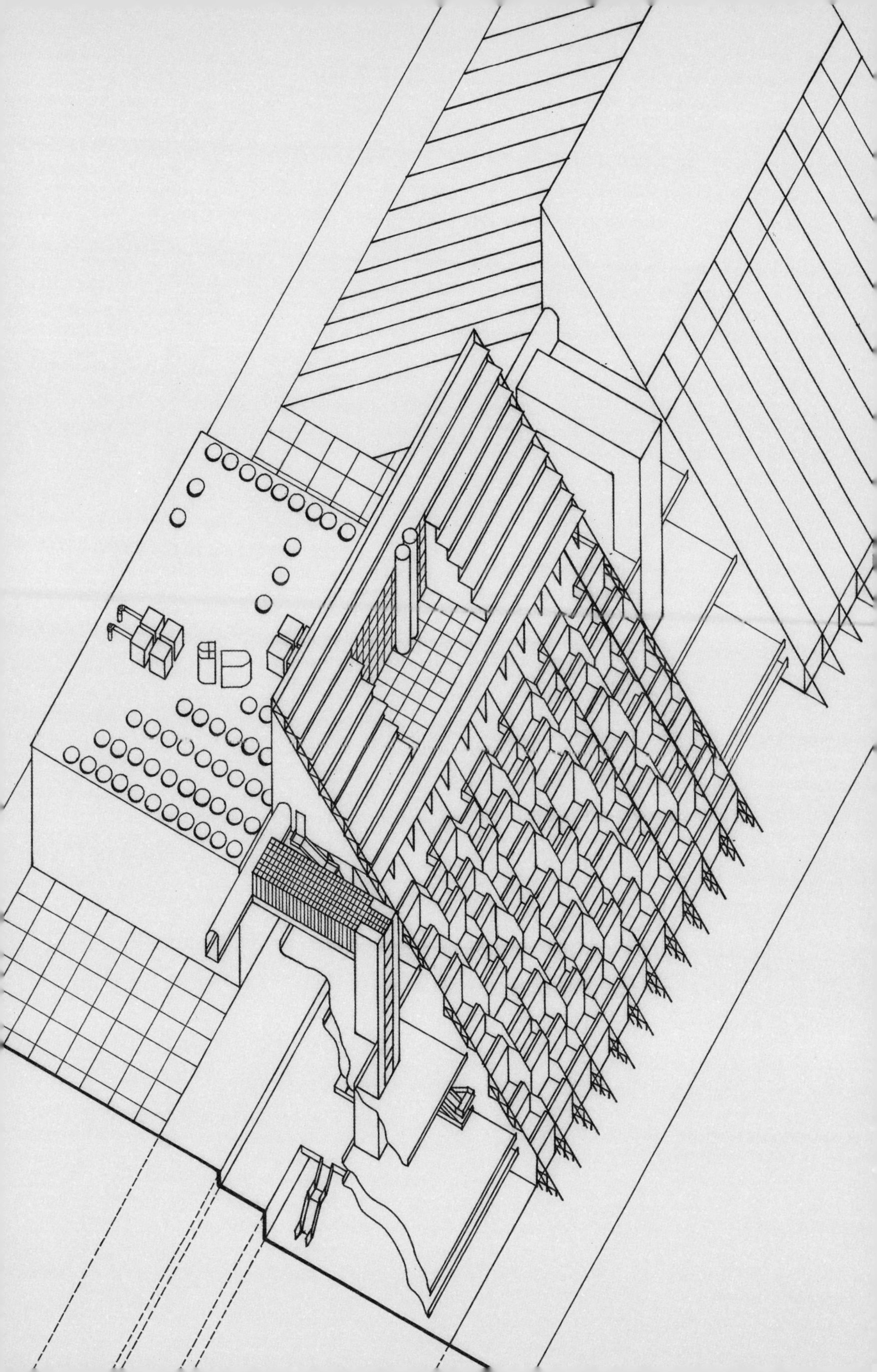

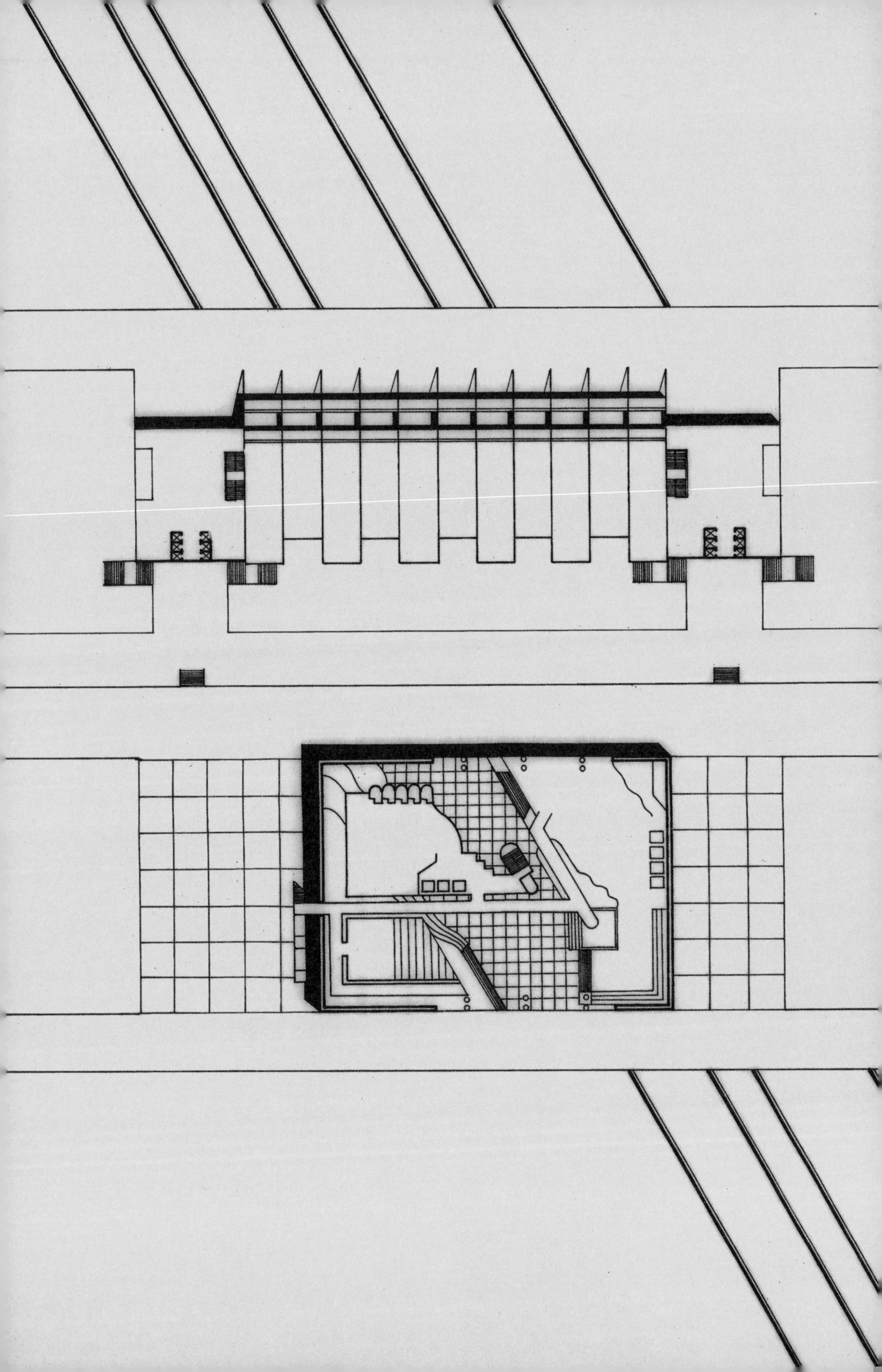

Ghaleh Morghi

Location:
Tehran, Iran

Year:
1980 (not built)

Program:
Independent Community

MEMORY AS INDICATION OF URBAN SYNTHESIS

For Ghaleh Morghi we propose an independent community. The area—the former Tehran military airport—already appeared as a space-structure, with a definite, drawn, readable ellipse shape. The space was available to complete, in relationship with the old context, the old bazaar, the train station, and immediate neighborhood. The elliptical, asphalt, track of the past became the founding and regenerating furrow of the new residential structure: the morphology of the whole was determined as a real presence, but also as a memory to be preserved. It indicated the new unity of the whole, the unifying sign of the articulations of its interior. Here, the bazaar was recreated as an equipped rout, that integrated many spaces, all different: the theater, the library, the houses, the schools, the garden, the market square, the shops, the factory, and the palace of the administration, all in an organic, continuous, complicated complex. It acted like the old city in the spirit of the contemporary new territory which we can call "Not City."

Collaboration with, H. Navvabi and M. Baghai of the Comp. course Arch. V of prof. Breschi AA. 1979-80

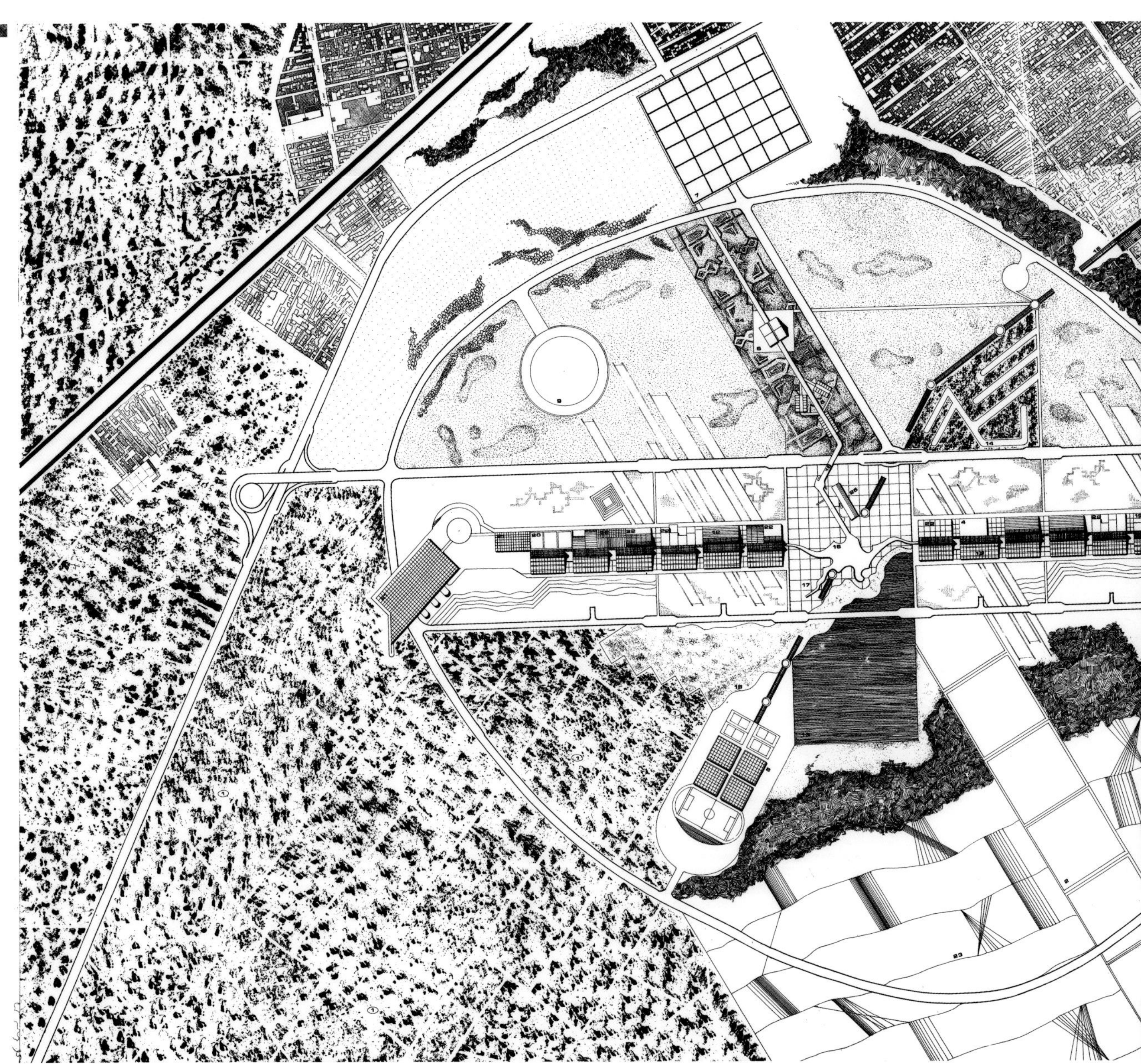

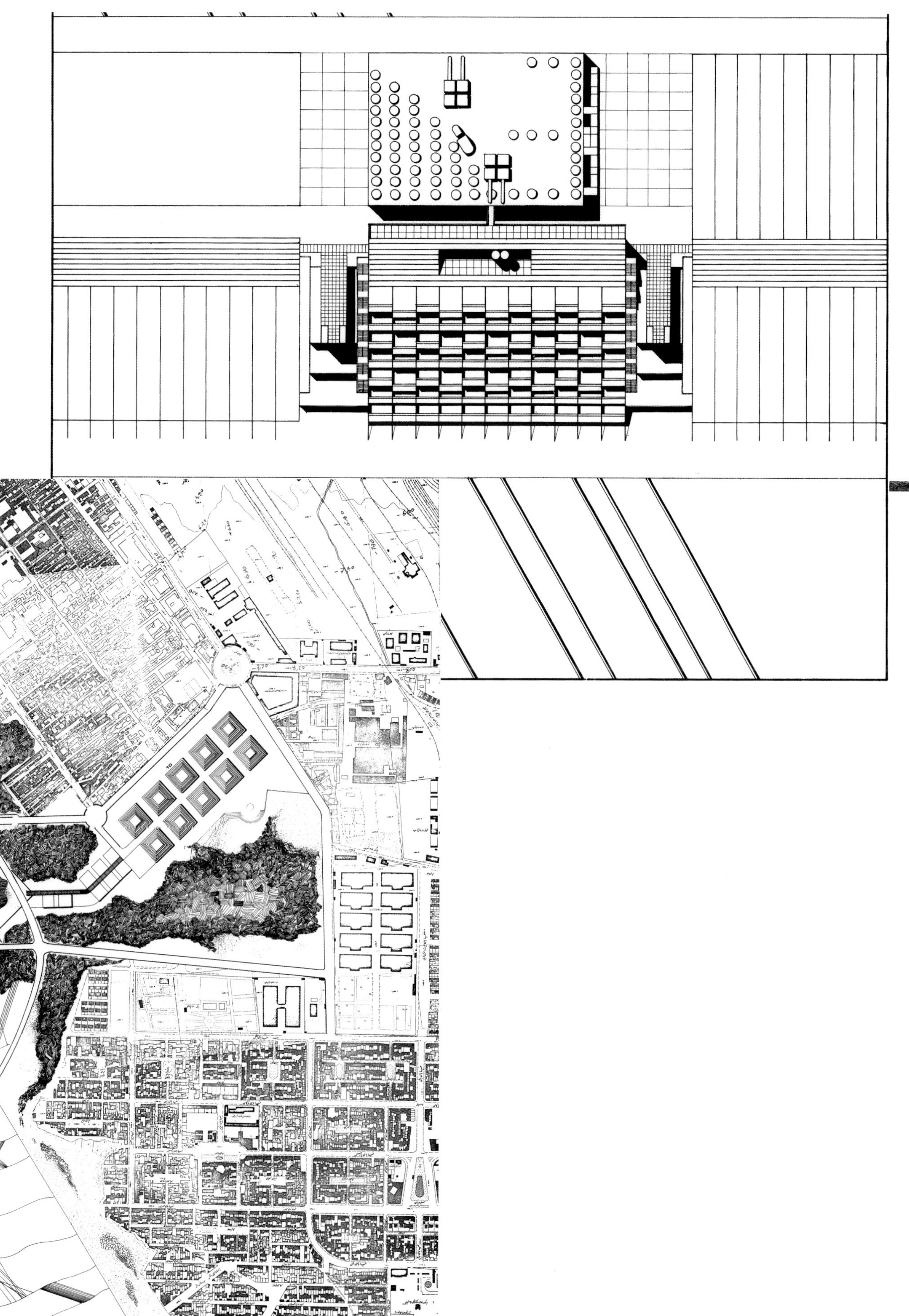

Ristoro

Box
Ricerca Scientifica

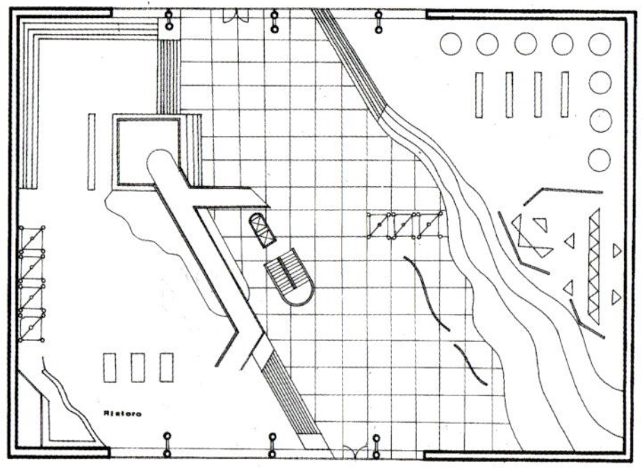

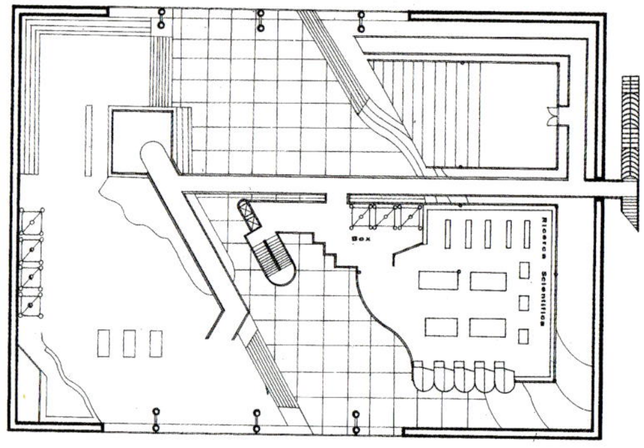

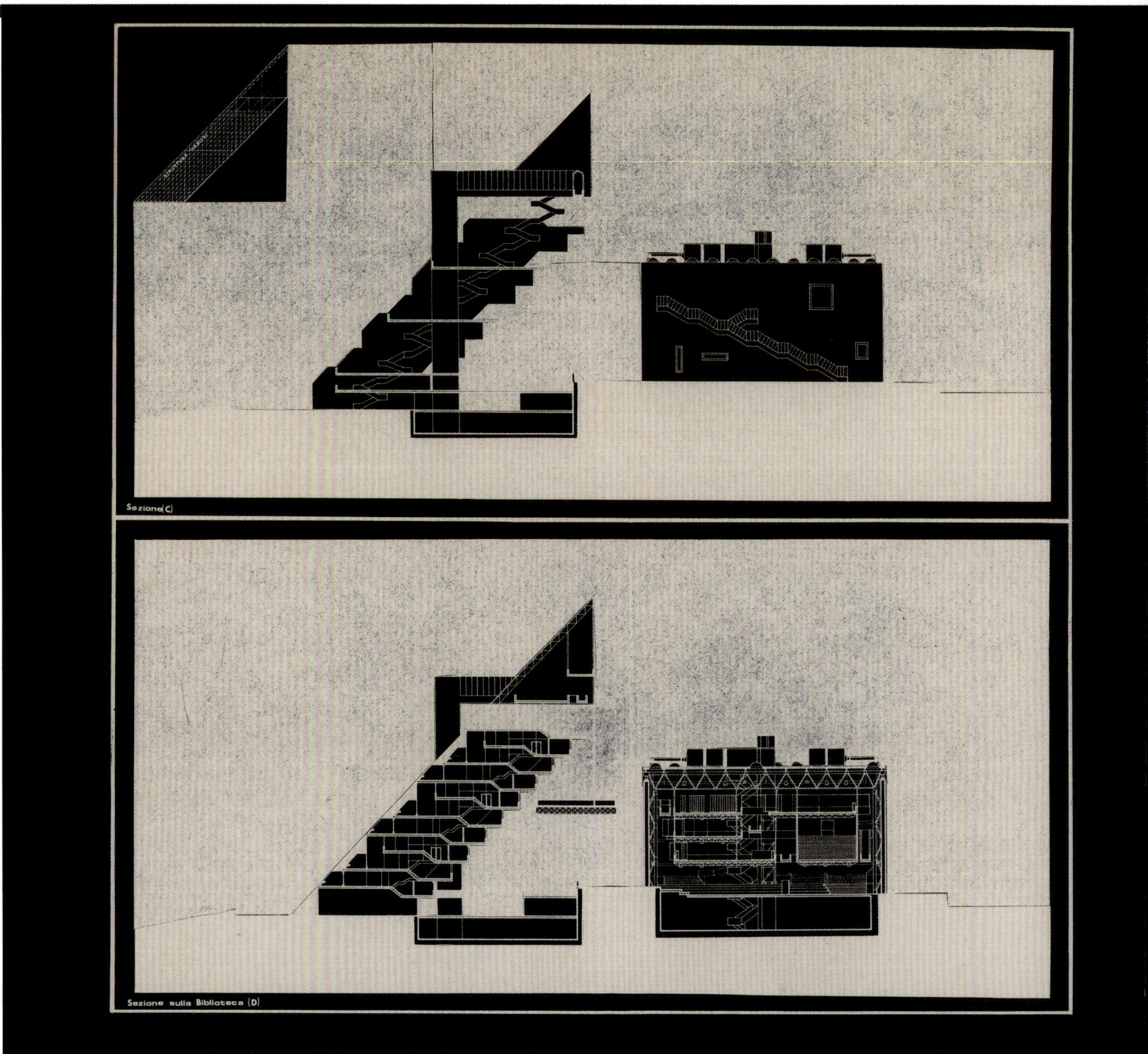

Sezione (C)
Sezione sulla Biblioteca (D)

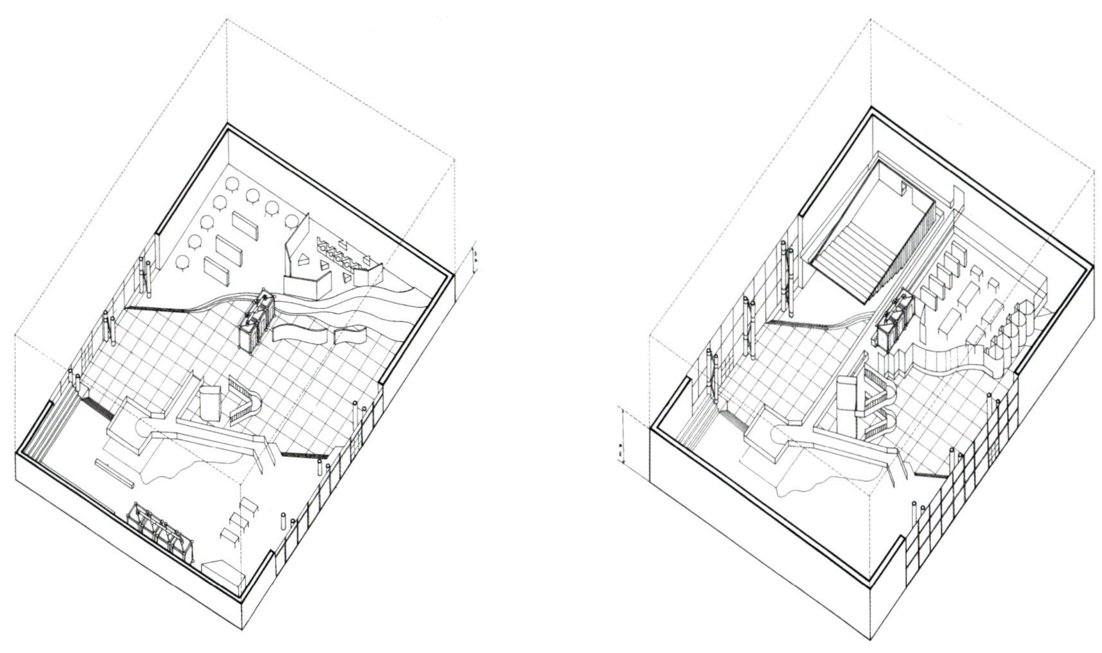

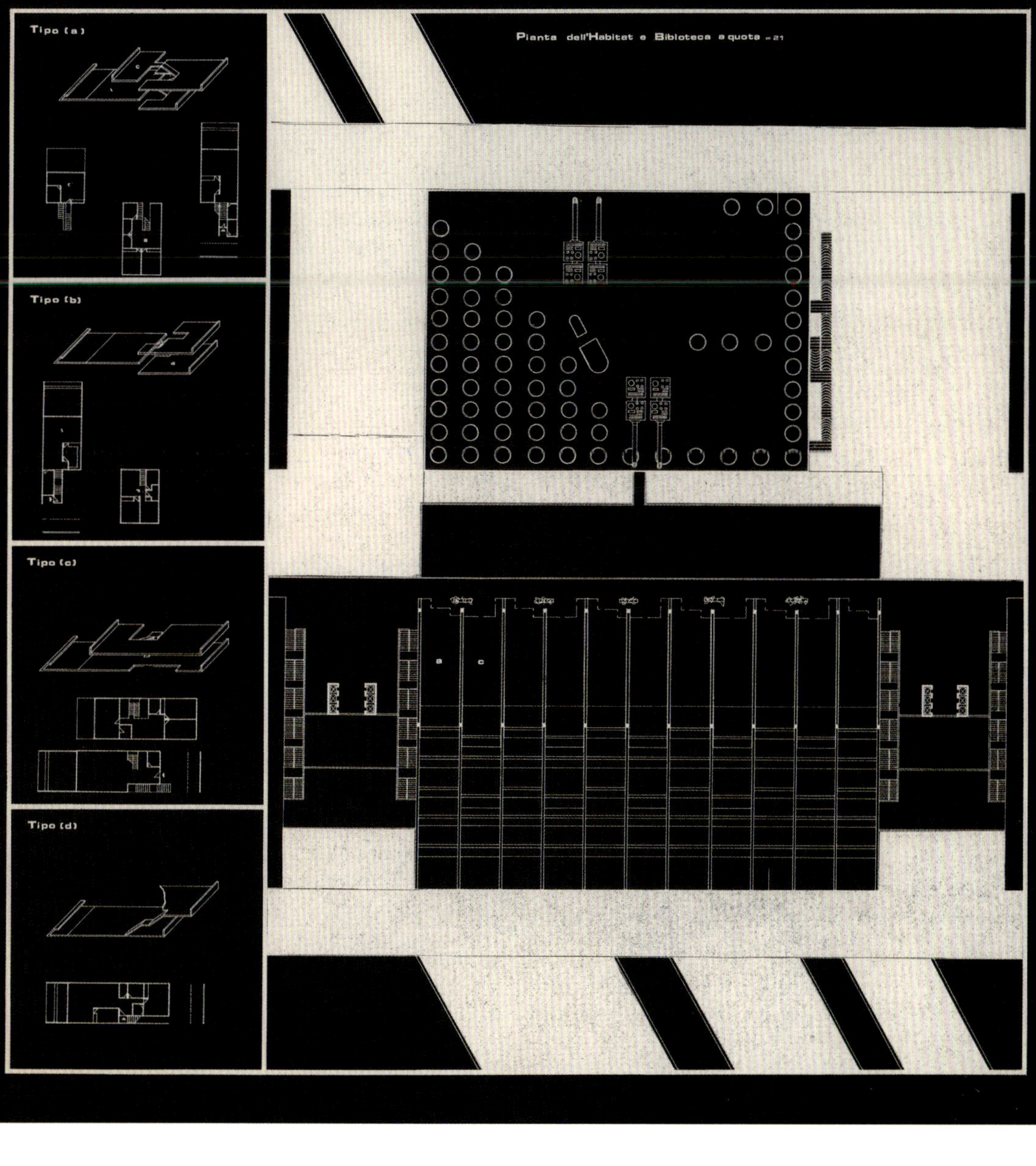

Tipo (a)

Tipo (b)

Tipo (c)

Tipo (d)

Pianta dell'Habitat e Biblioteca a quota +21

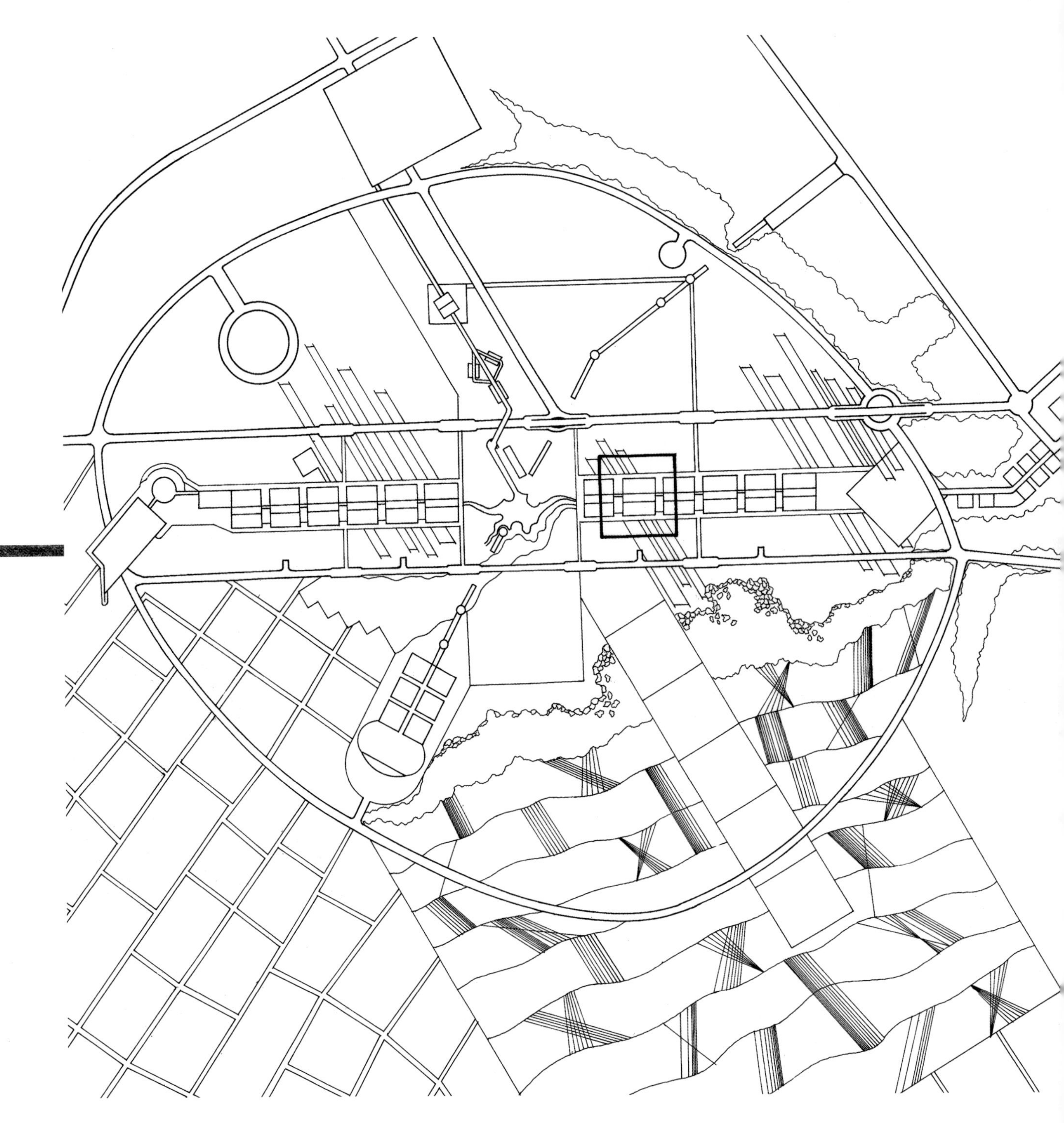

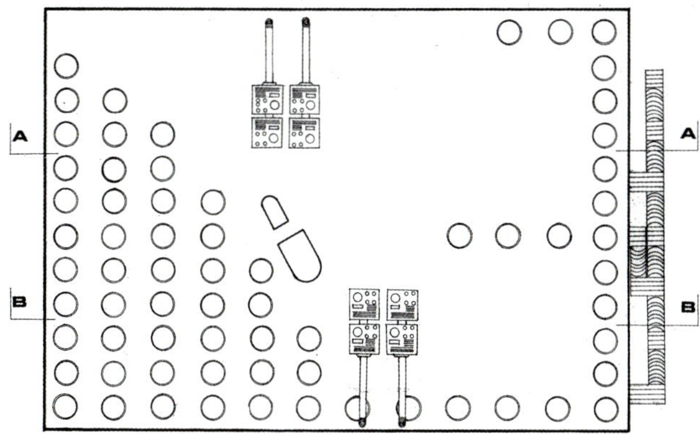

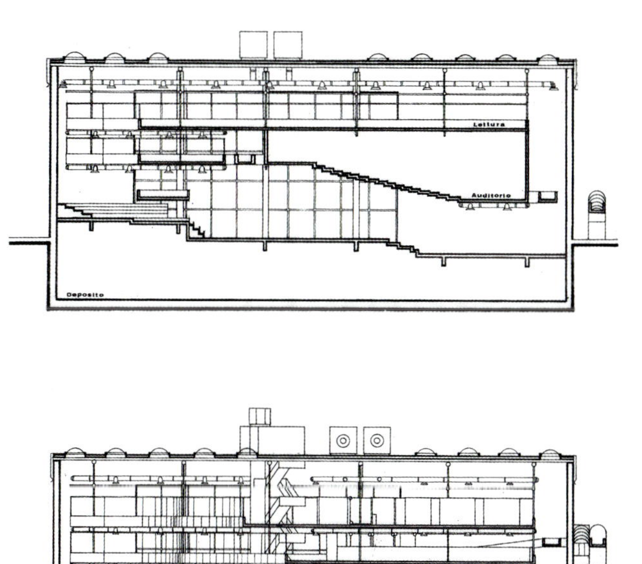

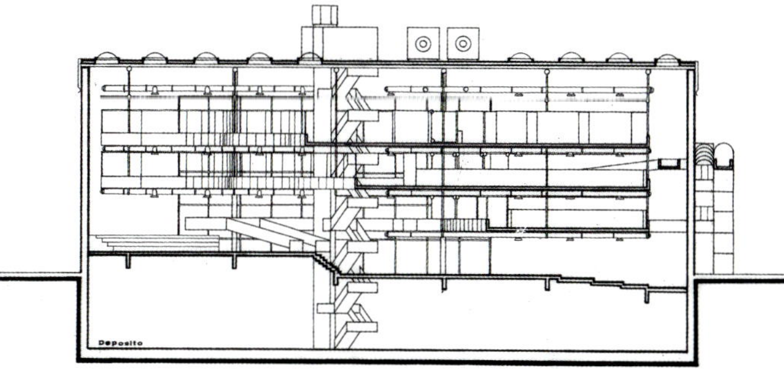

LA MEMORIA QUALE INDICAZIONE DI SINTESI URBANA

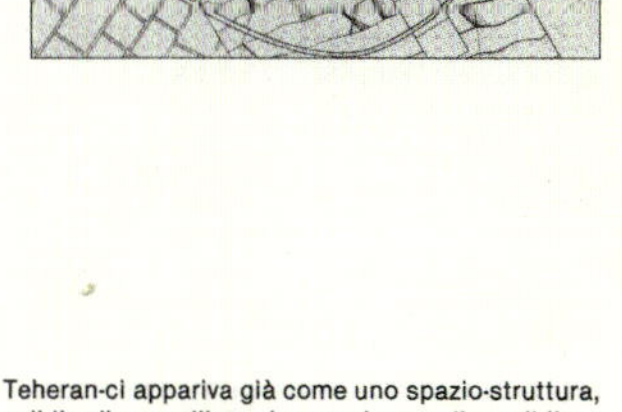

Fig. 28 - Planimetria generale del progetto per un'habitat urbano integrato nell'area dell'ex aereoporto a Teheran; studenti M. Baghai Ruddsari, H. Navvabi, M. Saee del corso di Comp. Arch. V del prof. Breschi A.A. 1979-80

"L'area-l'ex aereoporto di Teheran-ci appariva già come uno spazio-struttura, dalla forma definita, disegnata, leggibile di una ellisse. Lo spazio era disponibile a completarsi, cercando un rapporto con i vecchi contenitori in disuso, il vecchio bazar e la stazione ferroviaria, vicini. La traccia ellittica, d'asfalto, della pista d'un tempo, diventava il solco fondatore e rigeneratore della nuova struttura residenziale: la morfologia dell'insieme era determinata come presenza reale, ma anche come memoria da conservare, come suggerimento. Essa indicava la nuova unità dell'insieme, il segno unificante delle articolazioni del suo interno. Qui, si ricreava il bazar: cioè un percorso attrezzato, che integrava molti spazi, tutti diversi: il teatro, la biblioteca, le case, le scuole, il giardino, la piazza col mercato, le botteghe, la fabbrica, il palazzo dell'amministrazione, in un complesso organico, continuo, complicato, come nella vecchia città"

Dalla relazione degli studenti del corso di composizione V del prof. A. Breschi

57

Michele Saee is, therefore, like the platypus...
Essay by Luigi Prestinenza Puglisi

Michele Saee is part of that talented minority of architects who try to find a close relationship between body and space, even at the cost of deconstructing it. And, therefore, they are not satisfied with the white or colored boxes that minimalism and rationalism produce today in large quantity. In order to deal with this issue which—I assure you—is not at all simple, he has all the credentials: he is Iranian; he studied in Italy; he works in California; and he travels around the world, favoring France, Paris in particular, and China.

Good architecture never arises from a pure and simple formula. It is always the result of hybridizations in the ingredients. In our case there are three. The first ingredient comes from the Persian civilization: it is the sense of earth, of material, of the rhythmic decoration of a millenary tradition. The second comes from Italian culture: it is an obsession with history and tradition, albeit filtered through the avant-garde openings of Superstudio, a collective with which Saee connected during his years of training in Italy. The third ingredient is the explosive fluidity, not without sculptural spans, of an engaging space developed by the Los Angeles culture and, in particular, by Morphosis, where Saee worked at the beginning of his career, never forgetting the almost religious idea of a complex cosmos sensed by Eric Owen Moss.

Michele Saee is, therefore, like the platypus of which the philosopher and semiologist Umberto Eco spoke, is a particularly interesting hybrid that scientists find difficult to classify: he is an Asian who loves the body, a Mediterranean who plays with forms, a deconstructivist who challenges the Cartesian space. He is a designer who is always suspended between matter and abstraction, two opposites that, however, can only be the faces of a single reality.

The drawing by Gian Piero Frassinelli

In order to understand Michele Saee's point of view, I believe that we must completely abandon both the Renaissance point of view, which postulates a privileged point of view, through which the unity of space is contemplated, and the idea of the modern movement of the architectural promenade.

According to the latter idea, good architecture is a succession of different points of view united by a continuous thread, a walk around and inside of a building. In fact, in Saee's best works, the points of view do not proceed in an orderly fashion along a clear, defined route (think of Le Corbusier who almost imposes an ordered sequence), but they try to apply themselves freely and simultaneously.

The eye is stimulated to gaze into space in an effort to not ever lose its bearings. And it is through this continual mediation (or better: vibration) between the multiple visions that the object transmits its own charge of energy. Another particularly interesting aspect of Saee's work is the relationship between the building and the surrounding environment: an always open dialectic, also because the building refuses to be closed in itself. In this sense, it involves strongly ecological architectures where, however, the word "ecology" means much more than creating buildings with a low energy impact.

Nature is "the other" of architecture, but not "the stranger." That is the dimension from which it flees (civilization does not come forth unless fleeing from nature) but toward which it perennially aspires to return. And it is in this secret affinity that the value of a good spatial configuration is measured, which, only in this way, is transformed into the metaphor of our civilization.

Editions

Publishers of Architecture, Art, and Design
Gordon Goff: Publisher

www.oroeditions.com
info@oroeditions.com

Published by ORO Editions

Author: Michele Saee
Introduction: Claude Parent
Book Design: Weestar Studio / Xingyu Wei, Hongbo Yue
Managing Editor: Jake Anderson
Photography: Tim Street Porter, Marvin Rand, Peter Cook, Chen su, Luc Boegly
Raymond Koch, Richard Rubins, Lane Barden, Alisina Saee Nazari
Joel Reis, Greg Frost

10 9 8 7 6 5 4 3 2 1 First Edition

ISBN: 978-1-951541-29-3

Color Separations and Printing: ORO Group Ltd.
Printed in China.

ORO Editions makes a continuous effort to minimize the overall carbon footprint of its publications. As part of this goal, ORO Editions, in association with Global ReLeaf, arranges to plant trees to replace those used in the manufacturing of the paper produced for its books. Global ReLeaf is an international campaign run by American Forests, one of the world's oldest nonprofit conservation organizations. Global ReLeaf is American Forests' education and action program that helps individuals, organizations, agencies, and corporations improve the local and global environment by planting and caring for trees.